W9-BUT-992

THE ROYALS

KITTY KELLEY

THE ROYALS

WHEELER
PUBLISHING, INC.
ROCKLAND, MA

★ AN AMERICAN COMPANY ★

Published in Large Print by arrangement with Time Warner Books, Inc. in the United States and Canada.

Wheeler Large Print Book Series.

Set in 16 pt Plantin.

Library of Congress Cataloging-in-Publication Data

Kelley, Kitty.
   The royals / Kitty Kelley.
     p. (large print) cm.(Wheeler large print book series)
   ISBN 1-56895-529-4 (hardcover)
   1. Elizabeth II, Queen of Great Britain, 1926– —Family. 2. Queens—
Great Britain—Biography. 3. Windsor, House of. 4. Large type books.
I. Title. II. Series
[DA590.K39   1997]
941.085`092—dc21

97-47197
CIP

To my husband John,
who makes dreams come true.

"... Once in a while a family has to surrender itself to an outsider's account. A family can get buried in its own fairy dust, and this leads straight, in my opinion, to the unpacking of lies and fictions from its piddly shared scraps of inbred history...."

From *The Stone Diaries*
by Carol Shields

"I believe in aristocracy though, if that is the right word and if a democrat may use it. Not an aristocracy of power based upon rank and influence, but an aristocracy of the sensitive, the considerate and the plucky. Its members are to be found in all nations and classes and all through the ages and there is a secret understanding between them when they meet. They represent the true human tradition, the one permanent victory of our queer race over cruelty and chaos."

From a 1941 essay by
E.M. Forster

AUTHOR'S NOTE

February 13, 1997

If a cat may look on a king, as the English proverb goes, so can a Kitty. The ancient king had been succeeded by a modern queen by the time I started to take my look. So I wrote to Her Majesty Queen Elizabeth II as a matter of courtesy and said I was researching a book on the House of Windsor. I respectfully requested an interview, but her press secretary replied that the Queen does not grant interviews.

"Our policy," Charles Anson wrote on Buckingham Palace stationery, "is to try to help bona fide authors writing serious books on the Monarchy and the Royal Family with factual information on matters of public interest. I shall, therefore, be happy to do this for you if you can first give me some indication of the theme of your book and the specific areas in which you would like to put questions to me."

He asked me to submit an outline. "Naturally, I would treat this in complete confidence," he wrote. This puzzled me. Did he mean that he wouldn't show the outline to anyone, including the Queen and the rest of the royal family? Or was he going to keep it from the British press, which had been reporting (incorrectly) that I was writing a biography of the Queen's husband, Philip, the Duke of Edinburgh?

Already the Duke was getting agitated about the prospect of someone writing a book about him that he had not authorized. In 1994, according to British reporters traveling with him, he threatened to sue me. While visiting New York, he was asked about "the book that Kitty Kelley is writing," and he was quoted as saying, "I will protect my good name." His pronouncement caused a stir in the British press. "Never before has a member of the royal family personally issued such a blunt warning," wrote Chris Hutchins in Today. "Prince Philip says he is prepared to sue and Buckingham Palace lawyers are already `on full alert.' " The Daily Star reported the exchange as "Prince's Threat over Kitty Shocker: I Will Sue If Your Book's Too Saucy."

The stories prompted numerous calls to my office in Washington, D.C., from men and women claiming to be the illegitimate offspring of royalty. From Argentina, Australia, England, Wales, and New York, people called to tell me of their royal parentage. They volunteered to send photos of themselves, extracts from family diaries, and letters from distant relatives to substantiate their claim, but none produced a birth certificate. Yet even without authentic documentation, they remained convinced that they had been sired outside of marriage by a member of the British royal family.

When I wrote back to the Queen's press secretary, I told him that I wanted to interview as many people as possible who could speak with authority on the House of Windsor. As an American writing for an international audience, I asked the Queen's press secretary to help me develop an accurate record on a subject of intense public interest. Many books have been written about the Windsors, but most contradict one another. Eminent historians differ on basic details. Few agree on anything except how the family spells its name.

Since I was still in the process of acquiring information, I explained that the form of the book was dictated by chronology, from 1917, when the royal family was renamed, to the present day. Instead of an outline, I submitted two pages of questions about marriages, finances, and knighthoods. In response, Mr. Anson sent me a 632-page book entitled The Royal Encyclopedia.

We exchanged more letters as I traveled back and forth between Washington, D.C., and London to do research. In 1995 I was in England for the commemoration of V-E Day, May 8—the day in 1945 when the Allies announced the surrender of German forces in Europe. Again I contacted the Palace with more questions and renewed my request for interviews. On this visit I spoke with Mr. Anson on the phone.

We discussed the stirring ceremonies that had been staged to celebrate the fiftieth anniversary of victory over Nazi Germany. We talked about the moving scene of the previous day, when the ninety-five-year-old Queen Mother stepped onto the balcony of Buckingham Palace to wave to the fifty thousand people assembled below. Fifty years earlier she had stood in the same place to accept the tribute of a grateful nation. Then, as now, she was flanked by her two daughters. But missing from the historical tableau in 1995 were her husband, King George VI, and his Prime Minister, Winston Churchill, both of whom had stood beside her in 1945. Still, the sight of her on the balcony reminded everyone of Britain's indomitable spirit during the war.

"These sorts of occasions," the Queen's press secretary told me, "are very unifying for the country.... They show that the monarchy is an arrangement that suits the British people...."

After I returned to Washington, D.C., to begin writing the book, Mr. Anson did not answer any more questions. He seemed concerned that I might be misinterpreting his cooperation so I could market my book as an authorized biography. He need not have worried. But he conveyed his anxiety to a reporter from the royal family's favorite newspaper, the London Daily Telegraph, which headlined its story "Palace Alarm over U.S. Book on the Queen."

The Palace press secretary was quoted in the story as saying: "Ms. Kelley has not been given any special cooperation, nor will she be.

We have answered one or two factual questions put to us, as we do with any author writing on the royal household. This does not denote any special access."

Days later I received my last letter from Charles Anson. "I should emphasize at this point," he wrote, "that if the limited help we have given is misrepresented in any way in future, we will consider taking appropriate action." This, too, was reported in the British press. The Guardian's story—"Action Stations at the Palace"—ran under a cartoon of two corgis guarding the Buckingham Palace kennels. With bared teeth, one dog growled: "Kitty! Grrrr...Even the name makes me angry."

Despite the well-publicized warning from the Queen's press secretary, I have been able to interview several hundred people over the last three years, many of whom are current or former members of the royal household. Because I never pay for information, I gave no one money, but I did guarantee confidentiality to those who feared retaliation from the Palace. Most members of the royal household sign confidentiality agreements when they are hired, so I knew they took great risks in speaking to me. If identified, those in royal service could lose their jobs; those retired could lose their pensions. Charles Anson had made the point in one of his earlier letters to me: "We take very seriously here any breach of confidentiality or of the undertakings given, for example, by employees of the Royal Household concerning their employment with the Royal Family."

Yet with the unattributed help of many people, including past and present employees, friends, and relatives, I was able to get an inside look at the British royal family and how they live. I started at Kensington Palace, a few miles from Buckingham Palace in the heart of London.

During a time when Princess Margaret was traveling abroad, a member of her staff, whom I already knew, offered me a personal tour of her living quarters. I accepted gratefully because I had never been inside a palace. When I showed up at the front gates, I was surprised to be waved through by cheerful security guards. They did not ask my name or question my purpose, probably because I was greeted by someone familiar to them.

We began with the apartments known as Grace-and-Favor Residences, which are given to select employees by the sovereign. Some of these small apartments looked like monk's cells. They're clean but cramped, with just enough room for the essentials—bed, chair, couch, table. In some, the space is so limited that the private toilet is across the hall from the bathtub. But, as one appreciative employee pointed out, "They are rent-free."

When we walked into the residence of HRH the Princess Margaret, I gawked in disbelief; because I was standing in the home of the sister of the wealthiest woman in the world, I had probably anticipated something grander, more imposing. I half expected diamond-studded walls and floors inlaid with rubies.

Instead I saw plastic flowers arranged in vases on the windowsills and an electric heater with a badly frayed cord. A collapsible aluminum tray was stashed behind the door of the drawing room. I was told that it was placed in front of the television set when the Princess dined alone. Two large blackamoor statues guarded the entrance to the vivid blue room, where she displayed her vast collection of loving cups, crystal goblets, and pitchers. Lining the walls were porcelain plates and dishes embellished with great globs of gold. On a mahogany dumbwaiter by her desk, she had placed a collection of tiny porcelain boxes. One, circa 1800, carried an inscription: "May the King Live to Reward the Subject Who Would Die for Him."

My guide showed me through the rooms of the palace and patiently answered my questions about the royal family—the Queen, the Queen Mother, the Duke of Edinburgh, Princess Margaret, Princess Anne, Princes Andrew and Edward, and the Prince and Princess of Wales. When I asked about Sarah Ferguson, Duchess of York, I was told curtly, "She's not royalty." I gazed at the portraits and photographs, including the framed picture of Princess Margaret and her former husband, Antony Armstrong-Jones, at a White House dinner with President and Mrs. Lyndon Johnson. The photo, signed by the Johnsons, hangs in the bathroom.

The path from Kensington Palace to Buckingham Palace beckoned intriguingly as my research into the House of Windsor led me up and down the class system. Downstairs I interviewed footmen. Upstairs I conversed with courtiers. I listened to members of the House of Lords and House of Commons. I interviewed Tory and Labor Members of Parliament about the dominating influence of the monarchy.

At a meeting of women that I attended, actress Glenda Jackson, a Labor MP, said, "My constituents are angry about where their country is going, but you would never know their concerns from the press coverage, which is obsessed with royalty." The Tory MP Rupert Allason, who writes spy novels under the name of Nigel West, wrote to me about his high regard for the monarchy. "I am rather old fashioned about the Royals. Some of it may be unattractive but it serves the country well and…[it]…is regarded over here as a cherished if anachronistic institution."

Lord Jacob Rothschild was more mischievous. Over dinner at the River Club in London, he mentioned he had dined recently at Buckingham Palace. "You are never supposed to say if you dine at the Palace. But what's the fun of knowing the royals," he said with a wink, "if you can't talk about them?"

His wife tried to shush him. She shook her finger at me for taking notes. "You must not write a book," said Lady Rothschild. "We have to protect our royal family from themselves.…We don't need a book by an objective American. You're not supposed to be objective about royalty."

My research also included tea with titled ladies married to gentlemen with a string of initials after their names. These abbreviations indicate the honors they've received from the Crown. In their country manors, I saw the ermine-edged robes they wore to the coronation and the little gold chairs they sat on during the ceremony in Westminster Abbey. Many had known the Queen since childhood. She attended their weddings and wrote them "Dear Cousin" letters. "In this circle," explained one aristocrat, "everyone is considered a relation." (Even with the help of Debrett's Peerage, the bible of the nobility, I stumbled on the intricacies of British social precedence. More than once I fumbled a title or jumbled initials in addressing a letter, but my gaffes were graciously forgiven. "You're an American, dear," said one Countess. "You cannot be expected to know.") Royalists all, these aristocrats believe firmly in the Crown and maintain that the monarchy will survive as long as the White Cliffs of Dover. I'm grateful to all of them for their time and consideration.

Their insights contrasted sharply with those of republicans I interviewed. They believe the days of the monarchy are, or should be, numbered. Escorted by the writer Anthony Holden, I attended a meeting of the Common Sense Club in London, where British writers, editors, and scholars consider proposals for dismantling the monarchy, including a written constitution for the country that would terminate the House of Lords and separate church from state. The Common Sense Club takes its name from the pamphlet Thomas Paine wrote in 1776, urging a declaration of independence. The son of a Quaker corset maker, he was arrested, convicted of treason, and outlawed from England. His revolutionary spirit still inspires Mr. Holden and his republican colleagues, who combine immense charm and wit with their politics. I enjoyed my time with them and appreciate their efforts to educate me.

Marc Pachter, Counselor for Special Projects to the Secretary of the Smithsonian Institution, has conducted monthly seminars for the Washington Biography Group, which I attend for his wise advice. He believes that biography is a life lived and observed from the outside peering in. He tells us, "Write with your nose pressed to the window." So I have tried.

For expertise on British royalty, I turned to several social historians who lecture at the Smithsonian Institution in Washington, D.C. Particularly enchanting were Virginia W. Newmyer; Stanley Weintraub, Evan Pugh Professor of Arts and Humanities, Pennsylvania State University; Edward Keefer, U.S. Department of State; Marlene Eilers; Roland Flamini, formerly diplomatic correspondent, Time magazine; Catherine A. Cline, professor of history, Catholic University; David Cannadine, professor of history, Columbia University.

For answers to my historical queries, I'm

indebted to several librarians: Eugene Weber, manager of the Press Association of the United Kingdom, and his helpful staff: Adrian McLeay, Richard Peacock, and Katarina Shelley; Linda Amster, New York Times; Paul Hamburg, Simon Wiesenthal Center; Garner Shaw, the New York Observer; Gwen Odum, Palm Beach Daily News; Steve Glatter, Miami-Dade Public Library; Don Osterweil, Vanity Fair; Jeanette Brown, USA Today; Merle Thomason, Fairchild publications; Paul Cornish and Janet Bacon, British Information Service; Lisa Brody, American Film Institute; Terri Natale, New Statesman; Charles Seaton, the Spectator; Rodney Smith, New Orleans Public Library; Polly Townsend, Desmond-Fish Library, Garrison, New York; Janet Lorenz, National Film Information Service of the Center for Motion Picture Study, Academy of Motion Picture Arts and Sciences; Margaret O'Sullivan, Putnam County [New York] News and Recorder; Patrick Wagner, Smithsonian Residents Program; the reference librarians at the Alexandria, Arlington, and Fairfax, Virginia, Public Libraries; the Washingtoniana Room of the Martin Luther King Library in Washington, D.C.; the Foundation Center Library in Washington, D.C.

For documents and records on the British royal family, I'm grateful to the British Naval Office; the Office of Population Censuses and Surveys, St. Catherine's House, London; and the presidential archivists and researchers at the libraries of Franklin D. Roosevelt, Harry S. Truman, Dwight D. Eisenhower, John F. Kennedy, Lyndon B. Johnson, Richard M. Nixon, Gerald R. Ford, Jimmy Carter, and Ronald W. Reagan; the National Archives and the Library of Congress in Washington, D.C.; the State of New York Department of Law; the Freedom of Information Act Offices at the Department of State, Department of Justice, including Federal Bureau of Information, Department of Defense, and Central Intelligence Agency. Reaves West did commendable research at the British Library in London. For advice on protocol, I turned to Jean P. Inman, American Embassy, London, and appreciate the assistance of the staffs at the British Embassy in Washington, D.C., and the embassies of Sweden, Denmark, Norway, Canada, and Australia.

Some people provided information for the book; others provided hospitality for the author. Both are greatly appreciated. I extend thanks to the staff of the Athenaeum Hotel, where James A. Brown, Sally Bulloch, Alex Serra, and Donald Birraine made the first of many research trips to London so enjoyable. I'm particularly indebted to them for introducing me to the President of South Africa, Nelson Mandela, who also was staying at the hotel. The hour I spent with this man was my first encounter with nobility.

Writers become unbearable while writing books and so they owe the deepest thanks to those who will put up with them. My list is long of people who saw me through the ordeal. For the last ten years my research assistant, Melissa Lakey, has brought her bright mind and huge heart to every task she's been given. Professionally and personally, she's a treasure. I also value the family she's extended to me in her mother, Jeannette Smalling, and her brother, Walter Smalling. Her relatives have supported this project with love and patience and I'm indebted to all, especially Ray Rhinehart; Paul, Martha, and Allyson Gibson; Stephen and Margaret Gibson; Roger, Anne, Jeannette, and Rachel Buchholz; Jean, Bill, Mike, Doug, and Jon Lakey. I'm grateful to Melissa's husband, Bryan Lakey, for his patience with her long hours as she labored to deliver this book before the arrival of their first baby, Drew Edward Lakey.

My sisters, Mary Cary Coughlan and Adele O'Toole, provided loving encouragement throughout the writing, as did my dear friend Margaret Engel, director of the Alicia Patterson Foundation. Members of the International Women's Forum were extraordinarily helpful, particularly Sheryl Marshall, Joni Evans, Shirley Nelson, Peggy Czyzak-Dannenbaum, Martha Teichner, Barbara Hosking, Pam Garside, Susan Greenwood, Willie Campbell, Maureen Kindel, Mary Lehman, and Fruzsina Harshani. I'm also grateful for the support of I.W.F. friends like Patricia Gurne, Michele Hagans, Sandra Taylor, Mitzi Wertheim, Lilia Ann Abron, Alexandra Armstrong, Esther Smith, Patricia Bailey, and Patricia Goldman.

I appreciate the efforts of Bill Chaput of the Lotos Club in New York City; Rich Salke; Erna Steiner; James Henderson; Fabiola Molina; Germaine Attebery; Susan Nicholas; Silvia Costanos; Joan Worden; Deborah Cohen; Russell Kott; Eunice and Mones Hawley; Susan Mickelwaite; Patti Pancoe; Carolyn Telman; Forrest Mac Cormack; and Samuel Melman of Justine Melman, Inc.; Eliane Laffont, president of Sygma Photo News; and Mr. and Mrs. Louis J. Appell Jr., whose flat in Lenox Gardens became my London home.

For various research projects, I had expert help from Melissa Goldblatt; Aura Lippincott; Helaine R. Staver; Jacqueline Williams; Anne Whiteman, ABC News; Audrey Sands; Ray Boston; Barry Phelps; Sue Harmer; Mary Aylmer; Simon Nathan; Daphne Srinivasan; Lilly Lessing; Roger Law, Spitting Image; Pamela Warrick, Los Angeles Times; Ellen Warren, Chicago Tribune; Wade Nelson; Rachel Grady; Abby Jones Pauley; Emily Greines; Rebecca Salt, Reed Consumer Books, London; Phoebe Bentinck; Edda Tasiemka, the Hans Tasiemka Archives; Ann Geneva, Yale University Press; Ted Richards, Olsson's Books; Tim O'Connor, Palm Beach Polo Club; Frank Tenot, president, Hachette Filipacchi Presse.

For tapes and documentaries I received generous assistance from Howard Rosenberg of CBS News and Richard W. Carlson, president and CEO of Corporation for Public Broadcasting.

For foreign-language translations I relied on the expertise of Vivian Glick, whose linguistic skills encompass French, German, and Italian. Maria de Martini assisted with Spanish interviews.

For investment analysis of royal finances, I was guided by Marvin H. McIntyre of Legg Mason Wood Walker in Washington, D.C., and his staff: Colleen Bradley, Kim Dexter, Don Metzger, Bob Parr, Swati Patel, A. J. Vector. I'm also grateful to Arnold H. Koonin of Coopers & Lybrand; and Steve Weisman and Tracy Noble of Weisman, Noble and Moore.

For legal advice I relied on Marc Miller of McLeod, Watkinson and Miller; Robert Wald, Michael Nussbaum, and Benjamin Zelenko of Nussbaum & Wald, Washington, D.C. My favorite lawyer is still my ninety-three-year-old father, William V. Kelley, of Witherspoon, Kelley, Davenport & Toole in Spokane, Washington.

In recent years I've spoken to many people about the House of Windsor. Among those generous with their time, knowledge, and insights were Peter and Pamela Evans; Robert Lacey; Sue Townsend; Michael Cole; Linda White; Steve Aronson; Patricia Bosworth; Peter and Kit Hammond; Barbara and Ken Follett; Mara Berni; Lecia Crystal; Ericka Barty-King; Andrew David Ball and Judith Ball; Nancy, Barbara, and David Morowitz; Bob Glick; Sheila and Dobli Srinivasan; Cissy Finley Grant; Lionel Epstein and Elizabeth

Streicker; Lynette and John Pearson; Anthony Holden and Cindy Blake; Rosie Boycott, Esquire; Ross Benson, Daily Express; Peter McKay, Evening Standard; Gordon MacKenzie, Daily Mail; Hal Robinson; Michael Bywatter; Peter Kazaris; Roberta Ashley; Richard Cohen; David Patrick Columbia; Fiammetta Rocco, Independent on Sunday; Sue Crewe; Phyllis Stirman; Eric Weil, Buenos Aires Herald; Ivanna and James Whitaker, Daily Mirror; Barbara Cartland; Tim Heald; Giles Gordon; Christopher Hitchens, Vanity Fair; Francis Wheen, the Guardian; Ian Hislop, editor of Private Eye; Matthew Evans; Caroline Michel; Larry Adler; Larry and Mary Devlin; Daryll Bonner; Nancy Pollard; Mark Hollingsworth; Norman Douglas Hutchinson; Anthony Summers; Muriel Fox and Shep Aaronson; Ken Burrows and Erica Jong; Bonnie Goldstein, ABC-TV; Jim Grady; Myuki Williams; Jacqui and Jeff Weaver; Maurice Weaver, Daily Telegraph; Betsy and Ira Silverman; Monica Worth; Christopher Gulkin; William Norwich, New York Observer; Marian Lear Swaybill; Heather Perram; Richard Hough; Franklin Johnson; Fleur Cowles; Dominic Lawson, the Spectator; Margaret Gardner; Ken Jennings; Rex Reed; Eunice Roberts; Wendall (Sonny) Rawls; G. H. Hutchinson Smith; Geoffrey Bailey; Geoffrey Harley; Joyce Hopkirk; Emily Malino Scheur; Bevis Hillier; Veronica Forwood; Laura Zelenko; Rory Knight Bruce; Robin

Knight Bruce; John Davey Beverton; Noreen Talor; Rosalind Miles; Richard Johnson, the New York Post; Richard Turley; Carlos Anessi; Nina Myskow; Grant McCahon; Mary Kyreakowdis; Carinthia West, Marie Claire; John Teenan; Philip Benjamin; Taki Theodoracopulos; Margaret Holder; Michael Thornton; Lady Colin Campbell; Sylvia Wallace; Jonathan Engel, Reuters; Michael Nagel; Geoffrey Acquilina Ross; Kevin Dowling; Jean Ritchie; Nicholas Haslam; Caroline Kennedy; John Barratt; Stephen Maitin; Lindka Cierach; Una Mary Parker; Jeanette Walls, Esquire; Majorie Wallace; Wendy Leigh; Richard Ingrams; Christopher Silvester; Jack Hedley; Willie Hamilton; Kenneth Jost, Congressional Quarterly; James Bellini; Philip Knightley; Andrew Rosthorn; Paddy Crerand; Desmond Ellott; Gant Gaither; Jody Jacobs; Sharman Douglas; Achtar Hussein; Arlene Dahl; Pamela and Ronald Kessler; John Prince; Fornida and Nang Sang, People; Wanda Baucus; Mark Gisbourne; John Woods; Tony and Audrey Charles; Felicity Green, Daily Telegraph; Sheila Hailey; Geraldine Sharpe Newton, CNN; Susan Yerkes, San Antonio Express News; Ian Coulter; Angus Coulter; Heather Elliott; Gordon Graham; Marco Pierre White; Victoria Mather; Penelope Mortimer; Desmond Elliott; Ian Gordon; Michael Bloch; Ingrid Seward, Majesty magazine; Stephen Birmingham; Bob Jerome; Andrew Neil, the Sunday Times; Susan

Watters, Women's Wear Daily; Judy (Demetra) Green; Roberta Klein; Charles Higham; Julie Schoo; Lissa August, Time; Connie Bransilver; Lester Hyman; Ann Landers; Lucy Scardino; Kevin McMannus, Town & Country; Warren Rogers; Joe Laitin; Lilla Pennant; Leslie Linder and Norma Quine; Tim Heald; Nicholas Monson; Stephen Haseler; Lindsay Mackie; Roy Greenslade; Hugh Bygott-Webb; Magdalene de Blaquier; Nicki McWhirter, Detroit News; James Reginato, Women's Wear Daily; Maxine Champion; Leslie and Andrew Cockburn; Robert Sam Anson; Martin Peretz, the New Republic; David Hume Kennerly; Norman Mailer; Annie Groer the Washington Post; Toni Aluisi; C. Wyatt Dickerson; Terry Lichstein, ABC-TV; Ed Curran; Barry Everingham; David Kogan, Reuters; Carolyn MacDonald; Gilbert Mathieu; Maxine Mawhinney, GMTV; Joan Worden; William Keating; Barbara Dixon; Susan Tolchin; Marianne Means, Hearst newspapers; Al Eisele, The Hill; Evangeline Bruce; Dr. Nelson Lankford, the Virginia Historical Society; Priscilla Baker; Robert M. Eisenger; Gillian Pachter; Ronnie and Arnie Pollard; Ricki Morell; Nancy A. Poland; Penelope Farthing.

I also wish to thank my literary agent, Wayne S. Kabak of International Creative Management, who combines brilliance and good humor, even in the midst of crisis. He brings to mind Chaucer's "verray parfit gentil knight." I value his counsel and the friendship extended by his wife, Marsha Berkowitz, and his children, Victoria and Benjamin. His I.C.M. staff makes the writing life less burdensome, especially his extraordinary assistant, Laura Blaustein. I'm also grateful to the London office of I.C.M. where Duncan Heath and his assistant, Lucy Morrison, were so helpful.

I salute Warner Books and its dynamic C.E.O. Laurence J. Kirshbaum, Chairman of Time Warner Trade Publishing; Maureen Egen, President and Publisher and C.O.O.; Chris Barba, V.P., Director of Sales and Marketing; Emi Battaglia, V.P., Director of Publicity; Jackie Joiner, Assistant to the President; Harvey-Jane Kowal, V.P., Executive Managing Editor; Diane Luger, Executive Art Director; Martha Otis, V.P., Director of Advertising and Promotion; Karen Torres, Director of Marketing; Nancy Wiese, Subsidiary Rights Director. My thanks to Sona Vogel for expert copy editing and Vincent Virga for compiling the photographs.

Writing is tough, so writers need mentors. Mine continues to be Mervin Block, who sets the standard of excellence. After twenty years of friendship, I still marvel at his skill and intelligence. Humbling as it was, I'm mighty grateful for the red pen he wielded on my rough drafts and his insistence on making the contents shorter, sharper, stronger.

When the manuscript was completed, my publisher sent me a treasure in Carolyn

Blakemore, who arrived in Washington, D.C., determined to turn hopsack into velvet. She departed with my affection and gratitude.

My deepest appreciation goes to my husband, Jonathan E. Zucker, to whom this book is dedicated. He came into my life five years ago and continues to fill my heart with joy.

THE ROYALS

ONE

Princess Margaret strode out of the theater. She had barely managed to sit through the opening scenes of *Schindler's List*. She began squirming as soon as she saw the Jewish prayer candles burn down, leaving only wisps of smoke to evoke the ashes that would follow. She crinkled her nose at the sight of the captive Jewish jeweler being tossed a handful of human teeth to mine for fillings. As the nightmare unfolded, she stiffened in her seat.

On screen, the streets filled with screaming Jewish prisoners, brutal Nazi soldiers, and snarling police dogs quickly emptied, except for the scattered suitcases of those Jews who had just been hauled off to the death camps. At that point the Princess bolted out of her seat.

"I'm leaving," she said. "I refuse to sit here another minute."

Her friends were aghast but immediately deferred to her displeasure. They left their seats and accompanied Her Royal Highness back to her servants in Kensington Palace.

"I don't want to hear another word about Jews or the Holocaust," said the Queen's sister. "Not one more word. I heard enough during the war. I never want to hear about it again. Ever."

Margaret's friends later wondered why, feeling as she did, she had suggested going to the movie in the first place. She had to know that *Schindler's List* would depict the horrors of genocide. What they didn't understand

1

was that the Princess had read reviews of the movie and been taken with the portrait of the good German, Oskar Schindler, who had come to reap the spoils of war and ended up as a selfless hero who saved countless lives. That was the story she wanted to see enacted on screen.

For more than sixty years Margaret Rose had been a princess of the royal House of Windsor, reared to renounce her German roots, to deny the mix of Saxe-Coburg-Gotha blood that coursed through her veins, to repudiate the lineage of Wurttemburgs and Schleswig-Holstein-Sonderburg-Glucksburgs that haunted her ancestors.

She was not disturbed by searing childhood memories of Britain during the Blitz. When war broke out in 1939, she was nine years old. At sixty-four the Princess rarely reflected on the shattering bombs, the blackouts, or the deprivation that she felt she and her older sister, the Queen, endured to serve as public examples for others who were suffering much more. She no longer complained as much as she once did about being deprived of a normal childhood.

During those years, her royal image had inspired a thirteen-year-old Jewish girl in Amsterdam who was hiding from the Nazis. To remind herself of a better world, Anne Frank had pasted pictures of Princess Margaret Rose, and her sister, Princess Elizabeth, on the wall of the attic where she hid with her family for two years. But then the family was betrayed to the Gestapo and herded off in windowless boxcars on the train bound for the Bergen-Belsen concentration camp. Anne died there one month before Europe was liberated. When the Anne Frank House was opened to the public after the war, the pictures of Britain's little Princesses, yellowed with age, still smiled from the wall.

Princess Margaret was proud of her performance during the war and that of her earnest sister and her gallant parents, who had made sure that they presented the world with an image of royalty at its finest.

What Princess Margaret resented about *Schindler's List* and "those other tiresome movies about the Holocaust" was the lingering stench of Germany that continued to hang over her family. Their secrets of alcoholism, drug addiction, epilepsy, insanity, homosexuality, bisexuality, adultery, infidelity, and illegitimacy paled alongside their relationship with the Third Reich. Those secrets, documented by captured German war records and family diaries, letters, photographs, and memoranda, lay buried in the locked vaults of the Royal Archives at Windsor Castle, safe from the prying eyes of scholars and historians. Few people remembered that Margaret's mother and father had been disinclined to oppose Hitler and preferred Chamberlain over Churchill as Prime Minister. Most people had forgotten that the Princess's favorite uncle had embraced Nazi Germany as Europe's savior and her princeling cousin had run a concentration camp, for which he later stood trial as a war criminal. Margaret Rose remembered but knew that these facts—some secret, some sinister—were best left buried.

Yet the Princess was not averse to expressing her opinions, which sounded astoundingly ignorant coming from a woman who professed to read as much as she did. Despite her public participation in the arts and her devotion to ballet and theater, Margaret Rose remained closed-minded to the world beyond her privileged view. She made no apologies for her prejudices. In a discussion of India, she said she hated "those little brown people." Shortly after the IRA assassination of her cousin Lord Louis Mountbatten, she denounced the Irish. "They're pigs—all pigs," she told the Irish American mayor of Chicago while visiting the city. When the Princess was introduced to the respected columnist Ann Landers, Margaret looked at her closely. "Are you a Jew?" she asked. "Are you a Jew?" The columnist said she was, and the Princess, no longer interested, moved on. She dismissed Dr. Cheddi Jagan, the President of Guyana, as loathsome. "He's everything I despise," she said. "He's black; he's married to a Jew; and furthermore, she's American."

After walking out of *Schindler's List,* which she described as "a tedious film about Jews," she advised her butler not to waste his money on the Academy Award-winning film.

"A movie like *Schindler's List* just incites morbid curiosity," the Princess said when her butler served her breakfast the next morning. "I couldn't stand it. It was so thoroughly unpleasant and disgusting that I had to get up and leave."

The butler listened patiently, as always. Then he bowed his head and returned to the pantry. Later he repeated the conversation to an American, who asked if he were not offended by Princess Margaret's remarks. He seemed puzzled by the American's question.

"Oh my, no. You don't understand. The Princess is royalty. *Royalty,*" he said, pronouncing the word with reverence. "The Princess belongs to the House of Windsor—the most important royal house in the world. She's the daughter of a king and the sister of a queen. That's as exalted as you can possibly be on this earth."

"Do you mean to suggest that royalty, especially British royalty, can do no wrong? That just because she's a princess, she's immune to criticism?"

"She is royalty," repeated the butler.

"And therefore above reproach?"

"Royalty is royalty," he said. "Never to be questioned."

TWO

Once upon a time...the House of Windsor was a fantasy. The figment of a courtier's imagination. The dynasty was created in 1917 to conceal the German roots of the King and

Queen, and the deception enabled the monarchy to be perceived as British by subjects who despised Germany.

Until then, many English kings never spoke the King's English. They spoke only German because for almost two hundred years, from 1714 until this century, a long line of Germans ruled the British empire. By 1915 England finally had a king, George V, who could speak English without a German accent. Although he was a German from the Saxe-Coburg-Gotha line that had ruled England for eighty years, he considered himself to be indisputably British. His subjects, who hated Germany, Germans, and all things Germanic, were not convinced.

For years, especially in the early 1900s, the English had become increasingly afraid of Prussian militarism. They felt threatened by the Kaiser's oppression. And they were "sore-headed and fed up," as George Bernard Shaw wrote, with Germany's rattling sabers. They viewed World War I as a war against Germany.

Newspapers carried eyewitness accounts of revolting cruelty by the Germans, who bombed undefended towns and killed civilians. Those actions shocked the world in 1915. In England, editorials denounced "The March of the Hun" and "Treason to Civilization" as German U-boats sank British ships. The mounting death tolls on French battlefields caused hardships in England, which exacerbated Britain's hatred of foreigners.

King George V was disturbed as he watched

his subjects stone butchers with German names and burn the homes of people who owned dachshunds. Pretzels were banned and symphony conductors shunned Mozart and Beethoven.

This antipathy was not unique to Great Britain. Blood hatred of everything German had infected all of Europe and spread to America, where Hollywood produced a string of hate films such as *To Hell with the Kaiser, Wolves of Kultur,* and *The Kaiser: The Beast of Berlin.*

The King of England deplored the "hysterical clamor," calling it "petty and undignified," but few listened. The image of the hideous Hun as a fiendish torturer who raped, pillaged, and murdered innocents had gripped the public imagination.

The King became so concerned about the reaction of his volatile subjects that he was afraid to protect his relatives of German descent. Instead he stood by silently as his beloved cousin Prince Louis of Battenberg was vilified simply because of his German name. When war had threatened, Battenberg as the First Sea Lord of the Royal Navy mobilized the Admiralty with speed and efficiency, so that when war broke out, England was ready. But Battenberg, a naturalized British subject, became a target for abuse: his name was German, he was born in Germany, he spoke with a German accent, he employed German servants, and he owned property in Germany.

Despite his total loyalty to the Crown, he was forced to resign his military position and relinquish his princely title. The final humiliation occurred when the King told him to change his name. Shattered, Prince Louis dutifully anglicized Battenberg (*berg* is "mountain" in German) to Mountbatten to make it acceptable to the English.

The King tried to mollify his cousin by making him a British noble. Louis accepted the title of Marquess of Milford Haven because he wanted his children to be noblemen, but he never recovered from the shame of renouncing his ancestry. Somehow, though, he kept his sense of humor. He wrote in his son's guest book: "June 9th arrived Prince Hyde; June 19th departed Lord Jekyll."

His younger son and namesake, Louis, was shocked by the news of his father's resignation. "It was all so stupid," he recalled years later. "My father had been in the Royal Navy for forty-six years. He was completely identified with England, and we always regarded ourselves as an English family. Of course, we were well aware of our German connections; how could we not be? It certainly never occurred to any of us to be ashamed of them— rather the contrary. We are a very old family, and proud of it....My father had worked his way to the top of the Royal Navy by sheer ability and industry. And now his career was finished—all because of the ridiculous suspicion that he might be in secret sympathy with the very people he had come to England to avoid!"

Next, the King moved to cleanse the rest of his German family. Like the monarchs of mythology who bring magic clouds with them wherever they go, King George V waved his royal wand. Overnight, one brother-in-law—the Duke of Teck—became the Marquess of Cambridge, and the other—Prince Alexander of Teck—became the Earl of Athlone. One stroke of the royal quill eradicated all traces of Mecklenberg-Strelitz, Hesse, and Wettins from the King's lineage: the ugly German ducklings were transformed into beautiful British swans. The royal family's Teutonic dukes, archdukes, and princelings instantly became English marquises.

But the King felt he still needed to make the monarchy appear less imperial to survive. He decreed that members of the royal family could marry into the nobility. So, for the first time in history, royalty could marry commoners, whether they were titled or not. This paved the way for his second son, Albert, known to the family as "Bertie," to propose to a sweet-faced Scottish girl, reared as an Earl's daughter, although her mother has been rumored to have been one of the Earl's Welsh servant girls (these rumors, never officially acknowledged, have yet to be borne out by any evidence). Ironically, Bertie's marriage in 1923 to the commoner, Elizabeth Bowes-Lyon, brought stability to the British throne and propped up the dynasty for several generations.

During the First World War, concern was

voiced over the bloody role of the King's German cousin Prince Albert of Schleswig-Holstein, who was in charge of British prisoners of war in a camp outside Berlin.

"He's not really fighting on the side of the Germans," said the King defensively. "He was only put in charge of a camp of English prisoners."

"A nice distinction," Prime Minister Asquith later observed to a friend. His successor, Lloyd George, was even more blunt. When he received a royal summons to the Palace, he turned to his secretary and said: "I wonder what my little German friend has got to say to me." The Prime Minister's antipathy spread to his staff, who kept the King's private secretary, Lord Stamfordham, waiting on a wooden chair in the hall and refused to rise when he entered their office. The private secretary ignored the discourtesy. "We are all servants," he told shocked courtiers, "although some are more important than others."

As the devoted secretary to Queen Victoria, Lord Stamfordham was by far the most important of the King's men. He had served Victoria's heir, King Edward VII, who had put him in charge of his own son, George, at an early age. "He taught me how to be a king," said the master of his servant.

It was Lord Stamfordham who received the unenviable job of telling King George V about D. H. Lawrence, who had been hounded into hiding because he married a German woman. The once revered writer had married the sister of German military aviator Baron Manfred von Richthofen, the legendary Red Baron, credited with shooting down eighty Allied planes during World War I. After their wedding, Lawrence and his bride, Frieda, were forced by public hostility to seek refuge in the English countryside, where they hid in barns like animals.

This news was unsettling to the King, who also had a German wife. But the clever Queen—Mary of Teck—speaking English with a slight guttural accent, began referring to herself as "English from top to toe." The King immediately stopped addressing Kaiser Wilhelm II of Germany, the commander of the German forces sweeping across Europe, as "sweet cousin Willy." His German-hating subjects, who avoided references to sex, began referring to the male member as a "Willy."

Still, the hatred of Germans became so intense in England that the King's mother begged him to remove the Kaiser's honorary flags from the chapel. "Although as a rule I never interfere, I think the time has come when I must speak out," wrote Queen Alexandra. "It is but right and proper for you to have down those hateful German banners in our sacred Church, St. George's, at Windsor."

The Queen Mother sent her letter to "my darling little Georgie" after the *Daily Mail* had excoriated him for allowing the eight flags of "enemy Emperors, Kings and Princes" a place of honor at Windsor. "As long as the offending banners remain, their owners will be prayed for," thundered the newspaper. "What *are* the King's advisors doing?"

The King ignored the criticism until it came from his "darling Mother dear." Then he yielded and had the banners removed. "Otherwise," he told a friend, "the people would have stormed the chapel."

The King then threw himself and his family into the war effort. He dispatched his sons to the western front, sending the Prince of Wales (Edward, but known to the family as David) to France, while Prince Albert (Bertie) served on the battleship HMS *Collingwood*. The King banned alcohol and began strict rationing at the Palace to set a national example.

In March 1917 his cousin the Emperor Nicholas II of Russia ("dear Nicky") was forced to abdicate, in part because he, too, had a German wife whom the King blamed "for the present state of chaos that exists in Russia."

The King's equerry was more brutal on the subject: "The Empress is not only a Boche by birth, but in sentiment. She did all she could to bring about an understanding with Germany. She is regarded as a criminal or a criminal lunatic and the ex-Emperor as a criminal for his weakness and submission to her promptings."

That was all the King needed to hear. Concerned about the survival of his throne, he withdrew the warm friendship he had once extended to his "beloved cousin." When the Czar appealed for asylum for himself and his family, the King refused, prohibiting them entry

12

into England. The King felt he needed to separate himself from Russian imperialism, especially when wrapped with a German ribbon. So he wrote his cousin that he did not think it "advisable that the Imperial Family should take up their residence in this country." He suggested instead Spain or the South of France. At that point the revolutionaries in Russia realized that the King would not use military force to save his relatives. Thus abandoned, the Czar and his family were seized and sent to Siberia.

The King was more determined than ever to hang on to his threatened monarchy. He resented references to his German ancestry and raged over the caricatures of Max Beerbohm, who drew him as a comical and lugubrious figure. He lost his temper when a Labor Member of Parliament called him "a German pork butcher," and he erupted again when H. G. Wells branded him a foreigner. In a letter to the *Times,* the British journalist and novelist called for an end to "the ancient trappings of the throne and sceptre." He damned the royal house of Saxe-Coburg-Gotha by calling it "an alien and uninspiring Court."

"I may be uninspiring," boomed the King, "but I'll be damned if I'm an alien."

He resolved then and there to rid himself and his royal house of what he saw as its dreadful German taint. With the greatest sleight of hand since the sorcery of Prospero, he asserted his divine right and rechristened himself with the most euphonious, melodious British name

13

conceivable. His courtiers had spent weeks searching for just such a name that would reestablish the monarchy as thoroughly English.

Finally, Lord Stamfordham found it and secured his place in history by proposing the name of Windsor. That one word summoned up what the King was looking for—a glorious image that resonated with history, stretching back to William the Conqueror. For Windsor Castle, the most thoroughly British symbol extant, had been the site of English monarchs for eight hundred years. Although no king had ever lived there, several had died in Windsor Castle, and nine were buried in its royal crypt. The name was enough to redeem a tarnished crown.

The proclamation of the House of Windsor was announced on July 17, 1917, and appeared the next day on the front pages of England's newspapers. The British press dutifully reported that the King had renounced his German name and all German titles for himself and all other descendants of Queen Victoria and that henceforth he and his issue were to be referred to as the House of Windsor.

In the United States, news of the British royal family's reinventing itself was reported on page nine of *The New York Times*. In an editorial, the *Times* noted "the unnaming and renaming" was approved in a meeting of the largest Privy Council ever assembled and suggested that the name of Windsor, an Anglo-Saxon fortress where the legendary King

Arthur sat among the Knights of the Table Round, might have been selected for its "sense of continuity, of ancientness." America's newspaper of record praised England's King for choosing "a venerable name for his house."

In Germany, the news was reported with less reverence. The Kaiser laughed at his quixotic cousin and said that he was looking forward to attending a performance of that well-known play *The Merry Wives of Saxe-Coburg-Gotha.* But the Kaiser appreciated the political necessity of accommodation. As he pointed out, "Monarchy is like virginity—once lost, you can't get it back."

Still, he exacted revenge nineteen years later when the King died by sending the Duke of Saxe-Coburg-Gotha to his cousin's funeral in Windsor Castle. The Duke wore his Nazi uniform.

George V never expressed any qualms about his actions. He pragmatically buried his German roots to save his throne and then systematically ostracized his foreign relatives. He did this without compunction, even after receiving news from Russia that the Czar and Czarina and their four daughters and young son, who were moved from Siberia and Ekaterinburg, had been massacred by the Bolsheviks.

"It was a foul murder," he wrote piously in the diary he kept for posterity. "I was devoted to Nicky, who was the kindest of men and a thorough gentleman."

By keeping his distance, the King of England had held his crown in place. He then proceeded to rule the House of Windsor for the next two decades with probity. There was no scandal attached to his reign, and like his grandmother Queen Victoria, he excelled at the virtues the English prize most: duty and punctuality. His subjects saw him as a simple, decent man whose plain tastes reflected their own.

The King had started his adult life as the Duke of York and spent seventeen years shooting grouse on the moors of Sandringham. He became the heir apparent when his older brother, the Duke of Clarence, died. Even then the King kept the clocks at Sandringham set forward an hour to provide more time for shooting. A proper country squire, he enjoyed tramping across his twenty-thousand-acre estate in Norfolk. He adored his wife, indulged his daughter, and terrorized his five sons. "I was frightened of my father, and I am damn well going to see to it that my children are frightened of me," he said.

Poorly educated, he rarely read, shunned the theater, and did not listen to classical music. He ignored the arts, letters, and sciences. For recreation he licked postage stamps and placed them with childlike precision in blue leather stamp books. By the end of his life he had compiled an enormous collection of stamps from places he never wanted to visit. Known as "the Sailor King," he did not travel for education or pleasure. "Abroad is awful," he said. "I know because I've been there."

16

Except for touring military installations, he took few trips. He made an exception in 1911 to go to India for his coronation and in 1913 to visit relatives in Germany.

"My father, George V, took quiet pride in never having set foot in the United States," said his eldest son.

"Too far to go," said the King.

What he was, his children would become. In later years his eldest son, the Prince of Wales, who became the Duke of Windsor, was so humiliated by his father's ignorance that he reneged on an agreement to write a book of royal family reminiscences. He confided the reason to his publisher: "I'd hate for the world to know how illiterate we all were." The Prince of Wales embarrassed himself at a dinner party by not knowing the name of the Brontë sisters, who in their short lifetimes wrote *Jane Eyre* and *Wuthering Heights*, both considered classics of the English novel. The Prince of Wales, who rarely read, did not know who they were or how to pronounce their name. "Who are the Bronts?" he asked.

Unenlightened about mental illness, the Prince of Wales considered the condition of his youngest brother, Prince John, a source of shame. The last of the monarch's six children, John was mentally retarded and an epileptic. He was secretly removed from the family at an early age and lived on a farm on the Sandringham estate, where he died in 1919 at the age of thirteen.

As uneducated as the King was, George V

won wide respect from his subjects for his conscientious performance of royal duties and for his numerous military uniforms and the obvious pleasure he took in wearing them in royal parades. His subjects looked up to him as the father of their country and the personification of their values. England had gained enough land by conquest during the First World War to give her dominion over a quarter of the globe and a fourth of the world's inhabitants, thus making George V the last great Emperor King. During his reign, the sun truly never set on the British empire.

By the time King George V died in 1936, his beleaguered country was on the brink of another world war with Germany, which would end Britain's imperial power. And the House of Windsor, which he had built on the quicksand of illusion, started sinking under the weight of scandal.

For the last two years of his life, the King agonized over his heir. He dreaded leaving the monarchy in the hands of his feckless son, who at the age of forty-one was still unmarried. Following a fourteen-year affair with another man's wife, the Prince of Wales was now besotted with a married American woman, once divorced, named Wallis Warfield Simpson. Already Mrs. Simpson envisioned herself as the next Queen of England. The concept of a divorced person in royal circles was considered such sacrilege in those days that the King refused to receive his son's "unholy lover." He forbade his son to bring a woman defiled by divorce into his royal presence. When the King realized he was dying, he made his wife swear that she would never receive the despised Mrs. Simpson. The Queen, who regarded the King as more than her husband—"He's my almighty Lord and sovereign"—obeyed his command for the rest of her days.

At the end of his life, King George V cursed the laws of primogeniture that barred his solidly married second son from succeeding him. Although Bertie's stutter and stammer irritated him beyond bearing, he would have done anything to save the Crown from the Prince of Wales and his wenching ways.

"After I am dead," he said, "the boy will ruin himself in twelve months." In that the King proved prescient.

He wanted the throne to pass to his second son and then to his beloved granddaughter Elizabeth, who called him "Grandpapa England" because he referred to the National Anthem ("God Save the King") as his song. She sat on his lap, tousled his hair, pulled his beard, and plucked food from his plate for her Welsh corgi dogs. She also made him get down on his hands and knees to play "horsey" with her. The old King doted on his first granddaughter and held her in his arms on the balcony of Buckingham Palace so she could hear the crowd roar. "They're cheering for you, you know," he told her. Later he confided to an equerry: "I pray to God that my eldest son

[Edward] will never marry and have children, and that nothing will come between Bertie and Lilibet and the throne."

Critically ill for days, George V died on Monday, January 20, 1936, at 11:55 P.M. His end was hastened by Lord Dawson, who gave him a lethal injection of cocaine and morphine. The courtier wanted the King to die before midnight so that his death could be announced in the morning *Times* rather than in the less prestigious afternoon newspapers. The King, who had renamed the royal family, now lost his life to meet a newspaper deadline. Such was the legacy of the House of Windsor, which would eventually rise and fall as a puppet show for the media.

THREE

Winston Churchill puffed on his cigar and pondered the problem that was threatening a constitutional crisis: The new king, Edward VIII, wanted to announce his engagement to the American Wallis Warfield Simpson.

"Why shouldn't the King be allowed to marry his cutie?" Churchill asked.

"Because," retorted playwright Noel Coward, "England doesn't wish for a Queen Cutie."

The new King, who was forty-one years old and had never been married, intended to make his mistress his wife as soon as she got her second divorce. Upon his coronation he wanted her crowned as his consort. But he was up against the British establishment, which would not accept Wallis as Regina. Prime Minister Stanley Baldwin said it was outrageous to think that an American woman with two failed marriages could marry the King and become Queen of the British empire. The King insisted he would be supported by public opinion. The Prime Minister polled the Commonwealth and reported back the results: Either abandon Mrs. Simpson or abdicate.

"The throne," said the King, "means nothing to me without Wallis beside me."

Within ten months of his accession, the new monarch renounced the crown. He made public his abdication over the radio on December 11, 1936, in a speech that Churchill had helped him write. The evening broadcast from Windsor Castle was relayed around the world wherever the English language was spoken. In New York City cabdrivers pulled over to the curb to listen to the King say he could not continue to reign without the help and support of the woman he loved. The British public, which had learned of the crisis only weeks before, had sent telegrams and cables to Fort Belvedere, pleading with the King: "Stay with us!" and "Please don't desert us!" Now they wept as they listened to him give up his throne. "He Wuz Robbed!" said the Beaverbrook press. Journalist H. L. Mencken wrote, "It was the greatest news story since the Resurrection."

When the King married Mrs. Simpson six

months later, Queen Mary wrote in her diary, "To give up all this for that!!!!" The Prime Minister repeated a music hall joke: "He was Admiral of the Fleet, but now he's the third mate of an American tramp."

The man known to his family as David was born HRH the Prince Edward Albert Christian George Andrew Patrick David. For twenty-five years before becoming King, he was the most popular Prince of Wales in history. In every country he visited he was hailed as gallant and charming, a mesmerizing knight with shining gold hair and sad blue eyes. He bestowed the magic of royalty wherever he went, and people bowed eagerly in his presence. He was one of the most adored heirs ever to grace the British empire.

"Probably no one in our history has ever had so marked a power as this young Prince to rivet the ties of emotion and sympathy between the Mother Country and the millions of men, women and children in the outlying commonwealth of nations," wrote Frances Donaldson in her definitive biography of Edward VIII. "The emotions felt for England could never be explained merely by political or economic advantage, and there is no doubt that the monarchy was the greatest single influence in welding these disparate nations together...."

Women were especially thrilled to be in the company of such a man. Even meeting someone who had met him was exciting. This gave rise to a popular lyric of the time: "I danced with a man who danced with a girl who danced with the Prince of Wales."

One of those women was the daughter of a Scottish earl, Lady Elizabeth Angela Marguerite Bowes-Lyon. As the ninth of ten children, she was pampered and spoiled by her indulgent father. Like other women of her generation, she was formally uneducated but well versed in the arts necessary to marry well. Yet at the age of twenty-three she was still single while most of her aristocratic friends had husbands. Then she met the Prince of Wales, the most dashing man of the era. She relished the attention she received when the *Daily News* of January 5, 1923, reported:

"Scottish Bride for Prince of Wales. Heir to Throne to Wed Peer's Daughter."

The paper did not identify her by name, but she was obviously the young woman in question. "The future Queen of England is the daughter of a well-known Scottish peer, who is the owner of castles both north and south of the Tweed."

"We all bowed and bobbed and teased her, calling her 'Ma'am,'" Henry "Chips" Channon wrote in his diary. "She is more gentle, lovely and exquisite than any woman alive, but this evening I thought her unhappy and distraught."

She knew the rumor of romance was untrue, and to her chagrin, the newspaper printed a royal retraction a few days later. "We are officially authorized to say that this report is...devoid of foundation...."

Only in her old age did she admit to a friend that she was one of the many young women in the 1920s who had fallen in love with the Prince of Wales. "He was such fun," she said. *"Then."*

At the time, the Prince was interested only in other men's wives who were thin, streamlined, and looked as androgynous and anorectic as he did. He was not in the least attracted to the dumpling fullness of Elizabeth Bowes-Lyon. In fact, years later he and his wife mischievously nicknamed her "Cookie" because of her unfashionable plumpness and fondness for food.

In April 1923 Elizabeth married Bertie, the Prince's younger brother, the Duke of York, who had proposed to her after Lady Maureen Stanley had rejected him. He suffered from such excruciating nervousness that he stuttered, blinked incessantly, and could not control the muscles around his mouth. "Elizabeth Bowes-Lyon was determined to marry into the royal family," said biographer Michael Thornton, "so after his third proposal, she settled for the runt of the litter. I say this because I interviewed the Duke of Windsor to chronicle the blood feud between the Duchess of Windsor and the Queen Mother. I asked him why the Queen Mother continued to be so implacable toward his wife in later years, so unrelenting in her hatred of the Duchess.

"'Jealousy,' he said. 'To put it politely, she wanted to marry me.'

24

"Now, of course, so many years later, her friends deny this, but that's what the Duke told me a few years before he died."

Upon the abdication of King Edward VIII in 1936, his younger brother, Albert, known to the family as "Bertie," ascended to the throne. To keep continuity with the reign of his father, he became King George VI. His wife, who as a little girl had dressed up to play queen, now became a real one. The news was delivered to the public by newsreels and radio, but the coronation on May 12, 1937, was not broadcast. The ceremony in Westminster Abbey was considered too sacred to be aired. The Archbishop of Canterbury feared men in pubs would listen with their hats on.

Upon his accession, the new King, George VI, was determined to keep his older brother out of England to avoid competing with a second court. Churchill recommended the Duke of Windsor be appointed Governor of the Bahamas. But the King objected because the Queen felt that even that insignificant position was too good for the Windsors.

"She wanted them banished and completely stripped of all status," said Michael Thornton. "She was so vengeful that she wrote a letter to the Secretary of State for the Colonies, Lord Lloyd, and said that to make the Duchess of Windsor, a divorced woman with three living husbands, the wife of the Governor of the Bahamas would result in a disastrous lowering of standards."

Sir Walter Monckton, the royal courtier

who acted as intermediary, also recognized the Queen's motivation. As he wrote in his diary:

...I think the Queen felt quite plainly that it was undesireable [sic] to give the Duke any effective sphere of work. I felt then, as always, that she naturally thought that she must be on her guard because the Duke of Windsor, to whom the other brothers had always looked up, was an attractive, vital creature who might be the rallying point for any who might be critical of the new King, who was less superficially endowed with the arts and graces that please.

Despite the Queen's objection, the appointment was made. "She wreaked her sweet revenge later by making sure the Duchess of Windsor never received a curtsy or was addressed as Her Royal Highness," said Thornton. "The Queen helped institute the Letters Patent, which bestowed upon the Duke of Windsor 'the title, style, or attribute of Royal Highness' while withholding such title, style, or attribute from his wife and his descendants."

The King referred to the Duchess as "Mrs. Simpson," while the Queen disparaged her as "that woman."

Together, Their Majesties instructed the Lord Chamberlain to wire their new ruling to all Government House officials. His telegram from Buckingham Palace read:

You are no doubt aware that a lady when presented to HRH the Duke of Windsor should make a half-curtsey. The Duchess of Windsor is not entitled to this. The Duke should be addressed as "Your Royal Highness" and the Duchess as "Your Grace."

The Duke of Windsor drafted a passionate, bitter letter of protest to Winston Churchill:

...I am up against the famous Court ruling...whereby the King (or shall we say the Queen?) decreed that the Duchess shall not hold Royal Rank....I am quite sure that had your wife been the target of the vindictive jealousy...you would have the same repugnance to service under the Crown that I have....

Until this time, every wife automatically enjoyed the status of her husband. Now the rules were suddenly changed to deprive the Duchess of Windsor of royal acceptance. If the twice divorced American was not fit to be Queen of England, then she certainly was not fit to be a member of the royal family or admitted into their exalted circle. So no member of the House of Windsor ever received her until her husband's death, and even then she was accorded only minimal courtesy. "They were polite and kind to me," she said, "but they were cold. Very cold." The Duchess of Windsor died several years later at the age of ninety, alone and shriveled by infirmity.

Long before she became Queen, Elizabeth and her husband had assumed responsibility for restoring the royal family's reputation. Stolid and middle-class, they had drawn a stark contrast between themselves and the Champagne-swilling heir to the throne who cavorted at Fort Belvedere with his married lovers. The Yorks, or "Betty and Bert," as some newspapers called them, embodied domesticity. Elizabeth fostered this image by posing for pictures pouring tea and walking her corgis in the park. She invited Lady Cynthia Asquith to write *The Married Life of the Duchess of York,* a book whose cover announced that it was "Written and Published with Personal Approval of Her Royal Highness." After the birth of her first child, she allowed Miss Anne Ring, a former member of her staff, to write *The Story of Princess Elizabeth, Told with the Sanction of Her Parents.* With these frothy concoctions, she began establishing a myth that would elevate her beyond reproach.

"All done with mirrors," was how Noel Coward described the cunning mystery of mythmaking. But Elizabeth did it with feathers, a dazzling smile, a soft voice, and a tiara. With these ingredients she produced her soufflè of magic.

She was born in 1900 during the reign of Queen Victoria and lived through many monarchs and prime ministers. She survived two world wars and watched the British empire shrink to a small commonwealth. As she aged, she was celebrated as a befeathered emblem of a glorious past. She was history—the continuum that linked generations to their best memories of courage and duty and steadfastness.

From the beginning she understood the enduring power of image on the public imagination—the curtsies, the uniforms, the prancing horses, the movie star waves from the golden coach. She instinctively knew the value of such pageantry in stirring people's hearts. She was a genius at marketing herself and her husband, especially during the war years, when she propped up the weak, faltering man she had married and made him look like a king.

As the first commoner to marry into the House of Windsor, Elizabeth Bowes-Lyon showed the country how royalty should behave. She ingratiated herself as the Duchess of York with twirly little waves and gracious smiles. But she earned mass adoration as Queen during World War II when she stayed in London during the Blitz. She was photographed standing with the King in the bombed-out ruins of Buckingham Palace. "I'm almost happy that we've been hit," she said. "It makes me feel I can look the blitzed East End in the face."

Endearing herself forever to her embattled country, she refused to flee England to seek safety for herself and her children.

"They could not go without me," she said. "I could not possibly leave the King, and the King will never go."

When she and the King toured London's East End to inspect the bomb damage, a Jewish tailor advised the monarch "to put the empire in the wife's name." She became such a morale booster that Adolf Hitler called her the most dangerous woman in Europe. After the war, a grateful soldier rhapsodized:

> She put on her finest gown, her gayest smile and stayed in town, while London Bridge was falling down.

A photograph of the Queen in her crown was turned into a Christmas card during World War II and sent to every man and woman serving in the armed forces. It was a cherished keepsake from the monarch to his subjects.

Elizabeth was so ingenious at humanizing the royal family that she became an international media sensation in the newsreels shown in movie houses before the advent of television. Her radio speeches inspired hope throughout Occupied Europe as she told her listeners: "Wherever I go, I see bright eyes and smiling faces. For though our road is stony and hard, it is straight, and we know that we fight in a great cause." The sight of her smiling in the face of German bombardment inspired patriotism.

She put a caring face on the monarchy by visiting bombed sites throughout England. Beforehand, she had consulted with her couturier, Norman Hartnell, to make sure she was properly dressed. She would not wear anything as masculine as a military uniform, and she knew better than to appear imposing and regal. After urgent discussion, she decided she must never wear black—the color of mourning—or red, which would be too festive in wartime. Instead, as Hartnell wrote later, he designed a series of "combat frocks" in "the gentle colours—dusty pink, dusty blue and dusty lilac...because she wished to convey the most comforting, encouraging and sympathetic note possible."

Walking through bomb damage, she always wore her hat and her jewels. When asked if it was appropriate for her to wear her best dress while visiting the bomb-stricken areas, she smiled. "Of course," she said. "They would wear their best dresses if they were coming to see me."

She, in turn, despised Germans and declared she would shoot them before ever surrendering. Having watched the sorry parade of fallen kings and queens limping into London after their countries had been invaded, she vowed to defend herself and her crown. So she started taking revolver lessons every morning and insisted the King do likewise. "I shall not go down like the others," she declared.

She and the King became incensed by the Windsors' public admiration of Hitler. In April 1941, the Duke was reported as saying, "It would be very ill-advised of America to enter the war against Germany as Europe was finished anyway." The Duchess agreed. "If the U.S. entered the war, this country would go to history as the greatest sucker of all times." Then the Duke told the editor of the U.S. magazine *Liberty*, "...it would be a tragic thing for the world if Hitler was overthrown."

The Queen became more irate after seeing newsreel footage of the Duchess of Windsor traveling by luxury liner while people in England stood in freezing queues to collect morsels of fresh fish and bread. With her hand-tooled Hermès handbags, the Duchess traveled in high style during the war. She wore emeralds as big as eggs and enough furs to carpet a room, while war-rationed Britons mended old coats to stay warm. The Queen became especially agitated by a newspaper story about the Duchess flying first class from the Bahamas to New York just to get her hair done.

The Queen had demonstrated stout resolve in facing other obstacles in the past; the most pressing was her inability to get pregnant during the months after her wedding. The fertility problem stemmed from the "nervousness" that afflicted her husband, producing his debilitating stutter, distracting twitches, rickety legs, and bleeding ulcers. Most disturbing to the new bride was his inability to impregnate her. This was a disorder he shared with his older brother. When the Duchess of Windsor was asked why she had no children with her husband, she joked about the disability: "The Duke is not heir-conditioned."

Neither was his brother. For two barren years the Duchess of York was unable to conceive. She consulted several gynecologists and obstetricians about the problem. Finally, on the advice of her doctor, Lane Roberts, she and her husband submitted to the unorthodox science of artificial insemination. The arduous procedure of mechanically injecting his sperm into her uterus finally enabled her to get pregnant. Only because of this manual fertilization was she able to produce her first child, Elizabeth, in 1926, and her second, Margaret Rose, in 1930. The only comment recorded from her doctors after the birth of Elizabeth referred to the delivery by cesarean section: "A certain line of treatment was successfully adopted." Beyond that, the deferential British press did not report that the future Queen of England was a product of artificial insemination. "This was well-known in our circles at the time," said a royal family friend whose mother was a goddaughter of Queen Victoria. "My mother and the Duchess of York talked about it because they shared the same gynecologist.... The Duke had a slight...problem...with...a...his 'willy.'..."As George Bernard Shaw wrote: "Monarchs are not born; they are made by artificial hallucination."

As a commoner, the Duchess was respected for accepting the royal responsibility of producing an heir and a spare, even if it meant being artificially seeded. "Our family knew that Princess Elizabeth and Princess Margaret were born by artificial means," said a relative of the Earl of Arran. "It was revolutionary at the time, but it was not discussed publicly and probably never should be...."

By the end of the war, the Queen Mother had become a living saint to be praised and preserved. Because the country lionized her, the press followed suit and never printed a negative word about her. Even when every intimate detail of the royal family became newspaper fodder, she alone remained immune. The media respectfully refrained from reporting that as a result of intestinal surgery she wore a colostomy bag. Her incessant drinking, which might be described as incipient alcoholism in anyone else, was dismissed as mere tippling. Her propensity for gambling was never reported as an addiction, just an innocent pastime of a sweet old lady who happened to have installed in her house her own personal "blower," or bookie wire, to receive up-to-the-minute race results. Her support of white minority rule in Rhodesia was tagged not as racist, but rather as a right-wing political quirk. By the standards of her time, she was excused for calling people of color "blackamoors" and "nig nogs." "She is not fond of black folk," wrote Paul Callan in the *International Express*, "but these are, of course, traits typical of her age and class."

Even the satirical television program *Spitting Image* held back on lampooning the most beloved member of the royal family. "For the first show, we had prepared a sketch of the Queen Mother arm-wrestling Princess Margaret over a bottle of vodka," recalled Roger

Law, "but the producer, John Lloyd, refused to let us debut with that skit....We had to wait until the public accepted the show. The shock was that we treated the royal family as an ordinary family...."

"The Queen Mother was so untouchable by 1994 that I was prohibited from alluding to the possibility of her death in a piece of fiction," said writer Sue Townsend, author of *The Queen and I.* "When I adapted my book to be a play, the artistic director of the Royal Court Theater, Max Stafford-Clark, refused to let me use the scene of the Queen Mother's funeral. He was afraid of the public outcry and what might happen to him as a result. So I had to rewrite that part. I went along with it because I was in awe of the director and wanted the play produced."

When another writer reported some harmless remarks the Queen Mother had made over lunch, he was called a scoundrel. "I was denounced...as a cad for repeating the old lady's conversation," said A. N. Wilson, who broke the taboo of never repeating the unrehearsed words of a royal personage.

Writing in the *Spectator,* he reported the Queen Mother's merry recollection of an evening during the war when she met T.S. Eliot. She was worried that her children were not receiving a proper education, so she asked that a poetry evening be arranged at Windsor Castle.

"Such an embarrassment," she recalled. "We had this rather lugubrious man in a suit, and he read a poem...I think it was called 'The Desert.' And first the girls got the giggles, and then I did and then even the King."

"'The Desert,' ma'am? Are you sure it wasn't called 'The Waste Land'?"

"That's it," said the Queen Mother. "I'm afraid we all giggled. Such a gloomy man, looked as though he worked in a bank, and we didn't understand a word."

"I believe he *did* once work in a bank," said the writer. He was roundly criticized for presenting the beloved Queen Mother as a philistine. By then she had become an icon.

"Perhaps the most loved person in the Western world," suggested Sir Edward Ford, former assistant private secretary to the Queen.

"She is the embodiment of what royalty should be," said writer Robert Lacey.

She solidified her pedestal with more than seventy years of royal engagements: cutting ribbons, visiting regiments, christening ships, and laying cornerstones. That's how she earned her keep, which eventually cost British taxpayers about $1 million a year. She waved gaily, tilted her head coquettishly, and smiled sweetly.

"Work is the rent you pay for the room you occupy on earth," she said.

To the British, she was worth every shilling they paid to support her one butler, two drivers, two security guards, three castles, four maids, four ladies-in-waiting, eight footmen, ten servants, and fifteen stable personnel (to look after her fourteen horses).

"The Queen Mum is my love—the only one in the royal family I care about," said artist Fleur Cowles. "I don't know any of the others and I don't care to." Opening the door to her London drawing room, she pointed to a plush velvet love seat. "When Her Majesty Queen Elizabeth the Queen Mother comes for dinner, that's where she sits. And when she leaves, she always turns in the doorway, kicks up her heels like a chorus girl, and throws her arms in the air. It's such a cute exit."

The soft, cuddly appearance and sunny manner concealed layers of duplicity. Underneath the Queen Mother's feathers was flint. Stout-hearted and tough, she protected royalty's mystique by keeping its secrets. Throughout her life she was the warden who ensured that anything detrimental to the sweet myth was destroyed or buried forever. She had helped rescue the House of Windsor, and she intended to keep it standing. Even when she was well into her nineties she exercised enough influence to keep the British government from releasing the remaining evidence of the Windsors' sub-rosa contacts with the Third Reich. For more than fifty years she had guarded documents that detailed the Duke of Windsor's proposed separate peace agreement with the Nazis. She had kept sealed in the vaults of Windsor Castle all the King's papers, including the captured German war documents that summarized the Windsors' 1937 visit to Germany to meet with Hitler.

Within those documents were notes of a plan to return the Duke of Windsor to the throne after Germany's conquest of Europe. In July of 1940, as he was considering the invasion of Britain, Hitler decided to kidnap the Windsors and hold them in Berlin, from where the Duke would appeal to the British people to change governments and seek peace with Germany. Once the treaty was signed, the Duke and Duchess would be restored to the throne as puppet monarchs. Although the plan was never enacted, the Windsors' possible complicity with the Third Reich continued to taint the royal family.

The Queen Mother sailed into old age, smiling and undaunted. When she was ninety-six years old, she had hip replacement surgery. A few weeks after her hospitalization, she put on her blue silk hat, grabbed a walking stick, and visited an old age home. "I'm the oldest one here," she told the enfeebled pensioners. She bestowed smiles and sweet words and then departed, leaving the elderly residents feeling almost blessed.

"She has tremendous charm," said one woman. "All she says is 'I know, I know' and you feel rewarded. What a marvelous phrase. She changes inflection for every occasion: if she approves, she smiles and says, 'I know. I know.' If she's consoling someone in grief, she pats the person's arm and whispers, 'I know. I know.'"

Few people—only her household staff and her immediate family—ever see the iron frame under the marshmallow.

"A steel hand within a velvet glove," was how her husband's Foreign Secretary, Lord Halifax, described her.

"She was tough and ruthless," said historian John Grigg.

She herself agreed. "You think I am a nice person," she once confided to a friend to whom she was speaking about the Windsors. "I'm not really a nice person."

She had become the Crown's most ferocious custodian, and having invested her life in the monarchy, she would protect it until her death. She became more royal than royalty in guarding their mystique. Over the years she became the keeper of the secrets. She had learned early from her father.

For years she had shrouded the details surrounding her own birth. She airily dismissed questions about why her father, after eight children, missed the six-week deadline for registering her birth. He then put his historic name as fourteenth heir of the Earl of Strathmore to a lie. In doing so, he risked life imprisonment, which in 1900 was the extreme penalty for falsifying an official document. Instead he paid a fine of seven shillings and sixpence and stated that his daughter was born at St. Pauls Walben Bury, the family home in Hertfordshire. The Queen Mother maintained she was born in London.

This conflict gave rise to rumors over the years that after producing eight children, her thirty-nine-year-old mother finally had had enough. Some people have suggested that her father may have had an affair with a Welsh maid who worked at Glamis Castle in Scotland, and that this union produced the baby know as Elizabeth Bowes-Lyon. No evidence has been found to verify the suspicion, which may have arisen because of the unorthodox way her father filed her birth certificate.

"It really doesn't matter where she was born or if there were inaccuracies," said a Clarence House spokesman. "Strathmore did the evil deed and he is dead. If he did wrong, it didn't show."

The Queen Mother deflected scrutiny of her lineage to hide her family's hereditary defects. For generations the Strathmores had been haunted by the Beast of Glamis, which according to legend was the misshapen creature born to her grandfather's brother. Shaped like an egg with twisted spindly legs, this baby boy supposedly grew into a grotesque monster covered with long black hair. He was locked away in the castle for decades, his existence known only to his brother and three other people. The family covered their shame with secrecy. "We were never allowed to talk about it," said Elizabeth's older sister, Rose. "Our parents forbade us ever to discuss the matter or ask any questions."

This attitude toward physical deformities and mental illness was prevalent around 1920 when Elizabeth's young nieces were born. Katherine and Nerissa Bowes-Lyon, both retarded at birth, were secretly locked away in the mental hospital in Redhill, Surrey,

40

where they lived for decades. So great was the disgrace felt by the family that they recorded the two women as dead in 1941 in *Burke's Peerage,* the bible of British nobility.

"If this is what the family of the Bowes-Lyon told us, then we would have included it in the book," said Harold Brooks-Baker, editor of *Burke's Peerage.* "It is not normal to doubt the word of members of the royal family. Any information given to us by the royal family is accepted, even if we had evidence to the contrary...."

Such deference to the Crown helped the Queen Mother conceal any secrets that might have shamed the royal family. She hid the alcoholism of her husband and the homosexuality and drug addiction of his brother, Prince George, who eventually married and became the Duke of Kent. After the war she buried an explosive military report to King George VI from Field Marshall Montgomery and two confidential reports from Lord Mountbatten, which he described in a television interview as "too hot and uninhibited" to publish. She knew that these three documents, if ever made public after her husband's death, would reflect unfavorably on his stewardship during the war.

"The King was told everything," she admitted to Theo Aronson in 1993, "so, of course, I knew about everything as well. That is when I learned to keep things to myself. One heard so many stories, I became very cagey. And I have been very cagey ever since...."

FOUR

The Yorks, now the King and Queen of England, cultivated important American friendships in hopes of influencing public opinion in the United States. They wanted America to enter the war before it was too late for Great Britain.

In the spring of 1939 the King and Queen had invited Joseph P. Kennedy, the U.S. Ambassador to the Court of St. James's, and his wife, Rose, to spend a weekend at Windsor Castle. Over dinner in the Garter Throne Room, the Queen seated herself between the British Prime Minister, Neville Chamberlain, and Ambassador Kennedy. She had told the Ambassador how much she and the King had enjoyed their recent trip to the United States and how charmed they were by President and Mrs. Roosevelt, who entertained them at Hyde Park with hot dogs and beer.

That royal visit had caused a political ruckus in America, especially among upper-crust Republicans, who venerated Great Britain as "the mother country." One grande dame became so upset by the prospect of the monarchs' being subjected to the President's informal hospitality at Hyde Park that she appealed to the British Foreign Office to cancel that part of the visit.

"There is no proper arrangement for Secret Service men and police even in ordinary times," she wrote. "The house has no proper suites and rooms, etc., and the service represents a scratch lot of negroes and white, English and Irish. The Footman is a lout of a red-haired Irishman, and should only be carrying wood and coals and polishing shoes...."

The President, who was widely suspected—correctly—of trying to take America into a European war, was facing a tough reelection campaign in 1940. The Neutrality Act, then being debated in Congress, would limit America's ability to supply Britain with arms in case of war as well as limit Roosevelt's powers as President under the Constitution. Roosevelt hoped the act would be revised.

Roosevelt wanted the royal visit to be a public relations success so that Americans would be positively disposed to Great Britain and see the wisdom of giving military aid. But the President was almost stymied by the snobbery of Britain's class system, even among servants. He had tried to help the Hyde Park staff prepare for the royal visit by dispatching two black ushers from the White House. This incensed his mother's English butler, James, who refused to work with men of color in serving the monarchs. He insisted on taking his annual leave during the royal visit.

"Oh, but James," said Sara Roosevelt, "that's just when Their Majesties are going to be here."

"Madam," replied the butler, "I cannot be a party to the degradation of the British monarchy."

The King and Queen had requested that eiderdown comforters and hot-water bottles be provided for their ladies-in-waiting, which amused the President: the monarchs were visiting in June, when the weather was usually hot, even unbearably humid. He was also surprised by the attitude of his mother's butler, but then he did not understand that British servants could be as haughty as those they served. The President laughed aloud when he heard that the footman to King Edward VIII had walked off his job three years before when he encountered his master behaving in what he called "a most unbecoming manner." The footman explained: "Well, the butler, Mr. Osborne, sent me down to the swimming pool with two drinks. When I got there, what did I see but His Majesty painting Mrs. Simpson's toenails. My sovereign painting a woman's toenails! It was a bit much, I'm afraid, and I gave notice at once."

Showing the same hauteur, the Roosevelts' English butler left for vacation the day before the King and Queen arrived at Hyde Park. When Their Majesties were en route, the U.S. Ambassador to France, William C. Bullitt, sent a confidential memo to the President:

> The little Queen is now on her way to you together with the little King. She is a nice girl—eiderdown or no eiderdown— and you will like her, in spite of the fact that her sister-in-law, the Princess Royal, goes around England talking about "her cheap public smile." She resembles so much the female caddies who used to

carry my clubs at Pitlochry in Scotland many years ago that I find her pleasant....The little King is beginning to feel his oats, but still remains a rather frightened boy.

The King and Queen had made a royal visit to Paris the year before that was a public relations success with everyone except the French Premier, Édouard Daladier. He privately denounced the King as "a moron" and said the Queen was "an excessively ambitious young woman who would be ready to sacrifice every other country in the world so that she might remain Queen."

Ambassador Bullitt's 1939 memo to the President advised Roosevelt not to mention the Windsors to the King and Queen because "about a month ago the Duke of Windsor wrote to Queen Mary [his mother] that Bertie [his brother, the King] had behaved toward him in such an ungentlemanly way because of 'the influence of that common little woman,' the Queen, that he could have no further relations with Bertie. Brotherly love, therefore, not at fever heat."

The King and Queen arrived with their valets, maids, dressers, and ladies-in-waiting, and the British servants immediately started squabbling with their American counterparts.

The King's valet complained about the food and drink, saying it was far below what he was accustomed to in Buckingham Palace, which supposedly was getting by on war rations. Although the public was led to believe that the King and Queen and the two little Princesses were depriving themselves of meat, bread, and butter like everyone else in the country and sharing England's bleak fare of boiled potatoes, gray Brussels sprouts, and powdered eggs, those behind the Palace gates knew differently. The King and Queen sidestepped the country's strict food rationing and regularly ate roast beef and drank Champagne. Butter pats were monogrammed with the royal coat of arms, and dinners were served on gold plates.

"During the war, when the King and Queen were in London and their daughters at Windsor, the Princesses used to order their own meals," recalled René Roussin, the French chef who worked for the royal family from 1937 to 1946. "A typical day's menu for them began with buttered eggs for breakfast; boiled chicken with sieved vegetables—even when they were both in their teens, they still liked their vegetables sieved—potato crisps, and hot baked custard for lunch; bread and butter, cake, jelly, and toast for tea; and just some kind of broth followed by compote of pear with whipped cream for supper."

In London, no restaurant was allowed to charge more than ten shillings for a meal. But at the Palace, the King ordered two eggs and six rashers of grilled bacon for breakfast every day and grouse in season for dinner every night. The Queen, accustomed to a full meal at teatime, continued having her daily oatcakes, a rich dessert prepared by the Palace chef, which caused her to gain twelve pounds in one year.

"Her Majesty will not give up oatcakes," said her maid, who admitted having to let out the seams of the Queen's gowns.

The Queen insisted her tea be a special blend of China and Ceylon, brewed with London water that she had shipped to the United States with her luggage in heavy casks.

The vast amount of royal luggage—bulky wardrobes, numerous suitcases, crates of hat-boxes, bins of shoes—surprised the President's domestic staff, which had assumed the British monarchs were abiding by the same restrictions on clothes coupons as their subjects. The British servants reacted defensively. They knew what the public did not know—that the King was dazzled by gold-braided military uniforms and spent hours with his personal tailor being fitted every day. This obsession with fashion had started early.

"Unfortunately, Bertie takes no interest in anything but clothes, and again clothes," his father had complained. "Even when out shooting, he is more occupied with his trousers than his game!"

Equally concerned about his wife's appearance, the King winced when he heard her described as "dowdy." So he summoned couturier Norman Hartnell to the Palace to design a flattering wardrobe for her. Although silk was banned from sale to the public and used only to make parachutes, exceptions were made for the Queen, and by the time she left for America, she was changing her outfits as least four times a day.

During one photography session with Cecil Beaton, she posed in a pale gray dress with long fur-trimmed sleeves and a gray fox fur collar. She changed into a ruby-encrusted gown of gold and silver with ostrich feathers, then appeared in a spangled tulle hyacinth blue dress with two rows of diamonds as big as walnuts. For the last pose, she appeared in a champagne lace garden party dress that had been hand sewn with pearls to match the pearls that she had strewn through her hair.

The Queen's dresser had a full-time job just laying out the Queen's various outfits for the day and coordinating the morning and evening jewels she wanted to wear with each ensemble. The royal dresser felt insulted when she was interrupted by a White House usher to relay a message from the Queen to a lady-in-waiting.

"I am Her Majesty's maid," snapped the woman, "not a messenger girl." The White House usher did not understand the difference. Britain's rigid class system extended from the top of society to the bottom, or "the lower orders," as they were commonly called. In the hierarchy of royal service, household servants came first. They even had their own sitting room and dining room in the Palace. From their lofty perch, they looked down upon the stewards, clerks, and stenographers and refused to perform duties they deemed beneath them.

The King and Queen seemed unruffled by the fuss among their underlings. They felt at home in the country atmosphere of Hyde Park, especially when they found a tray of cocktails awaiting their arrival.

"My mother thinks you should have a cup of tea," said the President. "She doesn't approve of cocktails."

"Neither does my mother," said the King, gratefully reaching for a drink.

When the King and Queen returned to London, they dined with the U.S. Ambassador, and the Queen related this and other homey details of the Roosevelts' picnic for them at Hyde Park. She mentioned the emotional farewell she and the King received when hundreds of people gathered at the train station and spontaneously started singing "Auld Lang Syne."

Ambassador Kennedy had read the glowing press accounts of the royal visit to America in 1939. "The British sovereigns have conquered Washington, where they have not put a foot wrong," wrote Arthur Krock in *The New York Times,* "and where they have left a better impression than even their most optimistic advisers could have expected."

"They have a way of making friends, these young people," said Eleanor Roosevelt.

Even Kennedy, an isolationist, was impressed. But over dinner, as the Queen inched the conversation toward American foreign policy, he flared.

"What the American people fear more than anything else is being involved in a war," he told her. "They say to themselves, 'Never again!' and I can't say I blame them. I feel the same way."

"I feel that way, too, Mr. Kennedy," said the Queen. "But if we had the United States actively on our side, working with us, think how that would strengthen our position with the dictators."

The President agreed with the Queen. Within months Roosevelt asked for Kennedy's resignation. When the President heard that the Ambassador had told his private secretary, "Roosevelt and the kikes are taking us into war," FDR told his wife, "I never want to see that son of a bitch again." By that time the Ambassador—he relinquished the position but never the title—was despised in England for his appeasement policies. "He left London during the Blitz," said Conor O'Clery, Washington correspondent for the *Irish Times,* "and the British never forgave him."

The Queen did not have to resort to a hard sell with her American show business friends. The feeling among artists and entertainers was that if Britain were involved in a war, the United States was bound to come in sooner or later, because living in a totalitarian world was unthinkable.

The Queen was naturally drawn to show business people. The American theatrical producer Jack Wilson enjoyed special access to the Palace because he was the close friend and business partner of Noel Coward, who was the Queen's favorite playwright and part of her high camp coterie. After the abdication, Coward had endeared himself by suggesting that statues of Wallis Simpson be erected throughout England for the blessing she had bestowed on the British. "She gave us you," he said, "and saved us all from the reign of King Edward VIII." So when Wilson telephoned the Queen to say hello in 1939, he was immediately invited for tea.

Jack Wilson arrived at Windsor Castle and was escorted through the grand dining room, where the King and Queen had hired an artist to paint the backs of the Constable, Reynolds, and Gainsborough canvases with the cartoon faces of Mickey Mouse and Donald Duck to liven up the gloomy atmosphere for their children. Wilson was amused when the King's footman confided this small detail of royal family life. The servant then tiptoed across the Aubusson carpet, reached up, and slyly turned over a gilded portrait of Charles II to reveal the goofy grin of Walt Disney's floppy-eared dog Pluto.

Wilson followed the footman into the Queen's sitting room, where her thirteen-year-old daughter, Princess Elizabeth, was playing on the floor. Wilson smiled at the youngster and greeted her pleasantly.

"Well, hello there, cutie pie," he said. "How're you doing today?"

The footman froze, unable to continue into the room. The youngster stared hard at the producer. Then she raised her arm and pointed to the floor.

"Bow, boy, bow," she told the forty-year-old man.

The teenage heir to the throne had been trained to demand her royal entitlements.

"And you know what I did?" said the producer, laughing as he recalled his introduction to the young woman who would become the sixty-third sovereign of the oldest royal house in Europe. "I bowed my arse off because that little girl scared the living bejabbers out of me."

The Lord Chamberlain had had a similar experience when he encountered the Princess in a Palace corridor.

"Good morning, little lady," he said.

"I'm not a little lady," she snapped. "I'm Princess Elizabeth."

Hearing the youngster's uppity tone disturbed Queen Mary, her grandmother. An hour later the elderly Queen Mother had her granddaughter in tow as she knocked on the Lord Chamberlain's door.

"This is *Princess* Elizabeth," announced Queen Mary, "who hopes one day to be a *lady*."

Days later the Princess, in a fury, demanded a favor of her governess. The governess said no, but the Princess persisted. Finally she shouted: "This is royalty speaking." Her mother remonstrated: "Royalty has never been an excuse for bad manners."

Still, the young Princess never learned to conceal her imperiousness. From the age of ten she had been reared as the next Queen of England.* Platoons of liveried butlers, footmen, and chauffeurs bowed to her whenever she entered a room, and maids, nannies, and dressers fell to the floor in obeisant curtsies. And whenever she entered or departed the royal houses of Buckingham Palace, Windsor Castle, Sandringham, Balmoral, and Birkall, the scarlet- uniformed guards at the gates snapped to attention and performed the stately exercise of "presenting arms"—saluting her with a rifle or saber.

This royal treatment fascinated her. The first time she discovered the attention she commanded, she slipped away from her nurse and paraded back and forth in front of the Palace guard, who clicked his heels, raised his rifle, and stood ramrod straight each time she passed.

Her name was given to bone china, to hospitals, and even to chocolates. Her wax figure, sitting on the white pony she received for her fourth birthday, stood in Madame Tussaud's Wax Museum. Flags were flown on her birthday, and her face appeared on a six-cent stamp in Newfoundland. Her portrait hung in the Royal Academy, and her picture appeared on the cover of *Time* magazine. This reverence worried her father, who wrote to his mother,

* Between themselves, the Duke and Duchess of Windsor referred to the winsome Princess as Shirley Temple, who was the most successful child star in Hollywood history. Responding on cue to her mother, who said, "Sparkle, Shirley, sparkle," the movie moppet sang and danced and shook her ringlet curls to become the biggest box office draw of her day.

Queen Mary: "It almost frightens me that the people should love her so much. I suppose it is a good thing, and I hope she will be worthy of it, poor little darling."

The young Princess had a few ordinary experiences, such as Christmas shopping at Woolworth's, riding in the top deck of a bus, and traveling incognito on the underground. But she had never ridden in a taxi or placed her own telephone call. She was so protected that she had never contracted the childhood diseases of measles or chicken pox.* Her usual transportation consisted of a horse-drawn golden carriage, where she sat with her mother and grandmother, or the royal train with its nine cream leather coaches, gold-plated ventilators, gold electric light fixtures, and gold telephone. She was always accompanied by her governess, Marion ("Crawfie") Crawford; her guardian and dresser, Margaret ("BoBo") MacDonald; and her nurse, Clare ("Allah") Knight.

"We used to say that the first thing Nanny teaches a royal is how to ring for service," said a Palace employee. The youngster, who called herself Lilibet, certainly had learned that lesson well. By the age of seven she also knew her place in the line of succession.

"I'm three and you're four," she told her younger sister.

"No, you're not," said Margaret Rose, who

---

*In 1971, when Queen Elizabeth was forty-five years old, she caught chicken pox from her seven-year-old son, Edward. In 1982, at the age of fifty-six, she had her first wisdom tooth extracted.

thought her sister was talking about their ages. "I'm *three* and you're *seven*."

Knowing that his oldest daughter, Elizabeth, would follow him to the throne, the new King decided that she should be better prepared for her role than he was for his. He had been traumatized by the prospect of giving up grouse shooting every day to become King.

Minutes before his brother's abdication, he told his cousin Louis Mountbatten: "This is the most awful thing that has ever happened to me. I'm completely unfitted [sic] to be King. I've had no education for it."

He said that would not happen to his daughter, whom he began tutoring at an early age. He instructed her in the ceremonial duties of being a sovereign, and he made her study on her feet so she would become accustomed to long hours of standing in heavy robes to have her portrait painted. He told her she must keep a daily diary and showed her how to review troops and take a salute. He also shared the red boxes containing top-secret state papers that were delivered to him every day. Soon she approached new tasks by asking: "Will I have to do this when Papa dies?"

The first time her younger sister saw the King's equerry call for Elizabeth and escort her to the King's study to "do the boxes," she was curious.

"Does this mean that you will have to be the next Queen?" Margaret asked.

"Yes, someday," replied Elizabeth.

"Poor you," said Margaret Rose, who was

disgusted when her father became King and the family had to move into Buckingham Palace.

"What?" Margaret had asked. "Do you mean forever? I hate all this. I used to be Margaret Rose of York, and now I'm Margaret Rose of nothing."

But Elizabeth was wide-eyed when she saw a letter on the hall table addressed to "Her Majesty the Queen."

"That's Mummie now, isn't it," she said, awestruck.

By 1939 Lilibet was prefacing her sentences with "When I become Queen..."

"She makes it very plain to the Queen [her mother] that whereas she, the Queen, is a commoner, she, Princess Elizabeth, is of royal blood," said the Duke of Devonshire.

Although four years separated the two Princesses, they were reared as twins, and until they were teenagers, their mother dressed them identically in matching brown oxfords, coats with velvet collars, and little hats fastened on their heads by elastic bands. Featured frequently in the newspapers and newsreels, they became the paradigm for how all little girls should dress, sit, walk, talk, and behave.

The two Princesses played games together and performed plays and pantomimes for their parents on the stage built for them at Windsor Castle. Their mother liked to sing dance hall songs, while the King enjoyed dancing in a conga line. Their world, once described by their father as "us four," was filled with dogs and horses and servants but very few friends. They listened to Bing Crosby records, took weekly dancing classes, played the piano, and sang constantly. Because their mother stressed music over mathematics, they excelled at the former and neglected the latter.

When Germany invaded Poland in 1939, Britain declared war. Soon women and children were evacuated from London. The two Princesses remained in seclusion at Windsor for the next five years, traveling to London only to see the dentist. The Palace issued a statement that Princess Elizabeth, the heir presumptive,* was discontinuing her German lessons and, in another ploy for American intervention, would start studying U.S. history. Nothing was said about the education of Princess Margaret because she did not count: she was only a spare to the heir. Later, when Margaret wanted to study history with her sister's Eton tutor, she was told, "It is not necessary for you." Margaret exploded, "I was born too late!"

The biggest investment of time and attention was made in Elizabeth as the future sovereign, and she became as orderly, dutiful, and responsible as her father. "She is exactly the daughter that plain, conscientious King George and matronly Queen Elizabeth deserve," said *Time* magazine. "And that is precisely what her future subjects want her to be." Elizabeth shared her father's passion for horses, grouse

---

*Because she is female and first in line to the throne, she is *presumed* to be the heir. If she were male (far more preferable), she would be called the heir apparent.

shooting, and deer stalking. Like him, she did not much enjoy going to church. When a minister in Scotland promised to give her a book, she thanked him and asked that it *not* be about God. "I know everything about Him," she said.

She inherited her father's broad vaudevillian sense of humor, and together they laughed at the exaggerated antics of slapstick clowns wearing droopy drawers and doing pratfalls. Margaret, more like her mother, preferred sophisticated comedy and drawing room repartee. She was so spoiled as a child that her servants found her "terrible" and "absolutely impossible," but her proud and indulgent parents saw her outrageous behavior as merely "entertaining and engaging." They didn't bother holding Margaret accountable because she was never going to be Queen. As she once joked: "I don't have to be dour and dutiful like Lilibet. I can be as beastly as I want."

Inside the fortress of Windsor Castle the two Princesses bickered on occasion but became each other's best friends for life, with the older sister assuming the mentor's role.

"Margaret almost forgot to say 'Thank you,' Crawfie," Elizabeth reported to her governess, "but I gave her a nudge, and she said it beautifully."

Yet when Elizabeth became patrol leader for her own troop of Girl Guides, she spared no one, including her chatterbox sister.

"Here," she told Margaret, "I am not your sister, and I'll permit no slackness."

Margaret stuck out her tongue, not at all intimidated by her future sovereign. "You look after your empire," she told her at one point, "and I'll look after myself."

Nor was Margaret above berating the future Queen of England for overeating, especially when she indulged in sweets.

"Lilibet," she said, "that's the fourteenth chocolate biscuit you've eaten. You're as bad as Mother—you don't know when to stop."

Mother knew best how to handle her outspoken younger daughter. She simply ignored her, declining to react to any of Margaret's taunts.

"Mummy, why are you wearing those dreadful hairpins?" Margaret asked her mother one day. "They do not match your hair."

"Oh, darling," said the Queen before gliding off with a smile. "Are they really so awful?"

The two little Princesses shared the small, isolated world of royalty, where everyone tried to entertain them because that's what the King and Queen wanted—especially the King, who felt guilty that the war was depriving his daughters of a normal life. "Poor darlings," he wrote in his diary, "they have never had any fun yet." So he seized every opportunity to amuse them.

When Noel Coward began filming *In Which We Serve,* the movie based on the heroic exploits of Louis Mountbatten and the ship he commanded, HMS *Kelly,* the King and Queen were invited to visit the set, and they took the two little Princesses, who were entranced by the world of make-believe.

The King enjoyed the company of the glamorous Mountbatten, despite his excessive ambition and blatant self-promotions. The King secretly envied his cousin's dashing style and easy charm as he sailed along the surface of life without dropping anchor. The King even tolerated Mountbatten's exaggerated vanity and seemed more amused than offended when he took his medals and decorations on tour, producing them with theatrical flourish from a custom-built box with stacks of trays: "Did I show you my Star of Nepal?" The Queen was not so impressed. She distrusted Mountbatten because of his continuing friendship with the exiled Duke of Windsor, and years later, when he was Viceroy of India, she blamed him "for giving away the empire." Nor did she like his sleek, elegant wife, Edwina, who had inherited an immense fortune from her father, including Broadlands, the family estate in Hampshire.

"She's only partly English, you know," the Queen told one of her ladies-in-waiting. "Her mother was half-Jewish." The implication was that the "half-Jewish" part accounted for Edwina's taste in jazz, fast cars, cocktail parties, and moonlight swims in the nude—all unacceptable to the Queen, who now saw herself as the embodiment of English respectability.

"The Queen was far too clever to slam with a sledgehammer," said John Barratt, Mountbatten's private secretary. "She despised Edwina, who was named one of the best-dressed women in the world and looked like a gazelle in her Chanel suits, while the Queen made her suits look like slipcovers on fire hydrants. But the Queen never overtly sliced Edwina up. Rather, her cuts were sly and deftly delivered, even in death. When Lady Mountbatten died in her sleep in 1960, the Queen, who by then was the Queen Mother, attended the funeral service in Romsey Abbey but returned to Clarence House to view the burial at sea on television. As Edwina's coffin was lowered into the water, she smiled and said: 'Oh, my. Edwina always did want to make a splash.'"

During the early days of their reign, the King and Queen felt insecure as they struggled to lift the weight of Edward's abdication from the throne. They worried that Winston Churchill was stealing their limelight. "K. and Q. feel Winston puts them in the shade," the Conservative MP Victor Cazalet wrote in his diary of June 1940. After visiting with the King's courtiers, he wrote, "We talk of K. and how Winston quite unconsciously has put them [King and Queen] in background. Who will tell him?"

The motives of Lord Mountbatten, or "Uncle Dickie," as he was known to the family, were even more suspect. The Queen objected when he started addressing the issue of her elder daughter's future husband. He first raised the subject when Princess Elizabeth was only thirteen years old; the Queen dismissed the discussion as premature, although her mother-in-law, Queen Mary, already had compiled a list of eligible young men to be considered. Her possibilities, all of royal blood, included Prince Charles of Luxembourg, who was considerably younger than Elizabeth, and Prince Gorm of Denmark.

Unfazed, Mountbatten persisted through the years by strategically placing his handsome nephew Prince Philip of Greece at various family affairs. He encouraged the young man, whom he treated as a surrogate son, to ingratiate himself with the King and Queen and to get to know Lilibet, who was his third cousin. Mountbatten suggested that Philip correspond with Elizabeth ("A card here, a note there, would be very nice, my boy") during the war, so by the time Philip was eighteen, he, too, was seeing himself as a potential prince consort.

When he went to sea, Philip shocked his navy skipper by divulging his uncle's scheme. Vice Admiral Harold Tom Baillie-Grohman was Captain of the battleship *Ramillies* in the Mediterranean during the summer of 1939. As a favor to Lord Mountbatten, he had taken on board the midshipman known as Prince Philip of Greece. He told the young man, who was born in Greece to a German Danish father of the house of Schleswig-Holstein-Sonderburg-Glucksburg and a German mother (Battenberg/Mountbatten), that he would not be able to advance in the Royal Navy as a Greek citizen. Philip understood and said that he wanted to become a naturalized British subject. He knew his career in the British navy would not progress if he didn't give up his Greek nationality. Greece was then a neutral country, and England could not risk having even a distant heir to the Greek throne (Philip was sixth in the line of succession) killed by enemy action while serving on a British warship.

"Then came the surprise," the Admiral wrote in his diary. "Prince Philip went on to say: 'My Uncle Dickie has ideas for me; he thinks I could marry Princess Elizabeth.' I was a bit taken aback and after a hesitation asked him: 'Are you really fond of her?'

"'Oh, yes, very,' was the reply, and 'I write to her every week.'"

The Admiral added to his diary entry in brackets: "I wrote this conversation down directly afterwards and so it is pretty correct."

Two years later, in 1941, Philip, twenty years old, was still corresponding with the fifteen-year-old Princess. During a holiday visit in Cape Town, South Africa, his cousin Princess Alexandra of Greece saw the midshipman bent over his stationery. She asked to whom he was writing.

"Princess Elizabeth of England," said Philip.

"But she is only a baby!"

"But perhaps I'm going to marry her."

Alexandra was crestfallen. "I suspect I was a little in love with Philip myself," she admitted years later. "In my teens, there was a prospect that I might marry him....Our families discussed it."

Philip had become the ward of relatives when his own family fell apart. His father, Prince Andrew, was the seventh child of George I of the Hellenes. His mother, Princess Alice, was the daughter of Prince Louis of Battenberg, First Sea Lord of England at the outbreak of World War I. His father was a professional soldier in the Greek army. When Turkey invaded Greece in 1922, Andrew was accused of treason for disobeying orders and abandoning his post under enemy fire. He was tried, convicted, and jailed. As he sat in prison facing possible execution by a firing squad, his wife appealed to her powerful British relatives to save her husband's life. The King, George V, remembered what had happened to his Russian cousin ("dear Nicky") and dispatched a ship to Greece to forcibly remove Andrew and his family. The Prince, accompanied by his wife, who was deaf, and their four daughters, boarded the HMS *Calypso*. He was carrying an orange crate that contained his only son, Philip, eighteen months old.

The platinum blond toddler had been born on a kitchen table on the Greek island of Corfu in a house, Mon Repos, with no electricity, no hot water, and no indoor plumbing. He learned sign language to communicate with his mother, who had turned deaf after catching German measles at the age of four. He also learned English, French, and German but did not speak a word of Greek. After being evacuated from Greece with his family, he spent nine years living outside Paris with his parents, who were royal but not rich. In disgraced exile, they lived in borrowed houses, wore shabby hand-me-downs, and accepted the charity of relatives and friends to feed, clothe, and educate their children.

Within nine months in 1930, Philip's four older sisters, who had been educated in Germany, married German noblemen. One was an SS Colonel on Himmler's personal staff, and the others were Princes who supported the Nazis during World War II. One sister, Sophie, named her eldest son Karl Adolf in honor of Adolf Hitler. With his four daughters securely married, Philip's father abandoned his borrowed home to live on the yacht of his mistress in Monte Carlo, where he became addicted to the gaming tables. He left behind his ten-year-old son. His wife—Alice, Princess of Greece—collapsed. After the separation she suffered a nervous breakdown, which in retrospect appears to have been a traumatic menopause. No longer able to care for her young son, she was institutionalized in Switzerland.

She emerged a few years later, found religion, and established the Christian Sisterhood of Martha and Mary, an order of nuns who helped the sick and needy in Greece. During the war she sheltered Jewish families in Greece and was posthumously honored for heroism by Israel. Even though she had been married and borne five children, she dedicated herself to celibacy. For the rest of her days she wore a gray habit belted by a white cord and with a veil and wimple.

While Philip's mother was incapacitated, his maternal grandmother, the Dowager Marchioness of Milford Haven, stepped in to care for the ten-year-old boy, who was sent to England. When she died a few years later, the responsibility for Philip fell to her oldest son, George, the Marquess of Milford Haven. His wife, Nada, who bathed her feet in Champagne, was as exotic as Edwina Mountbatten. Both were rich, restless, and reputed to be sexually adventurous. During the 1934 custody trial for Gloria Vanderbilt in New York City, a maid testified to seeing evidence of a lesbian relationship between young Gloria's mother and Nada. "She put her arms around Mrs. Vanderbilt and kissed her," said the maid. The lurid testimony about "kissing on the lips" was not reported in the British newspapers because the Milford Havens were close to the British royal family and the press would not report anything that reflected negatively on the monarchy. That royal protection extended to Nada's husband, George Milford Haven, who was bisexual and obsessed with pornography. According to his personal financial records, he spent more than $100,000 amassing a vast collection of albums of erotic photographs and sadomasochistic books dealing with incest, homosexuality, bestiality, and family orgies, where mother and son joined father and daughter in sexual relations. George invested a fortune in buying catalogs for artificial genitalia, aphrodisiacs, horsewhips, and instruments for self-flagellation. After his death, part of his pornography collection ended up in a private case in the British Museum. He was only forty-six when he died of cancer in 1938, and the task of looking after Philip fell to George's younger brother, Lord Louis Mountbatten. "That's when Uncle Dickie took over," said Philip. "Before that no one thinks I ever had a father....Most people think that Dickie's my father, anyway."

Within ten years Philip had attended four schools, all paid for by various relatives. One rich aunt financed his first two years at The Elms, a school for wealthy Americans in St. Cloud, near Paris. His British relatives paid for his next four years at the Old Tabor School, Cheam, in Surrey, one of England's oldest, most traditional preparatory schools. Then his sisters decided he should be educated in Germany, so at the age of twelve—in 1933—he was enrolled in Schloss Salem in Baden, a school run by a brother-in-law. "Scholarship was not important when Philip and I were going to school at Salem," recalled actress Lilly Lessing. "The emphasis then was on courage, honesty, and taking care of people who were weaker than you...and Philip, who was very athletic, excelled even then. He was very much influenced by Dr. Kurt Hahn—we all were—but Dr. Hahn was Jewish, so he had to leave Germany. He sought refuge in Scotland, where he started Gordonstoun, and Philip followed him a year later."

Kurt Hahn, who was described by some

former students as "strong and dogmatic, probably a repressed homosexual," ran an experimental school that became the fore-runner for Outward Bound. All discussion of sex was forbidden at Hahn's school, where the military curriculum included a rigorous regime of exhausting exercise, two icy show-ers a day, and bracing hikes before break-fast. Philip, who became one of Hahn's most devoted followers, thrived at Gordonstoun, earning good grades and excelling at sports. He became captain of the cricket and hockey teams.

In his five years at Gordonstoun, his family never visited him once, and without a home of his own, he was shuffled off to relatives for holidays. He received some spending money from one of his uncles, the Crown Prince of Sweden, but it was never enough to cover all his expenses. Frequently he had to borrow clothes from his friends, who remember scrambling to find him a suit, cuff links, and collar studs so that he could be dressed properly for the wedding of his cousin Marina to the Duke of Kent.

After graduation from Gordonstoun, Philip wanted to join the Royal Air Force and become a fighter pilot. But his uncle Dickie steered him into the navy, saying it was the only branch of military service acceptable to the aristoc-racy. "The RAF is for the working class....All of our best kings have served in the Royal Navy," said Mountbatten. "I firmly believe that a naval training is the best possible training for royal duties." So Philip enrolled in the Royal Naval College at Dartmouth.

He was quite candid about why when he met the political diarist Sir Henry ("Chips") Channon. While visiting his mother in Athens, Philip spoke openly to Channon about his reasons for not becoming a fighter pilot, and Channon recorded the conversation on January 21, 1941: "I went to an enjoyable Greek cocktail party. Philip of Greece was there. He is extraordinarily handsome. He is to be our Prince Consort, and that is why he is serving in our Navy."

By then the young midshipman knew his life's direction and was steering himself toward an arranged marriage to the future Queen of England. Yet three years before, he had fallen in love with the most photographed girl in the world. Her name was Cobina Wright Jr., and Philip was bewitched. He met her in Venice during a holiday visit to his aunt Aspasia, the widow of King Alexander of Greece.

Philip had grown up around royalty—in addition to his uncle the Crown Prince of Sweden, another uncle was the exiled King of Greece, who was married to Princess Marie Bonaparte. She had once been the lover of the Prime Minister of France and later a disciple and patroness of Sigmund Freud. Philip's cousin Princess Alexandra married the King of Yugoslavia, and his favorite cousin, Princess Frederika, granddaughter of the Kaiser and a former Hitler Youth member, became Queen of Greece. As a child Philip had spent time at

Kensington Palace in London, the royal palaces of Bucharest and Sinaia, and the royal residence in Transylvania, visiting his cousin Prince Michael of Rumania. He called Queen Marie of Rumania "Aunt Missie." He also visited another aunt, Queen Sophie of Greece, who was the Kaiser's sister.

Accustomed to White Russians with gray teeth and European royals with high cheekbones, Philip had never experienced the dazzling megawatt glamour of American movie stars. Cobina Wright Jr. was all of that and more. She was Hollywood *and* high society, which was America's version of royalty. A spellbinding blond beauty, she had appeared on the covers of *Life* and *Ladies' Home Journal* as part of the Brenda Frazier debutante set. "That was when society really mattered," said her mother, Cobina Wright Sr., a society columnist for the Hearst newspapers and a social mountaineer on the level of Philip's uncle Dickie.

"My little Cobina was more than just a mere starlet," she said. "After all, her father—my former husband—was a multimillionaire who was in the *Social Register*." Following a nasty public divorce, Cobina Sr. lost her lofty listing in the *Social Register*. Without her husband's money she was forced to earn a living, which she did by collecting the celebrities of her day—generals, politicians, movie stars, and those she breathlessly described as "the crème de la crème of society."

"Mother was—well, so boisterous, so aggressive, always striving so hard to get to know the most famous, the most important people, that it used to embarrass me," her daughter said.

An enterprising stage mother, Cobina Wright Sr. was grooming "little Cobina" for a career in the movies to be capped by an illustrious marriage. "Certainly, Cobina is the 'most' girl," she said in 1938. "Most photographed, most publicized, most sought after." By then her promotions had persuaded press agents to dub her eighteen-year-old daughter as "Miss Manhattan of the New York World's Fair," "the Best Dressed New York Supper Club Hostess," and "the Most Beautiful Girl in Palm Beach." She also made sure her daughter was described as "the darling of high society."

At the time Cobina Jr. met Prince Philip, she was singing in nightclubs, modeling for John Robert Powers, and working under contract to 20th Century-Fox, along with Linda Darnell and Gene Tierney, later the sultry lover of John F. Kennedy and future wife of Oleg Cassini.

Philip was attracted the minute he saw the stunning young woman sitting in Harry's Bar in Venice with her mother and an Italian Countess. He was struck by her blinding good looks. She had none of the stony haughtiness of his royal European female cousins and looked more beguiling than the snooty young women of the aristocracy who were pursuing him so aggressively. This young woman combined the sunny insouciance of California beaches with the sleek sophistication of Manhattan nightclubs. Blond, lithe, and graceful, she was as bright and shiny as a new American penny. Her long, lean, leggy beauty matched his own. He immediately left his cousin, Princess Alexandra, and strode across the room to Cobina's table, where he nonchalantly accepted the curtsies of the two older women, who jumped up as he approached. They had recognized him at once and were enthralled to be in his presence. Young Cobina did not know who he was, but she stood up anyway and started to curtsy like her mother. Philip quickly extended his foot as if to trip her.

"Don't you dare," he said. "I'm just a discredited Balkan prince of no particular merit or distinction. My name is Philip of Greece."

"Just Philip of Greece? No last name?" she asked.

"Just Philip of Greece," he said.

Little Cobina was intrigued as Philip tried to explain that, traditionally, royal princes did not have last names because everyone in the land was supposed to know who they were. Only the lower orders needed last names for identification. "Because there are so many of them," said Philip, smiling, "and so few of us."

He told her how he always crossed out "Mr." at the top of the Admiralty forms and wrote in "Philip, Prince of Greece." Somehow he managed to sound almost democratic and down-to-earth as he described the imperial prerogatives that separated royals from commoners. He dismissed the ceremonial rights as bothersome, and Cobina was charmed. Philip was so entranced that he stayed in Venice for the next three weeks to be her escort. They accepted every party invitation her mother engineered, dancing and dining and drinking other people's champagne. Later, Cobina Sr. said the couple spent "passionate" evenings in gondolas on the Grand Canal. "Afterward Philip followed me to London," confided her daughter.

Ignoring the marriage that awaited him with Princess Elizabeth, Philip gave his heart to the American beauty. He proposed to her, insisted they consider themselves engaged, and looked upon Cobina Sr. as his future mother-in-law. He even inscribed a photograph of himself: "To my dear Madre, from Philip." He vowed to pursue her daughter to the United States.

"I shall come to America and get a job," he said, "and take the name of Augustus Jenks."

Cobina Sr. was ecstatic that a prince was proposing marriage to her daughter. That he sprang from one of Europe's most discredited royal families and lived on charity was only a slight concern. "A prince without a principality" was how she described the handsome young Viking. With or without money, he was still royalty. So she was determined to encourage his affair with her daughter. She gleefully accepted his suggestion that he leave Venice to follow them to London, and she was flattered when he invited himself to share their invitation from British actress Bea Lillie for a weekend at her country home.

"Philip gave me an impression at the time of a huge, hungry dog," said his cousin Alexandra, "rather like a friendly collie who had never had a kennel of his own and responded to every overture with eager tail wagging."

After three weeks in Venice, Cobina and Philip spent another week in England, dining, dancing, and walking London's streets, hand in hand. They cried as they watched the French film *Mayerling,* a sad romance starring Charles Boyer and Danielle Darrieux. The night before Cobina and her mother sailed for America, Philip went to the Claridge Hotel to say good-bye. He gave Cobina a small gold bracelet with the words "I Love You" dangling close to a Greek flag. He cried again as he kissed her good-bye.

For the next three years he wrote to her twice a week. "They were impassioned love letters," said Gant Gaither, one of Cobina's lifelong friends. "He said he planned to woo her to marriage, no matter what. He desperately wanted to marry her, but Cobina Jr. just wasn't all that interested."

Other friends confirm the romance. "No question about it," said writer Stephen Birmingham, who spent hours with Cobina Jr. in 1973 to write an article for *Town & Country.* "She did have an affair with Prince Philip, and her mother wanted her to marry him, but she just didn't want to. She fell in love with

Palmer Beaudette instead and married him in 1941. Her mother never forgave her."

Cobina Sr. kept writing to the young Prince long after her daughter had discarded him to marry Beaudette, an heir to an automobile fortune. The resilient Prince, still serving in the Royal Navy, resumed correspondence with his cousin Princess Elizabeth of England. But for the rest of his life, he, like his father, would be susceptible to the charms of actresses.

"At that time, most girls had someone they wrote to at sea or at the front," recalled Elizabeth's governess, Marion ("Crawfie") Crawford. "I think at the start she liked to be able to say that she, too, was sending off an occasional parcel and writing letters to a man who was fighting for his country."

One day Crawfie noticed Philip's photograph on the Princess's mantelpiece.

"Is that altogether wise?" Crawfie asked. "A number of people come and go. You know what that will lead to. People will begin all sorts of gossip about you."

"Oh, dear, I suppose they will," the Princess replied.

The picture disappeared a few days later. In its place was another one of Philip with a bushy blond mustache and beard covering half his face.

"There you are, Crawfie," said the Princess. "I defy anyone to recognize who that is. He's completely incognito in that one."

Rumors started anyway, and soon the backstairs gossip ended up in a newspaper item that it was Prince Philip of Greece whose photograph graced the bedroom of Princess Elizabeth. Uncle Dickie was delighted.

"Dear Philip" and "Dear Lilibet" letters crisscrossed from Windsor Castle to destroyers in the Mediterranean, the Straits of Bonifacio, Algiers, Malta, Suez, Ceylon, and Australia. The midshipman, who had formally renounced his claim to the Greek throne, was promoted in 1942 from the rank of sublieutenant to lieutenant. The next year Philip returned to England and did not go back to sea for four months. During that time he was invited to Windsor Castle for Christmas. Years later he said he accepted the invitation "only because I'd nowhere particular to go." He told risqué jokes to Queen Mary, who pronounced him "a very bright young man." He regaled King George VI with reports of German aircraft dive-bombing his ship off Sicily and bragged about dodging mines and torpedoes, accentuating his part in helping win a great victory. "It was a highly entertaining account," the King said later. Knowing that Philip had been cited for valor, the King had listened attentively, but there was something about the brash young man with his loud laugh and blunt manner that irritated him. As an overprotective father, he could not envision his beloved Lilibet marrying any man, and certainly not one as rough as Philip. Even worse, he wasn't rich and didn't dress like a gentleman. "His wardrobe is ghastly," said the King. "Simply ghastly."

Lord Mountbatten's valet, John Dean, agreed. "Prince Philip did not seem to have much in the way of civilian clothing," he recalled. "His civilian wardrobe was, in fact, scantier than that of many a bank clerk....I think he had to manage more or less on his naval pay. He did not bring much with him when he came to London, sometimes only a razor....He did not have his own hairbrushes....Either he was not too well looked after in the navy, or he was careless, for often he did not have a clean shirt. At night, after he had gone to bed, I washed his shirt and socks and had them ready for him in the morning. I also did his mending."

Philip's father, sixty-two years old, died in 1944 in the arms of his rich mistress. He had not seen his wife or son for five years. Penniless, Prince Andrew left his only son an estate that consisted of a battered suitcase filled with two moth-eaten suits, a worn leather frame, and a set of ivory shaving brushes. Philip did not get around to collecting his meager inheritance until 1946. Then he had the suits altered to fit him so he would have civilian clothes to wear when not in uniform. But the shiny gabardine hand-me-downs did not impress His Majesty, who counted a man without tweeds or plus fours as a man without breeding. Elizabeth had insisted that her father invite Philip to join them for a grouse shoot at Windsor, but the King balked because Philip did not own plus fours. Philip didn't know what they were. The King explained that the trousers were so called because they were four inches longer than ordinary knickerbockers—the baggy knee pants that golfers wore.

"Then he can wear a pair of yours," Elizabeth said to her father.

The King grudgingly agreed. He still retained reservations about the young man who never wore pajamas or bedroom slippers, had no formal clothes, and was unembarrassed by his scuffed shoes. The King felt that Prince Philip had been reared as a commoner, not as a royal.

The King's private secretary, Sir Alan (Tommy) Lascelles, dismissed Philip as a hooligan. "He was rough, ill-mannered, uneducated, and would probably not be faithful," he said, according to writer Philip Ziegler.

The monarch marked a man by what he wore and could not understand his lack of interest in buttons and bows. While Philip was always courteous and deferential to "Uncle Bertie and Aunt Elizabeth," he was still too assertive and familiar to suit the King. As far as the Queen was concerned, Philip made himself *too* much at home; she rebuked him several times for ordering the servants around. Neither she nor her husband realized then that their gawky seventeen-year-old daughter had marked the young man for marriage.

"I realized they were courting long before it got in the newspapers," said Charles Mellis, who for twelve years was chef on the royal train. "I saw something of the way they laughed, teased, and looked at each other while traveling together. And I shall never forget the time I heard the Queen Mother call out to them, 'Now, you two, stop kicking each other under the table and behave properly.'"

Princess Margaret teased her sister unmercifully about having a crush on Philip, but the King and Queen seemed oblivious. They noticed that Elizabeth was growing up in 1944 when they attended a small dinner dance given by the Duchess of Kent. There they saw Philip dancing almost every dance with their eldest daughter and being photographed helping her with her fur coat. But they never considered the prospect of marriage until shortly after Elizabeth's eighteenth birthday, when Uncle Dickie nudged his cousin King George of Greece to broach the subject with her father. King George VI turned on Mountbatten, saying he "was moving too fast." Later, in a letter to his mother, Queen Mary, he wrote:

We both think she is far too young for that now. She has never met any young men of her own age....I like Philip. He is intelligent, has a good sense of humour and thinks about things in the right way....We are going to tell George that P. had better not think any more about it at present.

Philip's plotting uncle was not to be discouraged. He seized the promise implied by "at present" and began campaigning to get Philip to switch his citizenship and religion so he would be perfectly situated for a royal marriage later. With British troops engaged on the side of the Greek government in the civil war, Mountbatten was told that making Philip a British subject might be misinterpreted and indicate British support for the Greek royalists or, conversely, be misconstrued as a sign that Britain regarded the royalist cause as lost and was giving Philip some sort of sanctuary. So the issue had to be postponed until the Greek general election and plebiscite on the monarchy had been held in March 1946.

Mindful of the animosity toward his own German roots, Mountbatten worried about Philip's guttural surname—Schleswig-Holstein-Sonderburg-Glucksburg—and his ties to his sisters and their German husbands, who supported Hitler's Third Reich. Philip was especially close to his brother-in-law, Berthold, the Margrave of Baden. Mountbatten also fretted about Prince Philip of Hesse, for whom Philip had been named. That German relation was Hitler's personal messenger and functioned so effectively for the Führer that he was awarded an honorary generalship in the Storm Troopers. Until his death in 1943, another of Philip's uncles—Prince Christopher of Hesse—was the head of the secret phone-tapping service in Göring's research office; this unit eventually became the Gestapo, the Nazi's secret state police.

Mountbatten was determined to put as much distance as possible between Philip and his German roots. The wily uncle knew how crucial it was for his nephew to be accepted by the British establishment, so he wrote to the British Commissioner of Oaths, saying that Philip had lived most of his life in England and joined the Royal Navy before the war with the intention of making it his life's career. "He has been brought up as an Englishman who rides well, shoots well, and plays all games such as football with more than usual ability," wrote Mountbatten.

He then wrote to Philip, saying that he was proceeding "full steam ahead" on the naturalization process so that Philip would be "totally acceptable" to pursue his romance with Princess Elizabeth. Philip pleaded with his uncle to slow down.

"Please, I beg of you," he wrote, "not too much advice in an affair of the heart or I shall be forced to do the wooing by proxy."

Philip knew how upset the King and Queen were about the article that had appeared in *The New York Times* entitled "Marriage à la Mode" and asserting that the most likely candidate for the hand of Princess Elizabeth was Prince Philip of Greece. The story had been officially denied by the Palace. But factory workers in England, depressed by six years of war, were starved for romance. When their future Queen made her first public appearance after the unconditional surrender of Germany in 1945, the crowds startled her with their boisterous shouts: "Where's Philip?" "How's Philip?" "Are you going to marry Philip?"

"It was horrible," she later told her sister.

"Poor Lilibet," said Margaret. "Nothing of your own. Not even your love affair."

FIVE

By 1945 the House of Windsor had been remodeled. The Windsors had repainted their dark German foundation with bright British colors and fashioned the exterior with an attractive new facade. The false front concealed the family flaws and allowed the renovated German house to look decidedly English—so English that by the end of World War II, the dynasty designed by dodgery was never more popular. Having removed itself from politics and no longer in danger of being damaged by factional disputes, the institution stood as a model of respectability. The monarchy, personified by the royal family, symbolized duty, decorum, and decency.

After the Allies crushed Nazi Germany, Britons discarded their courageous wartime leader Prime Minister Churchill, but they embraced their shy little monarch. On the day Germany surrendered, crowds surrounded Buckingham Palace, cheering and shouting for their beloved King and Queen. The royal family, which embodied Britain's sense of high moral purpose, had become the center of life in the United Kingdom. As the royal couple stepped out onto the balcony to wave, a voice in the throng shouted: "Thank God for a good King!" Deeply moved, George VI stepped forward and stammered: "Th-th-thank God for a g-g-good people!"

With the war finally over, the King wanted to make up for lost time with his family, especially with his eldest daughter. He planned picnics at Balmoral and shoots, hunts, and deer stalks at Sandringham so she could take part in his favorite pursuits. Elizabeth enjoyed spending time with her father, but the nineteen-year-old heir presumptive, who had been confined to Windsor Castle for six years, longed to sample the swing music of London nightclubs.

The dutiful daughter was growing up. She had her own lady-in-waiting, her own bedroom suite, and her own chauffeur-driven Daimler. She had never gone to school or visited a foreign country and had yet to draw her own bath, prepare a meal, or pay a bill; but she was selecting her own clothes. While her future subjects were still restricted to clothing coupons and wearing skirts made of curtains and trousers cut down from overcoats, she had her own couturier and was ordering strapless satin evening gowns.

"I'd like a car of my own, too," she told a friend, "but there's so damn much family talk about which make I must have that I don't think I'll ever get one."

Everything pertaining to Elizabeth was subject to intense discussion. Her father was not a man of initiative. Afraid of putting the wrong foot forward, he worried constantly about appearances and what people might think. He did not feel secure about making a decision until he had consulted all his courtiers. His wife, who rarely worried about anything, could not always make up her mind about what was best for their older daughter. So whether it was a car, a fur coat, or a new horse for Elizabeth, it was never a casual decision for her parents.

"They wanted the best for her," recalled Crawfie, her governess, "and it is never easy for parents to decide what that best is."

The only topic the King and Queen quickly reached agreement on was Philip of Greece. They felt their daughter was far too interested in the navy lieutenant, but only because she had not met any other men. So they started organizing tea dances, dinner parties, theater outings, and formal balls so she could meet the eligible sons of the aristocracy. They also invited the single military officers stationed near Windsor Castle. Elizabeth pronounced the chinless aristocrats as "pompous, stuffy, and boring," and her sister dismissed the officers as afflicted with "bad teeth, thick lips, and foul-smelling breath." Her parents' diversionary tactic was not lost on her grandmother Queen Mary, who referred to the cluster of young officers suddenly popping up at the Palace as "the Body Guard." Queen Mary's lady-in-waiting thought the King was simply an overpossessive father who could not face the prospect of his elder daughter's falling in love. "He's desperate," she said.

In 1946, when Philip returned to England, Elizabeth invited him to visit the family at Balmoral. She had not seen him for over three years. It had been Christmas of 1943 when he had chased her through the corridors of Windsor Castle, wearing a huge set of clattering false teeth that made her scream with laughter.

"I once or twice spent Christmas at Windsor, because I'd nowhere particular to go," Philip admitted many years later. "I suppose if I'd just been a casual acquaintance, it would all have been frightfully significant. But if you're related—I mean, I knew half the people there, they were all relations—it isn't so extraordinary to be on kind of family relationship terms with somebody. You don't necessarily have to think about marriage."

At the time, Elizabeth had delighted in her cousin's* juvenile antics and practical jokes, especially when he offered her nuts from a can and a toy snake popped out or when he handed her dinner rolls and made what he called "rude intestinal noises." She had laughed so hard at the time, she couldn't continue eating. Drawn to Philip's broad slapstick humor and his handsome good looks, she could hardly wait to see him again. She began asking her governess about love and marriage.

"What, Crawfie," she asked, "makes a person fall in love?"

"I would try to explain to her the deep common interests that cannot only first draw a man and a woman together immediately, but hold them together for life," said the governess. "The Princess listened attentively."

*Philip and Elizabeth were second cousins once removed through King Christian IX of Denmark, third cousins through Queen Victoria, and fourth cousins once removed through King George III.

"I guess it really started in earnest at Balmoral [in 1946]," Philip said, recalling the pretty twenty-year-old Princess, who still laughed at his jokes.

"I still recall the occasions when Prince Philip was an honored guest of Princess Lilibet—as we all called her—at those after-the-theater parties when he was on leave from the navy," recalled René Roussin, the former royal chef. "Then I would be asked—as a special request from the Princess—to send up some lobster patties, of which Prince Philip was especially fond."

After Philip had spent several days with the royal family at their Scottish castle, the King felt he had overstayed his welcome. "The boy must go south," he told his favorite equerry, RAF Wing Commander Peter Townsend. So Philip left. He later invited Elizabeth to visit him at the Kensington Palace apartment of his aunt the Marchioness of Milford Haven and the Chester Street home of the Mountbattens. He also took Elizabeth to visit Mountbatten's older daughter, Patricia, and her new husband, John Brabourne, at their modest cottage in Kent.

"It was an absolutely foreign way of life for her," recalled Brabourne. "She had never lived that sort of existence, and she was enchanted, though her maid could not believe it when she saw where we lived."

Philip also took Elizabeth to Coppins, the home of the Duchess of Kent, in Buckinghamshire, where he had spent many of his shore leaves. The Greek Duchess, known as Marina, who had been imported to marry the homosexual Duke of Kent, was one of Philip's favorite relatives. After several visits to Coppins, Elizabeth trusted her enough to confide, "Daddy doesn't want me to see too much of Philip or anyone, so please don't tell him." The Duchess never did.

Philip's cousin Alexandra, who knew about the couple's secret visits to Coppins, remembered his passion for Cobina Wright Jr. and wondered if he was simply toying with Elizabeth.

"I only hope Philip isn't just flirting with her," she told Marina. "He's so casual that he flirts without realizing it."

"I think his flirting days are over," replied the Duchess. "He would be the one to be hurt now if it was all just a flirtation or if it is not to be. One thing I'm sure about, those two would never do anything to hurt each other."

Reflecting on their courtship many years later, Philip said: "I suppose one thing led to another. I suppose I began to think about it seriously...oh, let me think now, when I got back in 1946 and went to Balmoral. It was probably then that we, that it became, you know, that we began to think about it seriously, and even talk about it...."

After spending time at Balmoral in August 1946, Philip proposed and Elizabeth accepted—secretly. This was the first time she had acted on her own without first consulting her parents. She then caused the first real argument she ever had with them by insisting she wanted to marry the penniless Greek Prince. She knew that the Royal Marriages Act of 1772 specified that descendants of King George II had to get the permission of the monarch to marry and that permission had to be "declared in council" before the marriage could take place. Elizabeth wanted her father's permission, but he did not want to give it. He confided his discomfort to his equerry, who shared the King's opinion of the brash young man and agreed that the King should delay making any decision.

Elizabeth's only ally within the royal family was her grandmother Queen Mary, whose arranged marriage to King George V had grown into a loving union that had produced five children. So when Prince Philip was ridiculed in her presence, she was not receptive. She frowned when he was derided as a product of "a crank school with theories of complete social equality where the boys were taught to mix with all and sundry." Queen Mary said nothing and stared straight ahead.

"What sort of background would this be for a son-in-law to the King?" she was asked.

"Useful," she said curtly.

The cautious King consulted his courtiers about the possibility of his daughter's marrying Philip of Greece, and the courtiers reported back the results of a *Sunday Pictorial* magazine poll, showing that 40 percent of Britain's class-conscious readers did not favor the marriage because Philip was "a foreigner."

A century earlier, when Prince Albert came to England as Queen Victoria's husband, the courtiers called him "that German." They called his aides "German spies." Now, more than one hundred years later, the courtiers exhibited a similar xenophobia. They called Philip "Phil the Greek."

Philip labeled himself as Scandinavian, "particularly Danish," he told an interviewer. "We spoke English at home...but then the conversation would go into French. Then it went into German on occasion because we had German cousins. If you couldn't think of a word in one language, you tended to go off in another."

The daughter of the Duchess of Marlborough remembered her brothers mocking Philip behind his back for not being an aristocrat. "He did not know the country life," she said. "He came from the other side of the tracks, which attracted Elizabeth. That and the fact that he was dead glamorous, absolutely drop dead glamorous. Although he was never quite digested into the British establishment, he decided in time to become just as pretentious, dull, and stuffy as the rest of us, while pushing his own personality uphill."

Elizabeth stood fast against her father's disapproval. She argued that she hadn't asked to be born and that if she, as an accident of birth, had to spend her life doing her duty as Queen, the least he could do was let her marry the man she loved. "After all, you married Mummy," she said. "And she wasn't even royalty. Philip is." The King sighed and said he felt Elizabeth was too young to get married. The Princess invoked Queen Victoria. "She was only twenty years old when she married Prince Albert, and look how happy that marriage was."

The King was not persuaded. As a father, he fretted about Philip's commitment to fidelity. He had been apprised of some of the young lieutenant's shore leaves with his navy buddy Michael Parker and their visits to brothels in Alexandria; he did not like the sound of Philip's continuing relationship with his childhood friend Helene Foufounis Cordet, and he heartily disapproved of Philip's midnight crawls through London's West End with his cousin David Milford Haven. But the King was growing anxious over his daughter's increasing willfulness and determination to marry Philip. She knew that because she was heir presumptive, her marriage required her father's approval as well as that of the government and the Commonwealth. Yet she alarmed her father when she intimated that if he did not give her permission to marry Philip, she would follow the footsteps of her uncle, the Duke of Windsor, who abdicated to marry the person he loved.

The Princess's apparent willingness to put love before duty was noted even by the U.S. Ambassador to the Court of St. James's, Lewis Douglas, a close friend of the royal family. He informed the State Department in a 1947 memo:

...it was learned that Princess Elizabeth had determined to marry [Prince Philip] and declared that if objections were raised she would not hesitate to follow the example of her uncle, King Edward VIII, and abdicate. She has a firm character.

More than forty years later, one of the King's former aides quaked at the mention of the 1936 abdication by the Duke of Windsor, which is still considered a sacrilege within royal circles. "The Princess did not threaten to do that...*exactly*," the aide said in an effort to "clarify" the record. "She only indicated that she could understand the romance behind her uncle's rationale. That's a far cry from declaring her intention to abdicate."

In public, Elizabeth could no longer hide her feelings. Her adoration of Philip was so obvious that rumors began circulating, prompting the foreign press to report that the couple were "informally engaged." The British press did not dare to make such a conjecture. Still, nervous about world opinion, the King told the Palace to officially deny the report. Five such denials were issued in the fall of 1945.

After Philip proposed to Elizabeth, he applied for naturalization as Lieutenant Philip Mountbatten, RN. First he took his uncle's advice, then his name. Years later Philip discounted his uncle's influence. "I wasn't madly in favour [of the name]," he told a biographer in 1971, "but in the end I was persuaded, and anyway I couldn't think of a better alternative....Contrary to public impression, Uncle Dickie didn't have *that* much to do with the course of my life."

Having given up his royal title, Philip next renounced the Greek Orthodox Church to join the Church of England. On December 16, 1946, *The New York Times* reported on the front page that "only politics, which has blighted so many royal romances, is delaying the announcement of the engagement of Princess Elizabeth, heiress to the British throne, and Prince Philip of Greece." Again the Palace issued a denial.

The King was beside himself. Becoming increasingly irritable and bad tempered, he drank heavily from the whiskey decanter that he insisted be placed next to his plate at every dinner. His war-weary country, though, was still scraping by on rations for food and fuel. Besides these shortages, Britain was beset by another problem: with millions of military being demobilized, the ranks of the unemployed swelled. And with Winston Churchill banished in defeat, the King was forced to deal with a new Prime Minister in Clement Attlee and a Labor government that the conservative monarch considered "far too socialist." (When someone told Churchill that Attlee was a modest man, Churchill agreed: "He has every reason to be modest.")

The King wrote gloomily in 1946, "Food, clothes and fuel are the main topics of conversation with us all." He grew impatient with everyone, especially his cousin Dickie Mountbatten, who strutted like a peacock after the new Labor government appointed him Viceroy of India, where he was to oversee that nation's progress to independence. The Queen complained that Dickie was "showing off his medals again" and getting more coverage on Movietone News* than the King. Years later she would ridicule Mountbatten's two-column entry in *Who's Who* as overblown and characteristically pompous. She became especially annoyed when he insisted on having his own honors list so he could bestow knighthoods in India just as the King did in England. She expressed her objection to Prime Minister Attlee, who agreed with her. "No one in a century has had such powers," Attlee said, "but he insisted as a precondition to accepting the job." As irritated as the King was, he felt that his biggest problem was not Mountbatten but his nephew Philip and the

---

* Movietone News was a newsreel shown in movie houses before the advent of television. By buying tickets to a cinema, people could see the news before or after the featured film. Newsreels, created in 1909, were especially popular in the 1930s and 1940s.

The British writer Nigel Nicolson recalls watching a newsreel in London in 1947 with his friend Sibyl Colfax. They had come to see the Mountbattens' departure from India at the end of his term as Viceroy.

"They were seen off at the airport by [Prime Minister] Jawaharlal Nehru," said Nicolson.

"As the plane took off, Sibyl said to me, 'But what they didn't show was that Edwina at the last moment kissed Nehru full on the lips, which deeply shocked Indian feelings, undoing all the good that Dickie had done.' The woman sitting immediately in front of us turned and said, 'Hullo, Sibyl.' It was Edwina Mountbatten, and sitting beside her was her husband. They had come incognito to the cinema to watch themselves. There was little doubt that they had heard what Sibyl said. I whispered to her, 'Would you like to leave?' 'I think we'd better,' she replied. We left."

problems he posed as consort to the future Queen of England.

His beloved daughter was balking at having to leave her secret fiancé at home to accompany her family on a ten-week tour of South Africa, which would include her twenty-first birthday. But the King insisted. The trip had been planned for four months to thank the South Africans for throwing out their Prime Minister and supporting Great Britain during the war. The King believed that the wounds splitting South Africa could be healed by the balm of royalty. As the first monarch to travel with his family, he wanted Elizabeth by his side as he opened the Union Parliament in Cape Town. Expecting a royal reception from the Africans, he decreed a ration-busting wardrobe for himself and his family, consisting of pearls and diamonds, cloths of gold, and endless yards of silk and satin, which required weeks of fittings and interminable work by dozens of seamstresses. The ordinary Briton received an annual clothing ration of 48 to 66 coupons. But the royal family received 160 extra coupons a year. For their South Africa wardrobe, they were issued 4,329 coupons. *The New York Times* described the result as "the most sumptuous wardrobe ever worn by British royalty."

On her twenty-first birthday Elizabeth was to make a coming-of-age speech in which she, as the future monarch, dedicated herself to her countrymen. The speech was broadcast around the world. Dutifully she rehearsed it, but each time, she said, the solemn words made her cry:

I declare before you that my whole life, whether it be long or short, shall be devoted to your service and the service of our great Imperial Commonwealth to which we all belong.* But I shall not have strength to carry out this resolution unless you join in it with me, as I now invite you to do; I know that your support will be unfailingly given. God bless all of you who are willing to share it.

Finally, against his better judgment, the King relented. He agreed to allow his daughter to marry Philip, provided Philip, who changed his name, his nationality, and his religion, was deemed acceptable by the British establishment. His uncle quickly introduced him to Britain's most powerful press lords, who agreed that his relationship to Queen Victoria (he, like Elizabeth, was a great-great-grandchild) and his service in the Royal Navy qualified him as suitable. Still, the King declined to announce the engagement. He ordered absolute secrecy about any future

* The next year, 1948, the Labor government passed the British Nationality Act, making Commonwealth citizenship equivalent to British citizenship, thus giving every citizen of the Commonwealth a legal right to reside in the United Kingdom. When the Commonwealth was established, members agreed that the British monarch should be the "symbol of free association of (Commonwealth) nations and as such Head of the Commonwealth," regardless of whether a member country retained the British monarch as its head of state. By 1997, the Commonwealth had 53 member states with a combined population of 1.4 billion.

plans until after the tour of South Africa, hoping against hope that Elizabeth might change her mind. He instructed the Palace to keep denying the rumors swarming around the couple, and he demanded total discretion from Philip. He forbade him to be seen with Elizabeth in public until after the royal family returned in 1947. He had told Philip that he could not see the family off at Waterloo Station, and he could not go aboard their ship at Portsmouth to say good-bye. The King would not allow his future son-in-law to attend the bon voyage luncheon at Buckingham Palace with the royal household staff or to be at the pier to welcome the royal family home ten weeks later. He did say Philip could write his fiancée during the trip, and he allowed him to attend his engagement party with the royal family and Lord and Lady Mountbatten at their London home on Chester Street two nights before departure. There the two families secretly celebrated the announcement, which would not be made official for several months. That night the King drank heavily.

Aboard ship, the Queen took comfort in the kindness of Surgeon Rear Admiral Henry "Chippy" White, who accompanied the royal family to South Africa, where he retired the following year. "Chippy White, whose son was my uncle, was knighted for his service to the King," said Hugh Bygott-Webb, "but I don't think that KCVO [Knight Commander of the Victorian Order] included his affair with the King's wife. Now, I have no absolute proof of this love affair with the Queen, who later became the Queen Mother, but their romance, accompanied by love letters, has been assumed within the family for years and years. The letters remain in the family and always will."

In photographs taken during the South African tour, the Queen beamed while her daughter Elizabeth looked bored and distracted, except during the celebration of her twenty-first birthday on April 21, 1947, in Cape Town. Feted with salutes all day and a grand ball and fireworks in the evening, Elizabeth spent the morning opening birthday presents of extravagant proportions: a platinum brooch in the shape of a flame lily set with three hundred diamonds and paid for with one week's pocket money collected from forty-two thousand Rhodesian schoolchildren; a pair of diamond flower-petal earrings from the members of the royal households, who barely made 1,000 ($2,000) a year; a diamond-studded badge of the Grenadier Guards, her favorite regiment, of which she was the Colonel; and from her parents a twin pair of Cartier ivy-leaf brooches covered with two thousand pavé diamonds surrounded by two five-carat diamonds in the center. The state gifts from South Africa, worth more than $1 million at the time, were equally lavish: the King received a gold box full of diamonds to put on his Garter star, and the Queen was given an engraved twenty-two-karat gold tea service. Princess Margaret received a necklace of seventeen graduated diamonds, and Elizabeth was given a silver chest containing twenty-one graduated brilliant-cut diamonds, some weighing ten carats, interspersed with baguettes.

Laden with jewels, the royal family returned to England in May 1947. But the King still wouldn't announce his daughter's engagement. He excluded Philip's name from the Royal Ascot house party at Windsor Castle, but on July 8 Philip, who was teaching at the Royal Navy Petty Officers School at Kingsmoor, phoned the King. He asked permission to go to Buckingham Palace that evening to give Elizabeth a three-carat diamond engagement ring that had belonged to his mother.* The King consented and graciously invited his future son-in-law for dinner. Philip drove his sporty MG ninety-eight miles from Wiltshire to London. Two days later the engagement was announced by the same Palace spokesman who had been denying it for two years.

"We got engaged," said Elizabeth's dresser, Margaret "BoBo" MacDonald, on the day the betrothal was announced. So close was she to Elizabeth that she frequently talked of herself and her future sovereign as a single person. The Scotswoman, who had been with Elizabeth since she was born, would accompany her on her honeymoon and serve her morning coffee every day until BoBo died.

The wedding was set for November 20,

*The official engagement photograph shows Philip, handsome in his uniform, beside Elizabeth, her hands folded to display her platinum ring. A friend recalled how thrilled she was with the ring, which symbolized the end of her drab years and the beginning of a happy future. Elizabeth said, "It's like turning a page in a book."

1947, but again over the King's objections. Citing the coal shortage and the country's economic collapse, he suggested a quiet ceremony at St. George's Chapel in Windsor to minimize the expense of pomp and ceremony. But Elizabeth and her mother insisted on a big wedding. The King tried to stall the inevitable by suggesting June of the next year, when, he said, the weather would be warmer. Elizabeth said she didn't care if it snowed: she was getting married in November.

The British press reported the engagement as the love match of the century. "This is no arranged marriage," said the *Daily Mail.* "The couple is well and truly in love," said the *Daily Telegraph.* Skeptical Americans did not try to dispute the matter. "The world, seeing this pretty girl and young navy officer together, will like to think of this as a love match rather than as any union dictated by politics," declared an editorial in *The New York Times.*

Arranged marriages were not foreign to Philip. Until 1923 such marriages had been the rule for royalty, not the exception. Love was seldom an option, as he knew from the marriages of his parents, his two Mountbatten uncles, and all of his cousins, including Marina, the impoverished Greek Princess who had been imported to England to straighten out the homosexual Duke of Kent. Ever pragmatic, Philip, too, was marrying for a reason.

"Why do you think I'm getting married?" he asked Cobina Wright. "I'll tell you: It's because I've never really had a home. From the time I was eight, I've always been away at school or in the navy."

Almost a quarter century later, Philip admitted publicly that his marriage to Elizabeth had been arranged. "There was their excursion to South Africa, and then it was sort of fixed up when they came back," he told his biographer, Basil Boothroyd, in 1971. "That's what really happened." By then he had been married to Elizabeth for twenty-four years, provided a male heir to the throne, and become resigned to his role as Prince Consort. Beyond that, he had learned to be discreet about the life he led with other women.

"This is not to say that he wasn't fond of Elizabeth when he married her," said his friend Larry Adler, the American harmonica player who moved to England after being blacklisted as a suspected communist* in America. He belonged to Philip's male luncheon group known as the Thursday Club. "Was he in love with Elizabeth? No, but he had a great deal of respect for her."

So much so that when someone suggested Philip was marrying the ugly duckling and that Princess Margaret was far prettier than her sister, he flared. "You wouldn't say that if you knew them. Elizabeth is sweet and kind," he said, "just like her mother."

---

* "Philip, who has great humor, joked about my being blacklisted," recalled Larry Adler. "When we were served Wite Baits at luncheon one day, he said, 'In Larry's honor, the fish should be called Red Baits.' Philip also suggested that I be listed as 'a distant country subversive member.' He later talked to me about the blacklist and asked how I coped with it. He seemed to be very much against such a thing as a blacklist."

As soon as the engagement was announced, Uncle Dickie, writing from India, bombarded his nephew with advice about how to arrange the wedding and how the new household should be run. He offered Broadlands, his home in Hampshire, for the honeymoon, suggesting Philip and Elizabeth use Edwina's suite. It featured Salvador Dalí paintings and a magnificent four-poster Tudor bed with an ivory satin headboard and "those lurid pink satin sheets." Philip accepted his uncle's hospitality, but for only a few days. He said his bride wanted to spend most of the honeymoon at Birkall, the small royal house on the twenty-four thousand acres of Balmoral in Scotland. Then he cautioned his mentor: "I am not being rude but it is apparent you like the idea of being the General Manager of this little show, and I am rather afraid that she might not take to the idea quite so docilely as I do. It is true that I know what is good for me, but don't forget that she has not had you as Uncle *loco parentis*, counsellor and friend as long as I have."

Unperturbed, Mountbatten wrote to Winston Churchill and asked him to take Philip to lunch to impress upon him "how serious it was, marrying the heir to the throne." Churchill, who was out of office then, agreed to tutor the young man for the sake of the monarchy.

Already Philip had been shut out of the wedding plans. He was permitted to choose his cousin David Milford Haven as best man, but of the 2,500 invitations, Philip was allotted only 2. These he gave to his navy shipmate Michael Parker and to Helene Cordet's mother. Cobina Wright Sr., the mother of his first lover, appeared on the official guest list as the society columnist for the Hearst newspapers. Beyond that, Philip was not allowed to participate in the wedding planning. This was not simply a marriage ceremony, but an affair of state that would focus world attention on the British monarchy. Consequently the King and Queen told him that his sisters and their German husbands, some of whom had supported Hitler's Third Reich, could not possibly be included. So they remained in Germany and listened to the service on the radio in Marienburg Castle, south of Hanover. Princess Margarita of Hohenloe-Langenbourg, Princess Theodora, the Margravine of Baden, and Princess Sophie of Hanover telephoned their brother to congratulate him. "We sent him jointly as a present a gold fountain pen with our names engraved upon it," said Princess Sophie.

The Duke and Duchess of Windsor, who had visited Hitler in Germany, were also excluded from the invitation list. Although the exiled Duke was Elizabeth's favorite uncle, he had embarrassed the royal family earlier in the year by selling his memoirs and publishing *A King's Story*. The Queen suggested to the Foreign Office that the Duke and Duchess might consider scheduling a trip to America during November, which would preclude their attending the wedding. The Foreign Office delivered the suggestion, but the Duke replied that he and the Duchess did not want to be away at that time. The Palace insisted. Further, it instructed him that, if asked, he was to deny that he and the Duchess had not been invited to the royal wedding. In the end they went to America, where they pointedly did not listen to the ceremony.

After the Queen vetted the invitation list, she addressed the issue of Philip's mother, whom she considered "pleasant but odd...definitely odd." The plump, winsome Queen with her baby blue feather boas and rippling giggles contrasted sharply with the gaunt, somber Greek Princess in her stark religious garb. The two women never had established a rapport, although they shared similar traits of courage and conviction. During the war, both demonstrated bravery: the Queen by accompanying her husband from Windsor Castle to Buckingham Palace every day to risk being bombed like her subjects, and Princess Andrew by hiding a Jewish family in her Athens home during the German occupation of Greece. Years after her death, the Princess was cited for valor by the state of Israel. But the Queen, unaware of Princess Andrew's heroism in 1947, viewed her as eccentric and overly religious.

Concerned about appearances at the royal wedding, the Queen sweetly asked Philip if he thought his mother would be wearing her nun's habit. As mother of the bride, the Queen said she herself would be wearing a dress of apricot-and-golden brocade, gracefully draped and trailing. Philip understood immediately that his mother's dour gray robe, white wimple, cord, and rosary beads would have to be closeted for the occasion. So on the wedding day Princess Andrew sat with the royal family in Westminster Abbey, wearing a hat and a simple silk dress, which the Queen later pronounced "very pretty and most appropriate."

On the morning of his wedding, Philip expressed his apprehension about marrying a woman who was destined to become an institution. "We had breakfast together," recalled a relative, "and he said, 'I don't know whether I'm being very brave or very foolish.'"

King George VI and his Queen had turned their own wedding into a spectacle, so they knew better than anyone the importance of producing a grand ceremony for their subjects. They understood how to rouse the people with a fanfare of silver trumpets and golden coaches. They recognized that such a ritual of imperial monarchy would distract people from the misery of their humdrum lives and unite the Commonwealth in celebration. Everyone would feel joyously invested in the royal family, which, in turn, would strengthen the monarchy's emotional hold on its subjects.

The power of such pageantry was not lost on Winston Churchill, who described the impending nuptials in 1947 as "a flash of colour on the hard road that we travel." *The New York Times* noted the need for "a welcome occasion for gaiety in grim England, beset in peace with troubles almost as burdensome as those of war." The next day a little girl in Brooklyn broke her piggy bank to send the Princess a turkey as a wedding present "because she lives in England and they have nothing to eat in England."

With only four months in which to stage a wedding extravaganza, the King and Queen concentrated on the costumes—the heralds in medieval scarlet-and-gold livery, the cavalry in shining helmets topped with plumes, the glistening swords, the sparkling medals, the crimson sashes, the gleaming breastplates. All were removed from prewar storage bins, where they had been sitting since 1939. Once again, clothes dominated the royal family's discussions as ration coupons were collected from cabinet members to insure that Princess Elizabeth had a proper trousseau and a stunning wedding gown. She told her couturier, Norman Hartnell, that she wanted to walk down the aisle in something unique and magnificent. She swore him to secrecy and threatened to go to another couturier if descriptions of her bridal gown were leaked to the public before the wedding. The royal designer insisted his workers sign secrecy oaths and whitewash the workroom windows, which were curtained with thick white muslin so no one could look in. Hartnell, who said he was inspired by Botticelli's "Primavera," envisioned Elizabeth in acres of ivory satin and tulle embroidered with ten thousand seed pearls and small crystals, which required two months of work by ten embroiderers and twenty-five needlewomen.

During the wedding, two sewing women were to be stationed in the Abbey in case the dress needed stitching. The bride's tulle veil was fifteen yards long and contained one hundred miles of thread. So Elizabeth was given an additional clothing allotment of one hundred coupons, plus twenty-three extra coupons for each of her eight bridesmaids. She also received from various well-wishers three hundred eighty-six pairs of nylon stockings—a most precious commodity for young women living through England's postwar reconstruction.

Expense was not considered when Elizabeth selected her trousseau. For her wedding night she chose a nightgown and robe set from Joske's department store in San Antonio, Texas, that cost $300, twice as much as most Americans earned in a month. The pale ivory Georgette gown had forty yards of silk with satin roses embroidered across the bodice; the brocade robe was patterned with tiny lords and ladies bowing in minuet, all hand stitched. The head of the store's gift-wrap department scrubbed up like a surgeon before she touched the precious parcel.

At the wedding, the Archbishop of Canterbury declared that the ceremony for Princess Elizabeth was "exactly the same as it would be for any cottager who might be married this afternoon in some small country church in a remote village in the Dales: the same prayers are offered; the same blessings are given." The differences: the twelve wedding cakes at the royal reception, including one nine feet high that Philip cut with his sword, each slice containing a week's sugar rations for the average family; 2,666 wedding presents, including a Thoroughbred horse, a mink coat, a twenty-two-karat gold coffee service, a television set, a fifty-four-carat pink diamond said to be the only one of its kind in the world, and a plantation and hunting lodge in Kenya.

Led by a procession of eighteen horse-drawn carriages, the royal guests included six kings, six queens, seven princesses, one princess regent, one prince regent, one Indian rajah, one crown prince, one crown princess, seven counts, six countesses, eleven viscounts, fourteen dukes, and eleven duchesses, who accounted for most of the sixty-seven diamond tiaras worn.

"The jewelry at that wedding was staggering," recalled the Danish Ambassador's daughter, who attended with her father. "I was breathless and gaping at the stupendous display. It was prewar dimension. Everyone had gone to the bank to get their jewels out of the vault. Diamond tiaras looked like beanies, and the former Duchess of Rutland had her entire head wrapped in diamonds. She said it was her grandmother's belt. A woman wearing a turban made of pearls the size of cherries passed another lady weighted down with bunches of cabochon emeralds cascading down her shoulders like grapes on a vine. The Indians wore breastplates of rubies and diamonds and wrapped their arms from wrist to shoulder in sapphires."

Overnight, the impecunious bridegroom, who was earning eight guineas a week as a navy lieutenant, became a nobleman with rank, title, and position, entitling him to layers of shining gold epaulets. He acquired a valet, a social secretary, and an equerry, plus a royal residence at Clarence House with 50,000 (about $100,000) for refurbishments, and a castle (Sunninghill Park) for country weekends. Before the couple could move into the castle, the Crown property on the edge of Windsor Great Park went up in flames—the first of many unexplained fires to haunt the House of Windsor.

"Oh, Crawfie, how *could* it have happened?" Elizabeth wrote to her former governess. "Do you really think someone did it on purpose? I can't believe it. People are always so kind to us...."

The morning before the wedding, Philip knelt before the King, who unsheathed his sword and, tapping each shoulder, knighted his future son-in-law with the Order of the Garter. Within the British honors system, the cornflower blue sash and eight-pointed star of the Garter is recognized as the highest accolade* a monarch can bestow. In a letter to his mother, the King said he had given the honor

---

* In 1945 Winston Churchill declined the Garter. "I could not accept the Order of the Garter from my sovereign when I had received the order of the boot from his people," he said. Later Princess Elizabeth approached him. "If you are Prime Minister when I become Queen, I would like you to be my first Garter Knight." She kept her promise and made him a knight on April 24, 1953, and installed him June 14, 1954.

to Elizabeth eight days earlier so that she would have precedence over her husband.

Previously Philip had been reduced to the status of a commoner when he was forced to renounce his Greek name, title, nationality, and religion. Now he was rewarded with three exalted British titles—Baron Greenwich, Earl of Merioneth, and Duke of Edinburgh. The title of Prince of the Realm was withheld and would not be conferred until 1957. But before his wedding day Philip was granted the distinction of being addressed as His Royal Highness. This rankled some of the nobility, who still point out that Britain's dukes not born of royal blood are to be addressed as His Grace, not as His Royal Highness. But the King was determined to ennoble his twenty-six-year-old son-in-law so that his daughter would have the status of a peer's wife. The King also wanted to make sure that his grandchildren would be born of noble blood. "It is a great deal to give a man all at once," he said, "but I know Philip understands his new responsibilities."

On the day of the wedding, the bridegroom, suffering from a cold, swore off cigarettes at the request of the bride and promised never to smoke again. He arrived at the church early with his best man, who later wrote that both of them were so hung over from the previous night's bachelor party that they had had to steady their nerves with a gin and tonic.

The jokes had been rough and the drinking

serious that evening, particularly after Vasco Lazzolo, a portrait painter, who was convinced that Philip was marrying Princess Elizabeth to advance himself, rose unsteadily from his chair to propose a toast. He lifted his brandy glass and glared at the guest of honor. "For what you are doing, I think you are an absolute shit," he said. He threw his glass into the fireplace and lurched from the room.

"That was quite a party," recalled Larry Adler many years later, "and Philip certainly didn't enjoy it as much as the rest of us. He was just too scared. I remember him looking white as a ghost and shaky the whole evening. He was damned frightened. The King had laid down the law to him about a lot of things, from fast cars to other women.

"Philip had had a minor automobile accident shortly after the engagement announcement which made the papers. He was driving fast, skidded, hit a hedge, and banged himself up a bit. This caused excessive press comment at the time and made him look like a reckless, pub-crawling playboy. Naturally, the King was annoyed. Then there was the Helene Cordet affair, which surfaced right before the wedding, when she was described in the French press as the 'mystery blond divorcée' whom Philip had visited in Paris the year before. Since then, Helene is always the first name mentioned as one of Philip's mistresses and the mother of his illegitimate children. Of course, he and Helene claim that they're merely childhood friends who grew up together in

Paris. He gave her away when she married the first time in 1938, and he's godfather to both her children, so who knows?"

Adler smiles and shrugs when talking about his old friend's relationship with Helene Cordet, who worked in a Paris dress shop before moving to London to open a nightclub and become a cabaret singer. Her parents, staunch Greek royalists, had helped support Philip's parents during their exile in France when Philip was growing up. "Mercifully, he spared us the personal details of his relationship with Helene," said Adler in 1992. "But we made certain assumptions at the time, and whether we were right or wrong, we understood why the King was agitated about his daughter falling in love with a bounder like our old pal. As I told Philip then, be glad your zipper can't talk."

Despite his friends' insinuations, Philip stayed married to Elizabeth, but he conducted discreet affairs with many other women, most of whom were aristocrats or actresses. One mistress reportedly bore his child as a single woman and never divulged the name of the child's father. Her refusal to name the man whipped up more rumors. By 1989 the stories of Philip's alleged illegitimate children forced Helene Cordet's son, Max, to make a public statement.

"I have heard these rumors all my life, but they are ridiculous," he said. "My father—my real father—[Frenchman Marcel Boisot] lives in Paris and it is silly to say otherwise. This all goes back to my mother's childhood with Philip. Nothing more to it than that."

His mother admitted that Philip paid for her son's tuition at Gordonstoun, but she said it was because she was destitute, not because Philip was her son's father. By then, though, the rumors, repeated for so many years, carried their own currency.

"I don't care what Max Boisot says now," said his classmate James Bellini in 1994. "I went to Cambridge with him and we all thought then that he was one of Philip's bastards. We talked about it all the time. Before Cambridge, Max attended Gordonstoun, the same school in Scotland that Philip attended and to which he sent his sons, Charles, Andrew, and Edward. And don't forget, Philip was also godfather to Max, which traditionally is the way royalty stands up for its illegitimate children. This is their way of giving their bastard offspring a tenuous tie to royal circles. Take a close look at the royal godparents of the aristocracy and you'll see the bastard sons and daughters of the monarchy."

While Philip had been intimate with many women before his marriage, his relationship with Helene Cordet was never the passionate love affair that was alleged. She publicly denied having a romance with Philip, but her coy denials seemed calculated toward publicity to launch her career as a London cabaret singer. She later cashed in on her relationship with Philip by writing a book entitled *Born Bewildered*. She intimated that she had not been

112

invited to the royal wedding because she was the "mystery blonde" he had been romancing in Paris. Helene was not invited because she was divorced, and at that time, divorced persons were not allowed in royal circles.

Years later, Helene's granddaughter told her to stick to the story of the affair with the Queen's husband. "Don't keep denying that you and Philip had more than a friendship going," said her granddaughter. "I like people thinking I'm royal and Philip is my grandfather."

Elizabeth, a virgin when she married, was the pampered, protected daughter of Puritan parents, whereas Philip, the son of separated parents, was reared by relatives who had been exposed to an atmosphere of decadence and amorality. Elizabeth had grown up with the comforting scent of Palace beeswax and fresh roses, while Philip was accustomed to the itinerant smell of mothballs from borrowed clothes in storage bins and battered suitcases hastily packed and unpacked. The twenty-six-year-old bridegroom, who had traveled through Europe, Australia, and the Middle East, was marrying a twenty-one-year-old woman who had never been outside Great Britain until the royal family tour of South Africa. Poorly educated, she had never attended school and received hourly tutorials only in British history and heraldry. She had studied Walter Bagehot's writings on the monarchy and had mastered the hereditary peerage with all its complex titles of antiquities. She spoke excellent French* but barely understood mathematics and science and knew little about the natural world beyond dogs and horses. She disliked poetry, except for the rhymes of Rudyard Kipling and Alfred Lord Tennyson. The only poem she ever memorized was the childish verses of "They're Changing Guard at Buckingham Palace" by A.A. Milne.

"I was never able to imbue her with enthusiasm for modern verse," said her governess, Marion Crawford. "'Oh, do stop!' she would say while I was reading from the works of some modern poet. 'I don't understand a word of it. What *is* the man trying to say?'"

Outside the Palace, Elizabeth felt self-conscious about the gaps in her education. She once asked if Dante was a horse, because she had never heard of the medieval poet.

"No, no, he isn't a horse," was the reply.

"Is he a jockey, then?" she asked.

She blushed when told that Dante Alighieri was the Italian classicist who wrote *The Divine Comedy*, a masterpiece of world literature. Horses were what she knew best.

Elizabeth's husband-to-be was neither a prodigy nor a scholar, but he at least had accumulated twelve years of formal schooling, plus several years of naval training, and he

---

* Reports of Elizabeth's faultless French made her former French chef, René Roussin, smile. "I treasure the memory that I was one of the first Frenchmen to converse with her in my own language," he wrote in *Good Housekeeping* in September 1955.

"'Did I say that correctly, Roussin?' she used to say. And if her accent did not seem to me to be quite right, I never said so. For the only time I did criticize, her little face fell, and she looked so downcast I never had the heart to do it again."

114

never experienced her hesitation in talking to people. With confidence bordering on arrogance, he could walk into a room without introduction, breezily announce himself, and approach the prettiest girl to say, "Well, this is a much more attractive audience than the one I've just left." Philip chatted with anyone about anything, while Elizabeth worried constantly about what to say. "If only I could do it as well as my mother does it," she said.

Receiving lines made her uncomfortable as she tried to manufacture small talk. Faced with a moment of silence, she once said, "Well...I can't think of anything more to say about that."

Confiding in a friend, she said, "Believe it or not, I lie in my bath before dinner, and think, Oh, who am I going to sit by and what are they going to talk about? I'm absolutely terrified of sitting next to people in case they talk about things I have never heard of."

A few years later Philip, too, would acknowledge his ignorance. "I regret to say that all my degrees are honorary ones," he told students at the University of Delhi in India. Later he addressed the subject with students at the University of Wales. "My generation, although reasonably well schooled, is probably the worst educated of this age. The war cut short any chance there was of acquiring a higher education. I'm part of this lost generation trying to make up for what it missed between 1939 and 1945."

When he and Elizabeth received honorary

doctor of law degrees from London University, she, too, sounded humble. "There is one piece of fortune which we have never known," she said. "We have never known a university from within...."

The King, a simple, uneducated man, prized his daughter's lack of sophistication and wrote in his diary how much he would miss the charades, games, and parlor singsongs they had shared at Windsor Castle. At her wedding reception, he rose from his chair, raised his glass, and, pointedly ignoring the bridegroom, saluted his beloved daughter. "To the bride," the King said with tears in his eyes. A few days later he sent her a touching letter:

> ...I was so proud of you & thrilled at having you so close to me on our long walk in Westminster Abbey, but when I handed your hand to the Archbishop I felt that I had lost something very precious. You were so calm and composed during the Service & said your words with such conviction, that I knew it was all right.
>
> I am so glad you wrote & told Mummy that you think the long wait before your engagement & the long time before the wedding was for the best. I was rather afraid that you had thought I was being hard hearted about it. I was so anxious for you to come to South Africa as you knew.
>
> Our family, us four, the "Royal Family," must remain together with additions of course at suitable moments!! I have

116

watched you grow up all these years with pride under the skilful direction of Mummy, who as you know is the most marvellous person in the world in my eyes, & I can, I know, always count on you, & now Philip, to help us in our work....

Your leaving us has left a great blank in our lives but do remember that your old home is still yours & do come back to it as much as possible. I can see that you are sublimely happy with Philip which is right but don't forget us is the wish of

Your ever loving & devoted
Papa

SIX

A few months after their wedding Prince Philip complained that his young wife wanted sex constantly. He said he was astonished to find her insatiable. "I can't get her out of my bed," he said. "She's always there. She's driving me mad."

Philip made these complaints during his 1948 visit to the South of France while his wife remained in England. He was traveling with his cousin David, the Marquess of Milford Haven, who was his best man and closest friend. They were staying in the Monaco apartment of an English friend, who entertained them and other visiting British nobility. Philip's grousing shocked everyone, including his cousin, who criticized him in front of other guests for being indiscreet.

"Real swordsmen don't discuss their fencing partners," said Milford Haven.

"Prince Philip complained that he could not keep Princess Elizabeth out of his bed, that she was at him sexually all the time," recalled the Duchess of Leeds, who was also vacationing in Monaco.

The Duke of Leeds reported Philip's caddish behavior to his brother-in-law, Oliver Lyttleton, a leading Tory Member of Parliament, and strongly recommended an official sanction.

"We all thought that Philip was singularly unpleasant to discuss his wife in such an open manner," said the Duke of Leeds. "He was a disgusting man."

"My in-laws were stunned by Philip's total lack of discretion," said Nigel Dempster, the *Daily Mail* gossip columnist, who married the daughter of the Duke of Leeds. "It wasn't that Philip was lying, but that he was telling the truth too bluntly. My aristocratic in-laws couldn't deal with the image of the randy little sex-crazed Princess who would one day be their Queen."

Philip was partly forgiven that summer when the Palace announced that Princess Elizabeth was canceling her schedule for six months. The official bulletin of June 4, 1948, read, "Her Royal Highness the Princess Elizabeth, Duchess of Edinburgh, will undertake no public engagements after the end of

June." The message indicated that the Princess was pregnant.

"Royal decorum prohibited using the actual word," said biographer Anthony Holden. "You had to read between the lines to understand that she was pregnant. In those days, physicians referred to pregnancy as 'confinement,' and the due date of birth was the EDC, or estimated date of confinement. After the birth, she started breast-feeding, but that news wasn't reported either because the word 'breast' was taboo in relation to royalty. This antediluvian mentality was prevailing thirty years later when I wrote a biography of the royal baby Prince Charles and mentioned that his mother had breast-fed him. I submitted my manuscript to the Palace for corrections, and John Dauth, press secretary to the Prince, rang me up in near hysteria.

"'The sentence about breast-feeding must be deleted. Absolutely and at once.'

"'But why?' I asked.

"'One never mentions the royal breasts.'

"'Perhaps I could paraphrase and say, "The Princess fed the baby herself"?'

"'That still implies the royal breasts, and the royal breasts must never be exposed.'

"In the end," said Holden, chuckling over the prudish restraints of royal protocol, "I deleted the sentence."

When the heir became apparent, Prince Philip looked like a hero. Not only had he ensured the line of succession and the continuation of the monarchy, but he had also produced a boy. The future King, Charles Philip Arthur George, was born by cesarean section at Buckingham Palace six days before his parents' first wedding anniversary at 9:14 P.M. on November 14, 1948. He was taken by forceps and weighed seven pounds six ounces.

His mother had insisted he be delivered in her suite at Buckingham Palace and not in a makeshift hospital wing. "I want my baby to be born in my own room, amongst the things I know," she said.

When she was a child, Elizabeth had told her governess, "I shall have lots of cows, horses, and children." When the twenty-two-year-old Princess became pregnant, Crawfie could not quite believe that she was going to have a baby.

"Are your frightened at all, Lilibet?" she asked. "What do you feel about it?"

Elizabeth said she was looking forward to the experience. "After all, it is what we're made for."

One morning her governess found her depressed after reading a newspaper account about the divorce of an acquaintance of hers who had small children.

"Why do people do it, Crawfie?" Elizabeth asked her governess. "How can they break up a home when there are children to consider?"

Crawfie tried to explain that some personalities were incompatible and some homes unhappy, but the Princess, who had been raised in a royal palace by loving parents and servants, did not seem to understand.

"But why did they get married in the first place?" she asked.

Crawfie eased the subject back to her impending delivery.

"She said she did not mind whether her first child was a boy or a girl," said John Dean, valet to Prince Philip, "but I believe the Duke was looking forward to having a son."

The King was convinced that the baby was going to be a girl because female genes ran strong on both sides of the family: Philip was the only boy following the birth of four girls, and Elizabeth was one of two girls. The genetic probability of a girl worried the King, who wanted his grandchild to be given the royal treatment, which included the bows and/or curtsies that accompany the HRH style. Since the creation of the House of Windsor in 1917, that style—His Royal Highness—had been reserved for the boys of the sovereign and excluded the girls. Not being a gambling man, the cautious King would not take a chance. He issued an official proclamation* a week before his daughter gave birth (not wanting his grandchild to be a commoner) and decreed that *all* children born to Elizabeth and Philip would be considered royal: *all* must be given the royal appellation of HRH and styled Prince or Princess. That way he ensured himself a royal grandchild, even if she was a girl. When Elizabeth produced a boy, the King

---

* British Information Services, an agency of the British government, issued a six-page advisory on the birth of Princess Elizabeth's baby to resolve the complicated issues of the baby's rank and title.

was ecstatic, and his enthusiasm affected everyone around the Palace.

"It's a boy. It's a boy," shouted a policeman at the Palace gates. The gathering crowds sang lustily for hours as the country celebrated the birth of a future king. The royal baby was hailed with forty-one-gun salutes from His Majesty's warships around the globe. Winston Churchill said the birth of Prince Charles had made the British monarchy "the most secure in the world." Prime Minister Clement Attlee congratulated the royal family, who by their "example in private life as well as in the devotion to public duty, have given strength and comfort to many in these times of stress and uncertainty."

At Windsor Castle, the two-ton curfew bell, which rings only for royals on four occasions—birth, marriage, investiture, and death—tolled for hours. For the next week, London's church bells pealed day and night, bonfires blazed, and fountains spouted blue-for-boy water. More than four thousand telegrams arrived at Buckingham Palace the first night, and a dozen temporary typists were hired to handle the letters and packages that poured in from around the empire and beyond.

The day after Prince Charles was born, the King ordered laborers working on Clarence House to "stop taking so damned many tea breaks." He insisted they work overtime to get the residence ready so his daughter, his son-in-law, and his eventual heir could move from their cramped quarters in Buckingham

Palace. During World War II, the King had lent Clarence House to the British Red Cross. When he decided to give the bombed-out mansion—which had no heat, bathrooms, or electricity—to his daughter as a wedding present so she could live near him, Parliament allocated 50,000 ($200,000) for renovations. But work stoppages throttled England's postwar economy and stalled the project for eighteen months, and it ended up costing five times more than the war-drained treasury had allotted. Still, the King's subjects did not object. The royal family was so beloved after the war that the public willingly absorbed the cost of $1 million for remodeling the royal residence and installing crystal chandeliers, satin draperies, and gold faucets. Only the communist newspaper in London questioned the expenditures for the future sovereign at a time when the average weekly wage was less than $100 and scores of homeless families were shivering in abandoned military barracks.

The Queen addressed the misery of "all those who are living in uncongenial surroundings and who are longing for a time when they will have a home of their own." In her radio address on the occasion of Their Majesties' Silver Jubilee in 1948, she said, "I am sure that patience, tolerance, and love will help them to keep their faith undimmed and their courage undaunted when things seem difficult."

The King continued raging at the laborers working on Clarence House, his irascibility now exacerbated by failing health. At the age of fifty-three, his habit of chain-smoking cigarettes had clogged his lungs with cancer, although the word was never used in his presence. The deadly disease had blocked his bronchial tubes, which caused incessant coughing and shortness of breath. He relied on his doctor, Sir John Weir, a genial seventy-two-year-old homeopath, who dispensed more jokes than remedies while His Majesty's health deteriorated. Finally the amiable practitioner called in six other elderly specialists, who recommended surgery to remove the King's left lung. None of the doctors ever told the King of his spreading malignancy, and only one cautioned against cigarettes.

"Before we do this operation, we've got to cut down on the smoking," said James Learmonth, England's top expert on vascular disease. Learmonth did not have the nerve to tell his sovereign that he was killing himself with cigarettes, but by then nicotine had become the Windsor family curse: Queen Mary, the Duke of Windsor, and Princess Margaret were all addicted, and even the Queen smoked eight cigarettes a day, although never in public.

In addition to lung cancer, the King also suffered from arteriosclerosis, which caused him painful leg cramps. In 1949 he underwent lumbar surgery to relieve the pain and prevent gangrene, which would have meant amputating both his legs. Cardiac complications so weakened him that he had to curtail his schedule and postpone the royal tour of Australia and New Zealand.

The Queen wanted to hide her husband's illness, so she began applying makeup to his face to camouflage his pallor during public appearances. Each time she rouged his sunken, wan cheeks, she cursed the Duke and Duchess of Windsor. "None of this would have happened," she said, "if Wallis hadn't blown in from Baltimore!" On her orders, the Palace denied that the King was camouflaging his ill health with cosmetics.

The Queen possessed the most engaging personality of the royal family. She usually demonstrated intelligence and forgiveness. But since the abdication in 1936, she remained implacable in her animosity toward the Windsors. Now, filled with bitterness, she blamed them for leaching life away from her husband. "If only Bertie hadn't had to worry so much during the war," she wrote in a letter, bemoaning the abdication that put her husband on the throne. "If only he hadn't had to carry the weight of the world on his shoulders." In her mind, and that of her mother-in-law, Queen Mary, the cause of the King's alarming deterioration was directly attributable to "that damnable Simpson woman."

Distracted by her husband's failing health, the Queen did not pay close attention to a letter she received from *Ladies' Home Journal,* soliciting her comments and corrections on excerpts from a manuscript entitled *The Little Princesses* by Marion Crawford. She was stunned to learn that her children's governess was publishing a memoir about her seventeen years of royal service. The Scottish schoolmarm, who retired in 1949, said she had postponed marriage until she was forty years old to take care of the Queen's children. The governess said she waited until Lilibet, twenty-three, and Margaret Rose, nineteen, no longer needed her on a daily basis. Only then did she decide that she could in good conscience accept Retired Major George Buthlay's proposal of marriage. The royal family did not rejoice. In fact, Queen Mary was horrified.

"My dear child, you can't leave *them*," she told Crawfie. "You simply cannot."

The Queen, too, was appalled by Crawfie's intentions, especially when she said she was going to be married three months before the royal wedding. The Queen, whom Crawfie described in her book as "always sweet," "usually charming," and "unfailingly pleasant," stared at her coldly. After a moment of stony silence, the Queen recovered her composure.

"You must see, Crawfie," she said, "that this would not be at all convenient just now." Her dulcet tone had hardened into the sound of a woman discovering a dog's mess in the middle of her living room floor.

The King, who usually agreed with his mother and his wife, flew into an imperial rage. Only when Crawfie promised to stay through the royal wedding was he pacified. He agreed then to make her a Commander of the Royal

Victorian Order. This honor, established by Queen Victoria in 1896 for members of the royal household who had rendered extraordinary personal service to the sovereign, was not good enough for Crawfie, or so the Queen maintained. She said the governess had expected to receive the highest household honor—Dame Commander of the Royal Victorian Order, which truly separated the upstairs from the downstairs. Because she didn't receive that particular decoration, she retaliated by writing a memoir and two more books.

The Queen denounced Crawfie as a traitor and never spoke to her again. When Marion Crawford died in 1988 at the age of seventy-eight, no member of the royal family attended her funeral, wrote a condolence letter, or even sent flowers. As far as the Queen was concerned, Crawfie was dead* the day her book was published.

More than anyone else in the royal family, the Queen understood the power of the revealing detail and the humanizing anecdote. She knew the historical impact of a book like Crawfie's, and despite its loving prose and affectionate stories, she never forgave the governess. The Queen did not like Crawfie's

* The governess always nourished the hope that she would be forgiven by the royal family. She saved the letters the Queen wrote to her during the 1936 royal tour of Canada, as well as photographs of Lilibet and Margaret Rose in the royal nursery and the birthday and Christmas cards the little girls sent her. Rather than sell her precious mementos, she bequeathed them to Lilibet in her will. When Crawfie died, her box of treasures disappeared into the vaults of the royal archive at Windsor Castle, which the Queen controls.

rendering of her as a passive, uninvolved mother who cared little about her children's education beyond their ability to sing and dance. The Queen felt betrayed seeing herself using the governess as a psychiatrist to talk to her difficult daughter, Margaret. "I knew that my real work as Royal Governess at the Palace was over," wrote Crawfie, who had trained to be a child psychologist before entering royal service, "but in the new, busy life which Princess Margaret was leading, her mother thought an hour or two of quiet, unrestrained chat on general subjects might soothe her....I had to go daily to the Palace to sit with Princess Margaret and discuss whatever subjects came up."

Although Crawfie described the Queen as "one of the loveliest people I had ever seen," she wrote that the Duchess of Kent was an "exceptionally beautiful woman" who, unlike the Queen, had married "the best-looking of all the Princes."

The Queen also objected to seeing personal details in print, such as the King's "blue-green draped bed" in his own bedroom "separate and away from the Queen." She did not like the reference to Margaret Rose's looking like "a plump navy-blue fish" in her bathing suit, and she was livid to read about "Uncle David" (the Duke of Windsor) being so "devoted to Lilibet." She was miffed that Crawfie had allowed the world to eavesdrop on the transatlantic call that the King and Queen had made to their children in 1939: "We

128

ended the conversation by holding the Queen's corgi, Dookie, up and making him bark down the telephone by pinching his behind."

And the Queen never forgave Crawfie for telling the stories of Lilibet's nursery, which indicated the future Queen's compulsive disorder as a child.

"She became almost too methodical and tidy," Crawfie wrote. "She would hop out of bed several times a night to get her shoes quite straight, her clothes arranged so." The image of such an obsessive youngster, "too dutiful for her own good," was painful.

The Queen knew that *The Little Princesses* would make Marion Crawford the most quoted royal historian of the twentieth century, because no one before had been given such intimate access to the royal family. Afterward, any mention of the author's name caused the Queen to turn away with displeasure. Her slang for treachery: "to do a Crawfie."

The King and Queen ordered their lawyers to institute loyalty oaths* for all future servants. Anyone who dared to "do a Crawfie" was sued by the Palace and stopped by the courts. Because of Crawfie, the subsequent see-and-sell memoirs of the royal servants had to find their markets outside the United Kingdom. No British publisher would dare dishonor the

* The following notice was given to all members of the royal household: "Communications to the Press: You are not permitted to publish any incident or conversation which may be within your knowledge by reason of your employment in the royal service, nor may you give to any person, either verbally or in writing, any information regarding Her Majesty, or any member of the Royal Family, which might be communicated to the press."

monarchy by venturing into print with unauthorized recollections. To do so would show flagrant disrespect and, not incidentally, prejudice his prospects for a knighthood. Over the years secrets seeped out of the House of Windsor, stripping the monarchy of its mystique and deflating the fantasy. By 1994 the chimera had been so exposed that all deference was gone. Not even the threat of litigation intimidated royal servants. The fairy tale thoroughly dissolved when Prince Charles, the future King of England, went on television and admitted adultery. His valet then revealed the future King's romps outside his marriage bed.

"He was in the bushes with his mistress and there was mud and muck everywhere," said the disgusted servant, who said he had to wash the royal pajamas. "They'd obviously been doing it in the open air." The valet was forced to resign his $18,000-a-year job, but he said he did not care. By then it was no longer an honor to be a member of the royal household. The royal family had tumbled so far off its pedestal that even royal servants were dismayed. The power of royal displeasure no longer carried the punch it did in 1949.

At that time, King George VI had his hands full. While dealing with the international commotion over Crawfie's book, and his own precarious health, he was being pestered by his son-in-law for permission to return to active duty. Prince Philip, who aspired to becoming an admiral, wanted to quit his office job at the Admiralty, where he said all he did was "shuffle ships around all day," and resume his career in the navy. The King was resisting because he knew Elizabeth would want to accompany her husband during his two-year tour, and the King did not want her to go. Weeks of family negotiations ensured what Elizabeth should do; when she agreed to commute to London every few months, the King agreed to release Philip from his desk. The Duke of Edinburgh left in October 1949 for Malta, where his uncle Dickie Mountbatten, second in command of the Mediterranean Fleet, eventually gave him command of his own frigate, HMS *Magpie*. Respected, not loved, he was called "Dukey" by his crew.

As she promised, Elizabeth remained in England for a few weeks with her baby. Soon, though, she left the eleven-month-old infant with his nannies and grandparents. She skipped her baby's first birthday to join her husband in Malta for their second wedding anniversary.

"[The] Princess had no very clear understanding of the way people lived outside Palace walls," said her governess, Marion Crawford. "But...when she flew to visit Prince Philip in Malta, she saw and experienced for the first time the life of an ordinary girl not living in a palace."

Lady Mountbatten agreed. In a letter to Jawaharlal Nehru, she wrote: "It's lovely seeing her so radiant, and leading a more or less human and normal existence for once."

The Mountbattens turned over their hilltop

131

quarters in Villa Guardamangia to Elizabeth and Philip during her visits, and the Princess so enjoyed herself that she extended her stay to spend Christmas with her husband. So little Prince Charles spent the holidays with his nanny, his grandparents, and his great-grandmother Queen Mary, whom he called "Gan Gan."

"He is too sweet stomping around the room & we shall love having him at Sandringham," the King wrote of his two-year-old grandson. "He is the fifth generation to live there & I hope will get to love the place."

Elizabeth returned home only when her husband went to sea, and Lady Mountbatten accompanied her to the airport.

"Lilibet had left with a tear in her eyes and a lump in her throat," Edwina Mountbatten wrote to a friend. "Putting her into the Viking when she left was I thought rather like putting a bird back into a very small cage and I felt sad and nearly tearful myself."

Back home, Elizabeth discovered she was pregnant. So she returned to Malta in March 1950 to tell her husband the news and stayed with him for another month. She returned to London in May and did not see Philip again until he came home for the birth of their daughter, Anne, on August 15, 1950. He stayed for four weeks before returning to Malta.

Elizabeth rejoined him there in November for three months, again leaving her children with their nannies and grandparents. Accompanied by her maid, her footman, and her detective, she arrived on the island with her sports car, forty wardrobe trunks, and a new polo pony for her husband. She spent her days relaxing in the sun, shopping, lunching with officers' wives, and getting her hair done in a beauty salon. Occasionally she toured military installations, cut ceremonial ribbons, and visited nursery schools. She filled her evenings with dinner parties, dances, and movies. On later trips she traveled with Philip to Italy and Greece. The Maltese press reported the personal cruise as professional business: "Like the wife of any naval officer, she is joining her husband on his station." While she said she considered herself "just another naval wife," she never discouraged curtsies or formal introductions as "Her Royal Highness the Princess Elizabeth, Duchess of Edinburgh."

The Maltese were enchanted with her, and the *Times of Malta* ran several stories reporting her visits to the Under-Five Club, for children whose fathers were stationed in Malta. But the paper did not raise the question of why she, unlike other military mothers, had left her own children, under the age of five, in England. Often, photographs appeared of her smiling and waving, attending Champagne parties, visiting churches, warships, and horse stables. She was hailed as "the best-loved, the most notable naval wife ever to visit these islands."

Back home, her press coverage was not

quite so gushy. One newspaper story wondered how she could abandon her children for weeks on end, especially when her son came down with tonsillitis. Other newspapers took her to task for looking like "an Edwardian vaudeville queen." Carpings about her weight and wardrobe disturbed her more than criticism about her children, especially coming from her husband.

"You're not going to wear *that* thing," he said when Elizabeth walked into his room to show him a new dress. "Take it off at once."

"It was all very upsetting," wrote Geoffrey Bocca in an early biography. "The Empire had on its hands a Princess it adored passionately, but a Princess that was both overstuffed and overdressed....As a non-smoker she did not have the assistance of nicotine to hold down the poundage...[so] she went off starchy food and she took appetite-reducing pills—a blue pill for breakfast, a green pill at lunch, and a chocolate pill at dinner."

The amphetamines, like all other medications for the Princess, were bought by a servant to preserve her privacy. "When sleeping tablets were prescribed to help her get a good night's rest, I got them in my own name," said John Dean. "To avoid drawing attention to the purchase and to the fact that they were for Princess Elizabeth."

During Elizabeth's longest stay in Malta, her sister came to visit, and the prospect of the glamorous, pouty-lipped Princess with her long, ornate cigarette holder and strapless gowns excited the bachelor contingent stationed on the small island.

"Malta is only ninety square miles in size, and Princess Margaret's arrival was big, big news for the men, who just about went crazy," recalled Roland Flamini, a diplomatic correspondent for *Time* magazine. "I was a teenager then, and because my father was writing Malta's constitution, I later got to meet Princess Elizabeth. I didn't have the slightest idea what to say to her, so I blurted out something about Princess Margaret's visit, and said I hoped that she had had a good time.

"'I haven't the faintest idea,' said Princess Elizabeth in her high-pitched voice. 'The little bitch hasn't written to me yet, or thanked me.'*

"I knew then that there was more to the proper, prissy-looking Princess Elizabeth than met the eye."

Because of her father's failing health, Elizabeth returned to London, and Philip had to follow a few months later after resigning from the navy. On July 16, 1951, he bade farewell to his crew. "The past eleven months have been the happiest of my sailor life," he said. Five days later he flew to England, where he was

---

*Forty years later, when Flamini wrote Sovereign: Elizabeth II and the Windsor Dynasty (Bantam Doubleday Dell Publishing Group, 1991), he recorded his introduction to Princess Elizabeth but was forced to alter the dialogue slightly. "The publishing lawyers refused to let me quote the future Queen of England calling her sister a 'Bitch,' " he said. "Although I was there and heard what she said, the lawyers maintained that no one would ever believe Elizabeth referred to her sister that way."

greeted at the airport by his young son, Prince Charles, and one of his son's nannies. But Elizabeth was not there. She was at the Ascot races.

Three months later, in October 1951, she and Philip were called upon to represent the royal family on a tour of Canada, which, after a diplomatic prod from the British to the Americans,* included a short visit to the United States. Once again Elizabeth and Philip left their children in the care of nannies and grandparents. They missed Princess Anne's first steps and the third birthday of Prince Charles, but before leaving England, they selected gifts for him, which they left with the King and Queen to present. They embarked on their five-week journey with an entourage of four servants and 189 wardrobe trunks. One suitcase contained a sealed parchment envelope with the Accession Declaration in case the King died during the tour. They spent almost a month in the Dominion, where their purpose, as described by the British Foreign Office, was "to show the flag" to fourteen million people whom the King still considered his subjects. He had insisted on the royal tour after hearing Newfoundland's Premier say,

* U.S. diplomatic memos suggest that the official invitation to Princess Elizabeth and the Duke of Edinburgh had to be coaxed out of the State Department. The cable to the Secretary of State, dated July 5, 1951, states: "Were no official United States invitation forthcoming, it might be misunderstood in England. A press report of today from London quoted a Buckingham Palace official as saying that the Princess would decide whether to visit the United States if and when she gets an American invitation. It is recommended that an official invitation to visit...in the fall be extended at an early date...."

"The cords that bind us to the Mother Country are only silken cords of sentiment." The King wanted those cords strengthened, so the royal couple crisscrossed Canada twice, traveling more than ten thousand miles through North America and visiting every province, including Newfoundland. All along their route, Elizabeth phoned her parents.

"Are you smiling enough, dear?" asked the Queen.

"Oh, Mother!" said her daughter. "I seem to be smiling all the time!"

Afterward she said Canada was "a country which has become a second home in every sense." Philip pronounced the country "a good investment."

When the royal couple arrived in Washington, D.C., for their two-day visit, President Harry S. Truman greeted them at the airport. Such a gesture was unusual for the President of the United States, but Truman was grateful to the "fairy Princess," as he called Elizabeth, for entertaining his daughter, Margaret, in London. His only child had been received by the royal family at Buckingham Palace, so he reciprocated by welcoming Elizabeth with open arms. When she came down the mobile stairway, he was waiting for her. Ignoring royal protocol, he addressed her affectionately as "my dear" and casually waylaid her at the foot of the airplane for ten minutes so photographers could take pictures. While she and her husband waited, Truman told jokes.

"Hundreds of police were milling about,"

recalled John Dean. "They told me they were amazed that the Princess and the Duke traveled with so little protection. I shall never forget the ride [we] were given to Blair House...for on our high-speed drive we were escorted by motorcycle police, with sirens blaring all the time."

Lines of uniformed police surrounded the President and guarded his armor-plated limousine. Jerking his thumb toward the security force, Truman said, "I suppose you haven't got the tradition of nuts that we've got." Knowing that Puerto Rican nationalists had tried to assassinate the President the year before, Elizabeth and Philip appreciated Truman's humor. When he stood with them in a receiving line, he announced they were ready by telling his aide, "Bring in the customers." The royal couple's smiling faces appeared in the next day's newspapers, and the President sent the photographs to the King. In his handwritten letter, Truman pronounced the trip a resounding success: "We've just had a visit from a lovely young lady and her personable husband," wrote the President. "They went to the hearts of all the citizens of the United States....As one father to another, we can be very proud of our daughters. You have the better of me—because you have two!"

The King responded to the expression of paternal love by sending a cable from Buckingham Palace: "The Queen and I would like you to know how touched we are to hear of the friendly welcome given to our daughter and son-in-law in Washington. Our thoughts go back to our own visit in 1939 of which we have such happy memories. We are so grateful to you, Mr. President, for your kindness and hospitality to our children."

With the White House under renovation, Bess Truman tried to spruce up Blair House across the street. She had removed all the air conditioners, as the royal couple had requested, and although surprised by their desire for separate bedrooms, she prepared a suite for Princess Elizabeth and moved in the blue damask four-poster canopy bed that the Trumans shared. The First Lady also hung flowered curtains from the presidential bedroom in the Princess's guest room and prepared an adjoining green suite for Prince Philip. "We brought in a small Oriental rug, with a table and a few books, to make it more cozy," recalled White House usher J. B. West. "But the Princess still had to use the concrete bathtub."

The Princess's maid and dresser, BoBo MacDonald, inspected everything before Her Royal Highness arrived and declared the accommodations satisfactory. "Why, it's just like her bedroom at Windsor Castle," she said.

Elizabeth never complained about her accommodations on foreign visits. She left that to her husband. On a subsequent visit to Washington, the royal couple again stayed in Blair House and were awakened throughout the night by the comings and goings of Secret Service agents. The next morning, Philip objected to U.S. Chief of Protocol Henry Catto. "I say, Catto. Do you employ professional door slammers in this house?" Duly chastised, Catto immediately ordered all the doorjambs to be lined in felt.

The President's elderly mother, who was bedridden on the top floor of Blair House, was looking forward to meeting the royal couple. "She'll kill me if she doesn't get to say hello to you," Truman told the Princess. So Elizabeth and Philip followed the President up six flights of stairs. Infirm and almost deaf at the age of ninety-eight, Martha Truman had learned that Winston Churchill had been returned as Prime Minister on October 25, 1951. So she was primed for the royal introduction.

"Mother," bellowed Truman, "I've brought Princess Elizabeth to see you!"

The little old woman beamed. "I'm so glad your father's been reelected," she said.

Elizabeth smiled and Philip chuckled as Harry Truman threw back his head and roared.

The folksy President had won the affection of the royal couple, and Elizabeth wrote him a three-page letter of thanks: "The memory of our visit to Washington will long remain with us, and we are so grateful to you for having invited us. Our only sadness was that our stay with you was so short, but what we saw has only made us wish all the more that it may be possible for us to return again one day...."

British Paramount News filmed one thousand

feet of newsreel on the royal visit to Washington, because after the GI presence in England during the war, Britons were intrigued with America. They packed the movie houses to see the footage. The Foreign Office complimented the British Ambassador to the United States for a job well done, and the Ambassador wrote to the President: "I am so delighted with the success of the visit of Princess Elizabeth and the Duke of Edinburgh that I feel I must express my own deep gratitude to you. I know from what they said to us how much Princess Elizabeth and her husband enjoyed their stay at Blair House."

On their return home, Elizabeth and Philip were buoyed by the praise they received for improving Anglo-American relations. The King and Queen met them at Victoria Station with Prince Charles, who timidly approached his parents as if they were strangers. The photograph of Princess Elizabeth greeting her three-year-old son with a pat on the back would haunt her years later when the young boy grew up and, citing the picture, criticized her for being a cold and distant mother.

The King, who had undergone three operations in three years, said he felt so much better that he wanted to reinstate his visit to Australia and New Zealand. "An operation is not an illness," he said, "and a sea voyage would be beneficial." His doctors adamantly refused, so once again Elizabeth and Philip were pressed into service. The King received tentative permission from his doctors to plan a therapeutic cruise to South Africa in the spring, and the departure date was set for the next March. The country rejoiced over the King's recovery. "By then he was esteemed to the point of tenderness," recalled writer Rebecca West. A national day of thanksgiving was declared for December 9, 1951. Church bells pealed, the Commonwealth thanked God, and the King knighted his doctors. Five days later he celebrated his fifty-sixth birthday at Buckingham Palace.

Preparing for the rigorous five-month trip ahead, Elizabeth asked that a rest stop be added to the itinerary so she could see the wild animal reserves of what was then called "Kenya Colony." She and Philip wanted to see the Sagana Royal Lodge at Nyeri, which had been their wedding present from the people of East Africa.

The royal couple left London by plane on January 31, 1952, with a small traveling party. The King and Queen and Princess Margaret went to the airport to say good-bye. Aboard the blue-and-silver royal aircraft, the King turned to BoBo MacDonald, his daughter's personal dresser.

"Look after the Princess for me, BoBo," he said. "I hope the tour is not going to be too tiring for you."

He disembarked and stood at the bottom of the steps, hatless and haggard. Newsreel cameras captured him in an overcoat, standing in the bitingly cold wind. He waved to his daughter and watched the plane until it became a speck in the sky. He never saw her again.

Five days later at Sandringham, in the early hours of February 6, 1952, he suffered a coronary thrombosis and died in his sleep. That morning, as the Queen was drinking her tea, Sir Harold Campbell came to her room to tell her that the King was gone. She hurried to her husband's chamber, walked to his bed, and kissed his forehead for the last time. She issued instructions for a vigil to be kept at his open door. "The King must not be left alone," she said. "And Lilibet must be informed." Quickly she amended her sentence. "The *Queen* must be informed."

The equerry backed out of the room to relay the awful news to the young woman, who had departed England a Princess and would be returning as Queen. Campbell did not reach the royal party because a tropical storm had knocked out the telephone lines in Kenya. So he contacted Reuters, which he deemed the most responsible news service, and asked that the message be conveyed to the royal party. Elizabeth and Philip had spent the night at Treetops, the remote observation post in the African jungle, where they watched animals gather at a salt lick in the shadow of Mount Kenya. At dawn the exhausted couple returned to the Sagana Royal Lodge to sleep for a few hours. A Reuters reporter received the news flash from London and located the Queen's private secretary, Martin Charteris.

"I remember he reached for a cigarette with trembling hands before he could tell me the King was dead," said Charteris, who relayed the news to Michael Parker, aide-de-camp to Prince Philip. "Mike," he said, "our employer's father is dead. I suggest you do not tell the lady at least until the news is confirmed."

The British Broadcasting Company made a formal announcement at 10:45 A.M., February 6, 1952, and, in a gesture of respect, went silent for the rest of the day. Stunned crowds filled the rain-drenched streets of London, and motorists stood in the middle of the street by their cars, weeping. Church bells tolled fifty-six times, one for each year of the King's short life. England's sorrow echoed around the world. In Australia a member of Parliament said, "We have lost a great bloke." In America the House of Representatives passed a resolution of sympathy and adjourned. President Truman wrote in his diary: "He was a grand man. Worth a pair of his brother Ed."

That brother, the Duke of Windsor, received the news in New York City, where he and the Duchess were staying at the Waldorf-Astoria. Winston Churchill advised him to return to England at once but cautioned against bringing the Duchess, who would not be received with propriety. The Duke sailed for England by himself, looking like a forlorn little man who had fallen off a charm bracelet. He stayed with his mother at Marlborough House, although he resented Queen Mary's hostility to his wife.

In Kenya Michael Parker hurried to Prince Philip's room to wake him. "It was his job to tell the Queen," said Parker. "Probably the worst moment of his life. All he could say was, 'This will be a terrible blow.' He took her out into the garden and they walked slowly up and down the lawn while he talked and talked and talked to her....I've never felt so sorry for anyone in all my life. He's not the sort of person to show his emotions, but you can tell from a man's face—how he sets his features. I'll never forget it. He looked as if you'd dropped half the world on him....The rest of us flew into action and were out of that place in an hour."

Elizabeth received the news without cracking. She walked slowly back to the lodge, where BoBo MacDonald was shining her shoes. Her personal dresser dropped to her knees in a deep curtsy. "Oh, no, BoBo," she said. "*You* don't have to do that." Her lady-in-waiting, Pamela Mountbatten, rushed to give her a comforting hug.

"Oh, thank you," said the new Queen. "But I am so sorry that it means we've got to go back to England and it's upsetting everybody's plans."

Martin Charteris entered with the dreaded envelope containing the accession documents, which required the new sovereign's name.

"I did what I had to do," he recalled. "I addressed her: 'The only question I have to ask you at this stage is, what do you wish to be called when you're on the throne?'

"'Oh, my own name, of course. Elizabeth. What else?'

"'Right. Elizabeth. Elizabeth the Second.'"

Many years later Charteris characterized the new Queen's reaction to her accession: "I remember seeing her moments after she became Queen—moments, not hours—and she seemed almost to reach out for it. There were no tears. She was just there, back braced, her color a little heightened. Just waiting for her destiny.

"It was quite different for Philip. He sat slumped behind a copy of the *Times*. He didn't want it at all. It was going to change his whole life: take away the emotional stability he'd finally found."

Charteris summoned the press to make the announcement about "the lady we must now call the Queen." He asked photographers to respect her privacy by not taking her picture as she prepared to leave. The photographers complied and stood by the side of the road as she passed, holding their cameras limp in their left hands and their right hands held over their hearts. The people of Kenya lined the dirt road to the airport for a solid forty-mile line. Black Africans, brown Indians, and white Europeans, subjects all, bowed their heads in silent tribute.

"There was very little conversation on the flight back to London," recalled John Dean. "BoBo and I sat together, with the royal couple immediately behind....The Queen got up once or twice during the journey, and when she returned to her seat she looked as if she might have been crying."

She was wearing the beige-and-white sundress she had on in Kenya and refused to put on mourning clothes until the very last minute. Upon landing, the Queen looked out the window and saw Prime Minister Churchill waiting with a clutch of elderly men in somber ration-book black suits and black armbands. She gasped when she saw the long line of black Daimler sedans.

"Oh, God," she whispered to her lady-in-waiting. "They've brought the hearses."

Composed, but unsure of what to do next, she turned to her husband.

"Shall I go down alone?"

"Yes," he said, acknowledging her sudden preeminence. As his wife's subject, he now was required to call her "ma'am" in public and walk four paces behind her.

Tears trickled down Churchill's cheeks and he struggled for composure as he offered his condolences.

"A tragic homecoming," said the Queen, "but a smooth flight."

After shaking hands with the plane's crew, and thanking each one, she stepped into the family Daimler and was driven to Clarence House, where Queen Mary, dressed in black, was waiting to pay her respects.

"Her old grannie and subject must be the first to kiss her hand," said Queen Mary.

The eighty-five-year-old woman, who would die thirteen months later, set the royal standard for mourning. After burying her husband, King George V, and two of her five sons, she declared black to be the color of death and to be worn only for doing death's duty. So the women of the House of Windsor never wore black except when grieving. "On royal trips, we always packed something black in the luggage in case news of any death reached us," said John Dean. "That is how it happened that the new Queen returned from tropical Africa dressed appropriately in a plain black dress, coat, and hat."

The Queen greeted her grandmother as always: by kissing her on both cheeks and curtsying. Queen Mary frowned and shook her head, insisting that she be the one to pay homage. Despite crippling arthritis, she dropped to the ground in a deep curtsy to her twenty-five-year-old granddaughter, who was now her sovereign. Then, standing upright, the elderly Queen chided the new Queen.

"Lilibet," she said, "your skirts are much too short for mourning!"

After seeing her grandmother, the Queen was led to St. James's Palace, where she made a poignant accession proclamation. "My heart is too full for me to say more to you today than that I shall always work as my father did," she said.

At Sandringham her mother and sister waited for her, mired in their own grief. Princess Margaret had locked herself in her room, almost inconsolable. "It seems that life has stopped forever," she told her mother. "I wonder how it can go on." The fifty-one-year-old Queen, not yet in black, resisted wearing widow's weeds. She returned to her room and began writing letters. She knew that she was now consigned to the role of Queen Dowager, a title that made her shudder. Ignoring protocol, she insisted on being called Queen Elizabeth the Queen Mother. Her biographer, Penelope Mortimer, suggested that she had devised the title because she could not cope with the sudden demotion she suffered from her husband's death. "In this way," wrote Mortimer, "she managed to be called 'Queen' twice over."*

Almost forgotten inside the big, hushed house at Sandringham was the King's three-year-old grandson, Charles, who was playing by himself, sliding a green toy crocodile up and down the great mahogany staircase.

"What happened, nanny? What happened?" he asked his nurse, Helen Lightbody.

"Grandpa's gone to sleep forever," she said, bowing to the bewildered little boy, who was now Duke of Cornwall, Duke of Rothesay, Earl of Carrick, Baron of Renfrew, Lord of the Isles, and Great Steward of Scotland. As the Crown Prince and heir apparent, he now outranked his father. Nanny took her royal charge by the hand and led him to bed for his nap.

* In response to this author's query about the title of Queen Elizabeth the Queen Mother, the Buckingham Palace Press Office offered a different interpretation: "No other widowed Queen Consort in English history has held a title such as Queen Elizabeth the Queen Mother, as no widowed Queen Consort has either had a reigning Queen as a daughter or lived to see her daughter crowned."

Upstairs, the King's body was moved from his bedroom to the small family church of St. Mary Magdalene, where it was guarded around the clock by his estate workers, who wore the same green tweed knickerbocker suits they wore when hunting with their King. They laid his royal purple standard over the coffin they had built that morning from Sandringham oak. Next to it they placed a white wreath from Winston Churchill. In his own hand, the Prime Minister had written: "For Valour." The Queen's flowers for her father arrived soon after and were placed on top of the coffin with her card: "To darling Papa from your sorrowing Lilibet." When she curtsied to her father's body at the funeral, it was the last curtsy she ever made.

Historians assessed the King as an important symbolic leader for the British during World War II, but they noted that his reign marked the end of the British empire. No longer King and Emperor, George VI was reduced to head of the Commonwealth of Nations and sadly watched Great Britain evolve into a welfare state. But France's Ambassador said the King had left his daughter "a throne more stable than England has known almost her entire history." To his countrymen the King remained a hero worthy of homage, a sovereign deserving respect. Soldiers wore black armbands after his death, and people contributed money for a memorial fund. Parliament voted $168,000 to pay for an elaborate state funeral on February

16, 1952, which included spreading purple cloth on the pavements so the white nylon ropes binding the King's coffin to the catafalque would not touch the ground.

On that day, two minutes of absolute silence were observed in memory of the monarch. A man, who defiantly slapped his feet on the street, was arrested for insulting behavior. Crowds of angry Britons mobbed him as he fled to safety in a policeman's arms. In court that afternoon, he was fined $2.80 for breaking the King's silence.

From the moment she stepped off the plane in London, the new Queen was engulfed by courtiers and advisers and equerries, all urgently directing her on her father's formal lying-in-state at Westminster Hall, his state funeral in London, his burial in St. George's Chapel at Windsor Castle, and the long period of national mourning. She was briefed on the protocol for entertaining prime ministers and high commissioners of Commonwealth countries attending the funeral and greeting the seven sovereigns from other countries, including her uncle David, the Duke of Windsor, who posed a ticklish problem. He wanted to discuss continuing the $70,000-a-year allowance he had been receiving from her father since 1936. Because those personal funds were now hers, she had to decide whether to keep paying him.

The Duke's lawyer argued that the money was a lifetime pension and his brother's compensation to the Duke for renouncing his inheritance. The Duke knew the new Queen would discuss the allowance with her mother and Queen Mary. "It's hell to be even that much dependent on these ice-veined bitches," he wrote to the Duchess from London. "I'm afraid they've got the fine excuse of national economy if they want to use it."

They didn't need it. The Queen Mother said the Duke already had millions of his own, which the Duchess simply squandered on fripperies like satin pillows for her dogs and Diorissimo perfume, which she sprayed on her flowers to give them added fragrance. Queen Mary, who collected antiques—frequently while visiting friends' homes and then sending her servant to "inquire" (that is, collect) the pieces she admired—said the spendthrift Duchess would only waste the money on her addiction to shoes, pointing out that she had once bought fifty-six pairs during one shopping spree. The new Queen deferred to her mother and grandmother and decided not to pay the Duke.

Upon the King's death, all royal possessions passed directly to the new sovereign, including the King's palaces, his twenty mares, his courtiers, and his private secretary, Sir Alan (Tommy) Lascelles. So, technically, Elizabeth's mother and sister no longer had homes or horses or courtiers. Worse, their eviction from Buckingham Palace would mean that Elizabeth and Philip would have to leave Clarence House, something neither wanted, and move into Buck House, as they called Buckingham Palace.

"Oh, God, now we've got to live behind railings," she said.

"Bloody hell," said her husband. He dreaded exchanging the modern comforts of Clarence House for the drafty caverns of Buckingham Palace, with its 10,000 windows, three miles of red-carpeted corridors, 1,000 clocks, 10,000 pieces of furniture, 690 rooms, 230 servants, and 45-acre backyard. King Edward VII had referred to it disparagingly as "the Sepulchre." King Edward VIII, later the Duke of Windsor, complained of the "dank, musty smell," and the Queen's father, King George VI, called it "an icebox." So Prince Philip, who said he "felt like a lodger," proposed using the Palace as an office and place of official entertainment while maintaining Clarence House as their home. The Queen put the idea to Winston Churchill, who sputtered indignantly. He insisted that Buckingham Palace was the sovereign's home as well as the sovereign's workplace—a focal point for the nation, the locus of the monarchy.

Hesitant to argue with the venerable Prime Minister, the Queen acceded and dutifully scheduled the move. Her husband was so incensed that he had the white maple paneling stripped from his study at Clarence House and moved to his bedroom in Buckingham Palace. Churchill then recommended that the Queen consider exchanging residences with her mother and sister. The Prime Minister confided his concern over her mother's mental state. He said he had heard that in her

153

grief the distraught widow had turned to spiritualism and even participated in a séance to speak to her dead husband. Churchill was so disturbed by the notion of the Queen Mother spirit rapping with ghosts that he traveled to Sandringham to persuade her to come out of retirement. He said that the government needed her more now than when her husband was alive. He offered to ease her return to public life by making Clarence House her London home.

"The Queen Mother had always thought highly of the bright comfort in which her daughter and son-in-law lived at the modernized Clarence House," said John Dean, "and even envied it. But when it was suggested that she should take over Clarence House, she seemed reluctant to leave the Palace. This was very understandable, for her large suite there was rich with memories of a beloved husband."

The Queen Mother told Churchill that she did not like the color scheme at Clarence House. He offered to change it. Then she said she could not bear to leave her bedroom in Buckingham Palace because the marble fireplace there had been a personal gift from the King. Churchill offered to move the fireplace to Clarence House. Still, she resisted, saying she couldn't afford to live in such luxury anymore. Churchill said that her presence was so vital to the monarchy that the government planned to allocate $220,000 to refurbish the mansion for her and to provide a yearly allowance of $360,000, plus a staff of fifteen. She also was given two other palaces: Royal Lodge, an elegant Gothic house in Windsor Great Park near Windsor Castle, and Birkall in Scotland. In addition she purchased the Castle of Mey, surrounded by twenty-five thousand acres of heather in Scotland. Still, she hesitated accepting Churchill's offer. "I was going to throw in Big Ben," he said later, "but she yielded—in time."

And the new Queen agreed to everything. She sympathized with her mother's sixteen years of royal prerogatives suddenly yanked—the crown jewels, the palaces, the servants, the title. What the Queen did not realize was how much her mother missed sharing the power of the throne. The Queen understood better as soon as she saw the letter the Queen Mother wrote to her friend Lady Airlie:

Oh, Mabel, if only you knew how hard it has been; how I have struggled with myself. All through the years the King always told me everything *first*. I do so miss that.

The Queen quickly ordered a new red leather dispatch box to be emblazoned in gold with the words "HM Queen Elizabeth the Queen Mother."

But the Queen did not extend this extra-ordinary privilege to her husband. In fact, she denied Philip the honor of sharing the red dispatch boxes that contained the confidential documents of government sent for royal approval. In this she broke all precedents: Queen Victoria had shared her boxes with Prince Albert. And her son and heir, King Edward VII, even shared his boxes with his daughter-in-law because he was so impressed by her devotion to the monarchy that he wanted her to be prepared to play her part behind the scenes when her husband became King. When he did become King, George V continued "doing" his boxes with his wife, Queen Mary, and his successor, George VI, did the same with his wife. But Queen Elizabeth II declined to carry on the royal responsibility with her spouse. Her advisers were so startled by her refusal that they posed the question again of permitting Philip to have access. Her reply: "No to the boxes." To her husband she blamed her advisers.

A few weeks later her friend Lord Kinross, third Baron of Glasclune, wrote a profile of Philip in *The New York Times Magazine* and quoted the Queen on how to manage husbands:

"What do you do when your husband wants something very badly and you don't want him to have it?" Elizabeth asked a friend.

"Well, ma'am," the friend replied, "I try to reason with him and dissuade him, and we sometimes reach a compromise."

"Oh," Elizabeth said reflectively, "that's not my method. I tell Philip he shall have it and then make sure that he doesn't get it."

The Queen held so tightly to her royal prerogatives that she would not even let her husband enter the Wedgwood blue room in Buckingham Palace during her weekly audiences with the Prime Minister.

"Before...whatever we did, it was together," Philip said of his marriage before the accession. "I suppose I naturally filled the principal position."

No longer. The strong, dominant, take-charge husband was suddenly unmanned. He was no longer on an equal footing with his wife. Constitutionally he had no status, except what he received from the Queen.

"I remember attending a dinner for only ten people," said Evelyn Prebensen, the daughter of the dean of the Diplomatic Corps. "And even then poor Philip could not sit down if the Queen was still standing. She was very much the monarch in the early years and insisted on her royal prerogatives. If Philip came into the room after she did, he had to bow to her and say, 'I'm sorry, Your Majesty.'"

His friends watched helplessly as Philip sank into depression after Elizabeth's accession.

"You could feel it all underneath," ex-King Peter of Yugoslavia told his wife after the King's funeral. "I don't know how long he can last...bottled up like that."

"He used to say, 'I'm neither one thing nor the other. I'm nothing,'" recalled Michael Parker's wife, Eileen.

Philip, who had aspired to be an admiral,

recognized that his career in the navy was sunk. He locked himself in his room and spent hours shut away by himself, confiding only in his eldest sister, Margarita.

"You can imagine what's going to happen now," he said with foreboding.

The day after the King's funeral, the Mountbattens entertained their German relatives at Broadlands, where Uncle Dickie boasted that the House of Windsor no longer reigned. With a Champagne flute in hand, he proposed a toast to the new House of Mountbatten. He boasted that the blood of Battenberg had risen from obscurity on the banks of the Rhine to the highest throne on earth. His cousin Prince Ernst August of Hannover reported the conversation to Queen Mary, who was outraged. As someone who studied genealogy like a miner assaying gold, she knew that Philip's family descended from the House of Schleswig-Holstein-Sonderburg-Glucksburg-Beck. She ticked off his royal antecedents like a child reciting the alphabet.

"Philip's name is *not* Mountbatten," she said. "If he has any name at all, it is Glucksburg."*

She summoned Churchill and reminded him that her husband, King George V, had decreed in 1917 that the House of Windsor was to be the royal family's name forever, and she said no amount of posturing by that

* Prince Philip's family—through the marriage of King George I of Hellenes to Grand Duchess Olga, granddaughter of Tsar Nicholas I—includes sixteen kings of the House of Oldenburg, seven tsars of Russia, six kings of Sweden, and three kings from the House of Schleswig-Holstein-Sonderburg-Glucksburg-Beck.

"ambitious upstart" Dickie Mountbatten could change the royal edict. The Prime Minister listened respectfully and marveled at how effectively the elderly Queen had buried her German roots to become an icon of Great Britain. She told him she had always despised Hitler because his German accent was so horrible. "He never could speak the language properly," she said.

Churchill called a cabinet meeting to discuss Mountbatten's claim. The cabinet ministers, mindful of the two world wars England fought against the hated Huns, insisted that the new Queen make a public announcement: she must affirm herself a Windsor and proclaim that all her descendants would bear the Windsor surname. Churchill and his ministers felt that anything less would cause political insurrection, so suspicious were they of Mountbatten's dynastic ambitions and liberal politics.* The Queen was duly informed. Churchill told her that "the feeling of the government reinforced by public opinion was that Her Majesty should drop the Mountbatten name and reign under your father's name of Windsor." Philip argued strenuously for the House of Mountbatten and Windsor and, failing that, pleaded for the House of Windsor and Edinburgh. But she relied on her Prime Minister and his advisers, which thoroughly

---

* The liberal politics of the Mountbattens shocked their conservative household staff. When a vote canvasser for the Labor Party called on them, Mountbatten said: "Don't worry about us. It's the servants you want to work on."

humiliated her husband.

"I'm just a bloody amoeba," he was heard to cry. "That's all."

Many years later Martin Charteris said, "I've always taken that to mean Philip [figured he] was just there to deposit semen."

The Queen even deprived her husband of that function. Having let it be known the year before that she had wanted to have another child, she now changed her mind. But she was angry when she read newspaper reports hinting at her pregnancy. During a meeting with Churchill and members of his cabinet to discuss the name change, she said sharply, "I expect these rumors to stop!" The next day the Prime Minister was quoted as saying, "She may not be pregnant, but she is certainly regnant."

After the row about renaming the House of Windsor, Queen Elizabeth II, the fourth sovereign of that dynasty, dutifully announced on April 9, 1952, that unlike every other wife in the realm, she would not carry her husband's name.

"It was very hurting to Prince Philip that the one thing he felt he brought to his marriage, which was his name, was no longer possible," said Countess Patricia Mountbatten. "But Churchill was an old, very experienced man, and [Elizabeth] was a very young and new Queen, and, understandably, she felt...it wasn't her place to stand up to him and say, 'I don't want to do this.'"

Philip's position was uncomfortable. When

a man ascends to the throne and becomes King, his wife automatically becomes his Queen Consort and is crowned with him. Not so when a woman ascends and becomes Queen. Her husband, who will never be King, remains a prince.

Elizabeth tried to mollify her husband by elevating his position within the realm. She declared that "His Royal Highness, Philip, Duke of Edinburgh, henceforth and on all occasions...shall have, hold and enjoy Place, Pre-Eminence and Precedence next to Her Majesty." This declaration of rank put Philip ahead of everyone in the kingdom, including someone who had once been King (the Duke of Windsor) and someone who would become King one day—Prince Charles.

The Queen then promoted her husband from lieutenant to Admiral, which entitled him to wear the uniform and receive full honors as Admiral of the Royal Navy.* She also elevated him to the highest rank in each of the other military services, making him Field Marshall of the Army, Marshall of the Royal Air Force, and Captain General of the Royal Marines. Despite these honors—sudden and unearned—Philip had no authority: he was only background music for the melody. During the painful adjustment to his wife's accession, he learned what his father-in-law, King

---

* When Mountbatten was promoted to Admiral of the Fleet, he arrived at Buckingham Palace to be greeted by Prince Philip, also wearing the same uniform. Someone asked, "Who salutes whom when you two meet as Admirals of the Fleet?" Philip said, "We salute each other, but only one of us means it."

George VI, had meant when he said: "Being a consort is much more difficult than being a sovereign. It's perhaps the most difficult job in the world."

Days after moving from Clarence House to Buckingham Palace, Philip had an attack of jaundice, a liver disease his friends attributed to stress and depression. Engorged with bile, he was confined to bed for three weeks. His valet, John Dean, served him his meals— "all boiled and bland"—and the Queen visited him three times a day.

"The Duke's complexion went a sickly yellow, and he was very disgusted and depressed when told what he had got," said his valet. "I paid great attention to him all the time he was ill, doing my utmost to meet his every wish, because I felt so sorry for him in that gloomy room."

Prince Philip recovered his health gradually but continued to feel diminished in his marriage. A few months later he rallied for the coronation because his wife had put him in charge of the ceremony, but the bleakness of being the Queen's Consort nearly capsized him.

"People forget what it was like when the Queen was twenty-six and I was thirty, when she succeeded [to the throne]," he told writer Fiammetta Rocco. "Well...that's when things started...."

SEVEN

The black armbands disappeared three months after the King's death, and for the next year the coronation of the Queen seemed to dominate the country's newsrooms, barrooms, boardrooms, and drawing rooms. The event was set for Tuesday, June 2, 1953, at 10:30 A.M., and until that moment, everything revolved around regalia.

The coronation, which was to be England's reward for prevailing in the war, resonated with the memory of sacrifice and the hope of rebirth. The hyperbolic British press wrote reams about the advent of "the New Elizabethan era" and compared the country's advances under Elizabeth I with the wonders that would occur under Elizabeth II. Then she herself spoke up to dampen the extravagant effusions.

"Frankly," she said, "I do not myself feel at all like my Tudor forebear, who was blessed with neither husband nor children, who ruled as a despot and was never able to leave her shores."

In distancing herself from her predecessor, Elizabeth II wrapped herself softly in marriage and motherhood. Forty-five years later she would be respected as a dutiful monarch and the most traveled in British history, but lacking as a wife and mother. Elizabeth I, though, would still be admired for the skill, intelligence, and fortitude with which she guided her country.

Coronation fever rose in 1953, and the

holiday mood swept over London and into the farthest reaches of the British Isles and dominions. British housewives carried brown ration books that controlled their butter, cheese, margarine, meat, and sugar. But now sugar restrictions were lifted, and people who had been deprived of cake, candy, and cookies for fourteen years indulged in sweets. Tea was derationed, and so were eggs. Wartime preoccupation with rifles, gas masks, and helmets stopped as everyone discussed jeweled swords, tiaras, and coronets. In honor of what was trumpeted as the New Elizabethan era, London turned itself into a gigantic merry-go-round of triumphal arches and twinkling lights. Purple flags and gold pennants with elaborate designs of crowns and scepters decorated the main streets. Shields and medallions adorned office buildings, and lampposts on major thoroughfares were painted a giddy combination of yellow, lavender, black, white, and red. Festive streamers and bunting festooned the seven-mile coronation route the Queen would take after her crowning. Exotic flowers flown in from Australia filled the gigantic boxes in front of Parliament, and two thousand square feet of new carpeting was laid in Westminster Abbey to accommodate the 7,700 guests the Queen had invited to witness her enthronement.

Recognizing the global interest in this event, the British Broadcasting Company suggested televising the coronation, but the Queen's courtiers said no. They said they did not want television cameras recording an event that they felt should be seen only by the aristocracy. They argued that it would be a commercial intrusion on a sacred ritual.

"I don't see why the BBC should have a better view of my monarch being crowned than me," said Prime Minister Churchill.

"Quite right," said the Queen's private secretary, Sir Alan Lascelles.

The Queen was consulted and was expected to concur. Instead she started asking technical questions about transmitting the ceremony to the far corners of the earth, how many microphones would be required, how the sound system would work, and where the cameras would be placed in the Abbey.

"But...but...the great and blinding light," protested Lascelles.

And the Archbishop of Canterbury chimed in, "It would be unfair to expose you...to this searching method of photography, without the chance of correcting an error, for perhaps two hours on end."

The Queen listened but disagreed. "I have to be seen to be believed," she said.

Days later she sent her husband to the Prime Minister's office with her decision: The BBC would be allowed to televise the coronation, but with one restriction: no close-ups. The Queen's democratic gesture astonished the conservative Prime Minister, but he recovered and presented her views to his cabinet.

"Her Majesty believes all her subjects should have the opportunity of seeing the coronation," he said.

His ministers argued and tried to reverse her decision, but Churchill said there were no options.

"After all, it was the Queen who was being crowned," he said later, "and not the cabinet."

The Queen's decision enabled the world to watch seven and a half hours of continuous live reporting. The television audience was the largest ever at the time—three hundred million. Later, when she visited the BBC to view her coronation coverage, she was delighted by what she saw. "She enjoyed it so much," said Peter Dimmock, the BBC coronation producer, "that she knighted George Barnes, who was director of television at the time. She knighted [him] on the spot in Limegrove, where she watched the recording."

"Allowing television cameras into the sacred precincts of Westminster Abbey was a key decision of her reign," said writer John Pearson. "It meant that the coronation...would be unique in the annals of the monarchy, the first time in history a sovereign had been crowned with millions of close and fascinated witnesses to the strange and powerful event...."

No other country has a coronation so steeped in mystique and majesty, laden with history, and imbued with religion. The occasion is celebrated with a festive holiday that includes songs, fireworks, and street fairs. Vendors hawk royally embossed gewgaws such as tea strainers, egg timers, pocket combs, and napkin rings. The commercial hoopla precedes a high church ceremony that combines the solemnity of a Papal installation with the impact of a presidential inauguration. All that plus the romance of a crown, orb, scepter, and gilded coach.

Nothing in the world is as elaborate as the pageantry surrounding a coronation, and nothing better defines the British monarchy. So the Queen was determined to stage the most magnificent crowning in British history. And it cost her government over $6.5 million—about $50 million in 1996 dollars. She felt it was a necessary investment for her impoverished country because the monarchy was, in her view, its most precious possession and the symbol of its historic continuity. Most other monarchies had crumbled under the weight of the two world wars, but the monarchy of Great Britain still dominated the life of the country. As Queen, Elizabeth II would reign over a shrinking kingdom known as the Commonwealth, a group of nations that included Australia, New Zealand, Canada, a few ports in the Caribbean, and some parts of Africa. But even without an empire, her crown still tied the Hong Kong coolie to the Australian Aborigine and the Rhodesian farmer and the Welsh miner. As Winston Churchill said, "The Crown has become the mysterious link—indeed, I may say, the magic link—which unites our loosely bound but strongly interwoven Commonwealth of nations, states and races." He did not need to add that the Crown also represented the biggest draw for tourist dollars. With at least two hundred thousand overseas visitors expected for a week in London, spending an average of $8 a day, the total amount estimated was $1.6 million every twenty-one hours.

"More money will change hands during coronation week than most English banks handle in an average year," predicted the *Times of London*. The newspaper estimated $300 million would be spent at the time, including $28 million for coronation decorations, $280,000 for fireworks on coronation night, and $10 million for the coronation parade.* "The British—after 14 years of war, reconstruction and austerity—just don't care."

The left-wing *Tribune* criticized the expenditure: "It really should be possible to crown a constitutional monarch in a democratic country without giving the impression that Britain has been transformed into Ruritania." The editorial page of the *Chicago Tribune* shouted, "Wake up, Fairyland!" And the communist *Daily Worker* said, predictably, the coronation represented the worst excesses of "luxury and flunkyism."

Unperturbed, the Queen summoned her

---

* The coronation became the most expensive celebration in British history. The U.K. government spent more than twenty-five times as much as the U.S. Treasury spent on President Eisenhower's inauguration in January 1953. British subjects withdrew $25 million from private savings accounts in less than two weeks to spend on the festivities. The spending spree prompted a sober editorial in the *London Times* that chided the British for taking "a holiday from reality."

personal couturier, Norman Hartnell. She requested ten designs for the lavish white satin gown she wanted to wear. She wanted to emphasize her small waist, so Hartnell designed an underskirt with nine layers of stiffened net to give her the fullness she desired. Then she decided she wanted the emblems of the eleven Commonwealth countries embroidered on the gown and encrusted with semiprecious jewels. So Hartnell refashioned his design to include England's Tudor rose, Scotland's thistle, Ireland's shamrock, the leek of Wales, Canada's maple leaf, South Africa's protea, the lotus of India and Ceylon, Pakistan's wheat, Australia's wattle, and New Zealand's fern. Then he hired six young women, who spent two months embroidering the Queen's gown. Money was no object to Elizabeth in her role as sovereign, but as the mistress of her own home, she was cheeseparing. Even as she dickered over the details of a gown that would cost her government $1 million, she scrimped on curtains.

"I was at her side while she leafed through a sample book of Bon Marché fabric with pretty designs for draperies," said William Ellis, former superintendent of Windsor Castle. "The Queen saw the prices and lifted her eyes toward me, lowered her head, and said with regret, 'They are truly pretty, Mr. Ellis, but I believe they are too expensive for me. It will be necessary to find something better priced.'

"The same thing happened with the lighting," Ellis recalled. "She refused a great number of excellent lampshades. Reason: too expensive. All of the lampshades that I finally bought for her had to be purchased locally in town and could only cost a few shillings. The Queen is very prudent about money."

At her other country homes, she regularly inventoried supplies and foodstuffs. "I remember her checking the liquor levels on the whiskey bottles every time she came," said Norman Barson, her former footman. "And she counted all the hams in the larder, too. Everything was logged. She was very businesslike and could spot if something was missing. She'd want to know why the cigarette box she remembered as full was half-empty, even though she didn't smoke. Or she'd ask why the gin was empty and where had the angostura bitters gone."

Absorbed with the mind-numbing details of the coronation, the Queen rehearsed by walking up and down the halls of Buckingham Palace with sheets trailing from her shoulders so she could learn how to walk regally with a sixty-foot train. She sat at her desk and worked on her dispatch boxes wearing the crown of St. Edward to get used to balancing the seven-pound weight on her head. In choosing her coronation stamp, she examined sixty-three designs. And to select her most flattering picture for her official souvenir,* she examined 1,500 photos.

* The Queen chose the photograph of herself and her husband in the state coach being driven to the opening of Parliament on November 4, 1952. She had been agitated that day because the procession was late. And she became upset when photographers crowded around. Then Prince Philip said, "Darling, give them one of your best." That made her laugh, which produced a smiling photograph—one of the few that did not make her look like a vinegary schoolmarm.

The Palace issued strict orders about what to wear during the ceremony in the cathedral. Gentlemen were required to wear dress uniforms, full decorations, and knee breeches. The Foreign Office cabled a series of instructions to embassies around the world: "If black knee breeches are worn, they should be of the same material as the evening dress coat, and should have black buttons and black buckles at the knee. Black silk stockings should be worn and plain black court shoes with bows—not buckles." Women were told to wear head coverings—preferably a diamond tiara—or a shoulder-length veil that dropped no lower than the waist. The diplomatic cables specified: "Any colour excepting black can be used for this headdress and it should be made in a suitably light material such as tulle, chiffon, organza or lace. It can be attached by a comb, jewelled pins, flowers or ribbon bows—but not with feathers."

Within Buckingham Palace, the livery room worked to outfit the men of the royal household in black velvet knee breeches with white silk stockings, black waistcoats, gold-braided tailcoats, lace neck ruffles, and patent-leather pumps with silver buckles. Fifteen thousand policemen were brought to London to handle the coronation crowds, and twenty thousand soldiers were assigned to line the coronation route. In accordance with ancient custom, the troops were ordered to abstain from sexual intercourse for forty-eight hours before the sacred crowning. The six young women who wore white satin gowns and carried the train of the Queen's gown were required to be virgin daughters of earls—"unmarried and untarnished." They were described by the *London Sunday Times* as the Queen's maids of honor—"the girls the whole world envied."

No movie star ever had a greater hold on her fans than this beloved twenty-six-year-old sovereign had on her subjects. They remembered her as a young girl "digging for victory" in her vegetable garden at Windsor during the war and recalled her as a fourteen-year-old, reassuring them sweetly over the radio "that in the end all will be well." They believed her then, and now, as she became the sixth Queen of England in her own right in four centuries, they gave her their hearts. One besotted poet, who stood in line all night to wave to her on coronation day, wrote:

I did but see her passing by
Yet I will love her 'til I die.

Even the elderly Prime Minister fell in love with the young Queen. "'Gracious' and 'noble' are words familiar to us all in courtly phrasing," said Churchill on the eve of the coronation, "but tonight they have a new ring in them because we know they are true about the gleaming figure which Providence has brought to us in a time when the present is hard and the future veiled." He was so enraptured with the photograph of the Queen smiling from her carriage window with her left arm raised in a wave that he ordered a large print, which he had framed. He hung the picture over his bed at his country estate, Chartwell.

The Archbishop of Canterbury also succumbed to the monarch's considerable charm. "On Coronation Day," he recalled, "this country and the Commonwealth were not far from the Kingdom of Heaven."

The *London Times* wrote: "The Queen represents the life of her people...as men and women, and not in their limited capacity as Lords and Commons and electors."

To her subjects, the Queen was an exemplar of respectability and the epitome of rectitude. She and her handsome husband and their two young children personified the ideal English family with simple values and ordinary virtues. In 1953 Britons revered their sovereign as someone ordained by God. Someone entitled to devotion. Someone they would lay down their lives for without hesitation. Allegiance to the monarchy filled a basic human need to believe in a cause beyond self-interest—something grand and momentous that excited the fervor of religion and patriotism. During the darkest days of the war, the royal family had made people feel good about themselves and the sacrifices they were making. When the King and Queen drove from Windsor to London every day during the Blitz to share with their subjects the risk of being bombed, they inspired fortitude. They fulfilled the fantasy of royalty, which was to always behave splendidly. To be above mere mortals. To be as noble as the legend of King Arthur and his Knights of the Round Table. By meeting these grandiose expectations, the King and Queen brought reverence and respect to the House of Windsor and bestowed a magic on the monarchy that made it unassailable.

The magic of the throne, heightened by the glamour of palaces and heart-stopping pageants, was so enchanting in 1953 that hordes of foreigners swarmed into London for the coronation, hoping for a glimpse of history. Americans, especially, were drawn by the allure of shining armour, prancing horses, and gilded coaches. They flocked to London in droves, captivated by the prospect of dancing at Hampton Court or attending a tea party at Buckingham Palace. The young Queen was so well liked in America that in a U.S. popularity poll she topped President Dwight D. Eisenhower, the most revered man in the country. In 1952 *Time* magazine named her "Woman of the Year," an honor previously bestowed on only one other woman—Wallis Warfield Simpson in 1936.

Major American newspapers, news services, and networks sent reporters to cover the coronation. The *Washington Times-Herald* sent a young woman named Jacqueline Bouvier, whose fascination with royalty eventually revolutionized fashion in the United States.*

* Upon her return from England, Jacqueline Bouvier became engaged to John F. Kennedy. They married on September 12, 1953. Seven years later he was elected President of the United States. His First Lady decided to wear hats "just like the Queen of England." She appointed her own couturier like

To cover the coronation, she crossed the ocean on the SS *United States* and reported back to her newspaper, "The passenger list aboard this ship reads like the *Mayflower* in reverse." She cited names like Freylinghusen, McLean, Reventlow, Arpels of Van Cleef & Arpels, CBS correspondent Walter Cronkite, Whitelaw Reid (publisher of the *New York Herald Tribune*), and the Duke and Duchess of Windsor. The Windsors were traveling with five pugs, two valets, and the Duchess's homosexual lover, Jimmy Donahue, the thirty-seven-year-old Woolworth heir. He was accompanied by his maid, his valet, his chauffeur, and his mother.

"Passengers stare at the Duke," reported Jacqueline Bouvier, "aware that if he had not abdicated, they would not be sailing to the coronation of his niece. Sometimes children ask him for autographs, which he gives cheerfully."

The Duke and Duchess were among the few passengers on board *not* going to England for the Queen's coronation.

"Why should he?" asked the Duchess. "He didn't go to his own."

The Windsors disembarked at Le Havre, France, took the train to Paris, and watched the ceremony on television at a party in the home of an American, Margaret Thompson Biddle. The Duke had received $100,000 for

the Queen and issued orders that she wanted her dresses, like to Queen's, to be originals. "Just make sure no one has exactly the same dress I do," she wrote to her designer, "or the same color or material." For her husband's inauguration, she imitated the Queen by wearing a white gown with a scaled-down version of the Queen's coronation cloak.

writing a ten-thousand-word article on the coronation for a U.S. magazine.* He also sold exclusive rights to United Press to photograph him watching the ceremony on television. At the party, he explained the long, complex ritual to the Duchess, providing historical details on the six phases of the ceremony— the recognition, the oath, the anointing, the investiture, the enthronement, and the homage. He sang all the hymns and identified the dignitaries as they moved across the screen, pointing to his friends and cursing his enemies. Seeing a close-up of the Queen, whom he affectionately called Lilibet, he complimented her regal carriage and pointed to her necklace of diamonds, which were as big as quail eggs.

"A Queen enjoys a marked advantage over a King on such an occasion," the Duke wrote, "when a combination of humility and resplendent jewelry play so important a role. A woman can go through the motions far more naturally and gracefully than can any man."

On the eve of the coronation, the Queen received the news that after several attempts the British had scaled Mount Everest.† She later bestowed a knighthood on Edmund Hillary of New Zealand for placing the Union

---

* While Britons were shamed by the abdication of King Edward VIII, Americans were enthralled, and so, naturally, the Duke and Duchess of Windsor spent a great deal of time in the United States. They became pert of New York's café society and what passes for high society in Palm Beach.

† The conquest of Mount Everest so captured the four-year-old imagination of Prince Charles that he climbed over the largest pieces of furniture in the Palace, announcing that he was "mountaineering." He snatched the towels from most of the Palace bathrooms to make "base tents."

Jack atop the world's highest mountain. In 1953 this summit of 29,002 feet was the last outpost on earth unknown to man. For a kingdom reduced from empire to commonwealth, and one suffering awful deprivation, the conquest of Everest triggered a national celebration. Months before the coronation, a census disclosed that 4.5 million people in England had no bathroom plumbing, and more than 900,000 Britons had no running water. Relatively few families had a car, a refrigerator, or a television set.

Peers of the realm attend the coronation as their traditional right to recognize, acclaim, and do homage to the new ruler. This was one of the few times when they wore their coronets and robes of rank and, for a few hours, relived times past when the power and privilege of the peerage predominated. In 1953 Great Britain was so impoverished that most of its 860 peers and peeresses could not afford to spend $600 for new coronation robes of red velvet trimmed with ermine. Some patched up old robes that had been used in 1937 for the coronation of King George VI, but most of the lords and ladies resorted to renting cotton velveteen capes stitched with shaved rabbit. The white fur trim was officially called miniver* to make it sound richer and more imposing. For the coronation parade, the country's cavalry, which had to sell most of its horses during the war, borrowed 350 dray

---

* Miniver was a plain white fur esteemed in the Middle Ages as part of a costume.

horses from breweries and rented 100 horses from Alexander Korda's film company.

Coronation Day arrived under gray skies, but when the Queen left Buckingham Palace and stepped into her gold state coach,* the rain stopped briefly. The huge carriage, weighing four tons, swayed back and forth as the eight gray horses, led by one named Eisenhower,† cantered down the Mall. The Queen, who had rehearsed every detail of this day for the past year, sat next to the Duke of Edinburgh. When she saw the columns of people lining the street to honor her, she smiled. Some had camped out all night, enduring steady rain and freezing winds just to see her pass by. The Queen tilted her head from side to side, and as she had practiced, she recited the phrase devised by her courtiers to carry her through the two-hour procession to and from the Abbey so that she would look as though she were talking to her subjects.

As her coach glided past her subjects, she said, "So kind, so nice, so very, very loyal," and she raised her arm in an elegant wave. "So very, very loyal."

She repeated the refrain over and over as the Duke of Edinburgh, sitting by her side, smiled

---

* The gold state coach was built for George III in 1762 from a design by a Florentine artist, Giovanni Battista Cipriani, who was living in London. The coach, twelve feet high, twenty-four feet long, and eight feet wide, is gilded on the exterior and lined with crimson satin and has been used for every coronation since 1831.

† As Supreme Allied Commander in Europe, Dwight D. Eisenhower enjoyed a special relationship with the British royal family, fostered during the Second World War.

easily and returned the salute of soldiers standing at attention under the Admiralty Arch.

Inside the Abbey, the peers of the realm began their stately procession down the long aisle. The measured line was broken when the Prime Minister, stooped from the weight of his seventy-eight years, saw his old friend, George C. Marshall, former Chief of the U.S. General Staff in World War II and now chief of the U.S. delegation to the coronation. Marshall had been assigned the most prestigious seat in the Abbey out of respect for the rebuilding plan for Europe that bore his name and later won him the Nobel Peace prize. Churchill was so moved to see the seventy-two-year-old General that he impulsively broke ranks to clasp his hand. Flushed and happy, the Prime Minister looked like a big red tomato.

The lords and ladies took their places on their little gold chairs with tufted velvet cushions. Outside, the populace camped on the curb or sat in one of the $14 stadium seats erected to watch the Queen pass in her golden carriage, wearing her heavy crown and holding her orb, a jeweled globe, in one hand and her scepter, a jeweled rod, in the other.

Heralded by trumpets and the voices of four hundred young Westminster choirboys, the Queen made her way down the aisle of the Abbey to begin the ancient ritual of her coronation. Throughout the ceremony, the Duke of Edinburgh, sitting with the Princes of the

Blood Royal, the Duke of Gloucester and the young Duke of Kent, never for one moment took his eyes off her. At times he leaned forward tensely as she went through the elaborate ceremony.

The supreme moment of the day was timed for 12:30 P.M., when the Archbishop of Canterbury anointed Her Majesty with sacred holy oil and placed the crown on her head, proclaiming her Queen Elizabeth II of England "by the Grace of God, of the United Kingdom of Great Britain and Northern Ireland and of Her other Realms and Territories Queen, Head of the Commonwealth, Defender of the Faith, Sovereign of the British Orders of Knighthood, Captain General of the Royal Regiment of Artillery."

Those words enthroned the monarch, whose blood flows from the Saxon King Egbert through Henry VIII and Mary Queen of Scots, linking Elizabeth II to every English sovereign since William the Conqueror. As Queen, she became Supreme Governor of the Church of England and Defender of the Faith. Her royal prerogative gave her ten powers: dismiss the government; declare war; disband the army; sell all the ships in the navy; dismiss the civil service; give territory away to a foreign power; make everyone a peer; declare a state of emergency; pardon all offenders; establish a university in any parish.

As a constitutional monarch, she reigns but does not rule. Her only rights are to be consulted, to be informed, to encourage, and to warn, and even those are more limited than they were in the days of her ancestors. Her role is mostly ceremonial, and her activities—opening Parliament, signing legislation, appointing officials, bestowing medals and titles—are ritual. In practice, her official actions are no more than mandatory approvals of her government's wishes. Still, her symbolic power is considerable, for as "the Queen" she personifies Great Britain. The government is "Her Majesty's Government," not Britain's government. British passports are issued "in the Name of Her Majesty," not in the name of the state. Her face appears on stamps and coins. Her royal arms dominate the judiciary. Her royal insignia governs the church. Cabinet ministers are her ministers, state departments are her agencies, and those living within her realm are her subjects. There are no citizens, only subjects, in Great Britain, and the country's armed forces and the police serve "the Queen," not the people.

Her greatest power as Queen is the emotional hold she exerts on her people, who toast her health at every formal banquet and dinner and whose National Anthem beseeches God to protect her. As the fountainhead of such honor, she is a sacred symbol that elevates her above criticism. From this pinnacle she commands absolute fealty.

"Because of her exalted position," wrote the Duke of Windsor in his coronation article for an American magazine, "it is possible for the monarch by the influence of example and personality to impart a character and coloring to an era in a manner that lies quite outside the day-to-day functions of government."

After the Archbishop set the crown on her head, Prince Philip rose to be the first to pay her homage. In the full dress uniform of Admiral of the Fleet, he walked to the foot of the throne, took off his coronet, and bowed. He walked up the five steps and knelt at his wife's feet. She took his hands in her own as he said:

I, Philip, Duke of Edinburgh, do become your liege man of life and limb, and of earthly worship; and faith and truth I will bear unto you, to live and die, against all manner of folks. So help me God.

He touched her crown and kissed her left cheek before returning to his chair.

"It was a gesture which had all the humility of a subject and the tenderness of a husband," wrote a British journalist, "and for a brief moment the Queen pressed her cheek close and firm to her husband."

That night the young Queen paid public tribute to the man she had married. In a radio address to her loyal subjects, she pledged "with all my heart" to devote her life to the service of her people. "In this resolve," she said, "I have my husband to support me."

As the Queen departed Westminster Abbey to the shouts of "Vivat Regina!" trumpets sounded and church bells pealed. Enraptured crowds cheered as the stately coaches of seventy-four foreign powers made their way along the coronation route. Despite the downpour, Queen Salote of Tonga rode in an open carriage, the only head of state to do so. An enormous woman, she waved her huge, fleshy arms to greet bystanders and completely overshadowed the frail little man sharing her carriage.

"What's sitting across from her?" someone asked.

"Her lunch," said Noel Coward.

The Sultans of Brunei, Johore, Perak, Lahej, Kelantan, Selangor, and Zanzibar passed in colorful turbans, silk saris, and extravagant plumage. The native dress of the Zulus, Arabs, Indians, Chinese, and Nepalese dazzled bystanders. To heighten the drama of the parade, BBC technicians laid microphones on the ground to magnify the thundering beat of the horses' hooves and tape-recorded nightingales to sing continuously in Berkeley Square.

The emotion reduced some men to tears. "When her carriage went past, I felt as if my heart were bursting," said Richard Smith, a soldier on duty. "We were virtually crying as we presented arms to the Queen. We were no more than ten yards away, and I don't think I've seen anything as beautiful in all my life."

Similar feelings swept through the cathedral. "Although our preparation was intense, the one thing the rehearsals hadn't prepared us for was the emotion of the ceremony, especially the entry of the Queen and her procession," said a radio announcer, John Snagge. "I was overwhelmed: Handel's 'Music for Royal Fireworks' on the organ, everyone standing, then Parry's anthem—Oh, it was the most moving moment."

The BBC engineer, who was supposed to black out close-ups of the Queen during the coronation, was so transfixed that he could not censor her image.

"Gorgeous, she was," recalled the engineer, Ben Shaw. "I thought the close-up picture of her was so beautiful that I couldn't press the button."

As Queen, Elizabeth became the head of two separate churches—the Church of England, which is Episcopalian, and the Church of Scotland, which is Presbyterian. For her assumption of authority, she took the sacraments and worshiped in both churches. In England she prayed as an Episcopalian, and in Scotland as a Presbyterian. Having sworn to govern all her peoples according to their respective laws and customs, she traveled north soon after her coronation in London for a second coronation in Edinburgh to receive the ancient crown of Scotland.

"This was her first visit to Scotland as Queen, and, naturally, everyone expected her to come in her coronation robes," recalled Margaret McCormick, who attended the event. "I was in my Sunday best and was shocked when she appeared in a simple gray blue coat, because she looked so...so...so...ordinary. She should've honored the occasion more."

In St. Giles Cathedral, the Queen, who was surrounded by the Scottish peerage in their velvet cloaks and coronets, looked strangely out of place in black leather shoes, a gray blue felt hat, and a street-length coat, especially next to the Duke of Edinburgh, who was dressed magnificently in a plumed helmet and gold-braided uniform. The most jarring part of the Queen's attire was the big black purse she was carrying in the crook of her arm. To the Scots she looked like a middle-class housewife on her way to the grocery.

At the altar she stepped forward while the Duke of Hamilton and Brandon knelt before her in his coronation robes to proffer the crown of Scotland on a velvet cushion with gold tassels. As she reached toward him, her leather handbag, which was as large as a breadbox, almost hit him in the face. He quickly moved his head to avoid getting smacked by the royal purse.

In the official painting commemorating the ceremony, the Queen is shown receiving the ancient crown of the Highlands but without her handbag. The Scottish portrait artist deliberately left out the purse because he could not bear to render his sovereign looking like a commoner.

The atmosphere around the Queen was so reverential that no one dared utter a word of criticism about her attire, which was viewed by some in Scotland as insulting. She would

185

falter a few more times in her new role, but each misstep would be carefully papered over by her courtiers, whose mission in life was to burnish the myth that the monarch was perfect.

These courtiers, whose families had been in royal service for hundreds of years, were either military men or from the landed gentry. "The circle around the throne is aristocratic," editorialized the *Daily Mirror,* "as insular and—there is no other word for it—as toffee-nosed as it has ever been." The courtiers felt that their positions were ordained in the Book of Proverbs: "A scribe skillful in his office, he shall find himself worthy of being a courtier....Seest thou a man diligent in his business? He shall stand before kings." With a heightened sense of superiority, these courtiers did for the Queen what they had always done for her father: they determined what she would do and say publicly and whom she would see, from debutantes to diplomats. The courtiers also protected the Crown from stain, blemish, and disgrace. They did this by controlling the flow of information to the public.

In the beginning of Elizabeth's reign, the courtiers expected reporters to be deferential, and for the most part the press obliged. This fandango between press and palace enabled the courtiers to fabricate news, withhold information, and impose restrictions without question. The courtiers manipulated the press to mold public opinion, and some of their efforts to make the monarch appear worthy of respect seem ridiculous in retrospect, but their dedication was unquestionable and their loyalty unswerving. In the beginning of Elizabeth's reign, her courtiers sought to present her as grand yet genteel. They refused to admit that she enjoyed playing canasta or that for her first royal portrait sitting, she arrived carrying her tiara in an egg box. They reluctantly admitted that she loved horse races, a fact not worth denying because she was constantly at the track, but they claimed she never gambled.

"Her Majesty never bets, but she shows great delight when a royal horse wins," the Queen's press secretary told *US News & World Report*.

In fact, the Queen always bet on her horses and twice topped the list of money-winning owners on British tracks in 1954 and 1957. She even advised the Palace stewards when not to bet on her horses. Yet because gambling was illegal and something that the courtiers felt a revered monarch should not indulge in, they promoted the fairy tale that the Queen never wagered.

Within four years a critic denounced these courtiers as fusty, old-fashioned, and hidebound. The critic, Lord Altrincham, derided them as "a second-rate lot." Altrincham later renounced his hereditary title and became known simply as John Grigg. A historian, he achieved recognition as the man who publicly criticized the Queen as "priggish" and "poorly educated" and lambasted all the Queen's men as blinkered and inept.

At the time of the coronation, such criticism was so outrageous as to be blasphemous. The monarchy was still revered enough that even those who served it were considered untouchable. The only voice of dissent being heard came from within the Palace walls, and that was the irascible growl of the Queen's husband, who was appalled by the inefficiency he found all around him.

Pronouncing his wife's courtiers "creaky" and their administration of Buckingham Palace "medieval," Prince Philip scorched most of the 230 servants as "goddamned idiots who wait on each other—not on us." Insisting on naval efficiency, he regarded the 690-room Palace as a leaky old rust-bucket that he had to make seaworthy. Beginning with the footmen, he said the practice of "powdering" their hair with a messy mixture of soap, water, flour, and starch was "old-fashioned and unmanly." He stopped it. He pronounced the Palace communications system "hopelessly antiquated" and instituted a system to get rid of the "bloody pages running all over the place." He ordered a modern intercom installed so that with a flick of a switch the Queen could contact him, her secretaries, the children's nannies, even her chef. Next, the gadget-minded Duke ordered intercoms put in every office and two-way radios put in all royal cars. He introduced Dictaphones, tape recorders, and automated filing systems. He had washing machines installed in the Palace basement to replace the platoon of laundresses scrubbing overtime on washboards. He ended the Palace system of running several dining rooms at full steam all day long just so the servants could eat. He commissioned small pantries with hot plates and refrigerators to be installed in the royal suites so servants would not have to walk three miles of corridors just to take the Queen her coffee every morning. He did away with placing a fresh bottle of Scotch by the monarch's bed, a quaint practice that had been going on since 1910 when Edward VII asked for a whiskey to counteract a cold. No one had ever canceled the order.

He did allow the Queen to keep her bagpiper. In a tradition started by Queen Victoria, the Pipe Major of the Argyll and Sutherland Highlanders marches across the terrace of the Palace at nine o'clock every morning, playing the bagpipes.

For the hidebound courtiers, who preferred having young pages in silk breeches run messages by foot, as they had done in the days of Queen Victoria, Philip was radically disruptive. They protested his time-motion studies of the staff and objected to his heliport behind the Palace to save commuting time. They opposed his plan for marketing surplus peas from the farmlands at Sandringham and sneered when he installed bread slicers and carrot-washing machines. They objected when he ordered that Queen Victoria's orangerie at Windsor Castle be converted into a heated swimming pool. They especially disapproved of his mingling with the masses and said he didn't distinguish between commoners and aristocrats. They cringed when he entertained labor leaders and shuddered when he invited movie stars to lunch with the Queen. Allowing film stars into Buckingham Palace was worse than permitting untouchables into a shrine.

"Why, that German princeling," snapped the Queen's private secretary, Tommy Lascelles, who did not understand or appreciate Philip's efforts to keep his wife attuned to the real world.

"That man is no gentleman," said Commander Sir Richard Colville, the Queen's press secretary, fuming. "And he has no friends who are gentlemen." For a courtier whose honor was invested in being considered a gentleman,* this was a debasing insult, but the swipe was passed privately. As so-called gentlemen, the courtiers were careful to be correct in public because they could not afford to be openly hostile to the Queen's husband. On the surface they acted civilized, and in his presence they addressed him respectfully. Behind his back they savaged him. Philip, who cared little about being defined as a gentleman, barged ahead with his sweeping innovations.

* In 1995 anthropologist Geoffrey Gorer wrote a book, Exploring English Character, in which he questioned the beliefs, prejudices, and habits of mind of large numbers of the English middle class. He found that the English people as a whole are deeply obsessed with restraining any element of violence and rate gentleness very high as a virtue. They regard impatience and loss of temper as major sins. Being considered a gentleman means everything.

"It's our job to make this monarchy business work," he said. He functioned for the Queen in much the same way Eleanor Roosevelt had done for the President. She had been his eyes and ears, his emissary to the masses. Philip was determined to revitalize the Crown and make it relevant to people's lives. He accepted honorary positions with groups like the National Playing Fields Association and fought hard to establish the Duke of Edinburgh Awards Scheme, which rewards young people for outstanding achievements in sports, cultural activities, and voluntary service.

The Ministry of Education was highly suspicious of a scheme bearing the obvious imprint of Dr. Kurt Hahn, the German founder of Gordonstoun, which was Philip's alma mater. The Minister of Education was more than a little dubious about the Duke of Edinburgh. "I had a rather difficult interview," admitted Philip many years later. "As with all our organization, it worked on the 'not invented here' syndrome. Anything you haven't thought of yourself is bound to be wrong....But gradually, as they came to realize what the scheme was about, and that it wasn't a new Hitler Youth movement, people began to realize that there was some merit in it."*

* The Duke of Edinburgh Awards Scheme is operated in more than fifty-five countries, but under a variety of names: the Benelux Award in Belgium; the Crown Prince Award in Jordan; the Gold Shield Award in South Africa. In Australia, Jamaica, and New Zealand, it is called the "Dee of Ee." Prince Philip says, "I don't give a damn what they call it as long as it is compatible with the one that runs here."

With frenetic energy Philip toured plants and factories and schools, constantly asking questions: "How do you make that work? Can't you find a better way? Faster? More efficient?" He fought the courtiers at every turn, refusing to let them write his speeches and, worse, refusing to follow their advice to say nothing. He insisted on being heard, and to their dismay, he was.

As President of the British Association for the Advancement of Science, he hectored the members for being complacent.

"It's no good shutting your eyes and saying, 'British is best' three times a day after meals and expecting it to be so," he said. "I'm afraid our no-men are a thousand times more harmful than the American yes-men. If we are to recover prosperity, we shall have to find ways of emancipating energy and enterprise from the frustrating control of the constitutionally timid."

The courtiers worried about negative press reaction to Philip's outspokenness. Already overworked, they had been trying for months to squelch a potential scandal involving the Queen's twenty-three-year-old sister, Princess Margaret, and Group Captain Peter Townsend, the thirty-eight-year-old equerry who had served her father since 1944 and was now working for her mother as Deputy Master of the Household. For months the courtiers had been denying rumors of a romance, but a newspaper photograph taken during the coronation showed the Princess flicking a piece of fluff from Townsend's shoulder. The intimacy of that small passing gesture revealed the truth and threw the Palace into confusion.

A fighter pilot in World War II's Battle of Britain, Peter Townsend had received the Distinguished Flying Cross and the Distinguished Service Order for valor. He then became the King's favorite equerry. With the same gentle appeal of Leslie Howard playing Ashley Wilkes in *Gone with the Wind*, Townsend was a charming man with humor. He was not robust and swaggering like Prince Philip, but slightly fragile and emotional. He stammered, which was one reason the King, who also stammered, loved him. Townsend had suffered a nervous breakdown in the RAF and had been grounded occasionally because of his incurable nervous eczema. To everyone who met him, he appeared graceful and considerate, the paradigm of an officer and a gentleman. "We were all in love with him," said British novelist Angela Lambert. "He was handsome, brave, romantic and discreet," wrote Francois Nourissier in *Le Figaro* upon his death in 1995. "He was one of those men without whose heroism and sacrifice our lives would have been no doubt less free, less honourable. An England, which I hope still exists, invented a kind of complete man that was one of the successes of Europe. Peter Townsend was the last of this species, now threatened with extinction."

Townsend had known Margaret since she was fourteen years old and, as a favor to her parents, had escorted her to dances and horse shows. He had served as her riding companion and flown her plane in the King's Cup air races. By the time she was twenty-one she had fallen in love with him. She pursued him openly, and each time he resisted her advances, she resorted to her royal prerogatives.

Coming home from a dance one evening, she demanded that he carry her up the stairs. He demurred. She insisted. He still resisted.

"Peter, this is a royal order," she said, stamping her foot.

The handsome equerry laughed and scooped her into his arms. "Ever your obedient servant, ma'am," he said, sweeping her up the staircase of Clarence House.

"Margaret was quite blatant," said her friend Evelyn Prebensen, whose father, the Norwegian Ambassador, was dean of the Diplomatic Corps in London. "I spent a lot of time with her in those days and remember one Christmas when the King had promised Peter time off to be with his family. Margaret got it into her head that she wanted to play cards, and she insisted Peter play with her. So he was forced to forgo the holiday with his family and dance attendance on Margaret. No wonder his wife wandered."

In 1952 Townsend was granted a divorce on the grounds of his wife's adultery and received custody of their two sons. Although he was the aggrieved party, his divorce traumatized the Queen's courtiers, who still felt haunted by the 1936 divorce that had led to the only abdication in British history and resulted in exile for the disgraced King. Divorce was considered such an abomination that the Lord Chamberlain,* Head of the Queen's Household in England, had to insure that no divorced person was ever allowed into the Queen's presence.† He even excluded from the royal enclosure at Ascot such a distinguished figure as Laurence Olivier, considered England's greatest actor, because of his divorce. In Scotland, Lyon King of Arms was the moral arbiter, and he, too, struck the names of all divorced persons from royal guest lists. One Scottish nobleman protested his exclusion from a royal visit to Edinburgh because he had been divorced.

"My marriage was annulled," said the nobleman, "and I've been remarried in the church."

"That may well allow you into the Kingdom of Heaven," said the Lyon King of Arms, "but it will not get you into the Palace of Holyroodhouse."

In 1953 Princess Margaret's love affair with Townsend, a divorced man, shook the British establishment, and the government, the

---

* In later years the Lord Chamberlain's duties were modified so the Queen could visit her divorced cousins, her divorced sister, her divorced daughter, and her two divorced sons, including the heir to the throne.

† The restrictions on divorced persons being allowed to share the same air as royalty were relaxed slightly after Peter Townsend's divorce. Only those divorced persons who were legally blameless for their divorce were admitted into the company of royalty. This policy allowed Townsend, who was wronged by an adulterous wife, to continue in royal service. From 1950 to 1953 he acted as head of the Queen Mother's household. For the rest of his life, even in exile, his name was listed in Witaker's Almanac as an extra equerry to Her Majesty the Queen.

church, and the royal family became intensely embroiled in the romance. As a royal princess, Margaret Rose, who was third in line to the throne, was excused for falling in love, while Townsend, a commoner, was condemned for crossing class lines.

"What cheek!" said the Duke of Edinburgh. "Equerries should look after the horses!"

The Queen's courtiers were equally outraged. They believed in the supremacy of the class system as defined by the doggerel they had learned as children:

God bless the squire and all his relations.
And keep us in our proper stations.

When Peter Townsend confided he had fallen in love with Princess Margaret, the Queen's private secretary, Alan Lascelles, snapped, "You must be either mad or bad." Lascelles quickly conferred with the Prime Minister.

"Captain Townsend must go," declared Winston Churchill. "He simply must go."

In desperation the courtiers decided to follow Churchill's advice and banish Townsend from England. They foolishly believed his relationship with the Princess would founder under the separation, not realizing that distance might lend enchantment. They cared only about buying time until Margaret's twenty-fifth birthday. Until then she was not allowed to marry without her sister's permission, and as head of the Church of England, her sister could never allow her to marry a divorced man. By separating the couple, the courtiers also quashed the publicity that threatened to overshadow the Queen's first royal tour of the Commonwealth.

Townsend, who was scheduled to accompany Princess Margaret and the Queen Mother on their 1953 tour of Rhodesia, was suddenly yanked out of royal service and dispatched to the embassy in Brussels as an air attaché. "I came here because the position was impossible for us both," he told a reporter. "I cannot answer questions because I am not the prime mover in the situation. My loyalty to Princess Margaret is unquestionable. I would undergo any difficulties because of that loyalty."

Townsend was banished so quickly that he did not have time to prepare his sons, boarding at a prep school in Kent, for the news. Margaret pleaded frantically with her sister to reverse the decision, but the Princess was refused. The sisters had a terrible row.* Margaret took to her bed for three days and lived on sedatives. When she got up, she sat at her piano and poured her misery into her music. "I composed a lament, words as well as music," she told biographer Christopher Warwick. "That was after Peter Townsend and I knew we couldn't get married." Townsend had left

---

* Years later Princess Margaret said, "I have only twice ever had a row with the Queen. These were probably both about men." She explained to the historian Elizabeth Longford, "In our family we do not have rifts—a very occasional row, but never a rift."

the country immediately upon his return from Northern Ireland with the royal couple and was last seen in England on the tarmac, shaking hands with the Queen and Prince Philip.* He returned quietly to visit the Princess twice before her twenty-fifth birthday, meeting her secretly at the homes of friends.

In October of 1955, a few weeks after her twenty-fifth birthday, Margaret went to Windsor Castle to talk to the Queen and Philip. In an emotional meeting they told her that the government of Sir Anthony Eden was implacably opposed to the marriage, as was the Archbishop of Canterbury.

"You are third in the line of succession," said Philip.

"I can count," Margaret snapped.

"You've caused a constitutional crisis," continued Philip, pointing to the lead editorial in the *Times,* which stated that a sister to the Queen, Governor of the Church of England, Defender of the Faith, had to "be irrevocably disqualified from playing her part in the essential royal function" if she married a divorced man.

"If you persist in your plans to marry," said the Queen, "you will not be allowed a church blessing." She went on to say that

* In his discreet autobiography Townsend wrote that he had been prepared to like Philip but... "When I went into exile in 1953, he did not exactly walk me to the door and say goodbye. ... He is a German but he does not look very German. He is certainly trenchant and his views are trenchant. I would say he is intelligent without being an intellectual ... he could be abrupt and he has this staccato way of talking, although he will often end things up with a joke or a quip."

the wedding could not take place in Britain, that the couple would have to live abroad, that Margaret would lose her title and her annual allowance and be forced to abandon her place within the royal family. The Princess left in tears.

To avoid an unpleasant scene, her mother had withdrawn to her Castle of Mey home in Scotland. As tough as she was, the Queen Mother shrank from direct confrontation. She could never abide personal collisions and avoided them by contracting bronchitis or taking to her bed with flu or a headache.

Without an advocate within the establishment, the couple were defeated. In anguish they bowed to the pressure and decided to part, knowing they could never see each other again. Townsend drafted a statement that the Princess approved, and her news was announced a week later when the BBC broke into its programming to read the text that was signed simply "Margaret":

I would like it to be known that I have decided not to marry Group Captain Peter Townsend....Mindful of the Church's teaching that Christian marriage is indissoluble, and conscious of my duty to the Commonwealth, I have resolved to put these considerations before others. I have reached this decision entirely alone.

The Duke of Windsor felt outrage toward the establishment that had forced his niece to make her announcement. "The unctuous hypocritical cant and corn which has been provoked in the *Times* and *Telegraph* by Margaret's renunciation of Townsend has been hard to take," the Duke wrote to his wife. "The Church of England has won again but this time they caught their fly whereas I was wily enough to escape the web of an outmoded institution that has become no more than a government department...."

Many others felt profound sympathy for the Princess, and a few letters of protest were published, but the vast majority of the public accepted the sad fact that she had done the right thing in putting duty first. The church was omnipotent. "A picture has been built up in some quarters that the church started bullying a lonely girl into doing something she did not want to do," said the Reverend Peter Gillingham, one of the Queen's chaplains. "That is false. All the church did was to make plain what the church's rules are."

Embittered, Peter Townsend returned to Brussels, resigned from the Royal Air Force, and remarried a few years later. He lived in self-imposed exile in Rambouillet, southwest of Paris, and vowed never to return to England. In his autobiography he wrote that he would like his ashes scattered in France. "And if," he concluded, "the wind, the south wind on which the swallows ride, blows them on towards England, then let it be. I shall neither know nor care." Thirty-seven years later when he was dying of cancer, he slipped into

London to have a quiet lunch with the Princess at Kensington Palace.

"It was a kind of good-bye," said one friend who was present. Townsend, then silver haired but still handsome at seventy-seven, was suffering from stomach cancer, which he gallantly dismissed as "a little gastric disorder." He died three years later with no regrets.

"Once a thing is behind you, you don't look back," he said. "Life might have been otherwise—but it wasn't."

The inflexibility toward divorce in royal circles had softened by then, but not the courtiers' attitude toward that particular romance. "Quite simple, really: Duty before diddling. Country before courting," said a former courtier. "We did what we had to do to protect the Crown, and, after that, we had to launch the first royal tour."

After her coronation, the Queen had agreed to spend six months traveling forty thousand miles around the world to greet 750 million of her subjects who inhabited one-quarter of the earth's surface and conducted one-third of the world's trade. She planned to visit twelve countries, six colonies, four territories, and two dominions. She would hear 276 speeches, receive 6,770 curtsies, and shake 13,213 hands.

Eventually she would become the most traveled monarch in British history. But in 1953 her first royal tour was a stupendous undertaking that had never been attempted by any head of state. The Queen wanted to be the first, because she was determined to present herself to her subjects as something more than a figurehead.

"I want to show that the Crown is not merely an abstract symbol of our unity," she said in her Christmas Day message from New Zealand, "but a personal and living bond between you and me."

"That tour was a grueling, merciless trip for everyone," recalled reporter Gwen Robyns, part of the small press contingent accompanying the Queen. "I was working for *Evening News,* the biggest circulation newspaper in the world at the time, and I watched the Queen every single day, every night, hourly sometimes. I can tell you that she could not have possibly survived that trip without the help of the Duke of Edinburgh."

Highly disciplined, Elizabeth could stand for hours in the sun and ride a horse sidesaddle for miles. But interacting with people and having to make small talk with strangers for any extended period of time was a burden. She had grown up alone at Windsor Castle, spending her time with her sister, their servants, and their governess. She was not accustomed to accommodating others and did not know how to be socially ingratiating. Her gregarious husband, though, enjoyed bantering with others, exchanging quips, and being flirtatious.

"Philip was perfect for her, and she was blindingly in love with him," said Gwen Robyns. "She was so young and unsure of herself as Queen. Very, very self-conscious as monarch. Painfully insecure. She did not know how to act or behave among so many people. But he was smooth and easy, more sophisticated. He'd jolly her into good humor, and warm her up for the crowds. She'd put on a grumpy face most of the time because she was overwhelmed, but he'd coax a smile out of her. He was disgusting to the press. 'Here come the vultures,' he'd say when he saw us. He threw peanuts at us in Malta, so we despised him, but we could see that he was truly marvelous for her. She brightened up around him. All he had to do was whisper in her ear and she glowed. Every time she was cross and sour, he charmed a laugh out of her. He made her look good. He really carried her on that trip.

"I remember in Australia when she was numbed into boredom by having to shake hundreds of sweaty hands in blistering 110-degree heat. She scowled and looked ugly until Philip turned and said, 'Cheer up, sausage. It is not so bad as all that.'

"In New Zealand, the little Maori children were fairly jitterbugging with excitement to do their 'party piece' for her by jumping off the riverbank. But the Queen didn't even look their way, and instead walked to her car. Philip saw what happened. 'Look, Bet [diminutive for Lilibet],' he said. 'Aren't they lovely?' The Queen turned and went back to look at the children.

"Philip was fiercely protective of her when her energy started flagging," Gwen Robyns said. "He would leap to her side and wave off photographers, if he thought they were getting too close or might embarrass her. 'Don't jostle the Queen,' he'd say. While he was great for her, he was boorish to others. I remember in South Australia the mayor of some little town was all got up in dreadful homemade robes of bunny rabbit fur to meet the Queen. He was about seventy years old, so sweet, so pathetic. He presented the Queen with a huge box, and in a quivering voice said: 'Your Royal Highness'—poor thing, he was supposed to say Your Majesty—'at this very moment, our Ambassador in London is presenting a similar box to your representative at the Palace.'

"'Oh, my God, man,' roared Philip. 'Don't you realize the ten-and-a-half-hour time difference between here and England? Your Ambassador is probably sound asleep right now.'

"The mayor wilted. He looked as if he'd been accosted. It was so sad to see him standing there in his sorry little costume, shaking and stammering apologies. 'I should have thought of that,' he said, berating himself. Here it was the day of his life and he's crushed by the Duke of Edinburgh. Philip acted like a bastard.

"Naturally, I couldn't report that kind of thing," said Robyns, "or any other personal details. When I noticed that the Queen always took her shoes off, which seemed endearing and human, I noted in one of my dispatches: 'The weary Queen slipped out of her shoes.' I got a rocket from my editors saying, 'Lay off the Queen. Buckingham Palace is furious with you.' Another time I wrote that the Queen looked tired. We knew that she was bored stiff with the flags and bunting and all that red, white, and blue every time she turned around, so I wrote that she looked fatigued like the rest of us. Another rocket: Lay off the Queen. So I had to stop reporting the human side of the tour...."

The vigilant Palace tried to protect the Queen from herself. "They wanted to hide her human side—or what there was of it," said the *Daily Telegraph*'s Maurice Weaver. "I remember a royal visit to Papua New Guinea when the Queen was watching the natives perform a dance in their grass skirts. They were wearing circular necklaces made out of bones and twigs and strange coins. She turned to her equerry. 'I feel these people need my effigy on their coins.' So he rounded up the British reporters and asked them for their sovereigns.

"I filed a light story about the whip-around for the Queen and how we had to rustle up some coins. When the equerry found out, he banged on my hotel door in the middle of the night and demanded that I spike the story.

"'It makes the Queen look poor,' he said.

"'Oh, rubbish,' I said. 'It's a frothy little piece, and besides, no one expects the Queen to be carrying money.'"

He said he had not written the real story, which was the Queen's pathetic noblesse oblige mentality about her poor benighted natives. So the froth stood. But he learned how sensitive the Palace was to the Queen's press coverage. "We were not allowed to write anything other than what the Queen wore and how she looked," he said. "The Palace press secretary would come out and feed us a description of Her Majesty in her green tulle gown, and we dutifully took it all down and reported it that way...."

As the Queen became more secure in her role, the Palace press office relaxed, but only slightly. "There's an unwritten agreement," said journalist Phillip Knightley, who accompanied the Queen on her first royal tour. "It's as if the Palace said, 'You need us to bring in your readers, most of whom love royal stories. We need you to tell the Queen's subjects what she's up to and what a wonderful person she is. So you can write anything you like about the royals—as long as you don't question the actual institution of the monarchy.'"

Yet a soupçon of deference was expected. In New Zealand only the American press could get away with mentioning the Queen's grammatical error. She had overheard two little girls arguing whether she was Queen Elizabeth or Princess Margaret. One said, "I tell you, it's Princess Margaret." The other said, "Is not. Is not. It's the Queen." With what *Newsweek* described as a "cavalier disregard for the Queen's English," the sovereign leaned over to the little girls and said: "No, it's me."

After years of travel the Queen eventually learned to carve a way for herself, but with great effort. "She was always proper, but never warm and ingratiating," said Gwen Robyns. "Still, stilted, and remote, she held herself at a distance so she would never make a mistake, never put a foot wrong. She was so insecure that that was the only way she could handle her role. She's not a woman who lights up in public like her mother, who on the surface is all bonnets, smiles, and feathers but underneath is steel—cold, hard steel with a marshmallow casing."

Despite obvious discomfort in the spotlight, the young sovereign starred in no fewer than three films that were spun out of the royal tour. Six months after leaving London, she returned home to a rapturous welcome from her subjects, who lined the riverbanks as she sailed up the Thames on the royal yacht, *Britannia*. They understood that she would never be the crowd-pleasing actress her mother was, but they still appreciated her solid commitment to duty. They roared their approval as the royal yacht approached, and the Queen acknowledged their cheers with a stiff little wave. She, too, knew how lacking she was compared with her charismatic mother. Like her stolid father, she depended on an appealing spouse. She later acknowledged as much to close friends when she paid tribute to her husband. "Without Philip," she said, "I could not have carried on."

EIGHT

The monarchy was a distant train that had been bearing down on Elizabeth since she was ten years old. Growing up, she always heard it approaching. She knew that one day she would have to climb aboard; she never dreamed it would arrive so soon. At age twenty-six she was in a marriage just starting to bloom.

Before her father's death forced her onto the throne, she had looked forward to being a wife and mother. After marrying, she said she wanted to have four children and devote herself to her family.

In the early years of her marriage, when faced with a choice between being a wife or mother, she always chose to be a wife. Her husband was her first priority—then. Before her son was born in 1948, she was quoted as saying, "I am going to be the child's mother, not the nurses." Yet when the role of mother conflicted with wife, she turned to the nurses.

She skipped her son's first birthday to be with her husband, who was on naval duty in Malta. Leaving the little boy at home with his grandparents and nannies for several months, she missed his first step and his first tooth. His first word was not "Mama," but "Nana," the person closest to him, his beloved nanny. Elizabeth raised her children the way that she had been raised. As an infant she had been left with nannies for six months while her parents toured Australia and New Zealand, so she did not hesitate to leave her own children in the care of others. Occasionally she expressed a twinge of guilt.

"I don't want someone else to raise my children," she said before the birth of Princess Anne in 1950. Yet when her daughter was three months old, Elizabeth left her in the Palace nursery so she could travel with her husband. When the little girl had her tonsils and adenoids removed, her nanny took her to the Hospital for Sick Children and spent the night at her bedside. Her mother, not overly concerned, stayed at Windsor Castle.

"Royalty regard their children like cattle," wrote John Gordon in the *Daily Express* after learning that the Queen stayed in bed the night Prince Charles was rushed to London's Great Ormond Street Hospital for an emergency appendectomy at midnight. "People didn't like the Queen's failure to go to Prince Charles's bedside when he was suffering," wrote Gordon.

In 1952, when Elizabeth became the new Queen, she struggled to make room in her life for her family, but she no longer had time to be a mother. Instead she dedicated herself to the Crown and postponed having more children.

As the new sovereign, she knew she had to reign—to travel the world, make state visits, welcome world leaders, consult Parliament, deliver speeches, accept salutes, cut ribbons, bestow knighthoods—and try to smile.

The obsessive-compulsive child, once described by her governess as "too methodical and tidy...too dutiful for her own good," took over as she buried herself in the duties of the monarchy. "I didn't have an apprenticeship," she said later. "My father died much too young. It was all a very sudden kind of taking on, and making the best job you can...." She became zealous about answering her mail, making her speeches, doing her boxes, which held the government documents sent to her every day.

"Oh, those boxes," said a former courtier many years later. "It was all too easy for her to say, 'I've got two red boxes upstairs, that's my constitutional duty, and I'd really rather do that than have a row with my son, daughter, or husband.' Red boxes are a marvelous escape from family problems."

Publicly Elizabeth looked like the ideal mother. Pictures of her with her handsome husband and her two young children appeared regularly in newspapers and magazines. She learned from her clever mother, who, as Queen, had authorized books such as *The Family Life of Queen Elizabeth*. She also arranged newspaper photo spreads called "Our Little Princesses at Home" and "Playtime at Royal Lodge" to foster the image of an idyllic royal family. Naturally Elizabeth grew up considering such orchestrated coverage a vital marketing tool for the monarchy. She felt that posing for photos was part of her job as Queen, and her husband felt the same way. "If you are really going to have a monarchy," he said, "you have got to have a family, and the family has got to be in the public eye."

Reordering her priorities, the Queen now placed the monarchy first, her marriage second, and her children third. "I think any idea of a family in the normal sense was knocked on the head by the Queen's accession at such an early age," said biographer Philip Ziegler. "I don't think it was ever in her nature to be a close parent, but in any case, it became impossible once she was swept up into the merry-go-round of royal activities."

Still, she tried not to give up all her maternal responsibilities. "I must have some time for the children every day," she said. She changed the hour of her weekly visit with the Prime Minister so she could see Charles, four, and Anne, two, before they went to bed, and she allowed them thirty minutes with her and Philip in the morning. Their nannies, Helen Lightbody and Mabel Anderson, took the children into the Queen's sitting room at 9:00 A.M. for this visit every day and promptly whisked them away by 9:30 A.M., when she sat down at her desk to work. Usually Anne did not want to leave, but her brother would pull her away, saying, "Anne, you must not bother Mummy. She's busy. She's queening."

The children spent the rest of the day with their nannies and nurses, the sturdy Scottish women with sensible black shoes and tightly permed hair, who fed them, dressed them, bathed them, and even slept in the same room with them. At 5:00 P.M.* every day, the nannies took the children back for another visit with their mother and father before taking them to the nursery for their baths and bedtime. The children saw their nannies more often than they ever saw their parents.

"A miserable childhood," recalled Prince Charles years later, blaming his parents, especially his father, for his upbringing. One of his saddest recollections was growing up alone. He said that his father was rarely present for his birthdays and missed the first five. Instead his father sent him notes.

"Loneliness is something royal children have always suffered and always will," said Lord Mountbatten, refusing to place blame on either parent. "Not much you can do about it, really."

The romance novelist Barbara Cartland could not bring herself to fault the Queen as a mother. Instead she damned her by implication. "Charles was born when his mother was very young, so she didn't spend an awful lot of time with him," she said. "He was such an unhappy little boy growing up."

The Queen Mother knew where to place the blame. "The papers continually accuse Philip of having been a harsh father," she confided

---

* "That particular hour was chosen more for the corgis than for the children," said the Queen's footman, explaining the Queen's daily ritual of feeding her dogs dinner in her sitting room. "One of us brings up a tray of bowls to Her Majesty every evening at that time, and the tray contains the individual diets prepared by the kitchen for the Queen's seven corgis." The silver bowls were placed on a plastic sheet on the floor, and the Queen mixed each portion with a silver knife and fork.

to a dinner partner. "If they only knew the truth....It was always Lilibet who was too strict and Philip who tried to moderate her."

Each time the Queen returned from one of her royal tours, she expressed surprise at how much her young son had grown and how noisy he had become. Unaccustomed to his energy, she felt overwhelmed around him. "He's such a responsibility," she said with a sigh.

Early on, she decided the children should be known in the household simply as "Charles" and "Anne" rather than "sir" and "ma'am." She decreed that maids and footmen no longer had to bow and curtsy to the sovereign's children, reserving that homage for herself and her mother. Like the staff, Charles, too, was required to bow to his mother before he left the room, just as he bowed to his grandmother, the Queen Mother.

"You always have to do as Granny tells you," he told a playmate, "or else she has no sweets in her bag."

"Why do you bow to her?" asked the playmate.

"It's what I have to do."

"Why?"

"Because Papa says so."

When his nanny insisted Charles wear a pair of tartan shorts beneath his kilt at Balmoral, he refused.

"I'm not wearing those," he said. "Papa doesn't."

"Papa" was the sun that shone on his childhood and warmed his days, despite occasional scoldings and spankings. "I think he has had quite a strong influence on me, particularly in my younger days," Charles said in later years. "I had perfect confidence in his judgment." Only when Charles was unable to live up to his father's expectations did he turn on Philip. Then Charles said his father was a bully, who ruled his childhood like a despot. He sniped to friends that there are two types of fathers: the first instills self-confidence in his children by offering praise when merited and withholding criticism when possible. "The second is the Duke of Edinburgh," he said. By then Charles had forgotten how he once idolized his father and imitated everything he did, right down to walking with his head down and his hands clasped behind his back.

"As a child, Charles begged to be with his father," recalled the Queen's footman, "and much preferred sitting on Prince Philip's knee than on the Queen's when we brought them for their morning visit....He was the sort of father any kid would adore....More so than the Queen, he has a natural, easy ability to come down to the simpler level of childhood without seeming either patronizing or condescending."

Members of the royal household recall Philip reading *Hiawatha* to the children and putting on the Indian feather headdress he had brought from Canada. Whooping and hollering, he performed war dances around the nursery, to the delight of his young son. "That's the game I love best of all," said Charles, clapping his hands.

Others see Philip through more jaundiced eyes. "He tolerated Charles, but I don't think he was a loving father," said Eileen Parker, whose former husband, Michael Parker, was Philip's best friend and equerry. "He would pick up Charles, but his manner was odd. He had more fun with Anne. I think Charles was frightened of him."

The little boy was certainly afraid of his mother, who appeared aloof, forbidding, and too busy for him. Years later he said he could not remember one incident of maternal love from his childhood, except for an evening when his mother came to the nursery before his evening bath. She sat on a gilt chair with a footman behind her and watched his nanny bathe him. "She didn't put her hands in the bathwater," Charles recalled, "but at least she watched the procedure."

He recounted for one of his biographers how his mother greeted him after her first royal tour. He had not seen her for six months, so he raced on board the *Britannia* to welcome her home. He ran up to join the group of dignitaries waiting to shake her hand. When the Queen saw her young son squirming in line, she said, "No, not you, dear." She did not hug him or kiss him; she simply patted his shoulder and passed along to the next person. A photographer captured the awkward greeting between mother and son, which the Queen later justified to a friend. "I have been trained since childhood never to show emotion in public," she said.

"Her dislike of physical contact is almost a phobia," wrote British columnist Lynda Lee-Potter. "By her inability to demonstrate love for her children, the Queen has made it difficult for them to give affection in return. She is a stoic and, like her mother, has a ruthless streak."

While the Queen seemed incapable of demonstrating affection, her husband appeared to be similarly aloof and reserved. "He doesn't wear his heart on his sleeve," said Michael Parker. "I always wanted to see him put his arms around the Queen and show her how much he adored her. What you'd do for any wife. But he always sort of stood to attention. I mentioned it to him a couple of times. But he just gave me a hell of a look."

Charles did not grow up seeing much physical affection between his parents; nor does he remember his mother kissing him after the age of eight. He wistfully told a friend that his nanny meant more to him emotionally than his mother ever did. He cited research done on baby monkeys deprived of a soft, motherly touch right after birth. He said they never recovered emotionally. They became impassive and withdrawn, not unlike the fearful little boy who wandered through the carpeted corridors of Buckingham Palace. When he became aware of scientific research that shows the loving interaction between mother and child charges the youngster's brain to be receptive to learning, Charles said he finally understood why he had been described as "a plodder."

A sickly child, he suffered from knock-knees like his grandfather and great-grandfather. His flat feet forced him into orthopedic shoes and he developed colds, sore throats, bouts of asthma, and chronic chest congestions.

"His Royal Highness was an earnest little boy," said a former courtier. "Correct, well mannered, but timid like his mother. He was uncertain on a horse and queasy on a boat. His sister, Anne, who was twenty-one months younger, was bold and rambunctious like her father, which is why she became his favorite child."

Philip worried about his son's frailties and tried to toughen him up. "I want him to be a man's man," he said. Fit, tough, and handsome, Philip played cricket and polo, crewed in yachting races, drove carriages, piloted planes, and shot grouse with zest. He wanted his son to do the same. Philip gave Charles a cricket bat for his first birthday and later taught him how to play. He gave him his first gun and taught him how to shoot. He taught him to swim, to ride, to sail, and to hunt. He later introduced him to painting and polo and arranged for flying lessons so he could pilot his own plane. Charles then survived strenuous naval training to take command of a coastal minesweeper, but he could not shed the image of a wimp.

A nail-biting child, afraid of the dark, Charles longed for his father's approval and overcame his fear of horses to ride and his sea-sickness to sail. He was not a natural athlete like his sister, but he pushed himself hard in sports, sometimes to the edge of reckless-ness.

Hardly an indulgent parent, Philip spanked Charles whenever he hit his sister or pulled her hair. And that was often. "When we were children, Charles and I used to fight like cat and dog," said Anne. Philip told Charles that he had to take his spankings "like a man."

"Act like a man," was his father's constant refrain. "Be a man." Once, after a mild scold-ing from his nanny, Charles ran to his father. "I'm so sick of girls, Papa," he said. "Let's go away and be men by ourselves."

Sometimes Philip's preoccupation with manliness bordered on homophobia. "I remem-ber when the Queen and Prince Philip were shown the newly done up Porchester house," said the British decorator Nicholas Haslam. "They brought Prince Charles with them but left him in the car when they went inside. The hostess asked, 'Wouldn't you like to let Prince Charles accompany us?'

"'Good God, no,' said Prince Philip. 'We don't want him knowing anything pansy like decoration.'"

Even so, the Queen's footman noticed a feminine effect on the young boy. "At the time he was first sent to school, Charles was already showing signs of succumbing to the cloying, introverted atmosphere that pervades the Palace," he said. "He was the object of considerable petticoat influence."

So many women exercising so much authority over his son annoyed Philip. "Nothing but nannies, nurses, and poofs," he said, referring to the household staff, which was mostly homosexual.* He insisted his son be educated outside the Palace. The Queen objected, but Philip pointed to her sheltered childhood and reminded her that she rarely met a commoner who was not a servant. "Charles must learn to mix with other lads on the same level," he said. The Queen preferred to continue her son's education inside the Palace with the private tutor, Miss Katherine Peebles ("Mispy"), who had been teaching Charles since he was five years old. Philip argued that while the small, spry Scotswoman was a nice person, she had no formal training and no university degree. Consequently he did not think she was qualified to educate a future king. She had proved adequate at taking Charles and Anne on field trips to the zoo, the planetarium, and the museums, but now that Charles was eight, he needed to get out of the Palace and begin his formal education. "That means school—a real school," said Philip.

The education of Charles became a matter of great debate inside and outside the Palace.

* Unhappy with so many homosexuals in the royal household, Philip cheered the footman who had been caught in flagrante delicto with a housemaid. "They sacked him," said the Duke of Edinburgh. "He should have been given a medal."

Regular newspaper headlines asked "Why Can't the Royal Children Go to School— Must It Always Come to Them?" and "Have We the Right to Cut Prince Charles Off from Normal Pleasures So Early in Life?"

The Queen reluctantly agreed to send her son to Hill House, a London day school. He arrived wearing a gray coat with a black velvet collar. The other children wore the school's uniforms. For the next year Philip suggested his own preparatory school, the Cheam School, where Charles would board, share a dormitory with nine other boys, and sleep on wood-slatted beds. Again the Queen resisted, but Philip badgered her. Finally she agreed and allowed her son to become the first heir to the British throne to go away to school like a commoner.

"We want him to go to school with other boys of his generation and to live with other children and absorb from childhood the discipline imposed by education with others," said Philip. The Queen told the headmaster at Cheam to treat the future monarch like any ordinary student but to address him as Prince Charles. He could be plain Charles to the other boys, some of whom made fun of their future monarch's soft pudginess by calling him "Fatty."

The little boy who had been dressed in silk dresses and ribboned bonnets for the first two years of his life now faced bamboo rod canings from the headmaster. "I was warned," Charles said years later, "that we would be beaten, and I got beaten [for dormitory horse-play]. I didn't do it again. I was one of those people for whom corporal punishment actually worked."

On the first day of school, Charles clutched his initial-embossed box of milk chocolates—his mother's parting gift. He did not know how to share with the other boys and was too frightened to try. Leaving the loving arms of his nanny, his nurse, and his governess proved painful for Charles, who was shy and unaccustomed to making friends.

"He felt family separation very deeply," said his nanny, Mabel Anderson.

"He would write Mispy every day," said his sister, Anne. "He was heartbroken. He used to cry into his letters and say, 'I miss you.'"

He wrote wistfully to his father. "Dearest Papa, I am longing to see you in the ship." He drew a sailboat like the one Prince Philip raced at Cowes, the world's biggest sailing regatta. He excelled in art and enjoyed drawing and painting pictures of his family. When he was six years old he drew a humorous Christmas card for his father, who was shown next to a vat labeled "Hair Restorer." Philip had been fretting about his receding hairline and encroaching baldness.

Soon after he started school, Charles was reprimanded for saying a naughty word. "He may have picked it up from one of the workmen," said Philip, "but I'm afraid he may equally have picked it up from me."

After five and a half years at Cheam, where

he failed mathematics and barely passed history,* Charles told his parents that he wanted to go to "Papa's school," which meant Gordonstoun, a Scottish citadel of cold showers and canings.

"I remember Philip discussing public [private] schools at one of our Thursday Club luncheons—those all-male get-togethers we had at Wheeler's Tavern in Soho," recalled harmonica player Larry Adler. "I told him I saw public schools as factories for manufacturing homosexuals. James Robertson Justice, a fine actor and a gruff Scotsman, joined the conversation.

"'Oh, God, Adler, are you on that dreary hobbyhorse of yours again?' he said. 'I was buggered my first week at Eton. Did me no harm whatsoever.'

"'Well, James,' I said, 'it was different with you, as everyone had to turn out to watch you being buggered because of the school motto: Justice Must Not Only Be Done, He Must Be Seen to Be Done.' Philip howled with laughter."

He felt that by sending his son to Gordonstoun in Scotland, he would protect him from the effete influence of the English public

* Charles, eleven, stunned his history teacher at Cheam by not knowing that Britain once had a Prince of Wales who became King Edward VIII and then abdicated to become the Duke of Windsor. Years later Charles shocked another history teacher by defending King George III, who suffered attacks of insanity because of the rare and incurable ailment of porphyria. "I happen to admire, appreciate and sympathize with a lot of things he did," said Charles of the British King who lost the American Colonies in 1783. "He was a marvelous eccentric."

school system. He also said that the school in Morayshire was far enough from London so that Charles would escape the daily scrutiny of reporters. "Eton is frequently in the news, and when it is, it's going to reflect on you," he told his son. "If you go to the north of Scotland, you'll be out of sight, and reporters are going to think twice about taking an airplane to get up there, so it's got to be a major crisis before they actually turn up, and you'll be able to get on with things."

Charles finally consented and chose his father's school, which he later regretted. "It was hell," he said. "I failed my math exams three times," he said. He also flunked German and struggled with science. He wrote sad letters every night, complaining about how his classmates treated him. "I don't get any sleep...they throw slippers all night long or hit me with pillows or rush across the room and hit me as hard as they can." Years later he blamed his father for sending him to Gordonstoun. Yet, at the time, Philip was not entirely comfortable about leaving his soft young son in the hands of Gordonstoun's taskmasters. After delivering Charles for his first term, Philip and the Queen returned to Balmoral, where they spent the weekend with their friends David and Myrah Butter. Philip, more than the Queen, seemed shaken by the sinking experience of leaving his firstborn at boarding school.

"Prince Philip came into the drawing room," recalled Myrah Wernher Butter, who has known him since childhood. "He was white as a sheet. I asked him what was the matter, but he just walked across the room and poured himself a drink, which was very unusual for him. Years later Charles was telling me about what he felt when he sent his son off to school. I told him I understood. He said, 'Oh, that's because you always cared so much. I bet no one ever cared that much about me.' So I told him the story about his father. He was stunned. He just couldn't believe it."

By the time Charles was ready to start school in 1956, his father was fed up. He was tired of fighting the Palace guard, especially for his wife's time and attention. He disliked the courtiers—he called them "old farts"—and resented his wife's dependence on them. She no longer consulted him on court matters, and her passivity to his suggestions infuriated him. "Come on, Lilibet. Come on," he would snap. "Just do it. Do it." Exasperated with Palace bureaucracy, he started spending more time with his pals from the Thursday Club. This only hardened the courtiers' opinion of him as a crude adolescent with a predilection for lavatory humor.

"The Duke of Edinburgh is very lewd, very Germanic," said one of the Queen's private secretaries. The haughty courtier attributed "Philip's vulgar German preoccupation with nudity" to his "Mountbatten origins." He cited the photographs that Lord Mountbatten had posed for with Cary Grant in Las Vegas. In the first picture, the two men faced the camera surrounded by gorgeous show-girls swathed in feather boas. In the second picture, the men turned their backs to the camera and so did the show girls, whose rhinestoned-thonged backsides were with-out feathers. Mountbatten found the picture of the bare-bottomed showgirls so amusing that he had it blown up and hung in the Queen's passageway on the royal yacht. Philip, who roared with laughter when he saw it, enjoyed showing it off and would not remove it, even for state guests. "That's his Germanic idea of art and entertainment—naked buttocks," said the courtier.

Philip started sharing the London apartment of actor Richard Todd with two other married men during afternoons to entertain young actresses. The three men called themselves "the Three Cocketeers."

"No, I can't talk about what went on in that apartment," said British actor Jack Hedley in 1993. "It's too dangerous to talk about those days—even forty years later."

Philip also used his equerry's flat on South Street. "Mike, or Parker-from-the-Palace, as we called him—that's how he always introduced himself on the phone—was living another life away from his wife and his family, and the parties at his flat were rousing affairs," recalled one man who attended many of the parties. "Yes, Philip was always there and he always had women, but nothing serious. As the French say, *les danseuses,* which are a rich man's indulgence. Philip usually came with

Parker and Baron Nahum, the court photographer, known by his first name. One night, Aristotle Onassis brought Maria Callas to dinner, and another night Prince Bernhard, married to Queen Juliana of the Netherlands, spent a riotous evening with us."

"I remember the dinner with Prince Bernhard," recalled Larry Adler. "That's when we all realized how much Philip hated his job as Prince Consort. Throughout dinner Philip kept jabbing at Bernhard: 'Boy, I really envy you,' he said. 'You can go anywhere you like and not be recognized. You can have all the girlfriends you like and no one knows. I can't go anywhere without press vultures and policemen following me.' Bernhard had to leave early that evening to get back to Holland before the airport closed and the field lights were turned off. As he got up to go, Philip bent down and gave him an exaggerated salaam. 'Give my regards to Her Imperial Majesty,' he said. He spat out the last three words with withering scorn. You could tell he identified with Bernhard, who, like Philip, was tied to a short royal leash."

By 1956 Philip had had a bellyful of "pomping," as he referred to court protocol. With his son starting school, his daughter too young to notice, and his wife too busy for him, he felt diminished. He decided to go off on his own for a while. He had been invited to visit Melbourne, Australia, for the opening of the 1956 Olympic games, so he laid out a forty-thousand-mile itinerary around this one event to include visits to The Gambia, the Seychelles, Malaya, New Guinea, New Zealand, Antarctica, the Falklands, Galápagos Islands, and the West Coast of the United States. He planned to travel for four months with Michael Parker. The two men had been navy shipmates, crewed on the same yachting team, and played cricket on the same team. Parker recently had separated from his wife, and Philip now wanted to be separated from his—geographically, if not matrimonially. So the two grown-up boys planned their trip to the South Pacific with the abandon of Huckleberry Finn and Jim rafting down the Mississippi.

"Philip was born with itchy feet," said the Queen, seemingly unperturbed by his plans. "It's a waste of time trying to change a man's character," she added. "You have to accept your husband as he is."

Her husband presented the cruise as a "diplomatic mission." "This is my personal contribution to the Commonwealth ideal," he said, announcing that he would leave England by air for Mombassa, Kenya, on the east coast of Africa on October 15, 1956, to meet the royal yacht, *Britannia,* with its crew of 275. He would be accompanied by his equerry, Michael Parker, and his friend Baron, the photographer.

Several weeks before they left, the forty-nine-year-old court photographer went into the hospital for hip surgery to relieve his arthritis. He wanted to be in good shape for the trip, but a few days after his operation, he died of a heart attack. His fiancée, actress Sally Ann Howes, who had begged him not to undergo the surgery, never forgave Philip.

"Baron was a wonderful guy—witty, debonair, and quite brave," said Larry Adler. "He belonged to the Thursday Club, and he gave Philip his bachelor party. He had been the official photographer for the royal wedding in 1947 and for the coronation in 1953. He felt that if he hadn't been Jewish, he could've married Princess Margaret. He took wonderful pictures of the royal family, and for all of that, he naturally expected a knighthood. But Philip wouldn't do a thing about it—he could have, I think, but he didn't—and the reason was the Queen did not approve of Baron. She thought he got Philip into trouble and helped Philip find girlfriends."

The Duke of Edinburgh, extraordinarily handsome at thirty-five, needed no help attracting women. He needed only privacy, which the cruise provided; it also kicked up a swirl of whispers. His trip to Australia became a sensitive issue for biographers who tried to investigate what happened and for friends who tried to defend him against scurrilous allegations. Even a devout monarchist like Barbara Cartland, who reveres the royal family, talks about a secret love affair that she learned of from Philip's uncle Lord Mountbatten.

"I know all about Philip's illegitimate daughter in Melbourne," she told an interviewer, "but I'm not going to talk about it."

"Look into the boathouse in Sydney that is owned by Lady Mary Ellen Barton," advised an Australian lawyer. "That's the place Philip used for his dalliances."

The stories of Philip's women and his trysts were as many and varied as his ports of call. "A couple of lady typists were flown out to join the boat in Singapore," reported the royal author Brian Hoey. "It was said they didn't do too much typing. They weren't the type."

The rumors dogged Philip from Melbourne to Sydney to Singapore, but as the Queen's husband he carried a certain immunity. No one could touch him without harming her, and no one in Great Britain, not even republicans, wanted to harm the Queen, who in 1956 was still considered inviolate. So despite his protestations to Prince Bernhard, Philip enjoyed a freewheeling life away from the Palace.

On the tour he managed to relax enough to joke about his second-class status within his marriage. In Australia a young couple were presented to him as Mr. and Dr. Robinson. Philip looked surprised until Mr. Robinson explained that his wife was a doctor of philosophy and much more important than he. "Ah, yes," said Philip. "We have that trouble in our family, too."

During the cruise, Philip and his equerry had a whisker- growing contest to see who could grow the longest beard; they shot alligators and were photographed tromping around in matching safari suits; they sat on the deck of the *Bri-*

tannia, sunbathing, painting at their easels in the afternoon, and drinking gin and tonics in the evening. Philip felt at home on the yacht, which appealed to his sense of neatness and precision. Navy stewards used a tape measure to set the table so that knives, forks, and spoons were lined up evenly with dishes. They wore felt slippers so they would not make noise while delivering his messages. The British press slammed the trip as "Philip's folly," calling it useless, unnecessary, and a luxury that cost the nation "at least two million pounds."* Estimating the tour's cost at $11,000 a week, they criticized Philip's "commando raft," created to unload the royal Rolls-Royce in places where no docking facilities were available for automobiles, and they carped about his traveling with his own sports car. "Who pays for it all?" asked one newspaper.

While decrying the expense of the cruise, no one dared publish a word about the women who were entertained on board ship. The Queen's husband was not an indiscreet man, and he certainly had no intention of embarrassing his wife. "He told me the first day he offered me my job," said Michael Parker, "that *his* job, first, last, and always, was never to let Her Majesty down." Still, the rumors persisted as Philip cruised the Indian Ocean, missing such family celebrations as his son's eighth birthday, his own ninth wedding anniversary, and the tenth family Christmas.

* About $6 million in U.S. dollars.

"The cruise was a brilliant idea of Prince Philip's and deserved much greater recognition," Parker said years later. "The object was to put *Britannia* to her greatest use in visiting beleaguered British people deep in the oceans around the world—Ascension, St. Helena, Gough Island, Tristan de Cunha, the Falklands, South Georgia, Chatham Islands, Deception Island, and some bases in Antarctica open only twenty days a year. It was quite a sacrifice for all—our first Christmas away from home since the war to boot."

Near Ceylon (now Sri Lanka), Philip and his equerry watched the world almost explode. Shortly after leaving England, the *Britannia* was put on emergency notice to stand by for nine days as the Middle East seemed poised for war over the Suez Canal. Egypt had seized the Canal in July 1956 after the United States withdrew its $56 million commitment to help build the Aswan Dam. The U.S. move enraged Egypt's President, Gamal Abdel Nasser, who then closed the canal to all foreigners.

"I look at Americans and say: May you choke to death on your fury!" Nasser roared. "The annual income of the Suez Canal is $100 million. Why not take it ourselves? We shall rely on our own strength, our own muscle, our own funds. And it will be run by Egyptians! Egyptians! Egyptians!"

Of the 1.5 million barrels of oil that passed through the canal each day, 1.2 million went to Western Europe. So, in nationalizing the canal, Nasser had choked off the chief source

231

of petroleum for England and France. Fearful for their survival and spoiling for retaliation, the two countries joined secretly with Israel, also menaced by the Arabs, to seize the canal. On October 29, 1956, Israel's armored tanks plowed across the Sinai and attacked Egypt, giving Britain and France the excuse they needed. The next day they declared that fighting in the Middle East threatened international navigation and demanded both sides withdraw from the Suez within twenty-four hours. Egypt refused, and on October 31, 1956, the British and French started bombing. Five days later they dropped fifty thousand paratroops on Port Said, Egypt, at the mouth of the canal.

The *Britannia,* officially designated as a hospital ship during war, suspended its cruise. Philip was in constant radio contact with the Palace, which relayed hourly news bulletins. He learned that most of the world opposed the Anglo-French alliance with Israel and their use of military force. At the United Nations, America, England's staunchest ally, denounced the invasion, and Britain's currency plummeted. Still, England and France continued to veto the UN's cease-fire proposals. Finally the White House made it clear that if they continued to use force, the United States would not support them. Just as terrifying to England, France, and Israel was the hectoring threat from Russia to "crush the aggressors" and "restore peace...through the use of force." With no U.S. support and the rest of the world

232

against them, they yielded and announced a cease-fire.

The Queen was too young and inexperienced to exercise her royal prerogative and advise her new Prime Minister, Anthony Eden. Instead she listened to him and accepted his proposals. She knew that he had been brilliant as Winston Churchill's Foreign Secretary but did not realize he was in over his head as Prime Minister. Struggling on five hours of sleep a night, he became addicted to amphetamines, which distorted his judgment. She was at the racetrack when his messenger reached her with an urgent proclamation requiring her signature, calling out army reserves. In between horse races, she signed. Britain was ready to go to war.

"In a few weeks' time," predicted Laborite John Strachey, "this country is going to wake up to the fact that we have marched into Egypt, marched out of Egypt, caused the canal to be blocked, stopped our oil, made every Arab in the world into an enemy, opened the Middle East to Russian penetration, split the Commonwealth, quarreled with the Americans, and ruined ourselves—all for nothing."

Prime Minister Eden collapsed and flew to Jamaica in December to recuperate. Randolph Churchill compared Eden's leadership to Hitler's in marching his troops to Stalingrad and leaving them there to freeze to death. "Except," said Winston Churchill's son, "Hitler, with all his faults, did not winter in Jamaica." Sir Anthony returned three weeks later to find gas lines blocking the roads as a result of emergency rationing brought on by the crisis. The next month he resigned as Prime Minister. As his replacement, the Queen chose Chancellor of the Exchequer Harold Macmillan.

The country was reeling from international humiliation. The British press lashed out at everyone connected with the debacle. Even Philip, thousands of miles away, was berated for not being at his wife's side. But the Queen said privately that she was relieved not to have her husband around. "I'm glad he wasn't here," she said. "All hell would have broken loose."

After four months on board the *Britannia,* Philip headed for a family reunion in Lisbon with his wife before their state visit to Portugal. First he had to stop in Gibraltar to say goodbye to his equerry, who was no longer allowed to be in the Queen's presence. Days before, news of Michael Parker's divorce had leaked and the press was full of stories that his wife, Eileen, was suing him for sexual misconduct and demanding alimony on the grounds of alleged adultery. He was forced to resign. Philip raged about the hypocrisy of a broken marriage being an impediment to royal service when the former Prime Minister, Sir Anthony Eden, had been married twice and divorced. Philip pleaded with his equerry to reconsider because he could not bear to lose the one person who was his friend and ally in the Palace, but both men knew, and Philip later admitted, that Parker "had to go," especially after the Townsend affair. The Queen's courtiers demanded that the equerry be put ashore before Philip's reunion with the Queen. Furious at having to follow their orders, Philip insisted on accompanying his friend to the airport in Gibraltar. "It's the least I can do," he said. He looked unhappy as he emerged from a government limousine with Parker. Philip walked him to his waiting plane, and in front of reporters,* he clasped his hand in silence. Parker forced a smile, bounded up the steps without a backward glance, and flew to London, where he held a press conference with his lawyer.

Waiting for him at the London airport was the Queen's formidable press secretary, Commander Richard Colville. The equerry brightened when he saw the courtier and approached to thank him for coming to run interference with the reporters. The press secretary cut him off before he could say a word and made it clear that he was not there to help him.

"Hello, Parker," said Colville. "I've just come to let you know that from now on, you're on your own." That said, Colville turned and walked away.

In Lisbon the Queen's plane circled the airfield because the Queen's husband was running late. On board the Viscount airliner, Her Majesty and her twenty-five passengers,

* Philip's rage over the press coverage given to his marriage and his equerry's divorce surfaced later at a reception. As an official pointed out Gibraltar's famous cave-dwelling monkeys, Philip asked in a loud voice: "Which are the press and which are the apes?"

235

including Foreign Secretary Selwyn Lloyd, and all her ladies-in-waiting, giggled as they pasted fake beards on their chins in preparation for Philip's arrival. He had sent the Queen a picture of himself after weeks without a shave. "It was the Queen's idea," said one of the women. "She has a wonderful sense of humor."

At the time, few people around the throne were laughing. The press in Germany, France, and Italy had published another round of stories about the Duke of Edinburgh's "bachelor apartment close to London's famous Berkeley Square" and questioned whether the weekly dinner parties of the Thursday Club that met "in the infamous Soho district" had been confined to Philip's male friends. On February 5, 1957, the *Evening Standard* of London had implied a less-than-happy marriage by reporting that Philip had ordered a new bed for his room at Windsor Castle. The bed was made to his exact specifications ("It's a *single* bed," reported the newspaper). Other than mentioning that the Queen "rode alone" in Windsor Great Park and opened Parliament "without her husband by her side," the British press had remained silent about the Queen's rocky marriage and relied on the American press to spread the bad news. On February 8, 1957, the *Baltimore Sun* delivered. The story ran on the front page under the headline "London Rumors of Rift in Royal Family Growing." Filed by the paper's London correspondent, Joan Graham, the article linked Michael Parker's resignation to whispers that the Duke of Edinburgh had had more than a passing interest in an unmarried woman and had met her regularly in the apartment of the late royal photographer, the Duke's friend Baron Nahum. Asserting that rumors about the splintered royal marriage "are now percolating down to the British masses, who only know about the royal family from what is printed in the British press," the dispatch concluded the real reason for the four-month cruise was that Philip "was being got out of the country to cool down."

The Queen, who according to people close to her had been troubled enough about her marriage to consult a psychiatrist three times during this period, acted stunned. "How can they say such terrible things about us?" she asked her dresser, BoBo MacDonald. The Palace courtiers became concerned, thinking the monarchy was being sullied. Commander Richard Colville, the Queen's press secretary, quickly denounced the story. "It is quite untrue that there is a rift between the Queen and the Duke of Edinburgh," he said. "It's a lie." His denial was reported around the world with a recapitulation of the offending story, which insured that the Queen's strained marriage now became international news.

The British press took exception. "We could not drag even a simple denial out of the palace for the British public," said an editorial in the *London Daily Herald*. "For Americans, a denial. For the British people, no comment. The Queen's subjects were evidently not supposed to know." The *Daily Mirror* blamed the Queen's courtiers: "They need lessons on how to handle a hot potato."

The next day the Queen put on her public face, and the United Press reported from London that she "was amused" by the rumors of a rift between her and her husband. "The Queen shrugged off the story," UP said, "and gave the impression that her reunion with the Duke in Portugal after the longest separation of their marriage would effectively squelch further gossip....Anyone with eyes to see will know then how wrong the stories are."

A horde of reporters and photographers swarmed into Lisbon to watch the royal reunion at the airport. Philip was already irascible about the press coverage he had received, which compared him—unfavorably—with Queen Victoria's husband, Albert. Victoria had included him in her meetings with ministers and allowed him to read her state papers. At first Philip joked about his lack of status. "Constitutionally, I don't exist," he said. But when he arrived in Lisbon and saw the press waiting for him, he stopped chuckling. "Those bloody lies that you people print to make money," he snapped. "These lies about how I'm never with my wife."

Running five minutes late, he bounded up the steps to the Queen's airplane two at a time. He was wearing a suit, a white shirt, a tie, and a bronze tan with a small white shadow around his chin where he had obviously just shaved off his beard.

An hour later he emerged from the plane with a faint smudge of lipstick on his cheek and smilingly assumed his position a few paces behind the Queen. They spent the weekend together on the *Britannia,* anchored in the choppy waters of the river Sado, which was a big concession on the Queen's part. Never a sailor, she was afraid of water and usually avoided the yacht because she was prone to seasickness, but on this weekend she was determined to accommodate her sea-loving husband. Knowing their schedule was set for the next two years, she decided that after their royal tour of Canada in 1959, she would concentrate on her ambition to have four children. She also would change the rules regarding her family name so that her descendants not in line for the throne would carry her husband's name and be known as Mountbatten-Windsor.

After their four-day state visit to Portugal, the royal couple returned to England, where the Queen made a rare public display of affection. She rewarded her husband for his service to the Commonwealth by issuing a proclamation that granted him the title and titular dignity of a Prince of the United Kingdom and Northern Ireland. She declared that henceforth he would be known as the Prince Philip* Duke of Edinburgh. She no longer wanted him treated as a mere adjunct or royal

* Although Philip had been born Prince Philip of Greece and Denmark, he renounced his title in 1947 when he became a British subject and assumed the name of Philip Mountbatten to marry Elizabeth. Upon his marriage, he became the Duke of Edinburgh. But most people continued to call him Prince Philip—incorrectly. Technically he was not a prince until his wife made him one.

accessory. Except for sharing her sacrosanct red boxes and her weekly meetings with the Prime Minister, she made her husband a full partner in her monarchy. She even insisted that when Philip attended royal functions alone, he was to get the complete first verse of the National Anthem, no longer the abbreviated version.

Feeling ennobled, Philip delivered a self-serving speech a few days later, to justify the four months he had spent away from his wife and children. "I believe there are some things for which it is worthwhile making personal sacrifices, and I believe that the British Commonwealth is one of those things, and I, for one, am prepared to sacrifice a good deal if by doing so, I can advance its well-being by even a small degree....I might have got home for Christmas, but I could not have entertained nearly 1,400 people in the Queen's yacht from Australia, New Zealand, and those remote communities at twenty-six lunches, dinners, and receptions, and thereby strengthened, I hope, the close links which exist between the Crown and the people of the Commonwealth."

Those close links were severely strained by the Suez invasion, which had so damaged Britain's reputation for morality in international politics that the Queen was forced to help pick up the pieces. She made four state visits during 1957 to Portugal, France, Denmark, and Canada. In October her new Prime Minister, Harold Macmillan, urged a visit to the United States to try to repair the damage she had allowed her country to wreak on that alliance. "A visit by the Queen is worth one hundred diplomats," said the Prime Minister, who was eager to mend relations between the two countries. And he wanted to persuade the Americans to share their nuclear weapons technology.

The Queen was not eager to add yet another state visit to her schedule until the Prime Minister shrewdly showed her a cartoon that had appeared in America after it became known that England had duped the United States by conspiring with France and Israel in the Suez invasion. The cartoon showed President Eisenhower sitting at his desk in the Oval Office. The former Supreme Commander of Allied Forces in Europe during World War II had said he always regarded England as "an old and trusted friend." Now, obviously distraught, he was holding his head in his hands. The cutline read "Great Britain Is No Longer Great."

The Queen did not hesitate. She agreed at once to make the five-day visit to America, with stops in Jamestown, Virginia; Washington, D.C.; and New York City, where she promised to address the UN General Assembly. She left England, in the words of historian Elizabeth Longford, "like a dove from a battered ark."

Queen Elizabeth and Philip arrived in the United States on Columbus Day, trailed by a press contingent of two thousand reporters and photographers who were not allowed to talk to her. Their instructions from the Palace included a "recommended" dress code. For women: no black dresses, gloves a must, and a curtsy would be nice. For men: a shirt, a tie, and a deferential bow from the neck. The Palace distributed press releases at every stop but ruled out personal interviews.

"How many people," asked Philip, "go to President Eisenhower's press conferences?"

"Up to three hundred," said the *Newsweek* correspondent.

The Duke of Edinburgh shook his head. "If we did the same thing, we'd get about two."

British reporters disagreed. "No dictator ever muzzled the press quite so tightly as the Queen of England muzzles hers today on every aspect of royalty," wrote Anne Edwards in the *Daily Mail*.

"We had our orders from Charlie Campbell at the British Embassy," said Warren Rogers of the Associated Press. "No direct questions to the Queen, no talking to the Queen, don't even look the Queen in the eye. So at the embassy's press reception, I talked to Philip, who held forth on a briefing he'd just received from the head of the Atomic Energy Commission. He was so full of himself, he sounded as though he could launch *Sputnik I* and *II* with his hands tied behind his back. The U.S. was smarting from getting beat the previous week in the space race by the Russians, who had launched the first earth satellites. So Philip's inanities on the subject were of timely interest, and I quoted him verbatim. We both got in trouble: he looked like an idiot for saying the things he said, and I caught hell from the [British] embassy for letting him say them. 'You should have protected him from himself,' I was told.

"At first, I was sympathetic to Philip and felt sorry for the guy having to drag along in his wife's wake. Not being a royalist, I certainly didn't expect to be impressed by the Queen of England, but after covering the royal tour for thirteen days and nights in Canada and America, I found him to be a pompous ass— and fell in love with her. She was so pretty and shy, so demure. I remember her walking down a cascade of white granite steps outside the U.S. Capitol—there must've been a thousand steps—and she never looked down once. I couldn't believe it. I thought for sure she'd fall on her face, but I guess they teach you how to walk down steps without looking at your feet in Queen School. Along with that funny little wave."

Americans were entranced by the royal visit. The *Chicago Tribune* hailed the Queen as "a charming little lady," and the *Louisville Courier-Journal* described her as an English rose "with a little of the morning dew still on the petal." Waiters and cabdrivers gathered at street corners to cheer her limousine, and the doorkeeper of the House of Representatives was so excited to see her that he hollered, "Howdee-do, ma'am." Women were captivated when she attended her first football game and appeared bewildered by men's passion for the sport. She didn't understand the concept of downs, or why the two teams huddled. "Why do they gather that way?" she asked. "Why are the goalposts behind the lines at the ends of the field? Why does one man leave the huddle first?" Pointing to the scoreboard, she asked what the numbers meant, and as the game dragged on, she inquired, plaintively but sweetly, "What is the duration of the game?"

Warren Rogers, the Associated Press reporter, who filed several stories a day during the state visit,* encountered further static from the British Embassy press office when he reported that Her Majesty and Gina Lollobrigida shared the same corsetiere. "The brassieres made for Gina were designed to maximize," recalled Rogers, "but those for the Queen, who had the same kind of prominent bosom, were designed to minimize. I wrote that this was the difference between movie stars and royalty. But I was taken to task by the British press officer for even mentioning the Queen's Hanoverian bosom. He said in oh, so lofty terms that I had crossed the line, even for a brash American. I had not demonstrated the proper amount of deference. 'After all,' he said, 'the Crown nevah, evah, evah shows cleavage.'"

---

* The three major U.S. wire services—Associated Press, United Press, and International News Service—filed four hundred thousand words on the royal state visit. The preceding week they sent out three hundred thousand on *Sputnik*.

NINE

Royal weddings invigorate the monarchy. With all their pageantry, they pump energy into the ancient rituals. They provide an epic pageant that stirs emotions. The romantic procession of a princess bride in a glass coach drawn by prancing horses to an enchanted life of happily ever after has no equal outside fairy tales. The crash of military drums, the blare of trumpets, and the roar of cheering crowds entrance the country like a shower of shooting stars.

Swept up in the excitement, people unite to celebrate. And, not incidentally, businesses prosper as couturiers design hats and gowns; hotels book guests; restaurants cater parties; concessionaires produce gewgaws; and tourists spend freehandedly. Next to a coronation, nothing enchants the British like a royal wedding, and by 1960 the monarchy needed one.

Reverence for the Crown had slipped since the coronation, and traditional deference had been displaced by a new press curiosity. While still submissive to the Palace, British reporters were finally disclosing how much it cost taxpayers to maintain royalty. The 1959 bill for upkeep of the royal yacht, *Britannia,* the two airplanes in the Queen's Flight, Prince Philip's two Westland helicopters, the royal train, and the Queen's four royal Rolls-Royces exceeded $1 million.

Reporters, far from being aggressive, were at least becoming more vigorous in covering the royal family. They still considered the sixty-year-old Queen Mother above reproach, so they rarely wrote a negative word about her, but they singed the Queen a few times for her lackluster style, her hidebound courtiers, her shaky marriage, and her absent (translation: philandering) husband.*

"What this family needs next year is a wedding," the Queen Mother told her oldest daughter during the royal family's 1959 Christmas holidays. She had consulted the court calendars to find the right time to announce Princess Margaret's engagement. She had decided to give her younger daughter a full-blown wedding with all the royal flourishes. She knew that such a state occasion would revitalize the monarchy, but the Queen resisted. She feared that an extravagant wedding would only bring more criticism for spending taxpayers' money, and she did not want any more criticism. Still, she would never oppose her mother—directly.†

The Queen Mother said Princess Margaret's engagement announcement would not interfere

---

* In 1959 Prince Philip made an extended trip to the Far East for almost four months. The Daily Express ran a series of articles entitled "The Woman of the World with an Absent Husband." Philip had made so many trips out of England that upon his return, one newspaper carried the headline "The Duke Visits Britain."

† The Garter King of Arms, who is in charge of the sovereign's heraldic ceremonies, wrote to the Queen to ask whether the entire College of Arms should attend Princess Margaret's wedding. The Queen shuddered. Her private secretary responded: "While Her Majesty appreciated the loyal feeling of the Officers at Arms, they would understand that for obvious reasons she did not want the wedding to be made more of an occasion of state than was absolutely necessary."

with the national celebration planned for the birth of the Queen's third child, expected in February. Ten years had passed since Princess Anne was born, and for the Queen, her current pregnancy would underscore the stability of her marriage and commitment to her family. Significantly, the birth was timed to coincide with changing the name of the House of Windsor to the House of Mountbatten-Windsor. The Queen had proposed the change the previous year and suggested the announcement to include her husband's name be made shortly before the arrival of their third baby.

Despite his misgivings, the Prime Minister agreed to present the matter to his cabinet. The traditional monarchists objected when he broached the subject, but the Prime Minister, Harold Macmillan, pushed for the Queen's position, saying how important it was to her that her husband's name be validated. The Bishop of Carlisle cooperated by announcing that he did not like to think of any child born in wedlock being deprived of the father's family name. "Why should Her Majesty be different from any other married woman in the realm?" the Prime Minister asked his cabinet.

"Why indeed," snorted one Tory minister, who suspected the ambitions of "that Battenberg buggerer" (that is, Louis Mountbatten) had more to do with the name change than the Queen's personal wishes.

The Deputy Prime Minister reported back to the Queen that several ministers suspected the strong hand of her unpopular husband. The

Deputy then wrote a confidential memo to the Prime Minister about his meeting, saying: "The Queen stressed that Prince Philip did not know of the present decision, on which she had absolutely set her heart."

So the Prime Minister went back to his cabinet and argued strenuously for the name change. The meeting was so acrimonious that papers dealing with the issue were not routinely released in 1990 under the thirty-year rule. The subject referred to within the cabinet as "the Queen's Affair" was so sensitive that the government ordered all pertinent documents be kept sealed for an additional twenty years.

After months of discussion, the Macmillan* cabinet finally acceded to the Queen, and the new name was intricately fashioned by lawyers to accommodate her wishes without sacrificing historical continuity. The hyphenated hybrid was confusing, but at least it gave the Queen and Prince Philip, not to mention "Uncle Dickie," some small measure of satisfaction. On February 8, 1960, eleven days before the birth of Prince Andrew,† Her Majesty announced:

---

* Three years later the Queen sadly accepted Macmillan's resignation as Prime Minister. In a letter, she thanked him for being "my guide and supporter" in international matters. "There have also been, I am afraid, a number of problems affecting my family... which must have occupied a great amount of your time. I should like to put on record my appreciation and gratitude for the unstinting care which you have taken in giving me your advice about them and helping me to find a solution."

† The Sunday Express, one of Lord Beaverbrook's three newspapers, acidly congratulated Prince Philip when the Queen was about to give birth: "We are edified that he was able at last to leave his bird shooting at Sandringham and rejoin his wife at this exciting moment of her life."

While I and my children will continue to be styled and known as the House and Family of Windsor, my descendants, other than descendants enjoying the style, title or attributes of Royal Highness and the titular dignity of Prince or Princess and the female descendants who marry, and their descendants shall bear the name Mountbatten-Windsor.

The reaction was immediate and scathing. "Only fifteen years after the second world war against Germany," fumed a columnist for the *Mirror,* "we are abruptly informed that the name of Mountbatten, formerly Battenberg, is to be joined willy-nilly with the name of Windsor."

Lord Beaverbrook, who owned the *Daily Express,* the *Sunday Express,* and the *Evening Standard,* blamed Mountbatten for pushing the Queen into a hyphenated name. "Small wonder that Lord Mountbatten, whose devotion to his heritage is little short of fanatical, has for many years nursed a secret ambition that one day, the name of the ruling house of Britain might be Mountbatten," he wrote. "The Queen could never see the name of Windsor, chosen by her grandfather, abandoned by the royal house. On the other hand, she sympathizes with her husband's feelings and more particularly with the overtures of his uncle."

The pompous Mountbatten was unperturbed. He was too busy celebrating. "My greatest happiness," he wrote in a letter to a friend, "is that in the future royal children will be styled by the surname Mountbatten-Windsor."

In January 1960 Lord Mountbatten had staged an elaborate wedding for his younger daughter, Lady Pamela, to interior decorator David Nightengale Hicks. Mountbatten invited all the crowned heads of Europe to make sure his daughter's wedding was as colorful and splendid as a royal wedding, prompting the press to describe him as "almost royal." Future Prime Minister Harold Wilson described him as "the Shop Steward of Royalty," but his future son-in-law said that Mountbatten was insecure about his status. "The trouble with Dickie," said David Hicks, "was that in spite of his brilliant achievements, he never really knew who he was. He wasn't a member of the aristocracy; he had royal blood, but he wasn't fully accepted in the royal family, so he held a peculiar position that somehow left him very insecure."

At first Mountbatten had been dismayed that his daughter wanted to marry a commoner far beneath her rank and station. For his own pride, he wanted her to make a more illustrious marriage like her sister's. In 1946 he had persuaded his older daughter, Patricia, his acknowledged favorite* and the one for whom he had secured his title,† to marry John Knatchbull, a strapping

---

* Mountbatten made no pretense about favoring his older daughter, Patricia. In 1953 he wrote her a letter saying, "You know how basically fond I am and always have been of Mummy, you know pretty well about my girl friends, but none of them have had that magic 'something' which you have." He said that he was fond of his second child, Pamela, "but the mainspring of my love [for her] is that she is *your* sister and *you* love her.

† In 1946 Lord Louis Mountbatten was created Viscount Mountbatten of Burma. The next year he was created Baron Romsey and Earl Mountbatten of Burma, with "special remainder" to his male heirs, and if no males, to his

aristocrat who was the seventh Earl of Brabourne. Mountbatten was proud to claim this man as his son-in-law; he was not at all pleased with the prospect of an impecunious interior decorator.

"David's effeminate profession, plus his sexual preferences, bothered Lord Mountbatten," said his former secretary John Barratt. "But he recognized that Pammy was already thirty years old and on the cusp of spinsterhood. She had never been proposed to before, so he tried to accept the situation and make the best of it."

Mountbatten's biographer, Philip Ziegler, agreed that Hicks* was not Mountbatten's idea of the perfect son-in-law. "An interior decorator," wrote Ziegler, "was not what he would have chosen as a recruit for his family."

"The English aristocracy are so two-faced about sexuality," said the writer Gwen Robyns. "It was absolutely hypocritical for Mountbatten, supposedly an old queen himself, or at least bisexual, to object to David Hicks. David never lied about himself or his boyfriends. He's always been quite open, and Pammy's very accepting of the men in his life.

eldest daughter and her male heirs. This special remainder, which allowed the title to pass to a female, was a rare concession by the monarch and granted only to military veterans with a record of distinguished war service. After the death of his wife in 1960, Mountbatten told his beloved daughter, Patricia, that he could not contemplate remarriage because he might have a son and disturb the plans he had made for her succession to his title.

* Mountbatten never developed deep affection for David Hicks and never accepted him as a surrogate son the way he did John Brabourne and Prince Philip. In 1972, twelve years after Hicks had married his younger daughter, Mountbatten wrote a letter to Philip in which he said, "Patricia and Pammy could not be sweeter or more affectionate daughters, but one does miss sons—so I am very lucky to have you and John who are both so affectionate and nice to me."

"I came to know Pammy and David quite well when I worked with him on a book about decorating," said the writer. "I dined with them many times, and there was always a beautiful young boy in attendance. I met several of David's boyfriends, and even interviewed them when I was writing his biography.* I do remember asking Pammy once how she could put up with all the men. And she said, 'Gwen, if you had parents like mine, you can put up with anything. Besides, David is a very good father and he's very nice to me. He runs the house, he orders the food, and he picks out all my clothes.'

"David told me that he was on the verge of bankruptcy in 1959," continued the writer. "A friend told him the only solution was to marry an heiress, but David didn't know any heiresses, so his friend invited him to a party to meet a few. That night David was taking his mother to the movies—he was living with his mother at the time. He left her in the car for a few minutes while he ran in to his friend's party to scout heiresses. Enter Lady Pamela Mountbatten. David didn't waste a second.

"'I saw an estate of five million pounds walk

---

* Mountbatten objected to his son-in-law's collaborating on a book. He phoned the writer and invited her for lunch. After a round of drinks he said, "Now, now, Miss Robyns. Be a good girl and give me those tapes." She refused. "I couldn't," she said. "I had all of David's old gay boyfriends on tape, saying terrible things about him, and I didn't think it right to release them." Mountbatten threatened to sue her. She gave in. "I couldn't fight a man with his money, so we ended up going to his lawyer's office and burning the tapes." Hicks waited until after Lord Mountbatten's death to contact another writer, June Ducas, to resume work on his life story. "June can write whatever she likes, warts and all," he said in 1995. "I don't give a damn."

through the door in white peep-toe shoes and the worst white pocketbook you've ever seen,' he told me. 'I immediately took her in my arms to dance and whispered, 'How many babies do you want?' Naturally, Pammy, who had never been courted before and was in danger of never getting married, was enchanted. She told me she went home and told her mother, who was pleased for her but rather puzzled.

"'That's wonderful, darling,' said Edwina, an heiress who inherited generations of heirlooms and never purchased furniture in her life. 'But what's an interior designer?'"

After conferring with the Queen's courtiers, Lord Mountbatten chose January 13, 1960, for his daughter's wedding because that was the only date that was convenient for the royal family. "Despite the snow and slush of a winter blizzard, he insisted on a January wedding because he wanted to have the royal family there," said Barratt, "and most of them attended, except for the Queen, who was in confinement at Sandringham for the birth of her third child."

Mountbatten took charge of his daughter's wedding like an impresario staging a theatrical production. He selected her royal bridesmaids—Princess Anne, the Queen's ten-year-old daughter; Princess Clarissa of Hesse; and Princess Frederica of Hanover. He summoned Owen Hyde-Clark of the House of Worth to design her wedding dress and promptly put his daughter on a diet so that she would look sleek and slim on her wedding day.

He relegated the incidental details to his future son-in-law, the decorator, who was eager to please his future father-in-law. Hicks decreed that everything should be white—"all white, all white"—from the mink cuffs on the bridal gown to the bridesmaids' coronets of hyacinth petals.

"As mother of the bride, Edwina was delighted to have her future son-in-law flying about attending to everything," said a friend, "because she was already overexhausted planning her charity excursion to the Far East. She left a few days after the wedding, and, sadly, died in her sleep on that trip while touring Borneo."

The press coverage of the Mountbatten wedding conveyed the impression of a glorious union between a nobleman's daughter and the common but worthy man of her dreams. The bride's entrance into Romsey Abbey was heralded by trumpets playing "O Perfect Love." And at the reception later, surrounded by members of the British and German royal families, the Duke of Edinburgh toasted the future of the bride and bridegroom.

"As long as they produce children and keep the bloodline going," said Gwen Robyns, "that's all that's required. Whether the bridegroom is homosexual, bisexual, or heterosexual doesn't matter, as long as the marriage looks good on the outside and is kept up for public appearances. It's worse for gay men within the aristocracy because it's the duty of the oldest male to produce an heir to pass on the family name, the property, and the title. So they've got to get married, no matter what their sexual orientation is, which accounts for the long established tradition in Britain of homosexual men marrying women simply to breed. Makes no difference what they do later on the side as long as they do it discreetly. That's the hypocrisy of it all."

In his memoir, *Palimpsest,* writer Gore Vidal reflects on the homoerotic preference of men for each other that is accepted as a fact of life in Great Britain, especially in public schools. "Most young men, particularly attractive ones, have sexual relations with their own kind," Vidal writes. "I suppose this is still news to those who believe in the two teams: straight, which is good and unalterable; queer, which is bad and unalterable unless it proves to be only a Preference, which must then, somehow, be reversed, if necessary by force." Within the British aristocracy, marriage was the force.

"The love that dare not speak its name" was the way Oscar Wilde's young male lover had described men's sexual preference for one another in 1895. At that time, men like Oscar Wilde, who married women but loved men, were considered degenerates whose sexual acts were punishable by imprisonment. Sixty-five years later nothing had altered that concept in England, and in 1960, after the announcement of Princess Margaret's engagement, homosexuality again became an issue.

The whispering started soon after the Queen Mother announced her daughter's engagement and impending marriage in May. Ordinary people were pleased that the twenty-nine-year-old Princess, who had partied aimlessly for five years since renouncing Peter Townsend, seemed to have finally found happiness. For the public, her marriage to a commoner would lower a class barrier between the monarchy and the people and bring them closer to the throne. For those within royal circles, the announcement caused an audible rumble in the tectonic plates that underpin the British establishment. Not only was the bohemian photographer a commoner whose parents were divorced, but he also had a mother who was Jewish. The white Anglo-Saxon Protestant aristocracy hardly considered him an appropriate suitor for the daughter of a king and the sister of a queen, a royal princess who was fourth in the line of succession to the throne.

"Princess Margaret has announced her engagement to Tony Armstrong-Jones," wrote Noel Coward in his diary on February 28, 1960. "Tony looks quite pretty, but whether or not the marriage is entirely suitable remains to be seen." He recorded further disapproval from the Duchess of Kent and Princess Alexandra. "They are not pleased over [the] engagement," he wrote. "There was a distinct froideur when I mentioned it."

Ronald Armstrong-Jones was shocked that his son was considering such a marriage. "I wish in heaven's name this hadn't happened," he said. "It will never work out. Tony's a far too independent sort of fellow to be subjected to discipline. He won't be prepared to play second fiddle to anyone. He will have to walk two steps behind his wife, and I fear for his future."

Tony's closest friends agreed. "I sent a telegram," said classmate Jocelyn Stevens, a former magazine editor, "and said: 'Never has there been a more ill-fated assignment.'"

The *Times* editorial page concurred. "There is no recent precedent for the marriage of one so near to the Throne outside the ranks of international royalty and the British peerage."

Even the *New Statesman,* a liberal publication expected to be enthusiastic, withheld approval. The magazine said that the suitability of this particular commoner to become a member of the royal family must be judged "with a leniency which only a few years before would have been unthinkable."

The Queen was the first sovereign in five hundred years to admit a commoner into her immediate family. She tried to remedy the situation by offering Mr. Armstrong-Jones a title, but he refused.* A year later, when his wife became pregnant, he decided he wanted his children to be titled, so he accepted the Queen's offer to become the Earl of Snowdon, also Viscount Linley of Nymans. The *Manchester Guardian* expressed a "tinge of disappointment

---

*When Angus Ogilvy, a commoner, married Margaret's cousin, Princess Alexandra, daughter of Marina, the Duchess of Kent, on April 24, 1963, he refused the queen's offer of an earldom. "I don't see why I should get a peerage," said Ogilvy, "simply because I have married a princess."

that the plain, honest Mr. Armstrong-Jones should have a title thrust upon him." *People* said the newly minted peer had lost his appeal. "As the husband of the Queen's sister, Tony Armstrong-Jones had one very big claim on the sympathy of the British people. He had no handle to his name. He was, in fact, one of us...now he has lost even that most precious asset which was his birthright."

Those close to the Princess were concerned that she was marrying on the rebound. They knew that Peter Townsend had written to her on October 9, 1959, to say that he was marrying a beautiful young Belgian tobacco heiress, twenty years old, whom he had met in Brussels soon after he arrived in exile. "She might be rich," said the Princess, trying to dismiss the news, "but she's not royal." Within hours of receiving that letter, Margaret had elicited a marriage proposal from Armstrong-Jones.

"It's true," Margaret admitted many years later. "I had received a letter from Peter in the morning, and that evening I decided to marry Tony. It was not a coincidence. I didn't really want to marry at all. Why did I? Because he asked me! Really, though, he was such a nice person in those days. He understood my job and pushed me to do things. In a way he introduced me to a new world." Margaret said she managed to keep Tony's proposal a secret for several months "because no one believed he was interested in women."

Described in the press as "artistic," "campy,"

and "theatrical," Antony Armstrong-Jones, thirty-two, was the only child of a lawyer. The father had long since divorced Tony's mother and remarried an actress, whom he also divorced. When his son's engagement was announced, Ronald Armstrong-Jones was living with an airline stewardess thirty years his junior. He quickly married her so as not to embarrass his son, who was only one year younger than his new stepmother. Years before, Tony's mother had married an Irish peer and was now the Countess of Rosse, which gave Tony a seat on the edge of the aristocracy. He attended Eton determined to become an architect and went on to Cambridge, but after a year he flunked out.

When he was sixteen he contracted polio. After hospitalization and several months in leg braces, he rehabilitated himself by designing a pair of skis with which he exercised to strengthen his leg muscles. He eventually developed a bouncy walk to hide his limp. Still, he identified with the handicapped and showed compassion for them. In later years he served on charity committees to raise money for medical research into disability. He also invented a wheelchair on a motorized platform to allow the incapacitated to move easily from room to room.

Tony's uncle was the theatrical designer Oliver Messel, who was a close friend to Cecil Beaton and Noel Coward. They encouraged the late court photographer Baron, who specialized in royalty and society, to take on

Tony as an apprentice. After working for Baron for several months, Tony opened his own photography studio in the Pimlico section of London, and with immense charm and ambition he began pursuing his own royal assignments. He photographed the young Duke of Kent and, after that sitting, photographed the children of the Queen's equerry. The Queen then asked him to come to Buckingham Palace to photograph Prince Charles and Princess Anne.

A few months later the photographer met Princess Margaret at the home of Lady Elizabeth Cavendish. The Princess, normally imperious, allowed herself to be approachable that evening, although she insisted that Tony address her as "ma'am," something she demanded of everyone because, as she said, it was her due as royalty. (A close friend, when asked what the Princess was like, said, "She needs to hear the crack of a knee at least three times before breakfast.") Tony cleverly appealed to her vanity by asking her advice about a fashion shoot he was doing for *Vogue* magazine. He later invited her to his apartment—and she accepted.

Although they came from far different backgrounds, the Princess and the photographer shared similar temperaments. Clever, witty, and sharp-tongued, both were petite rebels who chain-smoked cigarettes and slavered over pornographic movies. The photographer, barely five feet seven, longed to escape his class-enforced position, and the Princess, five feet tall in her platform heels, enjoyed flouting the strictures of society. Together they began a most unconventional love affair under the amused gaze of the Queen Mother. The Princess, disguised in a scarf and sunglasses, frequently sneaked out of Clarence House and was driven to the photographer's apartment in Pimlico, where he entertained her in his bedroom, which he had painted purple. Thriving on the glamour of show business, they socialized with the trendy celebrities of the day like Mick Jagger, David Frost, Peter Sellers, and the Beatles.

"Tone and Pet—their nicknames for each other—enjoyed exploring taboos—the strange, the dark, the bizarre—fetishes, that sort of thing," said a friend, who related how the couple dressed up in each other's clothes and posed for pictures.

As a little boy, Tony occasionally dressed up in women's clothes. One evening, with the encouragement of his stepmother, an actress, he dressed up as a parlor maid to serve dinner to his father and grandfather. He later attended parties in drag, and two years before his engagement, he entered the field of dress design. During his courtship he shocked Princess Margaret's footman by wearing her makeup and dressing up in her elaborate party dresses and veiled hats. "I gaped with astonishment," recalled the footman, "but Margaret's sides were splitting from laughter at the sight of Tony's bare legs with such spindly calves which showed out from underneath the Princess's maroon pleated skirt....His feet tottered in a delicate pair of the Princess's sandals with the laces untied."

The footman, David John Payne, wrote about this incident of cross-dressing in a book that angered the Queen Mother, who sued to prevent publication in England. She did not want the royal family embarrassed by the footman, particularly his allegation of having been the object of a sexual overture from Antony Armstrong-Jones. The British court issued an injunction in the United Kingdom, but the book was published in Paris, where readers of *France Dimanche* learned what were presented as intimate details of Margaret's courtship.

The footman, who resigned his position before the royal wedding, described an incident that he said left him shaken. He recalled leaving the Princess's Royal Lodge suite at Windsor Castle, where he had been helping her select records to take to London:

> I got up and left while she remained seated on the floor. I was halfway through the door when it burst open and Tony Armstrong-Jones came into the room. Seeing me, he exclaimed: "John, I've looked for you everywhere. Have a seat, darling."
>
> My heart stopped. Obviously, Tony hadn't noticed the Princess on the floor behind the sofa, which accounted for his familiar tone with me. He was interrupted

by the sudden rustle sounds of her skirt as she hastened to get up.

She looked at him, her face livid with anger. "'John, sit down, darling'? What does *that* mean? To whom are you speaking?"

Tony was totally caught off guard by these questions in a glacial tone. He blushed and began to sway from one foot to the other.

"Oh, madame," said Tony. "I didn't know...I didn't see you. I was looking for John."

"And what do you mean by 'darling'?" asked Margaret in a fierce voice.

"It's an expression used all the time in the theater, madame," he stammered.

Margaret said nothing to him, turned towards me, and in her most majestic voice said, "You may retire."

I left her still looking at Tony, who was nonplussed; she continued to look shocked. Then I left, and having closed the door, I realized I was soaked in perspiration.

Obviously unamused by her fiancé's familiarity with her footman, the Princess was relaxed about the dress-up games that Antony Armstrong-Jones liked to play. She joined him and assumed the male role by wearing suits and ties. They took turns photographing each other. She took a picture of him dressed as a child; he took a picture of her posing in his tuxedo, holding a cigar. Already they epitomized the swinging new decade of the sixties, in which the lines of sexual identity were blurred.

Because his mother was a countess, Antony Armstrong-Jones was considered privileged, but to aristocrats he was still a commoner who was now marrying above himself. This bold social leap, coupled with his artistic pursuits, subjected him to a certain amount of sniping in the press. Shortly before his marriage, *Newsweek* described him suggestively as "the uncommon commoner who once was set upon and de-trousered at a country house party by high-spirited male guests who saw him strolling with a camera round his neck. He weathered that indignity, chin up, just as he is making no apologies for his Bohemian cool-cat friends and showing no embarrassment in the unprecedented wave of pub and club innuendoes about his private life."

The bizarre sexual implications annoyed some of his friends, who emphasized that all-male dining societies are a tradition at certain English schools. "At some of the Oxford debauches, men regularly dress up as women in strapless gowns and high heels," explained one man. "The most notorious all-male dining society there is is the Peers Gaveston Society, named for King Edward II's catamite, who, by dictionary definition, is a boy kept for unnatural purposes. According to legend, the King's catamite was killed by being sodomized with a hot poker. So, in comparison, the little escapade of Antony Armstrong-Jones getting de-trousered is quite tame."

Without addressing the issue of sexuality head on, the press made snide insinuations about Tony's circle of male friends, who were described as "confirmed bachelors," a journalistic euphemism for homosexuals.

"Tony didn't know if he was Arthur or Martha," said the British novelist Una-Mary Parker. "We're not talking Adam and Eve; we're talking Adam and Steve."

"Not so," said one of Tony's Cambridge classmates. "I'd say he was more bisexual than homosexual. He'd never limit himself."

Another said, "Let's just put that subject under what Sir Osbert Sitwell called an enormous tolerance for the untoward or eccentric."

A few weeks before the wedding, Tony announced the name of his best man, and the press pounced like cats on a mouse. They reported that the best man, who was married, had been convicted of a homosexual offense eight years earlier.

"Prince Philip went wild. Tony was a little too swish for his taste anyway, what with his scarlet velvet capes and his long-haired friends who wore beards instead of shoes," said a friend. "But when Tony announced that Jeremy Fry was to stand up for him at his wedding, the Duke of Edinburgh exploded. Fry was flagrantly homosexual."

So, under pressure, Tony withdrew Fry's name, and the Palace quickly announced that the young man had come down with a case of jaundice and would be unable to take part in the wedding. A few days later Tony chose Jeremy Thorpe to be his best man, but Scotland Yard investigators informed the Palace that Thorpe might be the target of homosexual blackmail and, obviously, not an acceptable choice. The Queen's courtiers informed Tony that his friend could not be allowed to stand up for him in Westminster Abbey in the presence of royalty. Again Tony was forced publicly to retreat.

Because this would be the first royal wedding televised, the Palace insisted that a proper image be presented. The courtiers, whose responsibility was to protect the Crown from scandal, worried that people might think the Queen condoned "degenerate" behavior if she allowed a known homosexual to be part of the royal wedding party.

"Ridiculous, I know," said a friend of Tony's many years later, "especially since most of the royal household has always been homosexual, to say nothing of the aristocracy and the clergy; but that's how prickly the Palace was about the issue in 1960."

Tony was summoned to the Palace for a hurried meeting with the Queen's courtiers. Hours later they announced that the third choice for Tony's best man would be Dr. Roger Gilliatt, son of the Queen's surgeon-gynecologist. He was married to the magazine editor Penelope Gilliatt, for whom Tony occasionally had worked. He was hardly a close friend, as Gilliatt acknowledged. "Armstrong-Jones seems like a nice chap," he said, "but I don't know him very well."

Parchment wedding invitations engraved with the words "The Lord Chamberlain to Queen Elizabeth the Queen Mother is commanded by Her Majesty to invite…" were sent from Clarence House to two thousand people. The Palace did not release the names for fear of press inquiries regarding the marital status of some of the guests. The bridegroom's father and both his former wives, plus their husbands, were included in the guest list. Meanwhile the bride's disgraced uncle, the Duke of Windsor, and his twice divorced wife were pointedly excluded. "Ah, well, perhaps there'll be a funeral soon," said the Duchess of Windsor, blithely trying to bat aside the continued royal ostracism. Poking fun at herself, she added, "At least they can't say I haven't kept up with the Joneses."

As the only royal dynasty to stake its claim to the throne on its opposition to divorce, the House of Windsor could no longer preserve the pretense that divorce barred participation in royal events. Few people realized it at the time, but this royal wedding lowered the divorce barrier forever.

"They changed the guard at Buckingham Palace last night," observed the *Daily Mail* in describing the theatrical wedding guests who sat in the Poet's Corner of Westminster Abbey: playwright Noel Coward, ballerina Dame Margot Fonteyn, movie star Leslie

Caron, and actress Margaret Leighton. The newspaper listed the names of actors, actresses, couturiers, hairdressers, interior decorators, restaurateurs, choreographers, dancers, writers, singers, and songwriters—all friends of the bridegroom. "These are the people who will dominate the social landscape," the paper predicted, "not fusty aristocrats."

"This wedding marked a new chapter for royalty," said the *Daily Telegraph and Morning Post.* "Like the seventh son of the seventh son who eventually marries the beautiful Princess, the bridegroom was a new and magical link between Court and people. On pavement level, the marriage of Royalty with Royalty is a spectacle; but the marriage of a Princess with a photographer is a party."

Less enthusiastic were a few Scottish aristocrats north of the border, who watched the wedding on television. They professed astonishment when the young Prince of Wales walked down the aisle dressed as a Highland chieftain. The BBC broadcaster said he thought Prince Charles looked delightful in his green doublet, lace jabot, and Royal Stuart kilt, but several Scots pointed out that the eleven-year-old Prince was improperly dressed in evening attire. They became even more indignant when Antony Armstrong-Jones appeared at the Royal Highland Games at Braemar in Scotland wearing trousers instead of a kilt. The nobility of Scotland had looked down on the House of Windsor ever since the Queen showed up for her Scottish coronation wearing a street dress instead of her coronation gown.

For everyone else, the wedding was a dazzling spectacle of royalty, from the bride's diamond tiara to the five gold carriages transporting members of the royal family. Inside Westminster Abbey, the setting sparkled with more shades of gold than a Fabergé box. From the Queen's gilt chair to the Archbishop's polished miter to the solid gold altar plate, everything gleamed, reflecting immense wealth. A crowd of more than one hundred thousand people lined the procession route to cheer the Princess, whose wedding was the gayest and grandest ever staged by the royal family. Three million people watched on television, and schoolchildren were given the day off. For the first and only time in her life, Margaret was transported in a glass coach escorted by one hundred horsemen in gold braid. Awaiting her arrival, the crowds screamed: "We want Margaret! We want Margaret!"

Her state allowance was raised by Parliament from $18,000 to $45,000 per year. After a forty-four-day honeymoon in the Caribbean on the *Britannia,* which cost $30,000 a day, she and her new husband would return to a ten-room apartment in Kensington Palace that cost taxpayers $180,000 to renovate. British servicemen had had a portion of their wages deducted as a contribution toward a wedding present. The wedding itself had cost $78,000, which made the Queen uneasy. The Queen Mother shrugged off the expense, telling her daughter that she had to learn to live up to the lavish style people expected of royalty.

"There was nothing like it," wrote Eve Perrick in the *Daily Mail*. "I have been to highly publicised weddings before. I was outside the Abbey when the Queen married Prince Philip. I saw Prince Rainier marry film star Grace Kelly. The unique quality of yesterday's semi-state occasion was that it combined the best elements of both. It was a right royal affair."

"The Queen alone looked disagreeable," Noel Coward wrote in his diary. "Princess Margaret looked like the ideal of what any fairy-tale princess *should* look like...Prince Philip jocular and really very sweet and reassuring as he led the bride to the altar. The music was divine and the fanfare immensely moving. Nowhere in the world but England could such pomp and circumstance and pageantry be handled with such exquisite dignity...it was lusty, charming, romantic, splendid and conducted without a false note. It is *still* a pretty exciting thing to be English."

Noel Coward would not live long enough to realize that what he had just seen was the beginning of the end. Royalty was unraveling. Within a few years this wedding would push the House of Windsor into what it feared most.

TEN

The First Lady was sitting in her bedroom at the White House when her secretary entered with yet another dispatch from the British Embassy. For weeks diplomatic cables had been rocketing between London and Washington regarding the Queen's dinner party on June 5, 1961, in honor of the President and his First Lady. But she was exasperated.

"This is absurd," she said to her secretary. "It's not like I suggested inviting the Duke and Duchess of Windsor."

The First Lady had suggested inviting her sister, Lee Radziwill, and Lee's husband, the Polish Prince Stanislas Radziwill. But after the White House sent its proposed guest list to Buckingham Palace, the Radziwills were de-listed. By the Queen.

The Kennedys planned a stopover in London for a few days to attend the baptism of the President's godchild, Christina Radziwill, after the President's state visit to Paris. In London the Kennedys would stay with the Radziwills at their home on Buckingham Place, around the corner from the Palace. While there, President Kennedy wanted to meet informally with the British Prime Minister. Although Kennedy's visit was private and not official, the British government recommended that the Queen entertain the President and his wife. The Queen agreed. It was to be the first time an American president had dined with a British monarch in Bucking-

271

ham Palace since Woodrow Wilson was a guest in 1918.

A dinner party for fifty people was planned in the state dining room of the Palace, and the White House was asked to submit the names of people the Kennedys would like to attend. The First Lady proposed her host and hostess, the Radziwills, as well as Princess Margaret, whom Mrs. Kennedy wanted to meet; the President asked for Princess Marina of Kent, whom he had met during his year at Oxford. The Queen did not approve any of them.

Annoyed by the royal rebuff, the First Lady telephoned the British Embassy in Washington to speak to Her Majesty's Ambassador, David Ormsby-Gore, who was also a close Kennedy family friend. He explained gently the Palace policy on divorce, saying that because this was an unofficial visit, the Radziwills, both of whom were divorced—once for her, twice for him—could not be invited to the Palace. If this were an official visit and the Radziwills were part of the official group accompanying the President, they would have to be invited.

"But she's my sister," Jackie told the British Ambassador, "and they are our hosts."

The Ambassador sympathized and suggested that she call the U.S. Chief of Protocol, Angier Biddle Duke, to appeal the ruling through the U.S. Ambassador to the Court of St. James's, David Bruce.

"Oh, Angie," Jackie wailed, "you've got to help me."

The diplomat reassured the First Lady and promised to contact David Bruce. Jackie then called her husband in the Oval Office to tell him what she had done. The President was irked. He quickly called Ambassador Bruce in London to say he did not want to cause an international incident.

The Ambassador noted the President's conversation in his diary: "He wanted to make it clear that for his part he had no feeling about this incident, and any decision on the guest list must be the Queen's."

Her Majesty eventually relented and included the Radziwills; she even allowed them to be listed in the Court Circular for the occasion as "Prince" and "Princess." That was a great concession because the Queen had never granted Radziwill royal license to use his Polish title* in Great Britain.

"She did not like him," said Evangeline Bruce, the Ambassador's wife. "It had nothing to do with divorce. My husband was divorced, and the Queen loved him. She just didn't like Stash Radziwill...didn't approve of him and always referred to him and his wife as Mr. and Mrs., which irritated them."

"Anyway, the Queen had her revenge," Jackie later told Gore Vidal, her stepbrother once removed. "No Margaret, no Marina,

---

*When the Nazis invaded Poland, Radziwill fled Warsaw for London, where he became a British subject. Legally he forfeited the right to use his hereditary title of Prince of the Holy Roman Empire, which had been conferred on his family in the sixteenth century. His insistence on being addressed as Prince Radziwill remained controversial in Britain.

no one except every Commonwealth minister of agriculture that they could find. The Queen was pretty heavy-going. I think she resented me. Philip was nice, but nervous. One felt absolutely no relationship between them."

The Queen's resentment was real. She had read the press coverage of the First Lady's spectacular visit to Paris, where she had been hailed by the French newspapers as *"ravissante," "charmante," "belle."* Parisians had lined the streets, waving American flags and screaming, "Jacquiii! Jacquiii! Jacquiii!" The Mayor of Paris had given her a $4,000 watch and pronounced her visit the most exciting since Queen Elizabeth II had paraded through the city four years earlier.

"Queen Elizabeth, hell," presidential aide Dave Powers told the press. "They couldn't get this kind of turnout with the Second Coming."

Even the President was stunned by the excitement his wife had generated. Greeting reporters at a press conference in France, he introduced himself as "the man who accompanied Jacqueline Kennedy to Paris."

By the time the Kennedys arrived in London, Jackie fever had gripped the British, who lined the streets awaiting her arrival the same way they did for the Queen. One newspaper even dubbed the First Lady "Queen of America." Another ran a cartoon showing the Statue of Liberty with Mrs. Kennedy's face; one hand held the torch of freedom, the other clutched a copy of *Vogue*. The *Evening Stan-*

dard gushed, "Jacqueline Kennedy has given the American people from this day on one thing they had always lacked—majesty."

"The young President with his lovely wife and the whole glamour which surrounds them both caused something of a sensation," recalled Prime Minister Macmillan in his memoirs. "Normally, the visits of foreign statesmen do not arouse much enthusiasm...but the Kennedys were news on every level, political and personal."

The Prime Minister did not record Her Majesty's displeasure at having to entertain them. The Queen, who was forever proclaiming her disdain of glamour, scorned Hollywood and all that the film colony represented. Unlike her mother, her sister, her husband, and her uncle Dickie, who felt cinema was the highest art form, the Queen was not receptive to Hollywood or its celebrities. In fact, she was so contemptuous of associating with motion picture stars that she declined to attend Grace Kelly's 1956 wedding to Prince Rainier of Monaco. "Too many movie stars," she said.

As Queen, she resisted all attempts to dress up her image. When a BBC producer timidly suggested she show more animation during her first televised Christmas address, she snapped, "I'm not an actress."

For the same reason, she refused to wear a fur coat. "Absolutely not," she told footman Ralphe White. "I look too much like a film star in mink."

She acknowledged her dour image, saying

that unlike her mother, she was not a show stopper. At a subdued rally, she noted, "If it were Mummy, they would all be cheering."

Her husband shared her resolve that royalty must not descend to the level of movie stars. Like the Queen, he, too, would not sign autographs, and he resented efforts to make him perform. When he made a speech to the British Film Academy, he was heckled.

"Liven it up," shouted actor Tom Bell. "Go on, tell us a funny story."

The Duke of Edinburgh bristled. "If you want a funny story," he said, "I suggest you engage a professional comic."

Neither he nor the Queen recognized then that the British public wanted something more humane and spontaneous from their monarchy than an aloof wave from the royal coach.

"The Queen takes her Commonwealth responsibilities very seriously," explained Prime Minister Macmillan, "and rightly so, for the responsibilities of the U.K. monarchy have so shrunk that if you left it at that, you might as well have a film star. She is impatient of the attitude toward her to treat her as a woman, and a film star or mascot."

With the visit of the Kennedys, she was faced with entertaining the epitome of flash-bulb glamour. The Queen had admitted to her sister that she felt more comfortable with President Eisenhower's matronly wife, Mamie, than the mesmerizing Jackie, who was inciting the Queen's normally sober subjects to act like crazed fans. They clogged the streets of London for hours, clamoring for a glimpse of the U.S. President and his First Lady.

In preparation for the Kennedy visit, the Lord Chamberlain, who usually exercises his powers of censorship only on an objectionable word or sentence, had banned a theatrical review that lampooned the President's wife. The show, set to open in a Newcastle theater, was to have had a male chorus singing:

Here she comes, sing do re mi
Oh, what a change from old Auntie Mamie.

Then an actress was to appear in a black wig and impersonate Mrs. Kennedy in a satirical skit. Her routine, a string of barbed wisecracks, included the refrain

While Jack fumbles with Russia,
I use all my guile,
So the press and the public
won't guess for awhile,
He's just Ike dressed up Madison Avenue
*   style.*
I'm doing my best to be everyone's choice,
playing Caroline's mother with Marilyn's
*   voice.*

The mention of Marilyn Monroe prompted the censor's scissors. "The review deals unsuitably with a head of state's private life," was the Lord Chamberlain's official explanation, which only added credibility to the rumors of the President's intimate relationship with the Hollywood star.

Despite their differences, the Queen and the First Lady shared a similarity in their husbands, who were charismatic men. Extraordinarily handsome and witty, both were attracted to pretty actresses like fish to shiny metal objects. Neither man was hamstrung by romanticism, and both understood the social necessity of marrying well.

The Queen had not been impressed by the Kennedys' ascent from the Irish bogs to the White House. She still remembered her parents' antipathy toward the President's father, Joseph P. Kennedy. As Ambassador to the Court of St. James's he had opposed U.S. intervention on the side of the British in World War II, so President Franklin Roosevelt recalled him. Understandably the Queen was not enthusiastic about Kennedy's son.

She came around eventually, but she was a late convert. During the 1960 presidential campaign, she privately supported Kennedy's opponent, Vice President Richard M. Nixon. Publicly she remained silent, but her husband, who could and did speak out, made it clear. During a trip to New York City to open a British exhibition, Prince Philip showed a canny understanding of presidential politics. He did not overtly endorse Nixon, but he evoked the "special relationship" between America and England by saying, "The Queen was particularly delighted that our dear friend President Eisenhower agreed to join her as a patron for this exhibition." Then he toured the exhibit with the Vice President and New York Governor Nelson Rockefeller and posed for pictures. When photographers begged the Prince for more photographs, he insisted on posing with the Vice President. "We can't take a picture without Mr. Nixon," he said.

When Kennedy won the election, the Queen was smart enough to realize the political importance of good relations with the United States. So she followed her Prime Minister's recommendations to entertain the President and his wife at Buckingham Palace.

Jacqueline Kennedy later told Gore Vidal about the Queen's dinner party, where she sat between Prince Philip and Lord Mountbatten. During the reception before dinner, she talked to the Queen, whom she found chilly and standoffish.

"The Queen was only human once," she recalled. "I was telling her about our state visit to Canada and the rigors of being on view at all hours. I told her I greeted Jack every day with a tearstained face. The Queen looked rather conspiratorial and said, 'One gets crafty after a while and learns how to save oneself.' Then she said, 'You like pictures.' And she marched me down a long gallery, stopping at a Van Dyk to say, 'That's a good horse.'"

The Queen and the First Lady shared more than their mutual love of horses. Both were to become mythic figures and the most celebrated women of their era. Both were monarchs—Elizabeth in fact, Jacqueline in fantasy.

The crucial difference between them was politics. The First Lady disliked politics and was totally apolitical; not so the Queen.

"God knows she's supposed to be above politics," said her biographer Roland Flamini, "but everyone knows the Queen gets politically involved, especially if it concerns the Commonwealth, which is all she really cares about. Her political involvement is never talked about, of course, but everyone knows."

By March 1962 the Queen was embarked on a covert plan to influence the elections in Argentina. She did not realize then that doing her duty meant acquiescing to what her Prime Minister and Archbishop told her to do. Instead she wanted to affect policy. So she dispatched her husband to visit the British communities in eleven South American countries, ostensibly to promote British industry. In Argentina his real mission was to secure the presidency of a friend, Arturo Frondizi, who was in danger of being overthrown by supporters of exiled dictator Juan Perón.

The Queen and Philip had entertained Frondizi at Buckingham Palace earlier in the year, when he confided his fears about allowing Perón supporters to vote in the March elections. "Only my person," he said, "stands between order and chaos."

The Queen agreed and decided to do what she could to prevent a military overthrow that would lead to another dictatorship. Although Argentina was outside the Commonwealth, more Britons lived there than anywhere except the United States, and their imports and exports were important to British trade. At least, that was the Queen's rationale for her intervention. Her husband thought it was empire building, which, he said, was basic to the British: "They are always meddling in other people's business....That's why they're so successful at British charity work overseas. I think it reflects a hangover from the years of responsibility for the direct management of other countries."

Philip's trip to Argentina was the first time in thirty years that a member of the royal family had visited that country, but the Queen felt that her imperial luster would rub off on Frondizi.

In Buenos Aires the Argentine President hosted a state dinner for Philip, who used the occasion to lecture General Rosendo Fraga, Argentina's war secretary.

"Have you been a minister for a long time?" Philip asked.

"For almost one year."

"Tell me something," said Philip. "Do you enjoy it?"

"Yes, Your Highness."

"Another thing. Have you been in a war?"

"No, we haven't had wars recently in Argentina."

"Well," said Philip, wagging his finger in the General's face, "don't go and start one now."

In a speech, Philip referred to the good relations between Argentina and Great Britain: "The really remarkable part is that we are still on such excellent terms after so many years of intimate association. Perhaps it's a case of getting over the seven-year itch and staying good friends forever." (Diplomatically, he did not mention the epidemic of hoof-and-mouth disease that had spread to England in cans of Argentine corned beef.)

The next day young communists pelted Philip with eggs and tomatoes. The police arrested the young people, but Philip interceded. He was in Argentina to help lower political tensions, not stir them up. "Let them go," he said, "but tell them not to do it again. I haven't got an unlimited supply of suits."

This was the first (but not the last) time the Queen veered from her constitutional mandate to remain above politics. As monarch, she was forbidden to take part in the internal affairs of another country. So in Argentina she operated through her husband to influence the outcome of the elections. Unfortunately she miscalculated: Frondizi's opponents won, marched into Buenos Aires with machine guns, and seized control of the country.

Immediately Prince Philip was evacuated from Buenos Aires, and the Macmillan government moved to shield the Queen from responsibility and criticism. The government concealed her participation by sealing all documents pertaining to the trip. They refused to routinely release the 1962 cabinet papers under the thirty-year rule and stipulated secrecy until the year 2057. Most people assumed the secrecy was to cover up a sexual scandal involving Philip, who was forty at that time, and Señora Magdalena Nelson de Blaquier, the beautiful fifty-year-old widow who had been his hostess after the military takeover.

"Look into that story," advised Peter Evans, a prominent British journalist, "and you'll probably find a suspicious birth nine months after the Duke's departure."

"One of Philip's three illegitimate children is supposed to be the daughter of an Argentine polo player," said his biographer Tim Heald, "but I don't know the details."

It just so happens that the Duke of Edinburgh was blamed for a love affair he never had and a love child he never fathered.

"I didn't even know Philip until the Ambassador called and asked me to be his hostess," said Mrs. de Blaquier, whose vast estate, La Concepcion, is ninety miles from Buenos Aires. "I was called because my *estancia* is very secure and large enough to contain three polo fields. The government needed to get Philip out of Buenos Aires because there was so much danger. They couldn't take him any place within the city during that crisis, so he came to my estate in the country.

"He did not speak Spanish and I did not speak good English, so we conversed in French. He speaks the language fluently, like a Frenchman. I had been married thirty years when my husband died in 1960 in an airplane crash. We had nine children. Philip stayed with me and the children at the farm, and the couple who care for us. He was very *simpático*—very funny, nice, easy. He played cards with the children in the evening, and I organized four polo games for him at the level he could play. He's not a very good player, but he's passionate about the game. Passionate. He plays with a ten handicap, which is not very good, at least by Argentine standards, and I did not want him to feel slighted; so I found him players who would play his kind of polo, and he was very happy.

"During that time, he had three private meetings with Frondizi. Philip stayed with us six days and then was taken to the airport and flown to Britain. He did not allow any photographs during his visit, so I don't have pictures, but he did send me a very beautiful letter thanking me for his stay. I never more see him again for thirty-two years until I go to a polo game in Paris. I sent word to him that I was there with my sons and grandsons. He came over.

"'Are you the person who was my wonderful hostess?' he asked. I said yes, and he presented me to the Queen. He also introduced me to Prince Charles, who said, 'What did you do to my father? Whenever South America is mentioned, the only place he loves is Argentina because of the wonderful treatment you gave him at La Concepcion.'

"The reason, you see, is because of my polo fields. Philip said you can visit castles in Europe, but you can't play polo there. For polo—real polo—you must go to Argentina. That's why he loves our country so much. And Mexico, too."

In his role as Britain's goodwill ambassador, Philip took every opportunity to return to Argentina to play polo. He also visited Mexico several times, and again people assumed the magnet was a mistress—the beautiful Merle Oberon, who owned a sumptuous villa in Acapulco, a palace in Cuernavaca, and a huge estate in Mexico City. Married to the multimillionaire industrialist Bruno Pagliai, the former film star was celebrated in magazines as an international hostess who regularly entertained the ex-King of Italy, Greek shipowners, and Saudi Arabian princes. Her favorite royal guest was the Duke of Edinburgh.

"The Queen's husband was Merle's boy," said New York society columnist David Patrick Columbia. "He was her big social ticket. I had dinner with her at her Malibu Beach house in California with Luis Estevez, her favorite couturier, and she had framed pictures of really famous people all around. The pride of place was reserved for the personally inscribed eight-by-ten photograph of Philip, which she had in a large silver frame. She was always talking about 'when Philip visited us in Mexico,' and 'when Philip introduced me to the Queen,' and 'Philip this,' and 'Philip that.' I don't know whether they had an affair or not; I doubt it, only because Luis never thought so, and he would have known. In fact, Luis, who's homosexual, wondered if Philip wasn't just a little bit gay underneath that terminal macho facade of his. Luis was in Mexico with Merle several times when Philip visited, and contrary to what has been implied by others, Luis said he never saw anything romantic going on between them."

Despite Philip's attractiveness to women, he was also appreciated by men, especially in his younger days. "I think he far prefers the company of men," said a man who knew him in the navy. "There was the all-male Thursday Club before and after his marriage. The four-month cruise with his male equerry in 1956...." Another man, an internationally acclaimed writer and self-described homosexual, smiled mischievously when Philip's name was mentioned. The writer told another writer over drinks in the Oak Room Bar of the Plaza Hotel in New York City in 1994 that he remembered Philip well. "Ah, yes," he said wickedly, "I knew Philip when he was the girl."

With Merle Oberon, Philip appeared more beguiled by opulence than romance. Impressed by her extravagance, he enjoyed being cosseted in superlative comfort. She provided cashmere blankets, silk sheets, and a French chef who served superb cuisine with vintage wines. Although Philip was married to the world's richest woman, and accustomed to the highest level of royal service, he did not live sumptuously. His wife was frugal and accustomed to scratchy tweeds and sensible shoes. Her palaces were cold and drafty and required electric space heaters in every corner. Merle Oberon's estates had heated marble floors, heated towel racks, and gold-leafed beds swagged with silk tassels. Her house parties were rich, relaxed, and sunny, with sweet bougainvillea breezes.

Lord Mountbatten, who adored glamorous movie stars like Merle Oberon, had introduced his nephew to the legendary beauty when they'd visited Mexico fifteen years earlier. "I was on that trip," recalled John Barratt, who was Mountbatten's private secretary, "and I never saw anything to suggest an affair between the Duke of Edinburgh and Merle Oberon. Her husband was there, and he was our host."

The editor and writer Michael Korda disagrees. "Oh, c'mon," he said. "Everyone knows Philip had an affair with Merle. My uncle [film director Alexander Korda] was married to her from 1939 to 1945....No, I wasn't around then, and no, I never saw them together, but that's what I've always been told. Besides, if they didn't have an affair, they should have!"

Jody Jacobs, formerly a reporter for *Women's Wear Daily* and society editor of the *Los Angeles Times*, attended one of Merle Oberon's dinner parties in honor of Prince Philip. "It was during the [1968] Summer Olympics in Mexico City, and Merle, who was a stickler for royal protocol, insisted that everyone arrive before the Duke of Edinburgh and that the women wear long dresses. She invited Princess Lalla Nezha of Morocco and jet-setters like Cristina Ford, who was married to Henry Ford at the time, although he was not with her that evening; one or two Hollywood stars; and a few Mexican socialites whom Merle considered rich or aristocratic enough to be included. After dinner, when most of the other guests had left, I was part of a little group standing with the Prince near some French doors leading to the terrace and pool. There were two other women, including Cristina Ford, who was tan and tawny. This was the same Cristina Ford whose mad dancing at a White House dinner for Princess Margaret had made international news: Cristina, who was doing the twist, twisted herself right out of her white strapless gown. The top of her dress literally fell down. Now she was flirting madly with Prince Philip. They had danced a few times that evening. Suddenly she looked up at him and said, 'Why don't we go to the pool and go swimming? We (meaning the women) could leave our bras and little panties on.'

"Prince Philip blanched. 'Uh, uh,' he said. 'I think it's time for me to leave.' He smiled at Cristina and the rest of us. He was quickly surrounded by his group, which appeared from nowhere; he said good-bye to Merle and took off. I think in that setting, with a reporter listening in, he was being very discreet. Or maybe he just wasn't attracted to Cristina."

The Duke of Edinburgh was far too discreet to indulge in anything beyond harmless flirting in public. "Arrangements were made privately," said a Moroccan woman. "I was living in London in the late '60s and going to parties with a painter, Feliks Topolski, who had done a portrait of Prince Philip and become good friends with him. I told Feliks I thought Philip was quite handsome and I'd like to meet him.

"A few weeks later, Feliks said, 'I made a date for you to meet Philip. The Queen will be busy with the regatta. He has a flat on top of the hill and you'll meet him there at 10:30 in the evening.'

"'I'm not a one-night stand, Feliks,' I told him.

"'But you said you fancied him.'

"'Oh, I do but not to sleep with....' Feliks was taken aback and the date with the Duke of Edinburgh was canceled. I'm sure I wasn't the only woman propositioned in this way."

Philip certainly was not going to court criticism that might embarrass the Crown. The Profumo affair had already subjected the country to enough embarrassment. At the height of the Cold War, Britain's War Minister, John Profumo, shared a prostitute, Christine Keeler, with Soviet naval attaché Eugene Ivanov, and the scandal nearly toppled the government. The War Minister was forced to resign after he lied in a personal statement to the House of Commons. Years later the Queen knighted him. At the time, the sex scandal made the British the butt of international jokes, and the disgrace lasted for years, tarnishing the country's prestige.

Even before the scandal, the country seemed to be stumbling under the burden passed down from two world wars. "Britain still has shameful slums, obsolete housing, derelict dockyards," wrote John Gunther in *Look* magazine. "The rank and file of citizens seem apathetic about the future, despondent or confused."

Some citizens were angry. "Damn you, England," wrote John Osborne, the young playwright who transformed British theater with his blistering social drama. "In sincere and utter hatred...you're rotting now, and quite soon you'll disappear...untouchable, unteachable, impregnable."

Former U.S. Secretary of State Dean Acheson saw a country stripped of glory and floundering with no direction. "Great Britain has lost an empire," he said, "and has not yet found a role."

Even the weather aggravated the country's misery. The winters in England during the early sixties were so severe that power failed and people shivered. Then the impossible happened: the Queen was booed. She and her husband were attending a theatrical performance with King Paul and Queen Frederika of Greece when a group of Greek protesters in London yelled and hissed at her for associating with fascists.

Queen Elizabeth appeared not to notice. Having never encountered such criticism, she did not comprehend that the screaming was directed at her. She was equally unconcerned by the death threats she received when the Palace announced her plans to tour Canada in 1964.

"The Queen must not come," warned the *Toronto Telegram.*

"An innocent life is at stake," said the *Times of London.*

The *Daily Mirror* raised the specter of "a second Dallas" if the Queen ventured into Canada, where the French minority in Quebec railed against the English majority in Ottawa.

But she refused to cancel her trip. Canada was part of her realm and the largest member of the Commonwealth. "I am not worried about the visit," the Queen said, "and we are quite relaxed."

She had spent weeks preparing for the tour, including days of wardrobe fittings with her favorite dressmaker, Hardy Amies. For this trip she had allowed her hatmaker, Fredrick Fox, to make a dress. "Freddie was thrilled," recalled a friend. "He spends months designing the gown, makes it, and goes to the Palace for a fitting. Blue sort of sheath with silver bugle beads on the long sleeves. The Queen loves it. He does the fitting; she looks great. Then she presses a button. An old crone comes crawling in, hauling a box the size of Madagascar. The Queen opens it and removes an amethyst brooch as big as a plate. She lugs out diamonds the size of soup bowls and plops them all on her bosom. The style and creation of the dress is lost under the gargantuan crown jewels. Freddie rips everything off: the bows, the bugle beads, the whole lot. The Queen senses his distress. She says, 'But that's what they want to see.'" Someone later asked her an abstract question: "What do you think of taste?" The Queen said, "I don't think it helps."

On that trip to Canada, Her Majesty traveled to Quebec with her husband and grudgingly accepted the protection of bulletproof limousines and riot-control policemen. Philip chafed at so much security and, as always, spoke out. The Foreign Office patiently explained the political tensions building among French Canadians and noted that violence had become a terrible reality since the Kennedy assassination a few months before.

"Kennedy wouldn't have been shot," snapped Philip, "if it hadn't been for all the bloody security surrounding him."

Throughout Canada the Queen was trailed by armed guards and squad cars. She attended functions that required invitations and made her two speeches from secure television studios. Sailing up the St. Lawrence River aboard her royal yacht, frogmen checked the hull for explosives at every stop.

"Fancy having to put up with this sort of thing," said her dresser, BoBo MacDonald.

"Don't worry about me," said the Queen. "Nobody's going to hurt me. I'm as safe as houses."

She spoke English in Ottawa and French in Quebec, urging fraternity on both feuding factions. She praised Canada as "one of the older and most stable nations of the world." Still, she was hissed and booed, but despite the insults and screams, she never flinched.

After she left, Canadian television presented an hour-long show about her visit. "The question remains," concluded the commentator, "was it worth it? For all that was accomplished—the opening of a building here and making a speech there—was it worth the strife, the harsh words, oppressive security measures? We believe it was not. Good night."

In the past, the magnificent voice of Winston Churchill would have trumpeted the virtues of the British monarchy and drowned out such criticism. But that voice was gone. The Queen's first and favorite* Prime Minister had fallen into a coma in January 1965 and died nine days later. His death marked the end of an era for England and left the monarchy without its staunchest defender.

"The grandeur of Great Britain died tonight," the BBC reported on January 24, 1965. "The power and glory are gone."

The Queen wept privately. Then she composed herself and gave her revered mentor the first royal funeral ever accorded a commoner. Years before, Churchill had issued instructions for his burial: "I want lots of soldiers and

---

* The Queen admitted her preference for Churchill when asked, "Which of your Prime Ministers, ma'am, did you enjoy your audiences with most?" She said, "Winston, of course, because it was always such fun."

bands." His sovereign gave him all of that and more.

Attuned to Churchill's sense of history and theater, she instructed the Earl Marshall, who is also the Duke of Norfolk and in charge of royal pageants, to spare no expense. England was saying good-bye to its savior, and the Queen knew that the world would be watching this historic farewell on television. She wanted the spectacle to be as magnificent as the man himself.

She ordered that his body lie in state for three days and nights in Westminster Hall so that the million men, women, and children who had lined the streets to keep a vigil for him during his coma could pay their final respects. The floor of the great hall was lined in felt to muffle the sound of footsteps. Four guardsmen stood by the casket with four candles, providing the only light in the darkness. The Queen and her husband joined the long line of mourners filing past the catafalque, and for the first time in her reign, Her Majesty was not the center of attention. She was simply part of a tide of people. As *Time* magazine observed, "Before the casket of Winston Churchill, all mourners were equal."

On the cold gray day of the funeral, the Queen lent her carriage full of blankets and hot-water bottles to Lady Churchill and her two daughters. Her Majesty then paid special homage to her first Garter Knight by arriving in St. Paul's before his coffin and his official mourners, and not last, as is her due as Queen.

After the majestic five-hour funeral, the royal family joined the dignitaries from 110 nations* on the steps of the cathedral as Sir Winston's coffin was returned to the gun carriage for the final ride to his burial place in the little country churchyard of Bladon in Oxfordshire. The Queen's wreath was placed on the gravesite with a card: "From the nation and the Commonwealth in grateful remembrance— Elizabeth R." The great bells of St. Paul's pealed and the cannons reverberated as ninety salutes were fired—one for every year of Churchill's remarkable life. Dressed in his naval uniform, the Duke of Edinburgh, who had been a young lieutenant during World War II, stepped forward to give the old warrior a last salute.†

"There can be no leavetaking between Churchill and the people he served and saved,"

---

* The President of the United States was absent from the assemblage of five prime ministers, four kings, four presidents, three premiers, two chancellors, one queen, and one grand duke, who represented their countries at Winston Churchill's funeral. Lyndon Baines Johnson stayed in his bed at the White House and watched the funeral on television. "The President has a cold," asserted his press secretary, who added that Johnson's previous heart attack made his doctors especially vigilant. That Churchill was half American on his mother's side was a special source of pride to Americans, many of whom were embarrassed that their President did not attend the funeral of the country's most famous honorary citizen and did not send his Vice President to represent him. Instead the President dispatched his Secretary of State, Dean Rusk, who came down with a cold in London and could not attend. So the Chief Justice of the United States, Earl Warren, represented America. Former President Eisenhower attended the funeral because he commanded Allied Forces during World War II.

† Such an appropriate gesture contrasts with Philip's behavior the day after Churchill's death when he wanted to go on a shoot. Mountbatten said it was inappropriate during a period of national mourning, but Philip was unconvinced. "Well, I won't anyway," said Mountbatten, who refused to accompany him. Philip canceled the shoot.

said Lady Asquith in the House of Lords. "Many of us today may be feeling that by his going the scale of things has dwindled, our stature is diminished, that glory has departed from us.... Then I remember the words of his victory broadcast—when he urged us not to fall back into the rut of inertia, confusion, and 'the craven fear of being great.' And I knew that the resolve to keep unbroken the pattern of greatness which he had impressed upon the spirit of the nation is the tribute he would ask from us today."

Despite her ringing words, Britain had lost her greatness. The country was struggling to keep her footing in a cold war with a former ally, Moscow, while forced to make friends with a former enemy, Bonn. Four months after burying Winston Churchill, who had railed against "the hideous onslaught of the Nazi war machine with its clanking, heel-clicking, dandified Prussian officers," the Queen visited West Germany. It was her first trip to the country that had battered England in two world wars. Her husband had gone there many times before to see his sisters and his brothers-in-law, but because of the bitter anti-German sentiments in England, his trips had not been publicized. The Queen had wanted to accompany him, but each time her request had been denied by the conservative Tory government, which knew that the public would never accept a royal visit so soon after the war. Now under a Labor Prime Minister, who wanted to end the old hostilities, the

Queen was asked to make the trip in May 1965, the first time a British sovereign had visited Germany since 1913, when her grandfather, King George V, went to see his relatives.

At the time of Churchill's death, the German newspaper *Frankfurter Rundschau* recalled the Nazi invective against the British Prime Minister. "Nothing remains of the Nazi tirades," said the newspaper. "Those who authorized them have not only disappeared, but they have been proved wrong."

The newspaper repeatedly warned Germans against screaming out *"Sieg heil!"* when the Queen inspected the soldiers of the Bundeswehr and the airmen of the Luftwaffe. Instead they were told to wave the paper Union Jacks that would be distributed and to call out her name.

Newspapers and magazines stressed the theme of reconciliation by publishing the Windsor family tree with its German roots, including the names of Elizabeth and Philip's four hundred royal relatives still living in Germany: the princely Hanovers, Hohenzollerns, Brunswicks, and Glucksburgs dusted off their old decorations in anticipation of the royal visit.

"If we can't have our own Bavarian monarch back," said a city official in Munich, "at least we can borrow someone else's for a short while."

"After all," said his aide, "they are almost German, aren't they?"

For Germans, the Queen's presence meant

that England had finally forgiven them. Her words underscored her healing mission, despite the grimace she made when she first saw the ugly barbed-wire spikes on the Berlin Wall. "The tragic period is over," she said, her English being translated to German. "If we wish to preserve the best of our great heritage, we must make common cause....In the last twenty years, the problems facing our two peoples have brought us closer together again. It is now our task to defend civilization in freedom and peace together."

The crowds shouted, "Eee-liz-a-bet, Eee-liz-a-bet!" but the Queen did not smile or wave. In fact, she recoiled from the enthusiastic response. "I think she thought this was a bit too much of a good thing," said British Foreign Secretary Michael Stewart, "too reminiscent of ritual Nazi shouting. That was the only time I saw her perhaps at all put out."

With more dignity than warmth, the Queen went to ten cities in eleven days and was widely praised. "For the thirty-nine-year-old British monarch, theoretically above politics," said *U.S. News & World Report,* "it was a highly political performance."

Criticism toward the Crown had become increasingly strident. In 1957, after Lord Altrincham criticized the Queen as "priggish" and "a pain in the neck," he was slugged by a man on the street who considered his words blasphemous. A year later, when Malcolm Muggeridge, a leading British journalist, dismissed the Queen as "a nice, homely little woman" whose monarchy was "a transparent hoax," he was banned from appearing on the state-run BBC. Yet within ten years criticism of the Crown had become commonplace. Students in the sixties were apathetic toward the monarchy. To them the royal family seemed irrelevant, almost laughable. Movie houses had stopped playing the National Anthem because too many young people booed. The Oxford University Union debated the resolution: "The Monarchy should be sacked, Buckingham Palace given to the homeless, and the corgis put to productive work."

The monarchy could still count on the establishment press—the *Times* and the *Daily Telegraph*—to pay homage. Both newspapers published the Court Circular,* which lists the activities of the royal family and is delivered to the papers by Palace messenger every day. One day in 1966, according to a *Telegraph* editor, that delivery was jeopardized because of what the Palace perceived as a gross lack of deference.

"We cannot go on supplying you with the Court Circular," a Palace spokesman told the editor, "if you continue with your unjustifiable attacks on the Princess Margaret."

"What attacks?" asked the editor, who was embarrassed by his newspaper's subservience to the royal family.

"What attacks indeed?" said the Palace

* The first Court Circular was issued in the eighteenth century by King George III, who became annoyed by newspaper accounts about the royal family's activities. So the King appointed the Court Newsman to prepare a definitive document to be supplied to newspapers every day.

spokesman. "You know perfectly well that as a Princess of the Blood Royal, she is entitled to the word 'the' in front of her name."

The omission was duly rectified.

During the same period, the *Sunday Times* commissioned a Cambridge don to write a small biography of the Queen for a feature entitled "The 1,000 Men and Women of the Century." The biography referred to the Queen as belonging to the "regnum of mass consumption...like most carefully designed products, the Queen comes flavourless, harmless, beautifully packaged but a bit expensive....Cluttered with amiable feudal eccentricities...the monarchy survives to restore its earliest function, to celebrate the rite of fantasy."

The don's contribution was immediately rejected. A more respectful editor rewrote the piece and referred to Her Majesty as "charming, witty and wise...with beautiful eyes and a peaches and cream complexion."

Even the blinkered courtiers noticed a lack of deference among young people and tried to make the Queen appear more relevant. They announced she would honor the Beatles with the Member of the Order of the British Empire.★

"Wow," said John Lennon. "I thought you

★ "It's the lowest honor you can have from Britain," Paul McCartney told Newsweek thirty years later, explaining the honor bestowed no title ("not so much as a sir") and little prestige. The milkman, who delivered to the Prime Minister's official residence, received the MBE. This was not lost on Britain's biggest pop star. "It's the lowest," said McCartney. "But you can't sit around saying, 'God, I wish they'd make me a sir.' "

The Queen finally bestowed a knighthood on the Beatle in 1997, citing McCartney's "services to music" in her New Year's Honors List. Acknowledging the honor, Sir Paul said, "It's been a hard day's knighthood."

had to drive tanks and win wars to get the MBE."

Some people protested the award to the Beatles by returning their MBEs to the Palace, the first time such honors had ever been renounced. Lennon was furious. "Army officers received their medals for killing people," he said. "We got ours for entertaining. On balance, I'd say we deserve ours more."

Four years later he returned the medal to the Queen to protest British involvement in the Nigerian civil war and Britain's support of U.S. action in Vietnam. "Really should not have taken it," Lennon said of the honor. "Felt I had sold out...." One man who had sent his medal back to the Palace in protest of the Beatles' award now asked to have it returned.

When the four working-class lads from Liverpool arrived at Buckingham Palace in 1965 to receive their medals, they had to be protected by police from their screeching fans. Newspapers reported that they huddled in a Palace lavatory before meeting the Queen and smoked marijuana.

"We've played Frisco's Cow Palace, but never one like this," said Paul McCartney after the visit. "It's a keen pad."

"And Her Majesty?" asked a reporter.

"She was like a mum to us."

He paid amused homage to the Queen by writing a lyric in her honor entitled "Her Majesty's a Pretty Nice Girl, But Doesn't Have a Lot to Say."

The next year the Queen broke with precedent to knight a Roman Catholic, a black, and a rabbi. She even gave her divorced cousin the Earl of Harewood permission to remarry* when she found out his mistress was pregnant. Still, she was criticized for being out of touch with the times. Philip thought the problem was dull domesticity, which he said the Queen represented when she had another child in 1964. "Nothing more ordinary than a middle-aged Queen with a middle-aged husband and four growing children," he told a group of journalists. "I would have thought that we're entering the least interesting period of our kind of glamorous existence....There used to be much more interest. Now people take it all as a matter of course. Either they can't stand us, or they think we're all right."

In promoting the Firm, as Philip called the royal family, he traveled constantly to open British exhibits, push British products, support British trade. Always, the mystique of royalty had insured enthusiastic crowds for him and the Queen, especially in America. But by 1966 no one seemed to care. So when he agreed to tour the United States to raise money for Variety Clubs International, he summoned a Hollywood press agent.

---

* The Royal Marriage Act of 1772 requires that all relatives of the sovereign who might succeed to the throne—the Earl is seventeenth in line—ask for permission to wed. Reluctantly the Queen gave her divorced cousin permission to remarry, but he paid dearly—for years. He was ostracized from the court. He was not invited to the funeral of his uncle the Duke of Windsor or to the wedding of the Queen's daughter, Princess Anne. He was forced to retire early as chancellor of York University and had to resign as artistic director of the Edinburgh Festival.

"I was the lucky guy," said Henry Rogers of Rogers & Cowan, the Los Angeles-based public relations firm. "Although I've represented the biggest names in Hollywood, like Frank Sinatra and Rita Hayworth, I got a special thrill out of having a member of the royal family as a client....Before I got the assignment, I had to go to Buckingham Palace to meet with Prince Philip. He was polite, a bit reserved, but very gracious. Best of all, he was receptive to my ideas."

Rogers's first suggestion was for the Prince to hold a press conference in every city. Prince Philip laughed.

"Oh, God, Henry," he said. "I've never done a press conference* before. We never do things like that in the royal household. It's just contrary to our policy. But if you think we should have a press conference, then we'll have a press conference....But there have to be a few ground rules, and I would appreciate it if you would alert the press in advance to what they are."

The Duke of Edinburgh then explained his constrained role as Prince Consort. "First, make it clear to them that I am not in the British government. Press outside Great Britain are often confused about what role the Queen and I play in our country. Not being a part of the government, I cannot very well answer ques-

* The Palace press secretary was shocked when reporters suggested that Her Majesty hold regular press conferences. "It would be in keeping with a film star," said Commander Colville, "but not with the Queen. The monarchy doesn't need that sort of publicity."

tions about the British economy, the Tory versus Labor Party, the Prime Minister, the union problems, and inflation. Second, I will not handle any personal questions about the Queen. Outside of that, you can declare open season and let them fire away."

The press agent told the Prince not to worry. "All the questions will be inane," he said. And most were. But Philip handled them with breezy humor.

"Tell us about the London Symphony," said a reporter in Miami.

"It plays good music," said Philip.

"Have you considered sending your children to a U.S. school?"

"An absolutely truthful answer is no, but now you're making me think about it. Hmmmm. The answer is still no."

"What do you think of the success of the Beatles?* As an export product, don't they bring more money into Britain?"

"It's a very small return for some of the things imposed on Britain."

"Is this your first visit to America?"

"No," said Philip. "My first visit was during the reign of Harry Truman."

"Why is the Queen's birthday—"

---

* The Duke of Edinburgh was not a rock and roll fan. During a Royal Variety show, he scowled at the performance by Tom Jones and then asked the singer, "What do you gargle with—pebbles?"

The next day, in a speech to businessmen, the Prince mentioned the singer. "He's a young man of about twenty-five or something, probably worth about three million [$6 million]," said Philip. "It is very difficult at all to see how it is possible to become immensely valuable by singing what I think are most hideous songs."

"Don't ask me to explain why it is that she has an official birthday in June when her proper birthday is in April. You'll just have to accept it, like cricket, pounds, shillings, and pence, and other quaint British customs."

Reporters were amused by the Prince, and in every city he received laudatory press coverage. He raised a million dollars for charity and returned home convinced that the Palace needed the British version of a Hollywood press agent. The Queen rejected his idea as utterly preposterous, saying that she did not have to sell herself or her monarchy.

"My father never did," she said.

"He didn't need to," said her husband. "He had Winston Churchill and World War Two." This prompted a quarrel in front of the footman.

Philip again referred to the Firm in front of a group of journalists. "To survive, the monarchy has to change," he said. "No one wants to end up like a brontosaurus, who couldn't adapt himself, and ended up stuffed in a museum. It isn't exactly where I want to end up myself."

He continued to badger his wife about the problem, but she did not pay much attention—until the morning he stormed into her bedroom suite, waving his copy of the *Sunday Telegraph,* the conservative right-wing royalist newspaper he once jokingly called "the family bugle."

"You might be interested in this," he said, slapping the front page down in front of her.

The Queen put on her spectacles and read the article about the "marked change in the public's attitude toward the Crown."

Philip paced up and down in front of the Queen's footman.

Without comment she continued to read:

Most people care much less than they did—particularly the young, many of whom regard the Queen as the arch-square. They are not *against* in the sense of being *for* a republic. They are quite simply indifferent....The British monarchy will not be swept away in anger, but it could well be swallowed up in a great and growing yawn.

A few weeks later, when her press secretary, Commander Richard Colville, retired, an energetic Australian, William Heseltine, succeeded him. "When I took over, things were bound to change," he said. "The essence of the Queen's role is communication, and it needed improvement....During the sixties, the family had dropped from the news pages to the gossip columns. I wanted to rectify that by getting them back from the gossip columns onto the news pages where they belonged, and by making greater use of television."

Heseltine's first responsibility was to handle preparations for the investiture of Charles as Prince of Wales.* Years before, the Queen had promised the people of Wales that she would present her eldest son to them at Caer-

* The title Prince of Wales is reserved for the eldest son of the reigning sovereign, but it is not hereditary. The title is conferred only by the sovereign's personal grant.

navon Castle. She decided that Charles was ready to be crowned a few months before his twenty-first birthday. She agreed to have the investiture televised because she felt the miniature coronation ceremony was part of the continuity of the monarchy.

The BBC television producer suggested making a biographical film of Prince Charles, but the Queen and Prince Philip said no; they thought their son was too inexperienced to handle unscripted questions. The producer then suggested a film showing what sort of life Prince Charles faced as the heir apparent. Again the Queen and Prince Philip said no, but, influenced by the enthusiasm of Heseltine for television, they agreed to consider a documentary about the royal family and the work they do. The new Palace press secretary wanted to show the Queen, the Duke of Edinburgh, and their four children as something more than stiff cardboard cutouts. "No one knew them as people," he said. "We needed to make them more rounded and human for the general public." In this he was supported by Lord Mountbatten, who had recently filmed an eight-part series on his life for the BBC.

Still, the Queen resisted. She did not want the monarchy to have anything to do with show business, and she certainly did not want her family acting like television stars. "I'm not Jackie Kennedy and this isn't the White House," she said, referring to the First Lady's televised tour of the White House. The Queen disliked performing on television and could never relax in front of the camera. She dreaded having to televise her annual Christmas message, which was staged and carefully produced with makeup artists, technicians, and TelePrompTers. She could not conceive of having television cameras follow her around every day, recording her offhand remarks and actions.

"The Queen also questioned if it would be sensible to allow television to intrude into the family's private life," recalled Heseltine. "In the end, however, she agreed."

It took three months of negotiation to get her approval. "You know the proverb 'When elephants wrestle, it is the grass that suffers,'" said one man involved in the discussions. "There was Prince Philip to contend with; he kept saying, 'Most journalists just want the shot where you're seen picking your nose,' and Cawston [BBC documentary executive] kept saying, 'I'm not a journalist.' Then there was Mountbatten, who, of course, knew all there was to know about broadcasting, and Mountbatten's son-in-law, Lord Brabourne, who as a film producer actually did know something. He was the one who brought on Richard Cawston, head of the BBC's documentary department."

The Queen finally gave her consent to the film when she was assured total editorial control, including the copyright,* plus half the profits from worldwide sales.† She then agreed to allow

* Within a few years the Queen knew she had made a mistake in cooperating with the BBC to make Royal Family. Viewing the film is almost impossible in the United Kingdom. Since the Queen retains the copyright, she requires a viewing fee of approximately $70, plus written permission from the Palace. That permission is rarely, if ever, given.

† The film was shown three times in the United Kingdom, twice in the

the BBC's camera crew inside her office at Buckingham Palace during her weekly audience with the Prime Minister, which previously had been so privileged that even her husband had been excluded. She also invited the television crew into her home at Balmoral for a family picnic. To sell to the lucrative American market, she suggested a segment with President Nixon on his visit to London and another segment showing Walter Annenberg present his credentials as the Ambassador to the Court of St. James's. "We need something special," said the Queen.

But not so special as to create controversy. Her Majesty knew better than to allow cameras to accompany her to St. George's Chapel at Windsor on the morning of March 31, 1969, for the secret reinternment of her father. She knew the public might be jolted to learn that the King's body had lain unburied for seventeen years in an oak coffin locked in a small passageway under the castle. So she ordered the Windsor grounds closed to the public and summoned the royal family* to the chapel, where the Dean of Windsor, the Right Reverend Robin Woods, conducted the solemn burial service in private.

Throughout the filming, the BBC crew took direction from the Queen. At one point the producer suggested she exercise one of her

United States, and once in 124 other countries. The Palace declined to divulge the amount of money earned, but industry estimates placed the amount at $2.5 million.

* In deference to her mother, she did not invite the Duke of Windsor to his brother's burial.

corgis. Her Majesty insisted on exercising all of them. Her husband, who despised his wife's nipping dogs, exploded.

"They want one of the fucking animals, do you understand?" snapped the Duke of Edinburgh. "Not fourteen fucking dogs."

In the film, that scene showed the Queen without her husband but with all her corgis.

The BBC producer described the film as historic. "I'm sure people will find it fascinating because it will show the role of the monarchy, the day-to-day running carried on in private, and how the monarchy fits into the present day and age.

"It's terribly important people should understand it's not a film about ceremonies. What they really want to know about is what the Queen does, what goes on inside the Palace, what the job consists of....It won't be a formal type, but more of a film about people than buildings and ceremonies. The object of any documentary is to show people as they really are." He reassessed his view after seeing the effect of his film on people: "Monarchy *is* PR....Public relations—a focus for public interest—is what it is all about."

The anthropologist David Attenborough had told the producer that the documentary would kill the monarchy. "The whole institution depends on mystique and the tribal chief in his hut," he said. "If any member of the tribe ever sees inside the hut, then the whole system of the tribal chiefdom is damaged and the tribe eventually disintegrates."

The television cameras stayed in the Queen's hut for seventy-five days and even accompanied her on a state visit to Chile. More than forty hours were filmed at a cost of $350,000. The 105-minute* documentary, entitled *Royal Family* (but nicknamed *Corgi and Beth*), was seen by forty million Britons in June 1969. It was shown again in December, which is why the Queen canceled her annual Christmas Day message that year. "Enough is enough," said the Palace, but twenty thousand Britons disagreed and wrote letters protesting her not delivering the yuletide address.

"The most exciting film ever made for television" was how the BBC commentator introduced the show to viewers. Then they watched their Queen and Prince Charles prepare a salad at a family barbecue while Prince Philip and Princess Anne grilled sausages and steaks.

The Queen tested the salad dressing by poking her little finger into the mixture and licking it. She grimaced. "Oh, too oily," she said. She added more vinegar, pronounced the dressing perfect, and walked over to her husband. "Well, the salad is finished," she said.

"Well done," said Prince Philip. "This, as you will observe, is not."

In another scene, the Queen, known to her subjects as the richest woman in the world, fingers a fabulous necklace of rubies. She says how much she likes it and that it came to Queen

---

* The outtakes—more than thirty-eight hours of film left on the cutting room floor—were shipped to the royal archives at Windsor Castle.

Victoria from the ruler of Persia. Then, in a puzzled voice, she turns to her lady-in-waiting and asks, "I have actually worn this, haven't I?"

Minutes later the monarch, who supposedly never handles money, goes into a shop with her four-year-old son, Prince Edward, to buy him a sweet. She pays, saying she has just enough cash on her to cover the bill.

In another scene, the Queen laughs as she asks her family: "How do you keep a regally straight face when a footman tells you: 'Your Majesty, your next audience is with a gorilla'? It was an official visitor, but he looked just like a gorilla." The Queen said she could not hide her laughter.

"Pretend to blow your nose," advised Prince Charles, "and keep the handkerchief up to your face."

The Queen did not need to censor the film beforehand, although her husband worried that she might be concerned about the scene where Prince Charles shows his youngest brother how to tune a cello. In tightening the instrument, Charles breaks the A string, which grazes Edward's cheek, stinging him to tears. After screening the film, the Queen said, "It's the sort of thing that can happen to anyone." She pronounced the film fine just as it was.

Most of the critics agreed, including the *Times,* which editorialized about the importance of the documentary in showing the advantages of the British system of monarchy, especially when the sovereign is trained in the duties of royalty and is surrounded by a family with similar training and tradition of service.

"A romp with royalty," raved one critic. "Everyone deserves a bow for this show."

"The refurbishing of the royal image that has been going on for some time now has been managed with some skill," wrote William Hardcastle, a former newspaper editor, "and skill in this field involves judgment of when enough is enough. My guess is that 'Royal Family' is at the completion of a process rather than a herald of further revelations to come."

Little did he know. The monarchy had used television to enhance its image because it seemed like a good idea at the time. Only years later would it look like a blunder.

ELEVEN

Prince Charles peered at the poster on the dormitory wall with its photo of three young women sitting on an Edwardian sofa. The girls smiled invitingly under their slouch-brimmed hats. One long-haired beauty wore sandals; the other two were barefoot. The caption read "Girls Say Yes to Boys Who Say No." Proceeds from the sale of the poster supported the draft resistance.

"Appalling," said the Prince, shaking his head. "Bizarre and appalling."

The Prince of Wales was not a man of his times. While many Cambridge students were protesting the war in Vietnam, he was playing polo. He avoided political activists, whom he called "nutters." And he disliked hippies. He called flower children "freaks" and damned feminists as "idiotic man haters." He loved the Goons, a group of British comedians known for broad humor and brash antics. (Germans referred to the group as *Die Doofen,* or "The Stupids.")

Charles celebrated himself as old-fashioned. "I am proud to be a square," he said. While other young men streamed into singles' bars and took part in the sexual revolution, the Prince of Wales sipped cherry brandy and held on to his virginity. He stood ramrod straight during the swinging sixties and praised the sanctity of marriage. He declared he would not wed before the age of thirty.

By the time he was eighteen, the world's richest* teenager still hadn't gone on his first date. But three years later, in his last year at Cambridge, he was seduced by a young South American girl, who was a research assistant to the master of his college. Following his sexual initiation, Charles took a string of lovers, and he instructed each to call him "sir"—even in bed.

"I adore Prince Charles," said novelist Barbara Cartland, "and Lord Mountbatten, whom I was very fond of, always said Charles would make a great King. Dickie helped him become a man by giving him the privacy he needed at Broadlands [Mountbatten's estate] to discreetly entertain young women. Away from the prying eyes of the press."

---

* Charles received $500,000 a year from his Duchy of Cornwall properties, plus $125,000 salary as Prince of Wales. By 1995 he received more than $4 million a year from his Duchy properties and paid 40 percent in taxes.

Charles looked up to Mountbatten as "the most brilliant and kindest of great-uncles/grandpas," and Mountbatten reveled in that role. "Mostly, he enjoyed acting as royal procurer," surmised John Barratt, Mountbatten's private secretary. "We arranged several weekends at Broadlands for Charles to entertain young women—Lady Jane Wellesley, a direct descendant of the Duke of Wellington; Lucia Santa Cruz, daughter of the Spanish Ambassador; and Camilla Shand, whose great-grandmother Alice Keppel was the mistress of Edward VII, Charles's great-great-grandfather. Camilla later married Major Andrew Parker Bowles. She was quite pleasant and frisky, but Charles was a late bloomer.* Pity he was too inexperienced then to know that she would become the love of his life."

One young woman Mountbatten served up was his fifteen-year-old granddaughter, Amanda Knatchbull, the second daughter of Lord and Lady Brabourne.† Nine years younger than Charles, Amanda fired her grandfather's dynastic fantasies. Mountbatten saw her as the next Queen of England and, ever the scheming matchmaker, did all he could to foster her relationship with Charles, who was her second cousin. Mountbatten

---

* Camilla bragged to her brother-in-law that she had been the first woman to seduce Prince Charles. "She told me that she approached him [in 1971], but he didn't know how to have sex," said Richard Parker Bowles. "He didn't know how to do it. She laughed and said, 'Pretend I am a rocking horse.'"

† To illustrate the entanglement of British titles: Patricia Mountbatten, daughter of Lord Mountbatten—more correctly Earl Mountbatten of Burma—married John Knatchbull, who inherited his father's title and

invited them to spend weekends with him at Broadlands and threw them together on family vacations. After one such holiday in the Bahamas, Charles revved Mountbatten to new heights by writing, "I must say Amanda really has grown into a very good-looking girl—most disturbing." When Prince Philip learned of Mountbatten's matchmaking, he approved. "Good," he said. "It beats having strangers come into the family." Until Lady Amanda was old enough to be considered seriously, Mountbatten advised Charles to become "a moving target" for women. In a letter, he recommended taking many lovers:

> I believe, in a case like yours, the man should sow his wild oats and have as many affairs as he can before settling down but for a wife he should choose a suitable, attractive and sweet-charactered girl *before* she met anyone else she might fall for. After all, [your] Mummy never seriously thought of anyone else after the Dartmouth encounter when she was 13! I think it is disturbing for women to have experiences if they have to remain on a pedestal after marriage.

He advised Charles to shop carefully for a

became Lord Brabourne. Patricia Mountbatten Knatchbull then became Lady Brabourne. Her father, having no male heirs, asked the Queen to give his title to his eldest daughter. Upon Mountbatten's death, Lady Brabourne became Countess Mountbatten of Burma. Upon her death, her son, Norton Knatchbull, inherited the title. Until she died, he received the courtesy title of Lord Romsey.

wife. "A buyer must have a hundred eyes," said Mountbatten, repeating an Arab proverb. "He instructed him to choose only wealthy young women from the upper classes," said Barratt, "because their money and social position would insure discretion." When asked if it was true, as reported in a book, that Mountbatten had set up a private fund administered by a British lawyer through a bank in the Bahamas to pay off "troublesome conquests" and "one-night stands" who might embarrass the Prince of Wales by their disclosures, Barratt smiled. "Sounds absurd, but Lord Louie would have done anything to protect Prince Charles and the monarchy."

Mountbatten portrayed his protegé as the most eligible bachelor in the world, a sexual magnet to women. He compared him with movie stars like Warren Beatty and bragged to *Time* that Charles enjoyed "popping in and out of bed with girls." Privately, though, Mountbatten fretted about how emotionally immature the Prince was. "He falls in love too easily," Mountbatten told Barbara Cartland. "And he does cling so."

The press followed Charles whenever he appeared in public with a date, tracking him across Alpine ski slopes and Caribbean beaches. Some reporters even followed him when he did not expect press coverage. "I remember sitting in the bushes watching Charles attempt to make love to Anna Wallace on the beach of the river Dee at Balmoral," recalled journalist James Whitaker. "Moments before the royal wick was lit, he spotted us crawling on our bellies with binoculars. He jumped up and hid in the bushes, leaving poor Anna to pull up her knickers. He was a wimp that day. He hid and cowered and left the young woman unprotected. He shouldn't have done that— I was ashamed for him—but, of course, I didn't print the story. He is, after all, my future King."

On paper, HRH Prince Charles Philip Arthur George, Prince of Wales, Earl of Chester, Duke of Cornwall, Duke of Rothesay, Earl of Carrick, Lord of Renfrew, Lord of the Isles, and Prince and Great Steward of Scotland looked impressive.

But he was like the man Jane Austen described in *Sense and Sensibility:* "The kind of man everyone speaks highly of but no one wants to talk to." With his fusty manner and furrowed brow, he looked like a worried clerk. Uncertain and indecisive, he seemed overwhelmed by the weight of his titles and his country's expectations. Destined to become Charles III, the forty-first sovereign of England since 1077, he knew he was different.

"I am not a normal person in the normal sense of the word," he told the press. "I can't afford to be. I have been trained in a certain way, even programmed, if you like. My parents have always been most careful with this, obviously to the benefit of the throne of England. But this has tended to isolate me from normal life."

Sober and somber, the Prince exuded a heavy weariness—so much so that his classmates at

Cambridge wrote him off as a dolt and a plodder.* "He walks into a room like a dark cloud in a double-breasted suit," said one. Even his closest friends called him "the old soul."

"Charles is not a fast-car sort of man," said a Cambridge classmate. "He's all stick-out ears and bobbing Adam's apple—the little boy that grandmothers fancy."

A rapt listener, and extraordinarily polite, Charles, unlike his blunt sister, tried hard to please. But if he hadn't been Prince of Wales, he would have been ignored. Growing up with people bowing and curtsying and walking backward in front of him made him arrogant and haughty, but still he managed to maintain a certain earnestness that made him likable. He dressed in custom-made suits, starched shirts, gold cuff links, and silk ties; his shoes shone like mirrors. Like his great-uncle the Duke of Windsor, he was known for his sartorial splendor. Fastidious about how he looked, especially in uniform, Charles patted himself down before making public appearances and muttered his checklist: "Spectacles, testicles, wallet, and watch." Amused by the ritual, British Ambassador Nicholas Henderson said, "I gather this is part of the royal routine, at any rate for male royals."

Although Charles looked elegant and acted polished, he was ill at ease. He frequently twisted the gold signet ring bearing the three

* British students who want to enter a university take A-level examinations in subjects of their choice. The best students take four exams. Average students take three. Poor students take two. Charles took two.

plumes of the Prince of Wales that he wore on the little finger of his left hand.

"I think it was the ears," mused a former courtier to the Queen. "He never outgrew those unfortunate ears. A shame, really...." He said that the Prince's protruding ears became a source of amusement within the royal family, and he was teased constantly, which made him quite self-conscious. Princess Margaret urged her sister to let Charles undergo plastic surgery, but the Queen resisted. When Margaret's son, David, was three years old, she saw that he, too, was developing what she called "the Windsor flappers." So she sent him to a plastic surgeon at Great Ormond Street Hospital for Children to have his ears pinned back.

Mountbatten continually badgered the Queen and Prince Philip about getting their son's ears fixed, but they did nothing, so Mountbatten urged Charles to ask his parents about plastic surgery. "You can't possibly be King with ears like that," he said. The late photographer Norman Parkinson was so dismayed by the Prince's ears that during a sitting for a formal portrait, he pinned them back with double-sided sticky tape.

"Charles is not a common swashbuckler like his father," continued the courtier. "He's kind, sweet, but unsure of himself. Yes, I'd say it was the jug ears more than anything. It certainly wasn't parental neglect...at least on the part of the Queen."

The former courtier staunchly defends his

monarch as a mother while struggling to answer the question of how Charles grew up.

"His Royal Highness was a tentative little boy. Correct, well mannered, but rather timid like Her Majesty," said the courtier. "He was uncertain on a horse. His sister, who shared a similar upbringing, was bold and rambunctious, like her father....She should have been the boy, and Charles the girl."

"I was asked in Australia whether I concentrated on developing or improving my image—as if I was some kind of washing powder, presumably with a special blue whitener," Charles told reporters. He tried to be offhand and humorous but came across as clumsy. "I daresay that I could improve my image in some circles by growing my hair to a more fashionable length, being seen in the Playboy Club at frequent intervals, and squeezing myself into excruciatingly tight clothes....I have absolutely no idea what my image is, and therefore I intend to go on being myself to the best of my ability."

Reporters peppered the Prince with questions about what kind of woman he would make his Queen. They referred to his various girlfriends—slim, long legged, and usually blond—as "Charlie's angels," reporting that the world's most eligible bachelor sought safety in numbers. Charles admitted that he was afraid of marriage because he was not permitted to make a mistake. "Divorce is out of the question for someone like me," he said. "In my position, the last thing I could possibly entertain is getting divorced. Therefore, one's decision must be that much more careful."

Mountbatten had recommended a pragmatic approach to marriage that Charles now parroted back to the press. "If I'm deciding on whom I want to live with for fifty years—well, that's the last decision I want my head to be ruled by my heart," he said. "I think an awful lot of people have got the wrong idea of what marriage is all about. It is rather more than just falling madly in love with someone and having a love affair for the rest of your married life."

In fact, Mountbatten had cautioned him against falling in love. He said Charles could not afford that luxury. "I can still hear him say that falling in love is not an option for the man who would be king," recalled John Barratt. "'Leave that to your cousin,' Mountbatten advised." He was referring to Prince Michael of Kent, who was sixteenth in line to the throne when he fell in love with Baroness Marie-Christine von Reibnitz. She was hardly an appropriate choice for a man in the line of succession to the British monarchy. She was divorced, a Roman Catholic, and worse yet, a German, whose father had been a Nazi. The royal family has had other Nazis—the Duke of Coburg, brother of Princess Alice, Countess of Athlone, was a Nazi.

"Marie-Christine was tall, blond, and beautiful," continued John Barratt. "Lord Mountbatten thought she would add a bit of glamour to the House of Windsor. So he helped Prince

Michael get permission from the Queen to marry. The Queen consented, but she would not attend the wedding, even though it was not in a Catholic church. The Pope had forbidden that. So they had a civil ceremony, and Prince Michael* had to renounce his place in the line of succession." Charles hardly needed a more glaring example of a marriage going haywire than that of his aunt, Princess Margaret, who was creating an international scandal.

The Italian magazine *Men* ran a cover story on the "wild and intimate parties" of the Snowdons, citing an alleged passion for pornography. The article described the Duke of Edinburgh as being disgusted by what it called the disgraceful behavior of Snowdon, who, the Duke said, "entered society through the tradesmen's entrance."

The satirical television show *Spitting Image* featured the Snowdons in a sketch entitled "Nightmare Couples." "We paired the most horribly mismatched people we could think of," said Roger Law, the show's talented proprietor. "We had Margaret Thatcher and Johnny Rotten; Roman Polanski and Mae West; Diana Ross and Ian Smith. And, of course, Princess Margaret and Antony Armstrong-Jones."

Esquire magazine reported the Snowdons'

---

* While removing himself from the line of succession, Prince Michael retained the standing for his children. He said that any children of the marriage would be raised in the Church of England. So his son, Lord Frederick Windsor, and his daughter, Lady Gabriella Windsor, remain in the line of succession.

sniping at each other, especially over her insistence that even their closest friends observe protocol and treat her with the deference due royalty.

"You address me by my Christian name," protested a newspaper editor, who had known Margaret all her life, "so why can't I address you the same way?"

"You *can't*, that's all," said the Princess loftily. She insisted on being addressed as "ma'am" or "ma'am darling" and referred to as Her Royal Highness. She exacted abbreviated curtsies from women and small neck bows from men. Once she entered a room, no one was allowed to leave. And if she wanted to party until four in the morning, bleary-eyed guests had to dance attendance. No one sat in her presence without her permission, and if she wanted to sing, no one dared talk.

The Snowdons soon went their separate ways. Margaret built a home on the Caribbean island of Mustique, which her husband never visited. And he held weekend parties at his Sussex cottage, which she never attended. They maintained an open marriage with lovers on both sides. The Princess, who got a reputation as promiscuous, dallied with several of her husband's friends, including rock star Mick Jagger, writer Robin Douglas-Home, actor Peter Sellers, and photographer Patrick Lichfield, who was also a first cousin once removed.* "We're kissing cousins," she said. "So it's okay."

---

* Lichfield's mother, Anne, was the daughter of John Bowes-Lyon, brother of Queen Elizabeth, the Queen Mother.

Snowdon, too, engaged in extramarital affairs, including a year-long romance with Lady Jacqueline Rufus-Isaacs, the twenty-two-year-old daughter of the Marquess of Reading. But he objected to his wife's romance with the nephew of former Prime Minister Sir Alec Douglas-Home. The romance had started in December 1966 when Snowdon was traveling on a photo assignment for the *Sunday Times*. Upon his return, he learned that his wife had spent the weekend with Douglas-Home at his country estate. Snowdon flew into a rage, and Margaret quickly ended the relationship. The aristocrat fell further into alcoholism and drug addiction. A year later he committed suicide. He had begged the Princess to leave her dismal marriage, but she refused. In an exchange of letters with Douglas-Home, she wrote that she was too afraid of her husband:

Darling, I can't....I don't know what lengths he won't go to, jealous as he is, to find out what I am up to, and your movements too. Can I make you happy from a distance? I think we can, just by being there for the other. Promise you will never give up, that you will go on encouraging me to make the marriage a success, and that given a good and safe chance, I will try and come back to you one day. I daren't at the moment.

The Snowdons' marriage became a dog's bone as they wrestled it to the ground. They chased it, gnawed it, and bit it. At the beginning they had nipped each other like frisky pups; now they snarled like pit bulls.

Both chain-smoked and drank too much. Margaret, who suffered from migraines, started drinking gin and tonics for breakfast. She took pills to sleep and became so depressed, she went to a psychiatrist. Snowdon, who spent weeks at a time away from her, wanted a divorce, but she refused. She saw no need to disturb their life. Their enmity triggered vigorous sex, she confided to friends, and she relished it. She treasured the framed collage that Tony had made for her when they first became lovers. He had collected bits of leaf, a peacock feather, a coin, words cut out of a magazine, and a crown floating above a small pink satin bed. The puzzle, which apparently carried an intimate message, was signed with a picture of a pony. Crossing out the letter *P*, he had inserted *T* for Tony. Margaret hung the collage in her bathroom.

Devoutly religious, she believed a dreadful marriage was better than a divorce, especially for their son and daughter. At first she and her husband had not wanted children. "After we got married, Tony changed his mind," she said. "So I gave him two children." Now she wanted to keep the marriage together because of six-year-old David and three-year-old Sarah. Margaret also knew that a member of the House of Windsor was forbidden to divorce. And for her, divorce seemed inconceivable. "I do not say I don't

326

want a divorce," she told a friend. "But I believe it is my duty to keep my solemn vows—my duty to my family, myself, and my country." Snowdon appealed to the Queen, saying his marriage to her sister had become intolerable.

The Queen, who shied away from any kind of family confrontation, wouldn't address the subject of her sister's marriage until the *Daily Express* published rumors of a rift. Then the Queen's advisers recommended she meet with the Snowdons. Reluctantly the Queen invited the couple to Buckingham Palace after business hours on the evening of Monday, December 18, 1967. Margaret told a friend that the meeting was *"en famille"* and included Prince Philip and the Queen Mother.

Philip bluntly declared himself in favor of an informal separation. He compared the Snowdon marriage to a barnacle on the bottom of the monarchy. The only solution, said the seaman, was a wire brush. Margaret snuffled, and the Queen Mother, who avoided anything unpleasant, was teary but noncommittal. Her silent presence bolstered the Queen, who had said she needed everyone behind her for this decision. Snowdon, who wanted a clean break, sat silently. Tucked in his jacket were three of Margaret's love letters from Robin Douglas-Home. After listening impassively, the Queen said she wanted time to consult her advisers. With no decision reached, Snowdon left. Margaret stayed behind and later told her friend Sharman

Douglas that the Queen's parting advice was: "Why don't each of you go your own way— but please be quiet about it."

Snowdon felt trapped, and he reacted like a caged animal. With no escape in sight, he struck back with pitiless cruelty. He humiliated his wife at every turn, often in front of other people.

On a trip to Corfu, Greece, after a long boozy lunch with friends, he suggested that he and Margaret rest for a few hours before their dinner engagement. So they retired to separate bedrooms for a nap. An hour later the doorbell of their suite rang.

"Margaret told me that she called to Tony to answer the door, but he pretended to be asleep," said a friend. "The bell kept ringing, so finally she got up. She was in her nightie with her hair in rollers. Six people were standing at the door; they said that Tony had invited them for tea. Margaret realized that Tony had set her up simply to make her look foolish."

The Princess retaliated in London by tipping a pot of coffee over his negatives. "Oh, so sorry," she said with singsong sarcasm. At a New York City party given by Sharman Douglas, Margaret held court on one side of the room, Snowdon entertained friends on the other. The hostess, whose father was U.S. Ambassador to Great Britain in 1947, shuttled between them. Greeting Margaret, she inquired about the Queen.

"Which Queen are you referring to?" said

the Princess, waving her cigarette holder. "My sister, my mother, or my husband?"

At the end of the evening, the Princess wanted to thank the kitchen staff. She expected her husband to accompany her, so she sent an aide to fetch him.

"Sir, Her Royal Highness is ready to go into the kitchen."

Snowdon ignored the man and continued talking.

The aide waited. He cleared his throat and tried again. But Snowdon kept chatting. Finally the aide interrupted.

"Sir, I beg your pardon, but Her Royal Highness is ready to go into the kitchen."

"Really?" snapped Snowdon. "And what is she going to do in there? Scramble some eggs?"

A week later the Snowdons attended a private dinner party in London. "It was ghastly," recalled their hostess. "When we sat for dinner, Tony put a bag over his head. The first course was served. He did nothing. Nobody addressed a word to him, just pretended he wasn't there. Finally Princess Margaret said, 'Why are you wearing a brown bag over your head?'

"'Because I can't stand the fucking sight of you,' he said." He left a note on her dressing table headed "Twenty Reasons Why I Hate You."

No one was spared the bickering. In front of friends, Snowdon belittled his wife's appearance and her taste in clothes, especially her shoes, which she had custom-made to make her look taller.

"Oh, ma'am, what a pretty parachute silk," he said as she swept into their drawing room for a dinner party. She was wearing a flowing blue chiffon caftan designed to conceal her recent weight gain. He looked down at her high-heeled platform shoes. "Oh, and I see we have on our finest little prewar peep-toes." Later, he said, "You look like a Jewish manicurist."

At the beginning of their marriage, Snowdon helped his wife perform her royal duties, for which she received an allowance of $45,000 a year. "He was very good for me—then," recalled the Princess, who admitted that he charmed where she offended. She once shocked the head of a children's organization by announcing, "I don't want to meet any daft children." Later he chafed at the indignity of escorting her to hospital openings, ship launchings, and tree plantings. He especially resented the implication that he was a kept man. "I support myself," he told reporters. "I pay $2,500 a year in taxes."

By then he had resumed his career as a photographer with the *Sunday Times*. "Photograph by Snowdon" was a prized credit line for the newspaper. He enjoyed access to people unavailable to other photographers. The actress Vivian Merchant attributed this entrée to his marriage, not his talent. "Of course, the only reason we artistes let you take our pictures," she told him one evening at a dinner party, "is because you are married to her." She stabbed a finger toward Princess Margaret. Snowdon seethed.

His troubled marriage was known to journalists, who gossiped among themselves but never committed their stories to print.

"I remember going to Kensington Palace to look at a photo shoot," recalled a *Times* staffer. "Snowdon and I were sitting down, poring over proofs. I did not know the Princess had entered the room until I heard her high-pitched voice over our shoulders.

"'What pretty pictures,' she said.

"'Oh, God,' said Snowdon, hissing with irritation. He refused to stand up. Just jerked his head toward Her Royal Highness and said, 'Meet the chief Sea Scout.'*

"It was a biting remark, incredibly rude, and intended only to humiliate her," said the embarrassed reporter. "He then ignored the Princess for the next fifteen minutes until she finally left the room. He sighed with relief."

The couple's carping made their friends uncomfortable. "The marriage could never have worked," said one woman. "There was an evil fairy at Margaret's christening, and Tony, who is admirable and interesting, is hugely demanding. Both of them wanted to be stars, and their stars collided. He was more talented, but her appetite demanded constant attention, which he could not and would not

* The Sea Scouts are the maritime counterpart of the Boy Scouts. They tie knots and cook sausages in tin cans. Princess Margaret was their honorary patron.

give. She has a male ego in that it's voracious. He's got one, too, but he deserves his plaudits. She just demands hers." The British press maintained an official silence about the royal marriage because the Princess, then fifth in line to the throne, is the Queen's sister. "The British penchant for gossipy bitchiness cannot be offloaded on the monarch, who is inviolate, dull, and worthy," said British writer Andrew Duncan. "The younger sister, therefore, becomes the outlet for hypocrisy."

At first the stories that leaked into print protected the Princess more than the commoner she married. *McCall's* magazine reported the Earl of Snowdon had attended a party "wearing too much makeup." At another party, *Private Eye* reported him "racing across the room to Rudolf Nureyev and greeting him with a kiss full on the lips." The satirical magazine referred to Lord Snowdon as a dog on a leash: "The Princess is continually losing her husband. He slips off his lead and vanishes, often for weeks on end." The magazine suggested the Queen was so angry at her petite brother-in-law that she did not speak to him for eighteen months after his outrageous performance during the 1969 Christmas dinner at Sandringham: "It was then that the minuscule genius climaxed the evening by leaping onto the dinner table, crying, 'And now—it's Tony La Rue,' and commencing a lively striptease." The next year Princess Margaret went to Sandringham alone with her children while her husband spent the holiday in a London hospital having his hemorrhoids removed.

"The Queen has always been very fond of Lord Snowdon," said a member of her staff, dismissing the magazine's suggestion of displeasure. Years later, when Her Majesty met an Oscar-winning cinematographer, she asked him what he did in films. He said he was director of photography.

"Oh, how terribly interesting," the Queen was said to have replied. "Actually, I have a brother-in-law who is a photographer."

"How terribly coincidental," the cinematographer responded. "I have a brother-in-law who's a queen." Her Majesty moved on without saying another word.

Behind the rumors about the Snowdons' royal marriage lay a sordid mess of drinks, drugs, bright lights, and wild nights. "But worse than anything were the cracking rows," recalled a former lady-in-waiting for the Princess. "Dehumanizing to them and to those around them. Tony traveled on photographic assignments—Tokyo, Melbourne, New York—as much as he could to get away, and Margaret longed for him to go. But after a week without him, she'd get bored."

During a three-week assignment in India, Snowdon did not contact his wife. After the first week, the *Times* photo editor began receiving daily calls from the Princess, inquiring about her husband, who cabled the newspaper three times a day but didn't communicate with her. When the photo editor was unavailable, his assistant took the calls from Kensington Palace and left messages on the editor's desk: "HRH called," or "It's ma'am—again." By the end of the third week, the messages from the assistant reflected the maddening frequency of the calls: "*Please* ring the royal dwarf."

The disintegration of Princess Margaret's marriage put subtle pressure on Prince Charles, whose only responsibility in life was to marry well and reproduce. He was constrained by two pieces of eighteenth-century legislation: the 1701 Act of Settlement, which prohibits the heir from marrying a Roman Catholic; and the 1772 Royal Marriages Act, which requires the heir to receive the sovereign's permission before marrying, unless the heir is older than twenty-five. Then he must declare his intention to marry and proceed only if, after twelve months, both Houses of Parliament do not object. Born to be King, Charles knew that he needed to give the country a Queen and insure the continuation of the House of Windsor. Since he had been three years of age his future marriage had been a running story in the press, which did not hesitate to suggest suitable candidates for him. The need to make a perfect match was reinforced by every royal occasion during the seventies.

The death of the Duke of Windsor in May 1972 revisited the shame of the former King's abdication and the lonely exile forced on him—all because of an inappropriate marriage. Despite the hostility of his family toward the Windsors, Charles felt sympathy for the Duke and Duchess. He had accompanied his parents on an official trip to Paris and visited briefly with his great-uncle ten days before he died.

Knowing the seventy-seven-year-old duke was terminally ill, the Queen agreed to see him during her five-day state visit to France. Despite urgent calls from the Duke's doctor, the Queen would not rearrange her schedule. The doctor implored the Queen's secretary to relay how gravely ill the Duke was. "He's on the verge of death," said the doctor. The next day, the doctor received a call from the British ambassador, Christopher Soames, who was concerned that the Duke's death might interfere with the Queen's state visit.

"Now, look here, doctor," Jean Thin recalled the ambassador saying. "The Duke has got to die before or after the Queen's visit but *not* during the visit. Do you understand?"

A reporter questioned the Queen's secretary about Her Majesty's apparent callousness toward the Duke of Windsor. The Queen's secretary told the reporter, "You know he's dying. I know he's dying. But *WE* don't know he's dying."

Charles, who accompanied his parents to the Windsors' home in the Bois de Boulogne outside Paris, had been jolted by the sight of the fragile old man, wasted by lung cancer. Although racked and emaciated, the former King had insisted on getting out of bed to pay proper homage to his sovereign. Charles was touched by his gallantry.

The Duchess of Windsor, who had been reviled by the royal family, found the Queen cold and remote. "Her manner as much as stated that she had not intended to honor him with a visit," the Duchess told the Countess of Romanones, "but that she was simply covering appearances by coming here because he was dying and it was known that she was in Paris."

Upon the Duke's death, Charles wanted to extend kindness to the Duchess, who had been vilified for so long by the royal family. He graciously offered to meet her plane in London and to escort her to her husband's funeral, but the Palace said no. The Queen's courtiers explained that as heir apparent he would embarrass the throne by making such a royal gesture to a twice divorced commoner. "It might be misinterpreted," said the Queen's secretary. Charles realized that the obstacle continued to be the Queen Mother, and he could not offend his beloved grandmother. So the Earl Mountbatten of Burma was dispatched to meet the Duchess. She was invited to stay in Buckingham Palace, but only for the duration of her husband's funeral.

"Immediately afterward, everyone in the royal family went to Windsor and left the Duchess by herself," recalled one of the Queen's stewards. "I was working in the gold-and-silver pantry then and I remember them all—the Queen Mother, the Queen, and Princess

Margaret—planning to leave for the country without the Duchess of Windsor. It was despicable to treat her like that after all those years. I can still see her thin and withered face peaking out from the window sheers of Buckingham Palace after everyone left. She looked so alone and bereft."

For Charles, the importance of marrying well was again underscored in November 1972, when he and his sister held a dinner party to celebrate his parents' silver wedding anniversary. The country paused to honor the Queen's twenty-five-year marriage to Prince Philip in a celebration that lasted all day. Schoolchildren were given a holiday, and the Queen invited one hundred couples to attend a commemorative service in Westminster Abbey. Although the couples were all strangers, they shared Her Majesty's wedding date. So she invited them to pray with her. At the end of the service, the Duke of Edinburgh moved into the center aisle and crooked his arm to escort his wife out of the Abbey, just as he had on their wedding day. But Her Majesty was no longer looking in his direction, so the arm was not taken. The couple walked out side by side, smiling but not touching, a reflection of their marriage, which was an effective partnership—congenial, but not intimate.

Thousands of people poured into the City of London to hear the Lord Mayor praise the Queen as an unfailing example in public and private life. "Through the medium of television you have allowed us to look into your uncurtained windows more freely than any generation before," he said. "Of the many great services which you tendered to your subjects in these twenty-five years, that vision of this happiness in family life which you and your consort and your children so evidently enjoy yourselves must have strengthened the unity of every family in the land."

Even Willie Hamilton offered his congratulations. Parliament's most outspoken critic of the monarchy surprised people with his tribute. Seconds later, though, he criticized the commemorative plates and spoons being hawked on the street and slammed "the sordid, greedy commercialization of the event and the money-grubbing loyalists, who are busy cashing in on the irrational sentiment worked up on this unusual royal occasion." He suggested that the Palace should have stipulated all profits be donated to charity, particularly to children who were born deformed because their mothers had taken the drug thalidomide. The Palace ignored his suggestion.

"I looked like a crank then," he recalled. "Twenty years later, I looked like a prophet."

The Queen was so pleased to share her wedding anniversary that she ventured from her customary reserve and circulated among her subjects, trying to make small talk. People were agog; their sovereign had never been known to speak to ordinary people. This was the first royal walkabout London had ever seen, and flag-waving Britons cheered as the Queen, the Duke of Edinburgh, Prince Charles, and Princess Anne melted into the crowd, greeting people and trying to make the royal family appear less remote.

Stressing her commitment to family life, Her Majesty made a short talk of lace-capped innocence. "A marriage begins by joining man and wife together, but this relationship between two people, however deep at the time, needs to develop and mature with the passing years. For that, it must be held firm in the web of family relationships, between parents and children, between grandparents and grandchildren, between cousins, aunts, and uncles."

When she spoke those words, most Britons, according to a 1972 Harris poll, believed it was the monarchy that set the standard of morality for the country, even more so than the church. Such confidence in the Crown prompted the Queen to send a "gracious message" to Parliament asking for a pay raise. Although one million people were out of work at the time, no member of Parliament, except one,* wanted to deprive the sovereign of her tax-free allotment from the Civil List.

"Why should she get millions when old-age pensioners will die of cold and starvation this winter?" Hamilton asked from the floor

---

* Former MP Willie Hamilton told the author in 1993: "I was subjected to assassination threats when I demanded an investigation of royal finances....The Queen's advisers arrogantly told us to give them the money. 'Never mind what the Queen is worth,' they said. 'Never mind how rich she is. We want more money. You give us the money.' And we very tamely did. They knew they had a subservient government and that we were afraid of doing anything to offend the monarchy—then."

of the House of Commons. Outraged Tories rushed to their feet, shouting in protest. The Labor MP paid no attention. "And look at this," he thundered, waving a list of the Queen Mother's staff of thirty-three, including five Ladies of the Bedchamber and eleven Women of the Bedchamber.*

"What the blazes do they do? What size bedchamber is this? All right, the Queen Mother is an old-age pensioner and we say, 'Yes, she has always got a pleasant smile on her face.' But my God. If my wife got that pay, she would never stop laughing."

Tory members stamped their feet in protest. To criticize the expenditures of the Queen Mother sounded blasphemous to them. "This is an obscene speech," yelled one Conservative MP. But Hamilton pushed on, objecting to the raise proposed for Princess Margaret. "For this expensive kept woman?" he roared. "She should be sacked."

Not even Her Majesty was immune. Hamilton harrumphed: "There are one thousand women in my constituency who could do the Queen's job."

At first the Palace had tried to ignore Hamilton and dismiss him as a nuisance. "He's a bloody communist," said Prince Philip, who had been criticized in Parliament for saying

---

* The more socially elevated position is held by Ladies of the Bedchamber, who are married to peers. The Ladies are chosen for purely personal qualities and attend to the Queen Mother on specific public occasions. The Women of the Bedchamber work full-time shifts of two weeks at a time and attend to personal needs such as shopping and answering letters.

that England should worry more about its deserving rich than its hopeless poor. Outrage in the House of Commons★ over that comment forced the Prime Minister, James Callaghan, to remind critics of a long-established custom "to speak with respect of members of the royal family." There was no such rebuke from the Prime Minister after Willie Hamilton's attack.

"He's just a common† little Scotsman," said Princess Margaret, spitting out "common" like a fur ball. Her cut-glass accent sliced the word with contempt. For her, the rigid dictates of the class system ruled. People were defined solely by bloodline—not character, education, wealth, or accomplishment. Birth determined worth. And royalty stood at the top of humanity's ladder. Everybody else scrambled below with no hope of ascending. The Princess spared no one, not even her paternal grandmother. "I detested Queen Mary," she told Gore Vidal. "She was rude to all of us, except Lilibet, who was going to be Queen. Of course, she [Queen Mary] had an inferiority complex. We were royal, and she was not."

As royalty, Margaret did not carry cash. Nor did she pay her own bills. She didn't

★ "The Duke of Edinburgh is a useless, reactionary, arrogant parasite," said Arthur Latham, a Labor MP. "He's the most well-paid social security claimant in Britain simply for being his wife's husband."

† The Queen also used the word "common" as an indictment. She applied it with disdain to the actor who had played the role of King George VI in *Edward VII and Mrs. Simpson*, the television series. "Andrew Ray," said Her Majesty, "is far too common to have played my father."

even own a credit card. Her finances were handled by the head of her household, who managed her allotment from her Civil List. She complained constantly about her paltry allowance and was not above bartering.

"One Christmas someone gave her a huge gift basket with all sorts of bubble baths, perfumes, oils, and lotions that took two people to carry," said William C. Brewer, a former associate of Crabtree & Evelyn, the fragrance company. "The Princess and her lady-in-waiting came into our shop in Kensington the day after Christmas with the mammoth gift. I knew it was Princess Margaret from the springalator platform shoes. She had come to return the gift, and she refused to accept a store credit. 'I want cash,' she said. What could we do? Although it's against store policy, we gave her a cash refund because she's Princess Margaret. The lady-in-waiting took the money and the two of them walked out."

Margaret expects to be accommodated because she is royalty. Her mother and her sister have the same expectations. When they are invited to be houseguests (or, more accurately, when their ladies-in-waiting call their friends who have large country estates and inquire about the possibility of a royal visit), advance people arrive to make sure that the weekend premises will be suitable, not just for security, but for royal comfort.

When the Queen Mother visited British barrister Michael Pratt, he told friends that her lady-in-waiting arrived beforehand with a list of instructions: gin and tonic in the bedroom, no noisy children, and bronco paper fanned out in the bathroom. "Bronco paper is a heavy, rough, brown paper that is abrasive and good for cleaning motor oil off the linoleum," recalled one of Pratt's friends. "Most people want only the softest toilet tissue for their bums, but that old horse insists on having sandpaper wipes from World War Two when the country was on rations. They don't even sell bronco paper anymore. You have to special-order it on Walton Street, or else fake it by sloshing tea on white fax paper."

Princess Margaret's friends, who describe her as the houseguest from hell, also receive a list of instructions: tune the piano, get lots of Ella Fitzgerald records, import some young men who like to sing and dance, and have a recording of "Scotland the Brave" by the Royal Highland Fuseliers. Most important: provide potables—Gordon's eighty-proof gin and tonic for midmorning through midafternoon, and from midafternoon until midnight, Famous Grouse Scotch whiskey. "You must make sure she has jammy dodgers for tea," said one of Margaret's hostesses. "Jammy dodgers are little circular sandwiches cut out of white bread with raspberry jam in the middle. The raspberry preserve must be seedless because Her Royal Highness does not like seeds stuck in her teeth, so you have to purchase imported preserves.

"Royal weekends are such a nightmare. The worst pressure is if you have the Queen to stay. Then you must lock your cats in the stable because Her Majesty abhors cats. You have to have barley water for her because that's what she uses to cleanse her face. You have to send your children away because the royals can't stand children. My son hates when the royal family descends on us, especially Margaret. He says she's like the front of Notre Dame—all gargoyles—and should have water spouting out of her mouth.

"All members of the royal family believe the prestige they bring to their hosts justifies the inconvenience and expense of their visit. It's an arrogant assumption but indisputably valid because I don't know anyone within the aristocracy who has ever turned them down, myself included. Lord Douglas of Neidpath threatens to bar Margaret's next visit, but so far he hasn't."

The prospect of a royal visit can turn a household upside-down. "Every time that call came from the King's [George VI's] equerry or the Queen's [Elizabeth's] lady-in-waiting, my mother would go into a faint," recalled the daughter of a marquess. "'Oh, God, oh, God, they want to come for tea.' You couldn't say no. You just couldn't. So we'd rush around for biscuits, unearth the Earl Grey, and find some clotted cream. Then we got cleaned and scraped the horse muck off our shoes. We dreaded their arrival, but we were ready.

"In they'd ponce. The first visit I remember was King George VI, Queen Mary, the

Duchess of Athlone [Queen Mary's sister-in-law], Princess Elizabeth, Prince Philip, and Princess Margaret. I was eight, my brother was three. We stood to attention when they arrived. I had to curtsy to the floor and he had to bow with his neck, bringing his chin to his chest...."

Over the years Princess Margaret came to rely on the largesse of rich friends like the Aga Khan and Imelda Marcos to provide villas and yachts for her pleasure. She especially enjoyed visiting Italy and regularly invited herself to stay with Harold Acton at La Pietra in Florence and Gore Vidal in Ravello. She also expected to be paid to attend certain overseas charity events and demanded first-class accommodations—planes, hotels, limousines, hairdressers—in addition to a personal appearance fee. She acted as though this were her due. The royal presence deserved royal compensation, especially from rich Americans.

"I remember when one of her best friends arranged for Princess Margaret and Lord Snowdon to be guests of honor at a charity ball in New York," recalled writer Stephen Birmingham. "The Snowdons charged us $30,000 as their personal appearance fee, but we couldn't pay them because we couldn't raise enough money from ticket sales. They left New York feeling exploited and we felt robbed. Worse, the Princess never spoke to her friend again—all because of a lousy $30,000."

Even her friends described her as temperamental. "Margaret is operatic," said one man. "I've known her all my life. I've escorted her places, been entertained in her home at Kensington Palace, even stayed with her in Mustique. Yet I'm utterly dispensable. I'm there only for her entertainment and amusement when she needs to be entertained and amused. Beyond that, I'm nothing to her. I'm not otherwise acknowledged....I stayed up one night drinking and singing songs with her—God, how she loves to sing, fancies herself better than Barbra Streisand—and two nights later I saw her at the Palace for a big party. She walked in and strode past me as if I were a marble column. Not so much as a glance, nod, or a smile. That's royalty. It's beyond arrogance. It's total indifference to another human being."

Princess Michael of Kent* became known as the Pushy Princess after insisting that Thorn EMI (a record company) send her ten color television sets for her servants' quarters before she'd attend a cocktail party. The TV sets arrived—and so did the Princess-for-hire.

She showed a basic understanding for the commerce of royal patronage. Walking by Mozafarian Jewelers on Beauchamp Place in London, she spotted a decorative ivory bear

---

* The Queen and Prince Philip refer to the six-foot blond Princess as "Our Val" because of her strong resemblance to the Valkyries, warrior maidens of German myth.

When asked by a magazine what he would give his worst enemy for Christmas, Viscount Linley (son of Lord Snowdon and Princess Margaret) quipped, "Dinner with Princess Michael."

in the window. "It cost $1,000," said the owner's daughter, "and she wanted it. So my father said, 'Wrap it up for her.'" The Princess walked out with the fanciful object, and her personal secretary sent a thank-you note, which the owner then displayed in a gold frame.

The British royal family appears eccentrically tightfisted to the people who serve them. "Prince Charles doesn't like to spend money," said his former valet Stephen Barry, "and he moans about the price of everything."

Like his mother, Charles counts the chickens in the freezer at each one of his palaces and insists that leftovers be warmed and served, "night after night," according to one of his secretaries, "until there is no food left. He cannot abide waste." He also squeezes his toothpaste with a sterling silver implement called a mangle so he can get the last drop. Then he insists the tubes be recycled.

"All the Windsors are mean as cat's piss," said John Barratt. "All of them—from the Queen on down, and she's the leader of the miserly lot. They pay little to staff* because they think it's an honor for us to serve them. They give miserable presents—and then only at Christmas. The Queen once gave her laundress a bag of clothespins, which was her idea of a practical gift. She gave her seamstress a heavy horseshoe magnet to pick up the pins

---

* In 1994 the Queen's footman was paid $12,000 a year, plus a two-room apartment.

she dropped on the floor during fittings. Her Majesty does better for friends, of course, especially if they're famous. She gave Noel Coward a solid gold crown-encrusted cigarette case for his seventieth birthday, a bizarre present from someone who professes to hate smoking, but lavish. The usual present from the Queen is a photograph of herself or one of her with the Duke of Edinburgh in a sterling silver frame with the royal crest.

"When it comes to those who serve them, Princess Margaret gives the same kind of frightful present as the Queen. Margaret gave one of her elderly ladies-in-waiting a lavatory brush because the poor dear didn't have one in her loo when she visited."

The Princess spent weeks before Christmas choosing appropriate gifts for her family, her friends, and her staff and wrapped each present personally. She selects sensibly but has been known to splurge for special employees. One year she gave her detective a video compact disc player and her chauffeur two shirts from Turnbull & Asser. That same year her butler, who had been hired only a few weeks before, received a less extravagant gift. "It was a very nice silk tie from Simpson's," he said. "The Princess explained that I would have received a little something more had I been with her longer."

"The Queen gives the spare minimum," recalled Barratt, "blow heaters, bath mats, a shovel. She would ring up and ask what Lord Mountbatten would like. I'd tell her that he needed new spurs. So she'd give him spurs. It's a very useful way of giving a present, although it lacks spontaneity. But then spontaneity would be out of character for the royal family, where everything is programmed."

The Queen seemed hardworking to her subjects, who appreciated her frugality. They took comfort in her conscientiousness as she recycled her wardrobe and passed her castoffs to her sister and her daughter. They nodded approvingly when one of her corgis killed a rabbit at Balmoral, and she carefully presented the bloody hare to her chef. "We can eat this," she said. They saluted her practicality when she gave each of her staff at Sandringham a pot of chrysanthemums for Christmas with the instruction: "Give the pot back to the gardener when the plant dies." They approved of the memo she wrote to the Head of the Household to change the forty-watt light bulb in her bedside lamp to one of sixty watts— "but not until this one is finished." They liked her small efforts to conserve, especially during the droughts of the 1970s. When she alerted her households to save water, signs promptly went up in the lavatories of Buckingham Palace: "Don't pull for a pee."*

Her subjects accepted certain extravagances as basic necessities for the Queen such as her luggage—172 custom-made trunks of hand-

---

* Historians praised the Queen for her progressive "pee" signs, pointing out that her predecessor Queen Elizabeth I had been so backward that she'd refused to grant a patent for a water closet because she felt it would encourage impropriety.

tooled leather that carried her feather pillows, her hot-water bottles, her favorite china tea set, and her white leather lavatory seat.

Her arch, stilted manner was interpreted as dignified, even when she appeared to be totally out of touch. On a visit to Budapest she toured a homeless shelter and saw a line of unshaven men sitting on a bench outside. She said, "It must be so nice here in the winter." She tried to relate to a group of housewives in Sheffield, England, by saying, "I find it difficult keeping my floors clean, too."

Recognizing that Her Majesty's world was remote and rarefied, her courtiers instituted regular luncheons at the Palace to introduce her to interesting people. "It's supposed to be a hedge against high huckletybuck," said an actor who has been a regular guest, "but I haven't seen a change in ten years' time....She's still the Queen, who sent six half bottles of *non*vintage champagne to Winston Churchill on his deathbed...she's the wealthiest woman in the world, and this, of itself, tends to make one so aloof and distant as to be unapproachable. Poor woman cannot relate on a human level...just doesn't know how...making small talk pains her." The Queen's opening remark to one luncheon partner illustrated the vast distance between monarch and subject: "You can have no idea," she said, "how much work is involved in maintaining a private golf course."

The Queen was better on paper than in person, especially on matters of taste. When she received letters of protest objecting to a Danish director coming to England to film *The Love Life of Jesus Christ,* she, too, objected. Her press secretary said, "Her Majesty finds this proposal as obnoxious as most of her subjects do." The director was not allowed to film in the United Kingdom. When British newspapers offered huge sums of money for the life story of the Yorkshire Ripper, who had terrorized northern England for five years, killing women, the Queen registered her "sense of distaste." She wrote to the mother of one of the victims, who had complained about the murderer's profiting from his crimes. The Queen agreed, and the newspapers withdrew their bids.

Her subjects felt that Her Majesty was the best representative of the world's most prestigious surviving monarchy, and as such, she was entitled to extraordinary wealth. With the exception of the fiery Willie Hamilton, few people begrudged her her $400 million fortune.* So, with little dissension in 1972, Parliament voted to give her the tax-free raise she requested for herself—$3 million a year—and the tax-free raises for her family: the

*Mountbatten fretted about the negative impression forming over the Queen's fortune. In 1972 he wrote to Prince Philip: "Unless you can get an informed reply published [in an establishment paper like the *Times*] making just one point, the image of monarchy will be gravely damaged. It is true that there is a fortune, which is very big, but the overwhelming proportion (85%?) is in pictures, objets d'art, furniture, etc. in the three State-owned palaces. The Queen can't sell any of them, they bring in no income. So will you both please believe a loving old uncle and NOT your constitutional advisers, and do it." He did not do it.

Queen Mother was raised to $237,500; Prince Philip to $162,500; Princess Margaret to $87,500; and Princess Anne to $37,500. Because Prince Charles received an annual income from the Duchy of Cornwall, he was not included on the Civil List.

The pressure on Charles to marry grew in 1973 when Princess Anne became engaged to Captain Mark Phillips. Reporters suggested that Charles had been bested by his sister, who was marrying before him. Anne chose her brother's twenty-fifth birthday, November 14, 1973, as her wedding day, but Charles did not feel honored. He was aboard the frigate HMS *Minerva* when he received the news of her engagement in a letter from his father. "I was crestfallen," Charles admitted. "I reacted with a spasm of shock and amazement."

Growing up, he and Anne had become close, especially after their royal tours of Australia and the United States, when they represented the Queen. On those trips, Anne, who seemed selfish and arrogant, made Charles look good. He was ingratiating; she was dismissive. He tolerated tedious questions from reporters; she refused. He smiled for photographers; she swatted them like nasty flies. "Bugger off," she ordered, holding up her hand when cameras pressed too close. In Washington, D.C., Charles asked the Speaker of the House of Representatives why the bald eagle had been selected as the country's national symbol. Anne crinkled her nose in disgust. "Most unfortunate choice, isn't it?" she said.

1

Windsor Castle is the best-known symbol of the British monarchy. William the Conqueror chose the site for a fortress after his conquest of England in 1066. In 1917, when King George V needed to camouflage his German origins, he chose Windsor as the royal family's dynastic name.

Queen Victoria (far right) in 1893. After the death of her husband, Prince Albert, in 1861, she went into mourning and wore black clothes the rest of her life. Here she is pictured with her son the Duke of York, later to become King George V, and his wife, the Duchess of York, who became Queen Mary.

2

3

Prince Edward, who became King Edward VIII and later the Duke of Windsor, in 1909 with Czar Nicholas II, the last emperor of Russia, his son, and Prince George, who became King George V. As monarch, he did not dispatch the British navy to rescue his cousins during the Russian Revolution. The imperial family was executed by the Bolsheviks at Ekaterinburg in 1918.

4

Queen Mary sits with three of her five sons: Prince Albert, who became King George VI; Prince Edward (Duke of Windsor), who became King Edward VIII; Prince George (Duke of Kent), who died during World War II. Absent are Prince Henry, later Duke of Gloucester, and Prince John, who died in 1919 at the age of fourteen.

Britain's German royal family reinvented as the House of Windsor. At left, Princess Mary, the only daughter of King George V and Queen Mary, surrounded by four of her five brothers.

The first published photograph of HRH Princess Elizabeth, age two, in May 1928 with her governess, Nanny Knight. They are standing in front of No. 145 Piccadilly, then the home of the Duke and Duchess of York, who became King George VI and Queen Elizabeth.

6

7

"Britons hated that American woman," said the King's equerry Edward Dudley Metcalfe, recalling placards at the time of the abdication.

"I intend to marry Mrs. Simpson as soon as she is free to marry,"
King Edward VIII told the Prime Minister. "If I could marry
her as King, well and good. . . . But if not . . . then I am
prepared to go." He gave up the throne in 1936, and after her
second divorce, he married forty-year-old Wallis Warfield Simpson
on June 3, 1937, in France.

"Our family, us four," is how the new King, George VI,
described himself, his wife, Queen Elizabeth, and his two
daughters, Princesses Margaret and Elizabeth.

DUKE OF WINDSOR
SALUTES, CRIES
"HEIL, HITLER"

The Duke and
Duchess of Windsor
appear delighted to
meet Hitler in 1937.

DUKE OF WINDS
AND THE LETTE
OF A NAZI ENV

The King and Queen, accompanied by Prime Minister Winston Churchill, inspect bomb damage at Buckingham Palace during World War II.

Queen Elizabeth and Mrs. Franklin D. Roosevelt riding in the presidential limousine during a parade welcoming Their Majesties to Washington, D.C. The King and Queen visited the White House to appeal for U.S. intervention into World War II.

Princess Elizabeth became engaged to Lieutenant Philip Mountbatten on July 9, 1947, against the initial objections of her parents. Philip had renounced his Greek royal title and adopted his maternal grandfather's German surname.

15

On November 20, 1947, Princess Elizabeth married Prince Philip at Westminster Abbey. "I don't know whether I'm being very brave," the bridegroom told a relative, "or very foolish."

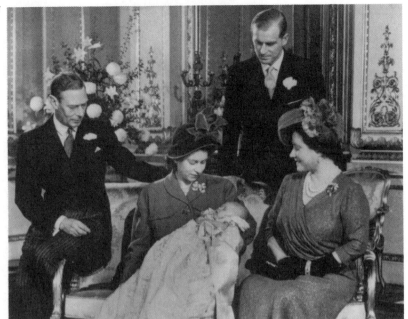

"IT'S A BOY," read the sign tacked to the gates of Buckingham Palace on November 4, 1948, to announce the birth of Prince Charles Philip Arthur George. The King and Queen, pictured with Princess Elizabeth and the Duke of Edinburgh after the christening of their first child.

After a three-month royal tour, Princess Elizabeth returns to London with her husband. She greets her young son, Charles, with a pat on the shoulder as Philip hugs her mother.

The grieving women of Windsor at the funeral of King George VI on February 6, 1952. The King's daughter, Elizabeth; his eighty-five-year-old mother, Mary, who died thirteen months later. The King's widow, Elizabeth, later styled herself as Her Majesty Queen Elizabeth the Queen Mother.

19

20

Surrounded by her family, Elizabeth II waves to her subjects from the balcony of Buckingham Palace after her coronation on June 2, 1953. After fourteen years of austerity from war, reconstruction, and rations, Britain spent $300 million during coronation week. The Queen's gown cost her government $1 million.

The new Queen meets her favorite Prime Minister, Winston Churchill. "He was always such fun," she said. Churchill admitted he had fallen "a little in love" with his monarch, whose portrait he hung above his bed.

21

22

Princess Elizabeth with her favorite U.S. President, Harry Truman, during her first visit to Washington, D.C., in 1951.

New York World-Telegram The Sun

7TH SPORTS
Wall St. Closing
LATEST RACING!

MEG WON'T WED PETER

Cites Duty to Church and Country

Rejects Civil Rites and Loss Of Succession

New York Post

Journal American

MEG SAYS 'NO'

EXTRA
Meg Won't Wed Peter

Decision Hers Alone

Dulles Asks U.S. Arms for Israel

23

24

Princess Margaret rebounds
from Peter Townsend with
Antony Armstrong-Jones, the
commoner who became the Earl
of Snowdon. They married on
May 6, 1960, and produced two
children, David and Sarah.

Roddy Llewellyn met Princess Margaret in 1973 when she was forty-three and he was twenty-three. Their public love affair caused the Queen to denounce her sister for having "the lifestyle of a guttersnipe."

25

26

HRH the Princess Margaret becomes the first member of the British royal family to divorce. She was not immune to the scandal she caused. She suffered a nervous breakdown and was hospitalized with gastroenteritis and alcoholic hepatitis. She also threatened suicide.

27

A QUEEN HAPPILY REUNITED WITH PRINCE OF THE KINGDOM

SUNDAY EXPRESS

FEBRUARY 17 1957 · · · Founded by LORD BEAVERBROOK · · ·

The Duke arrives late at the airfield to meet the Queen
—but he springs up the stairs two at a time

THIS SMILING DAY

A tiny smear
of lipstick
on his face

IT'S SO GOOD TO SEE THEM TOGETHER AGAIN

NEXT
a trip to
U.S. and
Canada?

London Rumors Of Rift
In Royal Family Growing

DUKE AWAY,
RUMORS PLAY

Rumors about the Queen's splintered marriage first surfaced in February 1957
in U.S. newspapers. The Queen's press secretary denounced the stories:
"It is quite untrue that there is a rift between the Queen and the
Duke of Edinburgh. . . . It is a lie." Yet, the royal couple,
who had been apart for four months, staged a very
public reunion for photographers.

28

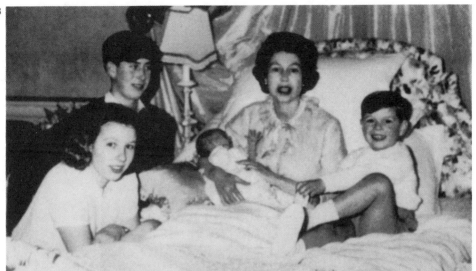

From the Queen's personal scrapbook: Her Majesty in bed with her children, Anne (age thirteen), Charles (age fifteen), and Andrew (age four, after the birth of her last child, Edward, in 1964. This photo appeared only once in England. After it was published in the *Daily Express*, the Palace announced: "Since the photographs are of such a personal kind, the Queen would naturally prefer that they not be published. For that reason, we are unable to approve their future publication."

29

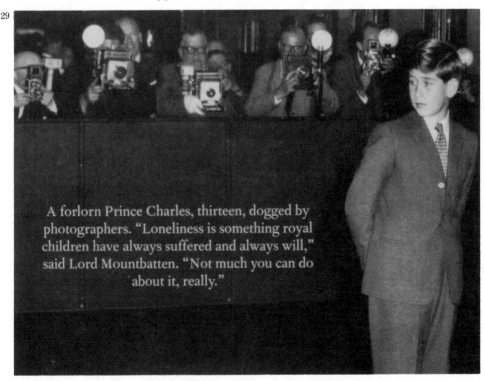

A forlorn Prince Charles, thirteen, dogged by photographers. "Loneliness is something royal children have always suffered and always will," said Lord Mountbatten. "Not much you can do about it, really."

The prettiest picture ever taken of
Queen Elizabeth II: no corgis, no purses,
no scowls.

American royalty meets British royalty in 1961 when Her Majesty and the Duke of
Edinburgh greet President John F. Kennedy and his First Lady, Jacqueline, at
Buckingham Palace.

The blond, blue-eyed prince who married Elizabeth and became the Duke of Edinburgh dazzled women.

Princess Alexandra, a married cousin of the Queen's, is a close friend of Prince Philip's.

The late film star Merle Oberon, another close friend, was Philip's favorite Hollywood hostess.

Helene Cordet, also a close friend, was the first woman publicly rumored to be a mistress of Philip's.

An extract from one of several letters the author received during the research of this book, offering to sell purported love letters written by Philip to other women on Balmoral, Sandringham, or *Britannia* stationery.

37

The royal family at Windsor in October 1972, celebrating the Queen's silver anniversary. Back row, standing left to right: The Earl of Snowdon; the Duke of Kent; Prince Michael of Kent; the Duke of Edinburgh; the Earl of St. Andrews (elder son of the Duke of Kent); Prince Charles, the Prince of Wales; Prince Andrew; the Honorable Angus Ogilvy and his son, James Ogilvy.
Seated on chairs, left to right: Princess Margaret, Countess of Snowdon; the Duchess of Kent (holding Lord Nicholas Windsor, her younger son); Queen Elizabeth the Queen Mother; Queen Elizabeth II; Princess Anne; Marina Ogilvy and her mother, Princess Alexandra.
Seated on floor, left to right: Lady Sarah Armstrong-Jones, Viscount Linley (children of Princess Margaret); Prince Edward; Lady Helen Windsor (daughter of the Duke of Kent). Photograph by Patrick Lichfield.

38

The royal family's love of blood sports: The Queen (center, holding her camera) and her shooting party at Sawai Madhopur, with the eight-foot-nine-inch tiger shot by Prince Philip (far left), who is president of the World Wildlife Fund.

39

Behind her back, the Queen Mother was called "Cookie" by the Duke and Duchess of Windsor because of her fondness for sweets. She, in turn, referred to the Duchess of Windsor as "that woman" and prevented her from having the status of Her Royal Highness. Their feud lasted a lifetime.

40

The Duchess of Windsor looking out the window of Buckingham Palace after her husband's funeral in 1972.

Charles and Lord Mountbatten, or "Uncle Dickie," as he was called by the royal family. He advised the young Prince to become "a moving target for women." He wrote: "I believe in a case like yours, the man should sow his wild oats and have as many affairs as he can before settling down. . . ."

41

Charles fell in love with Camilla Shand, but she married Andrew Parker Bowles.

42

Charles with the Earl Spencer's twenty-two-year-old daughter Sarah, in 1977, at Cowdray, Sussex, where he was playing polo.

43

Charles followed Mountbatten's advice to "choose a suitable, attractive, and sweet-charactered girl *before* she [meets] anyone else she might fall for." He became engaged to Lady Diana Spencer in 1981. Photograph by Snowdon.

44

45

The Prince and Princess of Wales after their wedding at St. Paul's Cathedral on July 29, 1981.

Diana's father, the Earl Spencer, with his second wife, Raine, in front of Althorp, the family estate.

Dame Barbara Cartland, the romance novelist, who is Raine Spencer's mother. "Her false eyelashes look like two crows flying into the White Cliffs of Dover," said Diana, who would not invite her stepgrandmother to the royal wedding.

48

Diana and her mother, Frances, who left Diana's father to marry Peter Shand Kydd. Accused of adultery, Frances lost custody of her children when her mother, Lady Ruth Fermoy, testified against her in the divorce.

49

50

Diana is estranged from her older sister, Jane, who is married to Sir Robert Fellowes, the Queen's private secretary.

Diana's brother, Charles Spencer, who inherited his father's title, was known in the press as "Champagne Charlie."

51

52

54

The young Princess of Wales in the fat and thin stages of bulimia before she conquered the disease and put herself under the fashionable tutelage of British *Vogue*.

55

56

57

58

59

60

The glamorous Princess became the most photographed woman in the world.

61

62

63

Diana becomes the first member of the royal family to touch a person suffering from AIDS.

"I am a humanitarian figure," said Diana during her 1997 visit to Angola, "always have been, always will be." After visiting amputee children, she criticized governments for continuing to manufacture lethal weapons and called for a worldwide ban on land mines.

"My biggest thrill," said Diana after dancing with John Travolta, the star of *Saturday Night Fever,* at the White House in 1985.

"The Prince nearly fell out of his chair," said the Royal Ballet's Wayne Sleep after Diana leapt on stage at Covent Garden in a white satin slip to surprise her husband. She had secretly rehearsed a dance routine that she performed in front of 2,600 people who had never seen royalty slink seductively across a stage. Charles later said her "exhibitionism" embarrassed him.

Diana with art dealer Oliver Hoare. Newspapers reported that for eighteen months the Princess peppered the married man with anonymous telephone calls and screamed torrents of abuse at his wife.

After Diana found out about her husband's affair with Camilla Parker Bowles, she began her own love affair with Army Major James Hewitt.

England's rugby captain Will Carling, another married man who became close to the Princess of Wales. His wife threatened to name Diana in a divorce suit for adultery.

British car salesman James Gilbey, whose telephone conversations with Diana were secretly recorded by a mysterious third party. In one transcript, Gilbey reassures the Princess, whom he calls "Squidgy," that she won't get pregnant.

"I never looked better," said Sarah Ferguson of her July 23, 1986, wedding to HRH the Duke of York, the Queen's favorite son.

"At one point, I weighed 250 pounds. I've always had a weight problem," said the Duchess of York, also known as Fergie. "I'd work out, but then I'd eat ten sandwiches with gooey mayonnaise." She later lost 100 pounds and became the spokesperson for Weight Watchers International.

Texan Steve Wyatt was "the love of my life," Fergie admitted. She was five months pregnant when they met. "He bored everyone to tears," said the columnist Taki, "by talking about diets and good karma and the rest of the bullshit modern Americans pollute us with."

"Glamorous at last," exclaimed Fergie in 1991 after months of strenuous dieting. Like the Princess of Wales, she, too, took lovers outside her marriage. Her excuse: her naval husband's absence. "He was away at sea all the time," she said. "But he's still my bestest friend."

Johnny Bryan, whose poolside romp with Fergie and her children in the South of France in 1992 was captured by paparazzi. The photos of a bare-breasted duchess and her toe-sucking financial adviser caused an international scandal.

"I like athletic men," said Fergie, who courted Australian tennis player Thomas Muster.

As single mothers, Diana and Sarah begin new lives. The Princess of Wales with her two children, Prince Harry and Prince William. The Duchess of York with her two children, Princess Beatrice and Princess Eugenie.

83

Sophie Rhys Jones with HRH Prince Edward, who asks to be called "Mr. Windsor" during the days he works for a living making television documentaries. In the evenings he insists that people address him as His Royal Highness. The Queen gave the couple, who met in 1993, permission to share Edward's rooms at Buckingham Palace.

The Queen Mother on her ninety-fourth birthday surrounded by most of the royal family. Back row, left to right: Anne, The Princess Royal; Commander Tim Laurence; Viscount Linley and his wife, Serena; Peter Phillips, son of Princess Anne; Sir Angus Ogilvy; Princess Alexandra; Prince Edward; Prince Andrew (head turned away from camera). Front row, left to right: Her Majesty; Zara Phillips, daughter of Princess Anne; Queen Mother; Prince William; Princess Margaret; Prince Charles; Prince Harry.

85

THE TROUBLES OF PRINCESS DI (REPRISE)
by Calvin Trillin

Oh Di, we try to keep your troubles high
On any list we make of tragic matters.
Egad, it's sad the *tsoris* that you've had:
The prince. Your health. A paramour who matters.

And now you vow to stick it out somehow,
So William would be king, and not his pater.
If so, let's go. If it would end this show,
We'd like to see it sooner, Di, not later.

87

88

Prince William, the man
who might be King.

"Anne was awful," recalled the wife of the Assistant Chief of Protocol in the Nixon administration. "She did not speak to anyone. Charles was stupid but rather sweet. During their visit to the U.S. in 1970, Charles asked the British Ambassador, 'Do the Catholics and the Protestants fight each other over here as much as they do in Britain?' The Ambassador cringed with embarrassment."

When Princess Anne was asked how it felt to have Buckingham Palace as a private property, she shrugged. "Don't know," she said, irritated by the question. "It's not private property. The Palace belongs to the Crown."

Charm eluded Anne, who didn't stifle yawns when bored or pretend to be amused when she wasn't. She had her father's blast furnace personality and his "the only good reporter is a dead reporter" attitude toward the press. She was terse, tough, and unemotional, a far cry from her grandmother. The Queen Mother preferred the sweet, malleable Charles to his blunt sister, but Anne won the affection of her aunt, Margaret, who envied her independent spirit.

"Anne's much more positive than I was," said Princess Margaret, who understood the difficulty of growing up as royalty's second child. "She's much tougher, too, and has been brought up in a different atmosphere, and went to school."

Charles, who valued his sister's no-nonsense strength, was heartsick to lose her to marriage. "I can see I shall have to find myself a wife pretty rapidly," he wrote to one friend, "otherwise I shall get left behind and feel very miserable!" To another he said: "Everyone is becoming engaged left, right and centre....I am now becoming convinced that I shall soon be left floundering helplessly on a shelf somewhere, having missed everyone!"

Prone to melancholy, the Prince of Wales fell into a deep depression, which he acknowledged in long, self-pitying letters to friends. "I suppose the feeling of emptiness will pass eventually," he wrote. He kept to himself as much as he could on board ship and poured his distress into his diary.

To his shipmates he tried to appear jaunty about his sister's engagement, but he could not conceal his resentment. "Anne couldn't marry her horse, so she's marrying Mark," he said about his future brother-in-law, an accomplished equestrian in the Queen's Dragoon Guards. Years later the writer Auberon Waugh described Phillips as "Princess Anne's grinning, speechless husband, who, if you whistle at him, wets himself." Charles agreed and called him "Fog" because he was "so thick."

The Duke of Edinburgh, whose letter to Charles had hinted at a mismatch between Anne and the army captain, had questioned his future son-in-law after the couple had been photographed kissing in public. The young officer professed honorable intentions toward the Princess, but Prince Philip cut him off.

"Balls," Philip retorted. "I just hope there's none of this premarital malarkey."

354

The Palace tried to claim the kissing photograph was a fake. They officially denied there was any relationship between the Princess and Mark Phillips. In fact, they claimed that the couple did not know each other. "They've never met," said the Queen's press secretary. He then asked Robert Edwards, editor of the *Sunday Mirror,* to run a story ending speculation about a relationship between Princess Anne and Captain Mark Phillips. The editor complied. Weeks later the Queen announced her daughter's engagement.

Marrying into the royal family at that time carried a certain responsibility for producing children. The Prince of Wales had not yet married and provided an heir, and his brothers, Prince Andrew (thirteen) and Prince Edward (nine), were too young to marry, so the prospect of children from Anne, fourth in the line of succession, became crucial. Mark Phillips was summoned to the Palace and ordered to provide a specimen of semen. When his potency was assured, the Queen offered him a title, which he respectfully declined. The Queen could not understand anyone's preferring to remain a commoner, so she tried again. But the young captain said no and was staunchly supported by Princess Anne. Later he turned down a desk job in the Ministry of Defense, preferring to be a country squire. So the Queen offered to buy Anne and Mark Gatcombe Park, a 500-acre estate in Gloucestershire worth almost $2million. Phillips accepted. "Very nice of her, indeed," he said.

"They're gold-plated parasites," roared Willie Hamilton in Parliament. "The lot of them. All parasites."

Four months later the surly Princess earned grudging respect from the public when she faced down a gunman threatening to kidnap her. Traveling down the Mall toward Buckingham Palace one evening, Anne was riding with her husband in a royal limousine. The blue light above the windshield indicated that a member of the royal family was inside, so pedestrians and motorists were stunned when the limousine was rammed by a small white Ford Escort. The Ford's driver jumped out with a pistol in each hand and started firing. The assailant ran toward the limousine, shooting the Princess's chauffeur, her protection officer, and a pedestrian. Then the gunman lunged toward a rear door to grab the Princess. Frightened but tough, Anne and her husband held on to the door from inside until the deranged man was subdued.

Acts of terrorism were so rare in England in 1974 that policemen did not carry guns* and people did not worry about getting shot. One man who rushed to Anne's rescue was more intent on manners than mayhem.

"My first thought was that the two cars had bumped each other, and that the driver of the Escort had lost his temper," recalled Ron

---

* So great was fear of public anger over the abdication that on the night of King Edward VIII's farewell address to the nation in 1936, the sentries guarding Buckingham Palace were issued live ammunition for the first time in history.

Russell, manager of a London cleaning firm. "Obviously he didn't realize he was embarrassing a member of the royal family. Someone should tell him. With this in mind, I pulled off the road."

The public was shocked by the attack on a member of the royal family but praised the composure of the Princess, who seemed to dismiss her assailant with the dispatch of Mary Poppins.

"The girl's got steel britches," a London cabbie told the *Daily Mail*.

Her father agreed. Anne had called him in Indonesia, where he was on a royal tour with the Queen. The Princess did not want to talk to her mother about the attempted kidnapping, only her father. "God help that cretin," Prince Philip said. "If he had succeeded in abducting Anne, she would have given him a hell of a time while in captivity." Upon her return to London, the Queen presented royal honors to the four men wounded while trying to protect her daughter. The Duke of Edinburgh commended his favorite child on scoring a public relations triumph. "Well done," he told Anne. "You saved the Civil List."

The royal allowances remained unchallenged until Princess Margaret let a fox into the chicken coop. With her penchant for weak men, she had become romantically involved with an effete young man who had lived with an avowed homosexual. Margaret was forty-three years old when she met Roderic ("Roddy") Llewellyn at a party. He was seventeen years her junior. As the second son of Sir Henry Llewellyn, he was an aristocrat, which was not insignificant to the Princess. His father seemed amused by their relationship. "You mean Roddy's new friend?" he asked. "Well, it makes a change from his usual Italian waiters." Margaret said the long-haired youth, who lived on a commune in Wales, reminded her of a younger version of her husband "back in the days when Tony was sweet." The Princess and the hippie began an affair known only to their friends. In deference to the Queen, the couple did not socialize in public.

Snowdon, who was involved in his own love affair, was desperate for a divorce. The Princess unthinkingly gave him grounds in 1976 when she took her young lover to Mustique. The couple were photographed there in a cozy island bar with another couple. A picture of Margaret and Roddy sitting on a wooden bench in their bathing suits was published on the front page of the *News of the World*. The other couple were cropped from the photograph so Princess Margaret appeared to be dining intimately with a man who was not her husband. Under the headline "Margaret and the Handsome Young Courtier," the article described the two lovers walking arm in arm on the beach, adding that "Roddy rubs suntan oil on her bronzed shoulders. She can suddenly look radiant in a way the public have not seen for a long time." In a later edition, the headline was changed to "The Picture a Husband Just Couldn't Take."

Even people who had suspected that Margaret's marriage was not perfect were grateful for the royal facade. For years the public made allowances for Princess Margaret, tolerating her minor transgressions such as smoking in public and showing up late for royal events. People said she had suffered extraordinary heartbreak when she was forced to give up Peter Townsend, so they relaxed the standards for her. They overlooked her imperious behavior and sympathetically referred to her as "poor Margaret." That gave her further license to be naughty. But now, on Mustique, she had gone too far.

No longer was there tolerance for a married royal Princess, who received $70,000 a year from the public purse, who left her children in England and flagrantly cavorted in the Caribbean with a raffish young man of ambiguous sexuality from a hippie commune in Wales.

"If she thumbs her nose at taxpayers by flying off to Mustique," said Willie Hamilton, "she shouldn't expect the workers of the country to pay for it."

This time another Member of Parliament agreed. "The Princess is a parasite," said Dennis Canavan, a Labor MP from Scotland. "She should not get any money at all."

Sensing the mounting public outrage, Snowdon pounced. He said he was humiliated by his wife's flagrant indiscretion and that continuing their marriage under any circumstance was intolerable. Alarmed by the uproar,

359

the Queen summoned Margaret to London, so she left Mustique—without her lover. The Palace told Snowdon to meet her at the airport for the sake of public appearance. He arrived in a royal limousine accompanied by his young son and thoughtfully carried Margaret's fur coat so she would not freeze in her summer cottons. In front of photographers, he kissed her on the cheek and draped the coat over her shoulders. Afterward she said, "Lord Snowdon was devilish cunning."

Two months later Kensington Palace issued a statement:*

Her Royal Highness, the Princess Margaret, Countess of Snowdon, and the Earl of Snowdon have mutually agreed to live apart. The Princess will carry out her public duties and functions unaccompanied by Lord Snowdon. There are no plans for divorce proceedings.

"I remember the night the announcement was made," recalled one of Margaret's friends. "The Princess was terribly upset. She kept running to the loo to cry, but we kept her going, took her to a premiere, and then to Bubbles [a nightclub] for Champagne. We stayed with her until four-thirty in the morning. She needed the support."

British law requires a formal two-year sep-

---

* The separation was issued from Kensington Palace because it is Princess Margaret's home, and according to royal protocol, she is the head of her family.

aration before granting an uncontested divorce. If one party objects, a five-year waiting period is imposed before the divorce can be granted. Margaret never believed that the separation would lead to divorce, but Snowdon was determined. He said he felt like a prisoner serving time and he wanted his freedom.

The Queen was so disturbed by what she saw as her sister's self-destructiveness that she didn't speak to her for several weeks. She said her sister was leading the life of a "guttersnipe," and the Queen's disgust soon led to snickering about Margaret's promiscuity. One joke making the rounds had the Queen and her lady-in-waiting driving in the country when the Queen's Rolls-Royce was overtaken by bandits. The gunmen, who did not recognize the passengers, demanded money and jewels but got nothing except an empty white handbag. So they threw the two women out of the car and drove off with the Rolls.

The Queen dusted herself off.

"Where is your beautiful ring?" asked the lady-in-waiting.

"I hid it," said the Queen.

"Where?"

"In a very private place."

The Queen looked at the lady-in-waiting and asked about her tiara.

"I hid it," said the lady-in-waiting.

The Queen raised her eyebrows inquiringly.

"Same place," said the lady-in-waiting.

The Queen looked at her and smiled. "Pity Margaret wasn't here," she said. "We could've saved the Rolls."

Despite the public derision, the Princess continued her relationship with Roddy Llewellyn because she said he was the only person who was kind to her. "I need him," she sobbed. "He's good to me." The Queen, aware of public opinion, begged her to reconsider. Margaret refused.

"That friendship may be in the modern trend," said Willie Hamilton on the floor of the House of Commons, "but it has turned the Princess into a royal punk." This time few members of the Tory Party rose to object. In fact, the only person to defend the Princess was her young lover.

"I would like to see Willie Hamilton or any of the others do all her jobs in the marvelous way that she does," said Roddy Llewellyn. "People love the monarchy and appreciate with their whole hearts the job Princess Margaret does."

By then the public had turned against the Princess. A national opinion poll reported that 73 percent of the country felt her way of life had harmed her public standing and that of the monarchy. So the Queen told her sister she must make a choice: either give up her lover or give up public life.

Margaret cursed the "prayer makers" in the church and mocked the establishment newspapers for their pious editorials against her. She called them all "slop buckets of hypocrisy." But in the end she caved in to public pressure and agreed to do her duty.

Looking worn and tired, she carried out her official duties but frequently arrived late or left early, pleading fatigue. Her doctors warned her to stop smoking and drinking, but she did not listen until she was hospitalized with gastroenteritis and alcoholic hepatitis. Even when faced with a lung operation, she continued smoking sixty unfiltered cigarettes a day, which she puffed through a tortoiseshell holder. She suffered a nervous breakdown, and shortly before the divorce announcement, she threatened suicide.

Margaret had not reckoned with her husband's determination to be rid of her. Despite their separation, she never believed they would divorce. So she was surprised when Snowdon asked to dissolve their marriage. She said she wouldn't stand in his way, especially if he wanted to remarry, but he said he had no such plans. He simply wanted a divorce. The announcement was made on May 10, 1978. But seven months later Snowdon remarried. His lover, Lucy Lindsay-Hogg, was pregnant. Margaret read about the marriage in the newspapers. "He didn't even have the courtesy to call me beforehand," she told a biographer, "and he never told the children."

The first royal divorce since King Henry VIII's divorce from Anne of Cleves in 1533 placed unremitting pressure on the Prince of Wales as he approached his thirtieth birthday. "This is the Year," headlined one newspaper, printing a photo montage of all the "suitable" young women Charles had dated and discarded. Another newspaper announced, "Prince Stranded Between Altar and Abyss."

Prince Philip teased his son about the press coverage. "You'd better get on with it, Charles," he said, "or there won't be anyone left."

Charles celebrated his thirtieth birthday on November 15, 1978, with a grand ball at Buckingham Palace attended by more than four hundred people. The invitations from the Queen and Duke of Edinburgh specified "no tiaras" the way other rich parents might specify "no gifts." The Prince took the tall, blond actress Susan George as his date, but he danced most of the evening with his friends' wives, Dale "Kanga" Tryon and Camilla Parker Bowles. As godfather to both their eldest children, Charles admitted he felt more relaxed with them than the eligible beauties pursuing him. "Married women are safe," he later explained to his fiancée. "Because of their husbands, they understand discretion."

As Prince of Wales, Charles was accustomed to adulation. He expected it and received it in full measure, especially from the wives of two of his friends. These married women gave freely and expected nothing in return, unlike single women, who required the time and attention of courtship. For Charles's married lovers, sharing his bed was like owning a wine cháteau or a Gulfstream jet: it added to their prestige. They enjoyed being whispered about as his "confidantes," and their husbands felt honored to share their wives with the future King. The arrangement enhanced their stature within the aristocracy.

"Poor Charles even feels more comfortable with bossy old women like me than he does with young single women his own age," said the sixty-five-year-old Viscountess he invited to Windsor for lunch a few days later. "I'm one of the old aristos who grew up with Her Majesty and Princess Margaret at a time in this tiny country when we all knew one another and understood our place. I'm part of a world no longer visible: the bloated upper classes where the echo of deference still lingers and allows for amiability toward our royal family, which is unfortunately German, and part of the vaulting arrogance of the middle class. We recognize them [the royal family] for what they are—they are undereducated and ill-informed Germans, and they need our help. We feel protective toward them, particularly the heir apparent, which is the reason Charles seeks me out.

"He was never more endearing than on that day after his thirtieth birthday," she said. "I arrived for lunch, and he said, 'Oh, God, I hope you are not very hungry. When Mummy's not here, nothing much happens. So my valet is making us a little omelet.' He eyed my dog. 'Thank God Mummy isn't here. Her corgis would've made a sandwich out of your Labrador. They're perfectly dreadful.'

"Charles is very sweet, but not too bright.

He has a slender understanding of the world. Humbly nice and well mannered, but there's a dimension missing. He said he'd become so set in his bachelor ways and habits that he didn't think he'd ever find a wife who'd fit in and want to share his life. 'Sad, isn't it?' he said. 'What woman would ever put up with all this? With me?'

"After lunch he showed me his horse, Mantilla, and then I left, feeling more protective than ever toward the future King of England, who seemed to have everything but actually had nothing. At least, nothing that mattered much."

TWELVE

Charles was in Iceland to fish when he received a call on August 27, 1979, from the British Ambassador. "Your Royal Highness," said the Ambassador, "I'm afraid I have some tragic news....Lord Louis has been...Sir, I'm so sorry....Earl Mountbatten of Burma is dead."

Charles was too stunned to cry. Stammering in disbelief, he asked for details, but the Ambassador said he knew only what he had heard on the BBC news flash. So Charles called his mother at Windsor Castle. She told him that "Uncle Dickie," on holiday in Ireland, had been blown up by an IRA bomb.

Mountbatten, seventy-nine, had been aboard his boat with his daughter, Patricia; her husband, John Brabourne; their fourteen-year-old twin sons, Nicholas and Timothy; and Lord

Brabourne's elderly mother. They were going lobstering in Mullaghmore harbor when the bomb was detonated. The explosion instantly killed Mountbatten; his grandson, Nicholas; and an Irish boat boy hired as crew. Lord Brabourne was severely wounded, and his wife almost died. She spent days on a life-support system and underwent several operations to save her eyesight, then weeks in intensive care. Their son Timothy was knocked unconscious but recovered; Lord Brabourne's eighty-three-year-old mother died the next day.

Prince Charles was heartbroken. He wired Mountbatten's private secretary: "This is the worst day of my life. I can't imagine going on without him." That night he poured his grief into his journal: "I have lost someone infinitely special in my life. Life will never be the same now that he has gone. ..."

Days later Charles met his mother and father for lunch at Broadlands to discuss Mountbatten's funeral arrangements. Still distraught, he said he didn't think he could get through the service without breaking down.

"He's gone now, Charles," said his father. "You've got to get on with it."

The Prince of Wales started crying and left the room. The Queen, who did not respond, just continued eating. She dropped bits of chicken from her salad on the floor to feed her corgis. Prince Philip threw down his napkin.

"I hope that has ensured that Charles will shed no tears when he goes out in public," he said. The Queen sipped her water and said nothing.

"Sounds cruel," recalled John Barratt, "but the Duke of Edinburgh was determined to put some steel in his son's spine. Her Majesty couldn't have given a tinker's cuss. Poor Charles was destroyed. He was so dependent on Lord Mountbatten. They spoke every day and wrote weekly. He was everything to Charles—his grandfather figure, his father, his tutor, his best friend."

Although Philip sometimes chafed at this closeness, he mourned his uncle's death and never forgave the Irish Republican Army. Two years later, during a tour of Australia with the Queen, he passed a group of IRA demonstrators. The Queen ignored them and stared straight ahead; Philip raised his hand to wave and gave them the finger.

On the day of Mountbatten's funeral, Charles stepped sadly onto the podium at Westminster Abbey to read the prayer that his great-uncle had selected years before when he planned his state funeral. The Prince of Wales had pinned to his own naval uniform all his ribbons and medals because, as he told his valet, that's what Mountbatten would have preferred. Tapping his chest, he said, "If the IRA want to get me through the heart, they'll have a hard job."

In a quavering voice, Charles recited Psalm 107 in memory of the Admiral of the Fleet: "They that go down to the sea in ships...These men see the works of the Lord and his wonders in the deep. ..." He struggled to keep his composure, but as the buglers sounded the last post, he broke and brushed away a tear.

His emotion contrasted starkly with that of his mother, who sat a few feet away, as impassive as stone. On the day of the bombing, ten days before the funeral, the Palace had issued a statement that Her Majesty was "deeply shocked and saddened," but she did not write a letter of condolence to Mountbatten's children, who were her cousins and her closest friends from childhood. Nor did she interrupt her vacation at Balmoral, where she was joined the next day by her daughter, Princess Anne, for a picnic. The Queen was seen walking in her garden with her corgis and playing with her two-year-old grandson, Peter.

Such ordinary activity in the face of tragedy jolted one royal reporter, who watched the scene through high-power binoculars. He said he was stunned to see the Queen skipping and laughing as if she didn't have a care in the world. "This was the day after Mountbatten had been blown to bits," he recalled, "and I've never seen Her Majesty so relaxed and happy* in all

* Although relations between the Queen and Mountbatten had always been warm, one subject caused them to cool: Japan. In 1971 Her Majesty invited Emperor Hirohito to Britain for a state visit. And she restored the seventy-four-year-old Mikado to the Order of the Garter. He had been stripped of it after Japanese forces attacked the Allies in 1941. His visit made Mountbatten furious. He was further enraged in 1975 when the Queen made a state visit to Japan. "You should have waited until I was dead," he told her.

Mountbatten, who had fought the Japanese for more than three years and served as Supreme Allied Commander, Southeast Asia, never forgave Japan its wartime savagery. But the Queen pointed to the passage of time since hostilites ended and what she saw as the need for reconciliation. "The Emperor is an old man now, Dickie," she said. Mountbatten snorted. "He's a doddering, incompetent old facist."

her life." Ever the loyal subject, the reporter filed a story for his newspaper, saying that the grief-stricken sovereign walked through the gardens of Balmoral in solitary sorrow.

Charles mourned his great-uncle's death for months and turned for guidance to Laurens Van der Post, a writer who had served as an aide to Mountbatten in India. Charles was in awe of the older man, who now replaced Mountbatten as his guru, spiritual mentor, and political adviser. Van der Post, a friend and biographer of Swiss psychoanalyst Carl Jung, talked to Charles about the concept of the collective unconscious, which is expressed through myths and dreams. He encouraged Charles to believe in the supernatural and to be open to the world of spirits. He accompanied the Prince to the Kalahari Desert in Southwest Africa to commune with the ghosts of bushmen. Charles was fascinated by the elderly mystic and soon sought the consolation of seers, mediums, and psychics. He dabbled in the paranormal, took part in séances, and consulted clairvoyants to communicate with the departed Mountbatten.

"Charles tried to summon the shade of Lord Louis on a Ouija board," said John Barratt, "but when the press found out, the Palace made him deny it because he looked barmy."

During this time, Charles became intensely involved with a beautiful Indian-born actress who had been the mistress of Hollywood director John Huston. Zoe Sallis, who gave birth to Huston's son in 1962, was a Buddhist and devoted to swamis. Her influence on Prince Charles disturbed the Palace. She espoused transcendentalism and the doctrine of many divinities, which is inconsistent with the Anglican belief in one omnipotent God.

Charles was enraptured by his new lover, who was ten years his senior, and he began practicing what she was preaching. She had given him a book entitled *The Path of the Masters* and said that her mission was to convert him to belief in reincarnation. To the dismay of his staff, she succeeded. He began talking about the transmigration of souls and speculated about the form that Lord Mountbatten might assume when he returned to earth.

The Prince's private secretary, Edward Adeane, became alarmed by what he saw as incoherent ramblings. The tough-minded barrister, whose father, Sir Michael Adeane, had been private secretary to the Queen, expected more of the future King of England than Charles was demonstrating. Adeane was dismayed by the hairshirt mentality, the do-good speeches, and the forays into alternative medicine. Mostly he was concerned about Charles's attitude toward religion. Adeane tried to redirect him back to the conventional teachings of the Church of England. He stressed the responsibility of the heir apparent to his future subjects, but Charles was not receptive. He was too enthralled by the message of nirvana. Under the influence of his new lover, he became a vegetarian and resolved (temporarily) to stop killing animals. "I want to purify myself," he declared, "and pursue a oneness with all faiths."

"It's got to be stopped," said Adeane to other members of the staff. Asserting himself, the private secretary told the Prince his relationship with the beautiful Buddhist was potentially harmful to the monarchy. Adeane felt the older woman's influence was warping Charles's perspective. He said Charles was destined to become Defender of the Faith—not, as Adeane put it, defender of many faiths. He recommended that Charles end the relationship, but Charles refused—until Adeane threatened to go to the Queen. Then Charles relented. At the age of thirty-one he was still afraid of his mother.

Charles ricocheted from casual dates to one-night stands and, in between, pursued brief relationships with tall, beautiful blondes whose fathers were rich landowners. "I fall in love so easily," he told reporters, trying to explain away the numerous women drifting into and out of his life. He proposed marriage twice—once to Davina Sheffield and again to Anna Wallace—but neither blonde accepted his proposal, and both fell out of favor once their pasts were revealed in the press.

"Oh, God," Charles moaned to his valet, "will I never find a woman worthy enough?"

During the summer of 1980, he found her sitting on a bale of hay. The fresh and lovely nineteen-year-old Lady Diana Spencer seemed too young and too innocent to have a past. Charles, who was fourteen years older, noticed her during a weekend house party at the country home of his friends Philippa and Robert de Pass. The Prince had met Diana in 1977, when he briefly dated her oldest sister, Sarah, and spent a shooting weekend with the Spencers at Althorp, their family estate in Northamptonshire, about seventy-five miles northwest of London. So she was not a stranger when he saw her three years later. He noted how much she had grown up from the sixteen-year-old girl he remembered. "No more puppy fat," he said.

Diana blushed, lowered her eyes, and looked down at her long legs. "I'm just taller now," she joked. "I've stretched the puppy fat."

Amused by her self-deprecating humor, Charles laughed and sat down to talk. They chatted about her sister, Sarah, who recently had married Neil McCorquodale, a former officer of the Coldstream Guards. Charles mused about how pleased he was to get away from his royal duties and be with friends. (The "never-ending bloody" burden of being Prince of Wales would become a constant refrain in the next few months, as Charles complained about his workload.) Diana listened sympathetically and told him how wonderfully he performed his duties. She mentioned how touched she had been watching him on television at Mountbatten's funeral.

"You looked so sad when you walked up the aisle at the funeral. It was the most tragic thing I've ever seen. My heart bled for you when I watched it. I thought: It's wrong. You are lonely. You should be with somebody to look after you."

She later recounted this conversation to her roommates and said that she had talked to the Prince as if he were one of her nursery school charges. She added that he drew close to her, just like the little children she looked after at the Young England kindergarten. Charles, leaving early, asked her to drive back to London with him, but she demurred, saying it might be impolite to her hosts.

"That was a good move on her part," said one of her roommates. "She didn't want to appear ill-bred, and she certainly couldn't look too eager."

For Diana, the courtship had begun. She was excited to be noticed by the Prince of Wales and told her roommates that if she had a chance with him, she would not treat him as dismissively as her sister, Sarah, had when she'd talked to the press. "I think of the Prince as the big brother I never had," Sarah had told a reporter. "I really enjoy being with him, but I'm not in love with him. And I wouldn't marry a man I didn't love, whether it was a dustman or the King of England. If he asked me, I would turn him down." Diana, who read the romance novels of Barbara Cartland, had fantasized about marrying a prince. She would never turn him down.

Diana confided her fantasies to her roommates, who started ransacking their closets to find the right clothes for her to wear on her royal dates. They never saw the future King of England because he never visited Diana's apartment. Nor did he pick her up when they went out. "There weren't many presents, either," recalled one roommate. "A book at Christmas, a watercolor he had painted at Balmoral, one bouquet after they got engaged that was delivered by his valet but without a card, and a little green plastic frog, which Diana kept on the dashboard of her car. She had teased Charles about not having to kiss any more frogs because she'd finally found her prince. I guess he agreed."

During their six-month courtship, Charles rarely telephoned Diana, and he relied on an equerry to issue his last-minute invitations. She was expected to provide her own transportation to wherever he might be. "We referred to him as 'sir,' " said one roommate, "because that's what Diana had to call him in the beginning....We helped her plot her strategy. It was great fun, and a bit of a game."

The young women, whom Charles referred to as Diana's "silly flatmates," shared an apartment at No. 60 Coleherne Court in London, near Harrods department store. Diana had bought the three-bedroom apartment with money she had inherited from her great-grandmother. "It was my coming-of-age present," she said. Like her two older sisters, she had received the money ($75,000) on her eighteenth birthday. Her mother advised her to invest in London real estate, so Diana bought the apartment. To meet the mortgage, she collected rent from three friends and assigned them cleaning chores. "Truth to tell, Diana did most of the housework," said one roommate. "She loved to clean. Pride of place and all that."

Growing up, Diana had been the meticulous member of the family. She spent hours cleaning and scouring, rearranging her dresser drawers, and hanging her clothes. She lined up her shoes by color and made her bed every day, tucking the corners precisely. She vacuumed constantly and learned to launder because she said she loved the smell of freshly ironed shirts. Like Cinderella, she worked cheerfully as a maid for her oldest sister, who paid her $2 an hour to clean her London apartment. Years later Diana told friends that her psychiatrist explained this compulsion to clean as an attempt to impose order on the chaos around her. Recognizing her obsessive nature, she avoided medications like tranquilizers, fearing that if she ever got started, she would become addicted.

Her family had been torn apart by divorce, alcoholism, and violence. For the first ten years of her parents' marriage, her father had blamed her mother for not producing an heir. "It was a dreadful time for my parents and probably the root of their divorce," said Diana's brother, Charles, "because I don't think they ever got over it."

Diana's father, Edward John Spencer, was known informally as Johnny Spencer. As Viscount Althorp, he was heir to a large fortune and a thirteen-thousand-acre estate, Althorp

House, which his ancestors had acquired in the sixteenth century. A former equerry to King George VI and Queen Elizabeth II, he was destined to become the eighth Earl of Spencer; when he inherited his title, he needed a son to pass it on. In 1954 he married Frances Roche, the beautiful blond daughter of the fourth Lord Fermoy. They moved into Park House in Norfolk, on the Sandringham estate. Their first child, Sarah, was born the next year, and two years later, 1957, they had another girl, Jane. Johnnie Spencer wanted a boy and insisted his wife be examined by specialists to find out why she produced daughters. Willing to try again, Frances became pregnant in 1958 and gave birth to a boy in January 1959. The baby was named John in his father's honor. "I never saw him. I never held him," Frances said. "He was an eight-pound baby boy who had a lung malfunction, which meant he couldn't survive." Ten hours after he was born, he died. Frances tried again, and eighteen months later, on July 1, 1961, she gave birth to a third daughter, whom they named Diana Frances. "I was supposed to be the boy," said Diana many years later.

Johnny Spencer started drinking too much and abusing his wife. He sent her back to London's Harley Street specialists to find out what was "wrong" with her. Three years later, when she was twenty-eight, she produced a son. "Finally," she said, "I've done my duty." The Queen was named godmother.

The heir, Charles Edward Maurice Spencer,

was known as the Honourable Charles Spencer, while his grandfather, the Earl Spencer, was alive. Upon the Earl's death in 1975, Johnny Spencer inherited his father's title and his son, Charles, then nine years old, became Viscount Althorp.

"Waiting for dead man's shoes," is how Frances bitterly described her husband's life before he inherited his father's title. By then she had fallen in love with a dynamic married man, who she said gave her life passion and purpose. Although Peter Shand Kydd, forty-two, did not have a title, he was wealthy and glamorous and had a wild sense of humor. Unlike Johnny Spencer, a courtier who approached royalty with reverence, Kydd was unimpressed. After dinner with the Queen, he told his children that Her Majesty "was as boring as ever" and "Buckingham Palace was a bit of a fucking Trust House Forte [hotel]."

Kydd was heir to a wallpaper fortune and a former naval officer who owned land in England, Scotland, and Australia. He was the father of three young children.

"That didn't stop Frances," said one of Peter Shand Kydd's sons. "She's tough—a predator. When she moved on my father, my mother didn't stand a chance."

Diana was six years old in 1967 when her mother left her father and moved into a rented apartment in the Chelsea section of London to be closer to her lover. Frances told her husband that she wanted a divorce and expected to receive custody of their children. Johnnie drunkenly raged at her as "a bolter" and beat her. When he sobered up, he sobbed and begged her to return home. She tried a reconciliation but said it was torture, so she moved out of Park House and returned to London.

Shortly after that, Mrs. Peter Shand Kydd sued for divorce and named Frances as correspondent. Johnny Spencer was so humiliated by his wife's adultery that he sued for custody. He was supported in court by Frances's mother, Lady Ruth Fermoy, a lady-in-waiting to the Queen Mother. Lady Fermoy testified under oath that the Spencer children appeared to be happier with their father than their mother. She also swore that she had never seen Spencer lose his temper.

"Ruth was an old royalist—humbly born in Scotland but incredibly snobbish—and she's been in royal circles all her life," said a Spencer family member. "I adored her and she was wonderful to me, but I must admit that she was rotten to her children, especially Frances. In the custody fight, Ruth sided with Johnny because, as she told me, and testified in court, she'd never seen him actually strike Frances. Ruth hadn't been around for the drunken thrashings, so she could swear without compunction that she'd never witnessed Johnny's physical violence. And Frances would never have told her mother about the abuse; she and Ruth weren't that close to begin with, and the subject wasn't one you discussed freely in those days.

"Ruth would never be party to anyone—let alone her own daughter—embarrassing one of the Queen's courtiers. But the real reason she turned on her daughter was to protect her grandchildren. She didn't want them living with a commoner when they could be living with an aristocrat. Frances never forgave her mother. They didn't speak for nine years and then just barely."

The writer Penny Junor concurred. "Lady Fermoy really could not believe that her daughter would leave a belted earl for a man in trade."

The court ruled in favor of Viscount Althorp, so Diana and her brother, who had moved to London with their mother, moved back to Park House to live with their father. Their two older sisters, Sarah and Jane, remained at boarding school. That year, 1969, Frances married Peter Shand Kydd, who was so torn about abandoning his children that he almost backed out of the marriage. "He never got over the guilt," said one of his closest friends, "and that, coupled with drink later on, probably led to the divorce from Frances in 1990."

A child of a broken marriage, Diana had trouble learning to read. Her brother teased her about being slow and dull-witted because she barely made passing grades. The only award she received in school was in the fourth grade when she won the Palmer Cup for Pets' Corner for being nice to her guinea pig. She loved to dance and spent hours in front of the mirror practicing toe, tap, and ballet exercises, but she was not scholastic. So she dropped out of school at the age of sixteen, and her father, who worried about her lack of education, enrolled her in a Swiss finishing school (Institut Alpin Videmanette in Gstaad). She went reluctantly and studied cooking and French halfheartedly. She spent most of her time skiing. After three months she said she was too homesick to complete the term. She badgered her father to let her come home, which, upon her grandfather's death, had become the grand Jacobean mansion of Althorp.

Her father continued to worry about her future, but Diana was unconcerned. After reading an article in the *Daily Telegraph* about academic failures who later became roaring successes in life, she clipped the story and slipped it under his door. Then she pestered him about moving to London. She wanted to get an apartment like her older sisters.

"I couldn't bear Althorp anymore," she said. "A hard Raine was falling."

Raine was the daughter of the flamboyant Barbara Cartland. More subdued than her mother, Raine, forty-seven, was known as Lady Dartmouth after her marriage. She was a Tory disciple in the lacquered mode of Margaret Thatcher. She had met Johnny Spencer at a local political meeting and invited him to dinner at her London apartment when her husband was away. Spencer, so lonely since his divorce, fed on her attention. Drawn to her strength, he turned to her for advice, especially about running Althorp. She advised him to renovate his estate and to pay for the work by selling off some of his family heirlooms, including three Van Eyck paintings. She suggested pitching an immense tent on the grounds, filling it with huge bouquets of plastic flowers, and serving tea in paper cups to paying customers. She recommended converting the stables into a gift shop and selling souvenirs. She even drew up a list of items to appeal to tourists, including rape whistles and her mother's romantic novels.

The Spencer children were aghast. "We didn't like her one bit," said Charles. "As a child, you instinctively feel things, and with her I very much instinctively felt things."

Diana was less direct than her brother but equally hostile. Behind her back she made fun of Raine's elaborate ball gowns, which were borrowed from film studios, and called her "Countess Come Dancing." Her sister Jane treated Raine like dust on the closet shelf, but Sarah was more outspoken.

"Since my grandfather died and we moved to Althorp," Sarah told a friend, "Lady Dartmouth has been an all-too-frequent visitor." When a reporter called asking to speak to the new Earl Spencer, Sarah said, "My father is in bed with Lady Dartmouth,* and I wouldn't dream of disturbing them."

*Raine's husband, Gerald Dartmouth, filed for divorce on May 29, 1976, and threatened to name Johnny Spencer for alienation of affections. When Raine admitted to adultery, her husband deleted Spencer's name from the public document and cited him only as "the man against whom the charge has not been proved."

Diana ran up and down the corridors of Althorp with her brother, chanting the nursery rhyme "Rain, Rain, Go Away." They called their father's lover "Acid Raine" and sulked in her presence. Charles refused to talk to her, and Diana deviled her with anonymous poison-pen letters and hang-up phone calls—a scare tactic she allegedly used on others years later. When Raine insisted on dressing formally for dinner, the children came to the table in jeans.

Like Frances Shand Kydd, Raine was still married when she began her love affair. She, too, was publicly humiliated by being cited for adultery in her husband's divorce action, and she also lost custody of her children. "It was quite a traumatic time for all of us," said one of her sons. "My father never forgave her."

Raine's husband, Gerald Legge—the Earl of Dartmouth—was so embittered that he commissioned an artist to paint her out of a family portrait; he replaced her with a tree.

By then Raine had moved into Althorp with her Vuitton trunks. The Spencer children pleaded with their father to send her away, but he was bewitched. In 1976 they married and she became the Countess Spencer.* None of their children attended the civil ceremony.

"We weren't invited," Sarah told a reporter. "Not grand enough."

* During a 1980 trip to New York, Raine corrected an American journalist who described her as the Countess of Spencer. Raine explained that she reflected her husband's title and he was the Earl Spencer, not the Earl of Spencer. She said that earls whose names are part of their title count for more socially than earls named for a place.

"The inference is unwarranted," snapped Barbara Cartland. "After all, my daughter gave up a sixteenth Earl for an eighth Earl. Hardly social climbing."

Raine relished the Spencer title, the fortune, and the estate. In fact, she loved everything about her new marriage, except the children. "I'm absolutely sick of the 'wicked step-mother' lark," she said years later. "You're never going to make me sound like a human being because people like to think I'm Dracula's mother, but I did have a rotten time at the start....Sarah resented me, even my place at the head of the table, and gave orders to the servants over my head. Jane didn't speak to me for two years, even if we bumped in a passageway. Diana was sweet, always did her own thing...and Charles, well, he was simply hateful."

Raine was more rancorous in the early months of her marriage. "Sarah is impossible, and Jane's all right as long as she keeps producing children. That's about all she is good for. As for Diana, how can you have intelligent conversation with someone who doesn't have a single 0-level? If you said 'Afghanistan' to her, she'd think it was a cheese."

The animosity between stepmother and stepchildren became even more vitriolic in September 1978, when Johnny Spencer suffered a near fatal brain hemorrhage. He lapsed into a coma for two months and lay in the hospital two more months. Raine visited him every day and sat by his bed, playing opera records and willing him to recover. She fought his children over his medical treatment and barred them from seeing him in a coma. She said she did not want them absorbing the life energy she felt he needed to recover. His doctors braced her for death, but she would not accept their diagnosis. She insisted her husband would live, if only he could be treated with a powerful new German drug (Aslocillin) that was not yet licensed in England. Citing legal restrictions, the doctors said they could not give him the drug, even if they could get it. So Raine moved her husband to another hospital and exerted her influence to get the drug imported for experimentation. She succeeded, and as she predicted, the Earl Spencer rallied and recovered, but not completely. He remained partially brain-damaged, which affected his speech and mobility.

"I could have saved my husband's life ten times over and spent all my money doing this," she told a writer, "but it wouldn't have changed anything in his children's attitude toward me.

"But I'm a survivor, and people forget that at their peril. There's pure steel up my backbone. Nobody destroys me, and nobody was going to destroy Johnny so long as I could sit by his bed...and will my life force into him."

Raine appreciated the opportunity for social advancement and welcomed Diana's new royal relationship. And her father felt flattered about his favorite daughter's catching the eye of the Prince of Wales. But her mother was troubled. Frances Shand Kydd had seen the royal brush swipe her oldest daughter, and she remembered the embarrassment Sarah had suffered when she was dropped from the royal guest list. Sarah, who was fighting anorexia while she was dating Charles, had treasured his invitations and hired a clipping service to send her all the stories written about them. She proudly started a scrapbook that chronicled her rise as one of the chosen few. After her "dustman" interview, there were no more articles and no more invitations. Now her younger sister was receiving them.

Prince Charles had been intrigued enough by his conversation with Diana during the weekend house party in July to invite her to the opera. He extended the invitation through his secretary and at the last minute. But Diana didn't care; she was thrilled. She accepted and pretended to share his appreciation of Verdi. Charles later invited her to watch him play polo at Cowdray, to watch him hunt at Sandringham, to watch him race at Ludlow. Diana accepted—and watched adoringly. "Mostly," she told her mother, "I just enjoy being with him."

Diana joined Charles aboard the royal yacht, *Britannia,* to watch the races at Cowes, and a week later she accepted his invitation to join his small party for dinner at Buckingham Palace. She admitted feeling intimidated by such friends of his as Nicholas "Fatty" Soames, who were so much older, but she managed to ingratiate herself with them and fit in. They especially appreciated her youthful adoration of the Prince. "She was clearly determined and enthusiastic about him," recalled Patti Palmer-Tomkinson, the wife of one of Charles's closest friends, "and she very much wanted him." Years later Diana's biographer, Andrew Morton, would state it more bluntly. "During their bizarre courtship," he wrote, "she was his willing puppy who came to heel when he whistled."

Diana was not discovered by the press until the autumn of 1980, when she was sitting beside Charles on the bank of the river Dee, watching him fish. The high-powered binoculars of newspaper reporter James Whitaker and his photographer, Arthur Edwards, spotted her through the trees. When she saw them watching her, she slipped away discreetly. They tracked her down in London, and days later, "the wicked Mr. Whitaker," as she teasingly referred to the leader of the royal tabloid pack, introduced his readers to "Lady Di."

"She was pretty, but not staggeringly so," he recalled. "She had charm, but no magic. Yet, before my eyes, she performed a miracle and transformed herself into the most glamorous woman in the world, worshipped by the media and the masses."

The portly reporter, who wore silk handkerchiefs in the breast pocket of gold-buttoned blazers, became to Diana what the fairy godmother had been to Cinderella. Whitaker waved his magic wand of publicity and, in story after story, presented her as "the most suitable choice for our future Queen." He praised her "innocence," her "delightful charm," her "blessed modesty." He rhapsodized about her "abundant freshness" and her "regal carriage." His colleagues followed his lead in varying degrees.

Within two months the Earl's sweet daughter had captivated the kingdom that wanted nothing more for its bachelor Prince than a beautiful blond princess. Diana was perfect. More British than Charles, who was her sixteenth cousin through King James I, she was an aristocrat with five lines of descent from Charles II. "She's also related to practically every single person in the French aristocracy," said Harold Brooks-Baker, editor of *Debrett's,* the bible of bloodlines. "She's even related to Napoleon's brother and eight American presidents, including George Washington."

Most important, Lady Diana Spencer was a Protestant without a past. Her virginity validated her as the most worthy candidate to become Queen and beget an heir. Even Prince Philip approved. "She can breed height into the line," he said as if she were a brood mare.

The British press was as beguiled as the public and couldn't get enough of the young woman they glorified as "Shy Di." They put her picture on the front pages of newspapers and magazines, with her head tilted coyly to one side or her eyes demurely cast down. "She's 19 and a perfect English rose," gushed the *Sun*. In her frilly blouses, she was the epitome of schoolgirl innocence. "*DI*vine" raved the *Mirror*. Reporters dogged her on foot, chased her small red car through traffic, and climbed over rooftops to photograph her. They pursued her every day down the street, on the phone, to her job.

"Darling, how do you put up with the bloody creatures?" Charles asked.

"I love working with children, and I have learned to be very patient with them," said Diana. "I simply treat the press as though they were children."

She gently reprimanded photographers who became too familiar. "Hey, Di," hollered one. "Cheat [turn] to the left."

She smiled sweetly. "My name is Diana," she said evenly. She never stopped smiling.

Unshakably poised at first, she gave way to tears when a posse of press cars almost drove her off the road. On another occasion, contrite reporters left a note on the windshield of her car: "We didn't mean this to happen. Our full apologies." She agreed to pose only after a photographer frightened the children at her nursery school by crawling through the lavatory window with his clattering gear.

"You've got two minutes," she told him sternly. He fired off four flashes, startling two nursery school tots, who clung to her for protection. The photographs became the world's first glimpse and most lasting impression of the winsome beauty. Balancing one child on her hip and holding the hand of another, she did not realize the sun was shining through her gauzy skirt and revealing what Prince Charles appreciatively described as "a great pair of legs." The caption was "Lady Diana's Slip." British newspapers called on Charles to make the guileless girl England's future queen.

The *Sunday Times* said she was perfect: "serious but not boring; sweet but not *too* sweet; funny, not silly; sporty, not horsey; and sexy without being brassy."

"I'm told she's ideal," said the *Daily Mail*'s Nigel Dempster. "She has been pronounced physically sound to produce children."

One headline advised, "Charles: Don't *DI*ther." Another screamed, "To Di For."

The press expected the Prince to propose on his thirty-second birthday in November 1980, when Diana spent the weekend with him and the rest of the royal family at Sandringham. So reporters camped out at the estate, waiting for an announcement. They watched Diana arrive on Friday and leave on Sunday. After her departure, Charles strolled by them as he walked his dog.

"Why don't you all go home to your wives?" he said. "I know you were expecting some news Friday, and I know you were disappointed. But you will all be told soon enough."

When the Prince did not propose, he was chided by an editorial in the *Guardian:* "The Court Circular that issued from Buckingham Palace last night," wrote the newspaper, "was profoundly disappointing for a nation which, beset by economic and political dissent, had briefly believed that the sound of distant tumbrels was to be drowned by the peal of royal wedding bells."

The romance was almost derailed on November 16, 1980, when the *Sunday Mirror* ran a front-page story headlined "Royal Love Train." The newspaper cited an unidentified police officer, who claimed that Lady Diana had spent two secret nights with Prince Charles aboard the royal train. The train, with its elaborate kitchen, sitting room, and bedroom suite, was used only by members of the royal family for travel on official business. The story alleged that Charles was spending the night aboard the train after engagements in the Duchy of Cornwall and had summoned Diana, who was secretly escorted through a police barricade in the middle of the night. The caption accompanying a photo of the secluded train in Wiltshire: "Love in The Sidings."

"Absolutely scurrilous and totally false," thundered the Queen's press secretary. "Her Majesty takes grave exception." The Palace demanded a retraction and an apology, but the editor, Robert Edwards, stood firm. He said he had a sworn statement from an eyewitness who saw a woman board the train on two nights, spend several hours with the Prince in his private bedroom compartment, and leave clandestinely. But the editor made one mistake: he identified the blond as Diana.

"It was Camilla Parker Bowles," said John Barratt. "She had started up again with Charles after Mountbatten's death, when she called to offer her condolences. I know because I was wrapping things up at Broadlands then and [was] in regular contact with the Prince. He did not hide the fact that Mrs. Parker Bowles was back in his life. He said she was helping him sort things out. They spent hours together—riding, hunting, shooting. She acted as his hostess at dinner parties, and arranged luncheons and country weekends, and, naturally, controlled the guest lists. Charles called her his Girl Friday.

"She was perfect for him—horsey and accommodating. Charles is like all the Windsor men, and I include Lord Louis and Prince Philip. They like women who look like men. Long legs in riding breeches. They want their tarts to look like their horses. Mountbatten's women, Philip's women, Charles's women— all cut the same, beginning with Sasha [the Duchess of Abercorn], who is the Queen's cousin. She was Mountbatten's before he passed her on to Philip, which is what they do in that family. Lord Louis and Philip also shared that chinless wonder [Barratt names a woman married to one of Prince Philip's close friends] whom Charles also inherited. Camilla was different. She didn't come in under Mountbatten or Philip before she got to Charles. She was under him from the start."

The Prince of Wales continued seeing Camilla during the time her husband, Lieutenant Colonel Andrew Parker Bowles, was posted to Rhodesia (now Zimbabwe)* to help the emerging British colony make its transition to independence. She did not accompany him on his overseas assignment.

"Charles said he couldn't bear for her to leave, so she didn't," said a friend who boarded her horses with Camilla. "It was no hardship for her husband not having her with him because Andrew Parker Bowles was already involved with another woman."

Diana did not realize the complexities facing her. She did know that Camilla was a constant presence whenever she turned around, and she wondered how the older woman always knew so much about her relationship with Charles. But she didn't feel secure enough yet to question the Prince about his former lover. She confided her discomfort to her roommates and her sisters but said nothing to Charles. She felt slightly reassured by his anger over the royal train incident; he lashed out at the press and called them "bloody vultures." When the editor refused to apologize and retract the story, Charles

---

* In March 1980 *Private Eye* published an item about Andrew Parker Bowles on duty without his wife, who elected to stay in England: "Andrew, 39, is married to a former (?) Prince Charles fancy, Camilla Shand, and if I should find the royal Aston Martin Volante outside the Parker Bowles mansion while the gallant Colonel is on duty overseas, my duty will be clear." The next month the *Daily Mail* reported that Prince Charles was to preside over the Zimbabwe independence celebrations. His official escort was "old flame, Mrs. Camilla Parker Bowles." Noting that Andrew Parker Bowles would be in England, the report said: "Buckingham Palace officials have always been happy to see Charles in the company of happily married women because such sightings cannot give rise to rumour."

insisted the Palace issue a second denial.

He left for India days later on a trip that had been planned for months, and Diana accompanied him to the airport to say good-bye. As he nonchalantly skipped up the steps of the royal plane without looking back, she burst into tears.

Reporters followed Charles on his visit to the Taj Mahal and asked what he thought about the great monument to passion built by a Moghul emperor in memory of his wife. "A marvelous idea," said Charles, "to build something so wonderful to someone one loved so very much." An Indian reporter asked about the Prince's own prospects for a wife, and Charles left him breathless with his odd response. "I'm encouraged by the fact that if I were to become a Muslim," he said, "I could have lots of wives."

The British reporters glanced at one another uncomfortably, wondering if the Prince was joking. None quoted him verbatim. Even with the arrival of Australian Rupert Murdoch and his tabloid papers, Britain's reporters remained deferential to royalty. They softened their stories on the Queen and her heir by withholding newsworthy details and, in this case, ignoring the revealing quotation. Instead they wrote as Her Majesty's obedient servants. They reported that Charles said: "I can understand that love could make a man build the Taj Mahal for his wife. One day I would like to bring my own back here."

In England, reverberations from the royal

train story were still rattling Diana, who became hysterical when she read the *Sunday Times* report of the "tawdry" incident. "Whatever the public expects of her," wrote the newspaper on November 30, 1980, "the monarchy demands that her copybook be unblotted. Part of Lady Diana's suitability is held to be the fact that she is, in the Fleet Street euphemism, 'a girl with no past'—that is, with no previous lovers."

Up to this point, Diana had carried her own pedestal wherever she went. Every word written about her had been laudatory. Now she was scared and called her mother in tears. Frustrated and angry, Frances Shand Kydd fired off a letter to the *Times,* deploring the "malicious lies" and "invented stories" printed about her daughter. She demanded that reporters stop harassing Diana, and her letter prompted sixty members of Parliament to draft a motion "deploring the manner in which Lady Diana Spencer is being treated by the media." An editorial entitled "Nineteen and Under Siege" followed in the *Guardian,* stating that no teenager deserved to be put through such an ordeal.

Fearing that her mother might have overreacted, Diana quickly called James Whitaker at the *Daily Star* to disavow the letter. She said she did not want to alienate the press but needed to proclaim her innocence.

"Diana wanted nothing more than to become Charles's wife," recalled Whitaker. "Everyone wanted it, the Queen included. Diana called me to deny that she had been involved in the royal train incident. 'Please believe me,' she said. 'I've never been on that train. I have never even seen it.' I ran the story and quoted her as saying she'd been at home all evening, watching television with her flatmates."

Most people, with the possible exception of her stepmother, assumed that Diana was as pure as Portia. She never proclaimed her virginity—directly—but years later her biographer Andrew Morton did it for her. He claimed that even as a young girl she had a sense of destiny about her future marriage. "I knew I had to keep myself tidy for what lay ahead," she supposedly said. Her stepmother thought she knew differently. Raine suspected that Diana's virginity had vanished in 1978 when she was dating James Gilbey, a member of the wealthy Gilbey's gin family. Lady Spencer had overheard conversations between her seventeen-year-old stepdaughter and the playful London bachelor, who occasionally stood her up to take someone else out. Diana got back at him by making a secret midnight run to his apartment building. His car was parked in front, and she and her roommate doused it with flour and eggs.

Raine had watched disapprovingly as Diana continued to pick up Gilbey's dirty laundry each week, lovingly wash and iron his shirts, and deliver them on hangers to his apartment. During an earlier infatuation, she had done the same thing for Rory Scott, a lieutenant in the Scots Guards.

Concern over Diana's tarnished image in the press was shared by Raine's mother, Barbara Cartland, who had made millions because she understood the importance of the soft lie over the hard truth: one fuels a fantasy while the other breaks your heart. She accepted the unspoken agreement between royals and commoners: they pretend to be superior and we accept the pretense. So the eighty-year-old novelist wrapped herself in pink marabou feathers and summoned a reporter to her house to declare Diana's innocence. She conducted the interview from her bed surrounded by five poodles in rhinestone collars.

"Prince Charles has got to have a pure young gel," she said, "I don't think Diana has ever had a boyfriend. She's as pure as one of my heroines. This is marvelous. Quite perfect."

Raine knew she needed more than her dear mother's breathless proclamation. She consulted a lawyer because she also was concerned about rumors that nude photos of Diana might surface in the press. "She particularly feared *Private Eye*," recalled the lawyer. Raine had remembered Diana's giggling on the phone with girlfriends about pictures* that had been taken of her at a pool in Switzerland, where she had taken off her bikini. The lawyer reassured Raine that an injunction might be obtained before such photos could be published. He then advised her to turn

---

* The nude photos of Diana were offered for sale in 1993 by a German magazine but were withdrawn and given to her. "They have no journalistic relevance for us," said the editor, "and could only be used to satisfy voyeurism."

to someone within the aristocracy to publicly proclaim Diana's good name. So Raine contacted Lord Fermoy, who was Diana's uncle, and asked him to uphold the family honor. The nobleman, a manic-depressive who would commit suicide four years later, readily agreed to talk to the press.

"Diana, I can assure you, has never had a lover," he told a reporter. "Purity seems to be at a premium when it comes to discussing a possible royal bride for Prince Charles at the moment. And after one or two of his most recent girlfriends, I am not surprised. To my knowledge, Diana has never been involved in this way with anybody. This is good."

"The consensus," declared *Newsweek*, "virtue is intact." The press coverage of the royal romance heated up as zealous reporters followed the Prince of Wales everywhere, pestering him about his intentions. By January of 1981 the royal family felt as if they were under house arrest at Sandringham, where reporters and photographers gathered outside.

"It's like a goddamned death watch," Prince Philip said to his aide as he looked out the window.

The Queen complained that she couldn't go riding without being pursued by "a ragtag band of reporters."

"Her Majesty, if you'll excuse me, behaved like a fishwife one morning and told me to 'eff off,'" said James Whitaker, who recalled the incident at Sandringham more vividly than he reported it. "I simply quoted the Queen as saying, 'Go away. Can't you leave us alone?' But she was more explicit than that.

"I was camped out with two photographers when she came out of her stables on the royal steed. She drove there to avoid the press and then rode out of the stables on her horse, but we were close enough to get to her. There were three of us: Les Wilson and Jimmy Gray, both photographers, and myself. The Queen galloped toward us, looked directly at me, and hissed. 'Get away, you fu——.' I started moving before she could finish the sentence.

"'Ma'am,' I said, 'I'm just about to do exactly that. To get away.' I scampered off and yelled over my shoulder for the two photographers to carry on. One froze, and the other reared back. 'If you think I'm going to knock the fucking Queen off her own fucking road to take her fucking picture,' he said, 'you're fucking crazy.' He ran off, too. None of us was brave enough to pursue the story."

When reporters approached Prince Philip later in the day to say "Happy New Year," he was just as vulgar. "Bollocks," he snarled. Putting his head down, he barreled through the swarm of reporters and photographers, swearing at them as he passed.

A reporter for the *Sun* said a hunting party that included Philip and Prince Charles peppered her car with shotgun pellets. And a *Daily Mirror* photographer was warned away from a public road near the family estate by sixteen-year-old Prince Edward. "I wouldn't stand there," the Prince said. "You could get shot."

Charles was incensed at being hounded, and when he encountered reporters, he struggled to be cordial. "May I take this opportunity to wish you all a very happy new year," he said through clenched teeth, "and your editors a particularly nasty one."

Diana arrived a few days later, prompting a commotion among photographers, who blocked the entrances to Sandringham, trying to get pictures. Exasperated, the Queen admonished her son, "The idea of this romance going on for another year is intolerable for all concerned." Prince Philip was more explicit. He told his indecisive son that he had to make up his mind one way or the other before he ruined Diana's reputation.

Always the more involved parent, Philip monitored the women Charles dated. He disapproved of his son's attraction to black women, and he ignored Charles's fling with a *Penthouse* centerfold. He knew about the affair with Camilla Parker Bowles and warned Charles that such an illicit relationship could endanger the monarchy. Pushing him toward marriage, Philip was concerned about the woman Charles would marry because that woman, whoever she might be, represented the future of the Firm. Philip had invested his life in the monarchy and intended to protect his investment. After Charles turned thirty,* his

* No other Prince of Wales since Charles II, three hundred years earlier, took so long to make up his mind about getting married. Only two others— James Stuart and Henry V from even earlier times—were still unmarried at the age of thirty.

father became especially vigilant and did not hesitate to say who was suitable, who was not. When Charles was dating Sabrina Guinness, from the banking side of the brewery family, he invited her to a house party in the country with friends of the royal family. The invitation was leaked to the press, and it triggered another spate of speculative stories about the new woman in Charles's life. "Is He in Love Again?" asked one headline. It so infuriated Philip that he called the hosts and instructed them to disinvite the young woman. To ensure that they did, he mentioned that he would be arriving at five P.M. that weekend. Mortified, the friends did as they were ordered and told Miss Guinness that she was "welcome to leave" by a certain time "to avoid confusion" with Prince Philip's visit.

Philip arrived early and met the young woman as she was leaving. He told her to join him in the drawing room. There were no break-the-ice pleasantries when she walked in and not so much as a perfunctory hello. As exacting as a guillotine, Philip told her to get out of his son's life. He said he never wanted to see her name linked with Prince Charles again. Philip tidied up the landscape by telling her to get out of the house. She fled in tears.

Philip spoke to his son in the same gruff manner about marrying Diana Spencer. He didn't tell Charles to marry her, simply to make up his mind. "Get on with it, Charles," he said.

"The difference between father and son,"

explained one of the Queen's secretaries, "is that Charles dithers, and Philip decapitates."

Charles spent the next four weeks agonizing over whether to marry Diana. He recorded his "confused and anxious state of mind" in his diary, and he consulted his mistress, Camilla Parker Bowles. She said she approved and described Diana to friends as "a mouse." In a letter to a friend, Charles wrote: "It is just a matter of taking an unusual plunge into some rather unknown circumstances that inevitably disturbs me, but I expect it will be the right thing in the end....It all seems so ridiculous because I do very much want to do the right thing for this Country and for my family—but I'm terrified sometimes of making a promise and then perhaps living to regret it." Years later he blamed his father for forcing him into a marriage that he was reluctant to embrace.

Yet despite his doubts, he proposed on February 6, 1981, in his third-floor quarters at Buckingham Palace over dinner for two. Diana accepted eagerly, and he apologized for not having a ring to give her. A few days later he contacted Garrard's, the Crown jewelers, who arrived with several black velvet trays filled with rings. Diana chose a six-carat sapphire surrounded by eighteen diamonds. Price: $50,000. "The Queen's eyes popped when I picked out the largest one," she said, giggling, "but I love it."

The engagement of the Prince of Wales to Lady Diana Spencer was officially announced on February 24, 1981. "I couldn't have married anyone the British people wouldn't have liked," said Charles. Most of the country joined the royal family in rejoicing. But Diana's mother, Frances Shand Kydd, was afraid for her daughter.

"I cried for six weeks after that," she admitted to a relative. "I had a terrible feeling about what was going to happen to Diana when she married into that family."

THIRTEEN

The prize for best performance in a supporting role should go to Lady Diana Spencer's gown—bold, black, and strapless.

When Diana wore it—barely—to London's Goldsmith Hall in 1981, she—and the gown—drew gasps. It was her first public appearance with Prince Charles since they'd become engaged, and the press pounced on them like condors on carrion. Flashbulbs popped and hydra-headed microphones closed in.

As the couple swept into the Royal Opera benefit, the BBC commentator stuttered as he tried to describe the eye-popping dress. He stumbled on the word "décolletage" and struggled not to look at Diana's cleavage. Spilling out of her low-cut gown, she smiled shyly. Off-camera, the BBC man whispered, "Now there's a bosom built to burp a nation." An American reporter whistled softly and quoted Raymond Chandler in *Farewell, My*

Lovely: "It was a blonde. A blonde to make a bishop kick a hole in a stained-glass window."

Diana had carefully selected her dress for the evening. The black taffeta confection, which sold for $1,000, was given to her by the designers David and Elizabeth Emanuel, who were making her wedding dress. She told them she needed to look "drop dead gorgeous" because she was meeting her movie star idol, Grace Kelly, at the benefit and dining with her later at Buckingham Palace. Diana did not realize that Her Serene Highness had probably been invited to the Palace only because she was performing for charity.

The Queen of England still considered the Princess of Monaco a bit of Hollywood fluff, who had married a poseur from a tiny principality. Her Majesty was not moved by the enthusiasm of her husband, Prince Philip, for the beautiful blond American, who also had been a favorite of Lord Mountbatten's. When Grace Kelly married Prince Rainier in 1956, the Queen declined to attend their wedding. "Too many film stars," she had said. As far as she was concerned, the Rainiers did not count as royalty, although Prince Rainier had reigned longer* than any crowned head in Europe.

"Her Majesty can be stuffy about that sort of thing," admitted one of her ladies-in-waiting. "Too many jewels, fur coats, and fast cars.

---

* By 1996 only Prince Rainier of Monaco and King Bhumibol Adulyadej of Thailand had reigned longer than Queen Elizabeth II.

Jet-setters, you know. Prince Philip, on the other hand, does not feel that way, particularly if the wife is pretty."

Diana, too, was fascinated by the former film star and sat spellbound through her poetry reading at the benefit. After the hour-long recital, Diana walked into the press reception rubbing her side. Someone asked if she had hurt her back.

"No, not at all," she said brightly. "It's just that I've pins and needles in my bottom from sitting still so long."

Her spontaneity charmed everyone. "She was enchanting then," said British journalist Victoria Mather. "So fresh and beguiling. At that reception, she spilled a little red wine on her gloves, held up the stain for us to see, and laughed. 'Oops,' she said, 'Guess I'll have to nip round to Sketchley's [a London cleaner].'"

Seconds later Diana showed off her engagement ring and offered to let an admirer try it on. "I'll have to have it back, though," she quipped. "Otherwise they won't know who I am."

The woman gazed at the ring on her finger. "Oh," she exclaimed. "It's beautiful. I've never seen such a large stone."

"I know," said Diana. "The other day I even scratched my nose with it. It's so big— the ring, that is."

Someone asked what it was like now that she had moved from Clarence House to Buckingham Palace. "Not bad," she chirped. "But too many formal dinners. Yuck."

A young man stepped forward. "May I kiss the hand of my future Queen?" he asked.

Diana smiled coyly and tilted her head. "Yes, you may," she said, extending her hand.

The young man kissed her wrist lightly and everyone clapped. He blushed with pleasure.

"You'll never live this down," Diana said, teasing him.

Delighted reporters crowded around her, and the cameramen bore in, jostling guests and pushing them to the edge of the room. Prince Charles headed off to greet someone, expecting the media to follow him, but they were taken with Diana. Feeling self-conscious about the disturbance she was causing, she excused herself and escaped to the powder room with Grace Kelly. The Princess-to-be confided her distress over the unrelenting press coverage and asked Her Serene Highness how *she* coped with it. The movie star who became a princess comforted the teenager, who would become royalty's movie star. Princess Grace, accustomed to unwelcome media attention, told Diana to treat it like the weather. "It'll get worse," she said with a warm smile.

And it did—the very next day. The tabloids were full of breathless reviews of Diana and her gown, accompanied by revealing photographs and suggestive headlines. "Lady Di Takes the Plunge," blared the front page of the *Daily Mirror*. "Di the Daring," exclaimed the *Sun*. "Shy Di Shocks," the *Daily Express* reported. Even establishment newspapers noted the dress that seemed so startling for the modest kindergarten teacher. "Shy Di R.I.P.," read the photo caption in the *Times*.

Diana was puzzled. "I don't know why everyone is making such a fuss," she said to Prince Charles's valet. "It's the sort of dress I would have worn anyway."

The valet lowered his eyes. "Well, it certainly caught everyone's attention," he said disapprovingly. He was fired a month after the wedding.

The *Daily Express* reporter praised Diana's decision to go strapless. "Her Gone-With-the-Wind dress...takes courage, and a lot more, to uphold it," wrote Jean Rook. "All Di must learn to watch, which the TV cameras noticed, is the ounce or two of puppy fat which boned bodices tuck under a girl's arms."

Diana cringed as she read the reviews of her "bounteous figure" and "blooming physique." She shrieked when she saw the television coverage.

"I look hideously fat," she wailed. "Fat as a cow. I can't stand it."

Charles, who never forgot the embarrassment of being called "Fatty" by his classmates, kidded her. Fanatic about staying slim, he exercised like a fiend and ate like a monk. On tours he carried snack bags filled with wheat germ, linseed, and prunes. His dinners at home consisted of two strips of dried fish or a yolk-free mushroom omelet. That was followed by green salad and a drink of lemon squash and Epsom salts, which Diana pronounced "revolting." Charles said he needed the concoction "to keep regular." He twitted her about her passion for sweets and called her "Plumpkin." As she agonized over her newspaper photographs, he teased her again. "No more puddings for you," he said. He had tossed off the remark casually, not realizing that she would plunge into bulimia. But after seeing herself on television, Diana was so distraught that she soon began bingeing and purging.

The eating disorder was seeded in the wreckage of her parent's marriage, which had thrown her oldest sister, Jane, into anorexia. As a young woman, Jane had starved herself to the frightening weight of a child, until her family forced her to seek help. Diana, too, reacted to her insecurities by secretly starving herself. But then she caved in to her hunger cravings and ate several bowls of cereal with sugar and rich Guernsey cream. She devoured bags of soft jelly candies, followed by vanilla cookies lathered with white frosting, which she quickly threw up.

She had moved into Buckingham Palace a few months before the wedding so she could learn the royal routine, and when Charles was traveling, she ate alone. Most of her meals were served in her room. At first she left her trays untouched, which concerned the chef, who felt he was not pleasing her. After he began asking, she flushed the food down the toilet.

"She nicked so many boxes of Kellogg's Frosties from the pantry," said royal reporter

Ross Benson, "that one of the footmen was accused of stealing and nearly lost his job. Diana stepped forward then and admitted she was to blame."

At first no one believed her. The staff was not ready to accept the image of their future Queen as a glutton who regularly gorged and vomited. "The picture of Lady Diana wrapped around the porcelain chariot—no, no, no," said a member of the royal household with a shudder. "That was inconceivable to us." The staff refused to see any dark shadows beneath the sunny exterior. "You've no idea how sweet she seemed—on the surface," said one of the Palace maids. "The few flashes of temper we saw we put to wedding jitters and worked harder to be of help." The staff did not believe that Diana was the culprit consuming the missing food. Even when she admitted it, they thought she was protecting a footman previously suspected of petty theft. They did not accept what was happening until the upstairs maids, who cleaned Diana's suite, reported evidence of her throwing up in the bathroom. Even then most of the staff did not accept it.

As Diana began losing weight, she increased the pernicious cycle of bingeing and purging until she was going through it five times a day. Within three months she'd lost twenty pounds. Charles was unaware of the problem because he was not with her all day every day.

For five weeks during the spring of 1981, he traveled on previously scheduled visits;

he toured the United States, New Zealand, and Australia, where he explored the possibility of a real job. The Queen and Prince Philip had been concerned for some time about the way Charles flitted from one cause to the next without direction. "He never sticks to anything," complained Philip, who once blamed his wife for being an inattentive mother. At a private dinner party attended by an American, Philip jerked his head toward the Queen and referred to Charles as "*your* son." Both parents despaired whenever he made impassioned statements about the jobless, the homeless, or the penniless. The Duke of Edinburgh, especially, had no patience with his son's concerns for the downtrodden and disadvantaged. "He wrings his hands like an old woman," said Philip after one of Charles's speeches. "Why can't he leave the weltschmerzen to the vicars?" Philip warned Charles not to become embroiled in politics and not to comment on "sacred cows" like the Church of England and the National Health Service. He said the one institution that could be insulted was the press—"I've relished doing it myself," Philip said—but nothing else. Charles ignored his father's advice. As Prince of Wales, he resented being cast as a pitchman for Britain. He wanted to be taken more seriously than a salesman who dressed up in gold braid and waved. "I'm not good at simply being a performing monkey," he said. His father disagreed. He thought Charles was perfect in the part.

Having enjoyed Australia as an exchange student, Charles was open to his mother's idea for a job there after his wedding. He and Diana would move to Canberra, the capital, and Charles would become governor-general. The position paid an annual salary larger than the premier's, but it did not carry great powers, other than commander in chief of the armed forces. Under the Australian constitution, it would enable him to summon and dissolve Parliament and carry the kind of responsibility that the Queen felt her son needed. She had discussed the appointment with her Prime Minister, Margaret Thatcher, who approached the Foreign Office in 1980; she reported back that Charles had permission to "informally explore the possibility" during his next Australian tour. But, on that trip, Charles decided if the position were to be offered, he would have to refuse because the Australian Prime Minister was too dour.

"The difficulty is that he does not have any humor," Charles told Diana in a phone call from Australia that was secretly taped. "He is terribly serious. I made a terrific effort to be amusing, but he just stared at me all the time."

That was just one of the five phone calls between Charles and his fiancée, and Charles and his mother, that had been recorded. The tapes, made by anti-British republicans within the Australian telephone company, were given to a freelance British reporter, who tried to sell them in England. Afraid of further straining relations with Australia, which had been threatening to break away from the Commonwealth, the Queen's courtiers moved swiftly. They called the Queen's lawyers, who claimed the transcripts were not authentic.* The Queen's courts agreed and issued an injunction to prevent publication of the transcripts in England. The Queen's lawyers then sought an injunction in West Germany, but they were too late: extracts had appeared in the magazine *Die Aktuelle* and were translated from German to English and published in the *Irish Independent*.

In one of the purported conversations, Diana mentioned her wedding preparations and complained about the behavior of her stepmother, Raine, who had appeared on British television. Standing alongside her beaming husband, Countess Spencer did all the talking. The Earl Spencer, who never completely recovered from his stroke, smiled benignly.

"She's got Daddy autographing photos and selling them in the gift shop," said Diana. "It's so embarrassing." She added that her stepmother was conducting paid tours. Priced at $2.50, the fee included tea with "the ghastly pink lady," as Diana now referred to Barbara Cartland. "The wedding," she said, "will be a catastrophe if Raine continues."

"Don't worry too much about that," Charles told her. "Edward [Adeane] can organize it

---

* Writing in the *Daily Telegraph* in 1993, Alastair Forbes challenged the royal denial and said the authenticity of the taped conversations had been "proved to me beyond doubt, despite the Palace's glib denial."

when we come back. You will see the Queen will be in a position to give the necessary instructions so that objections will not be possible."

"Yes, I know," said Diana. "But can I not have any say about my own wedding?"

"Naturally, but let your mother advise you."

"I will, I promise," said Diana. "I really don't want to complain, Charles, really not. I'm going to talk through everything tomorrow with Mummy. She has a very good feeling for things like this. She's very sensible."

The *Spectator* had already put out the call for Diana's mother to take over. Following Raine's television interview, the conservative magazine pleaded: "Come home, Mrs. Shand Kydd, your country needs you." In an editorial railing against the participation of Raine Spencer and Barbara Cartland in the royal wedding, Alexander Chancellor wrote: "If a special Act of Parliament is necessary, so be it. For it would be more than a little unfair on everybody if these two absurdly theatrical ladies were permitted to turn a moving national celebration into a pantomime."

Diana could do nothing about keeping her stepmother away from the wedding, but she was adamant about her stepgrandmother. "She struck Barbara Cartland from the guest list," said a former aide to Prince Charles, who tried to intercede. Six months later the aide was fired.

"It was so cruel to do that to Barbara," he said. "She was distraught, really deeply hurt, but there was nothing we could do. Diana had insisted her stepgrandmother not be allowed near St. Paul's Cathedral, and the Queen did not object. Barbara was so humiliated she wanted to go abroad for the wedding day, but her sons said that it would make it look as though she had been banished."

To save face, Barbara Cartland gave a party for the volunteers of the St. John's Ambulance Brigade. Forgoing her usual costume of ostrich feathers, she wore the tailored brown uniform of the Order of St. John and appeared on international television in a feature about the organization. She asserted that the St. John volunteers were devoted to providing "a Christian answer to the problems of a troubled and materialistic world."

By then even the spiritual participants were cashing in on the royal wedding. The Archbishop of Canterbury had divulged to the media details of a private conversation he had had with Charles and Diana.* And the three choirs of St. Paul's Cathedral had collected $1,200 each for 250 singers. By comparison, Barbara Cartland seemed positively benign.

During one of her conversations with Charles in Australia, Diana said she felt overwhelmed by having to learn so much in such a short time.

---

* Years later, after his retirement, the former Archbishop confided to his biographer that the Prince of Wales was severely depressed before his marriage because he was in love with another woman. He also described Diana as a "schemer."

"I'm so excited that I can't concentrate properly," she said. "I miss you very much."

"I miss you, too," he said, adding that he was late for a party but his hosts would have to wait. "I've done my duty all day and now I'm talking to my fiancée, whom I love very much." He told her about the Di look-alikes who had greeted him at the airport in Australia. "Not as good as the real thing," he said. She giggled. He complained about the press.

"During the whole trip, this guy had nothing better to do than to try to take photographs of the bald patch on my head."

Diana laughed. "I didn't know you had a bald patch."

"It's too stupid. I'm doing all of these things and the only thing they want are these ridiculous details."

"I think it's very funny."

"Yes. As children, we were all very amused at the way my father tried to hide his baldness."

"Oh, I really hope that yours is not as big as his," she said. "In any event, you seem to have much more fun than I do."

This was as close as Diana came to complaining about her royal tutelage. She pretended to Charles that she adored the Queen Mother but told friends she was "virtually ignored" for the few days she stayed with her in Clarence House. After Diana was moved into Buckingham Palace, she was given a small office near Oliver Everett, Charles's assistant private secretary. Everett was amused the first time she bounced into his office wearing headphones and workout tights. He soon learned that her weekly dance class took precedence over every other activity and that she loved rock and roll. "I actually wanted to be a dancer," she said, "but I overshot the height by a long way." She watched television day and night and was devoted to soap operas. The courtier began his classes in how to be a princess by giving Diana instructions on her royal engagements, which would average 170 a year and include Ascot, Trooping the Color, Badminton Horse Trials, Opening of Parliament, Chelsea Flower Show, Wimbledon, Garden Parties, Cowes Regatta, Hospital benefits, charities, and anything for the military.

The Queen's lady-in-waiting, Susan Hussey, helped Everett guide the Princess-to-be through the maze of royal rules: wear hats in public and bright colors to stand out; wave from the elbow, not the wrist; never use a public lavatory. "The worst thing about being a princess," said Diana years later, "is having to pee."

Everett hit his first snag when he recommended a course of study and gave Diana several history books to read about her future role as Princess of Wales. In the throes of bulimia, and lonely for Charles, she balked. When the equerry left the room, she told a friend that she threw the books on the floor. "If he thinks I'm reading these," she said, "he's got another think coming."

Weak from losing weight, she frequently cracked under the strain of preparing for one of the biggest ceremonies in British history. "I think I am realizing now what it all means," she told a reporter a few weeks before the wedding, "and it's making me more and more scared." She broke into tears in front of photographers at a polo match and had to be whisked away by her mother. "It was a bit much for her," Prince Charles explained to the press. Privately he told friends he was worried. "I wonder if she is going to be able to cope with the pressures."

An avid tennis player, Diana attended the finals at Wimbledon but left the royal box before U.S. tennis star John McEnroe won. He had objected to thirteen calls, shouted obscenities, and cursed the umpire. "I always get robbed because of the fucking umpires in this country," he snarled.

"The wedding's off now," said one television commentator, watching the abrupt exit. "Lady Di's ears are no longer virgin."

In the tea room below, Diana met the Wimbledon women's champion, Chris Evert, who asked why Prince Charles was not with her.

"He can never sit still," said Diana. "He is like a great big baby. But one day I hope to calm him down enough to enjoy it."

Diana admitted to the tennis star that she was nervous about getting married. "I assured her that marriage was great, and she had nothing to be concerned about," said Evert, then married to the British tennis star John Lloyd, whom she later divorced. "I told her to relax and think about other things."

The men who worked for Prince Charles also tried to be reassuring and help Diana ease into her future responsibilities. They showed her the daily and monthly events calendar and explained the tour schedule, which was planned six months in advance. Her only concern was the Prince's relationships with other women. His staff did not know how to deal with her persistent and personal questions. "I asked Charles if he was still in love with Camilla Parker Bowles," Diana said to Francis Cornish, "and he didn't give me a clear answer. What am I to do?" His assistant personal secretary lowered his eyes and changed the subject.

A few days later Michael Colborne, who was Charles's personal assistant, faced more uncomfortable queries. On his desk Diana had found a bracelet Colborne had ordered for Charles as a farewell present for his mistress. The gold bracelet with a lapis lazuli stone was engraved with the initials *G.F.* [Girl Friday]. Diana pressed Colborne about the gift and asked to know whom it was for. "I know it's for Camilla," she said. "So why won't you admit it? What does it mean? Why is Charles doing this?" Reluctantly Colborne acknowledged that he had ordered the present, but he refused to answer any more questions. He, too, lost his job shortly after the wedding.

Diana confronted Charles, who admitted that the bracelet from Asprey's was for Camilla Parker Bowles. He said he intended to give her the present in person to say good-bye. He maintained that the farewell gift would put a full stop to their affair. Diana didn't believe him. They quarreled, and she ran out of his office in tears. She later confided to her sisters that she didn't want to marry a man who was still in love with his mistress. "It's bad luck, Duch," said her sister Sarah, using the family nickname for Diana. "Your face is on the tea towels, so you're too late to chicken out now." For weeks feminists had been wearing buttons that warned, "Don't Do It, Di!"

The next day Diana retaliated by striking Camilla's name from the guest list for the wedding breakfast. She also crossed off the name of Lady Dale "Kanga" Tryon. She could not keep them from the wedding, but she insisted they be barred from the breakfast. Charles, who had grown up watching his father shuffle mistresses like a deck of cards, decided not to press the issue with his edgy fiancée. He told his private secretary that he didn't understand Diana's sudden moods and sulks, and her crying jags unnerved him. He also said he was alarmed by what one of his equerries had told him about her sitting hunched in a chair for hours with her head on her knees, absolutely inconsolable. Charles said he found such behavior to be irrational and unsettling. His private secretary dismissed Diana's behavior as wedding nerves.

Charles, never a decisive man, now reevaluated his decision to marry Diana. He visited his sister at Gatcombe Park and confided his doubts. Princess Anne, who was a month from giving birth to her second child, was in no mood for her brother's soul-searching whines. Airily she dismissed him as gumless. "Charles," she said, "you've got to play the hand you're dealt." She repeated Queen Victoria's advice to her daughter on how to survive the act of love: "Just close your eyes and think of England."

Still pondering his decision, the Prince visited a former lover, Zoe Sallis, in London. Her Ebury Street apartment was a few yards from the police station, where patrolmen watched Charles arrive and depart. He tried to disguise himself by wearing a gray fedora hat, which he pulled over his forehead. Several policemen, watching from a window, laughed at the royal camouflage. One said, "He looks like a bloke with big ears in a bonnet."

"Zoe told me later that Prince Charles had confided in her his misery and fear of marrying Diana," said *Time*'s Roland Flamini, "but he felt he had a duty to go through with it."

Resigned to prudence over passion, Charles visited Broadlands, where he planned to spend the first part of his honeymoon. "Five days before the royal wedding," said John Barratt, shaking his head, "Charles told myself and Lord Romsey [Mountbatten's grandson] that Camilla was the only woman he had ever loved. He told us, 'I could never feel the same way about Diana as I do about Camilla.' Lord Romsey simply assured him that his feelings would, most likely, change."

Although the bride was bulimic and the

bridegroom a bounder, they looked like an ideal couple. The public had been entranced by their romance: the Prince had *finally* found his Princess, and after their wedding on July 29, 1981, they would live happily ever after. Abracadabra, and bippitty boppetty boo. Most Britons needed to believe in this fairy tale to distract themselves from the awful reality of inner-city riots, IRA bombings, and widespread unemployment.

The Queen understood the spell a royal wedding could cast on an impoverished country. Despite more than three million people unemployed, Her Majesty did not hesitate to spend taxpayers' money. She felt any expense for ceremony (engraved invitations alone cost $10,000) was a hedge against hopelessness. Much as she disliked the whiff of show business, and the comparisons between royalty and celebrity, she staged an extravaganza worthy of Hollywood, complete with drums, trumpets, and coaches. Her production combined the romance of *High Society* with the magic of *Fantasia*. She had better costumes and more horses than *Ben-Hur*. The royal wedding she produced in 1981 gave the British monarchy its biggest ratings to date and British tourism its greatest revenues. The Queen knew that her crown and country depended on such moments of pageantry. "This is what we do best," said her Lord Chamberlain.

The site was St. Paul's Cathedral because it could accommodate more people than

Westminster Abbey. "I'm glad it's there," said Diana. "It would be too painful for me to marry Charles where my parents were joined for life." The wedding hymn she chose emphasized "the love that asks no questions, the love that pays the price, and lays upon the altar the final sacrifice."

The Queen sent 2,500 invitations* to friends, family, and heads of state, plus the crowned heads of Europe. King Juan Carlos of Spain declined his invitation when he learned the newlyweds would board the royal yacht at Gibraltar during their honeymoon. Spain had long disputed British occupancy of the little colony on the tip of the Iberian peninsula, and the King said Britain's decision to have Charles and Diana join the *Britannia* there was a diplomatic blunder. Face-to-face, Prince Philip told Juan Carlos he was an idiot. "We're fed up with the story of Gibraltar," Philip said, "and it is very expensive at that."

The President of the United States also declined the Queen's invitation, but only because his White House staff insisted. They told Ronald Reagan that his first foreign trip as President should not be to a glittering spectacle with British royalty. People might get the wrong impression. So his wife went without him. "I'm just crazy about Prince Charles,"

---

* The bride was allowed to invite one hundred people and her parents fifty. The bridegroom was allotted three hundred invitations, which he distributed to his beloved nanny, Mabel Anderson; former girlfriends like Sabrina Guinness and Susan George; and, of course, his mistress, Camilla Parker Bowles, and her husband, Andrew Parker Bowles.

said Nancy Reagan, who arrived with twenty-six suitcases, eleven hatboxes, seventeen Secret Service men, and one borrowed pair of diamond earrings worth $880,000.

The U.S. networks also invaded London, bidding up the price of window space along the parade route. The Palace press office issued regular bulletins about the ceremony to be telecast to 750 million people. Journalists, untutored in titles, learned that Lady Diana Spencer soon would outrank all other women in the realm, except the Queen and the Queen Mother. As an earl's daughter, she was below thirty-eight categories of British women who had titles superior to her own. But upon her marriage, she soared to the top of the social heap. The ancient title of Princess of Wales entitled her to deep curtsies from all other female royals, including her sister-in-law, the Princess Anne, and her husband's aunt, the Princess Margaret.

"Most definitely, that's the protocol," explained Princess Margaret's butler, "but not the reality. Never in your life would you see Princess Margaret drop a curtsy to anyone but Her Majesty or her mother. After all, Margaret was born royal; Diana was only marrying royalty. There's a big difference. And as for Princess Anne, well, as her father once said, 'If it doesn't fart or eat hay, she isn't interested.'"

The Palace press office announced the formal style for Lady Diana Spencer. "Following the wedding, she will be known as Diana, the Princess of Wales," said an aide. "She's not Princess Diana because she was not born a princess, and she's not the Princess Diana because only children of the sovereign are entitled to 'the' before their title." Americans, who did not understand titles or their subtleties, called her Princess Di.

In *Time,* British literary critic Malcolm Muggeridge sounded skeptical about the century's grandest nuptials: "Only fortunetellers, Marxists and Jehovah's Witnesses will venture to prognosticate whether Prince Charles and Lady Diana will actually one day mount the throne as King and Queen of England. In the course of fifty years of knockabout journalism, I have seen too many upheavals of one sort and another to feel any certainty about anything or anyone....Popularity, however seemingly strong and widespread, can evaporate in an afternoon, and institutions that have lasted for centuries disappear overnight. So I can but conclude by simply saying, 'God bless the Prince and Princess of Wales.'" Within fifteen years the critic looked like a visionary.

The night before the wedding, the royal family gathered on the balcony of Buckingham Palace for the largest display of fireworks since World War II's Blitz. British police estimated 175,000 people camped on the sidewalks around St. Paul's Cathedral to watch the procession of horse-drawn coaches. Crowds started forming the day before as aristocrats arrived at the Palace for the Queen's ball.

"That evening had a Waterloo feeling to it," said one titled British woman. "You could almost smell the formaldehyde from the mothballs. That was the last time I put on my tiara. It was gloriously dotty. We walked down the Mall with our diamonds and our gowns swirling and headed for an enormously grand occasion that everyone wished to be attending, except for those of us who had to go."

After the ball, Diana spent the night in Clarence House. Charles spent the night in the arms of his mistress. Camilla Parker Bowles later confided to her brother-in-law that she had slept with the Prince in his suite at the Palace. "She was cozy in the knowledge she had his heart when he married Diana," said Richard Parker Bowles.

The next day, as she recited her vows, the nervous bride transposed the order of her bridegroom's first two names: Charles Philip Arthur George became Philip Charles Arthur George. But even in error, she charmed. "Well," she said later, "with four names it's quite something to get organized." When the bridegroom pledged to share all his worldly goods, he, too, was nervous. He forgot to include the word "worldly." A prophetic omission, considering what he parted with fifteen years later.

The Princess of Wales was not resigned to giving up her husband to his mistress. Diana was determined to cement her marriage by getting pregnant. She packed accordingly for her honeymoon, taking a green bikini bathing suit that Charles liked, six satin lace teddys, and several sheer nightgowns. He took his fishing tackle. He also packed one book by Arthur Koestler on parapsychology and five scholarly books by Laurens Van der Post, which he said he wanted to share with his bride. She took two paperbacks by Danielle Steel, although she knew Charles disapproved. "He doesn't like me reading trash novels," she said. "But I love them."

Years later she read a psychological profile about the Unabomber, whose crimes were attributed to his being a loner. A mathematical genius at the age of ten, he took a book on vacation entitled *Romping through Mathematics from Addition to Calculus*. Diana said, "Sounds like Charles on his honeymoon."

Aboard the royal yacht, *Britannia,* the Princess charmed the crew of 256 navy men, especially the galley staff, whom she pestered for extra desserts. Near the royal stateroom, attendants wore rubber-soled slippers so as not to make any noise that might disturb the royal couple. "We were told to fade into the background," said seaman Philip Benjamin. "We were to act like air. Unless spoken to, we said nothing, just looked straight ahead. Bit difficult at times to look straight ahead with the Princess of Wales dashing about in her nightgowns.

"I remember her coming out of the royal suite one afternoon in a filmy white negligee with a pink satin bow at the bosom, which was untied and open. She was trying to lure the Prince away from his books.

"'Chulls,' she said in a sexy singsong, 'come here and do your duty.' He was reading in a deck chair and she wanted him to go inside and produce an heir. I was standing guard a few feet away and looked straight ahead. She giggled when she realized I had heard her, but she was unembarrassed. She just kept teasing Charles to go to bed with her. She teased him a lot. I never saw the awful moods that His Royal Highness complained about later."

Prince Charles told his authorized biographer, Jonathan Dimbleby, that he learned on the honeymoon his young wife was suffering from bulimia. Charles said it triggered sudden mood shifts, leaving Diana cheerful one minute and morose the next. After two weeks aboard the yacht, the couple joined the royal family at Balmoral. At times Diana felt overwhelmed by the heavy presence of her in-laws and excused herself from meals to throw up. Charles became so concerned about her eating disorder that he contacted Laurens Van der Post and implored him to help. The older man, whom Diana trusted, talked gently with her at each session, but he quickly realized that she needed more professional help than he could provide. He gave Charles the name of a psychiatrist, who made discreet visits to counsel the couple. The therapist met them in their suite at Balmoral at eleven A.M. for an hour every day. He spent thirty minutes with them together and then thirty minutes alone with Diana, trying to address her anxieties. Charles said he worried about her emotional state. "She's so high-strung," he said. He wondered whether or not his wife was suffering from manic-depression. "What else can explain the moods—vivacious charm in the morning and verbal assaults in the evening?" The therapist recommended tranquilizers. After the honeymoon, Diana continued psychotherapy in London but resisted taking sedatives. For eleven more years her bulimia haunted her.

"It's an insidious disease from which to recover," she said years later. "You inflict it upon yourself because your self-esteem is at a low ebb, and you don't think you're worthy or valuable. You fill your stomach up four or five times a day and it gives you a feeling of comfort. It's like having a pair of arms around you, but it's temporary. Then you're disgusted at the bloatedness of your stomach, and you bring it all up again....It's a repetitive pattern and very destructive."

Outside Balmoral, the international press had gathered, staking out the entrances and clamoring for photographs. Charles was incensed, saying they had enough photos from following the *Britannia* for two weeks with their snoopy long lenses. He was even annoyed at Patrick Lichfield, the Queen's cousin, for having taken a candid shot of the royal wedding party that he sold around the world. "He never even submitted the pictures to the Queen," Charles grumbled. Lichfield's unstaged photo showed the Prince and Princess of

Wales and their bridal attendants sitting on the Palace steps after the wedding, collapsed in laughter. Charles thought the photo taken in a relaxed moment made them look undignified. Having given Lichfield exclusive access to photograph the wedding, Charles felt used. He had not expected him to sell the photos without approval. "I can't believe Lord Lichfield could have let us down so badly," Charles said. Lichfield later made copies of the famous photograph and distributed them instead of business cards.

"He gave me one," said the Pulitzer Prize-winning photographer David Hume Kennerly. "He's an arrogant guy, but the picture of Charles and Diana is a great moment."

Charles was in no mood to placate the press, but by the fourth day of the Balmoral segment of the honeymoon, he had no choice. The royal family felt besieged, so the Queen dispatched her press secretary to negotiate a settlement: an interview with the newlyweds, plus photographs, in exchange for privacy. The deal was cut, and Charles, who groused, was required to cooperate.

The Prince of Wales was Colonel in Chief of the Gordons in Scotland, so for the interview he dressed in full tartan garb—knee-high socks, plaid kilt, and leather sporran (a pouch worn in front of the kilt). He appeared at the appointed hour to meet the newspeople, holding his wife's hand.

"Where do you want us to perform?" he asked.

"Right here is fine, Your Royal Highness," said a reporter.

Charles recognized him. "I hope you had a nice time going round the Mediterranean."

"Bit expensive," said the reporter.

"Good," said Charles with a tight grin.

The cameras whirred and clicked as the churlish Prince and his charming Princess chatted with the press.

"How was the honeymoon?"

"Fabulous," said Diana.

"And married life?"

"I highly recommend it," she said, beaming.

"Have you cooked breakfast for your husband yet?"

"I don't eat breakfasts."

Charles looked bemused. "This must be very exciting television," he said sarcastically. Diana lowered her eyes and smiled. Seconds later he kissed her hand, she laughed gaily, and the photographers grabbed their picture.

As the couple prepared to leave, one of the cameramen presented the Princess with a bouquet of flowers.

"Thank you. I suppose one of you puts them on his expense account," she joked.

Two months later, on November 5, 1981, the Palace announced the Princess was pregnant. She tried to continue her royal engagements, but frequent bouts of morning sickness forced her to cancel. Her husband explained to reporters.

"You've all got wives, you know the problems....It's better not to do too many things....After about three months, things are inclined to get better." Then, sounding officious, he added, "I am prepared to take full responsibility."

A few days later the Princess resumed her duties, but as she walked through crowds and accepted bouquets, she was hit by waves of nausea. She did not try to hide her discomfort. "This is terrible," she said. "Nobody told me I would feel like this." Seeing a pregnant woman in Derbyshire, she grabbed her hands in sympathy. "Oh, that morning sickness, isn't it dreadful!"

At every outing she was trailed by the press. She performed flawlessly in public, but each performance sapped her energy, leaving her emotionally exhausted. At home she flew off the handle. "It was tears and tantrums behind closed doors," recalled a Palace aide. Charles did not know how to cope with his wife's erratic emotions. He called his mistress for advice, and he played more polo. "I've got to get out," he'd tell his bodyguard. "Too many hormones."

The more elusive Charles was, the more upset Diana became. She accused him of sneaking away to visit Camilla, and he became so exasperated by her jealousy that he stalked out, which only infuriated her more. Angry over his absences, curious about his whereabouts, and frustrated by the prying lenses of photographers, Diana complained bitterly to the

Queen, who was unnerved by her daughter-in-law's hysterics. Blaming the press, the Queen summoned Fleet Street editors to tell them to leave the Princess alone. The royal press secretary, Michael Shea, met with them first.

"We expected that, following the honeymoon, press attention would wane somewhat," he told them. "But it has in no way abated. The Princess of Wales feels totally beleaguered. The people who love her and care for her are getting anxious at the reaction it is having."

The Queen entered the room to underscore the message. She said it was unfair of photographers to hide in the bushes with telephoto lenses to track the Princess without her knowledge. The Queen cited the picture published the day before of Diana with her arms around her husband's neck, smiling affectionately at him as they stood outside Highgrove, their house in Gloucester. Royally chided, the editors agreed to back off. In an editorial headlined "The Captive Princess," the *Times* declared, "It would be nice to think we are grown up enough not to imprison a princess in a palace." The truce lasted six weeks. Then Diana threatened to kill herself.

Shortly after the Christmas holidays at Sandringham, she warned Charles that if he left her alone again to go riding, she would commit suicide. As he stormed out, she threw herself down a short flight of stairs. The eighty-one-year-old Queen Mother heard the commotion and found the Princess in a heap, sobbing. Diana was led to her room by a footman, and her doctor was summoned. After his examination, he said she was fine, except for slight bruising around her abdomen; the fetus was unhurt. Hours later the footman sold the information about the Princess's fall to the *Sun*, proving that nothing weighs as heavy as a royal secret worth money. The tabloid ran the story on the next day's front page but did not say it was an apparent suicide attempt.

"The Princess just hated going to Sandringham for Christmas," said her hairdresser Richard Dalton. "She told me it was freezing cold and dinner had to be over by three o'clock: 'It's three and time to watch me on TV,' she'd say, imitating you-know-who. The royal family had to watch the Queen's Christmas message on television. Diana said it was a command performance."

The Queen Mother talked to her nephew John Bowes-Lyon about Diana's behavior, which seemed to be exacerbated by a physical malady. "She had fits which would last just a few minutes, during which she would go crazy and become uncontrollable," said Bowes-Lyon.* "And then it was all over as quickly as it began.

"At first, doctors thought her outbursts

* "John Bowes-Lyon had to apologize to Diana when it appeared in print that she was frothing at the mouth for a few seconds," said columnist Taki Theodoracopulos in 1993. "She has a slight disease that resembles epilepsy, which John Bowes-Lyon knew from the Queen Mother. He told me about it and I, of course, told Nigel [Dempster], who, like the dumb shit he is, used it in his book [*Behind Palace Doors*, written in 1993 with Peter Evans]. When the book came out, John had to write a note to Diana, saying, 'I apologize and I had nothing to do with that.'"

might have been epilepsy, but that was discounted because she didn't swallow her tongue or have other epileptic symptoms. Apparently what she suffers from can be hereditary, and there have been other instances in the Fermoy family, so the royal family have been told."

Over the next three years Diana would try several more times to take her life. Each was a desperate attempt at self-mutilation. "I tried four or five times," she told Dr. Maurice Lipsedge, a specialist in eating disorders at Guy's Hospital in London. She told him of the various attempts: she slashed her arms with a lemon slicer; she cut her wrist; she ran a knife down the veins of one leg; and she threw herself into a glass cabinet.

"When no one listens to you, or you feel no one's listening to you, all sorts of things start to happen," she said. "These attempts were my cries for help."

When the Queen saw the first signs of dissension between the couple, she proposed Charles and Diana take a trip. "In that type of situation, Her Majesty always recommends escape," said one of her friends. "Her solution is to get away together, sort things out, and everything will be fine. It's always worked for her. Why shouldn't it work for them?"

A few days later the Prince and Princess left for the island of Windemere in the Bahamas. "What Diana needs is a holiday in the sunshine," said Charles, "to prepare for the birth." Again the couple were followed by the long lenses of freelance photographers, who captured the Princess, five months pregnant, skipping through the surf in an orange bikini. Once again Diana was on the front pages of the tabloids, and the Queen was incensed. "This is one of the blackest days in British journalism," she said through her press secretary. The *Sun* later printed an apology and published the photographs a second time, just in case its five million readers wondered why the publication was saying it was sorry.

Her Majesty had been burned again by the *Sun* and the man who had come to dominate Britain's media through buying the *Sun*, the *Sunday Times*, the *Times of London*, and Sky TV. Rupert Murdoch was now teaching the Queen that her stingy wages were no match for his checkbook journalism. Every tidbit of royal gossip from inside the Palace was for sale, and he spent freely for sensational revelations. An Australian, unrestrained by deference to the Crown, Murdoch was no monarchist. So his irreverent publications zoomed in on the royal family and printed unprettified stories and candid photos. Without the protective blanket of reverence, the royals flapped and squawked like geese in a gunsight. The Queen lectured editors, demanded (and obtained) injunctions, and, finally, went to court to stop her servants from selling secrets. She called for press sanctions and sued for damages.

"Her Majesty became annoyed after a photo appeared of her six-year-old grandson, Peter, twirling a dead pheasant by the neck during a bird shoot," recalled a member of the royal household. "She ordered reporters and photographers off the estate at Sandringham and barred them from Windsor. She tried to keep them away from all family events, including the royal christenings."

Charles and Diana's first child, the forty-third heir to the British throne, was born on June 21, 1982, and the Hussars of the Royal Horse Artillery fired the traditional forty-one gun salute in honor of the new Prince. The blond, blue-eyed boy was called "Baby Wales" for seven days until his parents stopped fighting over his name. "We're having a little argument about what to call him," Charles admitted to reporters. The couple eventually settled on William Arthur Philip Louis in honor of William the Conqueror, the legendary King Arthur, the Duke of Edinburgh, and Lord Louis Mountbatten. Prince William ("Wills" to his parents) was to be christened on the Queen Mother's eighty-second birthday.

"It had been quite a difficult pregnancy—I hadn't been very well throughout it," Diana recalled in a television interview. "But I felt the whole country was in labor with me...so by the time William arrived, it was a great relief."

Britons rejoiced, except for William's crotchety aunt, Princess Anne, who was on a goodwill tour in the United States when Diana gave birth and resented the press queries.

"Your Royal Highness, any word about Princess Diana?"

"I don't know," she snapped. "You tell me."

"Your reaction to her having a son?"

She shrugged. "I didn't know she had one."

"This morning."

"Oh, good," she said sarcastically. "Isn't that nice?"

"How are you enjoying your visit to New Mexico?"

"Keep your questions to yourself."

"Ma'am, how does it feel to be an aunt?"

"That's my business, thank you."

The sourpuss Princess skidded to the bottom of the royal popularity polls. "Naff off, Anne," screamed the *Daily Mail,* which claimed she was envious of the fuss over Diana. Other newspapers dismissed the Queen's daughter as rude, surly, and miserable. Within ten years the pundits would change their minds. After her charity work for Save the Children, Anne would emerge as one of the most respected women in Great Britain. Some polls would show that the public thought her more worthy than Charles to ascend to the throne. But then, she was one of the most reviled people in the United Kingdom.

Within the royal family the relationship between the Princess Anne and the Princess of Wales was visceral: they loathed each other. Anne thought Diana was vain, dim-witted, and neurotic. "Too gooey about children," she said.

Diana dismissed her sister-in-law as a male impersonator. "I think she shaves."

"You forget," said a friend. "Anne was the only female competitor at Montreal Olympics [1976] not to be given a sex test."

"Results would've been too embarrassing," joked Diana. "She's Philip—in drag."

The Princess of Wales did not understand a woman like Anne, who appeared to be so determinedly unfeminine. She refused to wear makeup, pulled back her hair in a bun, and wore clothes that looked like thrift shop rejects. Diana had heard about Anne's adultery with a Palace guard but did not understand his sexual attraction. "What do men see in her?" she asked.

Blunt as a bullet, Anne did nothing to ingratiate herself with others, especially the press, which she detested. "You are a pest by the very nature of that camera in your hand," she snapped at a photographer who was trying to take her picture.

Charles agreed that Anne could be difficult but said she was his only sister and had honored him by making him godfather to her firstborn son. So he suggested that he and Diana return the honor by making Anne one of Prince William's godmothers. Diana refused.

"Darling, please," Charles said plaintively. "Please."

Diana was unmovable, and Charles, after a halfhearted struggle to change her mind, gave up. Days later they announced their choice of godparents: Princess Alexandra; the Duchess

438

of Westminster; Lady Susan Hussey; King Constantine II of the Hellenes; Lord Romsey; Sir Laurens Van der Post.

At the christening, the Archbishop of Canterbury poured water over the baby's head and handed a lighted candle to his father to signify the young Prince's admission into the church.

"The windows were open, the sun streaming in," Sir Laurens told *Horoscope* magazine. "Then the sky went grey as a great storm gathered. Just as the Archbishop handed over the lighted candle, a violent gust of wind blew through the windows. The candle flickered, but did not go out."

The sage saw that as a portent for the Prince and Princess of Wales, who both believed in mysticism. Van der Post said it was a good sign and explained that the flickering candle represented a crisis in Prince William's future, but one that he would survive.

Two years later, after the birth of their second son, Charles again suggested choosing his sister as a godmother, but again Diana refused. Instead she chose Lady Celia Vestey; Lady Sarah Armstrong-Jones, the daughter of Princess Margaret; and Carolyn Pride Bartholomew, her former roommate from Coleherne Court. As godfathers, Charles chose his brother, Andrew, the Duke of York; artist Bryan Organ, who painted flattering royal portraits; and Gerald Ward, a rich polo player.

The announcement of the baby's godparents sparked a furious row within the royal family. Prince Philip was so angry at Charles for bypassing Anne a second time that he didn't speak to him or visit his new grandson for six weeks. At the end of the year he fired off a memo, telling Charles he was not carrying his weight as heir apparent. Philip praised Anne, his favorite child, as the hardest-working member of the royal family. "She's represented the Crown at 201 events whereas records indicate you made 93 appearances and your wife 51. Taken together, these figures [for 1984] don't add up to your sister's efforts."

Three years later the Queen rewarded her daughter's dedicated service by naming her Princess Royal, the highest honor a sovereign can bestow on a female in the royal family.

But Anne was so humiliated at being passed over again as godmother that she declined to attend the christening of Prince Henry Charles Albert David ("Harry" to his parents). She said the date conflicted with a shooting party that she and her husband had planned. The Queen and Prince Charles moved the christening from Buckingham Palace to St. George's Chapel at Windsor so it would be closer to Anne's estate, hoping then she might change her mind. She didn't. The Queen's press secretary telephoned and begged her to reschedule her shooting party, saying that her absence would be interpreted by the press as a slight to the Princess of Wales.

"So what?" said Anne, who sent her children

in her place. "Peter and Zara will be there, and that'll be quite enough."

Michael Shea pleaded, but to no avail. As he predicted, the Murdoch press buried the Queen's daughter as petulant and vengeful. They canonized the Princess of Wales, and next to the Queen Mother, she was proclaimed the most beloved figure in the kingdom.

FOURTEEN

I'm fed up to the teeth with your bloody security," exploded the Duke of Edinburgh. "Let's get going."

"I'm sorry, sir," said the U.S. Secret Service agent, "but there's nothing I can do until the President's car moves."

The Queen and the Duke, touring California as guests of the Reagans in 1983, sat in the back of their limousine, waiting for the motorcade to move through the rainy streets of San Francisco. Philip strained with impatience.

"I said to get this car moving," he snapped.

"Sir, we're waiting for President Reagan's car."

The Queen stared straight ahead. Seconds passed. Bristling with anger, Philip grabbed a magazine from the seat pocket, rolled it up, and smacked the driver across the back of his head.

"Move this fucking car," he screamed, "and move it now!"

The Queen sat impassively and did not say a word as her husband whacked the agent like a horse. An hour later, after they had arrived at their hotel, she sent her embassy representative to the agent's room with an invitation to join the royal couple for a nightcap.

"No, thank you," said the agent. He made no attempt to disguise his anger over the treatment he had received from the Queen's husband as she said nothing.

"Please, sir. You must accept Her Majesty's invitation."

"I said, '*No, thank you.*' I will not be in their company any more than I absolutely have to."

The Queen's messenger appealed to the White House aide in the room. "Please, sir, I'm begging you. I cannot go back to Her Majesty and say her invitation was refused. I would lose my position. My tour of duty is up in six months and I can't afford to retire without my pension. I acknowledge the Duke of Edinburgh was beastly—rude beyond redemption—but I'm asking you as a personal favor to please accept this invitation."

The White House aide looked at the Secret Service agent, who stared at the anxious messenger—and reconsidered. "I want to make it clear," said the agent, "that I'm doing this for you, not for them."

The U.S. Secret Service had struggled throughout the visit to provide the highest standard of protection for the royal couple, but the Duke of Edinburgh balked at every security measure proposed. The night before, he had turned on the light inside his limousine.

"I'm sorry, sir," said the agent. "I must ask you to turn off that light. It makes you too easy a target."

"I'm damned if I will," snapped Philip. "Why do you think these people are out here? They want to see me, and I want to wave to them."

The U.S. Chief of Protocol, Selwa Roosevelt, interceded. "Sir, these men are only doing their job," she said. "If anything happens to you, it would be due to their negligence. Please do not take it out on them. They have their orders." As he got out of the car, Philip slammed the door in her face. Hours later, at a dinner, he apologized.

From San Diego to San Francisco to the Reagan ranch in Santa Barbara, the Duke fumed about the security. "They're bloody baboons," he groused to the Queen, who also chafed at extreme protection. Privately she agreed with her husband. Publicly she said nothing. She was on a goodwill trip—her fifth to the United States—and she was visiting at the express request of her government to solidify what the two countries now called their special relationship. The British Prime Minister, Margaret Thatcher, a political soulmate of Ronald Reagan, needed U.S. aid, so she fed the American appetite for British royalty by sending the Queen on tour.

Reagan had backed Thatcher when British troops landed in the Falkland Islands in 1982 to reclaim them from Argentina. The cost: 237 British servicemen and $3.7 billion. Most people had assumed Britain was too poor and too passive to mount such an attack, so the invasion boosted the country's prestige. Argentina's surrender in June 1982 allowed the forceful Prime Minister to emerge with a newfound respect as the Iron Lady. Prince Andrew, the Queen's favorite child, flew a navy helicopter in the war and returned home a hero.

The "special relationship" between London and Washington became strained after the United States invaded Grenada, a former British colony in the Caribbean, which had remained part of the Commonwealth. As Queen of England, Elizabeth II was also Queen of Grenada and not receptive to invaders, especially allies. "She is immensely displeased with President Reagan over this matter," said a Labor Party spokesman. The Queen summoned Margaret Thatcher to the Palace to explain why Her Majesty had had to hear the news of the invasion from the BBC and not from the Prime Minister herself. Mrs. Thatcher said she hadn't known about it until she called the President minutes before. "It's a benign invasion," Reagan had told her, asserting that one thousand Americans had to be evacuated from the island after a communist takeover. Mrs. Thatcher told the Queen that she, too, was upset, but Britain would not condemn the invasion. "We stand by the United States and will continue to do so in the larger alliances," said the Prime

Minister. "The United States is the final guarantor of freedom in Europe."

The Queen showed her displeasure during that meeting by not offering the Prime Minister a seat. Afterward she reported Thatcher's reaction: "Only two curtsies today." The exaggerated deference of the Prime Minister, who referred to herself as "we," amused the royal family. Prince Philip dismissed her as "the greengrocer's daughter" because she was born in a flat above her family's grocery in Grantham. The Queen, known for her wicked mimicry, relished telling Margaret Thatcher jokes. Her favorite was about the Prime Minister's visiting an old age home.

"Do you know who I am?" said the Queen, imitating Thatcher's grandiose accent as she shook the hand of an elderly resident.

"No," replied the befuddled resident, "but if you ask Matron, she'll tell you."

Once, however, a joke backfired. There is a story, probably true, about a Commonwealth diplomat who went to Buckingham Palace to present his credentials. When the Queen thought he had gone, she began to mimic him, then saw, to her distress, that he was still in the room. "Not bad, ma'am," he said courteously as he bowed himself out, "not bad."

The Queen's press secretary tries to humanize the monarch by emphasizing her sense of humor, which frequently lurks behind a stern facade. He disclosed that the royal family called the Queen "Miss Piggyface" when she looked bored or displeased. She, too, made fun of herself that way. Watching a video of the royal wedding, she called to her husband, "Philip, come here and look. I've got my Miss Piggyface on."

"Sometimes, certainly not always, Her Majesty enjoyed watching her puppet on *Spitting Image*," said her press secretary, referring to the satirical television show that used rubberized puppets to make fun of the royal family and other establishment figures. One sketch that amused the Queen featured a rubber caricature of the Prime Minister— heavily rouged cheeks, pointed nose, and hair plastered in place—talking to the Queen's puppet, dressed in a dowdy sweater set with a babushka tied over her crown.

"At least *we* don't strut around in ludicrous little hats," said the Margaret Thatcher puppet.

"But you'd love to, wouldn't you," retorted the Queen's puppet.

The Queen's relationship with Margaret Thatcher was always proper and cordial, but never as warm and cozy as the rapport she had enjoyed with Winston Churchill and Harold Wilson. Part of the problem was the Queen's preference for men. "She regards female inferiority as the natural order of things," said British historian David Cannadine. "The other part of the problem was Margaret Thatcher herself," Prince Charles told his biographer. "She was too formidable." The Prince described the Prime Minister to the editor of the *Sunday Express* as "a bit like a school ma'am." Charles eventually became so disenchanted with Thatcher's conservative policies that he sent a memo to the Queen, imploring her to do something before the Prime Minister ruined the country. The Queen, who came to agree with her son, could do nothing, but she occasionally shared her displeasure with Commonwealth leaders.

"Her Majesty was not at ease with Margaret Thatcher's policies," said Robert Hawke, the former Prime Minister of Australia. "She saw her as dangerous." During a dinner with Lord Shawcross, the Queen expressed anger toward her Prime Minister because Margaret Thatcher had reneged on granting the Shah of Iran asylum in England. "Once you give your word," the Queen said, "that's it."

Despite her negative feelings, the Queen did not withhold the Order of the Garter from her Prime Minister after Margaret Thatcher left office. Limited to twenty-four citizens, the Garter, the highest order of chivalry, is usually bestowed by the monarch on a retired prime minister who has not been defeated in a general election.

The Queen was just as politically suspect to Margaret Thatcher, who told conservative aides that Her Majesty was not "one of us." The Iron Lady clashed with the Queen over a Commonwealth statement opposing apartheid. She did not share the monarch's fervor for the Commonwealth; she cared more about Britain's stature in Europe. In fact, she dismissed the Commonwealth as a bunch of greedy beggars.

The Queen confided in Anthony Benn, a Labor MP, that she loathed the Common Market and considered its leaders rude, cynical, and disillusioned. In his diary Benn suggested that the Queen's negative attitude came from seeing there was no role for her in a European union. Benn, a republican, also derided the Queen, saying she was incapable of saying "Good morning" without a courtier's script.

Yet the Queen, despite her Prime Minister, remained devoted to her dominions. And she did everything possible to shore up the creaky concept of monarchy, especially in Canada and Australia, where republican sentiments ran high. By 1982 she had made twelve royal tours of Canada and nine of Australia. And she maintained the Crown's presence in both countries by regularly dispatching members of her family to visit. In 1983 she sent the Prince and Princess of Wales to Australia for six weeks, although the Princess at first refused to go. After considerable wrangling, she agreed, but she insisted on taking their nine-month-old baby and his nanny.

"You know how you felt," Diana told Charles. "You were miserable when your mother left you for months at a time, and you were older than Wills." She reminded her husband of what he had told her about his lonely childhood. Diana felt that he had been emotionally damaged by his parents, who were too busy for him because they were constantly traveling. "I will not do that to Wills," she said in front of her staff. She cited books she'd read about the first two years of a child's life being the time when a sense of self-esteem and security are implanted. "I know he's just a baby," she said, "but he still needs our attention."

Diana believed in tactile mothering or, as she defined it, "lots of hugs and cuddles." Frequently she startled the nanny, Barbara Barnes, by dashing into the nursery at odd hours when the baby was sleeping. "I just came to kiss him," Diana said, reaching for Wills and waking him up. An anxious mother, she hovered over his bassinet and worried about his crying. "Are you sure he's all right?" The nanny, whom Wills called "Baba," became exasperated with the Princess, who worried about being displaced. A few years later Diana felt that her child was having trouble distinguishing between "Baba" and "Mama," so she fired the nanny.

When Charles suggested taking the baby on the 1983 tour, the Queen was dubious. But he explained that Diana did not want to be separated from their child for six weeks. The Queen listened patiently and agreed to make the necessary arrangements with the Foreign Office so the couple could travel with their baby. Even so, she was concerned.

Diana's behavior had been worrying the Queen, especially since Diana's ski trip to Austria months before. The Prince and Princess had attracted throngs of paparazzi, who crowded the slopes, shops, and restaurants, causing pandemonium. Pushing and shouting to get closer to the royal couple, the press jostled a crush of tourists gathered to gawk. The resort town looked as if it had been invaded by lunatics, all carrying cameras and microphones. Photographers, desperate to get a picture of Diana, crashed through doors and broke shop windows as they chased after her. It took the police to restore order.

Once charming and cooperative with the media, Diana now refused to pose. She resented being followed every time she appeared in public. She hid her face in her coat collar, jammed her hands in her pockets, and lowered her head. She pulled her ski cap over her eyes, wore large goggles, and refused to smile.

On the slopes, Prince Charles begged her to cooperate. "Please, darling, please," he said. "Give them a smile and we'll get on with it." Diana stared at the ground.

"Please don't hide like that," he implored, leaning toward her. She stiffened and pulled away, keeping her head down.

"Diana, you're just being stupid," he said, irritated. "Please, darling, you've got to cooperate." She would not look up.

"Your Royal Highness," begged one photographer, "just a little smile. Like the old days." Diana buried her face in her hands and held her head for a full five minutes, further frustrating Charles and the cameraman.

Photographs of the sulking Princess and

her forlorn husband appeared in the British press with daily stories about the commotion she was causing: there were reports of one-hundred-mile-an-hour car chases of the Princess trying to dodge photographers and blond decoys she sent out to distract photographers; barricades thrown up and borders closed to the press; reporters roughed up and photographers driven off the road. When the Queen read about a British cameraman bloodied by a royal security guard, she sent a member of her staff to calm the disturbance.

Victor Chapman, a Canadian diplomat with a merry sense of humor, flew to Liechtenstein that afternoon with Francis Cornish of Charles's staff to deal with the Princess. During their meeting with the royal couple, Cornish began by reciting to Diana her obligations as royalty. He told her sternly that she owed it to Her Majesty to cooperate with the press people. Diana, who could no longer abide the courtiers, ignored Cornish, but she responded to the gentle flirtation of Chapman, who winked during the stern lecture.

"Vic was a lovely man," recalled one of his friends. "He'd been married twice and had five daughters. He loved women and knew just how to handle Diana. He flattered and cajoled and teased her."

At the time, the Princess of Wales was a psychological mess. But she looked stunning, having starved off the weight (fifty-three pounds) she had gained during pregnancy. She had shopped every day to keep her mind off her hunger, and the results were remarkable. Diana knew that style was the first priority of a princess, and she was determined to become the best-dressed Princess of Wales in history. She would show substance beneath the surface later; right now all she cared about was creating a lip-smacking first impression. She studied her photographs in the newspapers and read every word of commentary about her clothes. She consulted fashion editors and designers. She let them know that she intended to bring style and glamour to her role and distance herself from the rest of the Windsor women in their white purses, garden party hats, and sturdy platform shoes. With glistening blond hair and a year-round tan, she looked as bewitching as any movie star. "Gorgeous is the only word for her," sighed *Vogue* magazine. "Heart-stoppingly gorgeous."

Certainly few suspected that the Princess was bulimic or that she was suffering from postnatal depression. The Palace assumption was that she was merely acting spoiled and temperamental. She later confided to Chapman that she was bored with performing her royal duties and intended to get pregnant again as soon as she could. "I'd rather eat and have babies* than collect bouquets," she said.

"I quite agree, ma'am," he said, "but please

* Months later the Princess was pregnant and announced her news to the royal family at Balmoral. The Queen ordered champagne to celebrate. Within a week Diana had miscarried. She became pregnant a third time in 1983 and gave birth to Prince Harry on September 15, 1984.

let's not share that information with Francis [Cornish] just yet." Chapman achieved such a warm rapport with Diana that the Queen sent him on the royal tour of Australia in 1983.

"That's where he revolutionized Diana," said a woman also on the trip. "Vic showed her how to be a princess. He coached her: 'It would be lovely if you did a dance for the cameras with your husband,' he said before the night of the charity dance at the Southern Cross Hotel in Melbourne. Diana pulled a face, but he encouraged her. 'Have fun with it. Show them your style.' He flattered her, said that Diana was the best dancer he'd ever seen.

"'The best?' she asked.

"Vic laughed. 'The best—after Dame Margot Fonteyn. And that's only because she's got Nureyev.' Diana said she was stuck with Charles, who had admitted to all of us how much he dreaded having to get up at formal dinners and start the dancing. 'I assure you,' he had said, 'it makes my heart sink to have to make an awful exhibition of ourselves.'

"Vic was playful with Diana. He relaxed her. She mugged at him as her lady-in-waiting fussed with her jewelry that evening. Diana took the necklace and put it over her head rather than wait to have it clasped around her neck. She couldn't get it over the bridge of her nose. 'My honker's too big,' she said. Vic roared. 'Leave it there,' he said. 'It's young and fun, like you. Just be your wonderful self. They want nothing more than a beautiful princess. They'll love you.'"

And they did. The photograph of Charles and Diana dancing relieved Britons, who had begun to worry about their less-than-perfect Princess. With Queen Mary's emeralds wrapped around her head, Disco Di was a triumph.

When the tour was over, Diana gave her lady-in-waiting Anne Beckwith-Smith an expensive pair of earrings. The card read: "I couldn't have done it without you."

The problem of the Princess had been solved, but the solution upset the Prince. "We've got trouble," Chapman told his friend Carolyn Townshend when he returned to England. "She's *too* popular, and he doesn't like it a bit."

The Prince did not understand his wife's appeal. He expected his intelligence to be prized over her beauty and resented the adulation she stirred in crowds, who wanted to see her and not him. He smarted when people crossed the street to be on her side, not his. Because Diana looked like an angel and carried the aura of a royal princess, she fulfilled people's dreams in a way that he never could. And he was envious. She tapped into emotions that were deeply rooted in fantasy and nourished by fairy tales as an image of perfection, worthy of adoration. The title of Her Royal Highness, conferred by marriage, elevated her in people's eyes. Like a saint, she was automatically revered and considered deserving of worship. She packaged herself exquisitely, and her beauty, combined with natural warmth, made her magnetic. Charles, for all his worthy causes, looked dull, whereas Diana dazzled.

"One of the world's few true generalizations," wrote Simon Sebag Montefiore in *Psychology Today*, "is that all nations, including the British and the Americans, fight the boredom of everyday life by admiring and despising the flaws and glamour of their dynasties."

So, like Jacqueline Kennedy Onassis and Princess Grace of Monaco before her, the Princess of Wales became a decorative focus for the masses. Treated as a natural phenomenon, she became an object of mass hysteria. People lined up for hours to see her pass by. They reached out to touch her and felt blessed if she smiled in their direction. Unlike her earnest husband, she excited people. She possessed the incandescence of a movie star, and he couldn't stand it.

"Vic had seen the conflict developing in Australia," recalled Townshend, "so he tried to set things right for Charles. Vic suggested some jocular comments for the Prince to make at the farewell banquet in Auckland à la President Kennedy's wonderful line about being the man who had accompanied Jacqueline Kennedy to Paris and enjoying every minute. But Charles was not John F. Kennedy."

Whenever the Prince tried to be self-deprecating, he sounded strained and unnatural. Seeing someone wave a bouquet in Diana's direction, he offered to give it to her. "I'm just a collector of flowers these days," he said. His delivery suggested a sinner who sees redemp-

455

tion in self-inflicted humor but can't make the leap of faith. Although distinctly uncomfortable poking fun at himself, he made an effort. "I have come to the conclusion that it really would have been easier to have had two wives," he said. "Then they could cover both sides of the street and I could walk down the middle, directing operations."

Because he was the Prince of Wales, everyone laughed. But Chapman knew how hard it was for Charles to step aside and let his wife be the star.

"Vic stayed with us in the country," said Townshend, "and the calls came in late at night from the Prince of Wales, who was worried about some negative article that had appeared. 'There's nothing you can do about it,' Vic would say. The rest of the people around Charles would shuffle and shamble: 'Oh, yes, Your Royal Highness, you are absolutely right, sir. Such rubbish. It's an outrage. Indeed. Yes, sir. Yes sir. Three bags full, sir.' But not Vic. He shot straight and told Charles exactly like it was.

"Diana bit her fingernails to the quick because she worried about the tabloid stories displeasing the Palace. She once appeared in a new hairstyle that, unfortunately, upstaged the Queen, who was opening Parliament. Princess Margaret was furious and said something to Charles, who gave Diana unshirted hell. Poor thing, she quaked in those days. Her nails were the giveaway: if they were short and chewed, there was trouble."

The British press reported that for the first three years of her marriage, Diana said only five hundred words in public. She was too intimidated to make a speech or appear without her husband. Her first solo appearance was in France, not England, when she attended the funeral of Princess Grace of Monaco. On the strength of their one meeting, Diana had considered the Princess to be a close friend. "We were psychically connected," she told Grace's daughter Caroline. Diana, who believed in astrology and numerology, felt that she and the Princess of Monaco were born under the same star and shared mystical characteristics. In fact, both came from dysfunctional families. Both were third children. Both had married royal princes. Both became more famous than their husbands. Both paid a heavy price.

This was confirmed for Diana several years later, when Robert Lacey published a biography entitled *Grace,* which disclosed her excessive drinking, her fraying marriage, and her extramarital love affairs. Diana said the book substantiated her psychic intuitions. When Grace died in 1982, Diana had to fight to attend her funeral. The Palace did not want her to go, although no one else in the British royal family had volunteered. Diana said the glowing press coverage she received for going to the funeral had reassured her that she had done the right thing.

Charles was more concerned about receiving credit for his own good works. He said he had been the first member of the royal family to give blood, but no one paid attention. "I did this to reassure the country after the AIDS scare caused a drop in blood bank donations, but all the press cared about was Diana's frock," he complained to his equerry. "Journalists are creeps—bloody hacks, all of them."

His equerry realized how much the Prince of Wales longed to be appreciated as a humanitarian. "I wish I were Bob Geldof," Charles said after the Irish rocker was honored for raising millions for famine relief in Ethiopia.

Eager to please his master, the equerry phoned a reporter and mentioned that the Prince carried a donor card authorizing doctors to use his organs in a lifesaving operation. The reporter wrote the story, but it was barely noticed because Diana had appeared at a benefit the night before wearing a one-shouldered silver-spangled sheath, and her photographs dominated the news coverage.

Days later the dogged equerry called a BBC radio show to say the Prince had been studying the causes of unrest in inner cities. He said Charles had spent a night walking the dark streets of London, visiting shelters and talking to the homeless.

The polo-playing Prince saw himself as a man of the people, but his sister said he was far "too grand" for the role. She pointed out that his staff at Highgrove had to wear specially designed uniforms, including the feathers of the Prince of Wales, and bow every day when they first addressed him. When leaving the room, they usually backed out. His valet of twelve years concurred. "I was successful in knowing him well," said Stephen Barry, "but I could never forget that he was the master and I the servant."

Charles did not recognize the irony in preaching fuel conservation while driving a gas-guzzling ten-miles-to-the-gallon Bentley. He described himself as a gentleman farmer who was committed to urban renewal when not presiding over his country estate. Although one of the richest men in the world, he was passionate about the poor. He demonstrated his concern during a two-day visit to the United States: he spent the first day touring the slums of Pittsburgh and the second day playing polo in Palm Beach. He recuperated from both stops by flying to Switzerland to ski.

In England Charles craved a role in the public policy debate. He seized his opportunity in May 1984, when he addressed the Royal Institute of British Architects on their 150th anniversary. The architects expected to be praised, but the Prince of Wales lambasted them as elitists. He said their inhospitable designs ignored the feelings and wishes of ordinary people. He cited as an example the modern glass-and-steel annex proposed for the National Gallery of Art in London. Charles said the design was a "monstrous carbuncle on the face of a much-loved and elegant friend."

His speech made the front pages of Britain's newspapers, and he felt quite pleased, especially when the proposed plan was canceled. "I've fought hard for a role as the Prince of Wales," he told the editor of the *Sunday Telegraph* during a private lunch. "I feel I should do and say things in my position that, one hopes, can be a stimulus to the country's conscience, a bit of a pinprick." Some architects griped that he was less the first half and more the last half.

"I later felt obliged to challenge his opinion," said Gordon Graham, former president of the Royal Academy of British Architects. "I did it politely, but I did do it." Graham said he had experienced no royal repercussions after his speech, but his friends disagreed.

"Nonsense," said Ian Coulter, an international consultant who once worked for Randolph Churchill. "Gordon Graham gave up his knighthood with that speech. By directly challenging the heir apparent, he tilted at the biggest windmill of them all. If the Sun King turns his back on you, you're in his shadow. Royalty has patronage and support, and if it's withdrawn, you're a dead man."

Charles understood his power, but he did not understand criticism. He was accustomed to excessive praise, but for months now magazines and newspapers had ridiculed him, his wife, and his marriage. *Vanity Fair* said he was "pussy-whipped from here to eternity." His mistress had described his wife as a mouse, but others considered her a royal rat. She had purged his staff of over forty people who had either resigned or been fired. She retired most of "the pink mafia," as she called the homosexuals on Charles's staff, because she did not want them around her young sons. She even banished her husband's old Labrador because the dog was incontinent.

Diana was just as miffed as Charles by the tabloid stories of her "compulsive shopping" and the "exorbitant amounts of money" she was "squandering" on "high-style fashions." One newspaper estimated that after British *Vogue* started advising her, she spent $1.4 million in one year—for 373 outfits, complete with hats, belts, shoes, and purses. "It's not true, it's not true," she wailed. "In the beginning, I had to buy endless new things, of course, because on a tour you change three or four times a day. I *had* to buy new things. I couldn't go around in a leopardskin."

Since then her closets had expanded to six suites in Kensington Palace. One room was reserved solely for shoes: "Three hundred and twenty pairs," she gleefully told her friend Sarah Ferguson, "and that's not counting my trainers." Diana soon learned to send her bills to the British Foreign Office for the designer clothes she wore on royal tours. For a sixteen-day trip of Oman, Qatar, Bahrain, and Saudi Arabia, her clothing bill was $122,000.

She was distressed by the stories of how she had changed from a dewy-eyed virgin into a self-obsessed harridan. She was inaccurately blamed for turning her husband into a muzzy mystic, whom she no longer allowed to hunt and shoot.

Charles fretted continually about his media

coverage. He did not read the tabloids, which he called "the cheap and impertinent gutter press." But he complained that the quality papers he did read were not adequately reporting his worthy endeavors. Over a private lunch he grumbled to *Sunday Telegraph* editor Peregrine Worsthorne, "I sometimes wonder why I don't pack it in and spend my time playing polo."

Like politicians, who live and die by polls, Charles and Diana scrambled to find spin doctors. They asked everyone around them for advice, calling upon Tory Members of Parliament, discreet editors, and worshipful courtiers. They sought counsel from lawyers and media consultants, inviting them all to Kensington Palace to pick their brains.

"It was in November 1984 that I lunched with them," John Junor, former editor of the *Sunday Express,* wrote in his memoirs. "The Prince remarked that he hoped Princess Diana would begin to give interviews. But he added, 'Perhaps not just yet. It might be wise to wait until she has more experience.'"

The Princess agreed. "I just hate the sound of my own voice," she said. "I can't bear it. When I launched that new liner last week, I just couldn't believe it when I heard myself afterward. It just didn't sound like me."

The Prince laughed. "I felt exactly the same way. I just couldn't believe that yakkety-yak voice was mine. So upper-class."

Charles asked Junor for advice on how to handle public relations and combat "the idiotic stories" that appeared in the press. The Prince spoke at length about his concerns—the disadvantaged youth of the country, the inadequacy of the Church of England—and the editor listened. So did Diana, until Junor turned to include her in the conversation.

"Darling, I'm so sorry," said Charles. "I've done all the talking. Did you have something you wanted to say?"

The Princess nodded. Then she poured out to Junor her resentment about the way in which she had been attacked for influencing her husband and turning him against shooting and hunting.

The Prince broke in. "I'm angry about that, too. Because my wife is doing nothing of the kind. My wife actually likes hunting and shooting. It is I who have turned against it."

"It's all his own decision," Diana told another journalist. "I was brought up in the country and like shooting. I shot a deer at Balmoral on our honeymoon. I just think Charles has gone a bit potty."

Charmed by the Princess, John Junor had reservations about the Prince. "Charles was a serious, perhaps too serious, young man, obsessed with the idea of serving the nation, in some danger of overwhelming his wife, and in even greater danger of boring her."

After weeks of consultations with their advisers, including an astrologer, the Prince and Princess decided to go on television. They said they wanted to be interviewed ("by a respectful interviewer, of course," Charles stipulated) so they could present themselves to people without the subjectivity of newspapers. "Let people see us as we really are," said Diana. In exchange for the privilege of this interview, Independent Television gave them editorial control and assured them of soft lighting. "I wouldn't want my [bald] patch to blind viewers," Charles joked.

They called Sir Richard Attenborough, the film director, to coach them. Under his guidance they became world-class illusionists. Charles played the romantic lead; Diana was the pretty ingenue. The two little Princes, Wills and Harry, were the extras pounding the piano in the background. As the future King, Charles was to appear strong, resolute, and worthy of trust. As his consort, Diana was to sit by his side, sweetly and supportively. By October 1985 they knew their parts to perfection.

"People expect a great deal of us," Charles began earnestly, "and I'm always conscious— I'm sure you are, too, darling—of not wanting to let people down, not wanting to let this country down." Diana looked up at him demurely and nodded.

She was asked about her role. "To support my husband," she said, "and always be behind him and encouraging. And also a more important thing, being a wife and mother."

For forty-five minutes they performed flawlessly. She said she never dieted; he didn't even know what a Ouija board looked like. She denied being a shopaholic; he did not practice homeopathy. She professed the greatest respect for Princess Anne. He kept an open mind about architecture.

When the interviewer delicately approached the rumors about Diana's being a domineering wife and dictating her husband's taste, she looked surprised. "I might pick the odd tie now and then," she said, "but that's it." Later, she said Charles chuckled about that response, remembering her frenzied efforts to overhaul his appearance. She had spent days rummaging through his closets, discarding his solid blue shirts—"so boring"—and substituting Turnbull & Asser's stripes, tossing out single-button jackets in favor of double-breasted blazers, throwing away lace-up cordovans—"too fuddy-duddy"—and bringing in tasseled loafers. She even sent him to her hairdresser with instructions for blow-drying: "Cover up the patch." Because of his big ears, she told Charles not to wear hats. "You'll look like a Volkswagen with both doors wide open."

On television the royal couple shared an easy camaraderie and playfulness that dispelled rumors about their marriage. They bantered briefly, smiled frequently, and enchanted viewers. The interview was later shown on American television to coincide with their 1985 trip to Washington, D.C. This was to be Diana's first visit to the United States, so the Queen sent her Palace press secretary to the States to handle the media. Michael Shea briefed American reporters on how they were expected to behave, admonishing them to question only the Prince and not the Princess. "She will not answer," he said, "so don't even try."

Throughout the two-day tour Diana said nothing publicly. As they were leaving, she was asked how she liked Washington.

"Very good," she said softly, "I—"

Charles interrupted. "Speaking as her spokesman," he said in a booming voice, "she thinks it's wonderful."

Shea shot a reproving look at the reporter who had dared to address his question to the Princess instead of the Prince. The reporter rolled his eyes.

"Well then, sir," said the reporter, looking at Charles, "did the Princess enjoy the White House dinner?"

"I think you enjoyed it, didn't you, darling?" said Charles. "She would be an idiot if she did not enjoy dancing with John Travolta, wouldn't she?"

Days before the Reagans' dinner dance for the royal couple, the President's wife had instructed the Marine Band to rehearse the music from *Saturday Night Fever* so that its star, John Travolta, could twirl the Princess around the Grand Foyer of the White House. Knowing that Diana once dreamed of becoming a ballerina, Mrs. Reagan had seated her next to Mikhail Baryshnikov, director of the American Ballet Theater. The First Lady also invited Diana's favorite stars: Neil Diamond, Tom Selleck, and Clint Eastwood. Much as the Republican First Lady loved Prince Charles,

466

she did not invite his favorite movie star—Barbra Streisand—because she was a liberal Democrat. By happy coincidence, all of Diana's favorite stars were conservative male Republicans who had supported Ronald Reagan.

Still, the Princess was not impressed by the President and the First Lady. Diana privately referred to Reagan as "Horlicks," her slang for a boring old person, and she told Andrew Neil (editor of the *London Sunday Times*) that she considered Nancy Reagan a vulgar American. She said the only reason the First Lady had come to London the year before was to get her picture taken with the royal couple and Prince William.

At the White House the President claimed the first dance of the evening with the Princess, who had to bite her lip to keep from laughing when he flubbed her name during his after-dinner remarks. Standing up to welcome the couple, Reagan offered a toast to Prince Charles and "his lovely lady, Princess David." He quickly corrected himself and called her "Princess Diane."

"What did he say?" whispered ballerina Suzanne Farrell. "Did he call her Princess David?"

"Don't worry," replied actor Peter Ustinov. "He's just thinking of next weekend at Camp Diana."

The White House dinner in honor of the royal couple was touted as the most glittering party of the year. But the British press corps was unimpressed. They sniped at the Reagans and their tireless efforts to mingle with royalty and criticized the White House press corps as lazy. "They don't even know how to doorstep," said James Whitaker of the *Daily Mirror*. Whitaker and his colleagues prided themselves on dogging reluctant targets to their doorstep. Mrs. Reagan had barred press coverage of the dinner dance, so the British reporters followed the movie stars to their hotels. "We ambushed them to find out what went on," Whitaker said proudly. "The American reporters didn't care. They went home to bed. They were indescribably indolent." For their part, the American reporters said the British might sound cultivated but behaved like animals.

The BBC correspondent had set the scornful tone of British media coverage when he reported the royal couple's arrival at the White House: "President Reagan greeted the Prince and Princess wearing a plaid jacket that was remarkably similar to the carpet at Balmoral Castle."

That evening, after the royals and the Reagans had danced the first dance, the First Lady approached Travolta. "It's time now, John," she said. The movie star walked over to the Princess's table and asked her to dance. "I was thrilled," Diana said. Everyone stopped talking to watch them and completely ignored the Prince of Wales, who was dancing with Suzanne Farrell.

"The Princess got wind that it was a special

moment," recalled Travolta, "and she really seemed to take off. She had great rhythm. We did spins and turns. We did a kind of modern fox-trot, and she followed me very well. She's a good little mover."

The guests applauded wildly when the music stopped and Travolta escorted Diana back to her seat. The willowy Princess, flushed with excitement, wanted to dance again. She whispered to Clint Eastwood how much she would enjoy dancing with a man taller than she was. She confided to him that at five feet ten inches, she had been told to wear low heels so she would not tower over her husband.

"But you're over six feet tall," she said to the craggy-faced actor.

"I'd ask you to dance," Eastwood said, deadpan, "but you're too old for me."

"I'm only twenty-four," Diana said flirtatiously.

"Oh, all right," said the fifty-five-year-old movie star. "I'll make an exception."

Eastwood described his dance with Diana by paraphrasing a line he had made famous in his *Dirty Harry* movies: "She made my day."*

As dazzled as the celebrities were to meet Diana, she in turn was just as excited to meet them, including explorer Jacques Cousteau, skater Dorothy Hamill, artist David Hockney, Olympic gymnast Mary Lou Retton, and actress Brooke Shields. She told Baryshnikov

* When the author called the actor in 1996 to confirm the 1985 incident, Eastwood's agent said to delete the "made-my-day" quote: "We don't use that line anymore."

469

that she had gotten his autograph years before when he'd appeared at Covent Garden.

"I was one of those girls who was waiting for you for hours and hours after your performance," she said.

She asked Dorothy Hamill if there were gossip magazines and society magazines in America as there were in England. "They can be so nice," Diana said. "They ask you three lovely questions, and then they throw in a zinger question." She also inquired about television talk shows and wanted to know about Johnny Carson and the *Tonight* show.

"Of course, Joan Rivers's name came up," recalled Dorothy Hamill, who sat at Diana's table, "and Baryshnikov chimed in, 'No, don't do that! Don't go on Joan Rivers's show.'"

At a luncheon the next day in Upperville, Virginia, at philanthropist Paul Mellon's estate, the British royal couple were introduced to Caroline Kennedy and John F. Kennedy Jr. A few days later in Palm Beach at a charity ball, the Prince and Princess met Bob Hope, Gregory Peck, and Joan Collins, who had recently married a man sixteen years younger than she. Diana was fascinated by the fifty-three-year-old television star of *Dynasty* and cornered a reporter from the *Daily Mail* to pump him about Collins's latest wedding. "She's amazing," said Diana. "At her age. Husband number four."

In Washington and Palm Beach large crowds had lined the streets to welcome the royal couple. Young girls jumped up and down and screamed with excitement when they saw Diana. The Princess of Wales had become an international icon, who inspired the same kind of ear-splitting ruckus as a rock star. When she accompanied her husband to religious services in Washington's National Cathedral, more than twelve thousand people turned out. "I think it's her flying saucer hat," said Prince Charles.

In a lighthearted farewell toast in Washington, D.C., he said: "A gentleman of the press asked me, rather tactlessly, I thought, why there was a bigger crowd outside the cathedral than when I was last here on my own. The answer, of course, is that they all turned out to see my new clothes."

The audience responded appreciatively and laughed again when he referred to his wedding as a production of sanctified show business. "My wife and myself have been completely overwhelmed by the extraordinary, enthusiastic, and friendly welcome that we've received here," Charles said. "Perhaps it's the fact that we got married four years ago in a rather well-known ecclesiastical bull ring in London and it wasn't actually filmed in Hollywood."

Although most of the attention was focused on Diana with her youth and beauty, Charles, not surprisingly, charmed several older women. "I must admit I found him the more interesting of the two," wrote U.S. Chief of Protocol Selwa Roosevelt in her memoirs. "He was well read, spoke beautifully, had his father's charm and a great sense of humor." But President Reagan's daughter, Maureen, was more candid. "We all loved Charles," she said, "but Diana was stupid. Someone should tell her that it doesn't play well—that dopey looking-up-through-the-eyelashes bit of hers."

By the time she returned to London, the Princess of Wales had become a walking monument. British opinion polls said she was the country's greatest tourist attraction—a bigger draw than Trafalgar Square and the Houses of Parliament combined. One national survey calculated that from 1983 through 1985 she had generated $66.6 million in revenue from magazines, books, and tourists. She was hailed as the only member of the royal family to shake hands without gloves, to sign autographs, to kiss heads of state, and to embrace AIDS patients. She brought charm to the stolid House of Windsor, and on the evening of December 23, 1985, she also bestowed sex appeal.

She had accompanied Prince Charles to a benefit at Covent Garden for London's Royal Opera House. During the intermission, she excused herself. Leaving him alone in the royal box, she quietly slipped backstage to prepare a surprise.

When the curtain went up, a reed slim blonde twirled from the wings to center stage in a slinky white satin slip with spaghetti straps. People gasped audibly when they recognized the dancer, who was swaying to the pop music of Billy Joel's "Uptown Girl":

Uptown girl,
She's been living in her white bread world
For as long as anyone with hot blood can
And now she's looking for a downtown
　　man.

In her white satin heels, the Princess of
Wales (five feet ten) towered over her partner (five feet two), Wayne Sleep. The royal ballet dancer, who was in the *Guinness Book of
Records* for making more scissor-legged leaps
than Nijinsky, was hardly noticed. All eyes were
riveted on Diana.

She had secretly rehearsed the routine in
Kensington Palace as a Christmas present
for her husband. She presented it to him in front
of 2,600 people who had never seen royalty
slink seductively across a stage.

"The Prince nearly fell out of his chair,"
recalled Sleep, "especially when she did the
kicks over my head....That kick routine
brought the house down....I could not believe
how good she was. She was so confident and
so sure of herself that she even curtsied to the
royal box." Sleep gathered her up in his arms
and carried her off stage. "I was the one who
was nervous," he said, "knowing that I was holding the future Queen of England."

Roaring approval, the audience gave the
pop Princess a standing ovation. Then they
gave her eight curtain calls, and she took her
bows, looked directly at her husband, and
smiled. And she wanted to do an encore. "I
said no," said Sleep, "because they would

start nitpicking. She's a good dancer, but she isn't a professional. She started to do it again, and I had to drag her off. She loved it."

Diana returned to the stage months later to make a video of herself dancing to the theme song of *Phantom of the Opera*. After seeing the Andrew Lloyd Webber show six times, she told the manager of Her Majesty's Theatre in London that she wanted to be filmed dancing to the love song "All I Ask of You." She said it was to be a gift for her husband's birthday. Because it was a request from the Princess of Wales for the Prince, the theater manager agreed to make the stage and orchestra available to her. She admitted later that the video was never intended for Charles but, rather, for her own private use.

She did not object when the official photographer for the Opera House sold his pictures of her daring dance with Wayne Sleep for thousands of dollars. "It was the sexiest performance I'd ever seen at Covent Garden," said the photographer.

Unfortunately, the Prince, who had stood up to applaud his wife publicly, berated her in private for flaunting herself in an undignified manner. He rejected her gift of dance as a narcissistic exhibition and said it was just another one of her ploys to upstage him. He took no pride in her talent. Instead he felt humiliated and consoled himself in the comforting arms of his mistress.

FIFTEEN

Sarah Ferguson was one patient we never wanted to lay eyes on again. She was obnoxious—rude, demanding, and coarse," said Stephen Maitin, a London practitioner of homeopathy. "A few months before her wedding, she came to our Victoria Street clinic to be treated for obesity. She was brought in by her wedding dress designer, who was frantic to get her in shape.

"The designer, Lindka Cierach, was going through hell getting Sarah slimmed down—and calmed down. We treated her at the clinic with needles and prescriptions, and my partner also treated her at Buckingham Palace, where she was living. But, after a few sessions, we washed our hands of her. She expected us to be on call for her around the clock: if she was bingeing, we were supposed to drop everything and treat her. If she was overwrought, we were supposed to tranquilize her. If she was hung over, we were supposed to give her massages. Whether it was food, sex, or alcohol, her appetites were out of control; she did everything to excess—everything. She abused herself with too much cocaine, too many amphetamines, too much Champagne. Food, food, food, and sex all the time."

The spring of 1986 was a trying time for Sarah Margaret Ferguson, the twenty-six-year-old known as Fergie, who was engaged to marry Prince Andrew. "Sarah definitely needed help," said Lindka Cierach, "and I tried to get it for her....I would take her through the back door of the clinic and let her pay me for the treatments so no one would know."

The announcement of her engagement to marry HRH Prince Andrew had thrilled her family. The Prince's valet, James Berry, recalled her father's reaction when the news became public. "He hopped up and down on one leg in sheer happiness, chewing his fingers on one hand, and letting out shouts of joy."

"We did get quite emotional about it," admitted Sarah's stepmother, Susan Ferguson, who months later was still awestruck. The *Socialist Worker,* a British newspaper, had reported the news under the headline "Parasite to Marry Scrounger." The February announcement had jolted the Queen's press secretary, who had been advising reporters for months to disregard the relationship on the assumption that the exuberant Fergie would be just one more conquest for the Queen's twenty-six-year-old son.

Andrew, who had developed a reputation as a love-'em-and-leave-'em bachelor, seemed to prefer actresses and models, and freckle-faced Fergie certainly did not fit the mold.

"I remember Michael [Shea] inviting two of us onto the royal yacht, *Britannia,* for a briefing on the Andrew and Fergie romance," recalled Steve Lynas, then a reporter for *Today* newspaper. "Shea reassured us, 'There is no chance of these two becoming engaged.' We filed accordingly. But within a couple of days, the engagement was announced."

One cartoonist greeted the news by drawing the couple as Raggedy Ann and Andy dolls. They stood before a preacher. "Do you, Raunchy, take Randy Andy, to be your lawful ..."

Burke's Peerage, the bible of the aristocracy, was aghast that Prince Andrew, fourth in line to the throne, would choose a woman like Sarah Ferguson, "whose private life has, by the traditions of the royal family, been not only unorthodox, but well documented in the national press...six previous romances in six years...far more than Victorian in nature."

Sarah's father, Ronald Ferguson, a former army major, snorted with derision. "If she didn't have a past at twenty-six," he said, "people would be saying there was something wrong with her."

Precisely because of her background, some thought Fergie was ideal for Andrew, who defined making love as "horizontal jogging" and whose idea of playfulness was to jam a live lobster down the front of his date's bathing suit. His boisterous style puzzled his friends. "I asked him about this once," said Ferdie Macdonald, who knew the Prince as a young bachelor. "'Why are you always squirting girls with water, sir, and throwing things at them?' I said. He seemed baffled. 'They like it, don't they?' he said. 'When I squirt them with water they squeal. Doesn't that mean they like it?'"

Fergie, too, liked to play hard and play around. She made no apologies for her raffish love life. "I am a modern woman," she said. She swore easily, smoked a pack of cigarettes a day, and swapped dirty jokes with the boys. In one of her first television interviews, she used the word "prick." Wisecracking and raucous, she acted like the only dame dealt into the poker game. She said "yah" instead of "yes." When a BBC reporter asked what she had had for breakfast, she quipped, "Sausages and a migraine."

She said she suffered severe migraine headaches because of the frequent falls from her ponies when she was a child. A daredevil athlete, she won championship ribbons for skiing, swimming, and horseback riding. After competing in a steeplechase at midnight, she was awarded honorary membership in the Dangerous Sports Club, enabling her to wear the DSC badge of golden crutches. She was the only woman in the race. She never outgrew being the roughhousing tomboy who climbed trees and played pranks. She walked like a cowhand, with bowed legs and big strides, and she talked out of the side of her mouth.

Her classmates at Hurst Lodge, a boarding school in Sunningdale, Berkshire, remember her for her hearty appetite. They called her "Seconds" because she lined up twice for every meal. Expansive and enthusiastic, she was also generous, sometimes embarrassing her friends by sending them huge bouquets and expensive presents. To support herself, she worked odd jobs—sales clerk, messenger for travel agents, waitress, driver, and tour guide. To pay for ski trips to Switzerland, she worked as a chalet girl and cleaned hotel rooms.

Barely educated beyond high school, she took a course at Queen's Secretarial College in London. "She does not show the influence of too many schools," noted one of her teachers. When she finished at the bottom of her class, she bragged that she'd barely learned how to type. Shrugging happily, she said, "I'd rather ride than read."

Her father also preferred horses to books. When Major Ron, as he liked to be called, was accused of using his daughter's engagement to better himself, he insisted he did not need social advancement, especially through the royal family. "My mother was born Marian Louisa Montagu Douglas Scott, daughter of Lord Herbert Montague Douglas Scott, the fifth son of the sixth Duke of Buccleugh," he said. "To my amusement, Mother's family have always regarded their Buccleugh lineage as being socially superior to that of the Windsors!" Ferguson made sure the press knew that his family tree included four dukes and such ancestors as King Charles II and his mistress Lucy Walters. The Major was also a cousin of Robert Fellowes, the Queen's private secretary.

The *Times* wrote that Sarah Ferguson descended from landed gentry, landowners rather than aristocracy, with generations of service in the cavalry: "Every generation, down to her father, has held a commission in the Life Guards," the newspaper noted. "It is a family of old money, but not much."

The pursuit of money became a necessity

in 1970, when Major Ron accepted the unpaid position of polo manager to Prince Charles. Having flunked the examination to become a colonel in the Life Guards, which ended his advancement in the military, the Major resigned from the army. He opened an office in the Guards Polo Club in Windsor, where he tacked a pinup calendar on the wall. Even as a civilian he insisted on his military rank. "Most people address me as Major," he told a writer who had called him Mr. Ferguson. He entitled his memoir *The Galloping Major.*

The Prince of Wales was twenty-one years old when he offered Major Ferguson the honorary job of arranging his polo games, and Ferguson, a passionate polo player, accepted gratefully. He solicited corporate sponsors like Cartier and Rolex, who were eager to be associated with the Prince of Wales, and asked them to underwrite polo tournaments and cover the Prince's expenses. This lucrative patronage also included handsome compensation for the Prince's polo manager himself.

"Ronald was delighted to get the offer from Prince Charles," recalled his first wife, Susan. "It allowed him to spend a lot of time with the Prince, and it also enabled Ronald to stay in the world which interested him most, the world of horses."

Two years later, in 1972, the Fergusons separated when Sarah and her sister, Jane, were teenagers. Ronald Ferguson intimated to friends that his wife, Susan, had had a love affair with Prince Philip when the two men played polo together during the 1960s. Susan Ferguson, with her long hair and lean legs, was so sporty and elegant that designer Ralph Lauren once considered asking her to pose for a Polo ad. "She was definitely Philip's type," said her daughter. Publicly all Major Ferguson would say about his wife and Prince Philip was that the Queen's husband "certainly found my wife Susie's company much more enticing than mine."

Susan Ferguson denied having an affair with Prince Philip during her first marriage and swore that she had been faithful to her husband. "It was Ronald who had been seeing other women," she wrote in her memoir, "even while I was pregnant....His flirtations caused me a lot of suffering....I cried endlessly."

But she did not write about her relationship with Prince Philip *after* the end of her second marriage. Her daughter Sarah, though, frequently touched on the secret romance. She mentioned to acquaintances in New York City that her mother had been with Philip in Argentina during a World Wildlife Fund visit in November 1992. "It was the night of the Windsor Castle fire, which also happened to be the Queen's forty-fifth wedding anniversary," recalled one of Fergie's confidantes. "While Philip was with Susie in Buenos Aires, the Queen was by herself running pails at Windsor, trying to put out the fire." Ronald Ferguson was not surprised. "I always suspected that Prince Philip had an eye for Susie," he wrote in 1994. "Certainly, they remain friends to this day."

After sixteen years of marriage, Susan Ferguson left Ron Ferguson for another man and lost custody of her children. Her two daughters remained in England with their father in the Hampshire village of Dummer, sixty miles southwest of London. Once the divorce was final, Susan Ferguson married Hector Barrantes, a dashing Argentinian, who had been Ronald Ferguson's keenest rival on the polo field. The couple moved to Buenos Aires, where Barrantes raised and trained some of the world's best polo ponies.

"Major Ron remained bitter for years," said writer Nicholas Monson. "He was still bleeding about his divorce when I interviewed him in 1986, and asked if Argentina could not play England in polo because of the Falklands War. 'Hell, no,' he said. 'Argentina can't play here because one of those bastards ran off with my wife.'"

Major Ferguson admitted he was traumatized by his divorce. "It was a bit of a fright, to put it mildly, for everyone," he said. "It meant that at that vulnerable age my daughters didn't have Mother, so Father took over and did his best." He never forgave his wife. "That woman, you must remember, deserted her children," he told friends. He remarried in 1976 and started another family with Susan Deptford, the daughter of a wealthy farmer. Sarah jokingly introduced her to friends as "my wicked stepmother." The second Susan Ferguson soon learned that she, too, would have to contend with humiliation by a philandering husband.

"It's very acceptable behavior for some men," said Ronald Ferguson after he was caught patronizing a massage parlor employing prostitutes. "In fact, it's what I first liked about Prince Andrew. He had acquired quite a reputation as a ladies' man, for which I was rather relieved. He was a normal young sailor who had had a string of girlfriends; it all seemed very healthy as far as I was concerned."

Ever since Andrew's publicized love affair with the American actress Koo Stark, the Prince had been described in the press as "Randy Andy." During their romance, the tabloids had published nude pictures of Koo when she appeared as a lesbian in one of Britain's biggest-earning soft-porn films. These photographs showed her taking a shower with another woman. Months later the tabloids published pictures of Andrew as he skinny-dipped in Canada: "It's strip ahoy as naked Prince Andy larks about in the River." One downmarket magazine printed the photo-graph with a poem:

A rose is red
Koo is blue
Andy is Randy
What's HM to do?

On television, the satirical revue *Spitting Image* caricatured the handsome Prince as a nude pup-pet, holding up a glass of Champagne with links of sausage draped over his upper thigh. The Palace threatened to sue the show's producers, but the Director of Public Prosecutions urged royal restraint. "If I were you," he said to the Queen's lawyers, "I'd forget about it, because if you prosecute, they're going to turn up in court with that puppet." The palace backed off.

Weeks later, Faber & Faber, T. S. Eliot's publisher, announced plans to publish a book with the photograph of the naked Prince Andrew puppet.* This time, instead of threatening a lawsuit, the Palace tried the tactic of shame.

"The Queen's press secretary rang me up," recalled Mathew Evans, chairman of Faber & Faber, "and said, 'We are very disappointed that a publisher of your standing is marketing this tasteless book. We request that you do not reprint any more copies." Evans immediately upped the print order to five hundred thousand copies, and the book became a national best-seller.

"The Queen was hopping mad," recalled a secretary. "She said she didn't see any difference between the prestigious publisher of T. S. Eliot and the lurid Murdoch press."

Her Majesty had previously sued Murdoch's *Sun* for publishing breakfast-in-bed details about Prince Andrew's entertaining

* This image of Prince Andrew, as a highly eligible bachelor, appeared in *The Appallingly Disrespectful Spitting Image Book*. Entitled "Hot Dog," its caption read: "Andy is by far the dishiest royal, not having inherited many of the genetic disorders which mar the royal bloodline. Not for him the hump of Richard III, nor the babbling insanity of Canute but rather the legendary genitalia of Cuthbert the Ploughman (815-820) who, according to the legend, plowed a small furrow wherever he went."

women in his private apartment at the Palace. "The women were always young and fanciable," a former Palace pantry aide told the tabloid, "and Andrew was always so sure of his chances—so cheeky—that he would order double bacon and eggs the night before."

In selling his story, the former aide violated the confidentiality agreement he had signed as a condition of employment. The Queen was more incensed by his breach of contract than she was by his revelations. But Murdoch's paper paid the servant more than half ($3,500) of what he made in one year working for the Queen. So the former kitchen helper spilled the beans. He said Andrew's lover, Koo Stark, romped through the Palace kitchen in short skirts and skimpy T-shirts, wearing the bright red dogtags that Andrew had given her after the Falklands War. The actress, four years older than Andrew, issued orders to the staff, organized picnics for herself and the Prince, and helped herself to the Queen's favorite chocolates. The first installment of the story ended with a titillating headline about the Princess of Wales: "Tomorrow: When Barefoot Di Buttered My Toast."

The Queen, who was on tour, contacted her lawyers in London, and within hours they obtained a permanent injunction. The next day's headline: "Queen Gags the Sun." The Queen then sued Murdoch for damages, and the Palace justified the monarch's unprecedented action with a terse statement:

The servant has breached an undertaking of confidence which all palace employees sign. In this declaration, they agree not to make any disclosures about their work at the palace. It is a legally binding document under civil law.

"We might have to move toward some policy of sanction," the Palace press secretary warned royal reporters. "The line must be drawn between legitimate public interest, which all members of the royal family recognize, and prurient interest in their private lives." The Queen was awarded damages of $6,000. The *Sun* agreed to pay the amount to the Newspaper Press Fund, plus payment of the Palace's legal costs.

The Duke of Edinburgh phoned his son and told him that his love affair with Koo Stark was over. "It's finished, Andrew," Philip said sternly. The twenty-three-year-old prince did not even think of protesting. He was too afraid of his father and too afraid of embarrassing his mother. In love, but immobilized with fear, he did not know what to do. So he did nothing. Despite avowals of love to Koo Stark and a marriage proposal, he now drew back. He never apologized or explained. He simply did not call her or accept her calls.

"Koo Stark's life was ruined as a result of Andrew," said her friend Louise Allen Jones.

Although stunned and heartbroken, Koo Stark departed gracefully and maintained a discreet silence. She married months later and tried to resume her acting career. But she could never shed the identification with Andrew. Her marriage ended in divorce several years later, but she did not see Andrew again for years. Although he dated other women, he remained in love with Koo until the Princess of Wales decided to distract him with her friend Sarah Ferguson.

Diana had met Fergie at a polo match before her marriage, and they quickly became friends. They shared a fascination with astrologers, clairvoyants, and tarot card readers and compared notes on each of their sessions. During her marriage, Fergie regularly visited the basement apartment of a London faith healer known as Madame Vasso, who placed her under a blue plastic pyramid and chanted. Fergie said the Madame cleansed her while performing psychic cures.

Sarah had attended Diana's wedding and visited her several times in Kensington Palace when Diana was depressed, always making her laugh. She was the only person invited for lunch at Buckingham Palace on Diana's twenty-first birthday. "She's great fun," Diana told Andrew, who was her favorite in-law. She submitted Sarah's name to the Queen as someone young and single to include in the Windsor Castle house party for Royal Ascot week.

At the time, Fergie had hoped to marry Paddy McNally, a race car driver she had been living with on and off in Switzerland. She had proposed to him several times in their three-year relationship, but McNally, a forty-eight-year-old widower with children, kept saying no. Finally she issued an ultimatum: Either marry me or I'll leave. He offered to help her pack.

"She's been badly treated by men," said her friend Ingrid Seward, editor of *Majesty* magazine.

As her father had done to her mother, McNally frequently reduced Sarah to tears by openly pursuing other women. Now, hoping to make him envious, she waved the Queen's invitation for Royal Ascot. He responded by encouraging her to take advantage of the opportunity to socialize with the royal family. He even drove her to Windsor for the weekend and deposited her into the hands of a royal footman. McNally cheerily waved good-bye and told her to enjoy herself.

Over lunch before the races, Sarah and Andrew became acquainted. Rather, *reacquainted*: they had met as children, twenty years earlier, at a royal polo game. At this reunion he fed her profiteroles and she punched him in the arm, saying they were much too fattening. He tried to stuff them into her mouth, and she laughingly threatened a food fight. Both rowdy and rambunctious, they shared the same lavatory sense of humor and fondness for bodily noises—belches, burps, and grunts. "She whooped and hollered at all his fart jokes," recalled the waiter who served them at Windsor Castle. "As a joke, she later gave him an anatomically correct doll, and he displayed the ghastly thing in his suite at Buck House."

The gauche Prince, who banged his silverware on the table and helped himself to food before others were served, was described by some acquaintances as "Germanic, boorish, and a show-off just like his father." Others applauded him as the only one of the Queen's children "to pursue an honest-to-God job in the navy." He also studied photography and played golf like a pro.

Like his great-grandfather, his grandfather, and his father, Andrew had bypassed a university education to join the Royal Navy. When he went into the service, he was second in the line of succession, so he was accorded the privileges of royalty. He did not eat with the rest of the officers and insisted on having meals served to him in his private cabin. The chest patch on his flight suit read "HRH Prince Andrew." His nickname was "H" for Highness.

In 1981 he made a twelve-year commitment to the navy. The next year, during the Falklands War, he distinguished himself as a helicopter pilot. By the time he met Sarah in 1985, he was a lieutenant aboard the frigate HMS *Brazen*. A few days after Royal Ascot, he returned to his ship. But before going aboard, he sent Sarah roses and signed the card "A."

The Princess of Wales helped the courtship along by arranging to visit Andrew's ship with her four-year-old son, Prince William.

She invited Sarah as her lady-in-waiting, and the press turned out in full force to photograph them. Fergie was startled by the media clamor.

"God, what's this all about?" she said with a gulp as photographers pressed in.

"Keep smiling," whispered Diana as she held her son's hand. "Whatever you do, just keep smiling."

The Princess later invited Sarah and Andrew to spend private weekends at Highgrove, where the housekeeper remembers Fergie's pocketing the crested stationery and asking for more. "I've just got to send some letters on Highgrove paper," she said, giggling. "I promised a friend, who will be so *terribly* impressed." The housekeeper brought her extra stationery along with her clean laundry. "Ever time she came," the housekeeper recalled, "we had to wash and iron all her dirty clothes."

Most of the courtship was conducted on weekends in the privacy of friends' country estates, where guests remember an unmistakable physical attraction between the couple and incidents of exuberant horseplay. On one winter weekend in 1985, during a game of hide-and-seek, Andrew hid under a table, and Sarah, who was blindfolded, crawled around the floor looking for him. When she found him, she pinched his behind—hard. "Steady on!" he shouted. "You're not allowed to squeeze the royal bottom *yet!*" That evening he proposed.

Sarah replied, "When you wake up tomorrow morning, you can tell me it's all a huge joke."

The next morning Andrew proposed again and gave her a $37,000 ruby ring.

Sarah immediately called her father. "Dads, he's asked me to marry him," she yelled. "I made him propose twice, just to be sure." She cautioned her father not to say anything until Andrew received the Queen's permission to marry.

Intent on ingratiating herself with the royal family, Sarah spent weekends at Windsor when Andrew was home on leave. She took morning horseback rides with the Queen, something Her Majesty was never able to do with Diana, who was afraid of horses. Diana had been thrown as a child and broken her arm; since then she had not ridden. Unlike Diana, Sarah enjoyed playing charades and all the card games that Her Majesty liked. "Sarah cheats even more than my mother at Racing Demon," the Queen told Sarah's grandmother. The Queen called her future daughter-in-law by her Christian name. "It was never Fergie," recalled an aide, "always Sarah." Her Majesty enjoyed the spirited rapport between her son and his fiancée and observed approvingly, "He's met his match this time." Trading barbs with Prince Philip, Fergie laughed uproariously at his off-color jokes and asked him to teach her his favorite sport of competitive open-carriage driving. "I think she will be a great asset," Philip told the press. Prince Charles agreed. "She's so spunky, so enthusiastic," he marveled. "Delightful company. Just delightful."

Andrew was clearly besotted. "I know that the decision I made to marry Sarah was, and always will be, the best decision I have made, or ever will make in my life," he said. He felt especially reassured when she announced plans to take forty hours of flight training so she could share his career as a helicopter pilot. "She'll be a great navy wife," he told his family.

In Andrew, Sarah had finally found a man who treated her respectfully. "The most important thing that I felt...is his amazing ability to make one feel like a lady, like a woman....I just couldn't get over how in my life outside, as I call it, there were so many men strutting around thinking that they were so smart while they were being so foul to women."

Eager to prove herself, Sarah offered to accompany Andrew on one of his few royal duties. As the couple walked through the corridors of a convalescent home, she spotted the pool used for physical therapy and flippantly suggested that Andrew take a dip. She knew he was afraid of water and had not learned to swim. He smiled at her remark but looked slightly embarrassed. "Oh, dear," she told a patient, "he thinks I'm getting too excited."

Sarah raved to her father about her weekends at Windsor Castle. "She's either in love with Andrew or in love with the royal family," Major Ron told the press, "and I think it's the latter." The royal family welcomed Sarah

Ferguson into their midst, but other people questioned her suitability. Some patricians felt she would make royalty a roadkill. "Mark my words," predicted Ruth Fermoy, lady-in-waiting to the Queen Mother. "Nothing good will come from that common girl."

At least one Fleet Street editor agreed with the straitlaced aristocrat. "Fergie will topple the House of Windsor," predicted Brian Vine of the *Daily Mail.*

The fashion press took Sarah to task for being "stout," "full figured," and "Rubenesque." One columnist called her "the future Duchess of Pork." Another said, "She's as hearty and down-to-earth as a potato."

"I am not fat," she said defensively, "and I do not diet. I do not have a problem. A woman should have a trim waist, a good 'up top,' and enough down the bottom but not too big—a good womanly figure."

When hers was displayed at Madame Tussaud's Wax Museum, the sculptor, who had taken her measurements, would not divulge them. So one newspaper gleefully estimated 39-49-59 and said: "Here comes the bride, 41 inches wide." During a ride up an escalator, the wind blew Fergie's skirt above her knees as photographers snapped away. The picture was published over the caption: "Her Royal Thighness."

"Fergie is a jolly hockey-sticks type of girl," said one fashion editor. "A breath of fresh air. Lots of bounce. Yes, bounce. Very bouncy. Rather like a bouncing ball."

Without makeup and her hair in a ponytail, Fergie looked like the country cousin lost in the city. Snobbish fashion designers considered her a disaster—all freckles and frizzy hair—but the public embraced her freshness and accepted her oversize dresses and run-down heels. So did the Queen, whose only advice to her future daughter-in-law was to wave more slowly. Fergie imitated the Queen's wave, which she called "screwing in lightbulbs." But she was as herky-jerky as a week-old puppy, never learned restraint. Instead she bounded into crowds like a glad-handing politician. "Hi ya, hi ya, hi ya," she would say, pumping hands and collecting bouquets.

By then the Princess of Wales had become the darling of the British fashion industry, and in her designer clothes she radiated so much cinematic glamour that she was called the popcorn Princess. *Reader's Digest* called her "The World's Number One Celebrity." An international survey of magazines in 1986 reported her face graced more covers than that of any other woman, including Jacqueline Kennedy Onassis. Fergie in her baggy jumpers and horizontal stripes was relegated to covers of *Saddle Up* and *Weight Watchers*.

"Some of the clothes Sarah wore were awful," admitted her father, "but she would not be told." Understandably, she was wounded by the unkind fashion commentary, especially the comparisons with the Princess of Wales. "I don't want to be a Diana clone," she wailed.

"Not to worry," retorted British *Vogue*.

Fergie tried to pretend she didn't care about being svelte and elegant, but she begged her wedding dress designer Lindka Cierach to make her look beautiful. She felt the pressure of five hundred million people who would be watching the wedding on television.

On the morning of the wedding, July 23, 1986, the Queen invested her son with the titles of Duke of York, Earl of Iverness, and Baron Killyleagh. His bride, Sarah, became Her Royal Highness the Duchess of York. The title had not been conferred since 1936, when the previous Duchess of York became the consort Queen. She was now Queen Elizabeth, the Queen Mother, and at the age of eighty-six she remained the most beloved figure in the country. Sarah's sudden elevation to royalty entitled her to be addressed as Your Highness and to receive a respectful bob of the neck from men and deep curtsies from women, except for the only three in the realm who outranked her—the Queen, the Queen Mother, and the Princess of Wales. Fergie said she was "blissed out" by the title.

Always a stickler for protocol, she had mastered the rudiments of form by the age of twelve, when she insisted her father dismiss a butler who didn't know the difference between knickerbockers and plus fours. In a television interview after her engagement announcement, she was asked whether her uncle, who worked as a servant, would be invited to her wedding. "Of course he'll be invited," she said. "How absurd. But he'll know the form well enough not to come." Her comment was edited out of the interview. To a writer, she chided Prince Andrew for his less than elegant language. "He uses words that simply aren't on," she said. "He must have picked them up in the navy: mirror instead of looking glass; phone, mantelpiece, heads for lavatory—at least he doesn't say toilet!"

As the Duchess of York, Sarah expected the salutation of Your Royal Highness upon introduction. After that she was to be addressed as ma'am. "It rhymes with Spam," she said.

She knew she was entitled to a crest, so she designed one with a bumblebee and thistle and took the motto *Ex Adversis Felicitas* ("Out of Adversity Comes Happiness").

After her marriage, she insisted on receiving public formalities from her family, which meant her father had to bow and her stepmother curtsy. She exempted her friends but instructed her staff to advise strangers about royal protocol. On foreign trips, especially to the United States, she had a written sheet of instructions issued to those present before she made her entrances:

1. Do not speak unless spoken to.
2. Do not offer to shake hands unless she shakes first.
3. Do not instigate any topic of conversation.
4. Address her by her royal title, which is *not* Your Majesty, but Your Royal Highness.

As Duke of York, Andrew received a pay raise from the Civil List to $100,000 a year in addition to his annual naval salary of $20,000. He also received income from a $1 million trust fund his mother had set up for him. But Fergie kept her $35,000-a-year job as a publishing assistant. The Queen paid for the $350,000 wedding and presented the bride with a diamond tiara, a diamond bracelet, and a diamond necklace. Her Majesty also gave the royal couple five acres of land and paid for the $7 million construction of Sunninghill Park, their forty-six-room mansion, which was five miles from Windsor Castle. "I did it for Anne," said the Queen. "So of course I'll do it for Andrew." The rambling ranch-style house that Sarah and Andrew designed for themselves had twelve bedrooms, plus a swimming pool, a bomb shelter, and a medieval minstrel's gallery. There were two master bedrooms and a master bath with musical toilet rolls that played "God Save the Queen." The circular tub set in the middle of a white marble floor was so big that the builders called it HMS *Fergie*. Prince Philip said, "It looks like a tart's boudoir." The imposing residence was ridiculed as "a fifty-room pizza palace" and called "Southyork," after the Southfork ranch in the 1980s television show *Dallas*.

On the morning of the wedding, crowds began assembling early to watch the royal procession of coaches and celebrities. Major Ferguson marveled at the masses of people, who were standing ten deep in some places along the streets. "Just look at all these people," he said, "come to see my smelly little daughter."

America's First Lady, Nancy Reagan, had been preceded into Westminster Abbey by twenty-two U.S. Secret Service agents. Cosmetics tycoon Estee Lauder walked in behind movie star Michael Caine. Pop singer Elton John, in purple glasses and a ponytail, waved to the crowds, as did Prince Albert of Monaco. Minutes later Prime Minister Margaret Thatcher arrived, but she was booed for having sent in mounted police to settle a miners' strike.

The crowds erupted and cheered loudly when they saw the titian-haired bride, looking slim and lovely in her Victorian ivory gown. Royal trumpeters heralded her arrival as she stepped out of the glass coach. Trailed by 1712 feet of flowing satin beaded with anchors and the initial *A,* she proceeded up the steps of the Abbey. She halted at the top, unable to move. She turned around and yanked at her gown.

"Who the hell is standing on my train?" she yelled. The wedding dress designer dropped to her knees and quickly rearranged the folds of the gown. The bride then moved forward and grabbed her father's arm.

"C'mon, Dads," she said, "let's show 'em how it's done."

Major Ferguson nervously began the long walk down the aisle of the eleventh-century

Abbey with his daughter, who smiled nonstop. She made faces at one guest, gave a thumbs-up to another, and cracked jokes about the outlandish outfits she spotted among the 1,800 guests.

Major Ferguson was unnerved. "When we reached the archway leading to the chancel with the Queen and Prince Andrew gazing down expectantly," he recalled, "I had to say, 'Come on. You've got to be serious now.'"

Fergie tried to rein herself in, but the effort showed. At the altar, Prince Andrew stepped forward with his Falklands medals pinned to the breast of his naval lieutenant's uniform. "You look wonderful," he said.

"Thank you, darling," she said, smiling. "I forgot to pack my toothbrush."

"Never mind," said the beaming duke.

The Queen, who occasionally took deep breaths to control her emotions during the service, could not take her eyes off her son.

Princess Michael of Kent, who was married to the Queen's cousin, could not stop looking at the bride. "All that ghastly winking as she came down the aisle," she said. "So common."

The Princess of Wales seemed not to notice. Sitting with the royal family on pink-and-gold chairs, apart from the rest of the congregation, she looked sad and distracted, staring into space. She brightened up only when she saw her son, William, one of the four little pages. Dressed in a sailor suit, the four-year-old Prince tugged on his cap, wound the string around his nose, chewed it like taffy, and then pulled out his ceremonial dagger to bedevil the six-year-old bridesmaid next to him.

Having brought Sarah and Andrew together, Diana had looked forward to having a friend as a sister-in-law and to sharing what she called "the royal load." But she was unprepared for sharing the spotlight. The sudden media attention directed at Fergie jolted Diana, who was accustomed to being the focus of press interest. She slipped into second place temporarily. She tried to make light of her reduced status by joking to reporters. "You won't need me now," she teased. "You've got Fergie."

Sarah and Andrew's royal wedding was characterized most amusingly by an Italian newspaper, Milan's *Il G'iorno:* "And so to conclude, if it is true, as Flaubert asserted, that to be happy, it is necessary not to be too intelligent, to be a little bit arrogant, and above all, to have good health, then there is no doubt that the future of Andrew and Sarah will be among the best." And it was. Sublime. For a time.

SIXTEEN

The Prince of Wales was convinced that his wife was having an affair with her bodyguard. Barry Mannakee, a gregarious police sergeant, had been assigned to protect the Princess in 1985 when the Waleses' marriage started falling apart. He accompanied her wherever she went, and as Charles spent more time away from his wife, she turned to her personal detective for company.

"He was like all the protection officers for royalty,"* said the former head of Scotland Yard, who received a title when he retired. "They are selected for sensitivity and diplomacy. They're highly skilled at security and armed at all times, but they must also blend into any circumstance. This requires a range of social skills—skiing, sailing, horseback riding, hunting, even carriage riding. The royalty protection boys have expensive haircuts and wear Turnbull and Asser shirts. They're handsome, charming, and seductive."

The thirty-nine-year-old protection officer for the Princess of Wales was a married man with two children, so he got along well with three-year-old Prince William. "Barry was such a colorful and easygoing character," recalled the Highgrove housekeeper. "He was fun and everyone adored him. He was an ideal personal security officer for the Princess....She hung on to his every word, flirted with him outrageously, and pulled his leg in a way that suggested the two of them were very close. There have been many rumors about them having an affair, but I am sure that is com-

* The Royal Protection Unit of Scotland Yard provides full protection to the monarch, her husband, her heir, the Queen Mother, and all the monarch's children. Partial protection is provided to some of the Queen's cousins when they are performing public duties, but not to their spouses. "Most of the time, Prince Michael gets security," said the former head of security, "but *not* his wife."

pletely untrue. For Diana, Barry was simply a friend, someone she could rely on and trust."

The Princess's detective escorted her on her endless rounds of shopping and took her for long drives through the hills of Balmoral when her husband went fishing alone and she wanted to get away from the rest of the royal family. She turned to Mannakee when she was upset, which was often in those days, and he offered consolation and a strong shoulder to cry on. He comforted her when she became unstrung before public engagements.

"On one occasion, she kept saying she couldn't go ahead with it, and just collapsed into my arms," said Mannakee. "I hugged her and stopped her crying. What else would you have done?"

The policeman became the repository of Diana's secrets, including her suspicions about her husband and Camilla Parker Bowles. Diana told Mannakee she was convinced that despite Charles's promises to her before they married, he had gone back to his mistress. Diana said she confirmed her suspicions one weekend when she arrived at Highgrove and Charles was not there. His aide said he had left minutes before she arrived, roaring off by himself in his sports car. He did not say where he was going and didn't leave a number where he could be reached in case of emergency.

Diana went into his study and pushed the recall button on his mobile phone, which rang the Parker Bowles estate. When the butler answered, she hung up. She checked Charles's private calendar and saw a "C" marked on that date. She searched his desk drawers and told her bodyguard that she had found a cache of letters from Camilla. Some were chatty and some extremely intimate, addressed to "My Beloved."

After that, Mannakee felt even more protective toward the Princess, who tearfully asked him why her husband had turned away from her. "He's a fool," said Mannakee, shaking his head. "A bloody fool." Diana was touched by her detective's loyalty, and his working-class London accent made her smile. He became her close friend, her confidant, even her fashion consultant. She turned to him the way a wife turns to a husband, looking for approval. Servants recall many occasions when the Princess dressed for a public engagement and came out of her room to ask her bodyguard for his opinion.

"Barry, how do I look? Do you think these are the right earrings?"

"Perfect," he said. She twirled in front of him, smoothed down her evening dress, and applied more lip gloss.

"Are you sure?" she asked, looking in the mirror. "Do I look all right?"

"Sensational, as you know you do," he said with a laugh. "I could quite fancy you myself."

"But you do already, don't you?" she said flirtatiously.

Their easy banter disturbed Charles, who lived by a double standard: he confided in his gardener at Highgrove about the woeful state of his marriage, but he could not stand Diana confiding in her bodyguard. Charles accused her of lacking decorum and said her behavior with the staff was deplorable.

He was embarrassed that their marital fights, which had gone on behind closed doors, were now being waged in front of the servants. He blamed Diana for the open warfare because she had started to talk back. In the beginning of their marriage, she had been too insecure to speak up. But she gradually overcame her shrinking deference, and as her confidence grew with her popularity, she was no longer willing to defer.

Usually restrained in public, the Princess let loose in private. She railed about her husband's "toadying" friends, his preoccupation with polo, his dinner parties with "boring old men who smell of cigars," and his solitary trips to fish and paint and ski. She said his excursions were simply excuses to get away from her.

The Prince responded that he needed the trips to restore his peace of mind after enduring her neurotic behavior. He taunted her about her eating disorder, which caused fainting spells in public. "You're always sick," Charles said with disgust. "Why can't you be more like Fergie?" During meals, he chided her. "Is that going to reappear later? What a waste."

Diana struck back by accusing him of being selfish and stingy, and he yelled at her for being extravagant. "The meaner he got, the more she would spend," said interior designer Nicholas Haslam, a close friend of the royal family. "That meanness of his drove her crazy...but the royals love to play at being poor. Camilla is the same way; she can't abide spending money, and Charles adores that quality in her. They turn each other on with their stinginess. When Camilla comes in bristling about how much the cleaner costs, Charles becomes aroused and leaps in to exclaim about how much he had to pay for the same thing. Back and forth they go, banging on about the cost of having their clothes commercially cleaned. The two of them nearly expire with exasperation about having to spend their money on such a necessity. ..."

The Princess carped that his penny-pinching deprived her of a tennis court at Highgrove.

"You know it's the only thing I have ever wanted here," she told him.

Charles said he could not afford the $20,000 to build a tennis court.

"You cannot be serious," Diana shouted. "What about the thousands you pour into your precious bloody garden and anything else which takes your fancy? I don't think you realize quite the efforts I make to go along with what you want to do all the time. What about my wants?"

He shrugged and walked out of the room. Diana yelled at him through the closed door. That evening she did not show up for dinner. While he sat in the dining room waiting for her, she ate alone in the nursery, where she said she did not have to beg for love.

During their most heated arguments, they flung curses and objects. After one blistering row, Charles stormed out the door, jumped into his car, and roared out of Highgrove. Diana opened an upstairs window and screamed at the top of her lungs, "You're a shit, Charles, an absolute shit!" During another quarrel, she threw a teapot at him, stomped out of the room, and slammed the door, nearly knocking over a footman. She yelled over her shoulder, "You're a fucking animal, Charles, and I hate you!"

Soon Nigel Dempster, the *Daily Mail* gossip columnist, who said he socialized with royalty, denounced Diana in print. He called her a spoiled, fiendish monster who was making the Prince of Wales "desperately unhappy."

Her growing distrust of Charles and her jealousy over Camilla Parker Bowles marked Diana—in her husband's eyes—as irrational. Charles expected to do as he pleased—without objection from his wife. Her tearful outbursts about his long absences only convinced him of her instability. Worse, he was bored with her. He dismissed her interests—clothes, dancing, rock and roll—as trivial. He said her hospital visits were self-serving, and her humor, which he once found so delightful, grated on him.

A university graduate with intellectual pretensions, Charles was embarrassed to be married to a high school dropout who did not know the difference between Sakharov and Solzhenitsyn. During the taping of a television interview at Highgrove in 1986, she poked fun at herself for failing the college entrance exams. "Brain the size of a pea I've got," she chirped. Charles insisted her comment be edited out. Diana said he should have edited out his own comment about talking to the plants in his garden at Highgrove. "It's very important to talk to them," he had told viewers. She had told him, "People will think you're barking [mad]." That was the last television interview the couple did together.

But Diana was right. Charles's remark made him look slightly eccentric, if not ridiculous. "He's really not the nut-chomping loony you read about in the papers," insisted his brother Andrew.

"Charles sometimes complained to friends about what he considered Diana's coarse, even vulgar, sense of humor," reported journalist Nicholas Davies. "Once the couple were lunching with Charles's old friend, the South African philosopher Sir Laurens Van der Post. The two men were enjoying a weighty conversation about the problem of blacks and whites living together in South Africa when Diana suddenly put in, 'What's the definition of mass confusion?'"

The two men looked perplexed.

"Father's Day in Brixton [a predominantly black area of London]," Diana told them merrily.

"I can't believe you just said that," said Charles.

"Oh, well, if you two are having a sense-of-humor failure, I'll leave you to it," said Diana as she left the table.

Miserable, Charles wrote to a friend on March 11, 1986, that his marriage "is like being trapped in a rather desperate cul-de-sac with no apparent means of exit." He dipped into the poetry of Richard Lovelace (1618-1658) to describe his despair: "Stone walls do not a prison make, Nor iron bars a cage. ..." Diana's demands for attention exasperated him, and he was not willing to pump her up for every public appearance. In the past he had quoted Shakespeare's *Henry V* and told her (to) "Stiffen the sinews, summon up the blood. ..." Now he ignored her or else snapped with irritation, "Just plunge in and get on with it." He complained to his biographer about her self-absorption and extraordinary vanity, saying that she spent hours every day poring over newspapers and magazines, examining her press coverage.

Acknowledging Diana's preoccupation with herself, her friend Carolyn Bartholomew defended her to author Andrew Morton. "How can you *not* be self-obsessed," she asked, "when half the world is watching everything you do?"

Charles, previously controlled and gracious in public, started losing his temper. He clashed with Diana at a polo game when she posed for photographers while sitting on the hood of his 1970 Aston Martin convertible. The rare automobile, then worth $125,000, had been a twenty-first birthday present from his mother.

"Off, off! What are you doing to my wonderful car?" he shouted. "You can't sit there! Get off! You'll dent the bodywork."

Diana was mortified by his outburst. She quickly slid off the fender and slyly stuck out her leg to kick him. Startled, he grabbed her arm and pushed her against the car, but she slipped away and leaped inside. He started to cuff the back of her neck but realized that people were gathering around, so he pulled back. He smiled thinly and pretended the incident was a joke.

During another screaming argument, Charles threw a wooden bootjack at Diana. "How dare you speak to me like that?" he yelled. "Do you know who I am?"

At first he had responded to her outbursts with grim silence. Now he struggled to restrain his temper but was not always successful. Once he stalked out of the room, strode into his bathroom, and, in front of his valet, Ken Stronach, ripped the porcelain washbasin from the wall and smashed it on the floor. "I have to do it," his valet recalled him saying. "You do understand, don't you? *Don't* you?" The wide-eyed valet nodded.

Despite his violent outbursts, Charles denied ever striking his wife. In fact, he blamed her for throwing lamps and breaking windows. During one of their visits to Althorp, her family estate, they stayed in a newly decorated suite that Diana's father admitted

509

Charles and Diana left "somewhat damaged." An antique mirror was smashed, a window cracked, and a priceless chair shattered. "It was an almighty row," said the Earl Spencer, who added quickly that every married couple had fights. "It's nothing," he said. "Diana is still very much in love with Charles."

Diana stopped going to Althorp because of her father's wife. So the Earl Spencer had to go to London to see his daughter and grandchildren. After her brother's wedding, Diana said she could no longer bear the presence of "that woman [her stepmother]." The sight of Raine presiding over the Spencer ancestral home during a prenuptial party for her brother had incensed Diana. She felt that her mother, Frances Shand Kydd, had been slighted. Frances had recently been abandoned after nineteen years of marriage when her husband left her for another woman. Although she had left Johnny Spencer before he inherited Althorp, Diana and her siblings felt, perhaps without justification, that Raine had usurped their mother's rightful place. Even as adults they continued to revile their stepmother.

During a prewedding party for her brother at Althorp, Diana watched Raine go into the nursery and graciously pour tea for her husband's grandchildren. When Raine left the room and headed for the grand staircase, Diana followed her. As Raine started down the first flight of stairs, Diana lunged forward and knocked her over with her shoulder. The fifty-eight-year-old woman fell to her knees and tumbled down the steps, coming to a stop on the first landing. Diana walked around her and, without a word, proceeded into the party.

The assault alarmed the Countess's personal assistant, Sue Ingram. "I wanted to run upstairs and ask Her Ladyship if she was all right, but I was too embarrassed, not only for myself, but for her," she said. "The servants and I pretended that nothing had happened—we just looked away."

Later Raine mentioned the outburst to her assistant. "What has happened to Diana?" she asked. "Why such an occurrence? I just don't understand that girl."

Beset by her eating disorder and her husband's infidelity, Diana was volcanic and erupted frequently. After another of their incessant fights, Charles found her in tears in her bedroom, pouring out her heart to her detective about Charles's late night telephone calls to Camilla Parker Bowles and his unexplained absences. Charles was appalled by her lack of discretion.

Within days the detective, who had guarded the Princess for a year, was suddenly transferred into the Diplomatic Unit. A member of the Prince's staff told a reporter that the abrupt change was due to the sergeant's "over-familiarity" with the Princess.

"He's just punishing me," Diana told friends bitterly.

"I was transferred for domestic reasons," Mannakee admitted to the press, "but I have no intentions of discussing those reasons."

The Prince, who was polite but aloof with his servants, did not approve of his wife's familiarity with the help. He maintained a certain distance from the staff and expected her to do the same. But she treated her dresser, her detective, and her butler like extended family.

"Do not misinterpret the Prince's demeanor," said one of his equerries. "There's a seemly remove about him that comes from being reared as royalty."

Diana, who did not possess that royal remove, embraced servants like friends. She thought nothing of eating in the staff kitchen, where her first question upon arrival at Sandringham, Balmoral, or Buckingham Palace was usually, "What's for dinner?" She attended staff parties, brought records, and asked the servants to dance with her. Her husband rarely attended these employee get-togethers because he knew his presence would impose undue formality. Still, he regarded his wife's behavior as highly improper.

Her indiscriminate displays of affection also irked him. He said that she kissed everyone she met, even strangers. She did not discriminate between highway workers and heads of state. At polo games she kissed Major Ron Ferguson to say hello. After the royal wedding she kissed the Lord High Chamberlain to say thank you. On the honeymoon she kissed the President of Egypt, Anwar al-Sadat, to say goodbye. In New Zealand she rubbed noses with a Maori tribeswoman. When she returned home she kissed her servants.

When the royal family attended a grand ball at Buckingham Palace for the household staff, Diana circled the room in her tiara to greet everyone. She understood how much her title meant and how special people felt being in her presence. "I could see Charles watching her out of the corner of his eye," recalled Wendy Berry, who worked at Highgrove. "He looked on as she took the mother of one servant in her arms and kissed her expansively on the cheeks. Charles's expression was one of horror mixed with fascination that any wife of his could behave so normally with ordinary people."

Eight months after Barry Mannakee was transferred from the Royal Protection Unit, a car smashed into his motorcycle and he was killed. Charles was given the news immediately, but he waited twenty-four hours before telling Diana. When they were on their way to the airport to fly to France for the Cannes Film Festival, he turned to her moments before she was to get out of the limousine in front of photographers.

"Oh, by the way," he said, "I got word from the Protection Unit yesterday that poor Barry Mannakee was killed. Some sort of motorcycle accident. Terrible shame, isn't it?"

Diana burst into tears as the limousine pulled up to the royal flight. Charles pushed her out.

"Let's go, darling," he said sarcastically. "Your press awaits you."

Diana did not believe Mannakee's death was

an accident. She was convinced that her former protection officer had been assassinated by MI5 [Britain's intelligence agency] at the instigation of her jealous husband. She blamed herself for Mannakee's death and tried to summon his spirit through several séances. When a writer published a book suggesting a nefarious plot by MI5, Mannakee's father insisted his son's death was an accident. Diana eventually accepted that, but she never forgave her husband for the cruel way he broke the news to her. She told the story to friends to demonstrate his heartlessness and to show the diabolical pleasure he took in tormenting her.

Privately the fairy tale was over, but the public did not yet see the cracks behind the facade. The first glimpse came after a polo match when Charles kissed his wife in front of hundreds of people when his team lost; she turned her head quickly as if she had just been licked by a slobbering dog. Then she wiped his kiss off her cheek.

"I suppose I should've seen something askew in 1985 when I interviewed Prince Charles for my biography of the late poet laureate John Betjeman," said writer Bevis Hillier. "But I wasn't looking for a shadow on the romance. I'm in my fifties and grew up singing 'God Save the King.' I now sing 'God Save Our Gracious Queen.' The monarchy is like religion to me, and absurd as it might sound, I want it to survive. ...

"The Prince and I talked in his office at Kensington Palace, where a clock chimed every fifteen minutes. He was very messy—heaps of papers on the floor and red leather boxes with gold-embossed Prince of Wales feathers all over the place. But he was sweet and could not have been more pleasant.

"My last question to him was: Which was your favorite Betjeman poem? He flipped through the book of poetry and fell upon one dealing with the aging sex drive. He read the last stanza:

> *At all the thoughts that in us springToo*
> *long we let our bodies cling,*
> *We cannot hide disgust*
> *At all the thoughts that in us spring*
> *From this late-flowering lust.*

"He smiled ruefully and said, 'I'd like to choose "Late Flowering Lust," but I guess I better not.' Instead he chose 'Indoor Games Near Newbury.'" The Prince had carefully selected a poem about little children holding hands in a cupboard.

"I knew something was amiss in the fall of 1986, after an off-the-record interview with Prince Charles at Highgrove," recalled the London bureau chief of *Time*. "As a condition of the interview, I was not allowed to ask questions about his family. We talked in his study, where there were at least forty sterling silver-framed pictures—the Queen, the Queen Mother, the Duke of Edinburgh, King Juan Carlos, Mountbatten, Wills and Harry, the royal

515

horse, the royal dogs. But not one picture of the royal wife. Although Diana was the most photographed woman in the world, her picture was nowhere to be found in her husband's study."

The royal watchers on the tabloids noticed the strain between the Prince and Princess and reported that the couple had spent thirty-seven consecutive nights in Britain without once sharing the same bedroom. They noted that Charles returned early and alone from family vacations and that even when he and Diana were going to the same place, they arrived separately. She attended fashion shows and rock concerts with other people in London while he worked alone in his gardens at Highgrove, 113 miles west of the city. When he went fishing by himself at Balmoral, she remained at Kensington Palace with their children.

A Norwegian manufacturer capitalized on the discord and made the Prince and Princess of Wales role models for people too busy to cook. Billboards in Oslo featured the mournful faces of Charles and Diana looking at single-serving cans of pasta and beef stew marked *Middag for en*—Dinner for one. Yet Britain's establishment press did not take the rift rumors seriously. They dismissed the tabloid stories as "downmarket tittle-tattle" and called on establishment figures like Harold Brooks-Baker of *Debrett's Peerage* to dispel the rumors.

The reverent monarchist complied eagerly. "Outrageous, simply outrageous," said Brooks-

Baker. "These rumors of marital discord tarnish the royal family's image and diminish the monarchy. They must stop. There will never be a separation between the Prince and Princess of Wales, and there certainly will never be a divorce."

His denial did not dent the tabloids' credibility among royal servants. "Too much of the information was accurate and true," said one of Princess Margaret's butlers with dismay. "We knew that it had to be coming from someone on the inside. One of us. The royal family knew it, too. But there's nothing they can do about servants, who sell their stories, unless, of course, they catch them outright. Then we can be fired, fined, even imprisoned.

"The only people who knew that the Prince and Princess of Wales were no longer sharing the same bed were their personal maids. You don't think Her Majesty knew that. Or even wanted to know it. Princess Margaret used to say that she had to read the papers simply to find out what was happening in her own family. The floor-shaking fights between them [Charles and Diana] were known to their staffs, and the word traveled fast through the royal houses."

The butler offered an explanation for the disparity between the upmarket press, which proclaimed the marriage as solid, and the tabloids, which depicted the marriage as shaky. He said a footman at Highgrove had seen the Princess throw a teapot at the Prince and rush from the room in tears. Hours later the royal couple had composed themselves and appeared together in public at a benefit. Their smiling photographs in the *Daily Telegraph* made the teapot story in the *Mirror* look fabricated. "Actually, both stories were accurate," said the butler, "but the tabs ran the juicier bits."

Diana resented the press speculation about her marriage but did not know what to do. "Just because I go out without my husband," she protested, "doesn't mean my marriage is on the rocks." She had taken on more public engagements—299 in 1985, 70 percent more than her 177 in 1984—and more than half of those in Britain were without her husband. Heartened by her increasing commitment to performing royal duties, Prince Philip told her to ignore the rumors, and she tried.

"When we first got married," she said, "we were everybody's idea of the world's most perfect couple. Now they say we are leading separate lives. The next thing is I'll start reading that I've got a black Catholic lover."

The unrelenting pressure of having to appear in public and be gracious to a press corps that acted like a firing squad wore her down. During a visit to a children's nursery school, she was asked by the supervisor whether she wanted to accommodate the photographers clamoring outside.

"I don't see why I should do anything for them," she replied. "They never do anything for me."

The next day the *Sun* fired back with an editorial: "Princess Diana asks: 'What have the newspapers ever done for me?' The *Sun* can answer Her Loveliness in one word—everything! The newspapers have made her one of the most famous women in the world. They have given her an aura of glamour and romance. Without them, the entire Windsor family would soon become as dull as the rulers of Denmark and Sweden."

The burden of maintaining a sunny public image sapped the Princess's strength. "I got no help from anyone carrying this load," she complained to her lady-in-waiting. Like Diana's husband, the Palace expected her to do her duties without comment: show up and shut up. But Diana needed reassurance. Without Barry Mannakee beside her, she had no one to buoy her, to provide advice and offer affection. Her husband had come to regard her as a whiner. "Oh, God, what is it now," he'd say when she approached him. She felt increasingly isolated within the royal family and uneasy about confiding in her sisters, especially Jane, who was married to Robert Fellowes, the Queen's assistant private secretary.

Diana was also wary of Sarah Ferguson, who, she said, acted too eager to please Charles. Diana didn't want to disappoint her friends by admitting her fairy-tale marriage was a sham, so she said nothing. When her former roommate, Carolyn Pride Bartholomew, noticed her startling weight loss, Diana finally admitted her eating disorder and said she was throwing up four to five times a day because she was so unhappy. The Princess said her Prince was no longer charming.

When Mrs. Bartholomew was badgered by reporters in Australia about the state of the Waleses' marriage, she declined to comment. Pressed about the royal couple's separate quarters and separate vacations, she said nothing. One reporter pointed out the twelve-year age difference and suggested the twenty-six-year-old Princess was bored by her thirty-nine-year-old husband.

"Oh, no," said Mrs. Bartholomew.

"Well, what do they possibly have in common?"

"Well...uhmmm...uhmmm...they...uhmmm ...have their children."

Diana was at her most vulnerable in 1986 when she met Captain James Hewitt at a cocktail party. She had been lonely, neglected, and despondent. The twenty-seven-year-old bachelor knew how to flirt with a princess without overstepping the line. He was introduced as a skilled horseman with the Life Guards' Household Division. Diana told him that she had been afraid of horses since falling off her pony as a child. She said her fear of riding was a disappointment to her husband and his equestrian family, and she wanted to do something about it. The handsome cavalry officer smiled and offered to help her. Two days later she phoned him for riding lessons.

After graduating from Millfield, a private academy, James Hewitt received his military training at Sandhurst, joined the Life Guards, and made the army his life. He considered himself honored to be among the sovereign's elite personal guard. Out of uniform, the officer dressed like a gentleman in double-breasted blazers, Gucci loafers, and gold cuff links. He wore silk cravats, played polo, and cultivated good manners. And he listened to the wartime recordings of Winston Churchill to improve his enunciation. With wavy russet hair, full lips, and sleepy blue eyes, he was beguiling to women. "All I know," he said, "is horses and sex." Years later he boasted that he had shared both with the Princess of Wales.

Their love affair started in the stables of Knightsbridge barracks. For the first two months Diana arrived every week for her riding lesson, accompanied by her detective and her lady-in- waiting. Soon the lady-in-waiting was left waiting. And the detective remained discreetly in the barracks while the Princess and her riding instructor rode alone on the trails, laughing and talking. "Their horses," recalled the groom Malcolm Leete, "were hardly ever ridden." The groom later sold his recollections to a newspaper.

In James Hewitt, Diana had found a man her own age who thoroughly relished women and treated them with the same respect he accorded high-strung horses. He calmed and comforted them.

The Princess of Wales crossed class lines to find Hewitt, the son of a marine captain and a dentist's daughter. Diana described Hewitt to a friend as "my soul" and said that despite their backgrounds, they were very much alike. Both were graceful athletes, who reveled in their bodies and were extraordinarily vain about their appearance. They loved to dress up and spent hours getting ready to appear in public. Both were seducers who knew how to exploit their charms.

On a deeper level they bonded through the trauma of their parents' divorces. Diana said she was determined that her children would not suffer the same kind of childhood she had. Yet despite her best efforts, she was subjecting them to the same violent quarrels and tearful recriminations she had seen between her parents. Hewitt had avoided making those mistakes by not getting married. As the only son, he was spoiled by his mother and indulged by his two sisters, with whom he remained close.

Unlike Charles, Hewitt lapped up Diana's conversations. He listened attentively to her discuss her charity work and how much she enjoyed her royal duties when "they" (the Palace courtiers) left her alone. She felt as if she had a divine ability to minister to the sick and dying; she said this healing touch came from "spirits" that guided her. This enabled her to go beyond the ceremonial role of a royal princess visiting hospitals. She saw herself as Mother Teresa in a crown. She said she identified with victims and felt their pain. Although Hewitt did not understand her mysticism, he listened raptly and did not question her judgment—unlike the Bishop of

Norwich, who was startled by Diana's claims. When she told the cleric that she was a reincarnated spirit who had lived before, he looked puzzled. When she said she was protected by a spirit world of people she had known who had died, she said the Bishop looked horrified. But Hewitt was a simple man with no orthodox religion, and his silence encouraged her to keep talking.

She told him about her children, whom she called "my little knights in shining armor," saying they were the most important people in her life. Over several weeks she guided Hewitt through the swamp of her marriage, and as she revealed the dismal secrets—the bulimia, the suicide attempts, the separate bedrooms, and the mistress—he saw a woman reeling with rejection. Like most men who met Diana, he felt protective.

Wisely, he let her make the first move, which she did by inviting him to dinner at Kensington Palace when Charles was at Highgrove. She dismissed most of her staff that evening and greeted Hewitt excitedly at the front door. She led him to her private sitting room and handed him a magnum of Champagne. She said she rarely drank, but this was a special occasion. He popped the cork and filled the flutes as she sat on the apricot-and-white-striped sofa. Looking around the room, he chuckled when he saw the embroidered maxim on one of her scattered pillows:

If You Think Money Can't Buy Love

He appreciated her expertise at shopping London's finest stores because he'd been the lucky beneficiary of several extravagant sprees. He told her that members of his regiment had been impressed by the presents that had been arriving at his barracks. She lowered her eyes and giggled.

"Whether it's friends, lovers, or relatives, Diana is very generous," said interior designer Nicholas Haslam. "She's incapable of *not* giving presents. She always arrives at my flat with some kind of lovely gift—a tie, a plant, a book. Unlike the rest of the royals, she knows how to spend money on other people."

Among the presents Hewitt received from the Princess were a rust cashmere sweater from Harrods, four silk Hermès ties, and a pair of $1,500 hand-tooled leather riding boots from Lobb's, London's finest shoemaker. He also received a tweed hacking jacket with suede patches and leather buttons, three custom-made suits, ten Turnbull & Asser shirts with matching ties, two blazers, one dozen pairs of cashmere socks, two dozen silk boxer shorts, gold cuff links, a diamond-studded tie pin, and an eighteen-carat gold clock from Asprey, the royal jeweler.

Limited by his $50,000-a-year salary, the cavalry officer could not afford to reciprocate in the same grandiose style. "Instead I gave her the clothes off my back," he said lightly.

She asked him for his T-shirt to wear to bed and his cricket sweater to wear under her ski parka. She also asked for one of his down-filled jackets, which she wore frequently on walks. His most luxurious gift was a pair of diamond-and-emerald earrings, which he sent her as a reward for not biting her fingernails.

Following their first dinner at Kensington Palace, Diana served him coffee on the sitting room couch. She turned off the lamp on the side table and then slipped into his lap, putting her arms around his neck. Moments later, he told his biographer, she stood up and, without saying a word, led him into her bedroom.

For the next eighteen months their affair was vigorous and passionate and not conducted with utmost discretion. They visited Althorp, and according to Hewitt, they made love in the poolhouse. They stayed with Hewitt's mother in Devon and made love in her garden. They spent nights together at Kensington Palace with Diana's children and weekends at Highgrove when Charles was traveling. The young Princes became so accustomed to Hewitt's presence that they called him "Uncle James." He spent hours teaching them how to ride. He took them to his army barracks, where they were enthralled by the men in uniform. He taught the little boys how to march, salute, and hold a gun.

In turn, Diana invited Hewitt's father and his two sisters to London for a private dinner. James had confided in them about his relationship with Diana. She also accompanied him to Devon and spent many days with his mother, who ran a riding school. "She would always help carry the things out after lunch," recalled Shirley Hewitt. "She would wash up the dishes and, on one occasion, helped clear out a cupboard. She said, 'What is all this? It's disgusting!' and cleared the whole lot out and gave the cupboard a good wash." On those trips Diana endeared herself to Mrs. Hewitt with her girlish questions about James's childhood. Together they teased him as they paged through the family scrapbooks, looking at his baby pictures.

Hewitt said he had not intended to fall in love with the Princess, whom he described as emotionally vulnerable and distressed. "But," he admitted sheepishly, "it happened....We spoke a great deal about what the future may hold for us both. I think it was perhaps fun to fantasize and to believe in a situation which quite clearly might not be possible...the dreams of being able to spend the rest of our lives together."

Joking nervously about the Treason Act of 1351, he wondered aloud if he could be sent to the Tower and beheaded for sleeping with Diana. The archaic law forbids adultery with the wife of the heir to the throne to ensure that all heirs are legitimate. When the Princess's affair with her riding instructor was disclosed by Hewitt and confirmed by Diana, some royal biographers noticed a startling resemblance between the copper-haired Hewitt and rusty-haired Prince Harry. But Hewitt denied he was the father and staunchly maintained he did not meet Diana until two years after the birth of her second son. "In fact," stated *Private Eye,* "Hewitt first met Diana five years earlier—at a polo match in 1981, before her marriage."

The Princess did not exercise prudence in her relationship with the cavalry officer. Careful to disguise her voice when she called him on the pay phone at his barracks, she took few other precautions. In a sense, she felt immune from scandal because people were accustomed to seeing her at public events with escorts like Major David Waterhouse and the banker Philip Dunne. So the image of her in the presence of other men had already been established. She relied on the reservoir of goodwill she enjoyed as the Princess of Wales, knowing that most people would never suspect her of committing adultery, especially with the man in charge of the army's stables.

"It was simply too inconceivable," said one of her closest friends. "Even after she admitted on television that it was true—that she had been unfaithful with that cad, who cashed her in by writing a book—I still couldn't believe it."

Nor could her brother, Charles Spencer, who, despite contrary evidence, defended her against insinuations of promiscuity. "Hand to heart," he said, "my sister Diana has only slept with one man in her life and he is her husband."

Some of the men in Hewitt's regiment suspected the relationship from the beginning and nudged each other with burlesque winks about the Princess and her riding instructor, whom they had nicknamed the Red Setter. But none dared publicly to suggest anything improper. "Even when I saw them kissing and cuddling in the middle of the riding school, I was so shocked that I didn't tell anyone about it, not even my wife, for a year and a half, until after I left the army," said the former groom.

He described what he saw: "It was in the middle of November 1988 and Hewitt had been transferred to Combermere Barracks, not far from Windsor. I got the Princess's horse ready for her three-thirty P.M. lesson...and took it to the riding school because the weather outside was awful....The two of them met inside, and I stood on a mounting block to watch them. I saw his hands going up the back of her blouse. Her blouse was outside her jodhpurs. She was all over him. He was all over her."

As the affair progressed, Diana drew her former roommate, Carolyn Bartholomew, into her confidence as well as her friend Mara Berni, who owned the San Lorenzo restaurant in Knightsbridge, where Diana and Hewitt sometimes lunched together. She also relied on her detective, Ken Wharfe, who accompanied her with Hewitt, making their trips look like casual excursions rather than romantic outings.

Diana included her lover on the Queen's invitation list for a formal white-tie ball in November 1988 to celebrate Prince Charles's fortieth birthday. She knew without looking at the list of five hundred guests that Charles would invite his mistress. So she added the name of her riding instructor next to her favorite dress designer, Bruce Oldfield. Everyone in the royal family attended the ball at Buckingham Palace, except Prince Andrew, who was aboard the HMS *Edinburgh* in Australian waters. King Juan Carlos and Queen Sofia flew in from Spain to join the kings of Norway, Luxembourg, and Liechtenstein and the deposed king of Greece. The Dukes of Northumberland and Westminster danced and drank Champagne until three in the morning with rock stars, disk jockeys, and industrialists.

Charles had started his day by visiting the inner cities of Birmingham northwest of London, where the charity he founded in 1976, the Prince's Trust, employed disadvantaged young people. He arrived in the morning wearing a "Life Begins at 40" button, a gift from his children, and was cheered by crowds, who burst into a chorus of "Happy Birthday."

"When will you be King?" shouted a mechanic.

"Dunno," said Charles. "I might fall under a bus before I get there."

The inner-city celebration did not impress the chairman of the Labor Party. "It's just a way in which the benevolent hierarchy operates," said Dennis Skinner. "They have to push a few crumbs off the table for the poor and underprivileged...to ease their conscience and create an image of benevolence."

That evening's Palace party aroused even further indignation. "They'll spend as much on this celebration as many poor families would be able to spend in a lifetime," said Skinner. "Those on Easy Street, including the royal family, should take great care not to treat poor people with contempt. This party is like kicking sand in the faces of those people at the bottom of the ladder."

Charles said he would not be deterred by criticism, especially from cranks. "Now that I'm forty," he said, "I feel much, much more determined about what I'm doing." He considered his work for the underprivileged of Britain worthy of royalty but said his wife's patronage of AIDS patients was "inappropriate" and that the press coverage she received by visiting them was at times "sentimental" and "exploitative." He said her trip to visit AIDS babies in New York City's Harlem Hospital a few months later was totally unnecessary. When he refused to accompany her to Harlem, the capital of black America, she went by herself. He then dismissed the newspaper photographs of her hugging a dying black AIDS baby as "predictable."

Diana responded with calculation. On the return flight to London, she talked to a *Daily Mirror* photographer about her whirlwind tour, saying how tense she felt being whisked from one engagement to another. "I feel so sad when I think about how I held that little boy in my arms," she said. "It was so moving. Maybe it's because I'm a woman traveling alone. It never feels so bad when my husband is with me."

The Palace interpreted her comments as a veiled attack upon her husband and scrambled to issue a statement, which implied that she was overwrought: "Visiting Harlem Hospital was a very emotional experience for her. She has been working non-stop for two days and the full impact is only just catching up with her." That was the first shot fired in the media war between the wily courtiers and the willful Princess.

"Diana played the game of one-upmanship like a maestro," said London columnist Ross Benson. "When she and Charles visited a music college, he was prevailed upon to play a note or two on the cello. It was too good an opportunity for her to miss. While he was playing, she strode across the stage, sat down at the piano, lifted the lid, and struck up the opening theme of Rachmaninoff's Piano Concerto No. 2. Every camera swung around to follow her, leaving Charles beached and abandoned in his humiliation."

Diana had insisted on accompanying her husband, over his objection, to a birthday party for Annabel Elliot, the sister of Camilla Parker Bowles. The forty guests were part of what she dismissed as her husband's stuffy Highgrove set, so no one had expected her to attend. But she was determined to confront her husband's mistress.

"I remember meeting her at that party shortly after her Harlem hugging trip," recalled a London attorney, "and thinking she was either dumb or else jet-lagged because she couldn't carry on a conversation. She kept looking at Charles, who had left her and gone off in a corner all night with Camilla. I didn't get what was happening until later, when my wife explained it all."

Toward the end of the party, Diana approached Camilla and said she wanted a word with her in private. Diana waited until the last guests had left the room. Then, looking her rival in the eye, she spoke bluntly: "Why don't you leave my husband alone?" Taken aback, Camilla started to protest, but Diana cut her off, saying she knew all about their affair. She cited the telephone calls, the love letters, the foxhunts, the Sunday night visits. She said she knew that Camilla played hostess at Highgrove in her absence, and Diana resented Camilla's being in Diana's home. Diana blamed Camilla for turning Charles away from his children and ruining his marriage. That said, Diana walked out of the room and told Charles she wanted to go home.

The next morning she called Carolyn Bartholomew and told her what she had done. She also phoned James Hewitt and related every detail of the confrontation, relishing her bold performance. She said she finally felt free of Camilla's clutches. "Why, oh, why," she asked him, "didn't I say all of that to her sooner? What a difference it would have made."

Hewitt said she deserved a medal for bravery and inquired about Charles's reaction.

"Stone cold fury," Diana said proudly, "and 'how could I possibly.'"

Diana's father invited the royal couple to a sixtieth birthday party in honor of Diana's stepmother in May 1989. But Charles had planned a trip to Turkey and wouldn't cancel it. "I'll be traveling," he announced by memo, which was how he communicated with his wife to avoid bickering. He had quietly moved out of Kensington Palace and lived entirely at Highgrove, where his children visited him on weekends. He did not tell his wife that he would be going to Turkey with Camilla Parker Bowles and her husband, Andrew, but Diana found out.

When she told Hewitt about the trip, she said she no longer cared about Charles and Camilla and "Andrew Park-Your-Balls," the nickname she had picked up from *Private Eye** for Brigadier General Bowles. Hewitt suspected that she still cared very much and, despite her disavowals, wanted to revive her marriage. But he said nothing and jumped at the invitation to escort her to her father's ball. "With five hundred guests, we'll be safe," Diana assured him.

Soon after, Hewitt received transfer orders to Germany to command a tank squadron.

* Behind their backs, Diana referred to the royal family by their Private Eye nicknames: the Queen was Brenda, the Duke of Edinburgh was Keith. Princess Margaret was Yvonne, Charles was Brian; Edward was Cled (Peter Phillips's abbreviation of Uncle Ed), and Diana herself was Cheryl.

Excited by his promotion, he worried about telling Diana he would be gone from her life for two years. He later said she had berated him for leaving her and putting his career ahead of their relationship. For several months she did not take his calls, and he left for Germany without seeing her.

Within weeks Diana sought out the man she had been infatuated with when she was seventeen. This time James Gilbey was much more receptive. Over lunches and quiet dinners he listened worshipfully as she unfolded the saga of her miserable marriage. And he became her cushion. They had started seeing each other again after a private dinner party at the home of their friend David Frost, the television interviewer, and his wife, Carina. As Diana and Gilbey were leaving that evening, they were photographed in front of Frost's house, kissing good-bye. The kiss was so intense that the photographer decided to stake out Gilbey's apartment in London's Lenox Gardens, near Harrods department store. Days later the photographer was rewarded with a shot of the Princess leaving Gilbey's apartment at 1:15 A.M. Gilbey said they were playing bridge but added: "I suppose it wasn't that wise for Diana and I [sic] to meet in those circumstances."

From then on, Diana acted with much more caution. Instead of visiting Gilbey's apartment, she arranged to meet him secretly at Mara Berni's home, around the corner from the San Lorenzo restaurant. She also bought a shredder for her office at Kensington Palace. She used post office boxes for personal correspondence and talked on the phone in code. She preferred mobile phones because she thought they were more secure. But when she found out they were less secure, she stopped using them. When using the phones in Kensington Palace, she often closed the doors of her suite and turned up the television so servants couldn't eavesdrop.

Despite her efforts to avoid detection, her telephone conversation with James Gilbey on December 31, 1989, was intercepted by a stranger's scanning device and tape-recorded. When the British tabloids published the transcript three years later, they withheld an explicit ten-minute segment in which the Princess and her lover discussed masturbation. They also talked about Diana's fear of getting pregnant. "Darling, that's not going to happen," Gilbey said reassuringly. "You won't get pregnant." Diana said she was worried after watching a soap opera that afternoon in which one of the main characters had had a baby. "They thought it was by her husband," said the Princess. "It was by another man." She and Gilbey laughed.

"Squidgy [his nickname for Diana], kiss me....Oh, God. It's so wonderful, isn't it, this sort of feeling? Don't you like it?"

Diana replied, "I love it, I love it."

By the time the tape-recorded conversation known as Squidgygate became public, the Princess's pedestal had toppled into the ditch, and she was struggling to keep her head above the muck.

SEVENTEEN

The Duchess was teetering. She had veered from the path marked "Duty and Decorum" a few weeks before her wedding. And she was blamed for leading the Princess of Wales astray. The two women had been photographed at Ascot, poking a man's bottom with the tips of their umbrellas. Days later they dressed up as policewomen to raid Prince Andrew's stag party. With badges and billyclubs they barged into Annabel's nightclub and sat at the bar, drinking. The British press reported the incident in terms of class that Americans could understand: bush league vs. Junior League. Sarah was pilloried as the biker babe from hell. Diana, the sweetheart next door, emerged unscathed. They were like the fairy tale of the two Princesses: One opened her mouth and out came rubies and diamonds. The other one spoke and out came toads.

"The Princess of Wales escapes such censure because she is prettier," wrote *Sunday Times* columnist Craig Brown, "and less, well, *obvious* than the Duchess of York. It is the peculiar capacity of the duchess to mirror modern Britain, its gaudiness, its bounciness, its rumbustious lack of mystery."

Within the first year of her marriage, the Duchess of York became the Duchess of

Yuck. She took 120 days of vacation, yet she complained about overwork. She carried out 55 royal duties during the year, compared with 429 for Princess Anne. That earned Sarah Ferguson the title the Duchess of Do Little. When she gained fifty pounds during her first pregnancy, she was dubbed the Duchess of Pork. When she accepted free first-class plane tickets, free hotel suites, and free limousines, she became "Freeloading Fergie." She also accepted free watches from Cartier and free luggage from Louis Vuitton. As the Duchess of Dough, she expected payment for interviews and asked designers to give her expensive clothing. French couturier Yves St. Laurent agreed to, but British designer Zandra Rhodes turned her down flat, saying, "I don't need the publicity."

Sarah careened into controversy like a drunk with vertigo. She was seen in public playfully tossing bread rolls at her husband. On another occasion she emptied a salt shaker in his hair and squirted him with Champagne. As the auctioneer for a charity benefit, she exhorted bidders to pledge more money. "Come on, George," she hollered at one startled man, "your wife wants it *b-i-g*." At a private party for a Middle Eastern emir, she dropped to the floor in front of forty guests and screamed at a female stripper, "Take it off! Take it off!"

"Fergie thinks by throwing food around, she can identify with the lower orders, which only revile her vulgarity," said columnist Taki Theodoracoupolos. "If you want to clear a room in London and get rid of stragglers who've stayed on too late, just say: 'Oh, Fergie. At last. How are you?' People will start running. Whenever Philip wants to make the Queen laugh, he picks up the phone and says, 'What? You say that Fergie has been hit by a truck and run over?'"

The press even took potshots at her when she went deer hunting with the royal family in Scotland and bruised her forehead on the telescopic sight of her rifle. One columnist said she was sorry to hear that Fergie had hurt herself while "pursuing the innocent girlish pleasure of murdering a large mammal for sport."

"To a certain extent," admitted her father, "becoming Duchess of York did go to her head. She didn't always read the rule book properly. In the royal family, certain privileges are there for the taking, but there have to be limits. Sarah thought she could get away with much more than she did. In those early days, Andrew should have been strong enough to guide her and advise her, but he didn't."

Andrew did not hesitate to rebuke her in public when she acted up, especially if she had been drinking. Once, after he corrected her, she wheeled on him. "Why do you have to keep embarrassing me and pointing it out in front of other people when I get things wrong?" she asked. "It's not very charitable. Sometimes you're as bad as your father."

Fergie, who resented her negative press coverage, tried to ingratiate herself with reporters, while Andrew ignored them. "Don't talk to them," he advised her. "They're knockers. They create heroes and then knock them down."

"What can I do?" she said to a friend. "Andrew tells me to take no notice, but he's away on his ship, not in the midst of things."

The press criticism abated slightly in February 1988 when the Yorks agreed to a tour of Los Angeles to promote British arts and industry. Sarah, three months pregnant, arrived wearing French couture. But she quickly disclosed that her underpants were made in Britain.

"My knickers are from Marks and Sparks," she chirped, using the nickname for Marks & Spencer, the budget department store where middle-class British housewives shop.

In anticipation of the royal visit, Chinatown merchants had put up a banner: "WELCOME FERGIE AND WHAT'S-HIS-NAME." Andrew grinned at it good-naturedly. Stuffed into his pin-striped suit, he looked as if he had just won the all-you-can-eat contest. On his previous visit to Los Angeles, he had been called a royal brat after turning a spray-paint hose on the press. The British Counsulate had had to pay one American photographer $1,200 in damages and issue an apology.

"I was given the check to repair my cameras," recalled photographer Chris Gulken. "I was told: 'Her Majesty wishes you to know that this money comes from Andrew's personal funds and not from the public funds of the British people.'"

A Los Angeles television commentator reported Andrew's 1984 trip to California as "the most unpleasant British visit since they burned the White House in the War of 1812."

The Prime Minister was so distressed by Andrew's press coverage that she commissioned a confidential study from public relations specialists in the London office of Saatchi & Saatchi to try to tone down Andrew's image. Mrs. Thatcher's report was sent to the Queen, who refused to read it. She said, "I hardly think I need advice on family matters from that frightful little woman."

On this trip Andrew was better behaved. Arriving in Long Beach on the royal yacht, *Britannia,* he and Sarah spent ten days touring Southern California. They visited schools and supermarkets, where she blew kisses and he signed autographs. She appeared with tiny American and British flags in her hair and told photographers, "Check out the hair, boys." During their tour of Bullocks Wilshire, the Los Angeles department store, the couple visited the boutiques of several British designers. Andrew spotted a black suede jacket that he admired, so the president of the store had the jacket gift-wrapped for him. Andrew accepted the present and then decided he would prefer something more contemporary, like a navy blue suede bomber jacket. The store made the switch.

Schoolchildren, who had never met a duchess before, crowded around Fergie and peppered her with questions about living in a castle. She said the hardest part was going to the bathroom. The youngsters grew wide-eyed as she told them about the Queen's old-fashioned toilets. "You've got to pull up on the loo, not push down," she explained. "I always bungle it."

The British press branded her as coarse as a braying donkey. Once described as a breath of fresh air, she became a skunk at the garden party. "She's an international embarrassment," complained London's *Sunday Times*. "Americans will likely retreat to their more refined dinner parties, there to cap each other with anecdotes about the awful vulgarities of the British."

That evening the Duchess swept into a party decked out in the diamonds she had received from the Queen. Sparkling in her tiara, necklace, earrings, and bracelet, she quipped to onlookers, "Clock the rocks." When someone asked her whether she liked Gilbert and Sullivan, she said she preferred Dire Straits. One London journalist cringed. "We wanted a silk purse," he said, "and we got a sow's ear."

But Americans were charmed by the vivacious redhead, especially the movie stars, who lined up in Hollywood to meet her. Morgan Fairchild curtsied breathlessly, and Pierce Brosnan was speechless. "I didn't know what to say to her," he admitted with a blush. Jack Nicholson was not so reticent.

"She told me she was disappointed she wasn't sitting next to me," he said with a characteristic leer. "I told her that maybe she was lucky she didn't, because I didn't know what I might have done to her, if I had."

Fergie hurried up to John Travolta to tell him the Princess of Wales was still bragging about their dance at the White House. "She told me that Diana never stops talking about it," said Travolta, beaming.

At one gala dinner the Duchess appeared in a gown that looked like a playing field of pink tulle waffles topped with pink satin roses. London's *Sunday Times* commented disdainfully, "She looked like she came in third in a Carmen Miranda look-alike contest."

The next night, at the Biltmore Hotel, Sarah appeared in a long black gown wrapped with galloping puffs of orange silk. The designer Mr. Blackwell pronounced the dress "God-awful" and pushed her to the top of his Worst-Dressed List for 1988 as "the Duchess who walks like a duck with a bad foot." Her long red hair was twirled and twisted into a hive of fussy curls held in place by diamond combs with corkscrew ringlets cascading to her shoulders. The effect was startling, even by Hollywood's excessive standards.

As she approached the microphone that evening, she looked around at the audience of 750 people, who had paid $1,000 each to be in the presence of royalty. She winked broadly at Roger Moore, the master of ceremonies, and spotting the actor George Hamilton, she smacked her lips. "All these men around here," she said lustily.

An exuberant male guest shouted, "We love you, Fergie!"

She yelled back, "I'll see you later."

"That was it for Fergie," said columnist Ross Benson, shaking his head sympathetically. "That was the beginning of the end. I filed a story that she had been a great hit in the United States, but the rest of the British press turned on her with a vengeance. They said her behavior was disgraceful, and with the inherent snobbishness of this country, they dismissed her as the ill-bred daughter of a stable boy in a blazer."

The Yorks traveled from Los Angeles to Palm Springs, where they were weekend guests of Walter and Lee Annenberg at Sunnylands, the Annenbergs' 208-acre desert estate. The former U.S. Ambassador to Great Britain and his wife greeted the royal helicopter on their private runway. The Annenbergs had arranged for a flotilla of golf carts with Rolls-Royce hoods to transport the Duke and Duchess, their dressers, their aides, their guards, and their luggage.

Fergie hopped out of the helicopter with a large gold clasp in her hair fashioned like a guitar with the word "ROCK" on it. Andrew wore tasseled loafers. They jumped into two of the Annenbergs' golf carts and, like little children in bumper cars, drove up and down the runway with clownish abandon.

The next day they attended a polo game and a black-tie dinner party in the evening at the Annenberg estate. "Oh, it's just for a few friends," said Mrs. Annenberg of her party for one hundred people. U.S. State Department dogs sniffed for bombs as the movie stars and socialites arrived. Actor Michael York ("No relation," joked Fergie) took pictures, and the Duchess asked Frank Sinatra to sing her a song; he obliged with "The Lady Is a Tramp."

"I'm offended—absolutely—by the criticism the Duke and Duchess have received from the British press," snapped Los Angeles's Chief of Protocol. "Mayor Bradley found the Duchess to be great fun, and their royal tour of Southern California was a huge success."

Other Americans rallied to Fergie's side, finding the madcap Duchess immensely likable with her manic mugging and breezy asides. "It doesn't matter that Fergie's fashion statements sometimes end up with a question mark," said *USA Today*. "When a personality sparkles like hers, she could wear a lampshade and still light up a room."

Fergie, in turn, appreciated Americans. "I love visiting the United States," she told a National Press Club audience in Washington, D.C., several years later, "because Americans are so nice to me. I could've been an American in my last life." The audience cheered, apparently not realizing that the Duchess believed in reincarnation. She said she especially enjoyed her trips to New York City. "That's where I really load up," she said about her marathon shopping sprees. On one return trip to London, an airline charged her $1,200 for fifty-one pieces of excess baggage.

"Those U.S. jaunts began to cost her dearly in terms of her image here," said British journalist Ingrid Seward, who was also a personal friend.

But Sarah didn't care. With her husband away at sea, she was bored. So she began flying the Concorde to New York, where her presence triggered shameless jockeying among the nouveau riche. The social cachet of her title drew moguls and tycoons, who scrambled to meet her. "She's very pretty," said multimillionaire Donald Trump, "very bubbly, with lots of personality."

Sarah never failed to amuse and entertain. She regaled her new friends with anecdotes about the royal family. Citing the Queen's appreciation for bawdy humor, she repeated Her Majesty's favorite jokes and included the story of the state visit of Nigeria's General Gowon.

She said the Queen had met President Gowon at Victoria Station and was riding with him in a carriage when one of the horses lifted its tail and broke wind.

The Queen turned to President Gowon. "Oh, I do apologize. Not a very good start to your visit."

"Oh, please don't apologize," said Gowon. "Besides, I thought it was one of the horses."

After a few drinks Sarah continued with her repertoire of gamy jokes, her favorite being one about the Queen as a guest on a radio show called *What Is It?* The answer is given to the audience by a panel of experts before the guest appears. The guest gets twenty questions to figure out the answer.

The night the Queen appeared as a guest, the answer was "horsecock."

The no-nonsense monarch got down to basics with her first question. "Animal, vegetable, or mineral?" she asked.

"Animal," replied the panel.

"Can you kiss it?"

"Why, uhmmmm, yes...I suppose one *could* kiss it, if one were so inclined."

"Is it a horse's cock?" asked the Queen.

Sarah howled with laughter as she delivered the punch line, which startled one of her hostesses. "She certainly wasn't what I expected of a duchess," her hostess said carefully, "but she was lively and always sent us a thank-you." Sarah's letters, mailed from Buckingham Palace, arrived on her personal stationery, which featured a small crown atop a large "S."

An accomplished impressionist, Sarah also entertained her new friends with impersonations of her in-laws. She imitated Prince Philip by goosestepping around the room like a German soldier, barking out orders. Then she scrunched her face into a scowl and said, "This is Her Majesty when we call her Miss Piggyface." She mimicked the Queen's walk with her handbag dangling from her arm. Next, to the astonishment of her audience, she picked up a kitchen knife and knighted her host's dog. As she placed the stainless steel blade on either side of the pup's ears, she piped, impersonating the Queen, "Arise, Sir Rutherford."

The Duchess met her match for outrageous behavior at a New York City dinner party given by her first literary agent, Mort Janklow, who seated her across from author Norman Mailer.

"I've never read any of your books," she admitted, "so which one should I begin with?"

"*Tough Guys Don't Dance*," replied Mailer.

"What's it about?"

"Pussy," he said.

There was an audible intake of breath from the writer Tom Wolfe, but the Duchess did not blanch.

"You know, Mr. Mailer," she said, "the most interesting thing for me at this moment is watching everyone's face[s] at this table."

Mailer was impressed by her quick response. "She fielded it nicely," he said, recalling the evening with a tinge of regret. "I had a devil in me that night....I said the book had an interesting discussion of the differences between pussy and cunt. I must say she was terrific. A lot of people were offended, but Sarah Ferguson couldn't have been nicer about the whole deal, making a point of telling a lot of nice Nellies she wasn't the least bit offended, and I felt bad about it afterward because she got trashed in the papers, and I expect it didn't do her any good in England."

When Sarah returned to her office in Buckingham Palace, she was greeted by the unsmiling face of Sir Robert Fellowes, who had been promoted to the powerful position of the Queen's private secretary.* He walked in brandishing a pile of press clippings.

"Well, we didn't do very well again today, did we?" he said, shaking his head with disapproval. He dropped the stack of newspaper stories on her desk as if they were dead mice. She glared at him.

"Oh, Robert, really," she said with exasperation.

"This must be such a disappointment for you," he said, peering over his steel-rimmed glasses. Turning to leave, he added, "I know it is for Her Majesty."

Fellowes, or "Bellowes," as Fergie called him, was her father's first cousin and a man she came to detest. She dreaded his visits to her office. He always arrived looking dour and brandishing a pile of clippings that chronicled her latest misadventure. She told friends she got a stomachache as soon as she saw him approaching her door. "He could hardly wait to show me the story of the MP who said I was flagrantly abusing the royal name," she said.

"He was her Lord High Executioner," said

* In her reign, the Queen has had six private secretaries—all men. The first four were Sir Alan Lascelles: 1952-1953; Sir Michael Andeane: 1953-1972; Sir Martin Charteris: 1972-1977; Sir Philip Moore: 1977-1986. All were older than the Queen. The last two were younger: Sir William Heseltine: 1986-1990; Sir Robert Fellowes: 1990-.

By the 1990s the Queen's preference for men showed in her staffing of executive posts within the royal household. Out of forty-nine positions, only four were held by women, and one woman was forced to resign when she married a divorced man. Although much of the Commonwealth is black, the Queen has only ten blacks on her staff of nine hundred, and they hold menial positions.

a New York businesswoman whom the Duchess had adopted as her unofficial adviser. "Bad-news Bellowes, as we called him, made Sarah's life a living hell. She had to stand alone against that unremitting Palace machine which wanted nothing so much as to extinguish her delightful spirit. She had no one to help her. Not even her husband. As much as Andrew loved Sarah, he would not defend her against the courtiers. He was simply too terrified of them.

"She felt the weight and power of the monarchy crashing down on top of her; she knew she was in trouble, but she had no adult in her life to advise her. No one in the Palace wanted to help her. The Queen adored her, but the Queen is not the power in the Palace. Prince Philip runs everything, and once he had decided that Sarah was not worth the trouble she was causing, she was finished. Away at sea every week, Andrew was never there for her. Neither was the Princess of Wales, who saw her as a rival. Sarah's mother was dealing with a dying husband in Brazil. Her sister, Jane, was dealing with her own divorce in Australia. And Sarah's father was no help whatsoever after he became involved in a sex scandal. So, as her friend, I stepped in and tried to help."

The New Yorker advised the Duchess to improve her image by performing more royal duties and becoming active with charities for crippled children and the mentally retarded. "I told her to take a page from Diana's book," the adviser said. She explained the on-again, off-again friendship between the Duchess and the Princess as fraught with rivalry and petty jealousies. "Sarah felt that she was being sacrificed to make room for Diana as the future Queen. She resented the unfair comparisons in the press between them—Diana was depicted as a loving mother while Sarah looked like a wench who abandoned her children for months on end to go on luxury holidays."

Her ski guide in Switzerland, Bruno Sprecher, described her as a woman who did not like other women. "She could always ski well," he said, although she stopped every twenty minutes for a cigarette, "and was great chums with the men in the party, but she didn't like female competition."

Her New York adviser saw it differently. "Unfortunately, Sarah was too forthright for her own good. She admitted she never liked babies much before she had her own. Diana, of course, was portrayed as a madonna who adored children. But Sarah had reservations about Diana as a mother, especially when she tried to alienate her boys from Charles. She [Diana] constantly asked the little Princes, 'Who loves you the best? Who loves you more than anyone else in the whole world?' And the boys were supposed to say, 'You do, Mummy. You do.' Sarah felt that was troubling. She also did not agree with the hateful picture Diana painted of Charles, who, Sarah said, was just not *that* bad. Obtuse, yes, but definitely not the monster Diana said he was."

The New York adviser continued: "Sarah never publicly criticized the Princess of Wales—she wasn't that stupid—but there were many times when she felt badly used by Diana. For instance, the Princess was no comfort to her during the lurid business with her father. [In May 1988 Major Ron was exposed by the tabloids as a regular patron of massage parlors. *Private Eye* ran a competition for anagrams of "Ronald Ferguson." Winners were "organ flounders" and "old groaner's fun." Four years later his love affair with Lesley Player became public, and she admitted to aborting his child; and Prince Charles fired him as his polo manager. Diana shrewdly put as much distance as she could between herself and the Major, even ushering her children off the polo grounds so they wouldn't be contaminated by his presence. Sarah was hurt and humiliated by her father, but, as she said, Diana's family wasn't so exemplary that she could act holier than thou."

Shortly after his wedding, Diana's brother, Charles Spencer, called the *Daily Mail*'s gossip columnist to own up to an extramarital fling with a former girlfriend days before her story appeared in the tabloids. Spencer's story became a front-page scandal in Britain. "I have caused my wife more grief than I would wish her to have in a lifetime with me," he said, "and I accept full responsibility for the folly of my actions. Now, after the birth of our baby, we are deeply in love and our marriage is the most important thing in our lives."

He later said that his wife, the former model Victoria Lockwood, was deeply disturbed and suffered from anorexia nervosa and alcoholism. She required treatment at a detoxification center and was institutionalized for three months for what her husband described as "serious psychological problems." In a speech at his birthday party, Charles Spencer, known as "Champagne Charlie" before his marriage, said his father had advised him to find a wife who would stick by him through thick and thin. "Well," he told his guests, "those of you who know Victoria know that she's thick—and she certainly is thin." Within six years the couple, who had four children, separated.

Publicly the Duchess of York stood by her father after he was caught in the massage parlor, but she complained bitterly to friends that she felt soiled by his scandal. She said that his adverse publicity had affected her chances of attracting the charity work she needed to rehabilitate herself. She felt that "the galloping Major," as he began calling himself, made her look less respectable. Organizations seeking royal patronage, especially those that needed to raise money and maintain a worthy profile, avoided her. The Princess of Wales was patron to 120 charities; the Duchess of York had only fifteen.

"I had friends who were in drugs," Sarah said, "so I asked if I could join a chemical dependency movement." She became the patron of the Chemical Dependency Centre. "People tend to be very judgmental about drug users," she said. "But I see drug addicts as my equals." At the time, she, too, was a drug addict. "She had given her body over to these slimming drugs [amphetamines], and that was the beginning of her downfall," said seventy-nine-year-old Jack Temple, one of the many healers she turned to for help. "Slimming drugs fogged her brain. Her actions weren't normal."

From New York her American adviser watched in dismay as the Duchess was increasingly portrayed in the press as someone who advanced on the world with both hands extended like horseshoe magnets. She sold an exclusive interview to a British newspaper for $201,600. The newspaper complained that she had not been forthcoming and withheld part of her payment because she had denied that she was pregnant. The day the article was published, she admitted to a television interviewer that she was expecting her second child. "I forgot," she told the newspaper, insisting on full payment. She threatened to sue, but the Queen intervened, and Sarah backed down.

Sarah collected $500,000 for opening the doors of her home, Sunninghill Park, to *Hello!*, a large glossy picture magazine that caters to celebrities, especially royalty. The magazine, which pays huge fees for exclusives, was Sarah's favorite; over the next ten years she was featured on several covers. She sold exclusive interviews, plus photographs of herself, her husband, her children, her mother, her father, and her sister. In her debut issue she posed with her husband while they changed their babies' diapers. The magazine spread seventy photographs over forty-eight pages of the Yorks holding their two daughters, the Princesses Beatrice and Eugenie. And the cover boasted "The Duke and Duchess of York Grant Us the Most Personal of Interviews and for the First Time Ever Throw Open the Doors of Their Home and Invite Us to Share Their Intimate Family Moments." The Queen said it looked like a movie magazine launch for a Hollywood starlet. Even the novelist Barbara Cartland, whom Mrs. Thatcher's government had made a Dame of the British empire, expressed disgust. "We might as well have pictures of the Queen Mother taking her clothes off and climbing into the bath."

The Duchess's New York adviser had her hands full: "The newspaper stories about Sarah became so horrendous that I finally told her to stop giving interviews because her spontaneous comments were killing her. She would say something light and humorous that was invariably misinterpreted or came out sounding brash and stupid. So her secretary began telling reporters to submit their questions in writing. Sarah would fax the questions to me with what she'd like to say; I'd edit her comments and fax back what she should say. That worked for a while. ..."

The New York businesswoman tried to protect the Duchess from the press, but the Duchess's worst enemy was the Duchess herself. She didn't follow her friend's advice or learn from her own mistakes. Instead she bemoaned her public image and blamed everyone around her—the courtiers, the press, the Princess of Wales ("I know she leaks stories about me," Sarah said), her father, and even her husband, whom she now described to friends as "boring...a darling, but a boring darling." She complained that Andrew did not make enough money to maintain a royal lifestyle. Enthralled by the big-spending ways of her new American friends, especially Croesus-like Texans, she set out to augment her income.

During her first pregnancy, she decided to write a children's book, although she admitted that her best subject in school had been modern dance. Her headmistress at Hurst Lodge once described her in a school report as "an enthusiastic pupil who makes a cheerful contribution to life at the Lodge... [but]...consistently fails to do herself justice in written work."

Undaunted, Sarah said she didn't want to sound like a writer who swallowed the dictionary. So she put her name to a simple story about a helicopter called "Budgie" (slang for the budgerigar parrot) that is looked down upon by the bigger aircraft, until he does something heroic. "I sat down at the dining room table with a big pile of scrap paper, the backs of photocopied stuff and printouts," the Duchess told *Publishers Weekly*, "and started writing with just one pencil."

With that one pencil she made a fortune. She

received a $1 million advance from Simon & Schuster, and within three years she had produced four *Budgie* books; they earned more than $2.5 million from serial rights, foreign rights, and paperback rights. Later, with the help of her financial adviser, she sold merchandising rights, including rights to cartoons, wind-up dolls, T-shirts, hats, and lunch pails. The books became best-sellers in England, despite literary critics who dismissed them as "bland and ghastly" and "utter rubbish."

Sarah was so severely criticized for marketing her royal title that Robert Fellowes sternly suggested she consider donating at least 10 percent of her royalties to charity. She balked at first, saying *Budgie* was her only source of significant income. But she backed down as soon as she realized that the "suggestion" had come from Her Majesty. Sarah knew those royal demands usually came through the thin lips of Robert Fellowes. When she was accused of plagiarism,* she announced that she would donate† "a certain percentage." But, after making the public announcement, she reconsidered and kept the royalties. Then her *Budgie* books hit severe turbulence.

---

* The Duchess of York was not the first member of the royal family to be accused of plagiarism. In 1986 Princess Michael of Kent, who wrote *Crowned in a Far Country* (Weidenfeld & Nicolson), was accused of copying from the author Daphne Bennett. The Princess was forced to pay Bennett several thousand dollars.

† The Duchess of York did not acknowledge the author's written requests in 1993, 1994, and 1995 for conformation of her charitable donations from the royalties of *Budgie*. Her private secretary said, "She donated a certain percentage for so long, then it just ended."

An observant reader was struck by several similarities between *Budgie—The Little Helicopter* by HRH the Duchess of York and *Hector the Helicopter* by Arthur W. Baldwin, an Englishman who had died several years before.

Both books centered on the adventures of a little helicopter with eyelashes; both were similarly illustrated, and both told essentially the same story:

The adventures of Baldwin's Hector begin with the helicopter feeling "unwanted and forgotten" because he's left twiddling his thumbs in the hangar while all the other planes are traveling to exotic places. Budgie, too, feels dejected and twiddles his thumbs because all the planes in his hangar are going to an air show.

Hector falls asleep and has a "wonderful dream." So does Budgie. Upon waking, Hector goes for a spin. So does Budgie. Hector cheers up. "In the distance he could see the sea shining and sparkling in the morning sunlight." Budgie also "cheered up. The sea was sparkling and the cold wind whipped his cheeks." Both Hector and Budgie perform rescue missions that save people's lives; both little whirlybirds earn the respect of the big airplanes; and both live happily ever after.

The Duchess maintained that Budgie was her own creation—and she wouldn't budge: "The books are all me. Every page." The publisher holding the copyright for Hector was dubious but did not publicly dispute the Duchess. "It is difficult for us to say that anything has been literally 'copied,'" wrote Jane

Moore, group legal adviser of Reed International Books in a letter, "but if this was not a major source of inspiration for the 'Budgie' books then it is a remarkable coincidence." She did not say whether she thought the coincidence was accidental or significant.

During Sarah's second pregnancy in November 1989, she flew to Texas as the guest of honor of Lynn and Oscar Wyatt. The Wyatts' estimated wealth of $8 billion paid for a gold-plated life of private planes and French villas. Lynn, the Sakowitz department store heiress, was Oscar's fourth wife. Oscar, an oil tycoon, owned Coastal Corporation. Like little kids who collected Barbie and Ken dolls, the Wyatts collected celebrities—movie stars, models, artists, designers, and royals. "Grace and Rainier are our neighbors in the South of France," drawled Lynn Wyatt, making the Prince and Princess of Monaco sound like "just folks" on the nearby ranch. A petite blond beauty on the international best-dressed list, Lynn Wyatt thrived on socializing with the likes of Andy Warhol, Mick Jagger, Jerry Hall, Liza Minnelli, Nancy Reagan, Princess Margaret, and the Aga Khan.

"The Wyatts are walking wallets," Fergie told a friend, describing the international socialites and their free-spending style. She breathlessly recited the lavish details of the Monte Carlo Sporting Club Ball that Lynn Wyatt had decorated. "She flew in four thousand yellow roses," said Fergie, snapping her fingers, "and she didn't blink."

As the patron of the Houston Grand Opera, Lynn Wyatt had invited the Duchess to represent the royal family at a benefit salute to the British opera. She gave a dinner party in Sarah's honor and included her own two sons from her first marriage. Mrs. Wyatt seated her older son, thirty-six-year-old Steve, next to Sarah. He lived in London and worked in his stepfather's petroleum empire, dealing with sales to the Middle East. He flew from London to Houston solely to attend his mother's party for the Duchess of York.

Fergie fell hard for the tall, lanky Texan, who had thick dark hair, a year-round tan, and rippling muscles. He described himself as spiritual and attributed his spirituality to Madame Vasso, who later claimed that Sarah and Steve started their affair when Sarah was five months pregnant. The Madame offered this account to an editor at Little, Brown in New York in hopes of selling a book in 1996. But the editor turned down the book proposal, saying people were not interested in the Duchess's indiscretions.

Sarah, who regularly consulted astrologers, told one that she could not resist the Texan. She described him as "incredibly delicious...like a blue-eyed pudding." She also told her father that "Fred," her code name for Wyatt, was wild in bed. At first Major Ferguson objected to their relationship and told her to stop.

"Do you really feel that strongly?" she asked.

"Yes, I do," said the Major. "Stop. Now."

"You surely can't expect me to stay in on

my own night after night," she retorted. She didn't speak to her father for six months.

"Other people advised Sarah to stop seeing Steve Wyatt," admitted Major Ferguson, "and they weren't spoken to for months, either."

Steve Wyatt had been adopted by his mother's second husband after his natural father, Robert Lipman, was convicted of killing a woman during a drug overdose and served six years in prison for manslaughter. Steve idolized his freewheeling stepfather, Oscar Wyatt, and rarely referred to his natural father. If asked about him, Steve implied that Lipman had died before he was born. From his mother, Steve had learned the basics of moving in high society; he flattered rich wives and deferred to their rich husbands.

Steve and Sarah spoke the same New Age language of mystics and channelers and crystals full of electromagnetic fields that they fancied as healing and restorative. She told him about the voices she heard in her head and the spirits that protected her from harm. He told her he slept with one of Madame Vasso's pyramid shields over his bed to protect his psyche. He meditated every morning and ate a macrobiotic diet. "He bored everyone to tears by talking about diets and good karma and the rest of the bullshit modern Americans pollute us with," said the columnist Taki.

Wyatt despised cigarettes, so Sarah tried not to smoke in front of him. A physical fitness enthusiast, he said, "Mah body is mah temple." The Duchess said she'd like to start worshiping. Both laughed heartily.

The day after the dinner party, Oscar Wyatt proposed an aerial view of his 29,000-acre ranch near Corpus Christi; he flew Sarah in his private helicopter and allowed her to take over the controls. Steve marveled at her flying skill. "Did your husband teach you how to do that?" he asked.

"My husband doesn't have much time to teach me anything," she said.

"What a waste," said Wyatt. He was entranced with the Queen's daughter-in-law and let her know.

Sarah had given him her private phone number at the Palace and told him to call her when he returned to London. When he did, she immediately invited him over for drinks. He reciprocated with parties, restaurant dinners, and holidays. She visited him in his apartment in Cadogan Square. Weeks later she introduced him to her unsuspecting husband, and when Andrew returned to sea, she brought Wyatt into their Berkshire home. She invited him to their housewarming party, to their daughter's christening, and to dinner with her in-laws. She even gave him a place of honor next to the Queen.

Shortly after Andrew returned to his ship in January 1990, Sarah called him, saying she felt despondent. She asked how they could continue a marriage that was subjected to month-long separations. Andrew reminded her of what he had said before they married: he was a prince and a naval officer before he was a husband. He suggested she was feeling overwhelmed because of her pregnancy, but she insisted she wanted to escape from their marriage and the Palace courtiers. "I want to live in Argentina with my mother," she wailed. Their conversation was tape-recorded by a stranger, who had eavesdropped on his scanner, and sold the tape to a British newspaper.

Andrew rushed home for the March 23, 1990, birth of his second daughter and stayed six weeks. While he and the nanny took care of the new baby, Steve Wyatt flew Sarah and two-year-old Beatrice in a private plane to Morocco for a holiday. The next month Wyatt flew Sarah to the South of France, where his mother had rented a villa. Weeks later, in August 1990, he asked her to entertain Dr. Ramzi Salman, Iraq's oil minister, at Buckingham Palace. Sarah did not hesitate.

She invited her lover and his Iraqi business acquaintance to dinner in her second-floor suite at the Palace. Naively she did not consider the political ramifications of entertaining the representative of Saddam Hussein days after Iraq had invaded Kuwait. When Prince Philip found out what she had done, he sailed into her for poor judgment. For a member of the British royal family to publicly embrace Iraq when British soldiers might be going to war against the country was "unconscionable" and "just bloody stupid." Sarah blamed the courtiers. She said, "Someone should have told me."

After dinner that evening, she had taken her two guests to Le Gavroche, one of London's finest French restaurants, to join a small party hosted by Alistair McAlpine, former treasurer of the Tory Party. Lord and Lady McAlpine were friends of the Yorks and had dined at Sunninghill Park; they were fond of Sarah but were uncomfortable having to extend hospitality to Saddam Hussein's envoy. They were also disquieted by Sarah's blatant behavior with Steve Wyatt. "It was a display of mutual fondling I have never seen before in a three-star restaurant," said one of the McAlpines' guests.

"There is in the Duchess a free spirit," Alistair McAlpine wrote later, "an instinct she believes justifies whatever she may do, regardless of how ridiculous or unsuitable her actions are."

Surprisingly, Sarah, a master of what *Punch* magazine called "snoblesse oblige," did not comprehend the social liability of taking an American lover, especially one who sounded like Sammy Glick with a southern accent. It was a cultural clash of aristocrats versus armadillos on an island that defers to aristocrats. Despite his father's money, the Texan could not lasso a position within the British establishment. The social barriers were too high, even for an expert climber like Steve Wyatt. One American who had tried to scale the wall ended up living in exile—and she had married the King of England. "The attitude of most British people," said Harold Brooks-Baker, "is that Americans are savages."

By 1990 everyone knew that Sarah's marriage was over, except her husband. Her lover, who continued sleeping with other women, still reveled in her royal invitations. "For the Jewish boy from Houston, whose parentage was shrouded in scandal," wrote the *Daily Mail,* "there could have been no greater social triumph than his invitation from the Duchess of York personally to the December 1990 Buckingham Palace Ball to celebrate the birthdays of the Queen Mother (90), Princess Margaret (60), Princess Anne (40) and the Duke of York (30)."

Soon he had no more royal invitations. Through her equerries the Queen communicated her displeasure about the relationship and forced the Duchess to stop seeing the high-flying Texan. "There'll be nipples on a bull 'fore I'll embarrass that little lady," Oscar Wyatt told a business associate. Rather than offend Her Majesty, he cooperated with the Palace by having his son transferred to the United States. "It's very embarrassing," Lynn Wyatt told a gossip columnist. "Prince Andrew even called Steve to tell him how sorry he was about it all."

During the move from his apartment in Cadogan Square, Steve Wyatt left behind 120 photographs from his May 1990 holiday in Morocco with Sarah and her two children. A mover found the casual snapshots, recognized the Duchess of York, and sold the photos to a tabloid. Sarah was traveling to Palm Beach with her father and his mistress when she received the call from her husband prior to publication.

Andrew was aboard his ship when the Palace contacted him about the pictures. The Queen's press secretary suggested that the Duke tell his wife. So Andrew dutifully called Sarah, who took the call in the Palm Beach airport. She screamed at him for not defending her.

"It's not like you didn't know about those pictures," she said. "You saw them. You knew about the holiday. You wanted me to go. Why didn't you say that? Why do you never defend me to those bastards?" She slammed the phone down and that night got drunk. Very drunk.

She admitted overindulging when she addressed the Motor Neurone Disease Association the next day. "I had too many mai tais last night," she told the group. She brightened up during her visit to the Connor Nursery in West Palm Beach, where she posed for pictures with black children suffering from AIDS. That evening she attended a dinner party at the restricted Everglades Club in Palm Beach and the next day was severely criticized in newspapers for lending royal presence, even unintentionally, to a club that bars blacks and Jews.*

* "It [Everglades Club] represents in its policies the old-fashioned, albeit somewhat refined, bigotry which is no different in kind from the gutter-level bigot who wears a hood and sheet," said Arthru Teitelbaum, southern area director of the Anti-Defamation League, which monitors anti-Semitism. "We had alterted the embassy...with the expectation that it would sufficiently value the reputation and sensibilities of the royal family to advise the Duchess not to attend. They chose to turn a blind eye to the character of the club, which we find regrettable."

On her return flight to London, she started drinking again. After two glasses of Champagne she began throwing sugar packets at her father. She lobbed wet towels at his mistress and tossed peanuts around the cabin. "Then Sarah pulled a sick bag over her head," recalled the Major's mistress, "and started making telephone noises into it. We shrieked with laughter like silly schoolgirls." Other passengers watched the rumpus. Among them, three journalists taking notes.

"The way that story was embroidered," huffed Major Ferguson, "convinced me more than anything else that the press was out to discredit my daughter."

Two months later, on March 19,* 1992, the Palace announced that the Duke and Duchess of York were separating. The Queen's press secretary, Charles Anson, privately briefed the BBC correspondent, who reported, "The knives are out at the palace for Fergie." The BBC man said the Queen was very upset with the Duchess, and the rest of the royal family considered her unsuitable to be among them.

"I was furious," recalled her father, "and rang Sir Robert Fellowes, and told him how monstrous I thought it was...it was unforgivable."

The courtier responded coolly. "It's my job," he said, "to protect the family, and particularly the Queen. I have to."

---

* The Palace, which goes along with the Queen's superstitions, chose March 19 to announce the Yorks' separation. March 19 had been the date of Princess Margaret's separation announcement in 1976 and Sara and Andrew's engagement announcement was March 19, 1986.

"You don't have to go that far," said Ferguson.

Eventually the press secretary apologized to Sarah for his indiscretion and offered his resignation to the Queen, who did not accept it.* Rather, four years later, she knighted him.

"Vulgar, vulgar, vulgar." That's the word Lord Charteris used—in triplicate—to damn the Duchess. Charteris, the Queen's former private secretary, denounced Sarah in a *Spectator* interview with journalist Noreen Taylor. And a columnist for the *Sunday Times,* John Junor, condemned the Duchess as "highly immoral." He ran her down as the "royal bike"—ridden by everyone.

By this time she was thoroughly disgraced as a wife and as a mother. But even more disheartening for her was the news that the man she called the love of her life, Steve Wyatt, was leaving her life for another wife: he was marrying an American society beauty, Cate Magennis. When he told Sarah the news, she struggled to wish him well. But she admitted later that she almost cried. After the wedding she said, "I can't have the man I love because he's got married. What's the matter with me? Why wouldn't he marry me?"

In Wyatt's wake, another smooth-talking Texan was already circling in the waters. "If you want to ride swiftly and safely from the

---

* "The Queen didn't accept Charles's resignation," said Anson's good friend Maxine Champion, "because the Queen agreed with him. That's what he told us when he came to Washington, D.C. We had dinner with him one night and he told us all about the Fergie mess."

depths to the surface," Truman Capote wrote in a novella, "the surest way is to single out a shark and attach yourself to it like a pilot fish."

For the next three years it would be difficult to distinguish between the shark and the pilot fish, but the Duchess was about to embark on the ride of her life.

EIGHTEEN

He's absolutely brill about money," burbled the Duchess of York. "Really, really brill."

In her slangy way, Sarah was describing John Bryan to her husband as brilliant. She recommended they sit down with the thirty-five-year-old American to discuss their finances. "He can help," she said. "I just know he can."

By 1991 the Duke and Duchess were spending four times their annual income, and the Queen was balking at paying their overdrafts. Sarah, who spent wildly, refused to cut back. The worse her marriage became, the more money she spent, running up staggering bills. Her kitchen staples included caviar, raspberries (in season and out), a variety of imported cheeses, and at least thirteen flavors of ice cream. In one year she spent $102,000 for gifts and $84,560 on psychics. Then Steve Wyatt introduced her to his friend Anthony John Adrian Bryan Jr., known to his family and friends as "Johnny." He promised to come to her financial rescue. "Johnny stepped in," said columnist Taki, "and took over the Fergie account—so to speak."

A self-described financial wizard, John Bryan understood the art of making deals. He knew the intricacies of Swiss bank accounts and offshore tax shelters. He unraveled the mysteries of high finance and reduced complex transactions to simple logic. He reassured people like Sarah and Andrew, who did not know how to manage their money. After Bryan explained the tax advantages of incorporating Sarah's publishing ventures and funneling her *Budgie* profits through a corporation, Andrew and Sarah eagerly incorporated. Bryan helped set up ASB [Andrew Sarah Bryan] Publishing Inc. and, at Andrew and Sarah's insistence, became a member of the board.

Susceptible to gurus, astrologers, and fortune-tellers, the Duke and Duchess were drawn to the fast-talking American. Their goals were his goals: to make money—big money—or, as he put it, "megamillions."

During their first meeting, recalled a secretary who was in the room, Bryan endeared himself to the Duke of York by offering to restore the Duchess's image in the press. "Most everything written about her is rubbish," Bryan told them. Andrew nodded in agreement. Despite their marital problems, he remained devoted and wanted the rest of the world to see his wife as he did.

"Sir," Bryan said respectfully, "I want to show Her Royal Highness's commitment to charity and emphasize the good work she does which enhances the royal family." Sarah beamed as Bryan pitched his fastball without a pop. He spoke with quiet authority. As he later told one writer, he operated on the principle of "softly, softly...catchee monkey." Within fifteen minutes of their meeting, the organ-grinder had snared the Duke of York.

Andrew and Sarah sat spellbound as the American spun their debts into assets. He made their financial future look glowing. The bald sorcerer sounded as though he could sell toupees to Rastafarians. And he was such a fast talker that he made gypsy moths look like butterflies.

"He was clever, and he certainly knew business," said a British man who had known Bryan since he had moved to London. "But he was as ambitious as the Gordon Gecko character in [the movie] *Wall Street*. Johnny was hard charging, high energy; he lived on the edge. As you Americans say, he performed without a net."

John Bryan executed his high-wire act with style. He understood packaging and the importance of the first impression. He looked rich. He wore custom-made suits, hand-tooled leather shoes, and gold cuff links. He skied, golfed, and played squash in private clubs. He competed fiercely on the tennis court. He dated models and debutantes.

But there was little behind his fancy facade. He possessed none of the hallmarks of wealth— no property, no portfolio. He spent most of everything he earned—and more. When his businesses in New York City, London, and Munich ran out of money, and he became insolvent, he left town.

He did it first in New York City. Following graduation from the University of Texas in 1979, he received a master's degree in business administration from the University of Pittsburgh. He moved to Manhattan and started a small communications company with $1 million that he had raised from private investors. He promised them big profits, but after four years the company went broke.

"I lost over $50,000 on the guy," said Taki. "I based my investment on my friendship...and I have to say I'm deeply disappointed. He said it was a sure thing, we couldn't miss, and that my $50,000 would turn into millions. After the company failed, he went doggo for a while, and then turned up [in London] with Fergie."

The British Home Office wouldn't give him a work permit because it wasn't convinced he could support himself. His London apartment, which doubled as his office, was rented. So was his furniture. He also rented a country house in Gloucestershire. "That's where I met him," recalled journalist Rory Knight Bruce. "He was dressed in American tweeds and smoking a joint."

His leased car accumulated so many parking tickets that he was arrested and fined $800. After paying the fine, he continued collecting parking tickets. Finally police booted and towed the car, and he was reduced to taking cabs. He hired an occasional limousine that he charged to his business—before the business collapsed. He rarely paid cash for anything, except occasional cocaine.* "Fergie sniffed a lot, too," said Taki, who socialized with the couple. "I should know. I've done my share."

Although Bryan was described as a Texas multimillionaire, he was born in Wilmington, Delaware. But at the age of nine he moved to Houston when his father divorced his mother and married a Texas heiress, Josephine Abercrombie. During this second marriage, his father began an affair with (and later married) Pamela Zauderer Sakowitz, the wife of the Sakowitz department store heir Robert Sakowitz—who was Steve Wyatt's uncle.

Bryan bragged to one writer that he was part of "the American establishment" because his

---

* In My Story: *The Duchess of York, Her Father and Me* (HarperCollins Publishers, 1993), Lesley Player said John Bryan used cocaine. She wrote that Bryan invited her and another woman to his apartment, where he sniffed the drug. Bryan did not comment on the book, but Allan Starkie, his business partner in Oceonics Deutschland, a German construction company, denied Player's story. "I was there that night in John's Chelsea flat, and I certainly did not see anyone taking any drugs." Player indicated only three people were present that evening—she, a woman friend, and Brian.

Starkie, who accompanied the Duchess of York on her charity trips to Eastern Europe, was later arrested in Germany when Oceonics collapsed. He was held in a German jail for five months, pending a police investigation of the company that left debts of $15 million.

In 1995 Bryan, who had moved back to the United States, allegedly offered cocaine and prostitutes to entice investors into a Las Vegas real estate deal. The "investors" were reporters for the British tabloid *News of the World*, which published the story under the headline "Fergie's Ex in Vice and Drugs Shame."

godfather was Felix DuPont, and his mother, who had married three times, was listed in the *Social Register*. He boasted to girlfriends that his mother had once dated Frank Sinatra and that his British-born father had graduated from the Harvard Business School.

"It is perhaps no coincidence," said Pamela Zauderer Sakowitz after her divorce from Bryan Sr., "that Johnny's father seemed to single out wealthy, influential, and sometimes married women for conquests, me included." Although his father had married four times and very well, he had never married a duchess.

Skimming the surface of London society, John Bryan partied in expense-account restaurants and nightclubs like Annabel's and Tramps. When he became the Yorks' financial adviser, he moved into more rarefied circles. Still, the exclusive world of White's and Brooks's (private men's clubs in London) eluded him. To British aristocrats he looked like an American hustler on the make. To the Duchess of York he looked like a man on a white horse.

He had promised to make her rich and restore her image. He revered her title as much as she did and commended her for correcting Maria Shriver on camera when the NBC-TV interviewer addressed her as Sarah Ferguson. "I'm Her Royal Highness," Sarah pointed out. "I'm the Duchess of York." Bryan emphasized to her the value of her title in the marketplace. "Your image is all you have," he said over and over. "It is absolutely one hundred percent your biggest asset."

Capitalizing on Fergie, he made her his biggest merger and acquisition. Within days of her separation from Andrew, Bryan took over her life. "When Sarah moved from Sunninghill Park to a rented house, Romenda Lodge in Wentworth, John assisted with details like staff contracts, rental negotiations, security, confidentiality agreements," recalled her father, Major Ferguson.

After the move, Sarah said she would have a nervous breakdown if she didn't have a vacation. So "J.B.," as she and her children called him, arranged an extravagant six-week trip to the Far East. He planned the itinerary, complete with chartered flights, limousines, and luxury hotels. He said he paid for everything: $135,000. He joined the Duchess, her two children, their nanny, and their protection officers in Phuket, a resort island near Thailand, and traveled with them through Indonesia.

He was photographed traveling with the Duchess and described in the press as the unknown man who was seen carrying Princess Eugenie on his shoulders. He later explained that he was a family friend acting as a marriage counselor for the Duke and Duchess, trying to help them reconcile. He also said he had been asked by the Queen and Prince Andrew to handle Sarah's finances. "It's completely absurd to suggest that there is anything unprofessional in my friendship with the Duchess," he said. "I am acting in a purely professional manner."

Weeks later he and Sarah visited her mother

on her polo pony breeding farm four hundred miles west of Buenos Aires. Sarah wanted Bryan to advise Susan Barrantes on handling her husband's estate. Bryan told Susan he could make* her "megamillions" if she wanted to make a film about playing polo in Argentina.

Throughout the summer of 1992 he and Sarah were seen shopping in New York City, partying in London, and dancing in Paris. Still, he insisted their relationship was strictly platonic. When Clive Goodman of *News of the World* asked him about a romance, Bryan snapped, "Even such a suggestion is not just rude, it's impertinent and insulting." By then he had moved his clothes into her closet at Romenda Lodge and put his slippers under her bed.

With military precision he began organizing her finances. A big spender himself, he said he was startled by her spending, which he calculated at $81,000 a month. He told her she was spending almost $1 million a year— far more than she was making. She shrugged. She was still the daughter-in-law of the richest woman in the world. "It was madness," he said later, "spending for the sake of it, with no thought for the present, let alone the future." At the time, he joked about setting up a charity called Duchess in Distress.

* John Bryan also negotiated for Sara's sister, Jane Ferguson Luedecke. He sold exclusive coverage of her second wedding to *Hello!* magazine for $300,000, but Jane and her husband received only $217,000. They sued Bryan for the rest—$73,000. Sarah was outraged by the lawsuit. Siding with Bryan, she stopped speaking to her sister. A London judge ordered Bryan to repay the money, plus interest, and all court costs, a total of $82,500. But as of July 1996 Bryan had not paid. The next month he was declared bankrupt.

The financial adviser was captivated by his investment. When the writer Elizabeth Kaye compared him to Cinderella, John Bryan did not disagree. "I am like Cinderella," he said. "It's a kind of wonderful love story." He fully expected to marry the Duchess after her divorce, but his friend Taki was skeptical. "It'll never happen," Taki predicted. "He doesn't have enough money for Fergie."

Making himself indispensable, Bryan supervised her investments, her vacations, her wardrobe, even her diet. "It's very important to Johnny that Sarah look good and continue to keep her weight down," said his mother. Nothing escaped his attention. He even arranged her furniture. He called reporters regularly to tell them about her efforts for the Motor Neurone Disease Association. He said proudly that she generated 25 percent of the charity's income.

The grateful Duchess rewarded him with lavish gifts: a $1,500 Louis Vuitton trunk embossed with his initials; a Tag Heuer watch; Turnbull & Asser shirts with an oversize pocket for his mobile phone; a coffee machine from Harrods; silk burgundy boxer shorts; a trip to Paris; and a $20,000 birthday party under a canopy with a jukebox playing his favorite songs.

For her thirty-third birthday he reciprocated with $1,000 worth of lingerie, including a $330 teddy and a $22 garter belt.

"They tried to top each other with extravagance," said a friend, who decided that John Bryan won with his trip to Saint-Tropez in the summer of 1992. "At least in terms of radioactive publicity." He was alluding to the fallout from photographs that were secretly taken through the far-seeing lens of a long-range camera as the Duchess and her lover cavorted by a pool. She was without the top of her red-and-yellow-flowered bikini, and the pictures from that topless romp on France's Côte d'Azur produced a mouth-watering scandal.

Sarah was captured on film as she lolled on a chaise alongside Bryan, whose bald head gleamed in the sun. The camera caught him lifting her foot to kiss her instep. Click. He massaged her leg, nuzzled her shoulder, and rubbed her breasts. Click. Click. She slathered suntan oil on his bald head. He climbed out of his chaise and lay on top of her. Click. Click. Click. She put her arms around him and kissed him on the lips. Click. Click. They shared a cigarette. Playing alongside them were Sarah's two children; next to the children were their two royal protection officers, sunbathing. They later lost their jobs.

The embarrassing photos were published when Sarah was vacationing with the royal family at Balmoral Castle in Scotland. She had arrived with her estranged husband and their children for a week. On the morning of Thursday, August 20, 1992, the Duke and Duchess appeared for breakfast while the children remained in the nursery. Sarah and Andrew had been warned that the photos were to be published, but they had not seen them. So they were unprepared for the shock: the front page of the *Daily Mirror* featured John Bryan in swimming trunks lying on top of Sarah, who was bare-breasted. "Fergie's Stolen Kisses," blared the headline. The *Evening Standard* ran the photos under the banner "Duchess in Disgrace."

When Sarah saw the newspapers on the table, she went white. "I almost heaved," she recalled. Within seconds the Duke of Edinburgh was standing at her side. Months before, he had dressed her down for attending Elton John's fortieth birthday party when newspapers said the singer was involved in a sex scandal. He criticized her for lending her royal presence to someone who was the subject of lurid headlines. She felt vindicated when the rock star collected a $1.8 million out-of-court settlement from the *Sun* for falsely accusing him of using the services of a male prostitute. But by then Philip had moved on to blame her for embarrassing the royal family by going on a ski holiday during the Gulf War. So now Sarah braced herself for another blast.

But Philip, who was known to be a womanizer, looked at her with sympathy. "Look," he said softly, "you may like to know that there but for the grace of God go I." He straightened his shoulders and announced loudly that he intended to go grouse hunting with Charles and Andrew. Abruptly he turned and strode out of the room.

Sarah stayed at Balmoral for three more days until Sir Robert Fellowes pointedly suggested she "might feel more comfortable taking the children home." The suggestion carried the weight of an edict. Feeling the royal boot, she decamped.

Since her separation, she had been prohibited from representing the royal family in public. She had shrugged off her exclusion from events like Ascot and Trooping the Color by saying, "What the hell? I'll save on hats." But she stopped laughing when she found herself locked out of her office at Buckingham Palace. She blamed the courtiers, whom she called "the Queen's Rottweilers."

To her chagrin, newspapers around the world gave full play to her topless antics. "Monarchy in the Mud," blared Italy's *La Stampa*. The mass circulation *Bild* in Germany screamed, "Fergie Naked During Love Play." The *New York Daily News* ran the photo of John ("I was *not* sucking her toes, I was kissing the arch of her foot") Bryan under the headline "Toe Sucker and Duchess of Vulgarity." *USA Today*: "The Lens Doesn't Lie."

The editor of *The Washington Post* editorial page observed: "If your average American welfare mother had been photographed as she was, bare-breasted and fooling around with her lover in the presence of her toddler children, it probably would have been enough to get their caseworker a court order removing the kids from the home. We would have used words like 'disadvantaged' and 'sick.'"

But the Duchess's mother defended her— sort of. "Sarah is not sorry because she was caught topless with Bryan," Susan Barrantes told the Italian magazine *Gente.* "Being separated from Prince Andrew, she can do what she likes. But she is sad because she is sure...somebody...wanted to get at her and put her character in a bad light before the divorce."

John Bryan, who had tried but failed to get an injunction against publication of the photos, spun into action. "We'll turn this around," he promised Sarah. "You'll see. We'll turn this fucker around....I'm going to have those Palace bastards by the balls." He filed a $5 million invasion of privacy lawsuit in France against the photographer, who had dug a trench on private property and camped out for two days with his cameras' high-powered lenses. Bryan also sued *Paris-Match,* saying the French magazine had intended to damage the Duchess. "From being an admired figure," his lawsuit stated, "she has become a figure of ridicule." A French judge agreed and awarded her $94,000, which she announced would go to the British Institute for Brain-Damaged Children. "It's appropriate, don't you think?" she said. "Most journalists are brain-damaged, too."

Still, she knew she looked foolish in the world's press. "I've been criticized so much over the past seven years that I've lost all my confidence and self-esteem," she said. She cried over the photo caption: "Fergie—The Final Footnote." And she cringed when she saw sidewalk vendors in London selling chocolate toes. "It's hell," she told her father.

"I can't bear reading newspapers." One English reporter wrote that since she had become the Duchess of York, "covering the royal family is like riding down a sewer in a glass bottom boat." Some writers dredged history to draw mischievous parallels between Fergie and the fat, gaudy Caroline of Brunswick, who married the Prince of Wales in 1795. The English critic Max Beerbohm said of that promiscuous* Princess, "Fate wrote her a most tremendous tragedy and she played it in tights."

Sarah was not so carefree about her burlesque. She hid in her house for five days so she would not have to face people. One woman took pity and wrote a letter offering a "shoulder of friendship" to cry on.

"I simply felt, 'Poor thing!'" said Theo Ellert, who ran Angels International. The London-based charity raised money for children in Poland with leukemia. "The Duchess was at her lowest ebb, and when I suggested she come with me to Poland, she agreed instantly and said, 'I need to think of others to take my mind off myself.'"

John Bryan seized on the trip as an opportunity to repair her image. He was determined to showcase her as the do-gooding Duchess. "If we had to, we'd pay for the trip ourselves, so no one could accuse us of another Freeloading Fergie number," he said to her

---

*After Caroline was found in a compromising position with a naval officer, she was tried for adultery. "Was the man involved an admiral?" she was asked. "Oh, I don't know," she said. "He wasn't wearing his hat." She was not convicted.

secretary. "Forget the British press. We'll get this on American television where it counts....We'll give exclusive access to someone like Diane Sawyer on *Prime Time Live*...she's the best...she needs the ratings...but no personal questions...only a serious interview, substantive, about your work. ..."

With frenetic energy he started negotiating behind the scenes. "He used a husband-and-wife team to front for him," recalled the ABC-TV producer, "but he was definitely calling the shots." Bryan told Sarah he would control the interview and the questions she would be asked. Diane Sawyer does not share that recollection. Sawyer's producer recalled Sarah's major concern was being asked about her relationship with the Princess of Wales and the rest of the royal family. "That worried her more than the toe-sucking pictures," said the producer. At the end of the interview, Diane Sawyer slipped in a question about John Bryan. "What is the relationship? What can you tell us about him?"

Sarah was prepared. "He's done a wonderful job, helping me with all my financial work," she said on the air, "and he's been a fantastic friend."

"But he's not just a financial adviser," pressed Sawyer.

"I didn't say he was. I said he's been a fantastic friend, helping me with financial work."

Despite her plucky performance, Angels International dropped her. "She had a bad image and they didn't want her involved with them," said Theo Ellert. "I said, 'If you don't want her, you can't have me,' and my services were dispensed with." So Theo Ellert helped Sarah start her own charity, Children in Crisis, to raise money for youngsters in poor countries like Albania, Poland, and the former Yugoslavia. With this organization the Duchess finally had a vehicle for respectability. But she couldn't follow the road map. "Sarah has had everything," her father wrote in his memoir, "but she threw it away."

She tried to transform herself into a good-will ambassador like the Princess of Wales but was criticized as self-serving. "I cannot think of anybody else I would sooner not appoint to this post [United Nations High Commission for Refugees]," said the Tory MP Sir Nicholas Fairbairn. "She is a lady short on looks, absolutely deprived of any dress sense, has a figure like a Jurassic monster, is very greedy when it comes to loot, no tact, and wants to upstage everyone else." Fergie was not appointed.

The Royal Army Air Corps would not accept her as its honorary Colonel in Chief because, according to a senior officer, she was "dowdy and we didn't feel she had the right image."

When she took a group of mentally handicapped youngsters on a climbing expedition in Nepal, she was derided for checking into a suite at Katmandu's most luxurious hotel. During the trek, she toted only her bottle of Evian water, prompting the *Spectator* to snicker:

The grand old Duchess of York
She had ten thousand men,
She marched them up to the top of the hill
And she marched them down again.

When a twenty-two-year-old Sherpa accepted her invitation to leave his remote Himalayan village and return to Britain with her, she was accused of exploitation. "Perhaps the wayward duchess is simply keeping up the honourable aristocratic tradition of hiring a native and bringing him home," sniffed the *Daily Telegraph*. The Sherpa, who had cooked her meals and carried her rucksack when she went mountain climbing, found himself doing much the same thing at Romenda Lodge. One woman said, "She was using him like a dogsbody, and he wasn't being paid."

"He is a guest of the Duchess," said her spokeswoman. "She thought it would be nice for him to see another part of the world."

Sarah, who was convinced that the Palace courtiers would use anything to hurt her chances for a hefty divorce settlement,* sent her Sherpa packing. Bryan tried to allay her fears, vowing again to negotiate "megamillions" for her. Eager to create a sympathetic climate, he tried to discredit her husband.

He called *The People* newspaper, a British version of *USA Today*, and said Prince Andrew

---

* Sarah wanted a lump-sum payment of $10 million, plus $5,000 a month in child support and her title. She received $750,000 for herself and a $2.1 million trust fund for her children, and she lost her title.

was having an affair. "I know 100 percent he is going out with the girl, and I know she has spent the night a lot at South York," said Bryan. "I will produce a name. But I want $30,000 because I'm going to have to go through his personal address book...and I want it on goddamn publication, baby. I want immediate payment."

The paper drew up a contract, and Bryan amended it three or four times. When he finally produced the name of Andrew's alleged lover, the paper decided there was nothing to his story and didn't publish it. Instead they printed their tape-recorded conversation with him: "Jetset John Demanded £20,000 for Andrew Lie."

Barely embarrassed, Bryan asserted it was just a practical joke. He said he was setting up the newspaper. But Sarah was livid. "She screamed at me, 'You do not do that sort of thing to the Duke of York—it's totally irresponsible,'" Bryan confided to a friend as he recounted his regular rows with the Duchess. On that occasion she threw him out of the house. But days later they made up, and he moved back in. As a welcome home present, she gave him a silver globe of the world, inscribed "Together We Can Conquer It."

After the damaging photographs of their cozy romp on the Côte d'Azur had been published, the couple decided to be discreet. In the belief that they could conceal their affair, they no longer appeared in public together. When Bryan traveled from London to Sarah's house in Surrey, she sent a member of her staff to meet him at the train station. Disguised in a baseball cap and sunglasses, he hid in the trunk of her car and was smuggled into Romenda Lodge like stolen goods. Publicly Sarah professed to be confused about divorcing Andrew. She said she considered him to be "my very best friend." But privately she complained. "I think she felt she could never go to bed with him again," said Theo Ellert, "that their sex life had not been good from the beginning and couldn't be saved now." Mrs. Ellert made her comments after she and the Duchess had parted bitterly; she said Fergie had not supported her as chief executive of their charity. "I think she believed that I was deflecting the glory from herself."

Seeking guidance from everyone around her, Sarah consulted her circle of psychics, astrologers, and fortune-tellers. She called New Age mystics in Los Angeles, mediums in New York City, and channelers in London. She also consulted a Bosnian priest who was known at the shrine of Medjugorje as "the Eyes of Christ."

"Go back to your husband," Father Svetozar Kraljevic counseled her. "The best thing for you, for your soul, for your children, and for the royal family is for reconciliation."

"I can't," moaned Sarah. "If I did, I would have to lead the life of a nun."

The monk recommended she spend time with some nuns in a convent in Bosnia. "They will teach you how to lead a celibate life," he said.

Dismissing his stern advice, she turned to her friend Alistair McAlpine, who wrote about their private lunch: "She has often asked advice, thanked the giver profusely, but gone the way she wished in the first place. Perhaps she feels that those who give her advice will go away satisfied with just the honor of having had her ask. How terribly she misunderstands human nature."

Sarah told Lord McAlpine that she wanted to divorce her husband. "He is so boring," she said. "He only wants to play golf and watch science-fiction videos."

Lord McAlpine advised her against divorce. "It was at this point she informed me the Princess of Wales had had it in mind to leave her husband on the same day but had decided to postpone that event for a month or two, in the Duchess's words, 'to see how I get on.'"

While Diana stayed on the bus, Sarah decided to hop off. But she said she was nervous about public reaction and the way she would be treated by the royal family. McAlpine explained, "She meant, of course, financially."

Like a squirrel scampering to find nuts, John Bryan scurried in all directions trying to generate money for Sarah. He was never off the phone. Bombarding the media with proposals, he hawked her to the highest bidder: $25,000 for exclusive photo shoots, $50,000 to $200,000 for exclusive interviews. He dictated the rules to journalists: he provided the questions and demanded editorial control of the answers. When he negotiated a cover story with *Harpers & Queen* magazine, he insisted on their best fashion photographer, then demanded copyright to the photographs. "Do you know how many pictures she uses in a year?" he argued. "We send out a thousand, maybe two thousand pictures sometimes. She needs pictures for charity brochures, programs, book jackets, Christmas cards...She wants free and unencumbered use of the pictures for private purposes, to exploit them any way she wants to."

In his demands the deal maker became as noisy and disruptive as a high-speed water bike roaring up the Thames. "Mr. Bryan had everyone curtsying and making tea," recalled one frazzled editorial assistant. "He was remarkably quick to shout, 'Ma'am, if you please,' if one of us forgot for a moment to grovel to Her Royal Highness."

Put off by his hustle, the magazine finally withdrew from negotiations because Sarah would not be interviewed. She wanted her picture featured on the glossy cover but did not want to submit to questions. She phoned the editor, Vicki Woods, to try to change her mind. Miss Woods later wrote that she was exhausted from the round of "hideous telephone calls" she had been receiving from John Bryan.

"Poor you," Sarah told Miss Woods. "I know you think I just see myself as a celebrity...but I'm a serious person and I'm not doing this just so that I can get free Christmas cards or something...."

The editor told the Duchess she could make

her own arrangements with the photographer, but the magazine could not pick up the tab without getting an interview from her. Sarah pleaded Palace protocol. She told the editor: "It's always me who has to carry the can; it's always me who gets the blame for this kind of thing; it's always my fault, and I've had enough of it; that's why I want out of the whole thing, so I can get on with my own life….I'm so tired of carrying the can for all of them. I've been the scapegoat of the Waleses for the past four years."

After the photo shoot, John Bryan called to taunt the editor about the pictures. "This is the hottest set of photos I've dealt with ever," he said. "You really lost out….We were only ever gonna [sic] do this in our style. She's a goddamn pro. She's not some dead, common, fucking trashy little model."

Over the next sixteen months he jetted from New York to London to Paris, making deals for Her Royal Highness. He tried to sell her as a model, a writer, an ambassador. He courted publishers and producers to sell *Budgie—The Little Helicopter* as a television cartoon series. "That property was totally dead when I got hold of it," he recalled. "It had no credibility, nobody would deal with it—nobody would touch it with a ten-foot pole. …"

But he managed to sell *Budgie* for television, and then he sold commercial rights to *Budgie* trinkets: water wings, swimsuits, beach towels, greeting cards, gift wrap, night-lights, lampshades, balloons. The lucrative contract guaranteed the Duchess $3 million, plus a percentage of sales. The British media reported the transaction with a little awe and a lot of envy.

The Queen Mother heard the news as she sat in her drawing room at Clarence House, sipping a gin and tonic. She would have two more tipples before she picked up the telephone and called the Queen.

"I can assure you she was *not* drunk," said a former butler, offended by the suggestion. "Her Majesty Queen Elizabeth the Queen Mother does not get drunk. And on that particular evening, she wasn't even tipsy."

The Queen Mother listened carefully to the news report on television:

The Duchess of York is set to make eight million pounds [about $12 million]," intoned the broadcaster, "as her book, *Budgie—The Little Helicopter,* takes off on TV channels around the world. The Duchess has sold her book to be made into a television series. She also signed licensing contracts with thirteen American firms to market souvenirs ranging from tableware to lavatory seat covers.

"Lavatory seat covers? Did he say lavatory seat covers?" asked the Queen Mother.

"Yes, ma'am," the butler said with a sigh. "I'm afraid he did."

The Queen Mother motioned for another gin and tonic and requested the day's newspapers. Within minutes her drink was freshened from the table that served as a bar in her living room. Finding the newspaper took a little longer; she rarely read anymore because of the cataract in her left eye. The butler appeared with a copy of the *Daily Mail* of that day, April 19, 1994, and opened the paper to the story that concerned her.

She remained impassive as he read aloud the report of the Duchess's weekend visit to Cannes: Sarah had held what she described as a "power dinner" for two hundred key buyers attending the world's largest convention of television programmers.

"I'm absolutely delighted," Sarah was quoted as saying. "I've made merchandising deals all over the world from the little book I wrote in 1989."

The Queen Mother sighed but appeared benignly detached. She had never uttered a word of criticism about Sarah Ferguson—publicly. She had even feigned serenity when she heard about Fergie's clowning at her expense. The boisterous Duchess had been seen tearing through the food halls of Harrods department store in London, where she spotted a biscuit tin bearing the Queen Mother's likeness. She astonished onlookers by banging on the lid and shouting, "Are you in there, dear?"

During monthly planning meetings with her staff, Sarah further rattled sensibilities by referring to the death of the Queen Mother as a way of getting out of engagements she did not want to do. One participant recalled, "If there was a tricky commitment in the offing, she would say, 'Oh, well, look on the bright side—the Queen Mum might die and we'll have to cancel everything because of mourning.'"

From the pinnacle of public esteem, the Queen Mother gazed down on Sarah Ferguson. On the surface both women shared certain characteristics. Each was a commoner who had married the second son of a monarch to become the Duchess of York; each was the mother of two daughters. Both were friendly, ingratiating, strong-willed women who thrived in the spotlight; both were outrageous flirts who loved being the center of male attention. The Duchess gravitated to young heterosexuals, while the Queen Mother contented herself with elderly homosexuals. She called them "my knitting circle" and "the Queen's queens." So indulgent was she toward her high-camp coterie that she once buzzed the Clarence House pantry and said, "When you old queens stop gossiping down there, this old queen up here needs a drink."

The sixty years that separated the Queen Mother from the Duchess of York defined their differences. The older woman was traditional; the younger woman was modern. The former accepted the high price of membership in the royal family; the latter refused to pay the dues. Consequently the Dowager Queen was revered as a royal who retained the common touch; the young Duchess was reviled as merely common.

After the butler had read the Cannes story to the Queen Mother, he handed her the newspaper. But she waved it away in disgust. "Not even Wallis at her worst was this blatant," she said, referring to her implacable enemy, the Duchess of Windsor. She ordered another gin and tonic and picked up the telephone to call her daughter the Queen.

"That was the kiss of death for Fergie," said a Clarence House servant. "You can chart her downfall from that evening."

Most of Sarah's perquisites had already been stripped from her—the royal guards, the royal train, the royal duties, the royal invitations. Deprived of postal privileges, she was no longer allowed to send her letters free. She had been barred from accompanying her husband and their children to Windsor Castle over Easter, but the Queen felt bad about having to exclude her. As Sarah told her father, "I'm not going. Andrew's going. Apparently the Queen wants me, but the rest of the family don't."

Sarah had lost her seat in the royal box at Wimbledon, and her life-size wax figure had been yanked from Madame Tussaud's Wax Museum. Denied entry to the royal enclosure at Ascot, she looked pathetic as she stood on the side of the road, clutching the hands of her children and waving to the Queen as she passed in her royal carriage. Without Her Majesty's continuing tolerance, the Duchess would lose what little remained of her standing in British society. And she didn't stand a chance of retaining the Queen's affection without the goodwill of the Queen Mother.

Shunned by the Palace, the Duchess soon despaired. She sought help from a psychiatrist. But with no royal protection officers she no longer had privacy, and her psychiatric visits became public. A newspaper photographer followed her to the mental health clinic and snapped pictures of her arriving and leaving.

"It's been terrible," said Fergie. "All I can do is pray to the Lord for help."

At the age of ninety-four, the Queen Mother knew better than to waste time on the Duchess. At this point she was worth only a telephone call. After the Queen Mother had a word with Her Majesty, she felt confident that the family would finally be rid of the troublesome young woman, who had embarrassed them even more by announcing that she had been tested three times for AIDS.

The Queen Mother knew there was still the pesky matter of a $3 million divorce settlement, but that was only money. Once it was paid, the Duchess of York would be nothing more than a red-haired footnote to history. The elderly Queen knew better than to get distracted by a sideshow. As the center pole holding up the big tent, she stayed focused on the main event and conserved her dwindling energy for what was happening inside the three-ring circus.

NINETEEN

The sixty-eight-year-old Earl Spencer was ill with pneumonia in a London hospital, and Diana visited him the day before she left to go skiing in Austria. She hadn't spoken to her father for several months, and when she visited him, she took her children for their softening presence.

Unfortunately, none of the Earl Spencer's other children had been speaking to him at the time of his death. "It is a matter of great regret," said his son, Charles, "that no one was with him when he died." The children had been feuding over the renovations of Althorp and had publicly criticized their father and stepmother for their plans to pay for the $3.5 million restoration. The children had accused the Earl and his wife of flogging the family name and selling off heirlooms, including eleven Van Dyck paintings, to "tart up" the dilapidated estate, as Diana described the redecoration of Althorp. She was particularly incensed when she learned that her father had sold merchandising rights to the Japanese to make copies of her wedding dress. She told friends that she was thoroughly disgusted. And she said she was embarrassed by her stepmother's "tacky" decor and her father's "crass" commercialism. Then the family began slugging it out—on the front pages.

The Earl, who was devoted to his second wife, railed against his children for denigrating their stepmother's efforts to make Althorp profitable. He bitterly singled out Diana.

"I have given Diana a hell of a lot of money—between $750,000 and $1.5 million—to invest for Harry," he said, and disclosed Diana's concern about her second son's future. Her firstborn, William, destined to become Prince of Wales and eventually King, was guaranteed immense wealth. But not Harry.

"Diana doesn't understand about money," said her father. "She has no experience. She is too young." He accused all his children of "financial immaturity," said they were spoiled and "ungrateful," and said they did not realize what was involved in running a grand estate.* Soon the children stopped visiting Althorp and stopped speaking to their father.

Minutes after Diana learned of his death on Sunday, March 29, 1992, her lady-in-waiting dashed to the luggage room of the Swiss ski resort and removed the black dress, black shoes, and black hat that were customarily packed for royalty in case of death. Diana wanted to return home alone, but her husband insisted on accompanying her. She dug in. "It's too late for you to start pretending now," she snapped. He knew how unacceptable it

---

* The late Earl Spenser proved right. After his death his son struggled to operate Althorp, a fifteen-thousand-acre estate valued at $132 million. After four years the new Earl Spenser turned it over to a manager, who rented the property for corporate conferences for $5,262 a day. The young Spenser moved to South Africa with his wife and four children. He later separated from his wife but remained in South Africa. Like his father, he, too, exploited the Spencer name for profit. In 1996 he sold several of the family's honorary titles at auction to pay for new plumbing.

would be for her to return by herself. But she was adamant that he remain with the children, skiing. She resented his using her father's death to look like a loving husband.

The Prince's private secretary recognized the couple's impasse and called the Queen's private secretary. Only when Her Majesty interceded and called Diana did the Princess agree to return with her husband. The next day she got off the plane, looking red-eyed and stricken with grief.

"There was such dissension surrounding that funeral," said a relative, who ruefully recalled the misleading headline in the *Times*: "Earl Spencer Goes to Rest at Peace with His Family." In truth the family's antipathies had followed the late Earl to his grave. Johnny Spencer's bitter relationship with his father had forced Johnny to move off the family estate. He did not return until his father died. Johnny then repeated the acrimonious behavior in his relationship with his son, Charles, who was estranged from him at the time of his death.

The Spencer children accepted such acrimony as part of their life. They had grown up watching their father reject *his* father and their mother reject *her* mother. The children had seen nasty fights between their parents, which did not end with the divorce. Although both parents remarried, they continued to compete for the children's attention and affection by showering them with expensive gifts. "It makes you very materialistic," their son admitted later.

In his eulogy for the Earl Spencer, Lord St. John of Fawsley tried to make light of the family's discord. "Birds twitter and peck in their nests," he said, "even when they are gilded ones." He assured the congregation in the little country church of Northamptonshire that the Earl Spencer had loved all his family, especially the Princess of Wales.

Diana's floral wreath to her father was prominently displayed in front of his oak coffin with a card she had inscribed personally: "I miss you dreadfully, Darling Daddy, but will love you forever...Diana." Behind the coffin and barely noticeable was a tribute of flowers from the Prince of Wales, "In most affectionate memory."

In front of the press, the four Spencer children appeared cordial to their stepmother, with Diana reaching sympathetically for her arm at one point. "The sight [of that gesture]...made me feel quite sick," said Sue Ingram, who had worked for Raine Spencer for seventeen years. The assistant, who was fired by the new young Earl the day after the funeral, recalled what happened behind the scenes. When Raine, who had moved out of Althorp within forty-eight hours of her husband's death to make room for the new heir, sent her maid to collect her clothes, Diana and her brother were waiting.

The maid arrived and packed two Louis Vuitton cases monogrammed with the Spencer "S." Diana stopped her from leaving. "What have you got in there?" she demanded. "Those are my father's cases. They don't belong to you."

The maid explained that Raine had bought the luggage for a trip to Japan to match suitcases with the initials "R.S."

Diana ordered the maid to empty the Vuitton suitcases into black plastic garbage bags. The maid complied, and Diana snatched the suitcases. Her brother kicked the garbage bags down the stairs.

Days later, when Raine returned with a roll of red stickers to identify the pieces of furniture she wanted to move, she was confronted there by her stepson's lawyer. He told her she could not remove one single stick from Althorp until she supplied proof of purchase.

"She had to telephone the new Earl for details of the memorial service [held six weeks later in Westminster Abbey]," said her assistant, "and he told his solicitor to send her a fax." When her husband's ashes were placed in the Spencer vault, Raine was not invited to the family ceremony.

The last merchandising contract that the Earl Spencer had signed before he died was with the publisher of *Diana: Her True Story*. Having been assured that the book would portray his family positively, especially his daughter, he sold the rights to eighty personal photographs from the Spencer family albums. This time Diana did not object.

She wanted the photographs to illustrate a book, which she hoped would set her free from her marriage. Months before, she had given permission to a few friends to talk with the author, Andrew Morton. Through the eyes of her brother, her best friend, her lover, and her masseuse, she presented a shattered fairy tale: she had kissed a prince who turned into a toad. His love for another woman had driven her into bulimia and five attempts at suicide. She had been abandoned by his family, which did not appreciate her efforts to breathe life into their dreary dynasty.

An excerpt from the book ran in the *Sunday Times*. Its placement on the front page of the once respected newspaper had elevated its credibility above tabloid tittle-tattle. And its apparent endorsement by the Princess of Wales made it even more tantalizing. But it rattled the establishment. The Prime Minister, Members of Parliament, and the chairman of the Press Complaints Commission* denounced it as sensational and sordid. The Archbishop of Canterbury said it exceeded the limits of a society claiming to respect human values. Harrods refused to sell it. "Our customers would not expect us to stock such a scurrilous book," said the store's spokesman. The *Spectator* called it "a farrago of rubbish."

The book became an instant best-seller, but its author was dismissed by the British press as a former tabloid reporter whose father was

---

* The government can restrict journalists because there are no formal guarantees of freedom of speech in Britain. Rather than be restricted by law, British journalists decided to restrict themselves by establishing the Press Complaints Commission in 1991 to monitor their excesses. The commission of seventeen people includes, local, regional, and national newspaper editors. It has no enforcement power but is obligated to publish its findings.

a picture framer. From the snobbish commentary, it appeared that the author had compounded the misfortune of being born working-class: he was a republican in a country that revered royalty. "I asked Andrew Morton if he wasn't in danger of killing the golden goose which lays his eggs," said Michael Cole, the BBC's former royal correspondent. "He replied, 'Well, I can quite happily live on the ashes of the House of Windsor for the next twenty years.'"

Only two of Britain's eleven national newspapers ignored the published excerpt. The editor of the *Financial Times* said, "Not our subject matter." The *Daily Telegraph* editor said the subject matter was distasteful. "It's odious," he wrote in the *Spectator,* explaining why he would not permit coverage. The *Telegraph,* sometimes called the *Torygraph,* is the royal family's favorite newspaper, and its editor, Max Hastings, is a close friend of Prince Andrew. "The tabloid reporting of the Wales marriage," Hastings wrote, "makes lager louts look like gentlemen."

The morning the excerpt appeared, the Prince of Wales was reeling. "I'd say he was close to a panic," recalled his Highgrove housekeeper. Over breakfast Charles had read the serialization that his press secretary had faxed from London. Charles had known that a Diana-inspired book was going to be published, but he'd assumed that it would be nothing more than a self-serving account of her good works, plus pretty pictures. He was not prepared for her assault on him as a man, a father, and a husband.

When he finished reading, he left the table and went to Diana's room with the excerpts in hand. Like Richard III, he had one question for his wife: "Why dost thou spit at me?" Diana later compared their confrontation to the scene in *The Godfather* where Al Pacino berates Diane Keaton for humiliating him by trying to break free of their marriage. This was not the first time Diana compared the monarchy to the Mafia. "The only difference," she told her cousin, "is these muggers wear crowns." Minutes after Charles stormed out of her room, she left Highgrove in tears. Although she had denied having a hand in the book, he knew better.

"I can just hear her saying those things," he told his private secretary, Richard Aylard. "Those are her words, exactly."

Diana's grandmother Lady Ruth Fermoy visited Highgrove a few days later to console Charles. He embraced the frail eighty-three-year-old woman and asked her to walk with him in the garden. "Ruth never forgave Diana for causing the separation," said Lady Fermoy's godchild. "She felt that Diana had brought shame to her family by not remaining within her marriage. She didn't speak to Diana until the last few days of her life, and even then, Ruth told me, she could not forgive her for betraying the monarchy."

Charles was stunned that his wife had had the nerve to break the royal code of silence by revealing his mistress. Diana went further by calling Camilla "the Rottweiler" and describing her as a killer dog that had sunk her teeth into the Waleses' marriage and wouldn't let go. Television star Joan Collins said she wanted to star in a TV special of the royal soap opera: "I could play Camilla Parker Bowles," she said. "I could ugly up for that." The press unkindly described Camilla as "plain-faced" and "looking like her horse." The *Scottish Herald* sniffed, "She smokes, she jokes, and is capable of dressing for dinner after a day in the saddle without pausing to have a bath." The revelation that the Prince of Wales had long been in love with her so upset the public that when she went to the grocery, angry shoppers pelted her with bread rolls.

Charles had dismissed his wife's rantings about his mistress as adolescent jealousy. He didn't understand Diana's despair or her need to strike back. He had expected her to accept her loveless marriage in exchange for the privilege of being the Princess of Wales. He was taken aback when she balked and felt mauled by the book that made him look like a beast. Quickly the Palace went to his defense.

Sir Robert Fellowes phoned Diana before she left Highgrove. "I need to know the extent of your participation," he said sternly. His marriage to Diana's sister Jane had strained family relations on occasion. Diana replied tearfully that she had never met the author or granted him an interview. Her trembling voice convinced her brother-in-law that she was telling the truth. He didn't realize that she was simply panicked by the uproar that she had caused.

But she was rattled only momentarily. She later told one of her astrologers that she had no regrets about her decision to cooperate because her husband did not deserve to be protected by silence—least of all, she argued, because he was the Prince of Wales. "He's supposed to be a paragon to people," she said. "He's going to be the goddamned Defender of the Faith." After eleven years of marriage she had decided his infidelity deserved to be exposed. By entering into marriage, Robert Louis Stevenson had warned, "you have willfully introduced a witness into your life...and can no longer close the mind's eye upon uncomely passages, but must stand up straight and put a name upon your actions." If Charles wouldn't, Diana would. But even she was startled by what she had wrought.

She was appalled by the degree of detail in the book, and she felt betrayed by her brother, who had described her as a liar. He said she was someone who "had difficulty telling the truth purely because she liked to embellish things." He recalled, "On the school run one day, the vicar's wife stopped the car and said: 'Diana Spencer, if you tell one more lie like that, I am going to make you walk home.'" He related that one of her school reports asserted, "Diana Spencer is the most scheming little girl I have ever met."

She was also taken aback by James Gilbey's

remarks in the book, which she thought made her look like a suicidal maniac. She knew that Gilbey had spoken only with her approval and her best interests at heart, but she was dismayed by the pitiful picture of her that he painted. After publication, she closed the book on him.

Diana's assurances that she had had nothing to do with the book prompted the Queen's private secretary to fire off several protests to the Press Complaints Commission. He also drafted a public statement for her, disavowing the "preposterous" claims of her participation. He told her that anything short of an official denunciation would not be convincing. The public was prepared to believe the worst based on what they had read and seen in the past year.

Months before, Prince William was accidentally hit on the head with a golf club, which fractured his skull, necessitating emergency surgery. Diana, who was at San Lorenzo restaurant when she received the news, hurried to her son's side and spent two nights in the hospital with him until he could come home. Charles visited him for a few minutes after his surgery but did not otherwise interrupt his schedule. He said he had to attend a performance of *Tosca*. The press was appalled. "What Kind of a Dad Are You?" shrieked a *Sun* headline. Jean Rook in the *Daily Express* asked: "What sort of father of an eight-year-old boy, nearly brained by a golf club, leaves the hospital before knowing the outcome for a night at the opera?"

Charles blamed Diana for making him look

like a callous parent. Feeling slightly chastened, he made a point a few weeks later of being photographed riding a bicycle with his sons, but Diana told the press that Charles left the boys twenty-four hours later to go to a polo match. Jean Rook accused Charles of treating his sons like "well-fed pets who know their place in the world of their utterly self-involved parent. Certainly, it must hurt William and Harry to see their father more often on TV than in the flesh."

Photos appeared of Charles going to church with his sons at Sandringham, but when someone in the crowd asked him where the Princess was, he replied with a strained smile, "She's not here today, so you can get your money back."

Other photographs had also indicated friction between the couple. On a royal tour of India, Diana was shown sitting by herself in front of the Taj Mahal. That sad picture (which some reporters said was staged by the Princess) recalled Prince Charles's visit to India before his wedding. He had promised to bring his bride back to the seventeenth-century temple, a world-renowned monument to eternal love. But when he brought Diana in 1992 for a four-day tour, they were not speaking. They had arrived in India on separate planes; he flew from Oman, and she flew from London. They followed separate schedules. They stayed in separate suites on different floors of the hotel in New Delhi and communicated through their staffs. They smiled only in front of the cameras.

Then came a picture of Diana in front of the Pyramids—alone again. She had let it be known that while she was traveling on an official tour of Egypt, her husband was vacationing in Turkey with his mistress. More pictures followed of Charles playing polo while Diana visited leper colonies; Charles shooting birds at Sandringham while Diana consoled cancer patients in Liverpool; Charles partying with the Sultan of Brunei, the world's richest man, while Diana conferred with Mother Teresa, who ministered to the world's poorest people.

The Palace tried to counteract the discordant images of the Waleses and their marriage, but new disclosures kept popping up like frogs from a swamp. When police constable Andrew Jacques, a guard at Highgrove, disclosed that the Prince and Princess led separate lives, the Palace dismissed his story as tabloid fiction. The constable, who worked at Highgrove for four years, stood firm. "The only time they meet up is at mealtimes," he said, "and very often that ends in a blazing row for all to hear." He revealed that Prince Charles slept alone in one bedroom (with his childhood teddy bear in bed with him), while the Princess slept by herself in the master bedroom. "They never smile, laugh, or do anything together....In four years, I only ever saw him kiss her goodbye once, and that was a peck on the cheek."

Predictably, the establishment press called upon peerage expert Harold Brooks-Baker to respond to the constable's assertions, and, as always, the American-born royalist complied. "You can't break down a marriage that's been put up the way the press has put this one up," the peerage expert told *The New York Times*. "The press made a lot out of the fact that they were apart on her thirtieth birthday last month, but very little out of the fact that on the following weekend she and her husband were together; there was a birthday cake, and he gave her a lovely bracelet."

The former housekeeper of Highgrove disclosed that the gift from Charles was paste. In a diary she kept while working for the Prince and Princess of Wales, she noted that when Diana found out, she burst into tears. The Princess, accustomed to being consoled with expensive gifts, was distraught that her husband bestowed a diamond necklace on his mistress but gave her only costume jewelry. The housekeeper quoted Diana as saying: "I don't want his bloody fake jewels. I thought cheating husbands took great care to keep their wives sweet with the real things, saving the tawdry stuff for their tarts."

For her thirtieth birthday Charles offered to throw a party. But Diana didn't want to celebrate with him. So she said no and celebrated privately with her lover, James Hewitt, who had recently returned from the Gulf War. Charles was stung by press accusations that he had neglected the occasion of his wife's birthday, so he dispatched a friend to call Nigel Dempster to set the record straight. The gossip columnist obliged with a front-page story in the *Daily Mail* about the Prince's loving gesture. Diana responded the next day through a friend, who told the *Sun* that the Princess did not want a grand ball filled with her husband's "stuffy friends."

Princess Anne, disgusted by the newspaper sparring, confronted Diana about turning her marriage into a media free-for-all. "Before you joined, there were hardly any leaks," said the Princess Royal. "Now the ship is so full of holes, it's no wonder that it's sinking."

Diana stared hard at her sister-in-law without saying a word. But Anne didn't flinch.

"I wouldn't go telling too many tall tales if I were you," she warned. "They might just come back to haunt you one day."

After Anne's rebuke, Diana became convinced that the entire royal family was against her. She decided then to cooperate with Andrew Morton by giving her friends permission to talk to him about her dismal marriage. "Do what you think is best," she told her friends when they called her about the book. She made sure that nothing was said to the author about her love affair with James Hewitt.

Months later she could hardly disavow the book, so when Robert Fellowes called and read her the statement he had drafted for release, she withheld her approval. He insisted that she publicly disapprove the book, but she said, "I cannot be held responsible for what my friends say."

Waiting for the Princess to respond, the editor of the *Sunday Times* was getting jumpy.

"We thought she would break under all the pressure," recalled Andrew Neil. "We would not have been surprised had she committed suicide at that point. She was that unstable.

"Initially, I did not believe the book. Not for a minute. The Princess of Wales suffering from bulimia, throwing up in toilets, and attempting suicide? Impossible. But I grilled Andrew Morton, demanded to have the names of his sources, and independently interviewed all of them. Once I was satisfied the book was accurate, I decided to go with it, provided the two major sources, Carolyn Bartholomew and James Gilbey, signed affidavits backing up what they had said was true."

The newspaper's sensational excerpt appeared on the morning of June 7, 1992. That afternoon the Queen invited Camilla Parker Bowles and her husband to join the royal family in their box at Windsor to watch a polo match. Diana saw the gesture as one more kick in the teeth. Privately she questioned the Queen's sensitivity. "If she wants this marriage to work, why won't she help by acting like a decent mother-in-law?"

The next day the editor of the *Sunday Telegraph* said the editor of the *Sunday Times* was a scandal-monger who deserved to be horse-whipped. Andrew Neil published James Gilbey's statement:

"I can confirm that the Princess discussed with me on numerous occasions her attempted suicides, as she has done with other close friends."

The *Sunday Times* editor said he knew the monarchy was beginning to crumble when he received calls of support from aristocrats like Alan Clark, the former Tory Minister of State. "It's a shame," Clark told Andrew Neil, "but no great loss. The royal family is just a bunch of pasty-faced Germans."

An avalanche of news stories, editorials, and television commentaries questioned what was once accepted as unassailable—the future of the monarchy and whether Britain really needed a royal family. There were even questions about the dutiful monarch, who lavished more attention on her dogs and horses than on her children. Public opinion polls showed overwhelming support for the Princess, especially among American women. *People* magazine, whose twenty million weekly readers are predominantly female, put her on forty-one covers in sixteen years; and the issue featuring her with an excerpt from Morton's book was the best-selling cover in the magazine's history. The American writer Camille Paglia proclaimed the Princess a twentieth-century icon: "Diana may have become the most powerful image in world popular culture today."

Frustrated aides in the Palace press office strained to be civil. Their original denunciation of the book had been unequivocal: "outrageously irresponsible." Now they backtracked. "We have no further comment at this time." Their accents became more clipped, as if cut-glass enunciation would ward off further questions.

As the press office was trying to deflect

questions about the extramarital affair of the Prince of Wales, an internal memo surfaced that illustrated the standard of behavior the Queen expected from her servants. Her estate manager at Balmoral had issued a "gentle reminder" to any employee engaged in an illicit love affair. The reminder threatened eviction from Her Majesty's premises. "If you're living in sin," warned the Queen's manager, "you could lose your home." The Palace tried to dissociate itself from the tone. "Any correspondence on whatever is going on up there is totally private," said a press assistant. But Diana said the Queen should send a "gentle reminder" like that to her son. Although she had plenty to say about Morton's book privately, Diana said nothing publicly. With no response from her, the editor of the *Sunday Times* was worried. "I didn't know what to do to restore our credibility," said Andrew Neil. Within hours he was saved by an anonymous female caller. She told the Press Association, England's national news agency, that the Princess of Wales would be visiting the home of Carolyn Bartholomew. A photograph of Diana embracing her friend, a major source of information in the book, put the lie to skeptics.

When the picture was published, Sir Robert Fellowes knew he had been deceived by Diana. Having inaccurately reassured the Queen that Diana had had nothing to do with the book, he offered his resignation, but the Queen turned it down. She summoned Charles and Diana to Windsor on June 15, 1992, for a family conference.

With self-preservation on her mind, she insisted on a public show of unity, beginning with the Royal Ascot. Her husband objected. "Why the bloody pretense?" he snapped. "Let's be done with it." But the Queen had seen the crowds cheering Diana days before and waving placards: "Diana, We Love You" and "God Bless the Princess of Wales." The Queen knew those crowds would be angry if Diana was not part of the royal family's traditional carriage procession into Ascot. She stressed the importance of not disappointing people. Turning to Diana, she said, "Do you understand?"

Diana did not have the nerve—then—to openly defy the Queen, so she did as she was told. "I know my duty," she said, lowering her eyes. When the crowds saw her riding with the Queen Mother in the carriage, behind the Queen and Prince Charles, they roared wildly and gave the second coach more applause than the first. The Duke of Edinburgh scowled.

"He openly snubbed Diana that day," said reporter James Whitaker. "When she walked into the royal box, Philip turned away and would not speak to her. She sat by herself as he buried his nose in the program. He did not look up or acknowledge her presence, but she didn't seem particularly to care."

When someone mentioned the Duke's rebuff, Diana shrugged and said, "The man has the warmth of a snow pea." She was buoyed by the rousing cheers she had received, but her elation later evaporated as her confidence sagged.

During the meeting at Windsor Castle, the Queen had asked Diana what she wanted. "A legal separation," she replied. Instead the Queen recommended a cooling-off period. "We'll revisit the subject in six months," she said, adding that she expected the couple to proceed with their long-standing plan to tour South Korea. They agreed, but the trip was a public relations disaster. Diplomatic cables indicate almost as much tension between Charles and Diana as between North and South Korea. Press photos supported the top-secret cables flying back and forth from Seoul to London: they showed a dour Prince and a grim Princess, who clearly despised each other.

When the Queen saw the pictures, she called her son. "Charles, I don't understand," she said. The implication was that he was not trying hard enough.

"Don't you realize she's mad?" he said angrily. "She's mad!"

Before the Queen could respond, Charles had hung up on his mother.

Upon their return to England, Diana told friends that she did not think her husband was fit to be King. In the past she had said she knew she would never become Queen and that Charles would ascend to the throne without her. Now she questioned his ability to reign. She said she based her assessment on her instincts and her intimate knowledge of her husband. This raised questions about Charles, who was remembered as a shy little boy who always seemed fretful. Was he too timid to become King? asked an editorial under the headline "Unfaithful *AND* Reluctant?"

Charles wanted to respond but didn't know how best to defend himself. His zealous equerry urged him to cooperate with the journalist Jonathan Dimbleby on a book about his life. So the Prince decided to give the respected journalist unprecedented access to his private diaries and letters. The biography, to be preceded by an exclusive television interview, was timed to commemorate the twenty-fifth anniversary of Charles's investiture as Prince of Wales.

Such anniversaries gave the royal family opportunities to celebrate themselves with stirring parades and fireworks. But in 1992 the Queen, then in her fortieth anniversary* year on the throne, canceled plans for a grandiose celebration. She stopped the fund-raising for a $3.6 million fountain that had been planned in Parliament Square and said no to a military parade. "The past year is not one I shall look back on with undiluted pleasure," she said in a speech. "In the words of one of my more sympathetic correspondents, it has turned out

---

* To commemorate her forty years on the throne, the Queen authorized a BBC television documentary, Elizabeth R: A Year in the Life of the Queen. The film focused on her work as head of state and showed little of her family. "The Palace felt it was perhaps necessary to remind people what the Queen did and her enormous devotion to duty," said producer Edward Mirzoeff. "We deliberately tried not to reveal everything about her life." The New York Times described the film as "the most boring BBC import ever to make its way to American public television." The Queen loved it and knighted the producer.

to be an *annus horribilis.*" One newspaper headlined her remarks: "One's Bum Year." Another criticized her for using Latin to express travesties made all too plain in English throughout the year:

January: Publication of photos of the Duchess of York and Steve Wyatt on vacation in Morocco. The Palace denies there is a problem in the Yorks' marriage.

February: The Princess of Wales is criticized as unpatriotic when she exchanges her British-made Jaguar for a German-made Mercedes. "This is another example of the royal family showing contempt for British workers," says Dennis Skinner, a Labor MP. "They live off the fat of the land with taxpayers' money coming from British workers, and then they spit in their faces." At the Queen's insistence, Diana gives up the Mercedes—seven months later.

March: The Palace announces the separation of the Duke and Duchess of York.

April: After three years' separation, Princess Anne divorces Captain Mark Phillips. A paternity suit filed against Phillips by a New Zealand teacher who claimed she conceived after "a one-night stand" is settled. Without acknowledging fatherhood, Phillips agrees to pay the mother an undisclosed sum of money for "equestrian consulting services."

May: A love affair is reported between Princess Anne, forty-two, and thirty-seven-year-old Navy Commander Timothy Laurence. That prompts one newspaper columnist to exclaim, "Not Again, Anne!" Another warns: "Keep Your Hands off the Hired Help." The Palace denies the Princess is involved with her equerry. Seven months later she marries him in Scotland, where divorce is permitted. Some courtiers deem the match unsuitable, not because the royal bride is divorced, but because the bridegroom on his great-great-great-grandfather's side was Jewish. In 1826 the Laurence family had changed their name from Levy. Almost two centuries later this still prompts comment. One royal correspondent wrote, "One could not avoid the idea…[of]…his Jewish ancestors."

June: Prince Edward, the Queen's twenty-eight-year-old son, denies again that he's homosexual. He then denies that he issued the denial, which prompts a *Washington Post* columnist to observe, "The youngest son gets by far the best press, by Windsorian standards, which means that he merely needs to spend every second Tuesday denying in print that he is a woman."

July: Diana's masseur tells the press Diana wants to end "the inherent deceit, unhappiness, and dissatisfaction" of her marriage. "The situation has to end," says Stephen Twigg, who visited Kensington Palace regularly for three years to give the Princess holistic massages. "Otherwise there will be a tragedy." Hours later Diana fires the therapist.

August: Newspaper photos show Sarah Ferguson topless with John Bryan in the South of France. Days later the *Sun* publishes a tape-recorded telephone call between Diana and James Gilbey in which she complains about her treatment from the royal family. "My life is torture," she says. "Bloody hell. And after all I've done for this fucking family."

September: The Palace denies there is a problem in the marriage of the Prince and Princess of Wales.

October: The Queen is booed in Germany. Residents of Dresden throw eggs at her limousine shortly after the British unveil a statue in London to honor the memory of Air Chief Marshal Arthur "Bomber" Harris, who directed the fire-bombing of Dresden during World War II.

"November brought the worst," said the Queen. On Friday morning, November 20, 1992, the skies over Windsor Castle filled with orange balls of flame etched with black clouds of acrid smoke. A fire, started by a lamp that ignited the curtains in the Queen's private chapel, threatened to destroy what Samuel Pepys called "the most romantic castle in the world." Instead of sounding fire alarms, the staff called the castle switchboard for help. Prince Andrew, who was staying at Windsor for the weekend, rushed to save his mother's treasures. He joined the human chain of employees who passed pictures and tables and clocks from hand to hand until they were safe from destruction. Firemen poured a million and a half gallons of water on the structure, but the fire burned for fifteen hours.

"The Queen is devastated, absolutely devastated," Andrew told CNN television shortly after his mother arrived from London. "She is helping to take stuff out of the castle—works of art. She has been in there for thirty minutes."

Charles arrived the next day to survey the damage. He called it "a tragedy," then left for a shooting party at Sandringham. The Queen's other children, Princess Anne and Prince Edward, did not show up at all.

The sixty-six-year-old monarch looked worn and beleaguered as she tramped through the charred remains. Of all her royal residences, Windsor Castle, the symbol of her dynasty, was her favorite. It was where she had lived as a child during World War II. It also was the main repository of her art, considered the most important private collection in the world. Her holdings included works by Rembrandt, da Vinci, Holbein, Rubens, and Vermeer, as well as priceless porcelain, tapestries, furniture, and armor from William the Conqueror.

In her hooded slicker and rubber boots,

she bleakly surveyed the tangle of fire trucks, hoses, and ladders. It was her forty-fifth wedding anniversary, and her husband was in Argentina—with another woman. "Philip was traveling with us as president of the World Wildlife Fund," a member of his group reported, "and while I don't recall seeing him with Susan Barrantes [as her daughter, Sarah Ferguson, later alleged], there was talk about him and his secretary....What I remember most is the board of directors meeting the morning after the fire....We were all talking about the television coverage of the Queen and Prince Andrew at Windsor Castle, hauling out the debris. Philip walked into the room [in Buenos Aires] and started the meeting without mentioning a word about the fire, about his wife, or his son. We couldn't believe it. Not one word."

Britain's heritage secretary declared the fire a national disaster and expressed the nation's sympathy. He promised the Queen the government would restore her castle. But with no fire insurance, he said the cost to taxpayers would be about $80 million. He said people would be "proud" to carry the burden. England, though, was mired in a recession, and Her Majesty's subjects resented the implication that they should pay for the restoration.

"While the castle stands, it is theirs," wrote Janet Daley in the *Times*, "but when it burns down, it is ours."

The Palace argued that it was the government's responsibility to purchase the Queen's fire insurance.

"For the richest woman in the world?" boomed a Member of Parliament.

"She's *not* the richest," retorted a courtier. He flashed a recently published list of the country's wealthiest women, showing the Queen ranked tenth, with assets of about $150 million, which disputed previous estimates of her wealth at $7.5 billion. The Palace recognized the line between the "haves" and the "have nots"; and to some of her subjects, Her Majesty just had too much. So when *Business Age* magazine said she was the wealthiest person in Britain, the Palace protested to the Press Complaints Commission. The Queen's courtiers said it wasn't fair to lump in royal residences, art treasures, and crown jewels with her personal wealth. The commission agreed and said the evaluation should be lowered from billions to millions.

"I'm sure *that* will be immensely comforting to my unemployed constituents," said the MP.

The country's largest-selling tabloid, the *News of the World,* asked its readers to vote on the issue. Providing two telephone numbers, the paper said to call one number if "we should pay" and another if "she should pay." There were sixteen thousand calls, and fifteen thousand said "she should pay."

"She" struck a profitable pose. Like a business tycoon who recognizes there's money to be made in changing with the times, the Queen saw there was a dynasty to be saved. Not even the British monarchy could survive indefinitely in the thin air of unaccountable privilege. So she announced through her Prime Minister that she would start paying taxes. She also agreed to open Buckingham Palace to the public for two months a year. She said she would charge $12 admission to help finance restoration of Windsor Castle. And she would also help restore the castle with profits from the Palace gift shop, where tourists could purchase commemorative cup-and-saucer sets ($36) and crown-shaped chocolates ($6). Over the objections of her husband, she agreed to give up the royal yacht, *Britannia,* in 1997. That was when it was scheduled to be decommissioned to spare the taxpayer the expense of an overhaul.* Also, to the dismay of her relatives, she removed most of them from the public payroll and reimbursed the government for everyone but herself, her mother, and her husband. This gesture returned approximately $14 million to the taxpayers. But she kept herself on the Civil List for $11,850,000 a year, her mother for $972,000 a year, and her husband for $547,000 a year.

Perhaps to underscore his worth, Philip had agreed in 1993 to be profiled by journalist Fiammetta Rocco in the *Independent on Sun-*

---

* Six months before the *Britannia* was to be decommissioned, the Defense Minister announced that a new $100 million ship would be built in time for the Queen's golden jubilee in 2002. "The *Britannia* is a symbol of the Crown, the kingdom, and its maritime traditions," he said, "and should be funded by the nation."

day. His office had provided her with the phone numbers of fifty people to call. Her most interesting interview proved to be with the Duke himself. "I arrived at the Palace on the day of the Queen's *annus horribilis* speech," recalled the writer, who had to submit her questions in advance. "He had barred all personal questions about his family—his parents, his wife, his children. He only wanted to discuss issues, but not all issues. I couldn't ask about ordination of women in the church, but he would talk endlessly about the World Wildlife Fund."

During the interview, the reporter strayed slightly from the script. She mused that Philip seemed to be a man surrounded by many myths. He brightened slightly, so she proceeded.

"One myth is that you have had many mistresses."

He looked exasperated. "Have you ever stopped to think that for the last forty years, I have never moved anywhere without a policeman accompanying me? So how the hell could I get away with anything like that?" He stared straight ahead and waited for the next question. That subject was closed.

His response amused the former head of the Royal Protection Service, who chuckled when he read it. "The truth is our function is to protect the person, not his morals....If he's inside a woman's flat, we stand outside. We don't care what he's doing inside as long as he emerges unharmed...so he can get away with whatever he wants....We're not there to protect him as the Queen's husband, but to guard him as the

Duke of Edinburgh...there's a considerable difference. ..."

The British historian and writer Richard Hough, who spent time with Philip in the 1970s researching a book and traveling with him on the *Britannia,* acknowledged the other women in his life. "There were two secretaries on board ship, both very pretty," he recalled. "And I know that he keeps a mistress... somewhere in Notting Hill. But he was very discreet." Years before, Philip had underscored the importance of discretion when he was asked the secret of a successful marriage. "A home of one's own," he said, "*and* common sense."

The reporter did not push the point with Philip. "A second myth," she said, "is that Prince Andrew is not really your son. That he is the son of Lord Porchester [the Queen's racing manager]."

Philip did not flinch. Knowing that any reaction would be front-page news, he said nothing. He sat as impassive as stone. "Like a child with porridge in his mouth," the reporter later told a colleague. She had addressed the issue of his son's paternity because it had been raised weeks before by Nigel Dempster in *The New York Times Magazine:* "Get hold of a picture of Prince Andrew and then one of Lord Porchester at the same age," Dempster was quoted telling writer Christopher Hitchens. "You'll see that Prince Philip could never have been Andy's father."

The Palace did not challenge the published statement, and neither did Philip. When his silence became uncomfortable, Rocco moved on.

"The third myth is a rumor that you once had an affair with Valéry Giscard d'Estaing [former President of France]," she said.

Philip laughed. "Oh, Giscard is a delightful old boy, but I never stayed at the Elysée Palace when he was President. I would stay there when [Vincent] Auriol was President [1947-1954], and he was a frightful buggerer."

The reporter laughed, too, as if to acknowledge that her impertinent question deserved no more than his mischievous answer. A few days later a courier knocked on her door with an envelope. The thick heavy white stationery from Windsor Castle contained a curt message from HRH Prince Philip: "Do not use the Auriol anecdote on your tape." And her editor received a call from the Queen's press secretary, complaining about the reporter's impudence. Both journalists were summoned to the Palace for a meeting with Prince Philip's private secretary, Sir Brian McGrath. He reminded them he had provided the names and phone numbers of people whose recollections lent credibility to the profile. "At least, while those recollections remain on the record," said the courtier. The implication was clear. If the journalists used Philip's tape-recorded comment, they would lose their sources, who had agreed to be quoted because

Philip gave permission. Without named sources, the journalists knew the profile would lack punch.

They argued that the anecdote about the late President of France showed Prince Philip's sense of humor. The Palace was not to be conned. A deal was struck: the newspaper would not use the anecdote, and the Palace would not withdraw their sources.

Afterward Philip said he would never give another interview to a British reporter. But by then his personal life, once off limits to the press, had become vulnerable. The *Independent on Sunday* reported that he and the Queen slept in separate bedrooms. *Vanity Fair* said he kept a mistress. *The New Yorker* said it was a "succession of actress-mistresses who regularly appeared on television, prompting viewers in the know to smile and say, 'She's one of his.'" For those not in the know, the *Tatler* published "The Royal Collection," which provided the names, biographies, and photographs of thirteen women described as "the Duke of Edinburgh's fan club." The list included minor British stars but omitted major American ones like Jane Russell, Zsa Zsa Gabor, and Shirley MacLaine. The British aristocrats included two Princesses, one Duchess, one Countess, and five titled ladies, including the seventy-year-old wife of one of the Queen's former equerries. "That's an appalling image of my mother-in-law—in bed with Prince Philip," pooh-poohed the woman's son-in-law. "It's like *Love Among the Ruins.*"

"The [*Tatler*] list was a good lineup but hardly complete," said the columnist Taki. "Everybody knows that Sasha [the Duchess of Abercorn] is Philip's mistress....She's lasted the longest—six to eight years....He would take the *Britannia* to the Caribbean to attend an opening in St. Kitt's because she would be there." A private photograph from one Caribbean trip was sold to newspapers, showing Philip with only a towel wrapped around his waist. He had his arm around the Duchess, who was in her swimsuit. Her husband, James, who was standing a few feet behind her, was cropped out of the picture. "James is the nicest man in the world," said Taki. "He'd have to be to put up with Philip."

Before he died in 1993, John Barratt, who was Lord Mountbatten's private secretary for twenty years, also discussed Philip's extramarital love affairs. "The Duchess of Abercorn is Philip's now, but Mountbatten had her first—she was his godchild, and he loved her greatly, although she was forty years younger. Then he passed her on to Philip. ...

"The Queen can be very imperious and cold. Austere, really. So it's understandable why Philip goes elsewhere, and make no mistake about it, he does. But he hasn't had as many affairs as people think. Many women are social mountaineers who feed off the association with him. For them, it's a badge of honor to be perceived as a lover of the Queen's husband....I'd put Patricia Kluge in that category," he said, referring to the former soft-porn belly dancer from Liverpool. "Before her divorce from John W. Kluge, the American tycoon, she had him purchase an estate near Balmoral and obtain Philip's trainer to teach her carriage riding, which was his favorite sport....She was always ringing up to say, 'I'm having a party and would like you to come and bring some friends.' Through her husband, who was worth $6 billion, she was too rich for the royal family to ignore. Philip and Charles worked her for over $500,000 to sponsor the Royal Windsor Horse Show, but I seriously doubt whether Philip took a canter outside the rails for her. ..."

Barratt went on to say: "Now Princess Alexandra [the daughter of Princess Marina, who married the Duke of Kent] is different.... She and Philip have been long involved....She's the Queen's first cousin—a tall blond beauty who married Sir Angus Ogilvy....Her looks are reminiscent of Princess Anne, who is Philip's favorite child. You'll notice that many of his mistresses have his daughter's long, lean looks. The same horsey teeth, arched hair, Knightsbridge [slim] legs. ...

"Basically, Philip is not a happy man. He's solidly married, but not happily....He's blindingly energetic; travels constantly to fill the void of being the Queen's husband....He probably should've married some rich American woman, had a good time, and then divorced her. At least he'd have autonomy. Here, he looks like a kept man, and for someone as proud as he is, that's dehumanizing."

What the Queen did not see, she overlooked, and her husband pursued his flirtations with discretion. Except for the occasional actress, he confined himself to married women within the nobility. The aristocratic wives were impressed by his royal lineage and reveled in his attentions. The few who were not flattered pretended otherwise because he was married to the Queen. "It's a subtle form of blackmail," said one woman, who was subjected to what she called "an excessive overture" from the Duke of Edinburgh.

When one of the Queen's bankers was invited to Balmoral for a house party, he brought his very attractive wife. Philip insisted that she and the other female guests join him in a musical parlor game. He arrayed the women in a circle around him, and he stood in the middle. Placing a bottle of wine between his legs, he told the women they had to remove it without using their hands. The competition was to take the bottle away from him with their legs before the music stopped. "No hands, now," he warned the banker's wife. "No hands." Deeply embarrassed, she played the Duke's game because she said it would have been rude to decline.

"My wife felt the same way when he asked her to dance," said Robin Knight Bruce, an army officer. "Philip is Colonel-in-Chief of the Queen's royal Irish Hussars, and he comes to the regimental dinners to grope the officers' wives. When he did it to my wife, I went to my supervisor and said, 'Do not let the fucking

Duke of Edinburgh dance with my wife again or I'll kick him in the balls and so will she.'"

For a sophisticated man who spoke three languages, traveled the world, collected art, painted, and published numerous books, the Duke of Edinburgh could act like an oafish adolescent. One of his son's young girlfriends said she was "terribly embarrassed" by his juvenile behavior. Romy Adlington was sixteen years old when she spent her first weekend with Prince Edward and the royal family. She said that the sixty-six-year-old duke leered and winked, patted her bottom when she walked down the hall to her room, and ogled her cleavage during dinner. She did not realize that it could have been worse.

"If it's in his head, it's on his plate," said one of his former equerries, dismissing Philip's frank observations about women and sex. The former aide smiled as he described the Duke as "a man's man." In his defense, the aide offered a "boys will be boys" shrug. He laughed as he recalled Philip's comment at a film premiere when he saw Elizabeth Taylor in the flesh. As the Duke walked toward the star in a receiving line, he noted her revealing gown and her bosom, which he said, looked like two pillows. Turning to his aide, he said, "Hop in."

He theorized that the differences between men and women were best illustrated by women's ability to knit. "I do think it shows that girls have an ability to disassociate what they are doing with their hands from what they are doing with their minds," he told the writer Glenys Roberts. "It is why they are able to carry out repetitive production line jobs which intellectuals find so deadening. I once asked a girl in a factory what she thought about while she was working. She said she thought about her boyfriend, the shopping, the film she was going to see. Fascinating."

Philip scattered his opinions on a broad canvas, always colorfully, sometimes offensively. The Mother's Union of Great Britain took exception when he equated prostitutes with wives. In defense of hunting, he had said there was no moral difference between killing animals for sport and killing them for money. "It's like sex," he said. "I don't think a prostitute is more moral than a wife, but they are doing the same thing."

When a Member of Parliament asked him how he could justify being president of the World Wildlife Fund with his pursuit of blood sports, Philip snapped, "Are you a vegetarian?"

"No," replied the MP, Anthony Beaumont-Dark.

"Do you eat red meat?" Philip demanded.

"Yes, but that's a different matter from blasting poor birds out of the sky."

Philip disagreed. "It is like saying that adultery is all right as long as you do not enjoy it."

The MP smiled. "You, sir," he said, "might know more about that than me."

TWENTY

The Princess of Wales stood in the middle of her shoe closet and pointed to three rows of low heels. She waved her hand at the stubby shoes she had worn so she wouldn't tower over her husband. "You can throw out those dwarfers," she told her dresser. "I won't be needing them anymore." Within days she started wearing her highest heels—the ones with ankle straps and open toes that she called her "tart's trotters." She had been liberated by the Prime Minister's statement to the House of Commons:

> It is announced from Buckingham Palace that with regret, the Prince and Princess of Wales have decided to separate. Their Royal Highnesses have no plans to divorce and their constitutional positions are unaffected.
>
> This decision has been reached amicably.... The Queen and Duke of Edinburgh, though saddened, understand and sympathize with the difficulties which have led to this decision....

When the Prime Minister made that announcement, he looked like a man at a funeral forced to deliver the eulogy. His words had been crafted by the Queen's lawyers and courtiers to convey sad news without quite telling the truth. Despite the public reassurances, the couple *did* plan to divorce, their decision was *not* amicable, and their constitutional positions *were* affected. The Queen and Duke of Edinburgh were not saddened: they were incensed. And they did not understand or sympathize. Rather, they believed that the marriage should continue, no matter how miserable, for the sake of the monarchy.

Television programs were preempted on December 9, 1992, to carry the Prime Minister's statement, and when he rose to speak, the House of Commons fell strangely silent. Afterward the fiery Labor MP Dennis Skinner said, "The royal family has just pushed the self-destruct button." He was immediately barraged by indignant shouts. But he continued: "It is high time we stopped this charade of swearing allegiance to the Queen and her heirs and successors, because we don't know from time to time who they are....The reigning Queen could possibly be the last."

The Prime Minister bristled. "You do not, I believe, speak for the nation or any significant part of it."

But the Prime Minister was wrong. After his announcement, polls showed that three out of four Britons believed the House of Windsor was crumbling.

The Queen, who was at Sandringham, did not watch the announcement on television; she was walking her dogs. When she returned, her page was waiting to offer his sympathy. She nodded briskly and said, "I think you'll find it's all for the best."

Charles was more forthcoming with his

staff at Highgrove. "I feel a surging sense of relief," he told them. He had already started refurbishing the rooms that Diana had vacated. He ordered all the belongings she had not taken with her to be burned, including some of the children's old toys. On top of the bonfire was a carved wooden rocking horse that had been a birthday gift to Prince William from the President of the United States and Mrs. Reagan.

After the Prime Minister's announcement, reporters descended on Camilla Parker Bowles's manor home in Wiltshire, but she feigned ignorance about the Waleses' separation. "Obviously, if something has gone wrong, I'm very sorry for them," she said. "But I know nothing more than the average person in the street. I only know what I see on television." Fifty miles away, her husband emerged from his London apartment. The couple, who had been married nineteen years, lived apart quietly and saw each other only on rare weekends. When reporters asked his reaction, Andrew Parker Bowles kept walking. "Like everyone else," he said, "one feels sad about this." He scolded a reporter for suggesting that his wife had been instrumental in the breakup.

"No, it's not true," he said. "How many times do I have to spell it out? Those stories are pure fiction."

Some people on the street told reporters they felt betrayed. "The royal family is supposed to be better than us," said one middle-aged woman. "They're supposed to show us the way to behave. Otherwise, what's their purpose?"

Reaction split down generations. Those who had spent childhood nights huddled in London's underground during World War II looked to royalty as a beacon. But those who grew up listening to the Beatles, not to the bombs, viewed the royal family as a relic. To the postwar generations, especially those reared on video games, the monarchy just looked plain silly. One nineteen-year-old student from Liverpool said, "Just a bunch of out-of-date, out-of-touch richies."

But the royalist, Lord St. John of Fawsley, disagreed. He rationalized that the royal family was emblematic of the modern dysfunctional family. Next to the United States, the United Kingdom had the highest rate of divorce in the Western world, which was reflected in its royal family. "For this century the monarchy has been held up as an example of family rectitude," he said with a straight face. "Well, that can't go on. So the royal family will have to adapt itself to new circumstances. In some ways it will be nearer to the people because it will be sharing the family problems all of us have faced."

No dynasty had taught its subjects more emphatically to shrink from divorce—and no dynasty had given them more from which to shrink. Yet by 1992 all the monarch's married children were legally separated and headed for divorce. "Great weddings," observed writer Valerie Groves, "too bad about the marriages."

Half the country now believed that by the end of the twenty-first century the monarchy would be finished and that Britain would not suffer. The press reflected the public's sentiments. "Charles will not be King," predicted the *Sun*, "Di will not be Queen." The *Daily Mirror* said: "The latest royal mess is making a mockery of the monarchy. Unchecked, that mockery will destroy the monarchy itself."

Measured against people's expectations, Charles had fallen alarmingly far. Even Tory members of Parliament debated his right to the throne. Fearing a constitutional crisis, he called his friend Lord Arnold Goodman for advice. The eminent lawyer said that a divorce would not prevent him from becoming King—but a second marriage would. So Charles said he did not intend to remarry. He maintained stoutly, "I will be the next King."

The separation had international repercussions. In Germany wax museums moved the mannequins of Charles and Diana suitably apart. In Australia the government dropped all references to Queen Elizabeth II from its oath of allegiance. In Britain Labor MP Anthony Benn introduced a bill to abolish the monarchy. He suggested replacing the Queen with an elected president, separating church and state, and giving Wales and Scotland their own Parliaments. The Benn bill was never debated, but people who cared about monarchy were concerned.

From the United States, Prince Philip's onetime Hollywood press agent offered his services. Henry Rogers of Rogers & Cowan had orchestrated the publicity for Philip's 1966 trip to Los Angeles. The two men had met on the recommendation of Philip's Hollywood pal Frank Sinatra, a client of Rogers & Cowan. Now, twenty-six years later, Rogers offered to come out of retirement to help again. Philip thanked him in a handwritten letter from Windsor Castle:

Dear Henry,

Life appears to have changed out of all recognition. Whoever first said, "It never rains, but it pours" made a very profound statement!! So much happened at once and as bad luck would have it, it all took place against the sombre backdrop of the recession.

In spite of the dramatic media, we have had tremendous support through the mail from people of all kinds. I have every hope that things will get better this year.

But thank you all the same for generously offering your help. ...

The royal family appeared calm and tried to hold firm, especially the Queen Mother. She knew the country had survived bad kings, mad kings, weak kings, dumb kings, homosexual kings, even foreign-born kings. At the age of ninety-two she was not so acute as she had once been, but she was determined to help Charles, her favorite grandchild, achieve what she saw as his destiny. For she was a king maker. In her time she had rammed steel down the spine of her weak husband and made him look strong to his subjects. Now she longed to do the same for her beleaguered grandson.

But she opposed divorce—so much so that she would not let Charles move in with her after the separation as he waited for his apartment in St. James's Palace to be renovated. The Queen Mother had been reared during an era when divorce spelled social disgrace, and she remained convinced that the only real threat to the monarchy was divorce. She tolerated all kinds of deviant behavior in her family, from alcoholism to drug addiction. But she did not countenance divorce. She said that was the death blow to family stability, which she felt the House of Windsor must represent to survive. She resisted attending Princess Anne's second wedding in Scotland because she did not want to pay tribute to another divorce in the royal family. Despite her reservations, she eventually relented.

She dismissed those who said the monarchy was in crisis because royalty had stepped off the throne to marry commoners like Sarah Ferguson and Diana Spencer. As the most exemplary commoner of them all, the Queen Mother naturally disagreed with that. She said the problem was divorce and that Sarah and Diana were "unsuitable" because they were the children of divorce.

Both Sarah and Diana had grown up with mothers who had run off from their homes and abandoned their families to seek happiness with other men. Neither Sarah nor Diana had seen a marriage grow into a lifetime partnership that overcame adversity and boredom. Instead both had watched their mothers place personal satisfaction before duty and responsibility. To the Queen Mother, those were the hallmarks of royalty. Now the daughters were following their mothers' wayward footsteps by breaking their marriage vows. In doing so, they were betraying crown and country.

"You take in two girls from broken homes," the Queen had said, "and look how they repay you."

The Queen Mother agreed. She blamed Diana especially for allowing the world to see the "sordid" misery of her marriage. The Queen Mother had used that word in talking to her grandson. Charles had warned her about his wife's "instability" and her "confounded unreasonableness," but the Queen Mother was unprepared for Diana's unholy disclosures.

"The bulimia...the business of overeating and then vomiting—that thoroughly revolted her," said one of the Queen Mother's friends. "The image of the future Queen of England riding the porcelain chariot was, well...I'm afraid she couldn't get beyond the picture of the Princess of Wales crouched over a toilet bowl purging herself of puddings by throwing up."

"A traitor entered our house," the Queen Mother told Ruth Fermoy, her lady-in-waiting. Lady Fermoy agreed, but sadly—the "traitor" was her own granddaughter.

"Flesh and blood and family count for little when you're a royalist," said Ruth Fermoy's goddaughter, "and Ruth was a royalist to her core. She turned on Diana when she separated from Charles, whom she absolutely adored. She said it was the saddest day in her life. Despite what has been written about her and the Queen Mother engineering the marriage, Ruth told me that she didn't want Diana to marry Charles. She had warned her at the time of what she would encounter by joining the royal family. But Diana was helplessly in love and assured Grandma Ruth, as she called her, that she wanted to dedicate her life to Charles. ...

"Diana mended things a little before Ruth died—but just. I was there when she visited Ruth's flat in Eaton Square for the last time, and I felt sad for her when she left because Ruth said she still didn't forgive Diana for what she had done.

"But then neither did Diana's mother. She [Frances Shand Kydd] told me, and these were her exact words: 'I know Charles has hurt Diana terribly, but I love him and I refuse to take sides.' That's from Diana's own mother.

"And as for the Queen Mother...well, she unleashed her dogs, and it's been bloody hell for Diana ever since."

In public, the Queen Mother, who avoided any unpleasantness, never snarled, barked, or growled. For that, she "unleashed her dogs," who were the emissaries she designated to communicate her opinions to the press. She, like her daughter, insisted on maintaining the myth of never granting interviews, although both talked to favored writers. After the Prime Minister's announcement about the separation, Lord Wyatt stepped forward to comment on the behavior of the Princess of Wales.

He was identified as "a close personal friend of the Queen Mother," so readers of the *Sunday Times* were expected to know whose sentiments were being expressed:

> Princess Diana could never have won a university place, but she won a prince and failed to keep him. She is addicted to the limelight her marriage brought. It's like a drug; to feed her craving she will do anything, even if it meant destroying the throne she solemnly swore to uphold.

Within weeks Diana was portrayed as a woman more sinned against than sinning. A transcript of her husband's intimate telephone conversation with his mistress was published on January 12, 1993. The secret recording, known as Camillagate, was made on December 18, 1989, a few days before the secret recording of Diana's telephone conversation with James Hewitt, known as Squidgygate. Both conversations had been picked up by men, both hobbyists who claimed they scanned the airwaves in their spare time like ham radio operators. But those who tend to conspiracies hinted at something more sinister: they said that publishing transcripts three years after the conversations were recorded suggested more than mere coincidence. They speculated that the furtive interceptions had been carried out by Britain's domestic intelligence agency, MI5, to embarrass the royal family and destabilize the monarchy.

The embarrassment was profound. In the words of one writer, the public was "well and truly shocked" to hear the prospective Supreme Governor of the Church of England declare his passion for another man's wife. "I want to feel my way along you, all over you and up and down you and in and out...particularly in and out," Charles told Camilla. "I'll just live inside your trousers or something. It would be much easier...."

During the late night conversation, Charles proposed living inside Camilla as "a Tampax," which she found delightful. "Oh, what a wonderful idea," she exclaimed. He paused. "My luck to be chucked down a lavatory and go on forever swirling around the top, never going down." Sounding enthralled, she said she wanted him day and night..."desperately, desperately, desperately. ..."

The day the transcript was published, reporters surrounded Camilla's home. When she heard why they were there, she was stunned. "I can't believe it. I can't believe it," she said. "I must speak to my husband. He is on his way home." She closed the door and took the phone off the hook.

"6 Min Love Tape Could Cost Charles Throne" shrieked the *Sun,* but the *London*

Evening Standard asked, "So What's Wrong with a King Who Can Talk Dirty?" Charles said he was "appalled" by the publication of his private conversation and called friends to apologize for embarrassing them. They deplored publication of a private conversation that was taped, duplicated, sold, and printed in transcript form. "You might argue Charles and Camilla deserve the embarrassment," said his biographer Penny Junor, "but surely not their children."

Already nine-year-old Wills had been reported fighting with classmates at school, where he shoved a boy's head down the toilet. Deeply depressed by his parents' quarreling, he locked himself in the bathroom for hours, and his grades slumped. His younger brother, Harry, was seen sneaking cigarettes at school. Both children sucked their thumbs and wet their beds. Thomas Parker Bowles, the teenage son of Camilla and Andrew, was arrested for possession of drugs. He was not threatened with suspension from Oxford because he was off campus when apprehended by police for possession of cannabis and ecstasy pills. To escape the gibes of students, he began calling himself Tom Bowles. He did not admit that his middle name was Charles in honor of his godfather, the Prince of Wales.

Although the tabloid press condemned Charles as a knave, he found compassion in unexpected quarters: Peter McKay wrote in the *London Evening Standard* that the six-minute phone call was "silly, touching and filthy... [but it] made me think better of Charles....He comes out of it as a daft romantic, dying to leap under the duvet, fond of terrible sex jokes." The novelist Fay Weldon said she thought the transcript was moving. "What it's got to do with Charles being King I don't know. My opinion of him goes up no end because it shows he has some proper emotions. ..."

But most of the country was disgusted, and the next time he appeared in public, he was booed. At an official engagement, a man in the crowd shouted: "Have you no shame?" Opinion polls showed that only one in three Britons felt Charles was entitled to become King. Uncharacteristically, the English treated him like a politician, who could be deprived of his position because of his negative image. His friend and former equerry, Nicholas Soames, hastened to spell out the hereditary principle involved in succession. He explained that Charles's right to the throne did not depend on his popularity: barring abdication or an act of Parliament, Charles was not disposable. "The throne is his duty, his obligation, his destiny," said Soames. "It's not something he seeks, but it will be his....Twelve hundred years of British history are not going to be overturned by Mr. Murdoch's republican press, engaged in a circulation war. The heir to the throne will be the next King, and that's all there is to it."

Another close friend said: "It was a terrible moment, the worst moment of his life....He wanted to be taken seriously. He sincerely believed he had important things to say. And in six minutes of private conversation, a conversation that was nobody's business but his and the woman to whom he was speaking, his reputation was ruined....He really didn't deserve to be destroyed so publicly and so cruelly."

Even the far-off Fiji Islands were upset. The government announced it would discontinue celebrating Charles's birthday as a national holiday because he no longer represented greatness to them. In Australia the Prime Minister's wife would not curtsy to him, and the Deputy Prime Minister suggested that he not be invited to open the Olympics in the year 2000. "Let's have Prince William do it—anybody but his father."

If Charles had chosen one act, short of child molestation, he could not have alienated his future subjects more. Through The Prince's Trust he had established one of the country's biggest charities to benefit disadvantaged children, but no amount of grants to inner-city youngsters could make him look princely now. As his biographer Anthony Holden put it, "No one listens to do-gooding sermons from a man who is two-timing the world's most desirable woman."

Shaken by the crisis, Charles summoned six friends to Sandringham to advise him. Afterward one man was dispatched to tell the *Telegraph* that the Prince was prepared to make any sacrifice to insure his succession to the throne. The headline on the next day's front page:

"Prince of Wales Chooses the Celibate Life."

The attempt to win back public confidence did not work. Nothing could stop the sniggering jokes. "That'll be one pack of Charlie's," sang a London grocery clerk, ringing up a box of sanitary napkins. A cartoonist drew Charles's face as an egg cup with yolk dribbling down his nose. Greeting cards appeared with his caricature: "For your birthday, I'd like to treat you to a Chuck and Di margarita. It's cold, frosty, and it's on the rocks." The Palace finally intervened to prevent a safe-sex poster from appearing on British billboards. The proposed advertisement had shown a wedding picture of the Prince and Princess of Wales kissing on the balcony of Buckingham Palace in front of huge crowds. The caption read "Appearances Can Be Deceptive. Use a Johnny Condom." A spokesman for the British Safety Council resented the Palace interference: "We really could not care less what the royals think," said Fiona Harcombe. "The benefits far outweigh the offense it might cause to the Queen."

Charles was humiliated. "His Royal Highness didn't want to leave the grounds," recalled one of his security guards, "but his friends encouraged him not to retreat. 'Be seen helping people,' they advised. But he was scared. We saw it in his eyes. Like a rabbit in the clamp of a trap."

When Charles visited the scene of an oil tanker spill off Scotland's Shetland Islands, he imposed a "no children" rule. His aide explained: "They tend to ask awkward questions." The Prince arrived looking drawn and worried. His thinning hair was combed to conceal his bald spot, and he appeared stooped and defeated. He avoided the press as he tramped through oil-soaked fields, and he strained to make small talk with farmers whose fields and crops were buried in gunk. Later, at a midmorning reception, he passed on orange juice and ordered a Scotch whiskey. "We asked HRH [Philip] to visit the oil spill as president of the World Wildlife Fund," said the WWF's former communications director, "but Charles's staff didn't want him [Philip] there....They needed the sympathetic coverage for the Prince of Wales. But the WWF is the most prestigious conservation organization in the world, and we, too, needed a presence....We finally worked it out so both of them would go and pursue separate agendas. Charles said beforehand he would not respond to the press, but Philip agreed to answer questions. After the first one, though, he lost his temper."

A television reporter had asked Philip whether his visit had been overshadowed by headlines about his son's relationship with Camilla Parker Bowles.

"It's nothing to do with that," snapped Philip. Growing angry, he wheeled on the reporter. "I might have guessed someone like you would ask that question. Who do you represent?"

The reporter replied: "ITN [Independent Television Network]."

"Figures," said Philip, storming off.

The Duke of Edinburgh complained to the WWF communications director that the question was rude and boorish. "The ITN reporter wasn't disrespectful, just straightforward," said the WWF employee. "But the lack of deference shown in posing the question in the first place was not lost on HRH. ..."

That lack of knee-bending deference jolted the country in May 1993. More than five hundred people streamed into the Queen Elizabeth II Conference Centre in London to listen to a day-long debate by royalists and republicans on the future of the monarchy. The forum mirrored the mood of national anxiety as ninety speakers assembled. They discussed the Crown and why, or even whether, it continues to matter in twentieth-century England.

"Something has died," said Professor Stephen Haseler, "and that something is the enchantment of the British people for the monarchy." Historian Elizabeth Longford disagreed: she argued in favor of Prince Charles becoming King. But playwright David Hare recommended abolishing the monarchy because he viewed it as the fountainhead of falseness and snobbery. In between was Lord Rees-Mogg, former editor of the *Times,* who called himself a royalist but acknowledged the need for constitutional reform. He observed that an institution that had survived since the sixth century could be dislodged only by war or revolution. Because neither option was desirable for the country, he urged his audience to believe in the monarchy's ability to adapt.

But the Queen moved like moss. Less than three years after agreeing to pay taxes (on her public income, *not* on her private investments), she decided to fly commercial. By not using one of the eleven jets in the Queen's Flight, she saved taxpayers about $3 million on one trip. "Her Majesty took over the entire first-class cabin," said an Air New Zealand flight attendant, "but that's as it should be. After all, she is the Queen of England, not some bicycle monarchy."

But the Queen flew commercial only once. For comfort and convenience, she preferred the Queen's Flight. So instead she decided to economize on household expenses. She received $70 million a year in public funding for her travel expenses, her security costs, and the upkeep of her eight residences. She started trimming costs by eliminating her employee's traditional benefits: her chauffeurs, who earned $9,000 a year, had to start paying for their own shoe repair. Servants, paid $8,000 a year, no longer received free bars of soap. And the $60,000 a year courtiers who accompanied the Queen on foreign tours could no longer expect to receive a free suit. "They will receive a cash stipend in exchange," the Palace announced. "We want to make things work better and more efficiently."

As part of her cost cutting, the Queen

reconsidered giving cash bonuses to the two hundred employees at Windsor Castle who had helped save her treasures during the 1992 fire. Instead of money, she offered them a free tour of the castle library. Few accepted.

The royal family remained aloof from the debate about their future. Lord Charteris, the Queen's former equerry, said the idea of a republic never penetrated the Palace walls. Lady Longford, a friend of the Queen, disagreed. "They have been perfectly open about it," she said. As far back as 1966, when they toured Canada, they discussed the possibility of Britain's becoming a republic. If anything, they treated the subject lightheartedly. "We'll go quietly," the Queen said. Philip joked that he could be packed in a day, but she would need several weeks. "Too damn many corgis," he quipped. Walking into her office at Buckingham Palace one afternoon, he looked out the window and asked: "Have they got up the guillotine?"

The Queen, too, used humor in addressing a Commonwealth conference in Cyprus. She had arrived on the island in the fall of 1993 aboard her royal yacht. After dinner she relaxed with her guests. When she said she wouldn't wager on a similar Commonwealth conference in the next forty years, they knew she had studied the recent polls in Canada, Australia, and New Zealand that showed growing support for independence from the Crown. "The only safe bet is that there will be three absentees—Prince Philip, *Britan-*

nia, and myself," said the Queen without emotion. "But you never know....Nowadays, I have enough experience, not least in racing, to restrain me from laying any money down on how many countries will be in the Commonwealth in forty years' time, who they will be, and where the meeting will be held."

Within the royal family, the Queen did not need a trackside tip sheet to see who was running best in the mud and who was showing signs of weak knees. She read the opinion polls, which showed that her estranged daughter-in-law was winning the race while her son was still stuck in the paddock.

Charles stumbled along, trying to redeem himself, but even as he tried to make light of his predicament, he sounded more self-pitying than self-deprecating. As he autographed a soccer ball for youngsters at a London recreation center, he told them: "Now you've got my name on it. You can kick it all over the place." He gave up polo entirely; he cut ribbons, laid wreaths, inspected factories, visited troops in Bosnia, toured a former concentration camp in Poland.

But he could not compete with his wife, who radiated in the press like a movie star elevated to sainthood. As one headline put it: "The Princess Bids Halo and Farewell to Her Critics." She toured hospices and orphanages and Red Cross feeding centers. In India she touched untouchables. In Nepal she hugged lepers. She embraced amputees and ladled soup for starving refugees. People turned out in droves to see her, mesmerized by her warmth, her beauty, her glamour.

Although Charles could not draw crowds like Diana, his equerry said he was well rid of her. He said the Prince had grown more confidant because he was no longer saddled with the Princess and subjected to "superficial handshaking tours." Rather than belittle Diana, the equerry might have been better advised to announce that Charles had lashed himself to the steps of Canterbury Cathedral to do penance for his adultery, as his ancestor did to atone for the murder of Thomas à Becket. The public adored the Princess, and she reveled in the adulation.

She was regularly photographed visiting homeless shelters and talking to battered wives. She seemed especially taken with one woman, who admitted pouring gasoline on her husband and setting him afire as he slept. The woman, who said she had been driven insane by her husband, pleaded not guilty to murder and was freed. The Princess hugged her and said, "You have been so brave." Later, as Charles visited an inner-city housing project, he shook hands with a woman in the crowd who said she had met his estranged wife. He grimaced. "You lived to tell the tale, did you?"

Measured in newsprint, there was no contest between Diana and Charles. A media research firm measured the number of column inches allotted to each during the first six days of March 1993: Diana scored 3,603 inches of newsprint, Charles only 275.

One of Britain's prizewinning feature writers, Lynda Lee-Potter, advised the Prince to ignore the tally and stay out of the fray. "He should not play his wife's games," she wrote. "He should remain uncomplaining and dignified." She said Diana had declared open war on her husband. "She desires to be utterly vindicated. She yearns to diminish Prince Charles. She wants revenge, not merely justice. But the continuing public battle she plans can only take place if her husband and his family retaliate. If they do that, they may be defeated. If they refuse to fight, they will surely win."

By then the Princess had the Palace on the run. They appeared to support her charity work, but behind the scenes they sabotaged her. They kept her from becoming president of the British Red Cross and would not recommend her as head of UNICEF. They allowed her to make a few speeches but winced when she spoke about bulimia and depression. The courtiers, all middle-aged men, did not see her declarations of victimhood as a plus for a female whose poor self-image once made her feel as if she deserved to be dysfunctional. The courtiers said her speeches about self-esteem were silly and self-indulgent.

They sputtered with indignation when she spoke out on issues, especially AIDS, which they said were not in her domain. Diana paid no attention. She told a national AIDS conference: "It is doubly difficult to deal with AIDS in a country like Britain, where there is still an understandable reluctance to have frank and open discussions on emotional issues. We need to learn how to break through this barrier of inhibition. ..."

When the Princess was asked to deliver the prestigious Richard Dimbleby Lecture on the BBC to discuss her views on AIDS, the courtiers finally took action. The invitation was withdrawn.

What they did not take away from her, Charles did. He wanted her removed from public life with no access to the Queen's Flight, the royal train, the royal yacht, or any other privileged form of royal travel. In fact, he wanted her to be shorn of all royal trappings. But the Queen worried about isolating Diana and the effect it might have on her troubled mind. The monarch dispatched the Prime Minister to visit Kensington Palace to reassure the Princess that she had a continuing part to play. Her Majesty then authorized publication of the Prime Minister's visit in the Court Circular so the public and Diana would think she was still considered valuable.

The Palace allowed her to make a few goodwill tours, but, instructed by Charles, they cut back the honors she had once been accorded. No more high-level courtiers or official ladies-in-waiting. Her airline seating arrangements were downgraded from first class to business class, and the Palace banned playing the National Anthem upon her arrival in Nepal.

The tabloids, which revered her, reported the petty slights and wrote editorials calling for more dignified treatment for the mother of the future King.

But the courtiers were dropping the curtain on the star and inching her off stage. She was no longer invited to appear with the royal family at public celebrations like Trooping the Color. When the Queen did not extend an invitation to Royal Ascot in 1993, Diana took her boys to Planet Hollywood. The next day's newspapers showed a doting mother in blue jeans romping with her children alongside a stiff picture of the royal family waving from their carriages. One tabloid headline captured the contrast: "The Hugger and the High Hats."

Nor was Diana invited to the Queen Mother's birthday party in August of 1993. So she took her children go-carting. Again, her picture frolicking with her sons appeared on the front pages. When the Queen went to Hungary, her first visit to a post-communist state, Diana went to Paris to shop. The monarch's visit received minor coverage while Diana's was given the front pages. An *Evening Standard* editorial wondered: "Might it not be appropriate to place the Princess under house arrest when visits abroad by her less newsworthy royal superiors are imminent?"

Intent on being seen as an angel of mercy, Diana had wanted to attend the memorial service for two children killed by an IRA bomb in the Cheshire town of Warrington. But the Palace said no and sent Prince Philip instead. Diana let the Palace know that she understood how to play hardball: she phoned the grieving mothers of both bomb victims.

"I want to be there with you and give you a hug," she told them, "but I can't because they are sending my father-in-law."

Even Diana's critics felt the Palace looked petty and spiteful.

She saw the royal family siding with her husband and arrayed against her. He viewed it differently, saying he received more support from his friends than from his family. His father kept in contact by sending messages through his laptop computer, not all of which were appreciated. "Ah, yes, the Duke and his helpful bulletins," recalled one of Charles's aides. His arched eyebrows indicated the communications were unwelcome. The aide said nothing about the Queen, who maintained a cool distance from her heir. Sometimes the courts of mother and son clashed like fighting cocks.

"I nearly went mad trying to accommodate them," recalled the interior designer Nicholas Haslam. "The competition between the two circles is fierce and strangulating. There is no regard for the bond of mother and son: none whatsoever. It's a pitched battle: Her Majesty the Queen versus upstart Prince, who is the King-in-waiting. ...

"I came into Buckingham Palace in 1993 at the bidding of Prince Charles, who wanted me to do the decoration for a dinner he planned for the Royal Shakespeare Theatre. I surveyed a few rooms with one of the Queen's men and asked that the chairs be rearranged for a softer, more hospitable setting.

"'Absolutely not,' said the Queen's man. 'Her Majesty would not approve.'

"I asked another man for assistance with the lighting.

"'Her Majesty likes the lights as they are.'

"I inquired about moving some tables, saying that the Prince was having a dinner for three hundred people and we needed a bit more space.

"'Her Majesty prefers the tables to remain in place.'

"I was nearly around the bend with frustration," said the decorator. "I couldn't address the subject of candles because 'Her Majesty does not approve of dining by candlelight.'

"It was a disaster trying to represent Charles in his mother's domain, but I finally managed to pull it all together for him, and he was very gracious. He said that Buckingham Palace had never looked lovelier than it did that evening. Of course, I aged fifty years trying to negotiate arrangements with all the Queen's men...."

That evening, with his mother not in residence, Charles flew the Prince of Wales flag from Buckingham Palace. He endeared himself to his guests with his after-dinner remarks. "I've become quite familiar with the works of Shakespeare in the last year," he said. "I've lived through *The Merry Wives of Windsor, Love's Labors Lost,* and *The Taming of the Shrew*....It's about time for *All's Well That Ends Well.*" He brought down the house.

On occasion, Diana, too, poked fun at her plight. While visiting a London hostel for battered wives, she sat in on a therapy session and listened to the women talk about rebuilding their lives. When she was asked if she wanted to join in, she flapped her blouse and fanned herself: "I have a hot flush coming on."

Her regular tabloid press pack enjoyed her sly levities, especially when she targeted their counterparts in the upmarket press. "Oh, you're from the *Financial Times?* " she said to one man. "We took that at home. Yes, I believe we used to line the budgie's cage with it." One of her regular reporters complimented her on how fit she was looking. She startled the group by asking if they remembered her when she was younger and had had a large bosom.

"Oh, yes, ma'am, and weren't those the good old days," joked her favorite photographer, Arthur Edwards. He had covered her since she was nineteen and waiting for the Prince of Wales to propose. During that period she had ventured out the front door of her apartment at Coleherne Court and burst into tears when she found a horde of press men blocking her car. Edwards had barreled through the mob to help her. "Don't let them see you cry," he'd advised. "It's Queen Di for you, and when you finally get the job, it's Sir Arthur for me!"

After that, Diana rewarded the tabloid photographer with her sweetest smiles. When he fell ill, she took him medicine. "She calls me by my Christian name and has done [so] from the beginning," he said. "Prince Charles still calls me Mr. Edwards and is very formal. I think in this age it is out of place."

The *Sun* photographer did not flatter himself about why the Princess courted him. "The reason is most likely that thirteen million readers will see her at her gorgeous best," he said. "Funnily enough, it is always the papers with the highest circulation to whom Diana is the most cooperative."

Whenever the Princess appeared in a spectacular new gown, the photographer hollered approvingly, "You look lovely tonight, ma'am." When she wore something she had worn before, he complained. "Oh, not that one again."

She shot back, "Arthur, I suppose *you'd* prefer it if I turned up naked."

He countered, "Well, at least I could get a picture of you in the paper that way."

"I'll tell the jokes, Arthur," she said reprovingly.

He later used her retort as the title for his book of royal reminiscences. Diana let him know that she did not appreciate the exploitation. Withholding her usual smile, she asked, "How many books have you sold, Arthur?"

He smiled sheepishly. "I think you are wonderful, ma'am. I would never do anything to harm you."

Diana's father, the late Earl Spencer, once called her "pure steel inside," and Arthur Edwards occasionally felt her jabs. Commenting on a new hairstyle, he said if her hair got any shorter, she would look like Sinead O'Connor, the Irish pop star who shaves her head.

"At least I've got some hair," said Diana, looking at the photographer's bald head.

When she felt offended, reporters felt her sting. One young woman was pointedly ignored by the Princess when she wrote that Diana had worn comfortable but dowdy clothes on a royal tour. On the return flight home, Diana eyed the writer's ankle-length skirt and said, "She won't last long." Hearing the Princess discuss plans for making other overseas visits, the young reporter inquired, "Oh, more trips?" Without smiling, Diana said, "More trips and more dowdy clothes."

Usually Diana courted the media, especially after her separation, when she and her husband competed for coverage and used the press to take a poke at each other. Both had recruited national newspapers to carry his and her versions of their marital rifts. She received more sympathetic coverage because she befriended reporters: she gave cocktail parties for those who covered her royal tours, sent them notes when she was especially pleased by their stories, and remembered their birthdays. She regularly briefed the *Daily Mail*'s royal correspondent Richard Kay, who was photographed whispering with her in a car.

She invited media baron Rupert Murdoch to lunch at Kensington Palace and sent similar invitations to television personalities Oprah Winfrey and Barbara Walters. They all accepted. She ingratiated herself with Katharine Graham, chairman of The Washington Post Company, by visiting her in Martha's Vineyard and Washington, D.C. Diana also attended parties sponsored by *People* magazine, *Harper's Bazaar*, and *Vanity Fair*. She posed for *Vogue*. She was so accommodating to the photographers who accompanied her on ski vacations with her children that supporters of Prince Charles accused her of using the boys to look motherly at his expense. He countered with more exotic vacations for the children in Italy and on the Greek islands. She topped him by taking the boys to Disney World in Florida. Charles was determined not to be outdone. When he went with his sons to Balmoral for Easter, he gave them a set of soccer goalposts, a garden badminton set, two mountain bikes, a trampoline, guns for shooting rabbits and crows, and two mini-motorbikes that cost $3,000 apiece. But even his staged photo opportunities with his sons could not overcome the popularity gap.

"The big trouble with some of the royals is that they treat the press like telegraph poles," said Arthur Edwards. "They just walk round them and totally ignore them. That has been one of the reasons for the bad publicity they get....Diana has gone more than halfway to stop that."

She became the most photographed woman in the world, and photographers made thousands of dollars taking her picture. She was reminded what a valuable commodity she had become after receiving a call from Lady Elizabeth Johnston, a friend of the royal family, who lived near Great Windsor Park. She had heard from her hairdresser that Diana was being secretly photographed during her weekly workouts at the gym. Lady Johnston warned the Princess that the owner of the gym was the Peeping Tom.

"Oh, God," said Diana. "Am I decent?"

"As far as I know, you are."

"That's a relief. My mother-in-law would die."

The next day Diana asked her detective, Ken Wharfe, to check out the story. He talked to the owner of L.A. Fitness, Bryce Taylor, who denied taking pictures of the Princess.

"For chrissakes," said Taylor. "She's been coming here almost three years now. You're always with her. Have you ever seen a security problem?"

The detective satisfied himself by walking around the club. He did not inspect the premises thoroughly, but even if he had, he might not have noticed the hole cut in the ceiling panel.

Six months later a sneak shot of Diana appeared on the front page of the *Sunday Mirror* in spandex cycling shorts and a snug turquoise leotard. The newspaper had agreed to pay $250,000 for photos that showed her pushing a shoulder press with her legs spread wide apart. The poses were unflattering, even for a young woman as beautiful as the Princess, and the harsh angles emphasized her pelvis, revealing every bulge and fold and crease around her hips.

Looking at the voyeuristic photos made some people feel as if a dirty trick had been played on an unsuspecting maiden. Although Diana had borne children and taken lovers, she still retained an aura of demure innocence. People had seen photos of her plunging cleavage and her high kicks across a stage in a slinky satin slip; they had even seen her pregnant in a bikini. But they had never seen her looking coarse.

"It was a crotch shot, plain and simple," said one magazine editor. "Undignified and disgusting."

The royal biographer Brian Hoey said the pictures would never have been published in Britain if Diana had not been separated from Prince Charles. "She is now treated by the media with the same sort of disdain and contempt as film stars or...Fergie."

Diana felt bruised and abused. "I burst into tears when I saw that photograph," she said. "I felt insulted and humiliated and violated...."

The Palace and Parliament rallied to her side, deploring the invasion of her privacy. Her husband felt she got no more than an exhibitionist deserved, but her father-in-law urged her to sue. The furor over the pictures dominated the media for days, with politicians demanding press curbs and publishers protesting. The Mirror Group, the owner of the offending paper, withdrew from the Press Complaints Commission, and the editor admitted he was a "ratbag." But the gym owner was unapologetic.

"What I did was sneaky, surreptitious, and preplanned," said Bryce Taylor. "I don't make excuses....It was underhand....But if I told you I had an absolutely legal scam which didn't hurt anyone and would make you a million pounds, wouldn't you say yes?"

He hired a publicist and contracted with a photo agency to syndicate the eighty-two pictures of Diana he had taken. The Princess's lawyers obtained an injunction that froze the money Taylor was supposed to receive. With the full support of the Queen, Diana sued the newspaper and the photographer. She declared in sealed court documents:

> I was shocked when I saw photographs of myself exercising at the club as published in The Sunday Mirror on 7th November 1993 and The Daily Mirror on 8th November 1993. I was unaware that any such photographs had been taken and had at no time given my consent to being photographed at the club in any circumstances. I considered Mr. Taylor's conduct to be a betrayal of the trust I had vested in him.

The Princess intended to create a privacy law in England that did not exist and was prepared to testify in court. "I will do whatever it takes to achieve justice," she said. She issued a statement, expressing her gratitude to everyone who had condemned the actions of the Mirror newspapers. Within weeks the disgraced gym owner went broke trying to defend himself. But under Britain's legal aid system, he now qualified for expert counsel, because he was an indigent defendant in a case that sought to establish a new law. So he petitioned the court, and the presiding judge appointed one of the country's best-known lawyers, Geoffrey Robertson QC (Queen's Counsel), to represent him.

Suddenly, what had looked like a case weighted in favor of the Princess now became even odds. Robertson was well matched to the skills of Diana's lawyer, Anthony Julius of the law firm Mischon de Reya. The gym owner felt especially fortunate because Robertson was an Australian, known to be a republican, and not impressed by royalty. To Robertson, the Princess of Wales was merely a rich plaintiff named Diana Windsor. The sealed court documents show that he referred to her as Mrs. Windsor; Anthony Julius referred to her as HRH the Princess of Wales.

Within days Robertson's defense team had deposed employees who swore that the Princess actively encouraged attention in the gym by exercising in front of a window so the public could see her better. Several employees said she flirted openly with male club members and wore provocative, skintight clothes to show off her body. To them the Princess looked like a pickup.

Diana's lawyers countered that she wore appropriate exercise attire every time she went to the gym, but no matter what she wore, she was entitled to privacy. They produced a letter from Bryce Taylor dated September 25, 1990, promising to protect her from publicity.

His lawyers responded that by accepting a three-year membership as a gift, Diana was not entitled to the privileges of someone who had paid. They argued that by freeloading, she had forfeited her rights to privacy, especially when she agreed to be weighed and measured. They produced the personal data form she herself had filled out using the name of Sally Hughes, her former secretary:

Blood Pressure:	120/60
Height centimeters:	1.83
BMI (Body Mass Index)	60.5
Girth measurements:	
Shoulder:	40"
Chest:	35"
Right arm:	9 $^1/_7$"
Waist:	27"
Rt. thigh:	22"
Calf:	13 $^1/_2$"

The Palace became dismayed when they learned that some of Diana's sworn statements did not jibe with those of her personal detective. When Ken Wharfe was scheduled as a defense witness, the detective was swiftly transferred out of her service. Then Diana's chauffeur decided he wanted to work for Prince Charles. Diana had not been consulted about either move. Losing both men, who had been in her service for several years, left her shaken. Hours after being informed of the transfers, she arrived at a theater gala with red, puffy eyes. She stayed less than an hour before she ran out sobbing. The Palace said she was suffering from a migraine.

The next day's newspapers carried stories about "the tormented mind of a princess" and speculated she was suffering from a recurrence of bulimia. The employees' transfers were interpreted in the press as Palace plots to undermine her stability.

She tried to put the matter to rest three days later in a speech to charity workers: "Ladies and gentlemen, you are very lucky to have your patron here today," she said. "I am supposed to have my head down the loo for most of the day....I am supposed to be dragged off the minute I leave here by men in white coats."

Her audience applauded her good humor. "If it is all right with you," she concluded, "I thought I would postpone my nervous breakdown to a more appropriate moment." Smiling, she added, "It is amazing what a migraine can bring on."

By then the Queen had reconsidered her support for Diana's lawsuit. She questioned whether the emotional Princess could stand up to tough cross-examination. Further, she was troubled to learn that Diana's former lover James Hewitt was a houseguest of Geoffrey Robertson. The lawyer indicated he might subpoena Hewitt to establish just how averse the Princess really was to invasions of her privacy. The Queen was disconcerted to read Hewitt's comment to Robertson's wife, Kathy Lette, who asked him what the Princess was really like: "She's got bad breath," said Hewitt, "and she wants sex all the time."

The press was salivating over the prospect of a trial, and more than nine hundred reporters had applied for credentials in a courtroom with seventy-five seats. The Queen was concerned about the international media hoopla and did not want to see a member of the royal family take the witness stand. She recommended the case be settled out of court.

An overture was made to Bryce Taylor, but without a trial he would no longer be eligible for legal aid and would have to pay his own legal fees. So he had no incentive to settle. Now bankrupt, he was relying on a sensational trial to sell world rights to his story. The press agent he had hired said, "For him, it was always a matter of money—only money."

The Queen's private secretary contacted Lord Peter Palumbo, a close friend of Diana's, to say that the Queen wanted to spare the Princess the ordeal of taking the stand. Lord Palumbo understood. Although Diana wanted to proceed, the Queen did not. So Lord Palumbo negotiated with a few of the lawyers involved and worked out a confidential arrangement that benefited everyone: the Princess looked victorious; the newspapers avoided regulation; the Peeping Tom escaped poverty. The basic terms:

1. The Mirror Newspaper Group agreed to issue a public apology, pay $40,000 in damages to charity in Diana's name, and not to write about the case.
2. Bryce Taylor agreed to give Diana the photographs and negatives and issue a public apology. In exchange for agreeing never to discuss the case, he was to receive secret monthly payments totaling $450,000 from a blind trust. He did not know who provided the money but speculated on King Juan Carlos because the blind trust was incorporated in Spain. The final payment was made in June 1996. The trust also was to pay Taylor's taxes and his legal fees.
3. Part of Diana's legal fees were to be paid by the money that had been frozen by the court's injunction; the fees not covered by that money were waived by Lord Mischon's law firm.
4. All parties signed confidentiality agreements not to divulge the details.

When the settlement agreement was announced, the *News of the World* sighed in relief: "The Royal Family Is Safe." A rash of stories in London's other newspapers crowed mistakenly about "Di's smashing victory."

"I suppose we could've won," said a Mirror editor, "but it would've cost too much. Not in terms of cash, but in hatred from the public, especially from our downmarket readership, which adores Diana."

Although she looked like a winner in the media, the Princess knew she had been defeated. Most of her staff had resigned—her chef, her equerry, her dresser, her chauffeur, her detective. She struck back by firing her butler, Harold Brown, who had been with her since her marriage to Charles and stayed with her after the separation. Now she insisted he leave "as soon as possible" and give up his grace-and-favor apartment in Kensington Palace. When Princess Michael of Kent offered to hire the tall, courtly butler, who had spent his adult life in royal service, Diana said no.

Disturbed by her behavior, the Prince of Wales sent for the man. "I'm so sorry for what she's done to you," he said, "but I can't interfere...I can't even take you on myself. But I want you to know that I know what has been done. And the Queen has been informed about what the Princess has done."

The butler was eventually hired by Princess Margaret, who told him to keep his rent-free apartment. "The Princess of Wales dare not tell Princess Margaret whom she can employ," said a member of Margaret's staff. "After all, Princess Margaret is royal by birth. Diana is royal by marriage. There's a big difference. Even though Diana is senior to Margaret in terms of protocol, that's just on paper. That isn't the way it is. Princess Margaret is the Queen's sister, and Diana can't pull rank on someone who's really royal, like she can on Princess Michael of Kent."

By then Diana's royal duties had been curtailed and her husband had rejected her offer to reconcile. He said he would rather immolate himself than live with her again. She felt ostracized by the royal family and hounded by the press. So she decided to withdraw from public life. On December 3, 1993, again in tears, she publicly announced that she wanted privacy.

"When I started my public life twelve years ago," she told workers for the Headway National Head Injuries Association in a luncheon speech, "I understood that the media might be interested in what I did...but I was not aware of how overwhelming that attention would become, nor the extent to which it would affect both my public duties and my personal life, in a manner that has been hard to bear." Then she dropped her bomb: "I will be reducing the extent of the public life I have led so far."

The next day a tabloid screamed: "Ab-Di-Cation."

Her admirers bemoaned her withdrawal from public life as a tragedy for the country; her detractors disparaged her as a cunning actress who had milked the public's sympathy. Her royal retreat created reams of editorial commentary. Even the *Irish Times* sounded wistful. In the United States, writer Calvin Trillin

671

begged her to reconsider in an amusing bit of doggerel:

> *"Oh, Di," repentant tabloids cry,*
> *"Don't leave the role you occupy.*
> *For we can quickly rectify*
> *The misbehavior you decry.*
> *We need you, Di. We'll tell you why:*
> *The Prince is not the sort of guy*
> *Who causes lots of folks to buy*
> *Our papers. So we all must try*
> *To get along together, Di.*
> *So come now, be a sweetie-pie,*
> *We promise we'll no longer pry,*
> *Nor pay some sleazeball on the sly*
> *To photograph your upper thigh.*
> *So promise us it's not goodbye.*
> *Di?"*

TWENTY-ONE

Members of the British royal family were starting to look like impostors: they wore jewels, dressed up in gold braid, and rode in carriages. But they did not behave like royalty.

They tried to appear brave and true, but they were not even good-hearted. They did not understand royalty's obligation to behave with probity, to bestow kindness, to set a good example. The traditions of royalty passed on by literature and by art seemed to have bypassed them. They had forgotten the legends of King Arthur and his shining Knights of the Round Table.

Many of their loyal subjects, once enthralled by royalty, became disenchanted. Some became indifferent, some turned faintly negative, some were decidedly hostile. The public's respect, even reverence, for the Crown had eroded severely. Obeisance was no longer automatic. Only the Queen Mother, bobbing along in her feathers and veils, seemed capable of inspiring genuine affection.

The Queen, who had reluctantly agreed to pay taxes, trim the Civil List, open Buckingham Palace, and give up the *Britannia,* was barely accorded customary courtesies. In a breach of civility, she was not consulted when Britain's National Blood Service removed the crown from its insignia. Her representative was mooned in New Zealand by a Maori protester, who bared his tattooed buttocks and spat on the ground. And in South Africa she was asked by the government to return the Cullinan diamonds, which had been presented to her great-grandfather Edward VII.

The royal family was sinking in its own muck, and their problems were as unpleasant as rotting possums under the country's front porch. The press began fuming. London's *Sunday Times* summed it up for anti-royalists: "Gone With the Windsors." *The New York Times* was equally pun-ridden: "Windsors and Losers."

Monarchists looking for a morality play to guide them had been shoved into a lurid soap opera, complete with illicit sex, phone sex, foot sex, and, according to Charles's valet, garden sex. The valet, who sold his secrets to a tabloid, asserted that he had found the grass-stained pajamas the Prince had worn during a romp in the Highgrove gardens with his mistress.

The media, once monarchy's obedient servant, had become the master. So many rumors were circulating that the Palace broke its usual stance of "No comment" and began responding to the most salacious gossip. When scuttlebutt persisted about the health of Prince Andrew, courtiers denied that he was HIV-positive.

"Our stand on the rumors has been constant," a Palace official told the *Sun*'s royal correspondent. "Any suggestion that the Duke of York has AIDS is utter rubbish....He is in command of servicemen, and there is no way he would be allowed to continue his duties if there was any question about his health and fitness."

The rumors arose after Andrew's wife, Sarah Ferguson, had been tested for AIDS three times. Her previous drug use and her continued promiscuity with drug users raised concern about what she might have transmitted to her husband. His closest friends worried but said nothing to him. "We wouldn't dare," said a woman friend. "And we certainly would say nothing derogatory about Sarah. He won't hear a word against her."

Four months after the Palace denied that Andrew had AIDS, he resigned from the navy. He said that as a single father he needed to spend more time with his children. Others suggested the Lieutenant Commander was resigning after seventeen years because he was not qualified for promotion to commander. The navy quickly issued a statement saying that Andrew was a "highly competent and reliable officer."

Traditionally, military service validates male members of the royal family as manly and patriotic. The thirty-four-year-old Duke of York had served in the Royal Navy like his father, a decorated navy veteran of World War II, and his grandfather Prince Albert, who took part in the Battle of Jutland in World War I and later became King George VI. Andrew had distinguished himself as a helicopter pilot during battle in the Falklands. With his resignation from the military, no longer was a prince of royal blood serving in Her Majesty's forces.

His younger brother, Edward, had joined the marines, but after ninety days in uniform, he quit. His resignation disturbed his family greatly. His mother implored him to reconsider, saying he would no longer be allowed to wear a military uniform on ceremonial occasions. His sister, Anne, feared that he would be branded a quitter and a weakling. But Edward, then twenty-two years old, said he could not continue with the tough commando training. His father, honorary Captain General of the Royal Marines, shouted at him to pull himself together to spare the royal family embarrassment. The young Prince broke down and cried for hours. But the next day he resigned his commission. The headline in the *New York Post:* "The Weeping Wimp of Windsor."

Prince Philip wrote to the marine Commandant, expressing his dissatisfaction. "This is naturally very disappointing," he wrote, "but I can't help feeling that the blaze of publicity did not make things any easier for him. I think he now has to face a very difficult problem of readjustment."

When Philip's personal letter was published in a newspaper, the Queen sued the paper and won damages, but by then the country knew of the father's dashed hopes for his son. A comedian on British television announced: "Rumors abound that Prince Philip fathered an unwanted son who has threatened to embarrass him ever since. [Long pause.] His name is Edward."

When the young Prince decided to become an actor and joined Andrew Lloyd Webber's acting company, he was further ridiculed. Columnist Taki complained in the *Spectator* that Edward "is paid out of the public purse to pursue a theatrical career and assorted bachelors." The hint of the Prince's homosexuality, previously only whispered, was now hinted at in print. The press snidely characterized him as "the Queen's youngest son, a confirmed bachelor." The sexual innuendo became a japing bit of film dialogue in the Australian movie *Priscilla, Queen of the Desert,* when one transvestite asks another transvestite:

"Can the child of an old queen turn out all right?"

"Well, look at Prince Charles."

"Yes, but there's still a question about Prince Edward."

Whether an outrageous slur or a sly truth telling, the insinuation of homosexuality was treated as fact. When Prince William enrolled at Eton, the headmaster censored an article in the school magazine that claimed the royal family was "full of homosexuals." He said he did not want to upset the student Prince. But the insinuation resurfaced in *The New Yorker,* where novelist Julian Barnes wrote of "the seemingly unmarriageable Edward." In a lecture at the Smithsonian, historian David Cannadine opined: "The Queen is worried that Edward is *not* divorced. She thinks he's not normal." Writer Christopher Hitchens said in an interview, "Gay friends of mine refer to Prince Edward as Dishcloth Doris. 'Skirts down,' they'll shout, 'here comes Dishcloth Doris.'" Gore Vidal later corrected Hitchens. "He's not Dishcloth Doris," said Vidal. "He's Dockyard Doris." When gossipist Nigel Dempster wrote in the *Daily Mail* that Edward had a "touching friendship" with a male actor, the young Prince finally responded—angrily. During a visit to New York City, he snapped at reporters and said, "I am *not* gay."

When the Queen's thirty-one-year-old son started dating Sophie Rhys-Jones, their romance was disparaged by one newspaper as "arranged for public consumption." The tabloids speculated that the tall, blond Prince and his attractive girlfriend were decoys put forward by the Palace to divert attention from the rest of the family. Edward, always prickly about criticism, faxed London's news organizations and demanded that reporters "leave me and my girlfriend alone and give us privacy." The Queen obliged by letting it be known she had given permission for Sophie to spend nights with Edward in his apartment at Buckingham Palace. The Archdeacon of York scolded Her Majesty for allowing the couple to live in sin. "We still look to the royal family to set an example," he said, urging the Windsors to return to the values of "no sex before marriage." The Queen ignored the clergyman, and Prince Philip called him a pompous ass.

In June of 1994 the Prince of Wales yanked the loose thread of monarchy and watched in dismay as the ancient tapestry began unraveling. He admitted on television that he had been unfaithful to his wife. But, despite his adultery, he asserted that he would still be King. "All my life," he said, "I have been brought up to...carry out my duty."

The television interview conducted by Jonathan Dimbleby had been calculated by the Prince as his tit for her tat. His big bow-wow journalist would muffle the tinny arf of her tabloid lapdog. While Andrew Morton's book had put the camel's nose under the tent, Jonathan Dimbleby's book brought the tent crashing down. In presenting his version of his marriage, Charles had ignored proverbial wisdom: "If you seek revenge, dig two graves."

But Charles discarded the advice of his family, his friends, and his mistress, who had warned that nothing good could come of his candor. His beloved grandmother said she would have nothing to do with the project. But his private secretary, Commander Richard Aylard, had played to his pride and his vanity by arguing that he had to reclaim his status. "Put your side of the case, sir," he said. Aylard convinced him that his best chance was to cooperate with the journalist and give him unprecedented access to personal letters and diaries. The zealous equerry was determined to help the Prince get even with the Princess. He felt that Dimbleby would be the most devoted vessel—and vassal. Aylard envisioned a one-two punch, starting with a flattering documentary, *Charles: The Private Man, The Public Role,* followed by a laudatory book, *The Prince of Wales.*

In the television interview Charles tried to prove his worth as a statesman by tackling the touchy subjects of religion, politics, and sex. He presented himself as qualified to become philosopher-king: an Oxbridge graduate, artist, minesweeper skipper, organic farmer, businessman, philanthropist, sportsman, ambassador, humanitarian.

He complained about the media and "the level of intrusion, persistent, endless, carping, pontificating, criticising, examining, inventing the soap opera constantly, trying to turn everyone into celebrities."

He also spoke about the monarch's role as Defender of the Faith, saying he would prefer not representing one religion, but rather all religions. Most memorable, though, was his admission of infidelity.

"Gobsmacked," said the tabloids after hearing the Prince of Wales own up to adultery on television. While they pounded him, his supporters praised him. Historian Elizabeth Longford applauded his honesty, but most people were just plain appalled. The *Sun* set up a "You the Jury" telephone poll and reported that two-thirds of those who called said they did not want Charles to become King—ever. The *Daily Mirror* ran an editorial on the front page: "He is not the first royal to be unfaithful. Far from it. But he is the first to appear before 25 million of his subjects to confess."

The Scout Association considered altering its pledge of duty to God and the monarchy. "We extol the virtues of honesty, integrity, and the sanctity of marriage," said an Association spokesman. "But Prince Charles does not represent those virtues." Jonathan Dimbleby defended him on the radio as a deeply spiritual man. "He kneels to pray every night," said the biographer. Unmoved, one listener called in to say that kneeling down to pray is easy. "It's getting up to behave well that takes stamina."

The Queen had insisted on an advance viewing. She worried about what Charles would say on television, especially after his comment weeks before, citing the Scandinavian monarchies as "grander, more pompous, more hard to approach than we are." Now she watched the two-and-a-half-hour documentary without much comment. She shot the equerry a look when Charles recommended hiring out Britain's army to other countries like rent-a-cops. She raised her eyebrows when he complained about his staff's overworking him, and she sighed when he badmouthed her staff. "They drive me bonkers," Charles said of the Queen's courtiers.

Philip reportedly exploded when he saw the documentary. "Oh, God," he said, listening to the interview. He muttered something about his son's brain being sucked dry. Then he added caustically, "Maybe he's the 'missing link.'" Philip's comment referred to the unresolved mystery of the Piltdown Man, supposed to be the unknown connection between humans and apes.

"It would not have been appropriate then," said a man in the room, "to repeat to the Duke what he had once said: 'Every generation gets precisely the younger generation it deserves.'" The man was accustomed to Philip's outbursts. By way of defense, he said, "There's a saying that when your only tool is a hammer, everything looks like a nail."

The Queen was heard to say that she thought the interview had been "ill-advised." She appeared to disapprove of Charles's redefining the monarch's role as "Defender of Faith" rather than "Defender of the Faith." Charles had said that omitting "the" would embrace all religions, not simply Anglicans. "I belong to a hereditary monarchy," he said. "I understand the parameters, but I'm prepared to push it now and then because I feel strongly about things." His mother, who had forbidden him to attend the Pope's Mass during a visit to Rome, was not comfortable with her son's idiosyncratic attitude toward the Church of England. His father was convinced that his forty-five-year-old son had just set the record for stupidity.

The Palace did not comment on the interview, but almost everyone else did. *Time* headlined it as "Charles's Cheatin' Heart." And *Newsweek* reported it as "a bad heir day." *Newsweek* also characterized the documentary as "bad sex: painfully tedious foreplay followed by a lightning-quick climax." The *Daily Mail* headlined its story "Charles: When I Was Unfaithful," while the *Sun* said, "Di Told You So." One cartoonist drew the Prince of Wales in bed, grinning foolishly with his crown askew. Sitting between two women, he had his arms wrapped around both. The caption: "The Lyin' King." Another cartoon showed him standing before two stone tablets containing the Ten Commandments: he was scratching out the Sixth Commandment—"Thou Shalt Not Commit (nor admit) Adultery."

The Queen's former private secretary sighed. "In time it will fade," Lord Martin Charteris told writer Noreen Taylor. "People will forgive. There is an awful lot to be said for honesty." The courtier added sadly that this wasn't the first time the monarchy had gone through troubled times. "But the Queen is enough of a realist," he said, "to know there is nothing but to sit it out."

Sitting was her specialty. So she sat for weeks, dreading the biography that was to follow her son's television interview. Unfortunately the book was published on the eve of her departure for Russia. This was the first trip by a British monarch to that country since Edward VII had visited in 1908. Ten years after that, when the Queen's grandfather George V declined to send the navy to save his cousins, the Bolsheviks murdered the Czar and his family in a particularly gruesome crime. After the Russian Revolution, the British government turned down all invitations for a state visit to Moscow on the grounds that the communists had killed the monarch's family. Eventually some members of the royal family did visit the Soviet Union, but the Queen was not allowed by her government to go. Until now. The British government finally gave her permission after Russia's difficult transition from communism. She considered the trip to be the most important of her reign. But as she stood in Moscow's Red Square, extending her hand in friendship, she took a hit at home from her son—in that long-awaited book.

Through his approved biographer, Charles showed the Queen as a cold and uncaring mother. He said he had grown up "emotionally estranged" and craving affection that she was "unable or unwilling to offer." He depicted his father as an acid-tongued martinet and his Gordonstoun teachers as bullies. He described his estranged wife as a self-absorbed neurotic who was mentally unhinged. He said she was twisted with jealousy and temperamentally "volatile," "hysterical," "obsessive." In addition, she was prone to "violent mood swings," "black phases," and "bouts of gloom." He said the only reason he had married her was that his father had pressured him. The middle-aged Prince sounded like the hapless young man in the Danish ballet "The Young Man Must Marry," who was forced into marriage by his family and ended up betrothed to a girl with three heads. Through Dimbleby, Charles made it clear that Diana was nothing more than a hired womb.

His level of contempt disappointed people who expected their future King to be high-minded and big-hearted. Through Dimbleby, Charles tried to put his case forward and set right the real and imagined wrongs he felt had been done to him. But he came across as petty and small, and he offended his wife, his parents, his sister, his brothers, his children. He even managed to slight his favorite movie star, Barbra Streisand, whom he had once described as "my only pinup...devastatingly attractive and with a great deal of sex appeal."

Months before, the star had serenaded him in front of twelve thousand fans in London's Wembley Arena, her first public engagement in twenty-eight years. She sang "Some Day My Prince Will Come" and told her British audience that she was particularly fond of songs about imaginary princes. "What makes it extra special is that there's a real one in the audience tonight," she said, looking flirtatiously at the royal box, where Prince Charles was sitting. He beamed. She recalled their first meeting, saying she had not been very gracious. "Who knows, if I had been nice, I might have been the first real Jewish Princess—Princess Babs!"

She imagined the newspaper headlines that might have accompanied their romance: "Blintzes Princess Plays the Palace" and "Barbra Digs Nails into Prince of Wales." Charles laughed with everyone else and looked pleased when she sang "As If We Never Said Goodbye." The audience went wild and gave her a two- minute standing ovation. She raised more than $250,000 for The Prince's Trust. Yet in the Dimbleby book, Charles said her "attractiveness has waned a little."

He made it up to the diva several months later by inviting her to Highgrove for an overnight visit. But he almost withdrew the invitation after her secretary called to make advance arrangements. She told the Prince of Wales that the star wanted only white flowers in her bedroom and for breakfast an omelette of egg whites. Charles complained to his friend Geoffrey Kent. "She sounds daft," he said. But he sat up all night with Streisand, who, he said, arrived with eight suitcases. "We discussed philosophy," he reported to friends.

In the Dimbleby book, Charles described

his nanny and his mistress with the same words—"loving," "warm," "sympathetic," "gentle," and "caring"—words a child might use to describe his mother. He also admitted to three love affairs with Camilla: one before she married in 1973, the second after she had children, and the third in 1986, when he said his marriage to Diana had "irretrievably broken down."

His parents were greatly upset. "They had no idea what he was going to say," recalled a friend who had spent a weekend with the Queen and Prince Philip earlier in the summer. "I will not go into details because they did not go into details—they never do....A mention was made in passing about concern over a book—that's all. A book. We assumed it was James Hewitt's dreadful kiss-and-tell. ..." The Queen's friend waves a hand dismissively to indicate the book *Princess in Love,* which detailed Hewitt's five-year love affair with the Princess of Wales. "But the Queen didn't seem to care about Major Hewitt's tittle-tattle. Her concern was over what Charles intended to say. ..."

The Prince proved that his disclosures were every bit as sensational as those sold by his servants. Violating royal precedents of restraint, he astonished even those who were accustomed to gaudy sensationalism. "A Foolish and Sorry Authorised Version," was the *Guardian*'s opinion. The left-wing newspaper soon declared itself republican (opposed to a monarchy and committed to a republic), as did the *Inde-*

pendent on Sunday. The temperate *Economist* called the monarchy "an idea whose time has passed." Even the conservative *Daily Telegraph* chided the Prince for placing the book in the public domain. Columnist John Junor excoriated him as "wicked" and said he should feel "suicidal." *The Washington Post* called him "the Prince of Wails" for forgetting the cardinal rule of the monarchy: "The son never frets on the British Empire."

The Duke of Edinburgh also registered disdain—publicly. "I've never discussed private matters, and I don't think the Queen has either," he told reporters who asked for his reaction to his son's book. "I've never made any comments about any member of the family in forty years, and I'm not going to start now."

Charles's brothers and his sister criticized him for using the book to bash their parents. But the self-pitying Prince didn't see it that way. He rationalized that at his age he was entitled to a little happiness. He said he wanted to make a clean breast of it. "You'll see," he predicted. "At the end of the day, it will be for the best." This wasn't the first time he had been wrong footed.

His mistress's long-suffering husband was fed up. For years Andrew Parker Bowles had stoically endured gossip in his circle about the Prince's passion for his wife. "Actually, some people felt he rather enjoyed it," said Jocelyn Gray, a close friend of Prince Andrew. "Having your wife bonked by the future King of England lends cachet...in some circles." Barely suppressing a grin, British writer Anthony Holden explained on American television that some old-fashioned English men consider it an honor to share their wives with their monarch. "Comes from the French droit du seigneur and refers to the master of the house sleeping with his servants. ..."

When Andrew Parker Bowles saw himself derided in the press as "the man who laid down his wife for his country," he was angry. He had held back on getting a divorce two years before only because Charles had asked him to wait. The Prince had said that after his own separation he didn't think the monarchy could take another marriage scandal. "I'm afraid I've cocked up things a bit," Charles said apologetically. So his mistress's husband, who was also his friend and former aide, agreed not to start legal proceedings that might embarrass the royal family.

As Lieutenant Colonel Commanding the Household Cavalry, Andrew Parker Bowles held the honorary position of Silverstick-in-Waiting, which entailed accompanying the Queen on ceremonial occasions. Even after his love affair with Princess Anne in 1970, he had remained close to the royal family, particularly the Queen Mother. But after Charles made him nationally known as a cuckold, he felt he had no choice. "I can't keep on living someone else's life," he said. Although a devout Roman Catholic, he resolved to seek a divorce.

The year before, Andrew and Camilla Parker Bowles had celebrated their twentieth wedding anniversary with a big party at their country estate. Some of those invited had extended discreet hospitality over the years whenever one or the other wanted to entertain a lover. These same friends, part of Prince Charles's hunting and shooting circle, now professed surprise when the Parker Bowleses announced their plans to divorce. "We have grown apart to such an extent that...there is little of common interest between us," read the couple's statement. Their divorce was granted in January 1995, and less than a year later Andrew Parker Bowles remarried. Camilla sold their house and bought one closer to Charles.

Diana appeared unfazed by the divorce of her husband's mistress. She smiled at photographers as she made her early morning visit to her new gym. But away from the cameras, she seethed. She confided in the *Daily Mail*'s royal correspondent, Richard Kay, that she considered the Parker Bowleses' divorce part of a "grand scheme" to force her out of the public life she had gradually resumed. She worried about Camilla's influence on her children. She fretted about "enemies" out to get her. "They" wanted to harm her. She feared her phones were tapped at Kensington Palace, so she had her lines swept electronically. She talked of a "whispering campaign" against her conducted by friends of Charles such as Nicholas Soames and members of the Prince's staff at St. James's Palace.

Diana had summoned the *Daily Mail*'s

royal correspondent for a three-hour audience. She wore sunglasses and a baseball cap pulled over her eyes as she drove to meet him in London's West End, where he climbed into her car to talk. Whenever they met, she spoke freely and he quoted her as "a friend of the Princess." He published so many exclusives about her that he became known as her unofficial spokesman. Colleagues teased him about being "ma'am's mouthpiece." The tabloid reporter James Whitaker, who had helped engineer Diana's courtship, lamented his being "traded up." Realistically and without rancor, he explained why he had been replaced as her favorite reporter: "The *Daily Mail* is her crowd. That's what they read. It's more upmarket than my downmarket paper."

In fact, any story on the Princess of Wales appearing under Richard Kay's byline was assumed to come directly from her. He had reported her strong denials of an affair with James Hewitt. "We were *never* lovers," she swore to the reporter, although later she admitted on television that she had committed adultery with Hewitt. She denied to Richard Kay that she had had an affair with James Gilbey, although their taped phone conversation revealed her fears of getting pregnant. She also denied having an affair with England's rugby captain Will Carling, despite Julia Carling's public threat to name Diana in a divorce suit for adultery.

"I saw the Princess sneaking men into the back way of Kensington Palace," said a but-

690

ler in the royal household, "because she brought them round by my apartment....I couldn't help but see because she had to pass by my window."

The gamy insinuations swirling around the Princess inspired raucous jokes from late night comedians. In the States, *The Dana Carvey Show* lost two sponsors after the comic, performing as a prissy church lady, clucked disapprovingly about Diana's being a "slut." On the *Tonight* show, Jay Leno joked: "Princess Diana was in an accident today, but she's recovering. Soon, she'll be out of the hospital and flat on her back again."

In most of Richard Kay's exclusives, the Princess appeared as a paragon. When she told him how her phone call had saved a drowning man, Kay wrote dramatically: "She rushed to the water's edge and helped pull the unconscious tramp to the bank, where he was given mouth-to-mouth resuscitation." When she told him she had taken her children on a secret visit to a homeless shelter so they could see how others less privileged live, Kay's "exclusive" dominated the entire front page: "Princes and the Paupers."

Diana reveled in her role as a mother and felt threatened when Charles hired Alexandra Legge-Bourke to plan activities for the boys when they were with him. The former nursery school teacher, known as Tiggy, joined the Prince's staff a few months after his separation from Diana. Tiggy forged a close bond with the children, who enjoyed her rollicking enthusiasm. The Princess admitted feeling a "gut kick" the first time she saw Tiggy racing to embrace the children, whom she called "my babies." And Diana felt upstaged as "Mummy" after seeing pictures of the twenty-nine-year-old assistant skiing with the children at Klosters in Switzerland, grouse hunting with them at Sandringham, and deer stalking at Balmoral. Tiggy was quoted as saying: "I give the boys what they need at this stage—fresh air, a rifle, and a horse."

The Princess fumed. "She's undermining my boys," she said. She complained about Tiggy's cigarette habit and said she didn't want the young woman smoking in front of the boys. "What is it about Charles, who professes to hate smoking, and women who're addicted to cigarettes?" she asked, alluding to Camilla Parker Bowles, also a pack-a-day smoker. And when Diana read about Tiggy in the press as "warm and cheerful" and "a wonderful surrogate mother," she hit the roof.

Diana acidly pointed out to Richard Kay that if she employed a "surrogate father" to be with the Princes when they were at home with her, she would be criticized as a bad mother. Unlike her husband, who took Tiggy with him to events at the boys' schools and on all vacations with the children, Diana said she did not feel compelled to take a man with her when she visited her sons or took them on holiday. After seeing pictures of Charles embracing Tiggy on three occasions and greeting her with a kiss on the lips, the Princess speculated that the Prince was "probably having an affair with the little servant girl."

The kissing drew questions from reporters, but Commander Aylard dismissed the Prince's public displays of affection for his assistant. "Tiggy is a member of the household," said Aylard, "and an old family friend." He added that her mother was a lady-in-waiting to Princess Anne, her aunt was an extra lady-in-waiting, and her brother had been a page-of-honor to the Queen. When the Prince and Princess later started divorce negotiations, Tiggy called herself "Tiggy in the middle."

By then Diana felt displaced as a mother, so she fired off directives to her husband regarding Tiggy's role in the children's lives. The Princess banned the younger woman from the boys' bedrooms and bathrooms. She said Tiggy should stay in the background on any occasion when the boys were seen in public. "She is neither to accompany them in the same car nor be photographed close to them." She insisted that when the boys called her from Sandringham at Christmastime, they were to be taken to another lodge on the estate, where they could speak to her privately. "No one else, no staff or servants, is to be present during our conversations."

Diana publicly reinforced her image as the mother of a future King by talking to Richard Kay about her firstborn son. She bragged that at thirteen he was "taller than his father...and so very different." She belittled Charles by building up William: the son is "decisive"; the son has "sense and sensibility"; the son takes "people for what they are, not who they are." The son is handsome, "not burdened" with stick-out ears. "Tell him he's good-looking," wrote Richard Kay after visiting with Diana, "and Wills says he can't be because that would make him vain." In contrast with his father, the gentle son protected his mother. When he saw a tabloid story about her having a crush on Tom Hanks and bombarding the movie star with phone calls, she said she was prepared to laugh it off, but Wills had insisted she issue a denial. "As he crossly told a school friend later, 'It made my mother look like a prostitute.'"

When the Princess phoned the reporter on Saturday, August 20, 1994, she was distraught. "Someone somewhere is going to make out I am mad," she sobbed. She had just found out the next day's newspapers were reporting that for eighteen months she had been peppering the art dealer Oliver Hoare with anonymous telephone calls. She was suspected of making the crank calls to Hoare's home and hanging up when his wife answered. Sometimes the caller stayed on the phone without saying a word. Diane Hoare complained to her husband about the "silence" calls, which she found "unnerving." After a mysterious woman caller screamed torrents of abuse at her, Diane Hoare insisted her husband call the police. At first the art dealer, an expert in Islamic art, feared a terrorist threat against his family. So he insisted on answering the phone himself. But when the sinister silent calls continued, he realized that whoever was calling just wanted to hear his voice.

"I would be polite and say, 'Hello, who's calling? Who's there?'" he said. "But there was just silence at the other end. It was eerie."

After tapping the Hoares' telephone line, police traced the calls to Diana's and Charles's private lines at Kensington Palace, to Diana's mobile phone, and to Diana's sister's phone on the days Diana was visiting. An investigator from the Nuisance Calls Division speculated that the Princess was using different lines to avoid detection.

"Mr. Hoare went white as a sheet when he saw our report," said the investigator. "He never imagined in his wildest dreams that Princess Diana could be making the calls."

The Hoares, who were close friends of Prince Charles and had known Diana since their marriage, showed him the police report that logged the time of every call. A confidential extract from January 13, 1994, shows:

> 8:45 a.m. Phone rings. Silence. Hoare punches in the police code. The number that flashes up is a private office at Kensington Palace.
> 8:49 a.m. Phone rings. Hoare: "Who's there?" Code reveals Diana's private line.
> 8:54 a.m. Phone rings. Silence. Code reveals Charles's office phone at Kensington Palace. [Charles no longer living or working at Kensington Palace.]

2:12 p.m. Phone rings. Silence. Code reveals Charles's office at Kensington Palace.

7:55 p.m. Phone rings. Silence. Code reveals Charles's line from Kensington Palace.

8:19 p.m. Phone rings. Silence. Code reveals Charles's line from Kensington Palace.

The Prince shook his head sadly and expressed concern for his children. "They are the ones who will suffer from all this and will get it all played back when they return to school," he said. The Hoares declined to press charges, but someone in Scotland Yard leaked the story to the press, and the Princess looked pitiful. People began questioning her sanity. "Is the Princess of Wales going mad?" asked an editorial. "She's an hysterical woman," wrote a columnist, "clearly teetering on the edge of a nervous breakdown."

Her therapists explained her alleged pathological behavior as typical for a bulimic experiencing loneliness and isolation. "For a woman who has difficulty confronting people, and is struggling for control," said one specialist who treated Diana, "phone harassment gives a feeling of empowerment. It's a safe way to retaliate."

Then came a few tasty tidbits. The art dealer, a dashing married man and father of two children, apparently had extended friendship to the troubled Princess, and she had turned into an obsessive pest. But that was not entirely accurate, said Oliver Hoare's chauffeur, Barry Hodge. He spoke up after Hoare had fired him for unrelated reasons. The chauffeur asserted that Diana and the art dealer had been having an affair. He said the couple had set up a "love nest" in Pimlico, where they had been meeting three or four times a week for almost four years. The chauffeur said Hoare, who did not want to leave his wealthy, aristocratic wife, was very much taken with the Princess. And he said they dined secretly at the homes of friends such as Lucia Flecha de Lima, wife of a Brazilian diplomat. The chauffeur said the Princess "could phone [the limo] more than twenty times a day."

When Hodge's story was published, Diana contacted Richard Kay, who wrote that the chauffeur's "claims are said to have reduced the Princess of Wales to peals of laughter."

Oliver Hoare admitted that he had met with Diana on several occasions, but only to advise her and console her about her marriage. Still, his wife insisted on a separation, so he moved into a one-bedroom apartment in Pimlico. A few months later the Hoares reconciled and he moved back into their estate.

"All we know is that Mr. Hoare did not want to prosecute the Princess of Wales," said an investigator from London's Metropolitan Police Department. "He agreed to withdraw his complaint and said he would talk to the lady privately."

Diana denied making the harassing calls.

"There is absolutely no truth in it," Richard Kay quoted her as saying. She showed him extracts from her calendar, saying she was at lunch with friends or at the movies when some of the calls were made. "They are trying to make out I was having an affair with this man," she said, "or that I had some sort of fatal attraction....It is simply untrue and so unfair....What have I done to deserve this? I feel I am being destroyed."

He listened sympathetically. When she acknowledged that she and Hoare were "friends" and had spoken on the phone "occasionally," he asked if she had placed any of those occasional calls to him from pay phones.

"You can't be serious," she said indignantly. "I don't even know how to use a parking meter, let alone a phone box."

Her response made James Hewitt smile ruefully. He remembered many calls from Diana, who always disguised her voice when she called him at his army barracks. She told him she was dialing from a pay phone so the call would not appear on the phone bills that Charles examined. "I feel sorry for her," Hewitt said. "Very sorry."

Less sympathetic were the cartoonists, who lampooned her without mercy. One drew the Princess on the phone, saying: "Can you hold on a second? There's someone at the door. ..." Through a window, two men in white coats were approaching with nets and manacles. In another cartoon an old woman answers the phone. Hearing nothing but heavy breathing, she turns to her husband. "I think it's Princess Di for you."

Charles took advantage of the crack in his wife's stature. Having portrayed her as intellectually vacant and television addicted, he now said her only goal in life was to empty Chanel's boutiques and stock her closets at his expense. He complained loudly during a London dinner party about her expenses for travel and clothing and said she cost him $13,900 a month for "grooming." When Diana heard the comment she snapped, "I don't cost half as much to groom as his goddamned polo ponies." Days later people could decide for themselves when her yearly "grooming" expenses were itemized in the papers:

$25,000:	manicures and pedicures
$24,000:	hair, including color, cuts, and daily styling
$ 7,000:	fitness instructor
$ 4,400:	chiropractor
$ 4,300:	colonic irrigation
$ 4,290:	reflexology
$ 3,800:	osteopathy
$ 2,200:	holistic massage
$ 3,800:	aromatherapy, plus home visits
$ 1,000:	acupuncture
$ 2,000:	hypnotherapy
$65,000:	astrologers, psychics, and holistic counselors
$20,000:	psychotherapy

Again Diana rang up Richard Kay in dismay. "This is a deliberate attempt to discredit me," she said. She did not deny the therapies or their costs. Rather, she said that "someone" in the Palace wanted to make her look like a New Age flake who had her colon flushed every week because she was obsessed with being thin and didn't have anything better to do with her time or her husband's money. The reporter quoted "a friend of the Princess" as saying: "If the Prince had not treated her so shabbily, she would not have needed to turn to expensive therapists."

Her estranged sister-in-law, the Duchess of York, phoned to commiserate. She, too, felt persecuted by the Palace machine.

"They are out to get us—especially Bellowes," Fergie said, using her nickname for the Queen's private secretary, Sir Robert Fellowes, who was Diana's brother-in-law. "First me, now you....We're the bad girls and we must be punished."

During her protracted divorce negotiations, Fergie had been accused by the Palace of "insane extravagance" for running up expenses of $3 million. Details of her expenditures—$6,500 for twenty pairs of shoes and $85,000 for twelve dresses—were leaked to the press. After they were published, the Palace announced that the Queen would not pay the Duchess's bills. A spokesman said, "She lives beyond her means—and ours."

Fergie admitted she was "paranoid" about the courtiers. She started carrying a shredder with her wherever she traveled. And she stopped keeping a diary because she was afraid someone might expose her private life. "Andrew used to write me wonderful letters from the ship, but I haven't kept them," she told her friend David Frost, the television interviewer. "I did for a bit, in the bank, but then I thought the bank would be robbed."

Diana, who also used shredders for mail and scramblers on her telephones, subscribed to Fergie's conspiracy theory. She, too, distrusted the courtiers, including her brother-in-law, and believed they were trying to destabilize her. "They think we were crazy to start with," she joked to Fergie, "but we didn't get crazy until we married into this family...."

During their marital separation, both young women consulted psychiatrists, and both were put on antidepressants. Straining under the restrictions of being royal wives, both had taken lovers, who betrayed them for money. Now emotionally fragile and frightened about their future, the two women turned to their astrologers, numerologists, and spiritualists for help. But many of these celebrity-by-association gurus also sold them out. After Diana learned her beautician, her palmist, and her zone therapist were writing books, she stopped seeing them and told friends she could not rely on anyone around her. "She's alone, and she's so lonely," said fifty-three-year-old Lucia Flecha de Lima, who had become close to Diana after her 1991 tour of Brazil. "She doesn't know whom she can trust."

Fergie hired lawyers to stop publication of books by her former chef, her former psychic, and her former lover's business partner. But she was unable to prevent her former butler from selling his recollections of her and John Bryan splashing in the tub together. "Their lovemaking in the bath was always very noisy," the butler said. "Fergie would squeal her head off."

The Duchess and the Princess later joined forces to fend off the press. No longer members of the royal family or receiving public money, they fought for their privacy. They filed a criminal complaint and sought an injunction against photographers who trespassed on private property in the French Riviera to take pictures of them on vacation. They hired lawyers to notify Britain's Press Complaints Commission that they would not tolerate further invasions of their privacy, and Diana obtained an injunction against a freelance paparazzo she claimed was stalking her. She filed an affidavit with the court, saying: "He seems to know my every move. I shall suffer undue psychological pressure and become ill."

Feeling betrayed by everyone around them, both women kept track of insults in the press and made lists of reporters who could be trusted—short lists. They phoned each other when negative stories appeared and discussed what to do. Fergie usually chose the direct approach and called the offending writer.

"She rang me from London," said *New York Post* columnist Cindy Adams, "to bitch about my saying she'd been late for people her last visit."

In that case, the phone call was effective. On her next trip to New York City, the Duchess invited Cindy Adams to tea, and the columnist was elated. She told her readers: "I adored...Her Skinny Highness."

Still, the list of trustworthy reporters was shrinking. Diana, who had once complimented the *Daily Mail*'s Lynda Lee-Potter for her perceptive feature stories, dismissed her as a hack when she said the Princess was addicted to praise.

"She's off the list," said Diana. She also scratched Chrissy Iley of the *Manchester Evening News* for carping about her secret midnight visits to hospitals to comfort the sick and dying. The writer offended Diana by calling her "the super martyr" and "the husband stealer." When Noreen Taylor wrote an essay entitled, "Diana: A Princess in Love...with Herself," she, too, was dropped from the list of trustworthy reporters. Noreen Taylor had asked readers why, since the breakup of Diana's marriage, she allowed it to be known that she spent most of her Christmas alone. Noting that Diana had a mother, two sisters, a brother, and countless friends, the writer asked, "Is this another cry for attention from a public she believes is besotted by her?"

Diana called Fergie to complain.

"The women are the worst," moaned Fergie. "They're so bitchy." She made an exception for Ingrid Seward, the editor of *Majesty* magazine. "Ingie is okay, and her husband [columnist Ross Benson] is divine looking." Diana did not share Fergie's enthusiasm for Ross Benson because the columnist had declared himself firmly on the side of Charles in the war of the Waleses. She and Fergie agreed that they were much better treated by male writers than the females, except for gossip columnists such as Nigel Dempster. But both Diana and Fergie dismissed him as "an old woman."

When *Daily Telegraph* journalist Victoria Mather described Fergie in one of her "famous rump-straining sad floral prints," Fergie again picked up the phone and protested.

"This is the Duchess of York," she announced grandly, "and I'd like to talk about your sweeping judgments."

"Good afternoon, Your Highness," said the journalist, switching on her tape recorder.

Fergie asked, "Why did you write such a scathing article?" Without waiting for an answer, she continued: "I understand that journalism—that you have to do your job—but to talk about people's weight...and the size of their backsides and floral dresses...is so below the belt...so pathetic....I still do so much good work...so much good work....Nobody knows the good work I do. ..."

The reporter listened respectfully as the Duchess sounded ready to duke it out. She carried on for twenty minutes: "In this day and age, when the whole of Bosnia [is filled] with blind children and blind adults and you lower yourself to pull someone apart and [say] she's got a big bottom. I mean it's absolutely farcical...maybe you should come with me to Bosnia...and see then what is the real world and what real life is about. I mean, who cares whether someone is a size fourteen or size eighteen? Absolutely pathetic. ..."

Fergie cared desperately. She tried everything to lose weight—pills, diets, hypnotism. "I've even switched from white wine to red wine," she told a friend, "so I could cut down on drinking." Finally she sought out an "alternative healer" who gave her a nutritional plan and helped break her addiction to diet pills. After losing forty-two pounds, she emerged from his clinic—a hut in a field in Surrey—and announced her intention to become a professional model. "When I'm thin like this, my legs are better than the Princess of Wales's," she said gleefully. She hired a public relations agency and posed for photographers. Her picture, showing a newly slim and glamorously made up Fergie, appeared on the cover of *Paris-Match*. But London's *Sunday Times* was not impressed: "A little more mascara around the eyes," sniped the paper, "and the Chinese will be sending pandas to London for mating."

The pounding Fergie took in the press made her defensive and defiant. "They might hate us here," she told Diana, "but they love us in America." Both women enjoyed their trips to the States, where they were treated like royalty, not royal discards. Diana, who appeared regularly in the United Kingdom wearing sweatshirts emblazoned with "U.S.A.," skied in Colorado, shopped in New York City, and vacationed on Martha's Vineyard. But Fergie came to the States to prospect for gold.

After selling her *Budgie* rights to a consortium in New Jersey for $3 million, she set up a nonprofit charity in Manhattan. With Chances for Children, Inc., she tried to re-create herself as a humanitarian. She said the foundation was designed to give her a philanthropic presence in America. In one year it paid out $89,384 on expenses while disbursing $62,295 to needy children. The bare-bones operation, with its small budget, rented room, and part-time secretary, did not seem designed for substantial fund-raising. But the nonprofit corporation gave Fergie a way—legally—to raise money in the places where she liked to socialize: New York, Connecticut, Florida, and California. She said she enjoyed doing good while doing well.

During one of her visits to Greenwich, Connecticut, she appeared at a Champagne reception and dinner for which guests had paid $500. As she worked the room, her three assistants followed in her wake, toting copies of her book *Victoria and Albert: A Family Life at Osborne House*. They asked: "Would you like to buy the Duchess's book? It's $100. She'll sign it for you!"

Fergie insisted that she needed the money to support herself and her children. As she told the National Press Club in Washington, D.C., "It's rubbish to say that I'm rich....I can't afford to buy a house....I rent a pile in Surrey and have to be out with a month's notice....My husband pays only the school fees. I have to pay everything else....I'm Her Royal Highness the Duchess of York, but I'm not a millionairess."

She challenged critics who questioned her moneymaking schemes, including her $2 million advance from a U.S. publisher to write a manual for single working mothers. "The facts are that I'm a separated mother of two children and responsible for the finances of my family," she said. "Therefore, a great deal of my time has to be, *has to be*, occupied with commercial work. Believe it or not, that is the truth."

The unquestionable truth was that Fergie accepted the largesse of rich friends and eager admirers. Her rationale: She said she couldn't pay her own way. So she charged for personal appearances at benefits and theme parks. She picked up $75,000 for flying to Sydney, Australia, to launch Rupert Murdoch's pay-TV network. She flew to Beijing, China, for the opening of an $8 million restaurant because the owner paid her. Diana was more discreet, but she, too, freely accepted the gratuities that came her way as royalty. Both women were friends of the flamboyant founder of the Virgin empire, Richard Branson, and enjoyed free trips on Virgin Atlantic Airways and free holidays at Virgin Hotels, preferring Necker

Island in the Caribbean, which cost paying guests $15,000 a week. Fergie and Diana reciprocated by giving Branson their royal endorsements. They appeared at his openings, posed with him for pictures, and appeared in public wearing his company T-shirts.

Diana's friends, who preferred her association with the saintly Mother Teresa, warned her about the errant Duchess. "Free-loading Fergie is the worst friend you could have," wrote John Junor, but Diana decided that her sister-in-law was her only ally. "She's been over the same course," Diana said of Fergie.

In the past, the two young women had experienced edgy relations. Separated by competition and envy, they had avoided each other and sniped to friends about each other. During her taped conversation with James Gilbey, Diana dismissed Fergie as "the red-head" who was trying to cash in on her good image. For her part, Fergie thought Diana's good image was manipulated and undeserved. During her Mt. Everest expedition, the Duchess asked photographers who wanted to take her picture at a marker: "This doesn't look posed, does it? It doesn't look like those Taj Mahal pictures?"

When their marriages broke up, the two young women grabbed on to each other like the only survivors of a shipwreck. Ostracized by the royal family and "outside the net," as Diana put it, they took refuge in each other. They felt that no one else understood their problems as well as they understood each other. They talked constantly about the Palace machine that was grinding them down. They supported each other in standing up to the courtiers who had become their enemies.

After two years of legal separation, both of them could file for divorce, but neither wanted to look like the aggressor in ending her marriage.

"No mileage in it," said Diana, who clung fiercely to her position as a wronged wife.

"Especially without a signed financial," said the pragmatic Duchess, who was calling for a settlement of $10 million. She was also hoping to keep her status as Her Royal Highness. Fergie with no title was like Saudi Arabia with no oil.

Diana, too, was determined to hang on to her position, but her lawyers advised her to let Fergie lead the way through the divorce maze. They called the Duchess "the yellow canary" (referring to the bird that miners take underground to check for deadly gas; if the canary keels over, the miners back out of the pit).

Although both women were privately exploring financial settlements, they maintained publicly that they were very much married. "The subject of divorce has never come up between myself and my husband," Diana assured Richard Kay in the fall of 1995. By then the Princess was struggling to appear virtuous. Branded a home wrecker by Will Carling's wife, she was accused of breaking up the Carlings' marriage of less than a year. "This has happened to her before," said Julia Carling, who looked like a younger, blonder version of Diana, "and you only hope she won't do these things again, but she obviously does. She picked the wrong couple to do it with this time because we can only get stronger."

But within days the Carlings separated, with Julia Carling blaming the Princess. Reacting to reports that her husband had had an affair with Diana, Julia Carling told reporters: "I have always valued my marriage as the most important and sacred part of my life," she said. "It hurts me very much to face losing my husband in a manner which has become outside my control."

Diana's relationship with the rugby captain was headlined in the *News of the World* as "Di's Secret Trysts with Carling." So she called Richard Kay. She assured him that her "innocent friendship" with Carling had started only because of her rugby-mad sons. She summoned the *News of the World* 's managing editor to Kensington Palace and begged him to lay off. She also contacted the *Daily Mirror* and insisted her friendship with Carling was platonic. The paper quoted her as saying, "I don't need a lover." In distress, she phoned her friends— "endlessly," recalled one woman, who finally lost patience with the Princess. Diana also consulted her therapist, Suzie Orbach, who began seeing her on a daily basis.

"Through these sessions, Her Royal Highness determined to take control of her life," explained a friend who spoke with Diana during this time. The words sounded measured, as if they had been written in advance: "Eventually she desired a respectable forum to demonstrate that she was not deranged or mentally incapacitated....She felt she needed to answer her critics, reclaim her sanity, and prove her strength. ..."

Having pleaded for privacy two years earlier, Diana now sought the world stage. She decided the only way she could banish the image of herself as deranged was to give a television interview. She was encouraged by Fergie, one of the few people she confided in, who said that *she* had benefited from going on television and admitting her mistakes. So she urged Diana to do the same. Fergie agreed that *Panorama,* the award-winning current affairs program, was the proper vehicle to treat her seriously. But she cautioned Diana to keep her plan under wraps, because if the Queen found out, she would put the kibosh on the interview. Diana concurred.

Coached by her therapist and confident of her telegenic skills, the Princess met secretly with the BBC's Martin Bashir and his camera crew at Kensington Palace on November 5, 1995, to talk about herself, her husband, her marriage, and her life in the royal family. She had not sought permission from the Palace. And she informed the Queen only a few days before the interview was to be aired. The BBC announced its "world exclusive" four hours after playing the National Anthem to celebrate Prince Charles's forty-seventh birth-day. Diana's press secretary, who had not known of her plans, was so angry that he resigned the next day. Her private secretary, also unalerted and equally angry, waited a few more weeks to resign. And in a small display of spite, the Queen retaliated the following year by ending the BBC's sixty-year monopoly on carrying her Christmas broadcast. She gave the assignment to the commercial network for two years, after which she said the two net-works would alternate the production.

On the night of November 20, 1995, more than twenty-two million Britons gathered in front of their television sets to watch the Princess perform. "And it was a performance," said the royal biographer Penny Junor. "A bril-liant performance—totally plausible. Charm-ing, demure, and vulnerable...but a performance—an acting job."

Grid engineers had installed an additional power station to accommodate the expected national surge in electricity after the 9:40 P.M. program; they estimated the extra megawatts to be the equivalent of three hun-dred thousand teakettles being plugged in at once. When the show was broadcast worldwide, some two hundred million people in one hun-dred countries were watching.

Calmly and with poise, Diana discussed her postnatal depression, her suicide attempts, her crying jags, and her bulimia. She said she suffered because her husband made her feel useless and unwanted—a total failure. She said he had taken a mistress and then blamed her, his wife, for getting upset. He said she was an embarrassment to the royal family, and his friends, "the establishment that I married into," considered her unstable enough to be committed to a mental institution. She said her husband was jealous of her "because I always got more publicity, my work was more, was discussed much more than him." Yet she maintained she did not want a divorce.

She admitted having been unfaithful during her marriage. She denied having affairs with James Gilbey and Oliver Hoare but said she had been in love with James Hewitt. "Yes, I adored him," she said. "But I was very let down." She told the interviewer that she did not tell her children about her affair with Hewitt, but she did tell them about their father's adultery with Camilla Parker Bowles. "But I put it in gently," she said, "without resentment or any anger."

She faulted the press for its intrusions: "I've never encouraged the media. There was a relationship which worked before, but now I can't tolerate it because it's become abusive and it's harassment."

Conceding she would never become Queen of the country, she asked instead to be a queen of people's hearts. "I'd like to be an ambassador," she said.

The interviewer asked, "On what grounds do you feel that you have the right to think of yourself as an ambassador?"

Diana replied: "I've been in a privileged position for fifteen years. I've got tremendous knowledge about people and know how to communicate, and I want to use it."

Minutes later she was asked whether she thought her husband would ever be King. She raised her kohl-rimmed eyes to the camera and replied, "I don't think any of us know the answer to that. Who knows what fate will produce, who knows what circumstances will provoke?" She expressed hope that her tormented husband would find peace of mind. Without uttering an unkind word, she questioned his ability to reign. "I would think that the top job, as I call it, would bring enormous limitations to him, and I don't know whether he could adapt." Perhaps, she concluded, because of his "conflict" about becoming King, he should forgo the throne and allow the crown to pass directly to their son, Prince William, when he comes of age.

"You could almost hear the country's collective gasp," said a television commentator on the late news.

The next morning every one of Britain's newspapers devoted its front page to Diana. Every aspect of the interview was scrutinized: her clothes (tailored navy blazer, opaque black hose), her lighting (harsh), her demeanor (restrained), her vocabulary (impressive, according to *Time*, which reported she said "albeit" five times and "daunting" or "daunted" fourteen times).

Few people criticized her, but Nicholas Soames, Charles's friend, was outraged. His attack lent credibility to her charges. "The Prince has been wronged," Soames said. He pronounced her performance as "toe-curlingly dreadful" and said she was "in the advanced stages of paranoia."

But the working classes loved the Princess. The opinion polls showed public support for her running as high as 85 percent. The journalist and historian Paul Johnson declared her a heroine. He forgave her sexual indiscretions because "she was chaste when the Prince began the adultery game." In defense of Diana, he quoted Jane Austen's defense of Queen Caroline, the estranged wife of George IV: "She was bad, but she would not have become as bad as she was if he had not been infinitely worse."

The Charles and Diana camps formed along class lines. Elderly Tory squires and Anglican bishops backed the Prince, while a majority of working-class people, along with Catholic Church populists, supported the Princess. Emotions on both sides divided the country. And newspapers begged the Prince and Princess to put their marriage out of its misery. Tory members of Parliament beseeched the Prime Minister to consult with the Queen about a divorce. "We've become an international laughingstock," said one conservative MP. "A spectacle."

Within hours of Diana's interview, Olympus had prepared a full-page ad to promote its new camera. The commercial showed a picture of the Princess perched demurely on her chair in Kensington Palace. The photograph was cropped at the neck. The caption: "Avoid getting your head chopped off by the in-laws this Christmas."

In the United States Omnipoint Communications wanted Diana to launch its new mobile telephone network. "My idea," said the company's president, "is that she will hold a digital phone and declare, 'If I'd had one of these, I could have been Queen.'"

In Norway a condom advertiser featured Diana's picture at the precise moment she confessed to adultery on television. The caption: "It's hard to see on the outside whether someone has had casual sex."

The Queen was ready to listen to her Prime Minister. He arrived for their weekly meeting armed with the support of former Prime Minister James Callaghan and the Archbishop of Canterbury. The Prime Minister told the Queen that the uncertainty surrounding the couple's marriage had interfered with the country's business. Britain was losing face, and the monarchy was diminished. "I am only Your Majesty's adviser," John Major said respectfully. Then he recommended that the Queen step into the ring to stop the brawling.

On December 17, 1995, the Queen wrote to Charles and Diana, suggesting that for the sake of their children they resolve their differences "amicably and with civility." She asked them to agree to a divorce and to let her know their decision as soon as possible. She said she looked forward to the family's annual gathering during the Christmas holidays and assured them both of her personal affection and her continuing support in difficult times. She sent the letters by messenger and, two days later, authorized the Palace to confirm their delivery.

Diana was shocked by the Queen's public disclosure, which she felt was pushing her into a divorce she did not want. She called her lawyers, who advised her against making an immediate decision. They needed time to negotiate. She angrily canceled plans to join the royal family for Christmas.

Charles responded promptly to his mother's letter and agreed to a divorce, but only on condition that Diana agree, because he did not want a contest. He also declared he would not remarry.

The same day as the Queen's letter arrived, Diana received a letter from lawyers representing Tiggy Legge-Bourke, the young assistant who planned outings and activities for Wills and Harry. Tiggy sought a retraction of Diana's "false allegations" about her, plus acknowledgment that what Diana had said days earlier during a staff Christmas party was "totally untrue." The Princess had arrived at the Lanesborough Hotel for the annual holiday luncheon for the Waleses' employees. Instead of ignoring Tiggy, who was standing near the entrance, Diana walked over and confronted her.

"So sorry to hear about the baby," Diana said with a sneer.

The young woman was taken aback. Then she realized the taunt was based on gossip that she had become pregnant and had had an abortion. Crushed by Diana's accusation, Tiggy fled to a private room, where she was comforted by Prince Charles's valet. She returned to the party but confided her distress to Commander Aylard, who told the Prince of Wales. Charles counseled her to contact Peter Carter-Ruck, one of England's most widely known libel lawyers.

Two days after putting the Princess on notice, the lawyer sent letters to newspapers warning that the allegations were false. "Reports have reached her [Tiggy] and her family that a series of malicious lies are circulating in the press which are a gross reflection on our client's moral character. These allegations are utterly without the very slightest foundation."

With the full support of Prince Charles, Tiggy was prepared to sue Diana over her remark. But the Prince's friends cautioned him that the Princess would dig in her heels, even relishing the spectacle of the royal family in a courtroom fight. Charles agreed, and after lengthy talks with her lawyers, Tiggy decided not to sue.

Diana's oblique attack on Tiggy came within hours of being named Humanitarian of the Year. She attended the staff Christmas party upon her return from New York City, where she had received the prestigious United Cerebral Palsy award from former Secretary of State

Henry Kissinger. The seventy-two-year-old statesman seemed transfixed by the Princess in her low-cut gown and stared at her bosom like a high school boy. In his gushy introduction, he said Diana was a symbol to humanity of caring and compassion.

"She is here as a member of the royal family with which the USA has a long history of cooperation, friendship, and standing as allies," he said. "But we are honoring the Princess in her own right tonight, having aligned herself with the ill, the suffering, and the downtrodden."

Seven hundred people paid $1,000 each to attend the dinner and applauded Diana as she walked to the microphone, sparkling in diamonds. She spoke movingly of how her thoughts were with parents who were holding vigil at the bedsides of their desperately sick children, who might not live until the morning.

Then a woman called out from the audience: "Where are *your* children, Diana?"

"They're in school," replied the Princess, barely looking up. Then she resumed her speech. When she finished, the crowd stood up and cheered as if to drown out the rude interruption.

Afterward a reporter approached the middle-aged heckler and asked why she had yelled at the Princess of Wales, expressing surprise that someone would dare to yell at royalty. Without apology the woman replied: "I don't like being lectured on humanity."

TWENTY-TWO

A battle royal was brewing. For two months the Queen had been waiting for the Princess to respond to her letter. Her Majesty's private secretary had phoned Diana three times to nudge a response, but Diana kept stalling. Then Prince Charles wrote her. Finally she deigned to respond.

She called her husband and proposed a meeting with him: February 28, 1996, 4:30 P.M., in his office at St. James's Palace. She insisted they meet privately—no lawyers, no equerries, no secretaries. At the appointed hour, Charles and Diana were on the scene. His courtiers objected to the restrictions because they wanted to take notes, but Charles waved them off. As the last of his staff backed out the door, Diana sniped, "They'll probably bug the room anyway."

She later told Richard Kay of the *Daily Mail* that she had told Charles, "I loved you and I will always love you because you are the father of my children." But when Charles saw that statement in print he became angry. He told one of his aides that she had never uttered those words. What he clearly recalled—and said he would never forget—was his wife's threat months before. He quoted her as saying: "You will never be King. I shall destroy you."

When he read Diana's rendition of their private meeting as recounted in the *Mail,* he decided to get a gag order. He insisted a confidentiality clause be included in their divorce agreement to keep her from writing or speaking about their marriage. Diana accused him of extortion and demanded that he sign a similar pledge, but he resisted. He said his word of honor was enough.

During that meeting in his office, she had told him that if he made it clear to the world that he, *not* she, was requesting the divorce, she would agree to proceed with negotiations. She even offered to give up her royal status. Her title became a sticking point, but at first she said she didn't care about it. After the meeting she called the Queen to say she agreed to a divorce "with deep regrets." She told the Queen it was "the saddest day of my life."

Then her lawyers started haggling. They began by insisting on a lump sum payment of $75 million. His lawyers protested the amount and the method of payment: Charles wanted to pay less and in yearly installments rather than a lump sum. That way he could withhold money, in case Diana got out of line. But she refused. For her it was all or nothing. When he balked at paying her legal fees, which he said were "excessive," negotiations stalled. Her side reminded his side who wanted the divorce. She threatened to withdraw and force him to wait two more years to get a no-consent divorce decree. Then he would be able to get one automatically because their separation would have met the requisite five years. But, for the Queen, further delay was intolerable.

She intervened, and Charles paid his wife's legal bills—$120,000.

After five months of acrimony over almost every issue, the lawyers for both sides produced a document as intricate as a treaty between two warring nations. "The only element missing was a map delineating the deployment of troops," mused a man familiar with the agreement. "Everything else was covered—insignias, titles, possessions, even boundaries. [Diana was required to seek the Queen's permission to leave the country, unless on private holiday. With the Queen's permission, she could use the Queen's aircraft, but only if accompanied by her children.] Diana is entitled to keep all gifts of royal jewelry [the value of which is said to exceed $100 million] for her lifetime. She agrees not to lend or sell any jewels given to her by the royal family, including the thirty-carat sapphire brooch that was the Queen Mother's wedding present. Upon Diana's death, the jewelry passes to her son, William, for the future Princess of Wales. A codicil to her will nailing this down is attached to the divorce settlement."

The only area not disputed was the children: Charles and Diana agreed to share responsibility for raising their sons, including equal access and custody. Every other aspect of their contentious marriage was bartered down to the last square foot of office space Diana would be allocated. Charles agreed to pay her about $26 million, including her taxes, over a period of five years. In addition, he will pay $600,000 a year for her office staff, supplies, and equipment.* Diana retained use of her residence at Kensington Palace, until she chooses to move or remarry.

In the middle of the negotiations, Diana reconsidered her royal status. She said she wanted to keep her title "for the sake of the boys." Previously she had joked, "I don't need another title—I was born with one." But her friends emphasized that while Lady Diana might get a seat on the bus, Her Royal Highness the Princess of Wales could commandeer the bus, the driver, and all the curtsying passengers. They said the title of HRH gave her protection against being run over.

So important is the designation of royalty in a class-bound society that her friends don't want to see Diana curtsying to others. Nor do they want to see her lowered in public esteem like the disgraced Sarah Ferguson, who had been forced to give up her royal style upon divorce. Shorn of her HRH, the poor Duchess became a national punching bag. Frequently derided as greedy and moneygrubbing, she was roundly denounced after her divorce. A union flag raised to mark her thirty-seventh birthday was lowered after four hours when some union members objected; they said she did not deserve the honor. They placed a call to Buckingham Palace, which said the only official day that should be marked

---

* In 1997, Britain's annual survey of the 1,000 wealthiest people listed Diana as 916th with a personal fortune of $98 million.

was the Queen's birthday. "After all we've heard about Fergie's love life," said one union member, "they'd be better off flying a pair of knickers from the flagpole."

When the Duchess signed a $2.2 million book contract, one newspaper placed the story alongside a cartoon showing two men walking in the park. One man, hanging his head in shame, said: "I lied. I cheated. I betrayed my spouse. My boss. My friends. And my Sovereign. I sullied my reputation....I'm the lowest of the low...." The other said, "Call Fergie's publisher."

When Sarah sent Princess Margaret an extravagant bouquet on her birthday, the Princess pitched the flowers. Then she fired off a letter to Fergie: "You have done more to bring shame on the family than ever could have been imagined. Not once have you hung your head in embarrassment even for a minute after those disgraceful photographs. Clearly you have never considered the damage you are causing us all. How dare you discredit us like this and how dare you send me those flowers."

After published disclosures from former lovers and former employees, Sarah locked herself in her home for days, weeping inconsolably. Newspapers reported the Queen became so concerned, she placed her under a suicide watch. But the Palace denied the story, implying the Queen couldn't care less what her former daughter-in-law did to herself. The Palace reaction seemed to signal tacit permission to pile on. Days later the *Sun* ran a poll asking, "Who would you rather date—Fergie or a goat?" The goat won by a ratio of seven to one.*

Seeing what happened to Fergie when she lost her title, Diana objected to relinquishing hers. When Charles's lawyers suggested that she trade in HRH the Princess of Wales for the Duchess of Cornwall, she balked. Then they proposed that she be styled HFRH (Her Former Royal Highness). Diana turned to her supporters in the media, who debated the offer, pleading with the Queen to retain Diana's status and keep her within the royal family. They argued that as the mother of the future King she deserved no less. Historian John Grigg wrote, "The *reductio ad absurdum* is that, if she were to cease to be HRH, she would be obliged to curtsy to Princess Michael of Kent." And to her own sons.

Charles maintained that he did not care one way or the other about his wife's royal status. But he let it be known that his parents cared, particularly his father, who said that Diana was not entitled to be treated as royalty. In Philip's eyes she had betrayed the Firm, and her indiscretion and disloyalty barred her from any consideration other than bare civility. He was riled by her demand

---

* Ridiculed in Britain, Fergie came to the U.S., where she was treated like royalty. Her memoir, *My Story*, became a best-seller, earning her more than $3.7 million. She was paid $1.2 million to appear in a commercial for Ocean Spray Cranapple Juice and another $1 million to represent Weight Watchers International. Weeks after her lucrative American promotions, she amazed the Queen's bankers by paying off her debts of $6.2 million. "I love Americans," she said. "They give a girl a break."

that any future children she might have by another man be given an hereditary title. And she pushed too far when she proposed that Clarence House become her official residence upon the death of the Queen Mother. Philip insisted her title be lifted, and the Queen agreed.

"At the end of the day, it became clear," said one of Diana's representatives, "that the lamb was going to be fleeced." So Diana was advised to yield what was about to be snatched. Her lawyers tried to save face for her by negotiating a title that sounded like the one she had enjoyed during her fifteen-year marriage. They settled on Diana, Princess of Wales. They also inserted a clause into the final agreement that she would be "considered on occasion a member of the royal family." One skeptic familiar with the legal document realistically assessed such an "occasion" as "when corgis fly."

Diana said she stopped fighting for her title after talking to her fourteen-year-old son. She asked Wills if he would mind her not being called Her Royal Highness. "I don't mind what you're called," said the young Prince. "You're Mummy."

Yet by the standards of her world, she had been shorn of what had made her most valuable. Stripped of HRH, she lost her prized standing in society. As Diana, Princess of Wales, she was socially inferior to her own children. No longer royal, she resigned her patronage of more than one hundred charities and gave up her military regiments. Her friends worried about how she would survive such a blow. "I fear for her," wrote historian Paul Johnson, one of her staunchest defenders. "One society matron said to me yesterday: 'If I was publicly cast off like that, I really think I'd be tempted to do away with myself.'"

To the outside world, the thirty-five-year-old Princess still radiated royalty. Her sparkling beauty made her as lyrical as the "glimmering girl" of Yeats's poem who inspired the wandering aengus to pluck the "silver apples of the moon." But within her own world she was no longer a contender: "DI KO'd in Palace Rigged Title Fight" was one newspaper appraisal. Even anti-royalists, who sneered at social precedence, recognized that she had been flattened. "Throne for a loss," as one man put it. "She has lost something," wrote Stephen Glover in the *Daily Telegraph,* "which, according to the standards by which she lives, was infinitely precious."

The loss showed itself within days. Her once respectful press corps turned snippy. Photographers still showed up in full force to cover her because she remained the most famous woman in the world. But they started acting like hooligans, shouting in a way they would never have dared to do before. When she was royal they groveled: "Please, ma'am, one more shot." When she was no longer royal they were less respectful. One photographer, urging her to smile in his direction, hollered, "Hey, Di, cheat it to the left a little, will ya?" Unflattering photos began popping up: one caught her getting out of a car with mussed hair; another showed her skirt hiked up to her hips. Once adoring, some photographers acted as if she had personally offended them by losing her royal status. In retaliation they subjected her to the same harsh lens they aimed at pop divas and rock stars. Without the protection of her royal nimbus, Diana had been reduced to celebrity camera fodder like Mick, Michael, and Madonna.

Another indignity was inflicted on her while she was shopping in Harvey Nichols, her favorite London department store. A security guard directed a surveillance camera at her bosom and gathered footage of her cleavage. The guard was arrested for theft and taken into court, where the tape was produced. He was accused of video rape, but his female lawyer blamed Diana: "If a member of the public, whether royal or not, is willing to go into public showing a low cleavage, it ill behooves anyone to criticize the taking of a picture."

Weeks later a London tabloid published grainy photographs from a staged video that purported to be Diana in her bra doing a striptease for her former lover, James Hewitt, before jumping on top of him for a horsey-back ride. The photographs were published around the world. But the video was a hoax, and the newspaper apologized on page one. "We were conned by cunning fraudsters," said the editor, "and are sorry for any hurt or offense caused." What went unsaid was that Diana's previous behavior had been such that editors—and readers—were prepared to accept the trick as truth.

The royal divorce became final on August 28, 1996, and the *Sun* headlined the news triumphantly: "Bye Bye Big Ears." Even Mother Teresa was pleased. "I know I should preach for family love and unity," the eighty-five-year-old nun told a reporter in India, "but nobody was happy anyhow." Britain's Prime Minister acted swiftly to reassure the country that Charles had no "immediate" plans to marry again. Then he briefed the Queen, warning her that remarriage, especially to Camilla Parker Bowles, would be disastrous for the monarchy. Neither the Prime Minister nor the Queen acknowledged the irony: the Church of England had been established precisely because of King Henry VIII's desire to divorce one wife and marry another.

Charles had a talent for shooting himself in the foot. He let the press know that he had sent a letter to forty stores where Diana regularly shopped: "With effect from 2 September 1996, any expenditure incurred by or on behalf of Her Royal Highness the Princess of Wales, on or after that date should be invoiced directly to the Princess of Wales's Office, Apartment 7, Kensington Palace, London." Then he announced that he planned "to celebrate" his divorce at Highgrove—with a Champagne party.

The country's sentiment was best expressed

by the cartoonist who showed a huckster out-side Buckingham Palace hawking royal play-ing cards. Chomping a cigar, the hustler pushed a deck of cards on a hapless young man who looked perplexed. "It's just like an ordi-nary pack, son, without the Queen of Hearts."

The monarchy had lost its brightest star, but the Queen was determined that the show go on without her. She instructed the souvenir shops of Balmoral, Windsor Castle, and Buckingham Palace to remove all memorabilia with Diana's likeness—ashtrays, mugs, postcards. She also struck the Princess's name from the official prayers said for the royal family in Parliament. The move appeared "comically vindictive" to Tory MP Jerry Hayes. "To most people," he said, "it looks like they are trying to airbrush the Princess from the establishment in a Stalinist manner."

The *Sunday Mail* agreed. "Diana should still be in our prayers," stated an editorial that chastised Parliament for its "mean and venge-ful" decision. "They should recall that for-giveness is the first Christian virtue."

The final humiliation came when the Queen ordered the *London Gazette* to publish the Letters Patent: this was Her Majesty's official notice to her government, her embassies, and her diplomatic missions that both her for-mer daughters-in-law were toast.

"It's Wallis all over again, isn't it?" said the Queen Mother, shaking her head. She had received an advance copy of the notice that deprived Sarah Ferguson and Diana Spencer of their royal status without ever mentioning them by name. The Queen Mother had supported the move to strip "the troublesome girls" of their titles and was as complicit in the purge as she had been in depriving the Duchess of Windsor of her royal status. Now as then, the courtiers were as slick as seals. They dismissed the dry announcement as a routine matter of protocol: to inform people of the correct form of social address. But most everyone else saw the announcement as tactless and vengeful. They saw the monarch once again using the Letters Patent as a broom.

"First, you cauterize," said one of the Queen's advisers, "and then you heal." The scholarly adviser had written to the Queen, quoting the wisdom of England's sixteenth-century philosopher Francis Bacon, who said, "[He] that will not apply new remedies must expect new evils, for time is the greatest innovator."

But the seventy-year-old Queen did not feel she needed the advice. After forty-five years on the throne, she had developed her own endgame. Without a shrewd Prime Minister such as Queen Victoria had in Disraeli, Elizabeth relied on her courtiers. They believed, as she did, that she was anointed by God. With her position divinely ordained, she did not feel a need to respond to the whims of public opinion like a politician. She viewed the monarchy as a sacred destiny, not a popularity contest.

But when her authority was challenged, she showed that she understood the past was prologue. Her grandfather had built the House of Windsor on an act of expediency, which enabled the monarchy to survive during the First World War. By camouflaging his German ancestry and reinventing himself as English, King George V had appeased his Hun-hating subjects. "He knew and understood his people, and the age in which they lived," said C. R. Attlee, MP, "and progressed with them." The Bavarian nobleman Count Albrecht von Montgelas saw it differently. "The true royal tradition died on that day in 1917, when for a mere war, King George V changed his name."

The Queen understood the price her grandfather had paid to save the monarchy, and she intended to protect his investment. She made her initial concession to survival when she became the first British monarch of the twentieth century to pay taxes. Then she removed most of her family from the Civil List. When her subjects would not pay to finance the restoration of Windsor Castle, she opened Buckingham Palace to the public and charged admission. She even made a gesture toward the largest religious denomination in her country by visiting a Roman Catholic church. This was the first time in four hundred years that a reigning British monarch had done so. By 1996 the Church of England represented only 2 percent of the population, while Roman Catholics represented 43 percent of churchgoing Britons.

Despite the Queen's concessions, the monarchy looked vulnerable as it tottered toward the year 2000. Viewed as a golden coach, the institution that represented Britain to the world was tarnished and absurdly grandiose. The chassis wobbled and the wheels creaked. Shorn of its majesty, it barely limped along.

The Queen knew there would be a resurgence of fervor when the Queen Mother died. But she recognized the ardor would fade soon after the period of national mourning. As pragmatic as she was, she did not want to examine the elaborate plans for her mother's funeral.

"I don't need to address this now, do I?" she said, pushing aside the folder that contained the memorandum code-named Operation Lion. Its five pages outlined the procedures to be followed by the media after the Queen Mother's death. The Queen had determined that her mother would be accorded the grandest funeral since Winston Churchill's. She would lie in state for three days before being eulogized in Westminster Abbey. As a mark of respect, the broadcast networks had planned to suspend commercials. Their coverage of the funeral was to be solemn and stirring, featuring documentaries of the royal family during World War II. Historical footage would show King George VI and Queen Elizabeth waving from the balcony of Buckingham Palace with the two little Princesses—"Us Four," as the King had called them.

The services were designed to remind Britain of its glorious past when the country withstood Nazi bombs and the monarchy responded admirably. With full military honors, Her

Queen Elizabeth the Queen Mother would be laid to rest with the extravagant title she had styled for herself after her husband died.

Ordinarily unsentimental, the Queen resisted dealing with the harsh reality of her mother's eventual death, even after the Queen Mother reached her nineties. "My worst fear," the Queen told a friend, "is that Mummy will die, and then Margaret and I'll be left alone."

Her subjects' worst fear was that the Queen might die and leave them alone with Charles. Resistance to her heir had grown increasingly vocal since his divorce. Polls showed that he did not have the support of his prospective subjects. Most said they did not want him to become King, and the Members of Parliament who represented them did not want to sacrifice their offices for an unpopular heir.

"Charles is unfit to be King," declared the Labor MP Ron Davies on television. "He's an adulterer who does not practice the precepts of the church....He spends time talking to trees, flowers, and vegetables and...he encourages his young sons to go out into the countryside to kill wild animals and birds just for fun...."

The leader of the Labor Party, Tony Blair, who became Prime Minister in 1997 demanded the MP retract his remarks. So the MP reluctantly apologized for calling the future King a fornicating environmentalist who hugged trees and indulged in blood sports. Throughout his campaign, Blair had reiterated his party's support for continuing the monarchy. He could not afford to jeopardize his lead by threatening the country's natural conservatism with radical proposals. But his party, once firmly monarchist, was no longer unified. And a few rogue MPs, refusing to be silent, suggested eliminating the monarchy by an act of Parliament.

"The view that Charles is not fit to be King is shared by three-quarters of the people in the country," said Paul Flynn, a left-wing MP. "Forget the sycophantic drivel that the royals are somehow superior beings who have stepped out of a fairy tale. That has gone forever."

It looked as though the buzzards were circling the monarchy. Calling it an anachronism, another Labor MP demanded a referendum at the end of the Queen's reign on whether Britain should continue to have a hereditary head of state. The Press Association conducted a straw vote of the Labor Party and reported a majority favored an open debate on the future of the monarchy.

"I was threatened with assassination when I made that suggestion twenty years ago," said former Labor MP Willie Hamilton, reflecting on the dramatic change in attitude. "I was called a crank and a communist. It was easier to criticize God in this country than to criticize the monarchy. But no more."

"At such a turning point," asked the *Guardian* newspaper in 1996, "is it not also time seriously to consider the mechanisms for constructing the British Republic?"

The question seemed preposterous to those who judged the royal family by its entertainment value. "The American answer is simple," said a *New York Times* editorial, recommending that Britain retain its monarchy. "Of course they should keep it—for our amusement."

There were no more seasoned actors than the British royal family. Like an old vaudeville troupe, they filed on stage to go through their practiced routines. Looking like rouged curiosities, they performed at weddings and funerals. In costume, they still drew a few regular spectators, but they lost their biggest crowds with the departure of their ingenue Princess. They knew that they were viewed best from afar; up close, their imperfections showed.

They had learned the hard way, and perhaps too late, the wisdom of the eighteenth-century revolutionary Thomas Paine. "Monarchy is something kept behind a curtain," he wrote, "about which there is a great deal of bustle and fuss, and a wonderful air of seeming solemnity. But when, by any accident, the curtain happens to be open, and the company see what is is, they burst into laughter."

The colorful cast was ridiculed when Fergie starred as its vixen. But when she bowed out, she had left behind a prince who finally became charming. Through his failed marriage Andrew had learned to behave with dignity in the face of disgrace. No matter what his former wife did to humiliate him and provoke criticism, he remained blessedly silent, discreet, and steadfast.

His father continued playing his role of leading man, although he had faded slightly as a matinee idol. His handsomeness had disappeared beneath age spots, which emphasized his sharp features under taut skin and made him look like a hawk. Still, at the age of seventy-five, he managed to stir a few hearts when he marched alongside the elderly veterans of World War II. Instead of standing with the royal family during a Remembrance Day ceremony, Philip stood with his shipmates. His noble gesture brought tears to the eyes of many who remembered the dashing naval officer, kneeling before a young queen at her coronation and promising to be her liegeman for life. After fifty years of marriage (give or take a few mistresses), he was still at her side with his elbow crooked, ready to receive her hand.

Because of his constancy to the Queen, most people tried to overlook his gaffes. But it was difficult, especially when his boorish remarks caused international incidents. In France he infuriated half his wife's subjects by saying, "British women can't cook." During a trip to Holland he observed crossly, "The Dutch are so po'faced." In Canada he snapped at officials, "We don't come here for our health." In Egypt he complained about Cairo's traffic. "The trouble with you Egyptians is that you breed too much," he said. In Peru he was presented with a history of the town of Lima, which he thrust into the hands of an aide, saying: "Here, take this. I'll never read it." In Scotland he asked a driving instructor, "How do you keep the natives off the booze long enough to get them to pass the test?" In Hungary he spotted a British tourist in Budapest. "You can't have been here long," he observed. "You haven't got a pot belly." He warned British students in China, "If you stay here much longer, you'll get slitty eyes."

An avid hunter, Philip publicly criticized England's proposed legislation to crack down on handguns. During a discussion of the massacre of sixteen schoolchildren in Dunblane, Scotland, the Duke said guns were no more dangerous than cricket bats. Parents of the slain children were shocked by the comment, and the Queen's husband was taken to task by the nation's press. "Wrong again, Prince Philip," was the headline of the *Manchester Evening News* editorial that criticized him "for shooting his mouth off without regard to the feelings of others." The next day the Palace issued an apology.

But the Queen appeared unruffled by her husband's diplomatic pratfalls. She tolerated his curmudgeonly manner and made no excuses for his off-the-cuff humor. Charles was the one who cringed. He worried most about the family's declining popularity, and he accused the press of making them look like lumpen royalty. He urged his parents to address the future—his future—and consider ways the monarchy could prepare for the twenty-first century.

From the shadows of Balmoral, he let it

be known that the royal family was looking ahead. He indicated that he and his parents, his brothers, his sister, and his advisers were meeting twice a year. Their committee was called the Way Ahead Group, and their goal was to renovate the dilapidated House of Windsor. Under discussion were ideas that would radically reform the Crown. The most immediate was the family's intention to get off the public payroll. They agreed to end the annual Civil List payments (approximately $14 million from taxpayers) and suggested restoring to the Crown payments from the Crown Estates. These consist of three hundred thousand acres of prime London real estate, whose rents and revenues produce more than $100 million a year. They were surrendered to Parliament by King George III in 1760.

"Devilishly cunning," said a government minister who showed the respect of a pickpocket for a bank robber. He figured the arithmetic (more than $100 million) as a break for the public and a boon for the royal family. "This would spare taxpayers while manifoldly enriching the monarchy; at the same time, it removes the Crown from public scrutiny, which legitimately keeps the press at bay....How can the media justify invading their privacy when they are no longer supported by public dollars? Doubtful it would pass Parliament, but the proposal is admirable in its audacity."

Equally creative was the royal family's proposal to end the eleventh-century rule of primogeniture and allow women equal rights to succeed to the throne. They also committed themselves to downsizing: no more HRH aunts, uncles, or cousins. Upon the deaths of certain members of the royal family, the Firm would consist solely of the monarch, the consort, their children, and those grandchildren who are direct heirs to the throne.

The vote around the table at Balmoral was unanimous: Ditch the minor royals like HRH Prince Michael of Kent and his wife. The Kents had contributed their share of bad publicity to the royal family. She had been caught leaving her American lover's house disguised in a wig and sunglasses. He had cashed in on being the Queen's cousin; he appeared on television to hawk the House of Windsor Collection, a mail-order catalog selling ersatz royal trinkets. Within months the marketing scheme became a financial disaster, which caused further embarrassment. "We've got Ali Baba," joked one member of the royal family. "We don't need the Forty Thieves."

Charles recognized that an act of Parliament could deprive him of the throne, especially after he said that he did not want to be Defender of the Faith. Under the Bill of Rights and the Act of Settlement, the sovereign must swear to uphold the established Church of England and Church of Scotland. Charles was not in communion with either church. So the Way Ahead Group proposed separating the monarchy from the strictures of religion and dissolving the bonds of church and state.

As sovereign, Charles would have to commit himself to uphold the Protestant succession, which also troubled him. He did not understand why Roman Catholics had to be specifically excluded from succeeding to the throne. He said the rule, which also precluded a sovereign from marrying a Roman Catholic, was inherently unfair and discriminated against the 10 percent of Britain's 60 million people who were Roman Catholic. So he proposed eliminating the 295-year-old ban.

The heir was determined to acquire the throne. Although he had disappointed his future subjects by discarding a young wife and taking up with a weatherbeaten mistress, he would not step aside. Despite growing objections, he soldiered on. "I have dedicated myself to putting the great back into Britain," he said, "and that's what I intend to do." Yet even those who recalled the empire of Great Britain did not think he would become King.

Throughout the country people continued to stand for the loyal toast at formal black-tie dinners. They raised their glasses to salute the sovereign: "To the Queen," they would say in unison before sitting down. Even respectful republicans stood for the tribute. "No one is recommending a revolution," said Professor Stephen Haseler, chairman of Britain's Republican Society. "For most of us heading into the twenty-first century, the sentiment is: 'God save the Queen,' and then, 'Save us from her heirs.'"

To the professor, the monarchy looked as

if it were ready to be walked to the wall for one last cigarette. He predicted dissension throughout the land if the Prince of Wales ascended to the throne. "King Charles III will split the nation down the middle," he said. "The only solution, short of anarchy, which no one advocates, is an act of Parliament, agreed to by the Queen, that upon her death or abdication, the monarchy would end and a new head of state would be elected."

The republicans were asking the Queen to dissolve her dynasty. The royalists were spluttering. They warned that abandoning the monarchy would traumatize the country and cause great upheaval. They said it would require restructuring the entire system of government and creating a written constitution. And they predicted that the class system would disappear and the House of Lords would collapse. The republicans agreed and approved. They argued that the structural moves were necessary to revitalize the country. The national debate had begun, and words once considered treasonous were uttered without rebuke.

Crowded between republicans and royalists, though, was the majority. They wanted to retain the monarchy but bypass the future monarch. "It's as simple as ABC—Anybody But Charles," said one MP, recommending that the Queen move to make Princess Anne the next monarch. Polls showed great support for the idea. Others suggested skipping Charles and going directly to his older son, as Diana had proposed.

"The best hope is to jump a generation and appoint Prince William as the Queen's successor," wrote Paul Johnson in the *Spectator*. "That solution would eliminate the foolish and unpopular Charles and might prove a winner with the public."

Americans agreed. For their youth-crazed, celebrity-driven culture, the solution was ideal. *People* magazine described the young prince as "a looker just like his mom." *Time* put him on the cover and asked: "Can This Boy Save the Monarchy?" British commentator Julie Burchill expressed doubts. "I hope for the best for Wills," she said, "but I would be very surprised if he turns out to be normal, because that's the maddest family since the Munsters....We wouldn't be shocked if he turned out to be a cross-dresser who wanted to marry a corgi...."

Bookmakers began taking bets on whether the monarchy would survive into the next century. The odds soared to one hundred to one in 1994 but tumbled the next year to five to one. Assessing the imponderables in 1996, one London bookmaker from the William Hill firm predicted: "The smart money says Her Majesty steps aside at the age of seventy-five and turns the crown over to Charles. Right now, that's the only way she can ensure her heir succeeds her to the throne. Within the next five years, she works out a deal with the Prime Minister. Whether the government is Tory or Labor makes no difference because both parties have committed to supporting the monarchy. If the Queen makes the request, she won't be refused."

The "if" is operative. Some bookmakers are hedging their bets because they question the maternal instincts of the dutiful monarch. At best they see her as an inattentive parent, who is no longer inclined to give up her crown for her middle-aged son. "She is dedicated to her duty," said one London bookmaker. "She has described her job as a job for life. She'll never abdicate. Based on that, I'd give long odds on the Queen stepping aside before she goes to the angels."

Few criticize the Queen as a monarch. It's the mother who has failed. She has produced three children who are divorced and one who is still floundering. That's a sorry score for people whose only job in life is to live happily ever after. They are not evil, just venal. But being hapless and unheroic, they rubbed the luster off the House of Windsor and left it looking shopworn.

Many years ago, Farouk, the last King of Egypt, had predicted that most monarchies would disappear by the turn of the century. "By then there will be only five kings left in the world," he said. "The king of hearts, clubs, diamonds, spades—*and* the King of England." He, too, had been beguiled by the mystique of the British monarchy.

"In its mystery is its life," wrote historian Walter Bagehot more than a hundred years ago. "We must not let daylight in upon magic."

Since then the magic has been harshly

exposed. Yet the weight of history favors survival of an institution that continues to reinvigorate itself. Even as Britain reassesses its monarchy, the monarchy retains its genius for adaptability and compromise, almost defying destruction. Rooted mystically in religion and patriotism, it cannot be removed without leaving a gaping hole in the psyche of the country. As durable as the White Cliffs of Dover, the institution has existed for 1,200 years among people who have cherished pageantry and treasured mythology. The magic is not completely understood, even by devoted monarchists, who acknowledge that not all kings and queens have been good and noble and wise. But they have survived because their subjects had a need to believe in them. That yearning to look up to someone or something grand, even grandiose, still exists. Although the godlike luster has eroded and the institution has been diminished, even disgraced, the need for enchantment endures and the hope for renewal remains.

A Special Postscript

The House of Windsor went dark shortly after midnight on August 31, 1997, when Diana, the thirty-six-year-old Princess of Wales, died. Chased by paparazzi on motorcycles in Paris, she was killed when the limousine in which she was riding crashed into a concrete wall in a tunnel. The chauffeur, who died instantly, had been drunk, and speeding. French police said that the speedometer was stuck at 121 miles an hour. Diana's companion, Dodi Fayed, was killed on impact. The only survivor was the bodyguard, riding in the front seat.

The BBC announcement of the princess's dreadful death punched a hole in people's hearts. The British flag was lowered to half-staff and the national anthem, "God Save the Queen," was played in honor of her memory, although that tribute had been taken away from her only months earlier. "I feel as if the brightest star has been yanked from the sky," said a woman hearing the news, "and plunged us all into an awful darkness."

Fighting back tears, Britain's Prime Minister Tony Blair tried to comfort a nation convulsed in grief. "She was the people's princess," he said, "and that's how she will stay, how she will remain, in our hearts and in our memories forever."

Sobbing in the streets, people gathered to

remember Diana. In London, they prayed in churches, stood outside her gym, left flowers in front of her favorite restaurants. They thronged the grounds of Kensington Palace where she lived, heaping bouquets in front of the wrought-iron gates. "Born a lady, became a princess, died a saint," read one card. A hand-lettered sign said: "She now reigns as the Queen of broken hearts."

The President of the United States expressed his country's condolences, as did South Africa's President Nelson Mandela and Mother Teresa of Calcutta. In Washington, D.C., a capital without royalty, people treated the departed princess like a queen. Hundreds gathered outside the British Embassy to pay their last respects, standing in line for hours to sign the condolence book. At the U.S. Open in New York City, the tennis star Andre Agassi wore a black ribbon on his shoulder. And in Geneva, the International Red Cross lowered its flag to half-staff in memory of the princess whose last humanitarian mission had been to Bosnia to campaign against land mines.

Only weeks before, British opinion polls showed for the first time that a majority of the country no longer supported the royal family. Disappointment with the ill-behaved House of Windsor was widespread, especially among eighteen- to twenty-four-year-olds, who believed the country would be better off without them. "A hand full of gimme and a pocket full of much obliged," was one assessment.

Among the horde of mourners gathering in front of Buckingham Palace to pay homage to Diana, there was muted criticism of the royal family, who remained secluded in their castle at Balmoral.

"Just once," sobbed a woman kneeling in front of Buckingham Palace, "couldn't Her Majesty step down to comfort her subjects? It wouldn't impair her dignity....Just a word, a tear, some kind of gesture—just once—to show she cares." In those first days after the tragedy, the Queen was mum.

Obviously affected, Prince Charles flew to Paris with Diana's two sisters to bring her body home. He looked forlorn as he stood next to her coffin, which had been regally draped with the royal family's standard. An honor guard of the Royal Air Force hoisted the box and carried it into the chapel at St. James's Palace, the prince's private residence in London. Charles left immediately for Balmoral to be with his sons, William, fifteen, and Harry, twelve.

From his home in Capetown, South Africa, Diana's brother, the Earl Spencer, read an impassioned statement accusing the press of killing his sister. He said editors who fed off her image were bounty hunters with blood on their hands.

"I always believed that the press would kill her in the end," he said, "but not even I could imagine that they would take such a direct hand in the death, as seems to be the case."

No public reaction came from Diana's

mother, sixty-one-year-old Frances Shand Kydd, who lives alone in Scotland. Sadly, she and Diana had not been speaking. Their fragile relationship had fallen apart weeks before, when Mrs. Shand Kydd gave an interview to *Hello!* magazine. Diana complained bitterly to a friend that she felt betrayed. Her mother had talked to the magazine about Diana's childhood, her eating disorders, and her relationship with Prince Charles. Although she criticized both the Prince and Princess of Wales for their television confessionals, she would not take her daughter's side in the breakup of her marriage. Nor would she speak out against the Prince of Wales. She seemed oddly pleased that her daughter had been stripped of her royal title in the divorce, saying that liberation from the exalted status was "absolutely wonderful."

Diana expressed "complete shock" to the reporter Richard Kay about the private details revealed by her mother. And Diana said she was "bitterly disappointed and let down" by the magazine, which had not given her advance notice about the article. She felt she had a special relationship with the publication since 1994 after it bought—but never published—topless photos of her in Spain. Even so, she banned *Hello!* photographers from covering her next charity appearance. The *Daily Mail* reported her reaction on May 28, 1997. The front-page headline: "DIANA FURY AT MOTHER'S STORY."

A black man mourning her death recalled

the episode as he stood in front of Kensington Palace. "She was let down by everyone around her," he said. "Her husband, her lovers, her family—her real family and the royal family....I think we were the only ones—commoners like me—who truly valued her because she valued us." From a deck of playing cards, he had plucked out the queen of hearts and placed it on top of the carpet of flowers.

A young woman in a T-shirt and jeans approached in tears and left her offering: a picture of the princess in a tiara pasted above a few lines of poetry by W.H. Auden:

> I thought that love would last for ever: I
>   was wrong. [She] was my North, my
>   South, my East and West,
> My working week and my Sunday rest,
> My noon, my midnight, my talk, my song;
> I thought that love would last for ever: I
>   was wrong.
> The stars are not wanted now: put out
>   every one;
> Pack up the moon and dismantle the sun;
> Pour away the ocean and sweep up the
>   wood;
> For nothing now can ever come to any
>   good.

In between the flowers and stuffed animals was a smashed camera with a card that read: "This is the murder weapon that killed our beloved princess."

Some people had taken comfort from Diana's

relationship with the new man in her life, Emad Mohamed al-Fayed, known to friends as Dodi. She had been enjoying the last night of her fourth vacation with him in five weeks when both of them were killed in a true tragedy.

When their romance became public, the multimillionaire son of Mohamed al-Fayed, who owns Harrods department store in London and the Ritz Hotel in Paris, had his picture splashed all over newspapers. He was described by the *News of the World,* Britain's largest-circulation weekly, as a forty-one-year-old playboy, "unfit" to marry into Britain's aristocracy. "He excels at giving lavish parties, smoking expensive cigars and dating beautiful women," said the paper. "He is an unsuitable choice to become the stepfather of the future king of England." Noting the dismissive tone of the British press toward Diana's new suitor, *The New York Times* described Dodi as "a young, wealthy outsider in Britain's class-obsessed society."

His romance with Diana had started in July 1997, when his father had invited the princess and her two sons to spend time with his family at their villa on the French Riviera. The British press criticized her for accepting the invitation of a man who had been denied citizenship by the British government. Although al-Fayed, an Arab born in Egypt, admitted bribing Members of Parliament, he said the reason he was not accepted by the British was racial discrimination.

"Mr. Fayed is not the sort of person in whose debt a public figure such as the princess should knowingly place herself and her sons," pronounced the *Daily Telegraph*. The next day photographs of Diana with her arm around Mohamed al-Fayed aboard his yacht were spread across the pages of several newspapers. She was smiling happily, if not defiantly.

During that trip, she had approached the British reporters who dogged her to St. Tropez. She asked them for some privacy and then warned that they should prepare themselves for startling news. "You'll see," she said. "You are going to get a big surprise with the next thing I do....

"My boys are urging me to leave the country [England]. They say it is the only way. Maybe that's what I should do. They want me to live abroad. I sit in London all the time and I am abused and followed wherever I go. Now I am being forced to move from here. William is stressed. William gets really freaked out. I was hoping to keep this visit all covered up and quiet."

When the next day's newspapers reported that the princess planned to leave Britain, she disavowed her statement to the reporters. Despite their intrusion, she later told Michael Cole, the spokesman for Harrods, that she and her children had had an idyllic vacation. "I've never had such a wonderful time," he quoted her as saying. She told Richard Kay of the *Daily Mail* that she intended to bow out of public life to pursue her personal life. "She would then be able to live as she always wanted to live," he wrote, "not as an icon—how she hated to be called one—but as a private person."

Pictures of Dodi and Diana dominated the world's tabloids, and the grainy photograph of them kissing, captured by a telephoto lens, reportedly fetched $5 million. The *Sunday Mirror* told its readers that the couple had found soul mates in each other: "They are both outsiders who have clashed with the British establishment."

At the end of August, after a day cruising off Sardinia on his father's yacht, the couple flew to Paris on his father's plane to have dinner at the Ritz, his father's hotel. The next day, Diana was scheduled to fly to London to spend time with her boys before they returned to school. They had been vacationing with their father and the rest of the royal family at Balmoral. But she did not live to see her children again.

Days later, on Saturday, September 6, the young princes, William and Harry, were to stand with their father in Westminster Abbey to say good-bye to their mother. Diana was not to be accorded a grand state funeral, with gun carriages and muffled drums, although it was within the Queen's authority to give her such a tribute. Instead, the palace promised a farewell that would be "a unique ritual for a unique person." Two thousand people received personal invitations to be inside the abbey where English sovereigns have been crowned and buried for one thousand years.

Later, the princess was to be privately interred on the Spencer family's estate in the village of Brington. The mourners invited inside Westminster Abbey represented every facet of Diana's short bright life from royalty to reality. But outside, the hundreds of thousands of commoners who gathered seemed to represent a greater tribute to the young woman who gave more to the idea of royalty than she ever received in return.

In her death, Diana breathed life into the moribund British monarchy. Her inexplicable magic seemed to wrap itself around her son William like a giant halo. Hearts soared as the young man, who looked so much like his mother, was seen walking into church with his head bowed on the day she died. Touched by his sadness, people recalled her desire to see him become king. Nothing seemed more important on this day than to make that dream come true for the beautiful princess who had bestowed so much kindness on her country's dispossessed. For, as Shakespeare said, "Beauty lives with kindness."

More than any other member of the royal family, Diana had understood what it meant to be a princess in the twentieth century. She had reached out to those who needed help most. What she always extended to the poor and the sick was a golden hand—without the white gloves of royalty. Despite her position of privilege, she was never aloof. She shared her vulnerabilities and, in doing so, she gave people a measure of hope for their own lives.

She let people bask in her resilience so that they might believe that they, too, could rise above rejection, survive misfortune, and triumph over unhappiness. She did not dash dreams but, rather, she did what royalty was supposed to do. Her mere presence made people feel better about themselves. She brought light into every room she entered, which is why people around the world suddenly felt so desolate when she was gone. They realized that they had lost someone who was truly irreplaceable.

Kitty Kelley
September 1997

BIBLIOGRAPHY

Allison, Ronald, and Sarah Riddell, eds.: *The Royal Encyclopedia*, 1991.

Alexandra, Queen of Yugoslavia: *Prince Philip*, 1959.

Barker, Malcom: *Living with the Queen*, 1991.

Barr, Ann, and Peter York: *The Official Sloane Ranger Handbook*, 1982.

Barratt, John, with Jean Ritchie: *With the Greatest Respect: The Private Lives of Earl Mountbatten and Prince and Princess Michael of Kent*, 1991.

Barry, Stephen: *Royal Service*, 1983.

———: *Royal Secrets*, 1985.

Benson, Ross: *Charles: The Untold Story*, 1993.

Berry, Wendy: *The Housekeeper's Diary*, 1995.

Betjeman, John: *Collected Poems*, 1988.

Birmingham, Stephen: *Duchess: The Story of Wallis Windsor*, 1981.

Blackwood, Caroline: *The Last of the Duchess*, 1995.

Bloch, Michael: *The Secret File of the Duke of Windsor: The Private Papers 1937-1972*, 1988.

Blundell, Nigel, and Susan Blackhall: *Fall of the House of Windsor*, 1992.

Bocca, Geoffrey: *Elizabeth and Philip*, 1953.

———: *The Woman Who Would Be Queen*, 1954.

Boothroyd, Basil: *Philip: An Informal Biography*, 1971.

Boston, Ray: *The Essential Fleet Street*, 1990.

———: *Chronicle of the Royal Family*, 1991.

Boyle, Andrew: *The Climate of Treason*, 1979.

Bradford, Sarah: *Elizabeth*, 1996.

———: *The Reluctant King: The Life and Reign of George VI*, 1989.

Brendon, Piers: *Our Own Dear Queen*, 1986.

Brough, James: *Margaret, The Tragic Princess*, 1978.

Brown, Michele: *Prince Charles*, 1980.

Brown, Craig, and Lesley Cunliffe: *The Book of Royal Lists*, 1982.

Bryan, J. III, and Charles Murphy: *The Windsor Story*, 1979.

Buskin, Richard: *Princess Diana: The Real Story*, 1992.

Butler, David: *Edward the Seventh, Prince of Hearts*, 1975.

Campbell, Lady Colin: *Royal Marriages*, 1993.

———: *Diana in Private*, 1992.

Cannadine, David: *The Decline and Fall of the British Aristocracy*, 1990.

———: *Aspects of Aristocracy*, 1994.

Cannon, John, and Ralph Griffiths: *The Oxford Illustrated History of the British Monarchy*, 1988.

Cathcart, Helen: *The Queen Mother*, 1965.

Chester, Lewis, Magnus Linblater, and David May: *Jeremy Thorpe: A Secret Life*, 1979.

Clark, Alan: *Mrs. Thatcher's Minister: The Private Diaries of Alan Clark*, 1993.

Cooke, Alistair: *Six Men*, 1977.

Coolican, Don, and Serge Lemoine: *Charles, Royal Adventurer*, 1978.

Cordet, Helene: *Born Bewildered*, 1961.

Costello, John: *Mask of Treachery*, 1988.

Counihan, Daniel: *Royal Progress: Britain's Changing Monarchy*, 1977.

Cowles, Fleur: *Friends and Memories*, 1975.

Crawford, Marion: *Elizabeth the Queen*, 1952.

————: *The Little Princesses*, 1953.

Crossman, Richard: *Diaries of a Cabinet Minister*, 1975.

Davies, Nicholas: *Diana: A Princess and Her Troubled Marriage*, 1992.

————: *Queen Elizabeth II: A Woman Who Is Not Amused*, 1994.

Dean, John: *HRH Prince Philip, Duke of Edinburgh: A Portrait by His Valet*, 1954.

Debrett's Peerage Ltd.: *We Want the Queen*, 1977.

Delano, Julia: *Diana Princess of Wales*, 1993.

Dempster, Nigel, and Peter Evans: *Behind Palace Doors*, 1993.

Dempster, Nigel: *Princess Margaret: A Life Unfulfilled*, 1981.

Dimbleby, Jonathan: *The Prince of Wales*, 1994.

Donaldson, Frances: *Edward VIII*, 1974.

Duke of Windsor: *A King's Story: The Memoirs of the Duke of Windsor*, 1951.

Duncan, Andrew: *The Reality of Monarchy*, 1970.

Edwards, Anne: *Royal Sisters*, 1990.

Edwards, Ruth Dudley: *True Brits: Inside the Foreign Office*, 1994.

Everringham, Barry: *The Adventures of a Maverick Princess*, 1985.

Fairley, Josephine: *Crown Princess*, 1992.

————: *The Princess and the Duchess*, 1989.

Ferguson, Ronald: *The Galloping Major*, 1994.

Feldman, David: *Englishmen and Jews*, 1994.

Fincher, Jayne and Terry: *Debrett's Illustrated Fashion Guide: The Princess of Wales*, 1989.

Flamini, Roland: *Sovereign*, 1991.

Goldsmith, Barbara: *Little Gloria...Happy at Last*, 1980.

Graham, Caroline: *Camilla: The King's Mistress*, 1994.

Graham, Tim: *The Royal Year 1990*, 1990.

————: *The Royal Year 1992*, 1992.

————: *The Royal Year: A Present-Day Portrait of the Royal Family*, 1994.

Hall, Phillip: *Royal Fortune: Tax, Money & the Monarchy*, 1992.

Hall, Unity: *Philip: The Man Behind the Monarchy*, 1987.

Hall, Unity, and Ingrid Seward: *Royalty Revealed*, 1989.

Halle, Kaye: *Irrepressible Churchill*, 1966.

Hamilton, Alan: *The Royal Handbook*, 1985.

Harling, Robert: *The Great Houses and Finest Rooms of England*, 1969.

Harris, Kenneth: *The Queen*, 1994.

Haseler, Stephen: *The End of the House of Windsor: Birth of a British Republic*, 1993.

Hatch, Alden: *The Mountbattens: The Last Royal Success Story*, 1966.

Heald, Tim: *The Duke, Portrait of Prince Philip*, 1992.

Heald, Tim, and Mayo Mohos: *The Man Who Will Be King HRH*, 1979.

Henderson, Nicholas: *Mandarin: The Diaries of an Ambassador 1969-1982*, *1994*.

Heckstall-Smith, Anthony: *The Consort*, 1993.

Higham, Charles, and Roy Moseley: *Elizabeth and Philip*, 1991.

Higham, Charles: *The Duchess of Windsor*, 1988.

———: *Trading with the Enemy: An Exposé)¿ of the Nazi-American Money Plot 1933-1949*, 1983.

Hillier, Bevis: *Young Betjeman*, 1988.

Hoey, Brian: *The Princess Anne*, 1984.

———: *All the Queen's Men*, 1992.

———: *Anne the Princess Royal*, 1989.

———: *Mountbatten*, 1994.

———: *Charles and Diana: The 10th Anniversary*, 1991.

Holden, Anthony: *Charles: Prince of Wales*, 1979.

———: *The Tarnished Crown*, 1993.

Holt, Rinehart and Winston: *Lady Bird Johnson: A White House Diary*, 1970.

Hope, Alice: *Princess Margaret*, 1955.

Hough, Richard: *Edwina, Countess Mountbatten of Burma*, 1983.

———: *Born Royal*, 1988.

Hutchins, Chris, and Peter Thompson: *Fergie Confidential*, 1992.

Hutchinson, Roger, and Gary Kahn: *A Family Affair: The Margaret and Tony Story*, 1977.

Judd, Dennis: *Prince Philip*, 1981.

Junor, John: *Listening for a Midnight Tram*, 1990.

Keay, Douglas: *Elizabeth II*, 1991.

———: *Royal Pursuit*, 1983.

———: *Royal Wedding*, 1981.

Krin, Sylvie: *Heir of Sorrows*, 1988.

Lacey, Robert: *Majesty*, 1977.

———: *Princess*, 1988.

———: *Queen Mother*, 1987.

Laird, Dorothy: *How the Queen Reigns*, 1959.

Lane, Peter: *Princess Michael of Kent*, 1986.

Lefcourt, Peter: *Di and I*, 1994.

Liversidge, Douglas: *Prince Charles*, 1975.

Longford, Elizabeth: *Elizabeth R*, 1983.

———: *The Royal House of Windsor*, 1974.

———: *Oxford Book of Royal Anecdotes*, 1989.

———: *Queen Victoria: Born to Succeed*, 1964.

———: *Louisa Lady in Waiting*, 1979.

———: *The Queen*, 1983.

Lunt, W. E.: *History of England*, 1956.

Macmillan, Harold: *Pointing the Way: 1959-1961*, 1972.

Martin, Ralph: *Charles and Diana*, 1986.

————: *The Woman He Loved,* 1973, 1974.

————: *Jennie: The Life of Lady Randolph Churchill,* 1969.

Massie, Robert K.: *The Last Courts of Europe,* 1981.

Michie, Allan: *The Crown and the People,* 1952.

Mitford, Nancy: *Noblesse Oblige,* 1986.

Montague-Smith, Patrick: *Royal Silver Jubilee,* 1976.

Montgomery-Massingberd, Hugh, ed.: *Burke's Guide to the British Monarch,* 1977.

Moore, Sally: *The Definitive Diana: An Intimate Look at the Princess of Wales from A to Z,* 1991.

Morgan, Janet: *Edwina Mountbatten,* 1991.

Morrow, Ann: *The Queen,* 1983.

Mortimer, Penelope: *Queen Elizabeth,* 1986.

Morton, Andrew: *Diana: Her True Story,* 1992.

————: *Diana: Her New Life,* 1994.

————: *The Wealth of the Windsors,* 1989.

Mosley, Diana: *The Duchess of Windsor,* 1980.

Mountbatten, Earl: *From Shore to Shore: The Diaries of Earl Mountbatten of Burma, 1953-1979,* Philip Ziegler, ed., 1989.

Nesnick, Victoria Gilvary: *Princess Diana: A Book of Questions and Answers,* 1988.

Nicolson, Nigel: *The Great Houses of Britain,* 1978.

Orbis Publishing Limited: *The Royal Family,* issues 13-24, 1984.

Packard, Jerrold: *The Queen and Her Court,* 1981.

Parker, John: *Prince Philip: His Secret Life,* 1991.

Pasternak, Anna: *Princess in Love,* 1994.

Paxman, Jeremy: *Friends in High Places,* 1991.

Pearson, John: *The Selling of the Royal Family,* 1986.

People Weekly Extra: The Diana Years, spring 1996.

Player, Lesley: *My Story: The Duchess of York, Her Father and Me,* 1993.

Publications International, Ltd.: *Diana: The Story Behind Her Private Life,* 1992.

Ransford, Sandy: *When and Where to See the Royal Family,* 1988.

Regan, Simon: *Charles the Clown Prince,* 1977.

Roberts, Andrew: *Eminent Churchillians,* 1994.

Rose, Kenneth: *King George V,* 1983.

————: *Kings, Queens and Courtiers: Intimate Portraits of the Royal House of Windsor from Its Foundation to the Present Day,* 1985.

Roth, Andrew: *Sir Harold Wilson, Yorkshire's Walter Mitty,* 1977.

Russell, Peter: *Butler Royal,* 1982.

Russell, Peter, and Paul James: *At Her Majesty's Service,* 1986.

Seward, Ingrid: *Sarah: The Life of a Duchess,* 1991.

————: *Royal Children,* 1993.

Shute, Nerina: *The Royal Family and the Spencers,* 1986.

Solberg, Carl: *Hubert Humphrey: A Biography,* 1984.

Stenton, Doris Mary: *English Society in the Early Middle Ages (1066-1307),* 1951.

Taki: *Nothing to Declare,* 1991.

———: *The Greek Upheaval,* 1976.

Talbot, Godfrey: *Queen Elizabeth: A Birthday Tribute,* 1985.

———: *The Country Life Book of Queen Elizabeth the Queen Mother,* 1980.

Terraine, John: *The Life and Times of Lord Mountbatten,* 1968.

Thornton, Michael: *Royal Feud,* 1985.

Tomlinson, Richard: *Divine Right,* 1994.

Vansittart, Peter: *Happy and Glorious: An Anthology of Royalty,* 1988.

Varney, Michael, and Max Marquis: *Bodyguard to Charles,* 1989.

Vidal, Gore: *Palimpsest: A Memoir,* 1995.

Ward, Aileen: *John Keats: The Making of a Poet,* 1963.

Warren, Allan: *The Confessions of a Society Photographer,* 1976.

Warwick, Christopher: *Princess Margaret,* 1983.

Whitaker, James: *Royal Blood Feud,* 1993.

White, Ralphe M., and Graham Fisher: *The Royal Family: A Personal Portrait,* 1969.

Wilson, A. N.: *The Rise and Fall of the House of Windsor,* 1993.

Wilson, Christopher: *A Greater Love: Prince Charles's Twenty-Year Affair with Camilla Parker Bowles,* 1994.

Winchester, Simon: *Their Noble Lordships: Class and Power in Modern Britain,* 1982.

Wolfe, Jane: *Blood Rich,* 1993.

Woodham-Smith, Cecil: *Queen Victoria,* 1972.

Ziegler, Philip: *King Edward VIII,* 1990.

———: *Mountbatten,* 1985.

761

PHOTO CREDITS

1. UPI-Corbis/Bettmann
2. UPI-Corbis/Bettmann
3. UPI-Corbis/Bettmann
4. Archive Photos
5. Archive Photos
6. Archive Photos
7. author's collection (a.c.)
8. Archive Photos
9. Archive Photos
10. a.c.
11. Archive Photos/Express Newspaper
12. a.c.
13. Archive Photos/Express Newspaper
14. AP/Wide World
15. Archive Photos/Express Newspaper
16. Archive Photos/Express Newspaper
17. Archive Photos/Express Newspaper
18. Archive Photos/Express Newspaper
19. AP/Wide World
20. Archive Photos
21. UPI-Corbis/Bettmann
22. Harry S. Truman Library
23. Archive Photos
24. Archive Photos
25. Globe Photos
26. Archive Photos/Express Newspaper
27. a.c.
28. Archive Photos
29. Archive Photos/Express Newspaper
30. Archive Photos
31. John F. Kennedy Library
32. UPI-Corbis/Bettmann
33. UPI-Corbis/Bettmann
34. a.c.
35. Archive Photos
36. a.c.
37. Archive Photos/Camera Press
38. Archive Photos/Express Newspaper
39. Archive Photos/Express Newspaper
40. UPI-Corbis/Bettmann
41. Archive Photos/Express Newspaper

42. Archive Photos/Express Newspaper
43. Archive Photos/Express Newspaper
44. Snowdon/Globe Photos
45. Archive Photos/Express Newspaper
46. Archive Photos/Express Newspaper
47. Reuters/Russell Boyce/Archive Photos
48. Archive Photos/Express Newspaper
49. Archive Photos/Express Newspaper
50. Rex USA
51. Archive Photos/Express Newspaper
52. Archive Photos/Express Newspaper
53. Archive Photos/Express Newspaper
54. Archive Photos
55. Archive Photos/Express Newspaper
56. Archive Photos/Express Newspaper
57. Rex USA
58. Archive Photos/Express Newspaper
59. Reuters/Mike Theiler/Archives Photos
60. Archive Photos/Express Newspaper
61. Rex USA
62. Rex USA
63. Archive Photos/Express Newspaper
64. UPI-Corbis/Bettmann
65. Tim Rooke/Rex USA
66. White House Photo
67. Rex USA
68. Rondadswell/Rex USA
69. Globe Photos
70. Glenn Harvey/Globe Photos
71. Globe Photos
72. UPI-Corbis/Bettmann
73. AP/Wide World
74. Archive Photos/Express Newspaper
75. AP/Wide World
76. Rex USA
77. Rex USA
78. UPI-Corbis/Bettmann
79. Dave Chancellor/Globe Photos
80. AP/Wide World
81. Archive Photos
82. AP/Wide World
83. Archive Photos/BIG Pictures
84. Archive Photos/Express Newspaper
85. Archive Photos/PA News
86. Trog/The Observer/London/Cartoonists & Writers Syndicate
87. AP/Wide World
88. Calvin Trillin

If you have enjoyed reading this large print book and you would like more information on how to order a Wheeler Large Print Book, please write to:

 Wheeler Publishing, Inc.
P.O. Box 531
Accord, MA 02018-0531